Teach criminal investigations through real cases.

From the Case File chapter openers provide students with real cases to analyze and evaluate.

From the CASE FILE
An Internet Chat With an Undercover Officer

In December of 2008, Gary Becker, the fifty-one-year-old mayor of Racine, Wisconsin, population 80,000, brought his personal computer to work at city hall and asked a computer technician to see if he could fix the problems that Becker was having with it. While fixing the computer, the technician discovered what appeared to be child pornography on its hard drive. The technician contacted the police to alert them of his discovery. After obtaining a search warrant, investigators collected the images from the computer. Investigators were also informed that approximately two years prior, Becker had another of his personally owned computers serviced by a city computer technician, and a disk which contained files from the computer had been created by the technician who worked on the computer. When the investigator now examined that disk, another similar pornographic image was discovered. Investigators also discovered evidence of over 1,800 online chats, many of which were sexually explicit and appeared to involve juveniles. Investigators determined that the user's profile was "WISC_GARY" and that his screen name was "m reed." Subsequent to that discovery, on January 12, 2009, an investigator had an approximately two-hour online conversation with "m reed," except "m reed" thought he was conversing with a fourteen-year-old girl. Presented below is a transcript of that conversation (edited for length). Gary Becker is "m reed" and the undercover investigator is "Hope ulikeme14." (Warning: Disturbing content.)

4:10 p.m.:

m reed: how r u doing honey? Have u been a good girl lately?

No response

m reed: r u still teasing the men?

No response

m reed: how is sweet little hope doing today???

Hope Ulikeme14: hi reed sorry I was doing my homework b4

Hope Ulikeme14: lemme kno if u wanna chat later ttyl

Capstone CASE
The Coed Murders

The nightmare began on the evening of July 10, 1967, when nineteen-year-old Mary Fleszar did not return to her apartment, which was located just a few blocks from the Eastern Michigan University (EMU) campus in Ypsilanti, Michigan. Mary was a student at the university. As is the case in most missing person investigations, the first task for investigators was to determine when and where she was last seen. In reconstructing the last known whereabouts of Mary, an EMU police officer recalled seeing a girl matching her description walking near campus at about 8:45 p.m. the night before she was reported missing. She was alone. Another witness reported that he saw the girl at about 9:00 p.m. that same night in the same area, walking on the sidewalk. The witness reported that a car drove up next to her and stopped. According to report the witness gave, the only person in the vehicle was "a young man," and the vehicle was "bluish-gray in color, possibly a Chevy." The witness said that it appeared that the young man inside the car said something to Mary, she shook her head, and the car drove off. Shortly thereafter, the same car passed the witness's house again and pulled into a driveway in front of Mary, blocking her path. Mary walked around the back of the car and continued down the sidewalk. The car pulled out of the driveway and, with a squeal of the tires, drove down the street. At this point, the witness lost sight of Mary and the vehicle. Mary Fleszar was never again seen alive.

On August 7, 1967, a heavily decomposed nude body was found on farmland two miles north of Ypsilanti. Through dental records, the body was identified as Mary Fleszar. It was clear to investigators that, given the area in which the body was found (an open field) and the circumstances of her disappearance, the cause of death was certainly not natural, accidental, or suicide. In addition, given the area in which the body was found and the fact that no clothes were found in the vicinity, in all probability she was not killed where she was found. Her body had probably been dumped there. With the identity of the decedent determined and the crime established as a homicide, the next questions for investigators became, who killed her? And where was she killed? Matted grass around the body and the positioning of the body suggested that

A **capstone case** is presented at the end of the book so students can apply the knowledge they have gained throughout the course.

Evidence is key.

Criminal Investigations has more coverage of the strengths, weaknesses, and effectiveness of all major **forms of evidence** than any other title on the market.

••• Organized how you teach.

Strong foundational material

Chapter 1: The Investigation of Crime

Chapter 2: The History of Criminal Investigation

Emphasis on the role of evidence in criminal investigations

Chapter 3: The Role of Evidence in Criminal Investigations

Chapter 4: The Law and Criminal Investigation

Thorough discussion of evidence, identifications, and confessions

Chapter 5: Physical Evidence and the Crime Scene

Chapter 6: Interviews and Eyewitness Identifications

Chapter 7: Interrogations and Confessions

Coverage of additional sources of investigations

Chapter 8: Behavioral Analysis and Other Related Evidence

Chapter 9: Information from the Public, the Media, Electronic Networks, and Other Sources

Procedures for various types of criminal investigations

Chapter 10: Death Investigation

Chapter 11: The Investigation of Sex Crimes, Assault, Child Abuse, and Related Offenses

Chapter 12: The Investigation of Robbery

Chapter 13: The Investigation of Burglary, Vehicle Theft, Arson, and Other Property Crimes

Chapter 14: Digital Evidence and the Investigation of Fraud and Other Computer-Facilitated Crimes

Chapter 15: The Documentation and Presentation of Evidence

Current topics and the future of criminal investigations

Chapter 16: Terrorism, Technology, and the Future of Criminal Investigation

Appendix: Capstone Case: The Coed Murders

••• The Issue of False Confessions

A false confession is one where the individual is totally innocent but confesses to the crime, or where the individual was involved in the offense but overstates his or her involvement in the crime (Gudjonsson 1992). Why would anyone confess to a crime they did not commit? Three related explanations have been offered. The first is referred to as *stress compliant false confession*. With this type of false confession, a confession is offered "to escape the punishing experience caused by the adverse—but not legally coercive—stressors typically present in all accusatory interrogations" (Leo 1998b, p. 277). In this instance, the zealousness on the part of the police elicits the confession from the individual. The confession is an attempt on the part of the individual simply to end the misery of the interrogation.

The second explanation for false confessions is referred to as a *persuaded false confession*. In this instance, the suspect has "been persuaded (by legally non-coercive techniques) that it is more likely than not that he committed the offense despite no memory of having done so" (Leo 1998b, p. 277). In essence, the police are so convincing that the subject believes his or her guilt even though the subject has no memory of committing the crime. Numerous factors, identified in Leo and Ofshe (1998), increase the likelihood of a persuaded false confession:

- The interrogator repeatedly states his or her belief in the suspect's guilt.

- The suspect is isolated from anyone who may contradict the claims of the interrogator and is not told of other information that may lead one to believe that he or she did not commit the crime.

- The interrogation is lengthy and emotionally charged.

- The interrogator repeatedly claims that there is scientific proof of the suspect's guilt.

- The suspect is repeatedly reminded of previous instances of memory problems or blackouts. If these do not exist, then other factors are identified by the interrogator that could account for lack of memory of the incident.

- The interrogator demands that the suspect accept the interrogator's version of events and explanations for the crime.

- The interrogator induces fear in the suspect's mind about the consequences of repeated denials.

It is interesting to note that many of these factors are present in the interrogation protocol presented by Inbau et al. (2013). It is also noteworthy that *all* of these factors were apparently present in the interrogation of Michael Crowe discussed earlier. Of course, not everyone is equally susceptible to the influence of these tactics. Research has shown that the individuals most likely to provide such false confessions most often have several characteristics in common: an extraordinary trust of people in authority, a lack of self-confidence, and heightened suggestibility, which may be due to factors such as young age or mental handicap (Gudjonsson 1992). Research has shown that the one factor that both stress

MYTHS & MISCONCEPTIONS 1.2

The Role of Patrol Officers in Solving Crimes

Often much is made of detectives being the ones who are responsible for solving crimes and patrol officers being responsible for the countless other tasks of policing—everything from dealing with barking dogs to domestic violence incidents. However, it would be a serious error to minimize the importance and contribution of patrol officers in solving crimes. The activities of patrol officers during initial investigations are absolutely critical to the overall likelihood of the crime being solved. Studies have shown that about 20 percent of crimes are solved as a result of an arrest made during the initial investigation and that the overwhelming majority of other crimes that are solved are solved because of information that was discovered by patrol officers during initial investigations. Certainly, patrol officers are not just report takers, they play an extremely important role in the criminal investigation process.

Make teaching and learning easier.

Visit the password-protected instructor site at www.sagepub.com/brandl3e to access these resources:

- A Microsoft® Word® and Respondus electronic test bank with multiple choice, true/false and essay questions

- Microsoft® PowerPoint® slides, including figures from the text

- An annotated syllabus with media integration

- Lecture notes with brief summaries and detailed outlines of each chapter

- Instructor's manual for the coed murders case featured at the end of the text

- Lively and stimulating **ideas for class activities** that can be used to reinforce active learning

- Selected full-text **SAGE journal articles** with accompanying discussion questions

- Links to video and Web resources for use in class or with assignments

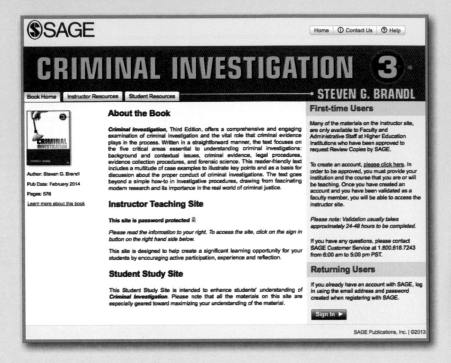

The FREE open-access student study site at www.sagepub.com/brandl3e features:

- **Video links** and mobile-friendly web quizzes to help you master chapter content

- Mobile-friendly eFlashcards that reinforce key concepts

- Web resources for further research on important topics

- EXCLUSIVE! **Access to full-text SAGE journal articles** that have been carefully selected for each chapter

Explore these additional titles from SAGE:

New! Coy H. Johnston, *Careers in Criminal Justice*

New! Kevin J. Strom and Matthew J. Hickman, *Forensic Science and the Administration of Justice*

New edition! Curt R. Bartol and Anne M. Bartol, *Forensic Psychology*, 4th edition

New! Curt R. Bartol and Anne M. Bartol, *Psychology and Law*

CRIMINAL
INVESTIGATION

*To the thousands of criminal investigation students that I have had
the privilege of instructing over the last 25 years.*

Make Justice!

CRIMINAL INVESTIGATION

STEVEN G. BRANDL

University of Wisconsin-Milwaukee

Los Angeles | London | New Delhi
Singapore | Washington DC

Los Angeles | London | New Delhi
Singapore | Washington DC

FOR INFORMATION:

SAGE Publications, Inc.
2455 Teller Road
Thousand Oaks, California 91320
E-mail: order@sagepub.com

SAGE Publications Ltd.
1 Oliver's Yard
55 City Road
London, EC1Y 1SP
United Kingdom

SAGE Publications India Pvt. Ltd.
B 1/I 1 Mohan Cooperative Industrial Area
Mathura Road, New Delhi 110 044
India

SAGE Publications Asia-Pacific Pte. Ltd.
3 Church Street
#10-04 Samsung Hub
Singapore 049483

Acquisitions Editor: Jerry Westby
Associate Editor: Theresa Accomazzo
Editorial Assistant: MaryAnn Vail
Project Editor: Veronica Stapleton Hooper
Copy Editor: Shannon Kelly
Typesetter: C&M Digitals (P) Ltd.
Proofreader: Dennis W. Webb
Indexer: Sheila Bodell
Cover Designer: Scott Van Atta
Marketing Manager: Terra Schultz

Copyright © 2014 by SAGE Publications, Inc.

Printed in the United States of America

A catalog record of this book is available from the Library of Congress.

ISBN 978-1-4522-7212-2

This book is printed on acid-free paper.

SUSTAINABLE FORESTRY INITIATIVE
Certified Chain of Custody
Promoting Sustainable Forestry
www.sfiprogram.org
SFI-01268

SFI label applies to text stock

16 17 18 19 20 10 9 8 7 6 5 4 3 2

Brief Contents

Detailed Contents

Preface

Criminal investigations are more complex now than ever before. Criminals are becoming increasingly devious, more is known about the problems and pitfalls of evidence and the importance of proper procedures in collecting it, forensic science continues to evolve and affect investigations in dramatic ways, and laws governing the collection of evidence continue to change and have made the process more complicated. As such, it has become extremely important that investigators have the requisite knowledge, education, and training in order to conduct competent criminal investigations.

Although it is not realistic to expect that this knowledge will be obtained in a single course (or from a single textbook) on criminal investigations, such a course (and textbook) can play an extremely important role in developing it. In general, there are five critical areas of knowledge in criminal investigation: background and contextual issues, criminal evidence, legal procedures, evidence collection procedures, and forensic science. Students of investigation must have competency in each of these areas, and each area should be adequately covered in a criminal investigation textbook. In this regard, *Criminal Investigation* provides a more complete and balanced discussion of investigative issues when compared to similar texts.

A focus on evidence in criminal investigations (e.g., the role and function of evidence, the collection of evidence, legal procedures as they relate to evidence collection) is especially important and is emphasized in *Criminal Investigation*. Criminal investigation and criminal evidence go hand in hand; they are inseparable. Criminal investigations are conducted in order to collect criminal evidence, and it is evidence that is used to establish proof in an investigation. As such, it is impossible to develop an adequate understanding of criminal investigations without an understanding of criminal evidence. An understanding of criminal evidence is not just for lawyers, therefore. Investigators must also understand the role and function of evidence, the strengths and weaknesses of various forms of evidence, how different types of evidence can be used to establish proof, the legal issues that relate to the collection of evidence, and best practices for the collection of evidence. *Criminal Investigation* provides this understanding.

Forensic science focuses most directly on the techniques and procedures of collecting and analyzing physical evidence, and it is important that investigators also have this knowledge. This material is included in *Criminal Investigation;* however, *Criminal Investigation* is not a forensic science text. It is not an instruction manual. Even in this era of DNA, other forms of evidence, such as information from witnesses and confessions, often have a more prominent role in criminal investigations than physical evidence. Further, technical instruction regarding the techniques of collecting physical evidence would be, arguably, most appropriately learned in investigative *training* courses delivered throughout a career. As such, the most important and complex forensic science procedures and issues are discussed in *Criminal Investigation* but not at the sacrifice of other, more important, material. Crime scene and physical evidence collection procedures, especially as they relate to the investigation of particular crimes (e.g., homicide, assault, robbery, burglary), are discussed in *Criminal Investigation*.

Criminal Investigation also emphasizes research findings that relate to criminal investigations. Like textbooks on other criminal justice topics, *Criminal Investigation* incorporates a discussion of research that has been conducted on the issue. Research findings provide a basis on which to identify and recommend best practices (procedures) to follow in criminal investigations. An understanding of research findings also allows one to develop a solid understanding of the issues under examination. One example (among many) is eyewitness identifications. *Criminal Investigation* devotes the better part of a chapter to eyewitness identifications. However, instead of just identifying how to conduct eyewitness identification procedures, *Criminal Investigation* provides a discussion of the empirical basis for the recommended procedures. To do so, the discussion draws upon the fascinating research on human memory, as well as the research on eyewitness identifications. As such, *Criminal Investigation* not only provides instructions regarding the collection of eyewitness evidence, it also explains *why* these procedures are important in order to collect valid evidence. Issues such as this receive minimal, if any, coverage in other criminal investigation texts. These deeper, more probing, questions are what lead to an adequate understanding of criminal investigation procedures. *The goal is to develop not only a technical competence in criminal investigations but to receive an education about criminal investigations.* Other topics this text covers in depth are the limitations of scientific evidence, the impact of the exclusionary rule, the impact of the Miranda decision, the effectiveness of the polygraph, the theory and effectiveness of psychological profiling, the complexities of false confessions and false convictions, the effectiveness of AMBER Alerts, crime pattern analysis and mapping, and the methods and motivations of offenders.

Just because *Criminal Investigation* puts research findings and criminal evidence center stage, this does not mean that the text is complicated or difficult to read. To the contrary; the text is very accessible to students and is written in a straightforward and understandable manner.

Criminal Investigation is of reasonable length for a one-semester course. Many instructors, including myself, have had difficulties teaching from the ever-expanding criminal investigation books, and students often have difficulties in learning from them. *Criminal Investigation* includes the most important material for students; I made decisions about what coverage was most important and what would be covered at appropriate places in the book.

A common and important method of learning and instruction in criminal investigation is the review and analysis of actual investigative cases. Case examples are often used as teaching tools in investigative seminars and in training. Investigators learn things from every investigation. *Criminal Investigation* also emphasizes this approach. A multitude of case examples is provided in the text in order to illustrate key points and to provide a basis for discussion about the proper conduct of criminal investigations. These detailed cases bring the discussion to life and make it interesting.

In short, *Criminal Investigation* offers several features to help establish an understanding of the complexities of criminal investigations:

- Detailed case studies (From the Case File) at the beginning of each chapter describe actual investigations as they were conducted. These case studies can be used to analyze how evidence is (or could be) used to establish proof and to evaluate how criminal investigations were conducted—what was done correctly and/or what mistakes were made in the investigation. At the conclusion of each case study is a section titled Case Considerations and Points for Discussion.

- Numerous other real-life investigative case examples (including Case in Point features) illustrate key points.

- Sections titled Myths and Misconceptions address some of the false information that is provided by the media and through other representations of criminal investigations.

- A Question of Ethics features require students to think about the importance of ethical conduct in criminal investigations.

- Detailed discussions are provided of the strengths and weaknesses, and the effectiveness, of all major forms of evidence: DNA and biological evidence, other forms of physical evidence, eyewitness identifications, confessions, and behavioral evidence, among others.

- Information on, and evaluations of, proper evidence collection procedures, from eyewitness identifications to physical evidence, is included.

- Important descriptive information is provided on the nature and content of criminal investigations.

With regard to the organization of the text, the first two chapters provide a discussion of the basic issues of criminal investigation (e.g., organization, design, history). Chapters 3 and 4 discuss the role of evidence in criminal investigations and the law as it relates to the collection of evidence. Chapters 5, 6, and 7 are the most important chapters of the book. These chapters discuss the "big three" types of evidence in criminal investigations: physical evidence, witness statements and eyewitness identifications, and confessions. The next two chapters examine other sources of information in investigations: Chapter 8 looks at psychological profiling and other forms of behavioral evidence, and Chapter 9 examines the role of the public, the media, social media, informants, gang intelligence, crime analysis, the Internet, and other electronic databases in investigations. Chapters 10, 11, 12, 13, and 14 focus on issues that are unique to the investigation of particular types of crimes. The book concludes with a discussion of the documentation and presentation of evidence (Chapter 15) and the future of criminal investigations (Chapter 16). Some important topics, such as issues associated with drug investigations and gang involvement in crime, do not have their own chapter but are discussed throughout the text. The appendix provides a longer and more detailed case study of a serial homicide investigation that occurred in the 1960s. The case involved the sexually motivated murders of seven mostly college-aged women in Michigan. This case can serve as a capstone discussion of many issues covered in *Criminal Investigation,* such as the basic problems of criminal investigation, the value of eyewitness identifications, the value of other evidence, the potential value of DNA evidence, and how proof can be established.

Criminal Investigation provides the reader with a substantial and necessary foundation on which to build an understanding of criminal investigation.

●●● Ancillaries

INSTRUCTOR TEACHING SITE

A password-protected site, available at www.sagepub.com/brandl3e, features resources that have been designed to help instructors plan and teach their courses. These resources include an extensive test bank, chapter-specific PowerPoint presentations, lecture notes, class activities, discussion questions, sample syllabi, video resources, links to SAGE journal articles with accompanying questions, and an instructor's guide to using the capstone case.

STUDENT STUDY SITE

An open-access study site is available at www.sagepub.com/brandl3e. This site includes eFlashcards, web quizzes, web resources, video resources, and SAGE journal articles for each chapter.

Acknowledgments

I am grateful for the kind and competent assistance of many people who assisted me in writing this book. Let me begin at the beginning: Professor Gary Cordner of Kutztown University was the push that got this book rolling. Throw in a whole bunch of enthusiasm from publisher Jerry Westby at SAGE and a lot of work from many other people and the book became a reality. The entire team at SAGE was a delight to work with. Jerry Westby in particular was beyond compare. His encouragement and guidance were instrumental in getting this book written. I would also like to acknowledge the kind assistance and competent work of the rest of the SAGE team, especially Theresa Accomazzo, who had nothing but great ideas for the book, and Shannon Kelly, whose skill with words made the copy-editing stage of the book productive and actually kind of enjoyable. I'm grateful to the many others who worked backstage at SAGE, including MaryAnn Vail, Terra Schultz, and Veronica Hooper.

Many law enforcement professionals also made important contributions to this book. I thank Chief of Police Ed Flynn, Inspector William Jessup, Detective Doreen DuCharme, and Officer Laura Kraemer of the Milwaukee Police Department; Chief of Police Thomas Czarnyszka and Lieutenant of Detectives Dan Herlache of the Glendale (WI) Police Department; Chief of Police Kenneth Meuler, Captain Timothy Dehring, and Officer Kelly Scannell of the West Bend (WI) Police Department; Chief of Police Peter Hoell of the Germantown (WI) Police Department; Chief of Police Peter Nimmer of the Burlington (WI) Police Department; Officer Mike Resineck of the Brown Deer (WI) Police Department; and Forensic Investigator Crystal Williams and Operations Manager Karen Domagalski of the Milwaukee County Medical Examiner's Office. These folks took the time and interest to answer my many questions and provide important information to make this an interesting book.

I would also like to thank graduate student Doug Mellom from the University of Wisconsin-Milwaukee. He was like a small army when it came to doing research for this book. Graduate student Rebecca Jaworowicz was also extremely helpful, particularly with regard to Chapter 4. And graduate student Meghan Wleklinski got going when the going got tough.

I would also like to acknowledge the input of numerous reviewers who helped improve the quality of the book: James A. Brecher, John Miller Brooks, Elizabeth C. Buchholz, John Edward Coratti, Gary Cordner, Stan Crowder, Joseph Davis, Robert Feliciano, Gerald P. Fisher, Ryan M. Getty, Melchor C. de Guzman, Mark R. McCoy, Gayle Mericle, John R. Michaud, Hal Nees, P. O. Patterson, Doug Shuler, J. D. Smith, David Striegel, Michael Tatum, Jason B. Waller, and Jay Zumbrun.

Finally, on a personal note, I thank Katy, David, and Laurie. You continuously remind me of what is most important.

1

The Investigation of Crime

Objectives

After reading this chapter you will be able to

- Discuss the evidence in the Unabomber investigation and explain how Ted Kaczynski was eventually identified as the perpetrator

- Define criminal investigation, criminal evidence, and forensic science

- Identify the goals of the criminal investigation process

- Discuss the three major problems with evidence in criminal investigations

- Identify two different types of criminal investigations (reactive, proactive)

- Define the four stages of the reactive criminal investigation process

- Identify the major undercover strategies (stings, decoys, undercover fencing operations)

- Discuss information theory and how it relates to the criminal investigation process

- Explain the role of luck, logic, and inference in criminal investigations and the associated pitfalls

- Describe the extent to which various crimes are solved and explain the reasons why more crimes are not solved by the police

From the CASE FILE
A 35,000-Word Clue

One of the longest criminal investigations in the history of the United States ended January 22, 1998, with a plea bargain that spared the life of Theodore J. Kaczynski, known in infamy as "the Unabomber." Ted Kaczynski, former professor of mathematics at the University of California at Berkeley, pled guilty to thirteen bombings that killed three people and injured twenty-three others. For more than seventeen years, a team of 100 Federal Bureau of Investigation (FBI) agents, along with scores of personnel from other law enforcement agencies, collected evidence in an attempt to solve the deadly bombings. During the course of the investigation, investigators gleaned much information about the bombs and how they were constructed, but they knew very little about the identity of the person or persons who made and sent the bombs. One thing that was clear was the bomber's modus operandi (MO), or method of committing the crime. Most of the packages were sent through the mail. The explosive devices were of similar construction, and they were often contained in a wood box or used wood as shrapnel. The word *wood* was sometimes used as part of the fictitious return address, the name of the sender on the package, or the name of the recipient. In addition, the bomber targeted similar groups of people—university professors (at University of Chicago, Northwestern

University, University of Michigan, Yale University, and University of California at Berkeley and San Francisco), airlines and airline executives (American and United Airlines), and computer technology firms. It was for the early targets, universities and airlines, that the FBI named this case *Unabom.* Over time, the bombs became more sophisticated and deadly. The early bombs often contained miscellaneous "junk," such as furniture pieces, plumbing pipes, and sink traps. For this reason the Unabomber was first known as the "Junk Yard Bomber." However, none of the components of the bombs were traceable.

In 1980, with the fourth bombing, forensic investigators discovered the letters "FC" engraved on a metal part of the spent bomb. In 1987, an eyewitness came forward, stating that she saw an individual placing what appeared to be a bunch of wooden boards, which later turned out to be a bomb, in the parking lot of a Salt Lake City computer store. This information led to the creation of the then-famous composite sketch of the Unabomber.

During the next several years, beginning in 1993, the bomber sent a series of letters to various newspapers (primarily the *San Francisco Chronicle* and the *New York Times*). Some letters identified the crimes as the work of the "FC" terrorist group, some made threats

PHOTO 1.1: In 1987, the FBI released this sketch of the Unabomber, which was based on an eyewitness's description. Ted Kaczynski was not identified and apprehended until 1996. The sketch did not assist in the investigation.

of more bombings, and one provided a social security number to authenticate future correspondence. As it represented a possible lead, the agents checked this social security number, and it belonged to a recently released convict from California who, strangely enough, happened to have a tattoo that read "Pure Wood." However, investigators quickly determined that this person had no knowledge of, or involvement in, the bombings. One of the letters had a handwriting impression that read "call Nathan R Wed 7 PM." As another possible lead, investigators checked 10,000 people with the name Nathan R in the United States, which yielded nothing. In April 1995, additional correspondence was made by the Unabomber to the *New York Times*. This letter provided a reason for a recent bombing, made more threats, and taunted the police (e.g., "The FBI is a joke"). In the letter, he also demanded that his "manifesto" be published. The Unabomber promised that if the manifesto was published, the bombings would stop. With the recommendation of the FBI, the 35,000-word article titled "Industrial Society and Its Future" was published in the *Washington Post* on September 19, 1995.

Later, the manifesto was read by a man named David Kaczynski. To his horror, he realized that the writing sounded very similar to the words and ideas of his brother Ted. Certain unique phrases used in the writing ("You can't eat your cake and have it too"), known to be used by his mother and by Ted, led him to the unbelievable conclusion that Ted was the author. In early 1996, David notified the FBI and told agents that his brother Ted, who was living in a shack outside of Lincoln, Montana, might have written the manifesto and might be responsible for the bombings. The FBI found Ted Kaczynski at his cabin in the midst of bomb design diagrams, explosives, other bomb-making materials, and a finished bomb ready to be mailed. After spending more than $50 million and a million work hours on the investigation, checking and rechecking 200 "good" suspects and hundreds of other suspects, conducting thousands of interviews, and fielding 20,000 calls placed to the FBI Unabomber hotline, Ted Kaczynski was apprehended uneventfully outside his Montana cabin. The rest, as they say, is history. Ted Kaczynski was sentenced to life in prison with no possibility of parole (Douglas 1996).

Case Considerations and Points for Discussion

- The Unabomber case provides an extraordinary example of the difficulties with evidence in criminal investigations. Identify and discuss the various false clues and true clues in the investigation. What was the most important development in the investigation?

- In your assessment of the investigation, does it appear that investigators made any significant mistakes in the investigation? What did they do right? What, if anything, did they do wrong? What was the biggest mistake of the Unabomber?

- What do you think should be the biggest lessons learned by the police as a result of the Unabomber investigation?

Also:

- See www.washingtonpost.com/wp-srv/national/longterm/unabomber/manifesto.text.htm to read the Unabomber's manifesto.

- Search YouTube for "The Unabomber Documentary" and "Inside Media: Hunt for the Unabomber, Parts 1–4" for additional details and perspective on the Unabomber investigation.

●●● Criminal Investigation, Evidence, and Forensic Science Defined

Simply defined, criminal investigation is the process of collecting crime-related information to reach certain goals. This definition has three important components: (1) the process, (2) crime-related information, and (3) goals. Each is discussed in the following paragraphs.

The process refers to the activities performed by the patrol officers, detectives, or other investigators who are responsible for the investigation. Criminal investigations usually consist of several stages, during which certain activities are performed prior to other activities. The activities performed may be extensive or minimal depending on the nature of the crime being investigated. The nature and seriousness of the crime determine the activities that are to be appropriately performed during the investigation. The most common activities performed during investigations, even the most routine ones, are searching for and interviewing victims and witnesses and reading and writing reports.

Crime-related information is criminal evidence. It consists of supposed facts and knowledge that relate to a particular crime or perpetrator. It is what is obtained as a result of investigative activities. It is used to establish that a crime occurred and that a particular person committed the crime. Evidence is absolutely critical to an investigation. In fact, criminal evidence and criminal investigation are inseparable; evidence is the basic substance of criminal investigation. Criminal investigations are conducted in order to collect evidence.

There are many different types of evidence in criminal investigations, such as fingerprints, eyewitness identifications, confessions, and psychological profiles. Some types of evidence depend on scientific analysis in order to be made meaningful and useful. For example, blood may be analyzed in order to develop a DNA print from it, human skeletal remains

PHOTO 1.2: Investigators discovered this chess piece at a homicide crime scene where a young woman was killed. At the time it was found, its relevance to the crime was unknown. Was it a clue from the killer? It turned out that it had nothing to do with the murder; it was just a chess piece in the road.

may be analyzed for clues about the cause of death, and bullets may be analyzed to determine the gun from which they were fired. These are issues that relate to the field of forensic science. Forensic science broadly refers to the field of science that addresses legal questions.

There are at least three potential problems with evidence in criminal investigations. The first is that at the time the information is collected, investigators may not know whether that evidence actually relates to the case at hand. Consider the information that was discovered during the course of the Unabomber investigation: the use of and reference to wood, the initials "FC," the composite sketch of the individual who was seen placing the wood boards/bomb in the parking lot, the social security number, and the "call Nathan R" note. As it turned out, none of this information was relevant or useful in the investigation or the eventual apprehension of Ted Kaczynski, although this was not known when the information was first discovered.

A second potential problem is that in some investigations the police may be overwhelmed with massive amounts of information but, again, its relevance may be unknown. Consider the difficulties associated with collecting, managing, and following up on the information that was obtained from the 20,000 phone calls placed to the FBI hotline in the Unabomber investigation.

A third potential problem with evidence in criminal investigations is that it may not be accurate. Again, however, this may not be known when the information is first obtained. Compounding this problem is that even inaccurate information can be quite influential in making a determination or in drawing a conclusion. Eyewitness identifications are perhaps the best example of this. Eyewitness identifications have been shown to be extremely influential in the minds of jurors (and also investigators and judges) in establishing that a particular person committed a particular crime; however, eyewitness identifications are often inaccurate. No question, these problems make the criminal investigation task much more difficult and complex.

The third definitional component of the criminal investigation process is that there are *goals* associated with the process. A goal is best considered a desired end or a future state. It is something that one wishes to achieve at some point in the future. Goals also assist in giving direction to activities to be performed. Various goals have been associated with the criminal investigation process: (1) to solve the crime, (2) to provide evidence to support a conviction in court, and (3) to provide a level of service to satisfy crime victims. Perhaps the most important goal of the three is to solve the crime. To solve the crime, investigators must (1) determine whether a crime has been committed and ascertain the true nature of the crime, (2) identify the perpetrator, and (3) apprehend the perpetrator.

Although the task of determining whether a crime has been committed and determining the true nature of the crime may seem straightforward, oftentimes it is not. Experienced investigators can provide many examples of when a crime was not really as it first appeared. In particular, "stories" told by certain victims, and incidents that involve certain circumstances, may be viewed as questionable in their truthfulness. For instance, did a burglary really occur, or is this a phony report to defraud an insurance company? Did the "victim" spend the money foolishly and then claim to have been robbed? In one notable case, an employee of a tire store stole cash from the store, buried the cash in a jar in his backyard, then returned to the store and hit himself over the head with a tire iron, causing unconsciousness. After other employees discovered the "victim" on the floor, lying unconscious in a pool of blood, a robbery was reported. After the detectives asked some questions of the "victim," the true nature of the crime became apparent. Even with the Unabomber case, the investigators probably questioned initially the true nature of the crimes. Was the individual who was injured in the blast really a victim, or was the victim the Unabomber himself? If investigators do not question the true nature of the crime, serious problems can result.

After verifying the occurrence and the nature of the crime, investigators must then identify who committed the crime, and, finally, the perpetrator must be physically apprehended. To identify the perpetrator is to know with some degree of certainty (i.e., probable cause) who committed the crime. To apprehend the perpetrator is to take this person into custody—to arrest the perpetrator. With the occurrence and nature of the crime verified, and the individual believed to be responsible for committing the crime identified and apprehended, the crime can be said to be solved. Often these three tasks—determining the occurrence and true nature of the crime, identifying the perpetrator, and apprehending the perpetrator—are related to each other and are worked on simultaneously.

A second goal often associated with the criminal investigation process is obtaining a conviction in court. The police are responsible for collecting the evidence that establishes that a crime occurred and that the person who was arrested actually committed the crime. The prosecutor may then present the evidence collected by the police in court to prove to a jury or judge, beyond a reasonable doubt, that the defendant is guilty of the crime for which he

MYTHS & MISCONCEPTIONS 1.1

CSI

There is something compelling about the drama of criminal investigation. Over the years there have been a multitude of television shows that have put detectives and the mystique of solving crime center stage. Some of the most popular shows have included *Starsky and Hutch, Miami Vice, Hawaii 5-0, Dragnet, Police Squad, Streets of San Francisco, Barney Miller, Columbo, Kojack, Law and Order,* and *Cold Case.* No show however, has been more popular than *CSI.* Since *CSI: Las Vegas* debuted in 2006, it has led to two spinoffs—*CSI: Miami* and *CSI: New York*—and has received numerous awards. In 2012, *CSI* was named the most watched show in the world for the fifth time. No question, *CSI* makes great television; however, unfortunately, it is not real. There is almost nothing about the show that accurately depicts the true nature of criminal investigations. Listed below are five things about *CSI* that distort the true nature of criminal investigations:

- The perpetrators are always calculating and clever, but *CSI* investigators are even more cunning and clever. The ensuing investigations are complex and sophisticated. However, no matter how complex the crime, it is solved and solved quickly. All evidence is relevant to the investigation, and all evidence proves the suspect's guilt. There are no dead ends in *CSI* investigations.

- The characters on the show are responsible for all facets of criminal investigations. The people who interrogate suspects also process crime scenes and analyze the evidence collected from crime scenes. Sometimes they even assist with autopsies. Interestingly though, patrol officers never have any investigative responsibilities.

- Physical evidence always plays a role, usually the most important role, in identifying the perpetrator and solving the crime. The most valuable of clues come from the most esoteric of evidence, from dandruff to bird eggshells to urine.

- Relatedly, crime solving depends mostly on scientific equipment and very cool technology. The results of scientific tests on physical evidence are obtained within minutes of when the evidence was first collected. The results are always clear and unambiguous.

- The police buildings, offices, and other equipment are state of the art. All the *CSI* investigators are attractive and engaging. The perpetrators and victims are equally attractive and sexy.

PHOTO 1.3: Although the popular television program *CSI* depicts crime scene investigators at work, very little about the show is realistic.

or she is charged. In this sense, the police and prosecutor are on the same team, working toward the same end. It is important to understand that solving the crime and convicting the defendant are separate, but related, outcomes. A crime can be solved without a conviction being obtained.

The third goal associated with criminal investigation is victim satisfaction. This outcome has taken on greater importance during the last few decades with the movement toward community policing. With the community-policing philosophy, the police are supposed to be more concerned with how they are perceived by citizens and how they treat citizens (Goldstein 1987). The idea is that satisfaction is a good thing and something about which the police should be directly concerned. After all, citizens provide the resources (e.g., pay taxes, provide information) necessary for the police to operate.

The *ultimate* goal of the criminal investigation process is a reduction in crime through either deterrence or incapacitation. To deter an individual from engaging in crime, punishment must be administered either to that person or to someone of whom that individual is aware. Of course, before punishment can be administered to a person, that person must be identified and apprehended. Similarly, before an individual can be incapacitated (by placement in prison or otherwise) and therefore rendered not able to commit future crimes, that individual needs to be identified and apprehended. Although deterrence and incapacitation are not within the complete control of the police, the police provide a critical ingredient in their achievement.

●●● Types of Criminal Investigations

Criminal investigations can be either reactive or proactive. Reactive investigations are the traditional manner in which police become involved in the investigation of crime. The crime occurs and then police respond or react to the crime. The police are typically in reactive mode when investigating crimes such as homicide, robbery, rape, and so forth.

REACTIVE INVESTIGATIONS

There are four stages to reactive investigations: (1) the discovery of the crime and the police response, (2) the preliminary or initial investigation, (3) the follow-up investigation, and (4) closure. With regard to the first stage, in the vast majority of cases, the victim contacts the police, and then a patrol officer is dispatched to the crime scene. In the most serious cases, such as bank robberies or homicides, detectives may also respond to the scene and conduct investigative activities.

Second, the preliminary investigation is conducted. The preliminary investigation consists of the immediate postcrime activities of the investigators who arrive at the crime scene. The specific activities performed by investigators are largely a function of the particular case at hand. All the information collected as a result of a preliminary investigation is then recorded in an initial investigative report and other related reports.

Third, if a perpetrator is not arrested during the initial investigation, the case may be selected for a follow-up investigation through a process of case screening. The screening decision is usually made by a supervisor and is based on two major factors: (1) the seriousness of the crime (based on factors such as the amount of property loss or the extent of victim injury) and (2) the evidence available as documented in the initial investigation report. Evidence is often referred to as solvability factors. Solvability factors are key pieces of crime-related information that, if present, increase the probability that the crime will be solved. If a case is selected for a follow-up investigation, then the investigators assigned to the case must decide what activities to perform during the investigation. Depending on the particular case, the follow-up investigation may involve a wide variety of activities, which can include re-contacting and re-interviewing the victim, submitting physical evidence to the crime laboratory, seeking informants, and/or questioning suspects. The information that is cultivated as a result of these activities is recorded in follow-up investigative reports.

Finally, at any time during the investigative process the case may be closed and investigative activities terminated. For instance, the case could be closed because of lack of leads or as a result of the perpetrator being identified and apprehended. In the latter situation, the crime would be considered cleared by arrest and primary responsibility for the case would shift from the police department to the prosecutor's office. However, the detectives assigned to the case may still have the responsibility of assisting the prosecutor in preparing the case for prosecution.

MYTHS & MISCONCEPTIONS 1.2

The Role of Patrol Officers in Solving Crimes

Often much is made of detectives being the ones who are responsible for solving crimes and patrol officers being responsible for the countless other tasks of policing—everything from dealing with barking dogs to domestic violence incidents. However, it would be a serious error to minimize the importance and contribution of patrol officers in solving crimes. The activities of patrol officers during initial investigations are absolutely critical to the overall likelihood of the crime being solved. Studies have shown that about 20 percent of crimes are solved as a result of an arrest made during the initial investigation and that the overwhelming majority of other crimes that are solved are solved because of information that was discovered by patrol officers during initial investigations. Certainly, patrol officers are not just report takers, they play an extremely important role in the criminal investigation process.

UNDERCOVER INVESTIGATIONS

Proactive strategies, which are often covert or "undercover," usually involve the police initiating investigative activities prior to the occurrence of a crime. Undercover strategies may be controversial, but they are necessary to effectively combat certain crimes, especially prostitution and drug dealing and trafficking. Covert strategies include stings, decoys, undercover fencing operations, stakeouts, and surveillance. Briefly, a sting involves an investigator posing as someone who wishes to buy (or sell) some illicit goods (such as drugs or sex) or to execute some other sort of illicit transaction. Once a seller (or buyer) is identified and the particulars of the illicit transaction are determined, police officers waiting nearby can execute an arrest. Undercover drug stings are often referred to as buy-bust operations in which an arrest is made after drugs are bought (or sold).

In a decoy operation, an undercover police officer attempts to attract crime by presenting the opportunity to an offender to commit such a crime. Once a crime has been attempted, officers who are standing by can make an arrest of the would-be perpetrator. A variant of this strategy involves the investigation into the Internet solicitation of minors for illicit sexual encounters. In this case an investigator poses as a minor in a chat room on the Internet. If a sexually oriented conversation develops and arrangements are made by the offender to meet with the "minor" for purposes of sexual relations, an arrest can be made when that meeting occurs.

Undercover fencing operations are another type of undercover investigative strategy. A fence is a business that buys and sells property that is known to be stolen. When the police go undercover and establish a fencing operation, word gets out that there is someone who is willing to buy stolen goods. The police make purchases, track the origin of the merchandise, and then make arrests. Other covert methods include surveillance and stakeouts. Surveillance usually involves watching a person to monitor his or her activities. Stakeouts most often involve watching a place and monitoring activities at that place.

When discussing undercover strategies, it is necessary to also at least briefly mention the issue of entrapment. Entrapment is defined as "the act of government officers or agents in inducing a person to commit a crime that is not contemplated by the person, for the purpose of instituting a criminal prosecution against him or her" (del Carmen 1995, p. 166). In essence, the police can provide an opportunity for a person to commit a crime but cannot compel or induce a person to commit a crime if he or she is not previously predisposed to committing such a crime. The offender's predisposition to committing the crime is critical; usually in an undercover drug buy-bust operation the undercover officer will make several buys from the dealer before making an arrest. Multiple buys helps establish predisposition.

MYTHS & MISCONCEPTIONS 1.3

"Are You a Police Officer?"

"Are you a police officer?" and "You're not a police officer, are you?" are probably the two most common questions asked of undercover officers by would-be offenders—or at least by *inexperienced* would-be offenders. Of course, this is not an effective way to identify a police officer. The police can legally lie and state that they are not police officers when in fact they are.

●●● Information Theory and the Criminal Investigation Process

Information theory is not so much an explanation of the criminal investigation process as it is a perspective from which to understand it. According to information theory, the criminal investigation process resembles a battle between the police and the perpetrator over crime-related information (Willmer 1970). In committing a crime, the perpetrator creates information that the police attempt to collect through investigative activities. For example, the perpetrator may leave fingerprints at the scene of the crime or may be described by an eyewitness to the crime. In each case, the original source of the information (or evidence) is the perpetrator and this evidence exists because the crime occurred.

If the perpetrator is able to minimize the amount of information available for the police to collect, or if the police are unable to recognize the information, then the perpetrator will not be identified or apprehended. The perpetrator wins the battle. On the other hand, if the police are able to collect enough "signals" from the perpetrator, then the perpetrator may be identified and apprehended. Critical to the process are mistakes. Evidence often comes to light because the culprit made a mistake. The police must capitalize on these mistakes and collect the corresponding evidence. Sometimes evidence is missed because the police make mistakes. In short, according to information theory, the source of all evidence is the perpetrator, and the fundamental task for the police in a criminal investigation is to find the evidence produced as a result of the crime.

Consider information theory in relation to the case of the Unabomber. Investigators had little information and few clues over the course of the seventeen-year investigation. Investigators knew of the "FC" initials and they had the composite sketch, the social security number, the "call Nathan R" note, and the reference to wood. The Unabomber was, apparently, good at minimizing the amount of relevant information available for the investigators to collect—until the publication of the manifesto in the *Washington Post*. The manifesto constituted a 35,000-word clue that came directly from the culprit. Indeed, the article proved to be the undoing of the Unabomber. The culprit made a big mistake by wanting the manifesto to be published, and the police capitalized on it. One can only speculate whether Ted Kaczynski would have been identified and apprehended if it was not for the publication of the manifesto.

The case of the so-called BTK Killer (bind, torture, kill) provides another example of how the actions of the perpetrator can lead to his or her apprehension (Case in Point 1.1).

●●● The Role of Chance, Accident, and Discovery in Criminal Investigations

It is common to hear discussions about the role of luck and good fortune in solving crimes and that the presence of good luck somehow diminishes the efforts of investigators in solving crimes (e.g., "Detectives got lucky in solving the crime"). The fact of the matter is that good luck should not diminish the work of the investigators or the quality of effort put forth during an investigation.

PHOTO 1.4: One basic task of a criminal investigation is to find and collect information (evidence) that was created as a result of the perpetrator committing the crime.

Accident and good fortune are natural ingredients not only in many solved crimes but also in many other discoveries and breakthroughs, including Post-it Notes, Velcro, Viagra, and even America, for that matter (see Jones 1991). The same sort of luck is often present in criminal investigations; see Case in Point 1.2.

CASE in POINT 1.1 — BTK and the Computer Disk

Beginning in 1974 and continuing over the course of the next thirty years, someone murdered ten people in Wichita, Kansas. The police had few good leads; the killer was very careful and was able to minimize the amount of information that was produced in committing the murders. Over the years, the perpetrator sent a series of anonymous letters to the police and media outlets taunting the police about his crimes. Some of the letters contained jewelry that was taken from the victims. To make it more difficult to trace the source of the letters, the killer sent copies of copies. However, the last letter the killer sent was on a computer disk, which turned out to be his big mistake. Through forensic computer analysis, investigators were able to trace the disk to a computer that was purchased by a church in Wichita. Investigators visited the church and found that a man by the name of Dennis Rader, the church council president, had access to that computer. Upon searching his church office, investigators found the original letters that were sent to the police and media. Rader was arrested on February 25, 2005. He pled guilty to ten homicides and was sentenced to life in prison.

CASE *in* POINT *1.2*

The Identification and Apprehension of Timothy McVeigh

On April 19, 1995, at 9:02 a.m., a bomb made of nearly 5,000 pounds of fertilizer and diesel fuel exploded at the front of the Alfred P. Murrah Federal Building in Oklahoma City. The explosion killed 168 people and injured 700. The bomb was so powerful that it completely destroyed or damaged more than 300 buildings and eighty cars in a sixteen-block area. The blast could be felt and heard fifty-five miles away. Three hours after the explosion, investigators from the FBI located a Ryder truck axle approximately 575 feet from the scene of the blast. It was figured that for this 250-pound piece of steel to be blown such a distance, it had to be at the center, or close to the center, of the explosion. Indeed, seconds before the explosion, a nearby security camera had filmed a Ryder truck in front of the Murrah building.

Upon examination of the axle, a vehicle identification number (VIN) was discovered. Through a check of the National Insurance Crime Bureau database of vehicle numbers and their owners, the truck to which the axle belonged was traced to Elliot's Body Shop in Junction City, Kansas. Wasting no time, investigators went to Elliot's and learned that the truck was currently rented to an individual named Robert Kling. They got a description and composite sketch of Kling from the people who worked at the shop. When investigators showed the sketch to people in Junction City, several individuals recognized the man, but no one had any further useful information about him—except the manager of a local motel who recognized the man in the sketch as her former guest. His name was not Robert Kling, she told investigators, it was Timothy McVeigh—or at least that was the name he used to register at the motel. With this name in hand, investigators checked a national criminal records database and learned that McVeigh was arrested two days earlier by a Oklahoma state trooper for driving without a license plate on his beat-up, yellow, 1977 Mercury Marquis and for carrying a loaded handgun. The news got even better—McVeigh was in still in jail awaiting a bail hearing for these offenses. A federal agent called the sheriff with an order to hold McVeigh for suspicion of bombing the Alfred P. Murrah Federal Building. Authorities had their culprit just forty-nine hours after the bomb exploded. If the agent would have waited another hour, McVeigh would have been free on bail and no longer in police custody (Serrano 1998).

PHOTO 1.5: In reviewing video surveillance after the Oklahoma City bombing, investigators noticed a Ryder truck that appeared shortly before the explosion. This discovery ultimately led to the identification of Timothy McVeigh as the perpetrator.

Just like with other discoveries, it is also quite common to find something when you are looking for something else. Have you ever misplaced your car keys and in the process of looking for them found something else you had been looking for earlier? The same phenomenon is present in criminal investigations. In investigating one crime, it is not uncommon to discover information that leads to another, totally unrelated, crime being solved. For example, consider the February 1993 explosion at the World Trade Center in New York City. The explosion killed six people, injured 1,042, and caused more than $500 million in damage. In investigating this bombing, federal agents discovered a different group of Muslim fundamentalists that planned to blow up various places simultaneously in New York City: the Holland and Lincoln tunnels, the United Nations building, and the Jacob Javits Federal Building. Through the use of surveillance and undercover infiltration, eight suspects were arrested and eventually sentenced to prison for this plot (Morganthau and Masland 1993).

••• The Role of Logic, Analysis, and Inference in Criminal Investigations

The task of criminal investigations has sometimes been likened to the process of assembling a puzzle where the final picture to be created is unknown. Some investigations have only a few pieces; some seem to have hundreds. Investigators who are working on many cases at the same time have potentially too much information to remember and keep straight. There is a lot to keep track of, a lot of things to remember, a lot of things to try to figure out, and a lot of decisions to make. In trying to figure things out, logic, analysis, and inference are necessary. Logic refers to the process of reasoning, of drawing conclusions from statements of fact. In using logic to solve problems, one is required to analyze the dimensions of the problem and to make inferences to draw accurate conclusions.

Because there are many decisions and judgments that need to be made in investigations, there are a lot of opportunities for investigators to make mental mistakes. The consequences of these errors may be an unsolved crime, a wrongful arrest, or even a wrongful conviction. D. Kim Rossmo (2006a; 2006b) discusses many of these mental errors or pitfalls. For example, coincidences may actually just be coincidences. In one case, a white female victim reported to the police that she had been sexually assaulted and described the assailant as an African American male. She told the police that one of the things he said during the attack was that he "had a white woman at home." Police discovered that in the apartment complex in which the victim lived there was a black man who lived with his white girlfriend. This individual immediately became the prime (and only) suspect in the case. The victim subsequently identified this man as the attacker in a photo array and then again in a live lineup. Only one big problem: DNA later proved that he was not the rapist. That the suspect lived in the same apartment complex as the victim and that he had a white girlfriend were simply meaningless coincidences.

Another mental error discussed by Rossmo (2006a; 2006b) is confirmation bias. This refers to the tendency of people to pay the most attention to information that confirms what they already believe to be true and ignore other evidence (the other possibilities). In the rape investigation discussed above, early on in the investigation the investigators learned of another African American male in the community who had just been released from prison for the attempted sexual assault of a white female. Witnesses also reported to the police that they saw this person in the area that the sexual assault took place at about the time the assault took place. The police ignored the evidence because they thought they already had their culprit.

Another potential pitfall is putting too much trust in potentially unreliable evidence. In the rape investigation, this evidence was the victim's identification of the wrong person. There

PHOTO 1.6–8: Investigators identified a possible suspect in a homicide investigation and conducted a consent search of his house. They found a collection of murder novels, bleach, and a knife under his bed. Incriminating evidence or a coincidence? As it turned out, the man had nothing to do with the murder.

are countless examples of investigations gone astray as a result of inaccurate eyewitness identifications. Indeed, eyewitness identifications are among the most persuasive forms of evidence, but they are also often inaccurate, especially when improper procedures are used to collect the evidence, as was the case in this investigation.

A final pitfall relates to the difficulty in changing one's mindset about the crime and who committed it once a theory about the crime becomes set and agreed upon, even in the face of mounting contradictory evidence. Once a crime is "understood," it is very difficult to consider other possibilities, to change the line of reasoning and the course of action. As seen in the rape investigation example, once the police believed they had their culprit, almost nothing was going to change their minds. Changing their minds would have required admitting mistakes and starting over. Investigators have to protect against involving their egos in the theory of the case and understand that the time and effort devoted to the case can lead to a mindset that is difficult to change. To avoid these pitfalls, an investigator must keep an open mind about the possibilities of the crime and who committed it, avoid getting personally invested in a particular theory about the crime, and be receptive to competing ideas and evidence.

Understanding the importance of logic, analysis, and inference in conducting criminal investigations also raises important issues about the necessary qualities and characteristics of investigators. What makes a good investigator? Surprisingly, little research has addressed this issue. According to Cohen and Chaiken (1987), the qualities most important in investigators are good judgment, stability, stamina, persistence, intelligence, initiative, teamwork, involvement, and dedication. Fundamentally, investigators should have common sense and should be able to think through a problem to its solution. In addition, motivation is widely perceived as one of the most crucial traits for effective investigators. This is in part because of the autonomy, or freedom, investigators often enjoy in performing their work. Because investigators are usually free of direct supervision, the opportunity for simply avoiding work is considerable. Integrity is also a critical quality. Cases can be lost when the honesty and integrity of investigators who collected the evidence during the investigation is effectively attacked by defense attorneys. Identifying the desirable qualities of investigators is a first step, and the easy step. The challenge is to develop valid and reliable measures of these qualities to make appropriate and well-justified job selection decisions.

In addition to these personal qualities and traits, Cohen and Chaiken (1987) also explain that investigators should have a wide range of previous experience in law enforcement, have solid street knowledge (i.e., knowledge of real-life criminal behavior), have knowledge of the law, and have excellent oral and written communication skills, as well as reading comprehension skills. The ability to read and write effectively is absolutely critical given the importance of reports in the investigative process. Reports provide continuity in investigations when several investigators are working on a case. They provide a basis on which to manage activities performed during the case, and they serve as the official record of how the investigation was conducted and how the information was collected. Well-written, complete reports are critical in securing arrests and convictions.

Similarly, much of investigators' time is spent interviewing victims, witnesses, and suspects, all of whom are important sources of information about a crime and who committed it. Consequently, effective oral communication and human relations skills are extremely important in being able to obtain information from people. Training may be used to develop or refine these skills among investigators. Training in these and other areas, such as forensic procedures, courtroom testimony, and legal updates, may be beneficial in conducting competent investigations (Kiley 1998).

●●● Criminal Investigation and the Criminal Justice System

The criminal justice system consists of three parts: police, courts, and corrections. By most accounts, the primary goal of the criminal justice system is to reduce crime, and this is to be accomplished through deterrence or incapacitation of offenders. To reach this goal, each component of the criminal justice system has a specialized function: the corrections component is supposed to maintain custody and control over offenders and to punish or reform them, courts determine the guilt or innocence of the accused, and the specialized function of the police as it relates to the overall goal of the criminal justice system is to identify and apprehend criminals. Sound familiar? Sounds like criminal investigation.

It is also important to take note of where the criminal investigation process falls within the criminal justice process. As seen in Figure 1.1, investigation is the second stage of the overall process. This is significant. If a criminal investigation is not successful (in this instance, if the perpetrator is not identified and apprehended), the rest of the criminal justice process is completely irrelevant. If the police are not able to identify and apprehend the perpetrator, then the courts cannot adjudicate, nor can corrections punish. In this case, criminals will not be deterred or incapacitated, and the amount of crime will not be reduced. No doubt, criminal investigation plays a critical and central role in the operation of the overall criminal justice process.

The criminal justice system can also be described as a filter or a funnel from which offenders (or cases) drop out as their cases progress through the system. Most relevant here are the cases that "drop out" because (1) they are not reported to the police and (2) they are not solved by the police.

As seen in Figure 1.2, the percentage of crimes reported to the police ranges from 32 percent for larceny-thefts to 83 percent for motor vehicle thefts.

So why are many crimes not reported to the police? The answer to this question relates somewhat to the type of the crime. For example, the most common reason given by rape victims regarding why the crime was not reported was that it was a private or personal matter. For robberies, the most common reason was that it was "not important enough." (Bureau of Justice Statistics 2003).

Many crimes, once reported, are not solved or cleared by arrest. There is significant variation in the success of the police in solving crimes: On the high end are murders, with approximately 65 percent solved; on the low end are motor vehicle thefts, with less than 12 percent solved (see Figure 1.3).

So why do law enforcement agencies not solve a greater proportion of crimes? This is a fundamental and important question that is explored throughout this book. There are likely a multitude of factors that explain police success (or lack thereof) in this regard. First and foremost may simply be the nature and structure of the crimes and how the police typically respond to them. The police are primarily reactive. Usually, it is only after a crime is committed that the police take action and, as such, the police are always trying to catch up to the culprit. In addition, given the structure of crimes, the necessary evidence to solve the crime may simply not exist. For example, given the way burglaries are typically committed and the fact that there is usually no significant evidence left as a result of the crime, it is difficult to solve such crimes. On the other hand, with a crime such as homicide or even assault, there are often witnesses to the crime. Furthermore, the perpetrator is usually someone known to the victim. These characteristics of the crime lead to a higher rate of solvability.

Another factor that may help explain the limited success of the police in solving crimes is that the police have to follow laws when collecting evidence. Perhaps the police would be more effective in solving crimes if the law did not prohibit the police arresting and interrogating citizens without reason or without limitations. As a society, we value our individual freedoms from government intrusion, but we must realize that this has costs.

A third factor may be that the police operate with resource (time and money) constraints. With limited person power, many crimes simply cannot be investigated as thoroughly as they could be. Perhaps with more money for more people and equipment, a greater number of crimes could be solved.

FIGURE *1.1*

Sequence of Events in the Criminal Justice Process

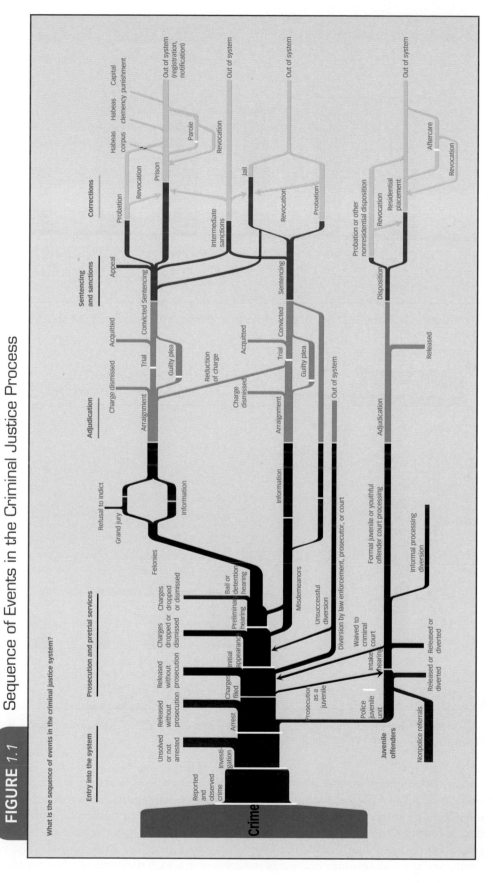

Source: President's Commission on Law Enforcement and Administration and Justice. 1967. "The Challenge of Crime in a Free Society."

Note: This chart gives a simplified view or caseflow through the criminal justice system. Procedures vary among jurisdictions. The weights of the lines are not intended to show actual size of caseloads.

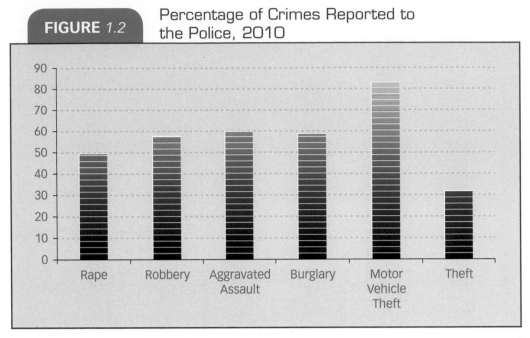

FIGURE *1.2* Percentage of Crimes Reported to the Police, 2010

Source: Bureau of Justice Statistics. 2011. *Criminal Victimization, 2010.* Washington, DC: U.S. Department of Justice.

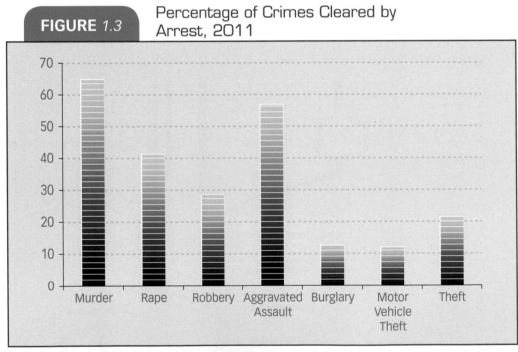

FIGURE *1.3* Percentage of Crimes Cleared by Arrest, 2011

Source: Federal Bureau of Investigation. 2012. *Crime in the United States, 2011 Uniform Crime Reports.* Washington, DC: U.S. Department of Justice.

Finally, investigators' mistakes may lead to offenders not being arrested. Investigators may overlook critical evidence, succumb to mental errors, or engage in questionable procedures in collecting evidence, such as conducting unlawful searches or mishandling physical evidence. Although all of these factors may help explain why more crimes are not solved, probably the most significant explanation lies in the structure of the crimes. The police simply are at a disadvantage because of the manner in which they typically become involved in investigations.

MAIN POINTS

1. Criminal investigation is the process of collecting crime-related information to reach certain goals: identifying the perpetrator, apprehending the perpetrator, providing evidence to support a conviction in court, and satisfying crime victims.

2. Criminal evidence is crime-related information. It consists of supposed facts and knowledge that relate to a particular crime or perpetrator. It is what is obtained as a result of investigative activities. It is used to establish that a crime occurred and that a particular person committed the crime.

3. Three problems associated with evidence in investigations are as follows: (1) it may be unknown whether the evidence collected is relevant to the investigation, (2) there is potentially much evidence to consider, and (3) the evidence may not be accurate.

4. Forensic science broadly refers to the field of science that addresses legal questions.

5. The television show *CSI* does not accurately portray the nature of real-world criminal investigations.

6. Criminal investigations can be either reactive or proactive (undercover).

7. The reactive criminal investigation process can be defined in terms of four stages: (1) initial discovery of the crime, (2) the preliminary or initial investigation, (3) the follow-up investigation, and (4) closure. The case screening process determines which cases receive a follow-up investigation.

8. Undercover investigations involve the use of various strategies, including stings, decoys, fencing operations, stakeouts, and surveillance.

9. The use of undercover strategies is sometimes controversial because of the possibility of entrapment.

10. According to information theory, the criminal investigation process resembles a battle between the police and the perpetrator over evidence. The perpetrator tries to minimize the amount of information produced as a result of the crime; the police try to find and collect the information that was produced. If enough evidence was created and the police are able to recognize and collect it, then the police win the battle.

11. Chance, accident, and luck can play an important role in criminal investigations, just like in other discoveries.

12. Criminal investigation plays a critical role in the criminal justice process. If a criminal investigation is not successful—that is, if the perpetrator is not identified and apprehended—the rest of the criminal justice process is completely irrelevant.

13. Many crimes, once reported, are not solved by the police. There is significant variation in the success of the police in solving crimes. On the high end of solved crimes are murders; on the low end are motor vehicle thefts and burglaries.

14. There are many reasons why more crimes are not solved by the police, including the nature and structure of crimes and that the police are reactive, have to follow legal rules, have limited resources, and may make mistakes.

IMPORTANT TERMS

Case screening

Confirmation bias

Criminal evidence

Criminal investigation

Entrapment

Forensic science

Information theory

Initial and follow-up investigation

Reactive criminal investigation

Solvability factors

Stings, decoys, undercover fencing operations, stakeouts, surveillance

Undercover criminal investigation

QUESTIONS FOR DISCUSSION AND REVIEW ●━━━━━━━━━━━━━━━━

1. What is a criminal investigation? What are the goals of criminal investigations?

2. What is criminal evidence? Why are criminal investigations and criminal evidence inseparable?

3. How does the television show *CSI* distort the realities of criminal investigation?

4. What are the three major problems with evidence in criminal investigations?

5. What is the difference between reactive and proactive (undercover or covert) investigations?

6. What are the four stages of the reactive criminal investigation process?

7. What are the major types of undercover strategies?

8. What is information theory? How does it relate to the criminal investigation process?

9. What is the role of luck and discovery in criminal investigations?

10. What is the role of logic and inference in criminal investigations? What are the pitfalls associated with the use of logic and inference in criminal investigations?

11. To what extent are crimes solved? Why are more crimes not solved by the police?

 STUDENT STUDY SITE

Visit **www.sagepub.com/brandl3e** to access additional study tools including eFlashcards, web quizzes, web resources, video resources, and SAGE journal articles.

Objectives

After reading this chapter you will be able to

- Discuss the Lindbergh baby kidnapping investigation, identify the critical evidence in the case, and explain how the perpetrator was eventually identified

- Evaluate the role of informers, thief-takers, and thief-makers in England in the 1700s and 1800s

- Explain how the designers of the detective position accounted for the problems associated with informers, thief-takers, and thief-makers

- Evaluate the role and function of detectives during the political, reform, and community problem-solving eras

- Compare the limitations of photography and Bertillonage as methods of identification, and the strengths of fingerprints

- Define the tactics of the "third degree" and the dragnet

- Discuss the creation and development of the FBI and its role in advancing the methods of investigation

- Identify the investigative strategies that are consistent with community policing

From the **CASE FILE**
The Lindbergh Baby Kidnapping

The date was March 1, 1932. The place was Hopewell, New Jersey, and the home of Charles Lindbergh, the famed aviator and the first man to fly over the Atlantic Ocean alone in a single-engine plane. Lindbergh was an American hero, a colonel in the U.S. Army Air Corps (the forerunner of the U.S. Air Force) and a wealthy aviation consultant. But on that day in March, he was the father of a missing baby. The baby was taken from his crib between 8 p.m., when his nursemaid, Betty Gow, last checked on him and 10 p.m., when she went to check on him again and discovered him missing. The baby's name was Charles A. Lindbergh Jr., and he was almost a year and a half old.

The Hopewell Police and the New Jersey State Police were immediately notified. Lindbergh reported to investigators that he and his wife were in the house between 8 p.m. and 10 p.m., but the only thing they heard was a "banging" noise at about 9 p.m., and it seemed to come from the kitchen area. They thought something fell off a countertop or chair. At the time, it seemed of little significance. On checking the scene, footprints were discovered in the mud below the second-story window of the baby's bedroom, but the police did not bother to measure, photograph, or take plaster casts of them. In the same area were two deep impressions in the ground, and next to these impressions lay a carpenter's chisel. Approximately 100 yards from the residence the police found a wooden ladder that was in three separate sections. It was believed that the deep impressions came from the legs of the ladder and that the ladder was used to gain entry into the second-story bedroom. On searching the baby's bedroom, an envelope was discovered on the window sill. Inside the envelope was a handwritten note that read

> Have 50000$ redy with 25000$ in 20$ bills 15000$ in 10$ bills and 10000$ in 5$ bills. After 2–4 days we will inform you were to deliver the Mony. We warn you for making anyding public or for notify the polise the child is in gute care. Indication for all letters are signature and 3 holes.

On the bottom corner of the letter there was a design that consisted of two interconnected circles and three small holes.

One week after the kidnapping, an individual by the name of John F. Condon placed a letter to the kidnapper in the *Bronx Home News* newspaper. The letter stated that he would be willing to serve as the go-between for the kidnapper and Lindbergh. The kidnapper agreed and so did Lindbergh. As instructed by the kidnapper, Condon then placed an ad in the *New York American* to notify the kidnapper that the

WANTED

INFORMATION AS TO THE WHEREABOUTS OF

CHAS. A. LINDBERGH, JR.

OF HOPEWELL, N. J.

SON OF COL. CHAS. A. LINDBERGH

World-Famous Aviator

This child was kidnaped from his home in Hopewell, N. J., between 8 and 10 p. m. on Tuesday, March 1, 1932.

DESCRIPTION:

Age, 20 months	Hair, blond, curly
Weight, 27 to 30 lbs.	Eyes, dark blue
Height, 29 inches	Complexion, light

Deep dimple in center of chin
Dressed in one-piece coverall night suit

ADDRESS ALL COMMUNICATIONS TO
COL. H. N. SCHWARZKOPF, TRENTON, N. J., or
COL. CHAS. A. LINDBERGH, HOPEWELL, N. J.

ALL COMMUNICATIONS WILL BE TREATED IN CONFIDENCE

COL. H. NORMAN SCHWARZKOPF
March 11, 1932   Supt. New Jersey State Police, Trenton, N. J.

PHOTO 2.1: With few leads to pursue in the kidnapping of the Lindbergh baby, investigators issued a poster asking for information. Notice that a telephone number to call was not included on the poster because most people did not have telephones at the time.

money was ready to be delivered. "Mony is redy" was the message. On March 12, Condon received written instructions delivered by a cab driver to meet the kidnapper in a particular cemetery to hand over the money. Condon followed the directions and met with the supposed kidnapper at the cemetery. Condon told the man that he could not give him the money until he saw the baby. No baby, no money. Condon later told the police that the man told him that his name was "John" and that he spoke with a German accent. On March 14, 1932, a second ransom letter was received that increased the ransom by $20,000. Subsequent to the new ransom demand, the baby's pajamas were received by Condon in the mail. On April 2, 1932, "John" and Condon met again at another cemetery to exchange the money for the child. Under the direction of federal treasury agents, the serial numbers of the

ransom bills had been recorded. At the meeting, Condon gave the money to "John" and Condon was given directions to a boat where they could find the baby. The boat was located but there was no baby.

On May 12, 1932, the body of an infant was found four miles from the Lindbergh home. It was believed to be the Lindbergh baby. The body was in an advanced state of decomposition. The autopsy revealed that the baby died as a result of a blow to the head and that death had occurred at about the time the baby was reported missing. Investigators suspected that the baby may have been dropped by the kidnapper as he was being carried down the ladder (which might have also explained the noise heard by the Lindberghs the evening of the crime). Meanwhile, the ladder was the focal point of interest and was analyzed by several experts. These experts were able to determine the kind of wood used to construct the ladder and the possible sources of the wood, but this information did not lead to any suspects.

Investigators theorized that an employee at the house might have been responsible for the kidnapping because of the timing of the crime: the Lindberghs normally would not have been at the house during the week that the baby was taken, but they decided to stay an extra day because the baby was not feeling well. With no other good leads, investigators focused their attention on Violet Sharpe, who was a maid at the residence. She did not have a solid alibi for the evening the baby disappeared and, according to the police, she appeared anxious when she was interviewed by them. With police pressure on her mounting, Sharpe committed suicide by drinking silver polish. The police later determined that she had been deceptive in answering their questions because on the night of the kidnapping she was on a date with another man, even though she was engaged to be married to the butler who worked at the Lindbergh estate. Condon was also considered a possible suspect, but after intense scrutiny he was determined not to be responsible either. The police began to be criticized for their handling of the investigation and their lack of progress in solving the most serious crime of the century. At this time, the FBI got involved as a result of Congress passing the so-called Lindbergh Law, which made kidnapping a federal offense and an FBI enforcement responsibility.

In mid-1934, ransom bills with the recorded serial numbers began to appear at various businesses in the New York and New Jersey area. The police recorded the locations in which the bills were being used, but this strategy proved to be of little help. The

PHOTO 2.2: The kidnapper used a homemade ladder to reach the window of the room where the Lindbergh baby slept.

investigation was still going nowhere. On September 15, 1934, the police got the break they were hoping for. An individual, described as speaking with a German accent, drove into a gasoline service station and proceeded to pay for his $.98 worth of gas with a $10 bill. The gas station manager thought this was rather strange and alertly wrote on the $10 bill the license plate number of the vehicle driven by the man. He then contacted the police. The police determined that the $10 bill was one of the ransom bills. Investigators checked the license plate number and found that it was for a blue, four-door, 1930 Dodge that was registered to Richard Hauptmann, a thirty-five-year-old German-born carpenter. The police staked out his apartment. When the police stopped and searched him, another ransom bill was discovered in his wallet. In his garage, the police found $14,000 of ransom money. On searching his home, police discovered a wooden rafter missing from the attic. The rafters were determined to be made from the same type of wood as the ladder, and the missing rafter appeared to be part of the ladder. With this evidence, Richard

Hauptmann was arrested and charged with the kidnapping and murder of Charles A. Lindbergh Jr.

During the trial, which was referred to at the time as the "trial of the century," the prosecution built their case on five critical pieces of evidence: (1) the money found in Hauptmann's garage was, as determined by the recorded serial numbers, part of the ransom money paid by Lindbergh; (2) the wood missing from the attic matched the ladder; (3) the handwriting on the ransom notes matched Hauptmann's handwriting; (4) witnesses reported seeing Hauptmann near the Lindbergh estate prior to March 1, 1932, the night of the kidnapping; and (5) Condon identified Hauptmann as "John," the person he met in the cemeteries. The fact that Hauptmann quit his job within days of when the ransom money was paid and that Condon's phone number was found written on a closet wall in Hauptmann's kitchen were also introduced at the trial.

The defense tried to counter several of these evidentiary items. They claimed the money found in Hauptmann's garage was given to him by a business associate before he left for Germany in 1933 (this man died before the discovery of the money by the police). It was claimed that because this individual owed Hauptmann money, Hauptmann decided to spend some of it. In addition, the defense questioned the handwriting match and the eyewitness identification. It was argued that the wood missing from Hauptmann's attic and used in the ladder was planted by the police.

After twenty-nine court sessions, testimony from 162 witnesses, and the introduction of 381 exhibits, the case was given to the jury for deliberation. After twelve hours, the jury returned a verdict of guilty. Richard Hauptmann was sentenced to death and was executed April 3, 1936, in New Jersey's electric chair (Fisher 1994; Waller 1961).

Case Considerations and Points for Discussion

- What was the most important evidence in the case that led to the identification of Richard Hauptmann as the perpetrator of the kidnapping? What was the source of this information?

- What do you think was the biggest mistake made by Hauptmann in committing the kidnapping? Why? What do you think was the most important action of investigators that led to this crime being solved?

- What do you think were the biggest lessons learned by the police as a result of this investigation?

Also:

- See "In Search of the Lindbergh Kidnapping" on YouTube for additional details on the investigation and prosecution of Richard Hauptmann.

••• The Importance of History in Understanding the Present and the Future

An understanding of history, and of the history of criminal investigations in particular, is important for at least four reasons. First, an understanding of history allows for an appreciation of how much or how little things have changed over time. Second, the present is a product of the past. To understand why things are the way they are today, we have to understand the past. Third, as the adage goes, those who do not remember the past are condemned to repeat it. To move forward, one must understand from where one has come. Accordingly, an understanding of history may provide insight into previous attempts and new methods of solving persistent problems. And finally, if history is cyclical, if it repeats itself, then we may be able to predict the future by knowing the past. It is with these understandings that attention is turned to the history of criminal investigations.

••• The Evolution of the Investigative Task: English Developments

Formal police departments were formed in the early 1800s in England. Soon after, the modern police detective was created. As discussed below, in designing the job of the detective, and to overcome public resistance to the idea of detectives, the problems associated with the predecessors to the police detective had to be addressed (Klockars 1985). The designers of the detective position took into account these issues in structuring the job.

INFORMERS AND PARLIAMENTARY REWARD

Parliamentary reward operated during the 1700s and early 1800 in England. With this system, a reward was offered by the government to anyone who brought criminals to justice or provided information that led to the apprehension of criminals; the more serious the crime, the larger the reward. Although this system may sound like a historical equivalent of a modern-day tip line, there were major differences, one of which was the laws at the time. During the time of parliamentary reward, more than 200 offenses were punishable by death. These offenses included theft, vagrancy, forgery, and even cutting down a tree without permission. The methods of execution included hanging, burning, and drawing and quartering. Many referred to the laws of the time as the *bloody code*. Most people, however, did not support the legal system nor did they believe the legal code was just. As a result, victims were often unlikely to pursue charges, witnesses often refused to testify, and juries were often not willing to convict. There was public sympathy for petty criminals who faced the possibility of execution (Klockars 1985). The problem was that by benefiting from providing information that would lead to the apprehension of petty criminals, informers were viewed with the same contempt as the legal system. Informers were not the answer, they were part of the problem.

THIEF-TAKERS

Thief-takers appeared in the early 1800s. A thief-taker was a private citizen who was hired by a victim to recover stolen property or to apprehend the thief. The fee that the thief-taker charged was most often based on the value of the property recovered, and the thief-taker only received compensation if and when the property was returned. As such, thief-takers were not likely to spend much time on crimes for which the property was not likely to be recovered or on thefts that involved small amounts of property (Klockars 1985). In essence, the thief-takers most often worked on behalf of the rich, not the poor. In addition to this problem, there was an even more serious problem with thief-takers: they often worked in cooperation with thieves. Some thief-takers even employed thieves (Klockars 1985). The thief would steal from the victim, the victim would hire a thief-taker, the thief would sell the property to the thief-taker, and the thief-taker would then "sell" the property back to the victim. Everyone prospered at the victim's expense. Thus the thief-taker arrangement was sometimes a corrupt one.

AGENT PROVOCATEUR AND THIEF-MAKERS

Along with thief-takers there were *thief-makers*. A thief-maker was an individual who tricked another person into committing a crime and then would turn that person in for the parliamentary reward. Thief-makers were often thief-takers who resorted to deception, seduction, trickery, and entrapment to apprehend criminals and receive the monetary rewards (Klockars 1985). These people essentially created criminals for their personal benefit. Not surprisingly, the methods used by these individuals were frequently viewed by citizens as outrageous and unacceptable.

LONDON METROPOLITAN POLICE DEPARTMENT

With the 1800s came the Industrial Revolution and the dramatic and rapid increase in the populations of cities, where people lived in order to be in close proximity to where they worked. Factory production was the basis of the new economy. With the Industrial Revolution also came an increase in wealth among some people and poverty among others. "Urban" problems were born—sanitation and health issues, ethnic conflict, and crime. With all the changes came political pressure on the government to institute a more formal, more sophisticated, and more effective system of property protection. In 1829 the London Metropolitan Police Department was established.

Introduced early in the London Metropolitan Police Department was the concept of the plain-clothes police officer—a detective to some, a police spy to others. In designing the job of detective, tremendous public resistance had to be overcome. The resistance was caused, in large part, because of the problems associated with earlier investigative arrangements—parliamentary reward, thief-takers, and thief-makers. To overcome these obstacles, and to allow detectives to be accepted by the public, certain features were incorporated into the design of the detective position (Klockars 1985).

First, to address the problems of parliamentary reward (when petty criminals faced unjust punishment because of the actions of informers), detectives were—in image, at least—linked to the crime of murder. There was no public sympathy for murderers. The architects of the detective position capitalized on stories of murder and offered detectives as a way to combat this horrible crime. In addition, detectives were to play a dual role. Not only were they to help bring punishment to the worst of criminals, they were also supposed to save the innocent from the worst of punishments (Klockars 1985). One can see very clearly the direct association between detectives and murder in early detective fiction (e.g., Edgar Allan Poe's *Murder in the Rue Morgue,* Arthur Conan Doyle's *A Study in Scarlet*), and this likely helped sell the idea of the police detective to a skeptical public.

Second, to address the problems associated with the thief-taker arrangement, the most significant of which was that thief-takers only worked on the behalf of the rich, detectives were to be given a salary (Klockars 1985). If detectives were given a salary, it was argued, they could work on behalf of the rich and the poor alike. Ideally, they could investigate crimes for which the property loss was small. In addition, given the profitability of working on crimes for a fee in a private arrangement, detectives were to be paid more than uniformed police officers.

Third, to address the problems associated with thief-makers, particularly the practice of thief-makers tricking people into committing crimes for the thief-maker's benefit, detectives were made reactive and were assigned cases (Klockars 1985). Only after crimes occurred were detectives given the responsibility for investigating them. As a result, there was limited opportunity for thief-maker trickery. Detectives were to be evaluated in terms of their

MYTHS & MISCONCEPTIONS 2.1

The Original CSI

As noted in Chapter 1, *CSI* is a tremendously popular television show that influences (and distorts) our views about how crimes are investigated and solved. Curiously, history has a way of repeating itself. In the late 1800s, Sherlock Holmes was the historical equivalent of *CSI.* Sherlock Holmes was a fictional detective created by author Sir Arthur Conan Doyle. He was featured in four books and fifty-six short stories. The first book, *A Study in Scarlet,* was published in 1887. Sherlock Holmes was legendary for solving the most difficult and complex murders. His most important crime-solving tools were his brilliant use of logic, his magnifying glass, and his uncanny ability to interpret clues from shoeprints, fingerprints, bullets, and handwriting. Sound familiar?

PHOTO 2.3: Sherlock Holmes was the historical (and fictional) equivalent of today's crime scene investigator. He solved complicated murders mostly by using his masterful grasp of logic and clues from physical evidence such as bullets and fingerprints.

success in solving crimes. As a result, detectives were given more control over how they were to spend their working time and more discretion in determining how to investigate the cases they were assigned. These features—being responsible for the most serious of crimes, receiving a salary, and being reactive—eventually neutralized public resentment toward detectives and paved the way for their incorporation into police operations.

●●● The Evolution of the Investigative Task: American Developments

At the time of the ratification of the U.S. Constitution, there were few federal laws and, accordingly, the policing function was almost exclusively a responsibility of local government. Policing was quite informal and consisted most often of volunteers assigned to the watch that guarded the village or town. Local control of the police function was a desirable feature of American policing because, ideally, it allowed residents (and politicians) to influence more easily how policing was conducted in their community. The desire for local control also helped explain why the creators of the Constitution were resistant to the idea of an all-powerful national police force.

THE FIRST AMERICAN POLICE DEPARTMENTS AND DETECTIVES

It was not until the mid-1800s that formal municipal police departments were created in the United States. The first police departments were located in the large and rapidly growing cities of the eastern United States, such as Boston, Philadelphia, and New York City. The Industrial Revolution created similar problems in America as in England. Of particular significance were the violent labor protests and the rioting that stemmed from clashes between immigrants and native-born Americans (Conti 1977). The mid-1800s to the early 1900s has been characterized as the political era of policing (Kelling and Moore 1988). Politicians, particularly mayors and ward politicians, controlled virtually every aspect of policing, including who got hired, what work officers performed, and who got fired. Besides political connections, there were few selection standards. Tremendous opportunities for corruption existed. Police supervisors were few, and their influence over beat officers was minimal because there was no way to provide for supervision. There was little ability for citizens to summon the police when needed because there was no means of communication. Officers patrolled on foot. The police made few arrests. According to Lane (1967), more than half of all arrests made at this time were for public drunkenness. This was an offense that beat cops could easily discover, and no investigation was necessary. The police simply did not have the capability to respond to and investigate crimes. When an arrest was made, it was usually as a last resort. Making an arrest in the late 1800s usually involved a lot of work; officers would literally have to "run 'em in"

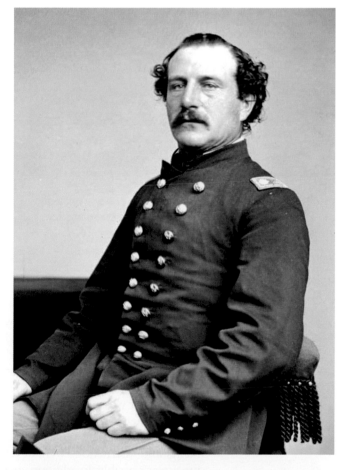

PHOTO 2.4: Police officers in the United States during the 1800s patrolled on foot and made few arrests for offenses other than public drunkenness.

PHOTO 2.5: Wanted posters, such as this one that related to the assassination of President Lincoln, were one of the few investigative tools of the 1800s.

to the police station. "Curbside justice" with a baton was often seen as an easier and more effective alternative by officers.

The political era of policing did not provide a large role for police detectives. Like the beat cops, detectives had limited capabilities in investigating crimes. During the late 1800s, Boston's politicians actually disbanded the police department's detective bureau because its contributions were so minimal (Lane 1967). Although important qualities for beat cops were size and fighting ability, the most important quality for detectives was a familiarity with criminals and their tactics. Many detectives were selected from the ranks of prison guards, and some were reformed criminals (Lane 1967). Due to their specialized knowledge, detectives received more pay than beat cops. Detectives also received extra compensation through witness fees, which were compensation for providing testimony in court. Detective work was often a clandestine activity. Detectives were sometimes considered to be members of a secret service (Kuykendall 1986). They depended heavily on criminals for information to solve crimes and often worked in an undercover capacity to collect this information. Detectives never wore uniforms. Rather, they often wore disguises, even in court, to protect their identities. Sometimes detectives submitted their court testimony in writing so as not to reveal their identity (Kuykendall 1986).

It was at about this time that identification systems began to be developed and applied to criminal investigations. The first technology that was used for this was photography. By 1858, the New York City Police Department had on file photographs of known criminals—a so-called rogues gallery (Dilworth 1977). Although photographs were commonly used in wanted posters and sometimes assisted in the apprehension of criminals, they were extremely limited in their usefulness because criminals could alter their appearance either deliberately or simply over time. Of course, to be useful, authorities first needed to have a photograph of the wanted person.

The most famous identification system of the time was the one developed by Alphonse Bertillon, a French criminologist who lived from 1853 to 1914. His system was known as Bertillonage, and it was considered a major improvement over the use of photographs. The premise of the system was that the bone structure of an adult did not change over the course of a lifetime. Bertillon identified eleven measurements (e.g., length and width of the head, length of the left foot, the length of the left middle and little fingers), and these measurements, it was suggested, could be used to identify people and to differentiate one person from another (Muller 1889). Bertillon estimated that the probability of two persons having the same eleven measurements was more than four million to one (Rhodes 1968). Instruments and instructions were developed by Bertillon to make the measurement process as precise as possible. In addition, an elaborate filing system was developed to classify individuals from whom measurements were taken. Because it was difficult for the police to take measurements of criminals on the street, Bertillon also developed a scaled-down version of his system. Although the technique enjoyed initial success in confirming the identity of suspected and known criminals and was used by police departments in many countries, by the early 1900s the deficiencies of the system were obvious. It was simply too cumbersome, prone to error, and limited in its applicability to be a viable identification strategy.

Along with the use of these identification methods, detectives at the time also used various investigative tactics to deal with crime and criminals. One common strategy was the dragnet roundup of suspects. When informed of a crime, the police would find and arrest all suspicious persons and would keep these people in custody until it could be determined that they did not commit the crime. In essence, the police would often resort to "rounding up the usual suspects."

Another commonly used investigative tactic at the time was the so-called third degree (Lavine 1930). The origin of the expression "the third degree" is not clear,

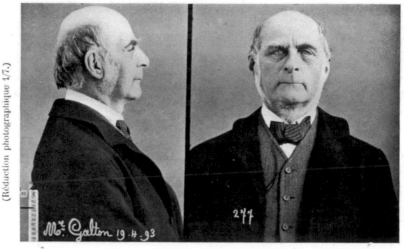

PHOTO 2.6: Bertillonage was a "cutting-edge" method of identification in the mid-1800s based on a person's bodily measurements. Today the idea of Bertillonage seems ridiculously primitive.

although some have speculated that the first degree was the arrest, the second degree was being transported to the police station, and the third degree was the interrogation (Kuykendall 1986; Skolnick and Fyfe 1993). Common methods of administering the third degree included beatings with a rubber hose (Haller 1976), placing a suspect in a sweat box for hours or days under constant questioning (Kuykendall 1986), drilling teeth, burning with lit cigars or cigarettes, and beating with blackjacks or batons (Lavine 1930). Many accounts suggest that the use of the third degree to obtain confessions was commonplace into the 1930s and beyond (Kuykendall 1986). In 1936, the U.S. Supreme Court ruled in *Brown v. Mississippi* that prolonged beatings used to extract confessions were no longer a legally acceptable police practice.

SHERIFFS, STATE POLICE, U.S. MARSHALS, AND THE BUREAU OF INVESTIGATION

While police departments were being developed in the major cities in the eastern portion of the country, other areas were most likely to be served by sheriffs and marshals. In the western portion of the country, U.S. marshals were often the sole police power (Ball 1978). Marshals often employed deputies who also served as sheriffs, deputy sheriffs, or constables.

With the appearance of automobiles, and due to corrupt and ineffective municipal police agencies and sheriffs' departments, state police agencies were created to assist. In 1905, Pennsylvania created the first state police agency. It was designed to provide a police presence throughout the state, to assist the local police, and to provide police services in less populated, rural areas of the state (Conti 1977).

Also of significance at this time was the development of the Bureau of Investigation, later known as the Federal Bureau of Investigation (FBI). In a highly controversial move, in 1908 President Theodore Roosevelt created a Bureau of Investigation by executive order. Twenty permanent and eighteen temporary investigators were hired (Murray 1955). During the first years of its operation, the bureau was entrenched in scandal. However, at the same time, it was slowly becoming accepted as a law enforcement agency and was assigned law enforcement responsibilities. For example, in 1910 Congress passed the Mann Act, which prohibited the transportation of women across state lines for immoral purposes. Responsibility for the enforcement of the law was given to the Bureau of Investigation. Other statutes followed that prohibited the transportation of stolen goods, vehicles, and obscene materials (Murray 1955).

In 1916, with war raging in Europe, the 300-agent bureau was given power to conduct counterintelligence and antiradical investigations. In 1919, the country experienced a series of bombings, with the targets ranging from police departments to banks. These actions were believed to be the responsibility of communists and others who were "un-American." In response to the bombings, Attorney General A. Mitchell Palmer established the General Intelligence Division (GID) within the Justice Department to increase significantly the ability to store information on radicals and those suspected of being sympathetic to radicals. John Edgar Hoover was named the head of GID.

PRIVATE DETECTIVES

In the mid-1800s and early 1900s, private detectives played an important role in criminal investigations. In addition, many corporations, such as railroads and iron and coal mines, hired their own police forces for the primary purpose of dealing with their labor strikes (Conti 1977). The most prominent private detective agency was Pinkerton's agency. In 1850, Allen Pinkerton quit his job in the Chicago Police Department and established his own private detective agency. At first, most of the work of the agency involved protecting several Midwestern railroads and railroad bridges from being sabotaged by the Confederates, as well as striking laborers. Pinkerton and his associates' preferred method of operation was to mingle with known rebels and criminals in taverns, hotels, and brothels to learn of their plans. Pinkerton was also hired to spy on the Confederacy, to collect information on their strengths and weaknesses, and to apprehend enemy spies. Also at this time, the Justice Department, having no investigators of its own, used agents from the Pinkerton agency. Pinkerton was able to operate without concern for cumbersome political jurisdictional lines. This capability made Pinkerton ideal for pursuing mobile criminals such as train robbers. Pinkerton also had a well-developed system of internal communication, records, and files on criminals. Police departments often relied on this information to learn what criminals were in their area. By the turn of the century, the agency had a system in place to share information with the investigative services of foreign nations (Conti 1977).

THE REFORM ERA

With the problems of the political era policing system well noted, efforts were made to reform the police—namely, to get the police out from under the control of politicians. To do so required a new way of thinking about policing. This effort took the form of police professionalism. This new way of thinking about policing was in direct reaction to the politics of before. According to Kelling and Moore (1988), policing from the early 1900s to the 1960s was known as the reform era.

The reform era was all about police professionalism and antipolitics. The police presented themselves as experts who had the specialized knowledge and capabilities to control crime. It was argued that if the police were able to distance themselves from citizens and politicians (i.e., have professional autonomy), they would be more efficient and effective. Crime control and criminal apprehension were viewed as the primary functions of the police. The new technology of the time contributed to and supported the ideals of the new way of thinking about policing. Examples of this technology included patrol cars, two-way radios, and telephones (see Walker and Katz 2007).

During the reform era, detectives became an important tool in police departments' efforts to enhance their professionalism and deal with crime. Detectives were the ultimate professionals. They were well paid and highly trained. The media at the time portrayed detectives as efficient and effective crime solvers. Similar to the police style in general, detectives often went about their work in a professional, aloof manner. *Dragnet,* a popular television show during the 1960s, captured this style well. The show was about two Los Angeles Police Department detectives and the investigations they conducted. They cut through the emotion of their work and became famous for their line, "Just the facts, ma'am."

MYTHS & MISCONCEPTIONS 2.2

The Mythology of the Federal Bureau of Investigation

The FBI has become the epitome of the scientific law enforcement agency. The agency has the highest prestige among many citizens, law enforcement officials, and even criminals. This is at least partially the result of the reverent media portrayal of the agency, even during its early years. For example, starting in 1935, a series of "G-Men" ("government men") movies was produced. Censorship laws only allowed gangsters in the movies if they were being captured or killed by agents of the FBI (Gentry 1991).

The FBI has done much to advance the methods of criminal investigation. It took the early lead in the development of fingerprints as a method of identification. It instituted stringent hiring standards for its agents. Today it operates the largest and most scientifically advanced crime laboratory in the world. The FBI operates the prestigious FBI National Academy. Over the years, the FBI has taken the lead in the most high-profile criminal investigations, from

the Lindbergh baby kidnapping to the terrorist attacks in 2001 to the Boston Marathon bombing in 2013.

However, justified or not, the FBI has also been criticized for its handling of several other high-profile investigations, including the catastrophic burning of the Branch Davidian compound in Waco, Texas, in 1993; the investigation into the 1996 bombing at Olympic Park in Atlanta; the investigation into the anthrax letters in 2001; the Foot Hood shootings in 2009; and the lack of information-sharing that might have prevented the September 2001 terrorist hijackings and the 2013 Boston Marathon bombings. The FBI crime laboratory has also been subject to criticism for its work in several cases (Kelly and Wearne 1998). Although the FBI continues to be an admired and well-respected law enforcement agency and is generally portrayed well in the media, it is not immune from criticism and error.

As a continuing attempt to provide control over officers and detectives, detective work became much more removed from interactions with criminals. With scientific advances, more emphasis was placed on getting information from science (and from victims and witnesses) as opposed to criminals. The rise of science was led in large part by the FBI. Through the 1920s and 1930s, several initiatives were embarked on by the bureau, each of which helped solidify its reputation as the top law enforcement agency in the country. Namely, it took the lead in the development of fingerprints as a method of criminal identification, it developed a scientific crime laboratory, and it established the National Police Academy (to be known later as the FBI National Academy) to train select local police officers in investigative and management methods. Selection for, and graduation from, the National Academy was, and continues to be, a prestigious law enforcement accomplishment. In the 1940s and 1950s, the FBI experienced dramatic growth. With the passage of federal laws, the FBI became responsible for domestic security investigations.

THE COMMUNITY PROBLEM-SOLVING ERA

The 1960s were a troubling time for many Americans and the police. In the 1960s, America was in the grip of the Vietnam War. There were war protests across the country. It was the time of the civil rights movement and its related demonstrations, marches, and riots. The police became viewed by many as an "occupying army" in the low-income, minority ghettos of urban cities. The police were "pigs." During this decade, President John F. Kennedy was assassinated, as were senator and presidential candidate (and former attorney general of the United States) Robert Kennedy and civil rights leader Martin Luther King Jr. American society was in turmoil. Fear of crime was increasing dramatically. Actual crime was also increasing; the crime rate doubled from 1960 to 1970. The police were experiencing a crisis, yet they were supposed to have the knowledge and capabilities to control crime successfully. If the situation was not bad enough for the police, the U.S. Supreme Court rendered several landmark decisions (e.g., *Mapp v. Ohio, Miranda v. Arizona*) that were seen as "handcuffing" the police. In the late 1960s and early 1970s, several major research studies were conducted to examine the effectiveness of police operations. The Kansas City Preventive Patrol Experiment (Kelling et al. 1974) concluded that random motorized patrols did not deter crime. The RAND study on detectives (Greenwood et al. 1977) concluded that detectives contributed little to solving crimes and that many detectives could be replaced with clerical personnel.

In the face of this multifaceted crisis, the police realized that the old ideas of professionalism no longer worked. They needed to get closer to the community to enlist citizens' support and assistance in fighting crime. This new realization instigated the community problem-solving era of policing (Kelling and Moore 1988). The reform era emphasized police-citizen separation; the community era emphasizes police-citizen cooperation.

The idea of police-citizen cooperation and community policing seems to be quite congruent with the task of criminal investigation. The basic task of the police in a criminal investigation is to collect information that will lead to the identification, apprehension, and conviction of the perpetrator of that crime. Much of the research on the investigative function highlights the role of the public as suppliers of information to the police. Simply stated, the police are dependent on the public, and the community problem-solving era makes this dependence explicit.

Strategies that provide an opportunity for community residents to share information with the police in order to solve crimes are particularly relevant in the era of community policing. For example, tip lines are quite common in criminal investigations today. Along the same line, school liaison officers are located in a setting where they are available not only to assist students with questions or problems that they may have, but also to obtain information about crimes from them. Similarly, police involvement with community watch groups provides a public service and also makes it easier for residents to contact and provide information to the police that may assist in investigations. These strategies make police dependence on the public explicit and are congruent with the ideals of community policing.

Along with a dependence on community residents for information, other developments in criminal investigation have occurred during the community problem-solving era of policing. Chief among these is DNA analysis as a method of identification. DNA analysis represents an extraordinary advance in science and in identification methods as applied to criminal investigations. The science of DNA, along with the introduction of computer technology to store, record, and match DNA prints across individuals, has the potential to revolutionize criminal investigative methods. In addition, other technology in the form of computer networks and databanks are also changing criminal investigations in dramatic ways. COMSTAT, an operational approach to policing which is based on "gathering accurate and timely intelligence, designing effective strategies and tactics, the rapid deployment of personnel and resources, and relentless follow-up and assessment" (Dabney 2010, p. 34) also has the potential to affect how criminal investigations are managed and performed. In addition, empirical research continues to be conducted on the criminal investigation process, the contribution of detectives in solving crimes, and the impact of forensic evidence on crime solving (e.g., Eck 1983; Brandl and Frank 1994; Baskin and Sommers 2010).

As in the past, the FBI is often considered to be at the forefront of technological changes in the criminal investigation process. Today, the FBI crime laboratory is the most scientifically advanced and well funded in the world. The FBI also operates the National Crime Information Center (NCIC)—a computerized network and storage system of crime information. The FBI continues to operate the National Academy and provides many other types of operational assistance to federal, state, and local law enforcement agencies, including psychological profiling.

During the course of history, police institutions and organizations have responded to a variety of external forces that have caused changes in their structure and function. From these changes has emerged the present criminal investigation function and investigative methods. Most people would argue that much progress has been made in criminal investigations. Ultimately, that is for the future to decide.

MAIN POINTS

1. With parliamentary reward, an investigative arrangement of the 1700s in England, a reward was offered by the government to anyone who brought criminals to justice or provided information that led to the apprehension of criminals; the more serious the crime, the larger the reward.

2. In the early 1800s, a thief-taker was a private citizen who was hired by a victim to recover stolen property or to apprehend the thief.

3. Also in the early 1800s, a thief-maker was an individual who tricked another person into committing a crime and then would turn that person in for the parliamentary reward.

4. The people who designed the detective position considered the problems that resulted from parliamentary reward, thief-takers, and thief-makers. To address the problems associated with parliamentary reward, detectives were associated—in image, at least—with the investigation of murder. To address the problems associated with thief-takers, detectives were to receive a salary and not be paid by victims. To address the problems associated with thief-makers, detectives were made reactive and assigned cases.

5. Detectives played a small and largely ineffective role during the political era. They relied on the technology of photography and Bertillonage and the tactics of the third degree and the dragnet.

6. During the reform era, detectives became an important tool in police departments' efforts to enhance their professionalism and deal with crime. Detectives began to incorporate science into criminal investigations.

7. In the community problem-solving era, citizens are important in criminal investigations as they can supply necessary and important information. With the development of computer technology and advances in science, investigations rely more on science than ever before.

8. Photography had many limitations as a criminal identification tool. To be even minimally useful, investigators needed photographs of criminals; however, criminals could easily alter their appearance.

9. Bertillonage provided a methodology for criminal identification, but the system was cumbersome to use and, at best, it was limited to verification of an individual's identity.

10. The FBI has a long history and has done much to advance the methods of criminal investigation. Some people say that there is a mythology to the FBI, given its role in high-profile investigations and favorable treatment in the media.

IMPORTANT TERMS

Bertillonage

Bureau of Investigation

Community problem-solving era
of policing

Dragnet

Federal Bureau of Investigation (FBI)

Informers

London Metropolitan Police
Department

Parliamentary Reward

Photography

Pinkerton Detective Agency

Political era of policing

Reform era of policing

Rogues gallery

Thief-makers

Thief-takers

Third degree

QUESTIONS FOR DISCUSSION AND REVIEW

1. Who were informers, thief-takers, and thief-makers
   in England in the 1700s and 1800s? What problems
   did citizens have with these people?

2. How does the position of detective today reflect the
   problems associated with informers, thief-takers,
   and thief-makers?

3. How did the role of the detective differ in the
   political, reform, and community problem-solving
   eras of policing?

4. What were the limitations of photography and
   Bertillonage as methods of identification, and what
   are the strengths of fingerprints in comparison?

5. What were the third degree and the dragnet?

6. What role did the FBI play in advancing the methods
   of criminal investigation?

7. What investigative strategies are most congruent
   with the ideas of the community problem-solving era
   of policing?

 # STUDENT STUDY SITE

Visit **www.sagepub.com/brandl3e** to access additional study tools including eFlashcards, web quizzes,
web resources, video resources, and SAGE journal articles.

3 The Role of Evidence in Criminal Investigations

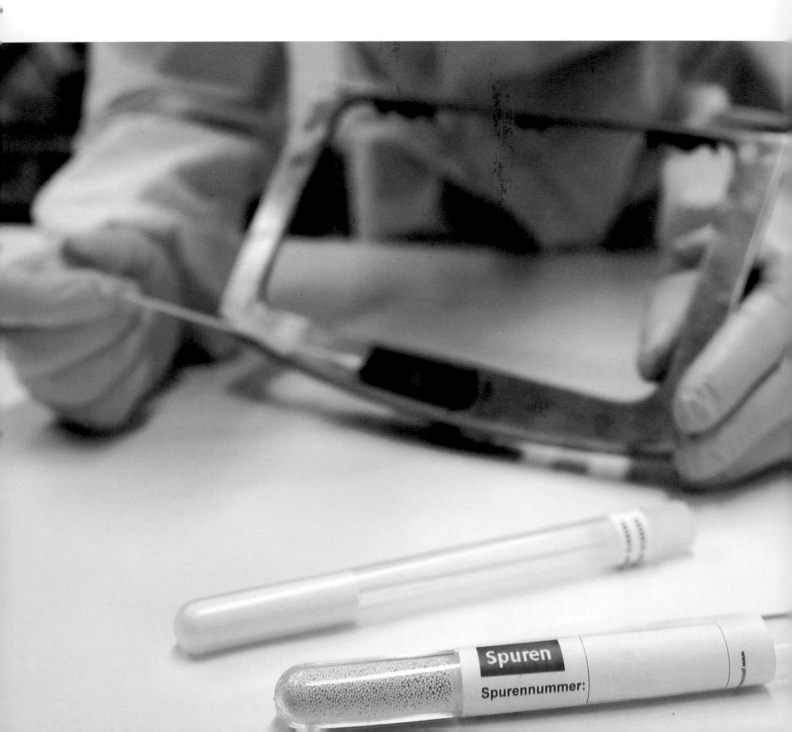

Objectives

After reading this chapter you will be able to

- Discuss the investigation of the death of Caylee Anthony. Identify the major evidence in the case and the probable reasons why Casey Anthony was found not guilty in the trial

- Differentiate between judicial evidence and extrajudicial evidence, as well as exculpatory evidence and inculpatory evidence

- Explain the various levels or standards of proof

- Compare direct evidence with indirect evidence and give an example of each

- Identify the various forms of circumstantial evidence

- Define testimonial evidence, real evidence, documentary evidence, and demonstrative evidence

- Discuss reasons for the hearsay rule and the exceptions to it

- Compare the role of lay witnesses with expert witnesses

- Provide examples of corpus delicti evidence, corroborative evidence, cumulative evidence, associative evidence, identification evidence, and behavioral evidence

From the CASE FILE
The Death of Caylee Anthony

On June 15, 2008, Casey Anthony, twenty-two, had a huge argument with her mother Cindy Anthony. Cindy discovered a photograph of Casey at a "no-clothes party" and was not happy about it. Cindy not only had concerns about the behavior of her daughter but also about the welfare of two-year-old Caylee, Casey's daughter and Cindy's granddaughter. Cindy told Casey she was unfit to be a parent and threatened to get custody of Caylee. Casey lived with her parents, Cindy and George, in Orlando, but for everyone involved, things were intolerable. The next day, June 16, Casey packed up and left the house with Caylee. She said they were going to Tampa and that she was going to get her old job back at Universal Studios. During the next thirty-one days, Cindy called Casey numerous times to see how Caylee was doing. Every time she called, Casey told her mother that Caylee was with the babysitter, Zenaida "Zanny" Fernandez-Gonzalez.

On July 13, 2008, Cindy and George received a letter in the mail informing them that Casey's car had been towed and was available for pickup at a particular tow lot. George went to get the car. In the car he found Casey's purse and Caylee's car seat and toys. Reportedly, he also noticed a strong odor coming from the trunk. Now Cindy was even more concerned. She eventually found Casey at her boyfriend's house and

brought her home. Casey explained to her mother that that she actually left Caylee with Fernandez-Gonzalez in Orlando on June 16 and that Gonzalez kidnapped Caylee. Casey told her mother that she had not seen Caylee since then.

On July 15, 2008, Cindy called the police to report Caylee was missing. Investigators questioned Casey. She told them a similar story to what she told her mother earlier: Caylee was kidnapped by her babysitter, Fernandez-Gonzalez. She told investigators that she left Caylee with the babysitter when she went to work at Universal Studios. She said that she did not tell the police about Caylee earlier because she was too afraid. Upon checking for a "Zenaida Fernandez-Gonzalez," investigators discovered that there was no such person. Casey had lied. After Casey showed investigators around the Universal Studios theme park, they discovered that she did not actually work there. She had worked there two years ago, but not recently. Another lie. Casey was arrested on July 16, 2008, for the neglect of a child, providing false statements in a criminal investigation, and obstruction of a criminal investigation. Investigators wondered what else she was lying about. She was released from jail on August 21 but was arrested and returned to jail on August 29 for check and credit card fraud.

Initially the investigation focused on trying to find Caylee, although investigators were not optimistic that they would find her alive. When Casey's car was examined, a cadaver dog alerted to decomposition in the trunk of the vehicle. Insects and maggots commonly associated with dead bodies were also found in the trunk. The examination also revealed a trace of chloroform in the trunk, and investigators recovered a hair that was microscopically similar to Caylee's hair (a sample of which was obtained from a hairbrush). Analyses revealed that the hair had certain characteristics that indicated that it came from a dead body. Computers in the Anthony house were seized and analyzed. On one of the computers the investigators found Google searches for the term *chloroform* made in March 2008. Upon checking the whereabouts and activities of Casey from June 16, 2008, to July 15, 2008, they did not find much except that on July 2, Casey got a tattoo that read "Bella Vita"—"beautiful life" in Italian.

On December 11, 2008, a meter reader found skeletonized human remains in a wooded area near the Anthony house; the remains were determined to be those of Caylee Anthony. Duct tape was found in the hair and around the skull. Investigators reasoned that Caylee died from suffocation as a result of the duct tape being placed over her nose and mouth. Duct tape that was the same as that found with Caylee was found in her grandparent's garage. A laundry bag that was the same type and brand as one found with Caylee's remains was found in the Anthony house. A

blanket that was recovered with Caylee's remains also matched Caylee's bedding at her grandparent's house.

In June 2011, three years after the disappearance of Caylee, the trial of Casey Anthony began. She was charged with first degree murder, aggravated child abuse, and aggravated manslaughter of a child. In a nutshell, the prosecution's theory was that Casey was a party girl and no longer wanted the responsibilities of being a parent. She used chloroform to incapacitate Caylee and then used duct tape to suffocate her. Her body was kept in the trunk of her vehicle. The Internet search for chloroform showed premeditation.

Casey's lawyers had a different explanation for the disappearance and death of Caylee, and they had alternative explanations for the prosecution's evidence. According to the defense, Caylee actually drowned in the family pool on June 16, 2008, and Casey's dad helped cover up the death so that Casey would not be charged with child neglect. Caylee's death was not the result of a murder; it was a tragic accident and then, unwisely, covered up to avoid police scrutiny. The attorneys further explained that Casey had an abusive childhood and was sexually abused by her father and her brother, so she got used to disguising and hiding her emotional pain. As for the evidence, through expert testimony the defense argued that odor analysis of the trunk was not scientific and was not accepted by the scientific community. A primary compound found in human decomposition was not present in the trunk. The guts of the maggots found in the trunk were not analyzed

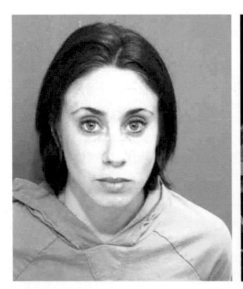

PHOTO 3.1–3.2: When she was being investigated as a suspect in the disappearance and death of her daughter, Casey Anthony provided several stories to investigators about her activities and the whereabouts of Caylee. These stories were shown to be false, and this, along with other evidence in the case, led many people to think Casey was responsible for Caylee's murder.

for DNA; therefore, it was not possible to determine what they had consumed, if human remains or other organic material, such as food or excrement. According to the defense, the source and reason for the presence of chloroform in the trunk was not adequately specified and did not prove anything. The hair in the trunk was presumed to be Caylee's, but this was not proven with certainty. Caylee's body was never in the trunk, it had nothing to do with her accidental death. The duct tape found on Caylee's skull was simply trash recovered with the body; it had no connection to or role in her death. The Google searches for chloroform were not conducted by Casey but by her mother who was actually searching for chlorophyll and then got sidetracked and searched for chloroform as well.

After thirty-three days of testimony, on July 5, 2011, the jury found Casey not guilty of first degree murder, child abuse, and aggravated manslaughter of a child. She was only found guilty of four counts of providing false information in a criminal investigation and check forgery. Casey did not testify at the trial.

Case Considerations and Points for Discussion

- Two fundamental questions are present in homicide investigations and trials: (1) Did a homicide occur? and (2) if a homicide occurred, did the suspect/defendant commit the homicide? What evidence in the Caylee Anthony investigation suggested that a homicide actually occurred? What evidence suggested that Casey Anthony committed the homicide?

- Since Casey Anthony was found not guilty of murder at trial, apparently the evidence in the case was unconvincing to the jury. Why? What other evidence may have helped to establish that Caylee was murdered and that Casey committed the murder?

- Many people think that Casey actually killed Caylee. What do you think? Was Casey found not guilty because she did not do it, or was she found not guilty for some other reason? Explain.

Also:

- See "Casey Anthony Trial: Police Tapes" on YouTube for additional details regarding the investigation and prosecution of Casey Anthony.

••• The Basics of Criminal Evidence

Broadly defined, criminal evidence is any crime-related information on which an investigator can base a decision or make a determination. It consists of supposed facts and knowledge that relate to a particular crime or perpetrator. Evidence is the product of investigative activities; investigative activities are performed to discover and collect evidence. In turn, evidence is used to establish proof that (1) a crime was committed and (2) that a particular person committed that crime.

A basic and fundamental distinction can be made between judicial evidence and extrajudicial evidence. Judicial evidence is evidence that is admissible in court and meets the rules of evidence. As such, it is often referred to as *admissible evidence*. In the Anthony case, the remains of Caylee, the hair recovered from the trunk of Casey's car, and the testimony of the computer forensic expert were all examples of judicial evidence.

Extrajudicial evidence is *any* information on which an investigative decision can be based but which is not allowed in court proceedings. It is often referred to as *inadmissible evidence*. An example of extrajudicial evidence may be the results of a polygraph examination taken by a suspect. It is certainly not unreasonable that investigators would consider the results of a polygraph examination when judging whether a particular person committed the crime in question. At the same time, however, this "evidence" would not be allowed by a judge to be introduced into court proceedings; it would not meet the rules of evidence. In this sense, such evidence can be quite useful, even though it may not be admissible in court.

Another basic but important distinction can be made between *exculpatory evidence* and *inculpatory evidence*. Exculpatory evidence is evidence that tends to exclude or eliminate someone from consideration as a suspect. If a witness described the perpetrator as being six feet tall and having black hair, that would tend to exclude a suspect who was five feet tall with blond hair. Inculpatory evidence is evidence that tends to include or incriminate a person as the perpetrator. For example, a lack of an alibi for a suspect may be inculpatory, as would a suspect's characteristics that matched the perpetrator's description. Through the course of an investigation, investigators will likely uncover both inculpatory and exculpatory evidence in relation to a particular suspect. It is a legal requirement that the police and prosecutor share not only the inculpatory evidence but also the exculpatory evidence with the defendant's attorney through the discovery process.

STANDARDS OF PROOF

Evidence is used to establish proof that a crime was committed or that a particular person committed that crime. To prove something (e.g., that Casey Anthony killed Caylee) is to eliminate uncertainty, or to eliminate some degree of uncertainty, regarding the truthfulness of the conclusion. Proof is not a one-dimensional phenomenon; there are various levels, or standards, of proof. For example, as discussed in more detail later, the police often need enough evidence to establish *probable cause* to justify a search or an arrest. Probable cause, then, is a standard of proof. Probable cause exists when it is more likely than not that a particular circumstance exists; generally speaking, the degree of certainty is greater than 50 percent. Probable cause is the standard of proof of most direct concern and relevance to investigators in solving crimes.

Another standard of proof is *beyond a reasonable doubt.* Proof beyond a reasonable doubt is needed in a trial to conclude that a defendant is guilty of the crime. With this level of proof, a jury (or a judge in a bench trial) may have a doubt about the defendant's guilt, but this doubt cannot be meaningful or significant. Beyond a reasonable doubt is the level of proof of most direct consequence to prosecutors, who have as their responsibility presenting evidence in court to obtain a conviction.

A third level of proof is *reasonable suspicion.* In order for police to legally stop and frisk a person, the police have to have a reasonable suspicion about that person's involvement in, or association with, a criminal act.

A fourth major level of proof is *preponderance of the evidence.* Preponderance of the evidence is the degree of certainty needed to prove and win a civil case. It is essentially the functional equivalent of probable cause but applies only to civil matters.

It is important to understand that all levels of proof are subjective in nature. The determination of what constitutes proof depends on the judgments of people. As a result, what constitutes probable cause for one judge may not constitute probable cause for another judge. One

TABLE 3.1	Standards of Proof in Criminal Matters

STANDARD	CRITICAL QUESTION	SITUATIONS OF RELEVANCE
Reasonable suspicion	Is there reason to believe that a particular circumstance exists?	To stop and frisk
Probable cause	Is it more likely than not that a particular circumstance exists?	To make an arrest To conduct a search
Beyond a reasonable doubt	Is the doubt about the defendant's guilt meaningful or significant?	To obtain a conviction

jury may find proof beyond a reasonable doubt, and another may find reasonable doubt. The weight and value of evidence in establishing proof is an individual determination.

●●● The Meaning and Nature of Probable Cause

Probable cause stems directly from the Fourth Amendment to the U.S. Constitution and constitutes a critical ingredient needed to justify a legal search, seizure, or arrest. In general, if probable cause does not exist to conduct a search or to make an arrest, any evidence collected as a result of that search is not admissible in court, nor is that arrest considered valid. Probable cause is critical indeed and, as such, is discussed in more detail here.

Probable cause exists when "the facts and circumstances within the officers' knowledge and of which they had reasonably trustworthy information are sufficient in themselves to warrant a man of reasonable caution in the belief that an offense has been or is being committed" (*Brinegar v. United States* [1949]). This is known as the "man of reasonable caution" or the "reasonable person" standard. In *United States v. Ortiz* (1975) the court ruled that police officers could legitimately draw on their experience and training in determining whether probable cause existed in a particular situation. As a result, what may look like innocent activity to the "reasonable person" may indeed be sufficient to establish probable cause for a police officer.

In *Aguilar v. Texas* (1964), the court established a two-pronged test to determine probable cause when information is given to the police by an informant. The two prongs were (1) the reliability of the informant and (2) the reliability of the informant's information. This is particularly relevant when the police obtain information from a person who has been engaged in criminal activity and has low credibility. The Aguilar two-pronged test was abandoned with *Illinois v. Gates* (1983) when the court ruled that the "totality of the circumstances" must be considered in establishing probable cause. So, with specific reference to this case, not only should the informant's tip be considered in determining probable cause, so too should the corroborating information from other independent police sources.

As a practical matter, establishing probable cause can be viewed as a process by which some evidence can lead to other evidence, which can lead to still more evidence. The accumulation of this evidence may eventually provide a basis on which probable cause can be established. Consider the case of the kidnapping and murder of seven-year-old Danielle van Dam in San Diego (see Case in Point 3.1).

●●● Types of Evidence

Various types of evidence can be used to establish proof. All evidence can be classified as being either direct or indirect, and all evidence can be classified as either testimonial, real, demonstrative, or documentary. Each type of evidence is discussed next.

DIRECT VERSUS INDIRECT EVIDENCE

Direct evidence refers to crime-related information that immediately demonstrates the existence of a fact in question. As such, no inferences or presumptions are needed to draw the associated conclusion. On the other hand, *indirect evidence,* which is also known as *circumstantial evidence,* consists of crime-related information in which inferences and

CASE in POINT 3.1

The Murder of Danielle van Dam and the Arrest of David Westerfield

During the early morning hours of February 2, 2002, a sleeping Danielle van Dam was taken from her home by David Westerfield, fifty, a neighbor of the van Dams. Upon being notified of the missing girl, the police, using police dogs, launched a massive door-to-door search of more than 200 homes in the neighborhood and interviewed all the residents. Reportedly, Westerfield was the only neighbor the police were unable to contact because he was not at home.

Westerfield returned home on February 4 and was then questioned by the police. He told the police that at about 3:30 a.m. on February 2 he began a 550-mile motor home trip to various places in and around San Diego and Imperial counties. The nature and timing of this trip was suspicious to the police. Police also found it unusual that a garden hose used to equip his motor home with water that was in front of his house appeared hastily placed there, as though he had been in a hurry before he left, but everything else appeared to be in perfect order. When checking his story about this trip, the police discovered that Westerfield got stuck in the sand in the desert and had to call a tow truck to get him out. According to the tow truck driver, Westerfield was in such a hurry to leave after getting pulled out of the sand that he left some of his equipment behind. The more investigators heard, the more suspicious they became. The police asked Westerfield to take a polygraph examination. He agreed but reportedly failed it, raising additional suspicions about his involvement in the disappearance of the little girl. All this information was used by the police to establish probable cause to justify a search warrant for Westerfield's property. In conducting the search, the police seized his sport utility vehicle, boxes of personal property, several computers (some of which contained images of child pornography), and his motor home. When investigators examined Westerfield's motor home, they found blood that matched Danielle's, along with her fingerprints and hair. Blood on Westerfield's jacket recovered from a dry cleaner also matched Danielle's (Dillon and Perez 2002; Roth 2002a; Roth 2002b). Based on all this evidence, probable cause was established to justify an arrest warrant for kidnapping and possession of child pornography. While in custody, Westerfield was charged with homicide after the decomposed body of the missing girl was found along a roadside west of San Diego. In August 2002, David Westerfield was found guilty of kidnapping, murder, and possession of child pornography and was sentenced to death. He is now on death row at San Quentin State Prison.

probabilities *are* needed to draw an associated conclusion. Of course, from an investigator's perspective, the ultimate conclusions that need to be drawn are that a crime occurred and that the suspect committed the crime; however, there may be other conclusions that would be useful to establish as well. In determining whether evidence is direct or circumstantial in nature, one needs to consider the conclusion that is trying to be established. For example, in the Caylee Anthony case, a hair that was microscopically similar to Caylee's hair was recovered from the trunk of Casey's car, and the trunk had an odor of human decomposition. These two pieces of evidence are best considered circumstantial evidence that Caylee's dead body was in the trunk of that car (because her hair was in the trunk does not necessarily mean that her dead body was in the trunk) and, further, that Casey killed Caylee (because the trunk smelled of decomposition does not necessarily mean that it was Caylee's dead body that produced that smell, nor does it mean that Casey killed Caylee). If a witness saw Casey kill Caylee, that information would be direct evidence that Casey killed the victim because no inferences would be needed to draw the conclusion.

Consider a case in which a knife, identified as the likely murder weapon, has the suspect's fingerprints on it. Are the fingerprints direct evidence or circumstantial evidence? Again, it depends on the conclusion trying to be established. The fingerprints on the knife would be best considered direct evidence that the suspect touched or held the knife but circumstantial evidence that the suspect murdered the victim with the knife.

MYTHS & MISCONCEPTIONS 3.1

Circumstantial Evidence Is Not Very Useful

Circumstantial evidence is often viewed as less valuable than direct evidence in establishing proof. It has been said that one cannot be convicted of a crime based on circumstantial evidence alone. This is just not true. Sometimes reference is made to a case that is "just" circumstantial. In fact, circumstantial evidence can be quite powerful in establishing proof—perhaps even more influential than direct evidence, especially if there is much circumstantial evidence that can be presented. No question, a person can be convicted of a crime based only on circumstantial evidence. See Case in Point 3.2 for an example of a case where circumstantial evidence played a critical role in an investigation.

It is important to understand that the distinction between direct and indirect evidence depends entirely on the need for inferences to draw the associated conclusion; it does not depend on the likelihood that the evidence is valid. For example, a statement from an eyewitness that she saw the suspect shoot the victim is best considered direct evidence that the suspect shot the victim, regardless of the possibility that the eyewitness is mistaken. The possibility that the eyewitness identification is wrong does not make the eyewitness identification circumstantial evidence.

There are many different types of circumstantial evidence. First, one's physical ability to commit the crime can be introduced as circumstantial evidence of guilt or innocence. For example, consider the trial of O. J. Simpson for the murder of his ex-wife, Nicole Brown Simpson, and her friend Ron Goldman. On June 12, 1994, at approximately 11:00 p.m., the two victims were found slashed and stabbed to death on the front walkway of Nicole's home in Brentwood, a wealthy section of Los Angeles. As there was substantial physical evidence associating Simpson with the homicides (see the introduction to Chapter 5 for a detailed discussion of the investigation), he was arrested and charged with the crimes. During the trial, the prosecution provided evidence to the jury about the nature of the crime and the nature of the wounds inflicted on the victims. In turn, the defense provided testimony about the poor physical condition of Simpson, which had resulted from the effects of arthritis caused by a career of playing professional football. The defense argued that whoever committed these homicides had to be of superior physical strength and abilities, and, as a result, it could not have been Simpson. The prosecution countered this testimony by introducing a recently produced commercial exercise video showing a physically capable Simpson engaged in an aerobic exercise routine. With this evidence, the prosecution argued that Simpson was capable of committing the crime, thereby allowing one to *infer* that he committed the crime.

Second, an alibi, or the lack of an alibi, may be best considered circumstantial evidence. An alibi is a claim on the part of a suspect that he or she was somewhere other than at the crime scene at the time of the crime. The primary issue associated with an alibi as evidence is its believability. Because alibis are often established by friends of the suspect or by the suspect's own account (e.g., "I was home in bed by myself"), they are often not believed by investigators or jurors. The lack of an alibi or an alibi that is not believable may be used to infer that the suspect committed the crime. From the suspect's perspective, one of the problems with alibis is that they are often inherently difficult to convincingly prove (Olson and Wells 2004). Consider the case of Steven Avery, who was wrongfully convicted of sexual assault in 1986 and spent eighteen years in prison before he was cleared of the crime through DNA analysis. Avery had sixteen witnesses (including friends, family, and clerks at a store) that corroborated his alibi, but the jurors did not believe them. They believed the

CASE *in* POINT 3.2

The Value of Circumstantial Evidence in the Murder Investigation of Laci Peterson

On December 24, 2002, a pregnant Laci Peterson was reported missing by her husband, Scott. Four months later, Scott was arrested and charged with the murder of his wife and their unborn baby. He was convicted and sentenced to death. The prosecution of Scott Peterson rested entirely on circumstantial evidence—a lot of it. Specifically:

- Approximately one month after Laci was reported missing, a woman came forward and reported to the police that she and Scott Peterson were dating. She did not realize while they were dating that Scott was married. She told the police that two weeks prior to Laci's disappearance, Scott told her that he had "lost" his wife and that he would be spending Christmas without her.

- Scott's alibi for the time that Laci went missing (Christmas Eve) was that he was fishing on his boat in San Francisco Bay. On April 14, 2003, a fetus was found on the shoreline of San Francisco Bay. The next day a partial female torso washed ashore in the same area. These were the bodies of Laci and her unborn child.

- Investigators discovered a hair of Laci's in a pair of pliers that belonged to Scott. The pliers were kept on his boat.

- Two days after Laci's disappearance, Scott had installed two pornographic television stations on his television.

- Shortly after Laci's disappearance, Scott sold her vehicle, and he wanted to sell the house they lived in.

- Just prior to his arrest, Scott drastically changed his appearance by bleaching his hair and growing a goatee. When he was arrested, he was in possession of numerous items, including $15,000 in cash, several cell phones, multiple credits cards belonging to family members, his brother's driver's license, and camping gear.

While any one of these "circumstances" could possibly have been explained, all of them together represented powerful evidence of his guilt. Scott Peterson remains on death row in the San Quentin prison. If you were Scott Peterson's defense attorney, how would you explain the existence of this circumstantial (and inculpatory) evidence?

PHOTO 3.3: Even before the bodies of Laci and her unborn child were found, investigators believed that Scott had potentially disposed of Laci in San Francisco Bay, where he said he had been fishing the day she disappeared. Here divers search for Laci's body.

victim who (incorrectly) identified Avery as the attacker. The Avery case is not unique. In many wrongful conviction cases, alibis are presented but not believed.

Third, MO, or the method in which the crime was committed, may be introduced as circumstantial evidence. In particular, if a series of crimes are committed in a particular manner, and a defendant has been linked to one of these crimes through other evidence, one could infer that the defendant committed the other, similar crimes as well. The reasonableness of the inference may depend strongly on the uniqueness of the MO. For example, if a series of burglaries took place in early afternoons in which entry was gained into the houses by breaking a window and only jewelry was taken, this might allow investigators to infer that whoever committed one of the crimes also committed the others.

Fourth, the existence of an identifiable motive (or lack thereof) may represent circumstantial evidence of guilt or innocence. Motive—a reason why the crime was committed—is an important dimension of identifying a perpetrator. If a motive such as anger, revenge, greed, or jealousy on the part of the perpetrator can be established, one may infer that the defendant committed the crime. It was suggested by the prosecutors in the Casey Anthony trial that Casey killed her daughter because she was not interested in having the responsibilities of being a mom. During the trial of Scott Peterson, his affair, his increasing debt, and Laci's life insurance policy were presented by prosecutors as evidence of motive for the murder of his wife.

Fifth, evidence concerning an individual's attempts to avoid apprehension after the crime occurred can be used to infer guilt. For example, that Scott Peterson changed his appearance and had items with him that suggested he was about to flee was presented as circumstantial evidence of his guilt. Similarly, there was a belief that Casey Anthony also attempted to elude the police prior to her arrest, although she claimed she was simply trying to flee from the media, not the police.

Sixth, if an individual is found to be in possession of the fruits of the crime, this evidence could be used to infer that that person is guilty of the crime. For example, if a person is found in possession of a cell phone that was taken in a robbery, it might (but does not necessarily) indicate that person committed the robbery. Of course, that person could have come into possession of the cell phone in some other way other than being the one who actually took it. If chloroform had been found in the possession of Casey Anthony, it would have been powerful circumstantial evidence that she killed her daughter.

Seventh, the existence of prior threats made by the suspect or similar prior behaviors of the suspect may be introduced as circumstantial evidence of that suspect's guilt in the crime. If Casey Anthony had previously done harm to her daughter, it would have been powerful circumstantial evidence that she killed her daughter.

Finally, character witnesses can be introduced to help establish the innocence of the defendant. Character witnesses are used by the defense to bring evidence to court that the defendant is incapable of committing a crime like the one in question.

••• Testimonial versus Real versus Demonstrative versus Documentary Evidence

Just as all evidence can be considered either direct or indirect, all evidence can be classified as either testimonial, real, demonstrative, or documentary. Each is discussed next.

TESTIMONIAL EVIDENCE

Testimonial evidence is evidence that is presented in court through witnesses speaking under oath when those witnesses would be committing perjury if they did not state what they believed to be the truth. Testimonial evidence often begins as statements made to the

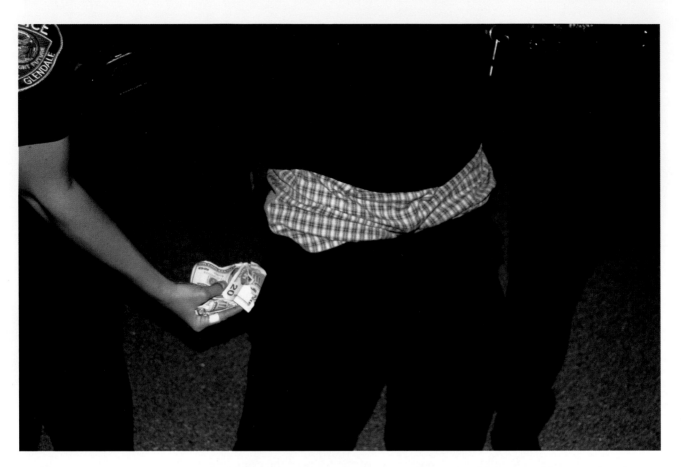

PHOTO 3.4: If a subject is apprehended with a pocket full of cash near a gas station that was just robbed, this means there is circumstantial evidence that the subject committed the crime.

police. Witnesses can be considered either lay witnesses or expert witnesses. Lay witnesses are individuals whose testimony is limited to the facts as personally observed. In some situations, lay witnesses may also offer judgments as they relate to the particular case at hand (e.g., "In my best judgment, the person I saw running through my backyard was about six feet tall").

Expert witnesses are persons who possess special knowledge about a particular issue or phenomenon under examination (e.g., post-traumatic stress disorder, DNA analysis, the characteristics of the odor of decomposition). Expert witnesses often hold academic or scientific positions and conduct research on the issue at hand. They are able to express their opinions about the issue in court and speak about hypothetical cases. Ideally, the function of expert witnesses is to help the jury or judge understand the complex issue under consideration—to basically educate the jury.

Associated with the admissibility of expert testimony are the Frye and Daubert standards. Briefly, the Frye standard holds that in order for the results of a scientific technique (and corresponding testimony) to be admissible, it must have gained general acceptance in its particular field. With the Daubert standard, the trial judge must screen the scientific evidence and testimony to ensure that it is relevant and reliable. In the Caylee Anthony investigation, the odor analysis presented by the prosecution was questioned on this basis. The meaning and implications of the Frye and Daubert standards are discussed in more detail in Chapter 4.

One form of testimonial evidence is *hearsay*. Hearsay is "an oral or written assertion . . . made or carried on by someone other than a witness who is testifying at a trial or hearing, which is offered in evidence to establish the truth of the matter asserted" (Waltz 1997,

p. 73). In other words, when someone repeats information that someone else said, it is hearsay. Hearsay is most often excluded from consideration in court proceedings because it is considered unreliable. The serious concerns about the reliability of hearsay are that (1) the person who made the original statement was not under oath and therefore was not obligated to tell the truth and (2) the person who originally made the statement cannot be cross-examined to test his or her perception, memory, veracity, and ability to be articulate (Waltz 1997). Simply stated, "Criminal cases cannot be made on gossip and secondhand accounts of what happened" (Waltz 1997, p. 82). To avoid the complications of hearsay, investigators need to get information "from the horse's mouth." For example, suppose a lawyer has a witness who has critical information about the crime, but this witness would not likely leave a favorable impression on the jury and probably would not be believed by the jury. The witness is sloppy, not very articulate, and is of questionable mental competence. Without the hearsay rule that excludes most hearsay evidence, the lawyer could have this witness meet with another individual who would have a much more favorable impression on a jury. This witness is bright, articulate, and attractive. The sloppy witness could tell the articulate witness the relevant points of the testimony and then the lawyer could call the articulate witness to testify. Obviously, this hearsay testimony could raise all sorts of questions about fairness and the discovery of the "truth" (Waltz 1997).

As with just about every legal rule, there are exceptions to the hearsay rule. There are instances when hearsay is admissible as testimony in court. For example, previously recorded testimony that was provided under oath and was subject to cross-examination is admissible as hearsay as long as the witness is no longer available. Under certain conditions, dying declarations of a victim may be admissible in court through hearsay. A defendant's previous admission and confession can be admitted into court as hearsay. An admission involves acknowledging some aspect of involvement in the crime (e.g., "I was at the gas station at about midnight"), whereas a confession involves acknowledging the actual involvement in the crime (e.g., "I robbed the gas station at about midnight"). Given a defendant's right to remain silent, the only way a defendant's statements may be presented in court is through hearsay, unless the defendant chooses to testify. Further, a claim on the part of a defendant that the statements were not subject to cross-examination would be strange.

Statements that relate to a witness's state of mind may be admissible as hearsay evidence as long as there is a question at hand about the person's state of mind at a particular time and the statements made were made in an apparently sincere manner. Excited utterances or spontaneous exclamations may be admissible as hearsay. Finally, statements regarding one's physical condition are often admitted as hearsay evidence. For example, a defendant's statement "I am so drunk" could be admitted through hearsay to refute a defendant's current claim that he or she was totally sober at the time of the crime and had a crystal-clear memory of the incident. There are several other, rarely encountered exceptions to the hearsay rule that are not discussed here. For an additional discussion of this issue, see Waltz (1997). See Case in Point 3.3 for an example of unusual hearsay evidence that played a critical role at trial.

REAL EVIDENCE

Real evidence is also known as *physical evidence, scientific evidence,* or *forensic evidence.* Real evidence refers to tangible objects that can be held or seen and that are produced as a direct result of the commission of a crime. Examples of real evidence would include blood splatters on a wall, semen recovered from a victim, and the knife used to kill a victim. In the Caylee Anthony case, the duct tape recovered from Caylee's remains was real evidence. In the Peterson trial, the hair found in the pliers was real evidence. All real evidence that is introduced in court must be accompanied by testimony that demonstrates that the evidence complies with the rules of evidence.

CASE in POINT 3.3 — A Homicide Victim's Letter to the Police

A husband was accused of killing his wife by poisoning her. She had suspected that he was going to kill her, and, as a result, she wrote a letter to a detective at the local police department. She then gave the letter to her neighbor with instructions to give it to the detective if she were to die. She wrote the letter on November 21; she was found dead in her home on December 3. The letter was admitted at trial as evidence as an exception to the hearsay rule. The letter read as follows:

Pleasant Prairie Police Department, Ron Kosman or Detective Ratzenburg—

I took this picture + am writing this on Saturday 11–21–98 at 7am. This "list" was in my husband's business daily planner—not meant for me to see. I don't know what it means, but if anything happens to me, he would be my first suspect. Our relationship has deteriorated to the polite superficial. I know he's never forgiven me for the brief affair I had with that creep seven years ago. Mark lives for work + the kids; he's an avid surfer of the Internet.

Anyway—I do not smoke or drink. My mother was an alcoholic, so I limit my drinking to one or two a week. Mark wants me to drink more with him in the evenings. I don't. I would never take my life because of my kids—they are everything to me! I regularly take Tylenol + multi-vitamins; occassionally [sic] take OTC stuff for colds; Zantac, or Immodium; have one prescription for migraine tablets, which more use more than I.

I pray I'm wrong + nothing happens . . . but I am suspicious of Mark's suspicious behaviors + fear for my early demise. However I will not leave [my two sons]. My life's greatest love, accomplishment and wish: My 3 D's—Daddy (Mark), [deleted] + [deleted].

Julie C. Jensen

DEMONSTRATIVE EVIDENCE

Demonstrative evidence refers to tangible objects produced indirectly from the crime that relate to the crime or the perpetrator. For example, diagrams or videos of the crime scene may be produced by investigators for evidentiary reasons and may be used in court, photographs of the victims (or victims' injuries) may be produced as a result of the crime and used in court, and radiographs showing injuries to the victim may be produced for medical reasons and introduced in court. Photographs, videos, diagrams, and medical records are all common forms of demonstrative evidence.

DOCUMENTARY EVIDENCE

As the name suggests, documentary evidence refers to any evidence that is in the form of a document or to evidence that documents some issue related to the crime. Included would be printed e-mails relating to the crime (e.g., in a conspiracy investigation), bank statements (e.g., in an embezzlement investigation), surveillance video relating to the crime (e.g., in a bank robbery investigation), or any other documents relating to the crime. The evidentiary value of documentary evidence is limited to the content of the document. For example, if a book is introduced as evidence because of the fingerprints on that book, the book (and fingerprints) would be best considered real, not documentary, evidence. However, if the book is introduced because of what the suspect wrote in the book, the book would best be considered documentary evidence.

Sometimes the lines are blurred between testimonial evidence, documentary evidence, real evidence, and demonstrative evidence. For instance, in Case in Point 3.3, the actual letter written by the decedent would be best considered documentary evidence, but what was said

PHOTO 3.5: Crime scene photos are best considered demonstrative evidence. The photograph here shows the inside of the garage shed at the home of Casey Anthony's parents. Duct tape that was found with Caylee's body was the same brand as the duct tape found on the gas can in the shed.

in the letter would best be considered testimonial evidence (hearsay). If there was a question about whether the victim actually wrote the letter, the handwriting would best be considered forensic (real) evidence. A video that captured a crime as it occurred would best be considered documentary evidence because the video was produced as a direct result of the crime. A crime scene sketch would be demonstrative evidence, not documentary evidence, because that evidence was produced only indirectly as a result of the crime, and only after the crime occurred.

●●● The Functions of Evidence

Evidence, be it testimonial, real, demonstrative, documentary, circumstantial, or direct, may serve various purposes or functions in establishing proof. In this sense, evidence can be classified as corpus delicti evidence, corroborative evidence, cumulative evidence, associative evidence, identification evidence, or behavioral evidence.

CORPUS DELICTI EVIDENCE

Corpus delicti evidence refers to evidence that establishes that a crime actually occurred. For example, a dead body with knife in its back is best considered corpus delicti evidence that a homicide occurred. The presence of semen recovered from a victim *may* help establish that a rape occurred (of course, the presence of semen does not always prove that a rape occurred, just as the absence of semen does not prove that a rape did not occur). A victim's statement that property is missing from his or her house and that no one had permission to take it establishes that a burglary occurred. In such cases, the dead body, the semen, and the victim's statement constitute corpus delicti evidence.

CORROBORATIVE EVIDENCE

Corroborative evidence is evidence that is supplementary to the evidence already available and which strengthens or confirms that available evidence. For example, a male suspect is apprehended near a burglary scene and his fingerprints are collected from the scene. The fingerprints would corroborate the statements of a witness who saw the suspect running from the house with a television.

CUMULATIVE EVIDENCE

Cumulative evidence is evidence that duplicates but does not necessarily strengthen already existing evidence. For example, cumulative evidence would be when investigators find five witnesses (as opposed to just one) who can provide the same details about the same incident.

ASSOCIATIVE EVIDENCE

Associative evidence is evidence that can be used to make links between crimes, crime scenes, victims, suspects, and tools or instruments. Evidence may also prove to be dissociative, showing a lack of association between crime scenes, victims, and so forth. Most evidence in criminal investigations is used to establish associations. For example, in the Anthony case, Caylee's dead body was associated with Casey via the odor of the trunk of her car and the hair found in the trunk of the car. Caylee's remains were associated with the grandparents' house (and by implication Casey) as a result of the duct tape found with the remains and the duct tape found in the garage.

IDENTIFICATION EVIDENCE

Evidence that leads to the identification of the perpetrator is considered *identification evidence*. Fingerprints most commonly serve this purpose. Fingerprints may be recovered from a crime scene and, through the use of an automated computerized search, the perpetrator may be identified. Dental evidence and DNA can also be used to make identifications, usually of dead bodies. The skeletonized remains of Caylee Anthony were identified through DNA analysis, as were the remains of Laci Peterson and her unborn baby.

BEHAVIORAL EVIDENCE

Behavioral evidence provides a basis on which to identify the type of person who may be responsible for a particular crime and considers directly the nature of the crime and how it was committed. Behavioral evidence constitutes the building blocks on which a psychological or geographical profile may be built or on which linguistic analysis may be conducted. Behavioral evidence and psychological profiles are discussed most often in relation to serial crimes—particularly homicides, rapes, and, to a lesser extent, arson. However, such evidence may be available in other crimes as well. For example, in a burglary, what could be inferred from the fact that the only property missing from a residence was an Xbox? This evidence might suggest that whoever broke into the house knew that the game was there (perhaps a neighbor or a friend). It might also suggest that the culprit was a teenager or young adult and that he was probably male.

In an apparent sexually motivated serial homicide (most serial homicides are sexually motivated to some identifiable degree), the behavioral evidence may be more elaborate. Experts sometimes differentiate between MO (modus operandi) and the signature of the criminal (Douglas 2000); both represent behavioral evidence. The MO refers to the mechanics of the crime—the circumstances of the crime and manner in which it was committed. *Signature* refers to that part of the crime that provides emotional satisfaction to the perpetrator. This and other types of behavioral evidence are discussed in more detail in Chapter 8.

MAIN POINTS

1. Criminal evidence is any crime-related information on which an investigator can base a decision or make a determination. Evidence is used to establish proof that (1) a crime was committed and (2) that a particular person committed that crime.

2. Judicial evidence is evidence that is admissible in court and meets the rules of evidence; it is often referred to as admissible evidence. Extrajudicial evidence is *any* information on which an investigative decision can be based but is not allowed in court proceedings; it is often referred to as inadmissible evidence.

3. Exculpatory evidence is evidence that tends to exclude or eliminate someone from consideration as a suspect. Inculpatory evidence is evidence that tends to include or incriminate a person as the perpetrator.

4. Probable cause exists when it is more likely than not that a particular circumstance exists. Probable cause is the standard of proof of most direct relevance to investigators in solving crimes, especially when conducting searches and making arrests. Beyond a reasonable doubt is the standard of proof needed in a trial to conclude that a defendant is guilty of the crime. In order for police to legally stop and frisk an individual, the police have to have a reasonable suspicion about that person's involvement in, or association with, a criminal act.

5. Direct evidence refers to crime-related information that immediately demonstrates the existence of a fact in question. As such, no inferences or presumptions are needed to draw the associated conclusion. On the other hand, indirect evidence, which is also known as circumstantial evidence, consists of crime-related information in which inferences and probabilities *are* needed to draw an associated conclusion.

6. Testimonial evidence is evidence that is presented in court through witnesses speaking under oath. Testimonial evidence often begins as statements made to the police.

7. Lay witnesses are individuals whose testimony is limited to the facts as personally observed. Expert witnesses are persons who possess special knowledge about a particular issue or phenomenon under examination. Expert witnesses are able to express their opinions about the issue in court and speak about hypothetical cases.

8. When someone repeats information that someone else said, it is hearsay. Hearsay is most often excluded from consideration in court proceedings because it is considered unreliable, although there are several exceptions to the hearsay rule.

9. Real evidence is also known as physical evidence, scientific evidence, or forensic evidence. Real evidence refers to tangible objects that can be held or seen and that are produced as a direct result of the commission of the crime. Demonstrative evidence refers to tangible objects that relate to the crime or the perpetrator and that are produced indirectly from the crime. Documentary evidence refers to any evidence that is in the form of a

document or to evidence that documents some issue directly related to the crime.

10. Corpus delicti evidence refers to evidence that establishes that a crime actually occurred. Corroborative evidence is evidence that is supplementary to the evidence already available and that strengthens or confirms it. Cumulative evidence is evidence that duplicates but does not necessarily strengthen already existing evidence. Associative evidence is evidence that can be used

to make links between crimes, crime scenes, victims, suspects, and tools or instruments. Evidence may also prove to be dissociative, showing a lack of association between crime scenes, victims, and so forth. Evidence that can be used to identify a perpetrator is considered identification evidence. Behavioral evidence provides a basis on which to identify the type of person who may be responsible for a particular crime and considers directly the nature of the crime and how it was committed.

IMPORTANT TERMS

Admissible evidence	Direct evidence	Indirect/circumstantial evidence
Associative evidence	Documentary evidence	Lay witness
Behavioral evidence	Judicial evidence	Preponderance of the evidence
Beyond a reasonable doubt	Exculpatory evidence	Probable cause
Corpus delicti evidence	Expert witness	Proof
Corroborative evidence	Extrajudicial evidence	Real evidence
Criminal evidence	Hearsay evidence	Reasonable suspicion
Cumulative evidence	Identification evidence	Standards of proof
Demonstrative evidence	Inculpatory evidence	Testimonial evidence

QUESTIONS FOR DISCUSSION AND REVIEW

1. What is the difference between judicial evidence and extrajudicial evidence?

2. What is the difference between exculpatory evidence and inculpatory evidence?

3. What is *proof*? What are the various levels or standards of proof?

4. What is the difference between direct evidence and indirect evidence? Is one type of evidence more useful than the other? What are various types of circumstantial evidence?

5. What are the differences between testimonial evidence, real evidence, documentary evidence, and demonstrative evidence?

6. What is hearsay? What is the hearsay rule? What are the major exceptions to the hearsay rule?

7. What are lay witnesses and expert witnesses? What is the role of each in court?

8. What are corpus delicti evidence, corroborative evidence, cumulative evidence, associative evidence, identification evidence, and behavioral evidence?

▶ STUDENT STUDY SITE

Visit **www.sagepub.com/brandl3e** to access additional study tools including eFlashcards, web quizzes, web resources, video resources, and SAGE journal articles.

4

The Law and Criminal Investigations

After reading this chapter you will be able to

- Discuss the qualities that evidence must have in order for it to be admissible in court

- Explain the chain of custody, its purpose, and why it is important

- Discuss the role of arrest warrants and search warrants in the criminal investigation process

- Differentiate between a frisk and a search incident to arrest

- Discuss the purpose of the exclusionary rule and explain the exceptions to it

- Evaluate the impact of the exclusionary rule on criminal investigations and the criminal justice process

- Identify the ways that the police may attempt to "get around" the 4th Amendment

- Define "interrogation" from the perspective of the 5th Amendment

- Identify the "Miranda warnings" and describe circumstances under which the police must notify suspects of their Miranda rights

- Discuss the impact of the Miranda decision on criminal investigations and the criminal justice process

From the **CASE FILE**
Ernesto Miranda's Confession

Miranda v. Arizona (1966) is perhaps the most well-known U.S. Supreme Court case ever decided. If a person knows of *any* Supreme Court case, this is probably it. It is also the case that is most applicable in law enforcement; in just about every investigation where a suspect is identified, Miranda applies. However, despite being so well known and frequently used, it is often misunderstood. For instance, as discussed in this chapter and also in Chapter 7, Miranda rights do not always allow a subject to remain silent when asked questions by the police. Sometimes they do, sometimes they don't. The Miranda decision was also extremely controversial, although it is considered less so now than in the years immediately after it was rendered. When Miranda requirements were first instituted, the police thought that suspects were never again going to confess to the crimes they committed. The police and many law-abiding citizens believed that the Supreme Court went too far in its protection of criminals' rights. Most incredibly, there were calls for the impeachment of the Supreme Court justices who were in favor of the law; it is difficult to identify another case where that happened. Given the prominence of the Miranda decision in the conduct of criminal investigations, it is interesting to consider more closely the details of the investigation that gave rise to the Mirada warnings.

In the early morning hours of March 3, 1963, in Phoenix, Arizona, eighteen-year-old Kathy Midare (not her real name) was on her way home after working the evening shift at a local movie theater. It was about 12:10 a.m. when she got off the bus to walk the remaining short distance to her home in the northeast section of the city. As Kathy was walking down the sidewalk, a car stopped about a block in front of her and a man got out of the car and walked toward her. The man grabbed Kathy, put his hand over her mouth, and dragged her to his car. Once in the backseat of the car, the man tied her hands behind her back and then tied her ankles. He drove for about twenty minutes to the desert and then raped her in the back seat of the vehicle. He took $4 from her then drove her back to the city and let her out of his car a half mile from her house. He then drove off.

The police were notified of the incident by Kathy's sister, who was home when Kathy arrived. Kathy told the police that the man appeared to be in his late twenties, was Mexican, had a scant mustache, was about six feet tall, and weighed about 175 pounds. He had short, black, curly hair and was wearing blue jeans, a white shirt, and glasses. She described the car as either a Ford or a Chevy and said that it was light green with brown upholstery. She noted that in the car there was a loop of rope hanging from the back of the front seat. Police initially had concerns about the truthfulness of the often confusing and conflicting statement provided by Kathy, but these concerns were lessened when they learned from her family that Kathy was mentally disabled and possessed the intelligence of a twelve- or thirteen-year-old. Nevertheless, the police administered a polygraph to Kathy to verify the truthfulness of her statements; the results of the polygraph were inconclusive.

On March 11, as the police were looking for the man who attacked Kathy, her brother-in-law notified the police that two days earlier, when he was giving Kathy a ride home, they saw a green car in the neighborhood that Kathy said looked like the one driven by the attacker. He told the police that the license plate number of the vehicle was DLF-312 and the make of the vehicle was a Packard. The police determined that the license plate number DLF-312 was registered to an Oldsmobile that could not have been the vehicle involved. On searching further, they discovered that license plate DLF-317 was registered to a green Packard, and the owner was a woman named Twila N. Hoffman who lived in Phoenix. When checking the address of the woman, it was learned that she and her live-in boyfriend had just recently moved out of the house. On March 13, the police tracked down the woman at her new address and found the green Packard in the driveway. In looking inside the car, an officer saw a loop of rope hanging from the back of the front seat, just as described by Kathy.

The police found Ernesto Miranda asleep in the house. Miranda was twenty-three years old and, it was quickly learned, had a long history of delinquent and criminal behavior. The police arrested Miranda, transported him to police headquarters, and placed him in a lineup with three other Mexican Americans to be viewed by the victim. Although Kathy thought that Miranda had similar features and a similar build as her attacker, she could not positively identify him as the perpetrator. In the interrogation room, police told Ernesto that he had been identified by the victim. After two hours of questioning, he confessed to the kidnapping and rape of Kathy Midare as well as two other recent crimes—a robbery of a woman and an attempted rape of another young woman. Police then provided a sheet of paper to Miranda on which to provide a handwritten confession. The following disclaimer was at the top of the paper: "I, (Ernesto A. Miranda), do hereby swear that I make this statement voluntarily and of my own free will, with no threats, coercion, or promises of immunity, and with full knowledge of my legal rights, understanding that any statement may be used against me" (Thomas

1998). The confession provided by Miranda was similar to the account provided by his victim.

At the trial, which took place June 20, 1963, the prosecutor presented Miranda's written confession, along with testimony from the victim, her sister, and the two police officers who found and questioned Miranda. The defense did not present any witnesses or evidence. The confession was admitted in court despite the objections of Miranda's court-appointed attorney, who argued to the judge that the confession was coerced and therefore inadmissible. The judge ruled that the case of *Gideon v. Wainwright* (1963) offered the benefit of defense counsel at trial, not upon arrest, and therefore that the confession was legally obtained and admissible. The jury found Miranda guilty of rape and kidnapping, and he was subsequently sentenced to a term of twenty to thirty years in prison.

Miranda's attorney appealed the conviction to the Arizona Supreme Court with the argument that the confession was not voluntarily offered. Meanwhile, during this time and while Miranda was serving his sentence in prison, the U.S. Supreme Court ruled in the case of *Escobedo v. Illinois* (1964). In this case, the court held that defendants have the right to an attorney at the interrogation stage of criminal proceedings. However, because Miranda had not requested an attorney at the time he was questioned by the police, the Arizona Supreme Court ruled that the Escobedo decision did not apply to Miranda. The court upheld the conviction.

In June 1965, a request for review of the case by the U.S. Supreme Court was made by Miranda's new defense counsel, attorneys who were hired by the American Civil Liberties Union but who worked pro bono. In writing the appeal, the attorneys framed the legal issue of the case as being whether a suspect needs to be explicitly informed of his or her right to counsel by the police or if suspects should simply know those rights without being advised of them. Arguments were made in front of the U.S. Supreme Court for three days beginning February 28, 1966. The court issued its decision on June 13, 1966. Chief Justice Earl Warren wrote the sixty-page opinion for the five-member majority. The court held that

> the prosecution may not use statements, whether exculpatory or inculpatory, stemming from questioning initiated by law enforcement officers after a person has been taken into custody or otherwise deprived of his freedom of action in any significant way, unless it

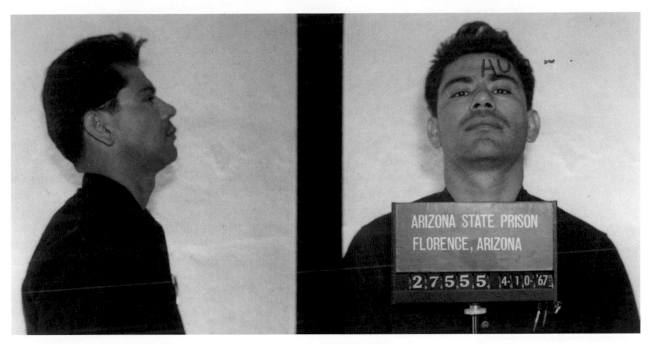

PHOTO 4.1: Ernesto Miranda, the man responsible for the Miranda warnings.

demonstrates the use of procedural safeguards effective to secure the Fifth Amendment's privilege against self-incrimination.

As for the procedural safeguards to be used,

> The person in custody must, prior to interrogation, be clearly informed that he has the right to remain silent, and that anything he says will be used against him in court; he must be clearly informed that he has the right to consult with a lawyer and to have the lawyer with him during interrogation, and that, if he is indigent, a lawyer will be appointed to represent him.

As a result of this decision, the conviction of Miranda was overturned, but Miranda did not go free. Prosecutors who won the original case against Miranda decided to retry Miranda on the rape

and kidnapping without the original confession as evidence. At the new trial, held on February 15, 1967, Miranda's common-law wife provided testimony that Miranda had earlier confessed to her about the rape (admitted as an exception to the hearsay rule). Ernesto Miranda was convicted again and received the same sentence of twenty to thirty years. Miranda was released on parole in 1972 after serving a total of nine years for the crimes committed against Kathy Midare.

During the following years, Miranda was cited on several occasions for driving and traffic violations and once for being in possession of a firearm. For this arrest (and violation of parole) he was sent back to prison for a year. In January 1976, after being released from prison, Miranda got into a fight in a bar, apparently over $5, and was stabbed to death. Ernesto Miranda was thirty-six years old. No arrests for his murder have been made (Baker 1983).

Case Considerations and Points for Discussion

- With regard to the investigation, what was the most important evidence in the case that led to the initial identification of Miranda as a suspect in the rape of Kathy Midare.

- What role did Miranda's confession to the police have in the investigation and the prosecution? From your perspective, how important was the confession in obtaining the initial conviction? Explain how prosecutors were still able to use a confession from Miranda in his re-trial.

- How did the two Supreme Court decisions of *Gideon v. Wainwright* (1963) and *Escobedo v. Illinois* (1964) relate to the decision made in *Miranda v. Arizona* (1966)?

- The Supreme Court provided two "qualifiers," or circumstances as to when the police must inform suspects of their rights. What are these two circumstances and why do you think they are important?

••• Basic Legal Terminology

Before proceeding to a discussion of the qualities of evidence and the legal procedures involved in collecting evidence, it is necessary first to understand some basic legal terminology. The concepts of arrest, arrest warrant, search, and search warrant are discussed here.

First, an *arrest* occurs when the police take a person into custody for the purposes of criminal prosecution and interrogation (*Dunaway v. New York* [1979]). When a person is under arrest, that person is in custody; however, it is possible for a person to be in custody of the police without being under arrest. When a person is under arrest (or in custody), the police deprive that person of freedom, if only the freedom to leave. All arrests must be based on probable cause that a crime occurred and the person under arrest committed it. The person that is arrested must understand that he or she is under arrest, either through police words or actions. Generally, if a person is free to leave, that person is not under arrest (nor is the person in custody). For example, a subject who is handcuffed in the back seat of a police car is probably in custody and may be under arrest. A subject who is told by the police that he or she is under arrest is most certainly under arrest. However, to make things more complicated, a person who is stopped by the police is also not free to leave but is not necessarily under arrest. Along with arrests and stops, there are also encounters, or nonstops. A nonstop is an encounter, confrontation, or questioning of a subject by a police officer that requires no justification. However, during a nonstop, the subject is free to leave.

Second, *Black's Law Dictionary* (Garner 2000) defines an *arrest warrant* as

> a writ or precept issued by a magistrate, justice, or other competent authority addressed to a sheriff, constable, or other officer, requiring him to arrest the body of a person therein named, and bring him before the magistrate or court to answer, or to be examined, concerning some offense which he is charged with having committed. (p. 1756)

The overwhelming majority of arrests made by the police are made without an arrest warrant because they are made in public. An arrest warrant is required when (1) the police must enter a home to make an arrest, although where there are exigent circumstances (*Payton v. New York* [1980]) or there is consent (*Steagald v. United States* [1981]), the police do not need a warrant to enter or to make an arrest, and (2) when the police seek to make an arrest of a subject in a third party's home (*Steagald v. United States* [1981]). In this situation, if there are exigent circumstances, the police do not need an arrest warrant to arrest the subject. Additionally, if consent is obtained from the third party to enter and search, the police do not need a search warrant to enter and search the home for the subject. By matter of policy, some police departments require that investigators obtain arrest warrants prior to making arrests in criminal investigative situations where time is less of an issue than when an officer is confronted with a criminal incident and suspect on the street. In any case, arrests and arrest warrants must be based on probable cause that a crime occurred and that the person to be arrested committed that crime. The arrest warrant must be issued by a neutral and detached magistrate, and it must name the accused or provide a specific description of the person so that his or her identity is not in question.

Third, a *search* can be defined as a governmental infringement into a person's reasonable expectation of privacy for the purpose of discovering things that could be used as evidence in a criminal prosecution (*Katz v. United States* [1967]). A reasonable expectation of privacy exists when a person believes that his or her activity will be private and that belief is reasonable (*Katz v.*

The Bottom Line

When Is an Arrest Warrant Necessary?

1. An arrest warrant is necessary when the police enter a home to make an arrest, unless there are exigent circumstances that make immediate police action necessary or the police obtain consent to enter the home.

2. An arrest warrant is necessary when the police enter someone else's home to arrest a subject, unless, again, there are exigent circumstances that require immediate police action. In addition, when the police enter someone else's home to arrest a subject, the police are also required to have a search warrant to enter that home and search for the subject, unless exigent circumstances exist or consent has been obtained by the third party to enter and search the home.

United States [1967]). A *seizure* is an act of the police in taking control over a person or thing because of a violation of a law. What is seized may constitute evidence and could include items such as contraband (e.g., drugs), fruits of the crime (e.g., stolen goods), instruments of the crime (e.g., weapons), and mere evidence of the crime (e.g., bloodstained clothing). Nearly all searches must be based on probable cause, although, as discussed later, some limited searches can be based on a lesser standard of reasonable suspicion.

Lastly a *search warrant* is similar to an arrest warrant except that it specifies the person, place, or vehicle to be searched and the types of items to be seized by the law enforcement authority. Similar to arrests, most searches are conducted without a warrant.

When obtaining a valid search warrant, several requirements must be satisfied:

- The search warrant must be based on probable cause (*Franks v. Delaware* [1978]).

- The facts must be truthful (*Illinois v. Gates.* [1983]).

- Probable cause cannot be based on stale information (*United States v. Leon* [1984]).

- Probable cause must be determined by a neutral and detached magistrate

- (*Coolidge v. New Hampshire* [1971]).

- The search warrant must be served immediately.

- The search warrant must identify what is to be seized and what is to be searched (*Maryland v. Garrison* [1987]; *United States v. Leon* [1984]).

The Bottom Line

When Is a Search Warrant Necessary?

A search warrant is necessary whenever an exception to the search warrant requirement does not apply. These exceptions can include incidents involving exigent circumstances, vehicles, other places and things, hot pursuit, search incident to arrest, stop and frisk, plain view, and consent (as discussed in detail later in the chapter).

PHOTO 4.2: The police need a search warrant to conduct a search unless the search involves a situation where a warrant is not necessary. Most searches involve one of these situations; as a result, most searches are conducted without a warrant.

In a search warrant application, there are generally three documents. First is the search warrant itself. Second is the affidavit that provides facts to establish the probable cause needed to support the warrant. Third is the search warrant inventory and return, which are completed after the search warrant has been executed and identifies the items seized. These documents are usually filed with the court that issued the warrant. An example of a search warrant used in the Caylee Anthony case is provided in Exhibit 4.1. This is one of several warrants that were executed during the investigation. This warrant authorized a search of the home that was owned and occupied by Casey Anthony's parents. The search was for the purpose of collecting evidence possibly associated with the murder of Caylee (as described in Chapter 3). The associated search warrant and inventory and return is shown in Exhibit 4.2.

Exhibit 4.1   Search Warrant Relating to the Murder Investigation of Caylee Anthony

ORANGE COUNTY SHERIFF'S DEPARTMENT

SEARCH WARRANT

DATE: AUGUST 5, 2008

Orange County Sheriffs Office

In The Ninth Judicial Circuit Court

In And For Orange County, Florida

In The Name Of The State Of Florida

To: Keven Beary

Sheriff Of Orange County Florida

And Of Any Of His Deputies

Whereas, complaint on oath and in writing, supported by affidavit attached hereto and incorporated herein by reference, having been made this day by the undersigned judge.

Whereas, said facts made known to me have caused me to certify and find there is probable cause to believe that certain laws have been and are being violated in and on certain premises and the curtilage thereof in Orange County Florida as described as follows:

4937 Hope Spring Drive, Orlando Florida 32818

Begin at the intersection of Curry Ford Road and South Chickasaw Trail in Orange County. Head south on S. Chickasaw Trail for approximately 1.7 miles to the intersection of Suburban Drive. Turn left to head east on Suburban Drive. Continue east approximately 2/10ths of a mile to the intersection of Hope Spring Drive. Turn right to head south on Hope Spring Drive. Continue south for approximately .29 miles

until you get to 4937 Hope Spring Drive. The residence will be on the east side of the street.

The residence is a single story dwelling with an attached two car garage. The residence is cream in color and the front door faces east towards the roadway. The numbers "4 9 3 7" are listed vertically to the right of the front door.

And being the premise occupied by and under the control of George and Cynthia Anthony.

And that there is now being kept in and on said premises and curtilage certain to include trace evidence to include DNA, blood, or other bodily fluid and the like that may be on said property along with clothing which may have been worn by the suspect Casey Anthony the day the child Caylee Anthony went missing.

Which are being kept and used in violation of the laws of the State of Florida, to wit; Florida State Statue 827.03(3)(C), 837.055, and 837.06 unlawfully commit the offense(s) of CHILD NEGLECT, OBSTRUCTION OF AN INVESTIGATION, and FALSE OFFICIAL STATEMENTS respectively.

Now, therefore you or either of you, with such lawful assistance as may be necessary, are hereby commanded, in the daytime, nighttime, or on any Sunday as the exigencies of the situation of the may require, to enter and search the aforesaid premises together with the yard and curtilage thereof, and any and all outbuildings and vehicles thereon, and any persons thereon reasonably believed to be connected with the said illegal activity, for the property described in this warrant, and if the same or any part thereof be found, you are hereby authorized to seize and secure same, giving proper receipt therefore and delivering a completed copy of this warrant to the person in charge of the premises, or in the absence of any such person, leaving a completed copy where the property is found, and making a return of your doings within ten (10) days of the date hereof, and you are further directed to bring said property so found and also the bodies of the person of persons in possessions thereof before the court having jurisdiction of the offense to be disposed of according to law.

WITNESS MY HAND AND SEALED THIS 5 DAY OF AUGUST 2008

JUDGE

ORANGE COUNTY, FLORIDA

NINTH JUDICIAL CIRCUIT OF FLORIDA

Exhibit 4.2 Search Warrant Inventory and Return Relating to the Search Warrant Provided in Exhibit 4.1

Search Warrant Inventory and Receipt

STATE OF FLORIDA

COUNTY OF ORANGE

ARTICLE	DESCRIPTION OF ITEMS SEIZED	LOCATION FOUND
1	"Zinc" size 5 pants	Closet of Casey Anthony's room
2	"Coolwear" size 5 skirt	Closet of Casey Anthony's room
3	"Mossamo" size 5 shirt	Closet of Casey Anthony's room
4	"George" XS shirt	Closet of Casey Anthony's room
5	"One Step Up" size M shirt	Closet of Casey Anthony's room
6	"Solution" size M shirt	Closet of Casey Anthony's room
7	"Quizz Again" size S shirt	Closet of Casey Anthony's room
8	"American Eagle" size 4 shirt	Closet of Casey Anthony's room
9	"American Eagle" size 2 shirt	Closet of Casey Anthony's room
10	"Old Navy" size 4 pants	Closet of Casey Anthony's room
11	"Old Navy" size 2 jeans	Closet of Casey Anthony's room

I, Detective Yuri Melich, the officer by whom the Search Warrant was executed, do swear the above Inventory and Receipt contains a true and detailed account of all of the property taken by me on said warrant.

Dated this 6th day of February, 2008

x _____

DETECTIVE YURI MELICH

ORANGE COUNTY SHERIFF'S OFFICE

RETURN OF SEARCH WARRANT

Received this Search Warrant on the 5th day of July 2008, and executed same in Orange County Florida, on the 6th day of July, 2008, by searching the property described therein by taking into custody the evidence described in the above inventory and receipt and by having read and delivered a copy of the search warrant and the inventory and receipt to the location.

_____

DETECTIVE YURI MELICH

ORANGE COUNTIES SHERIFF'S OFFICE

Sworn to and subscribed before me this ___ day of ___ , 2008

_____ _____

(Notary Public) or (Deputy Court Clerk)

●●● The Rules and Admissibility of Evidence

All evidence admitted into court for consideration by a judge or jury must have certain qualities. First, all evidence must be *relevant*. If evidence is relevant, then the evidence has some bearing on the case or on some fact that is trying to be established. For example, in the Casey Anthony case, photographs of Caylee and Casey were reportedly seized from the computer in the Anthony home but were never introduced at trial, presumably because the judge ruled them as not relevant to the murder investigation.

Second, all evidence must be *material*. Evidence is material if it is significant. Evidence is material if it makes the existence of a fact more probable than it appeared prior to the introduction of the evidence. If evidence is material, then it may influence the issue at hand—the point trying to be established. For example, testimony about the odor in the trunk of Casey Anthony's vehicle was ruled to be material in that it could influence the determination that a dead body was in the trunk. The determination as to relevance and materiality of evidence is made by judges and depends heavily on the particular facts of the case. Third, all evidence must be *competent*. Incompetent evidence is of questionable value. It is considered invalid or untruthful. There are three categories of incompetent evidence: (1) evidence wrongfully obtained (e.g., as a result of an illegal search or an involuntary confession); (2) statutory incompetency (e.g., when federal or state law prohibits the introduction of certain forms of evidence, such as polygraph results); and (3) court-established rule (e.g., hearsay evidence). If evidence is ruled incompetent, it is not admissible even if it is relevant and material.

With regard to statutory incompetence in particular, the rulings from two court cases are of importance. First, the *Frye test* relates to *Frye v. United States* (1923), when the U.S. Court of Appeals refused to admit novel evidence in court that was not generally accepted in the scientific community. The Frye test dominated the admissibility of scientific evidence for seventy years following the decision. In 1993, in the case of *Daubert v. Merrell Dow Pharmaceuticals* (1993), the U.S. Supreme Court replaced the Frye test for determining the admissibility of scientific evidence. The Frye approach was ruled too restrictive. The fundamental question for Daubert is, is the evidence and corresponding testimony based on scientific knowledge? Daubert provided some factors that should be considered by judges in making this determination:

- Whether the theory or technique on which the testimony is based is capable of being tested
- Whether the technique has a known rate of error in its application
- Whether the theory or technique has been subjected to peer review and publication
- The level of acceptance in the relevant scientific community of the theory or technique
- The extent to which there are standards to determine acceptable use of the technique

In addition to Daubert, another basis on which to exclude scientific evidence is constituted by Federal Rule 403 and its state court equivalents, which allow a trial judge to exclude evidence that is relatively weak or may cause confusion, consume too much time, or cause unnecessary prejudice to a party.

Fourth, the introduction of all evidence at trial must be *necessary.* Evidence must be introduced to establish a point. If the only purpose of presenting evidence is to arouse feelings or to be dramatic, the introduction of the evidence is not necessary. It may only prejudice a jury. Arguments regarding the necessity of evidence are often raised by defense attorneys with regard to the introduction of particularly gruesome crime scene photographs.

Finally, with regard to physical evidence specifically, the *chain of custody* must be maintained. The chain of custody refers to the record of individuals who maintained control (custody) over the evidence from the time it was obtained by the police to when it was introduced in court. At a minimum, it would likely include details about the collection of the evidence from the crime scene, the storage of the evidence in the police evidence room, and the transfer of the evidence to court for trial. The chain of custody is to ensure the security of physical evidence. If a chain of custody is not established, or if the chain of custody can be questioned, the value of the evidence itself may be questioned.

••• Constitutional Constraints on the Collection of Evidence

In order for evidence to be admissible in court, not only does the evidence have to have certain qualities but the police also have to follow certain legal rules in collecting it. These laws are intended to protect citizens from unwarranted governmental intrusion into their lives. These rules represent the civil liberties of citizens and, as far as criminal investigation is concerned, relate to the protections offered by the Fourth, Fifth, and Sixth Amendments to the U.S. Constitution. The procedures associated with arrests, searches, and seizures relate to the Fourth Amendment and courts' interpretation of it.

? A Question of Ethics

Fudging a Chain of Custody

As discussed, there is a legal requirement that physical evidence be collected and recorded in accordance with a chain of custody. The chain of custody is meant to ensure the integrity of the evidence. For sake of example, however, let's say that in a particular case, the shoes of a subject were collected as possible evidence (by way of consent), but a chain of custody was not established at the time they were seized; the detective really did not think that the shoes would be useful in the investigation, but he was not sure. Because he had a lot of other work to do, he put the shoes in his desk drawer and forgot about them. Later it was determined by the detective that the shoes, and the possible DNA on them, might actually be very important in the investigation. Upon realizing that he should have created a chain of custody for the shoes at the time they were seized, the detective made one up. The question is, since there was no intent on the part of the detective to tamper with or otherwise manipulate the evidence, was there a problem with the detective's conduct? Why or why not?

••• The Fourth Amendment

The Fourth Amendment reads as follows:

> The right of the people to be secure in their persons, houses, papers, and effects, against unreasonable searches and seizures, shall not be violated, and no warrants shall issue but upon probable cause, supported by oath or affirmation, and particularly describing the place to be searched, and the person or things to be seized.

Over the years, a multitude of court cases have defined (and redefined) the meaning of the Fourth Amendment. In essence, the intent of the Fourth Amendment is to protect individuals' privacy and protect against arbitrary intrusions into that privacy by government

The Bottom Line

What Is the Purpose of the Fourth Amendment to the U.S. Constitution?

The purpose of the Fourth Amendment is to protect individuals' privacy and protect against arbitrary intrusions into that privacy by government officials.

officials. As such, as interpreted by the courts, the Fourth Amendment offers protection in a variety of situations. For instance and most fundamentally, as stated in *Katz v. United States* (1967), searches are restricted wherever individuals have a reasonable expectation of privacy. In the case of Katz, this was during phone conversations in a public telephone booth. In this case, the Supreme Court ruled that the Fourth Amendment protects people not places, so the fact that the eavesdropping took place at a public phone booth was not an issue.

Other cases have further defined the parameters of the Fourth Amendment protections. For example, in the case of *O'Connor v. Ortega* (1987), it was ruled that a reasonable expectation of privacy exists in a defendant's desk and file cabinets. *Winston v. Lee* (1985) ruled that surgery constitutes a search and seizure. The use of a thermal-imaging device to detect criminal activity in a home represents a search (*Kyllo v. United States* [2001]), but a dog sniff of the outside of an automobile during a valid traffic stop does not (*Illinois v. Caballes* [2005]).

THE SEARCH WARRANT REQUIREMENT AND ITS EXCEPTIONS

The general rule is that the police need a search warrant to conduct a legal and valid search. However, there are many exceptions to this rule. In fact, as noted earlier, most searches conducted by the police are conducted without a search warrant, just as most arrests made by the police are made without an arrest warrant (del Carmen 2003). Generally speaking, probable cause (or reasonable suspicion, in some cases) is required in nearly all searches, regardless if conducted with or without a warrant, unless the search is conducted with consent when neither probable cause nor reasonable suspicion is necessary. When a search is conducted without a warrant, the burden is on the police to establish a valid and lawful reason for the search. Specifically, when a search is conducted without a warrant, police actions must relate to one of the exceptions to the search warrant requirement. These exceptions can be grouped into several categories:

- Exigent circumstances
- Vehicles
- Other places/things not covered by the Fourth Amendment
- Hot pursuit
- Incident to arrest
- Stop and frisk
- Plain view
- Consent

Notice that there is *not* a "crime scene" exception to the search warrant requirement. For the police to conduct a search of a crime scene, such as a house, the police either need a warrant or their actions must relate to one of the exceptions to the search warrant requirement.

EXIGENT CIRCUMSTANCES EXCEPTION

Exigent circumstances, or emergency situations, may require that the police conduct a search without first obtaining a warrant. In general, the rationale for the exigent circumstances exception is that without immediate police action, the suspect may destroy evidence; the suspect may pose a threat of danger to himself or herself, the police, or the public; or someone else may be in further danger of harm (see Pettry 2011; Hendrie 1998). Several Supreme Court cases define the exigent circumstances exception. For example, consider the case of *Schmerber v. California* (1966). Schmerber was hospitalized as a result of an automobile accident during which he had apparently been drinking. A police officer smelled alcohol on his breath and noticed symptoms of intoxication at the scene of the accident, as well as at the hospital. Schrember was placed under arrest and informed of his rights. On the officer's direction, and despite Schmerber's refusal, hospital medical staff took a blood sample. A chemical analysis of his blood indicated a blood alcohol level indicative of intoxication, and this evidence was admitted at trial. On appeal, the Supreme Court ruled that exigent circumstances existed in this situation because the alcohol in a person's bloodstream may disappear in the time required to obtain a warrant. As a result, obtaining evidence in this manner, under these circumstances, and without a warrant, did not constitute a violation of a defendant's constitutional rights.

A recent case that also relates to the prevention of the destruction of evidence is *Kentucky v. King* (2011). In this case, the Supreme Court ruled that if the police reasonably believe that a subject is destroying evidence, they can take immediate action without a warrant. In the case of King, the police kicked in a door to an apartment after pursuing a subject into the apartment building, smelling marijuana outside of the apartment, and announcing their intent to forcibly enter the apartment. The search was ruled as an exigent circumstances exception and the seized evidence was admissible.

The Supreme Court case of *Michigan v. Fisher* (2009) relates to the emergency aid rationale of the exigent circumstances exception of the search warrant requirement. The Supreme Court ruled that when the police encounter a situation where a subject is injured, may be about to be injured, or is in need of aid, exigent circumstances exist and a warrant is not necessary to enter a home, even if the police do not have "iron-clad proof" that a subject has life-threatening injuries (also see *Brigham City v. Stuart* [2006]).

In the case of *Payton v. New York* (1980), the Supreme Court ruled that there were no exigent circumstances and, correspondingly, that the warrantless search was unconstitutional. After two days of intensive investigation, New York detectives had assembled evidence sufficient to establish probable cause to believe that Payton had murdered the manager of a gas station. The next day officers went to Payton's apartment with the intent to arrest him. They did not have a warrant. There was no response after they knocked on the door. The police then used crowbars to gain entry into the apartment. No one was there. In plain view was a .30-caliber shell casing that was seized and later admitted into evidence at Payton's murder trial. Payton was convicted and he appealed. The Supreme Court ruled that in the absence of consent or exigent circumstances, the police may not enter a suspect's home to make a routine felony arrest or to conduct a search without a warrant. As a result, the evidence seized from the search was not admissible.

VEHICLE EXCEPTION

Vehicles (including motor homes; see *California v. Carney* [1985]) are not treated in the same manner as homes and other places in affording rights to privacy; people have a lesser expectation of privacy in vehicles. Moreover, vehicles are mobile and, as such, it is more difficult for the police to collect evidence contained in vehicles. Searches of vehicles may also be conducted to minimize the dangers to officers that may be associated with vehicle stops. Several cases have defined this exception to the search warrant requirement.

First, consider the case of *Chambers v. Maroney* (1970). Shortly after an armed robbery of a gas station, the police stopped the car of Chambers and three other men. The stop was based on information (including a description of the getaway car used by the perpetrators) supplied by the service station attendant and bystanders. The occupants of the car were arrested, and the car was driven to the police station. During the course of the search of the car at the police station, the police found concealed in a compartment under the dashboard two .38-caliber revolvers, a glove containing change, and cards bearing the name of a different service station attendant who had been robbed a week earlier. In conducting a warrant-authorized search of the petitioner's home the day after the arrest, police found and

The Bottom Line

When Does the Exigent Circumstances Exception to the Search Warrant Requirement Apply?

The exigent circumstances exception applies when the police are confronted with a situation where they have a reasonable basis to believe that their immediate action is necessary in order to prevent a suspect from destroying evidence; to prevent a suspect from causing a threat of danger to himself or herself, the police, or the public; or to prevent someone else from being in further danger of injury or harm.

PHOTO 4.3: Many court cases have defined the parameters of lawful vehicle searches. Because vehicles are mobile and people have a lesser expectation of privacy in them compared to homes, police do not generally need a warrant to search a vehicle.

seized .38-caliber ammunition. At the trial, the materials taken from the car and the bullets seized from the home were introduced as evidence. Chambers was convicted of robbery of both service stations. On appeal, the Supreme Court held that if probable cause exists that a vehicle contains evidence, and if that vehicle is mobile, an officer may search that vehicle at the scene or at the police station without a warrant. The search was valid and the evidence admissible.

In *South Dakota v. Opperman* (1976), the court ruled that when the police tow and impound a vehicle, even for a parking violation, a routine inventory search, without a warrant or without probable cause that the vehicle contains evidence, is reasonable. This procedure protects the owner's property, protects the police against claims that the owner's property was stolen while the car was impounded, and protects the police from potential danger. However, inventory searches conducted solely for the purpose of discovering evidence are illegal regardless of what is discovered during the course of the search. In addition, during an inventory search, it is reasonable for the police to search closed containers, such as a backpack, without a warrant (*Colorado v. Bertine* [1987]).

In *Michigan v. Long* (1983), the Supreme Court spoke of the dangers associated with roadside encounters with suspects and stated that this can justify searches of vehicles in such situations. It is important to note that in this case, a search was conducted *prior to* arrest. While on patrol in a rural area at night, two police officers observed a car traveling erratically and at an excessive speed. When the car swerved into a ditch, the officers stopped to investigate and were met by Long, the only occupant of the car, at the rear of the car. The door on the driver's side of the vehicle was left open. Long did not respond to initial requests to produce his license and registration. When he began walking toward the open door of the car, the officers followed him and saw a knife on the floorboard of the driver's side of the car. At that time, the officers subjected him to a pat-down search, but no weapons were found. One of the officers shone a light into the car and saw something protruding from under the armrest of the front seat. On lifting the armrest, the officer saw an open pouch that contained what appeared to be marijuana. Long was then arrested for possession of marijuana. A further search of the car revealed no additional contraband, but the officers decided to impound the vehicle. As a result of the subsequent search, more marijuana was found in the trunk. The marijuana was introduced at trial, and Long was convicted of possession of marijuana. On appeal, the Supreme Court held that if an officer has reasonable suspicion that a motorist who has been stopped is dangerous and may be able to gain control of a weapon in the car, the officer may conduct a brief, warrantless search of the passenger compartment even if the motorist is no longer inside the car. Such a search should be limited to areas in the passenger compartment where a weapon might be found or hidden. If contraband is discovered in the process of looking for a weapon, the officer is not required to ignore it. However, to look inside a closed container in a vehicle without a warrant, there must be probable cause to suggest that evidence is contained in the container (*California v. Acevedo* [1991]).

Similar to *Michigan v. Long* (1983), in *Knowles v. Iowa* (1998) the court ruled that as a result of a traffic stop made to issue a traffic citation, the police may order the occupants out of the vehicle, but to justify a brief search of that vehicle there must be a reasonable suspicion of danger to the officer. In *Brendlin v. California* (2007), the Supreme Court held that once a vehicle is stopped by law enforcement, all of the vehicle's occupants are subject to search (and seizure). A drug dog can sniff the outside of a vehicle in a traffic stop (*Illinois v. Caballes* [2005]). In any case, there must be a reason to stop a vehicle in which a search is executed. As held in *United States v. Ortiz* (1975), a search at a fixed vehicle checkpoint requires consent, probable cause, or a warrant. Random searches are not legally permissible. However, checkpoints where all vehicles are stopped by the police for the purpose of locating witnesses or to collect other information are permissible (*Illinois v. Lidster* [2004]).

Arizona v. Gant (2009) also has important implications for the searches of vehicles, although this case relates most closely to the searches of vehicles after an arrest is made (i.e., or incident to arrest). As such, this case is discussed below in the section on search incident to arrest.

Exhibit 4.3   Levels of Proof Necessary to Conduct a Vehicle Search

TYPE OF SEARCH/ACTION	MINIMUM LEVEL OF PROOF NECESSARY
To stop a vehicle	Reasonable suspicion/violation of traffic law
To order occupants out of the vehicle	Reasonable suspicion
To search occupants for weapons	Reasonable suspicion/fear of safety
To search occupants for evidence	Probable cause
To search the passenger compartment for weapons	Reasonable suspicion/fear of safety
To search the passenger compartment for evidence	Probable cause to arrest
To search closed containers in vehicle	Probable cause or an inventory search

The Bottom Line

The third exception to the search warrant requirement applies to other places and things that are not afforded Fourth Amendment protections. For example, consider *Oliver v. United States* (1984). Narcotics agents from the Kentucky State Police received information that marijuana was being grown on the farm belonging to Oliver. Upon arriving at the farm, the agents drove past the house to a locked gate that displayed a "No Trespassing" sign. A footpath led around the side of the gate. The agents walked around the gate and along the road for several hundred yards. At that point, someone standing in front of a camper on the property shouted, "No hunting is allowed. Come back up here." The officer shouted back that they were the police, but they found no one when they returned to the camper. The officers resumed their search without a warrant and found a field of marijuana approximately a mile from Oliver's house. Oliver was charged with, and convicted of, manufacturing a controlled substance. On appeal, the Supreme Court ruled that a reasonable expectation of privacy does not apply to open fields. "No Trespassing" signs around the property do not establish any reasonable expectation of privacy. Consequently, the police can enter the property without a warrant or probable cause.

Other decisions of the U.S. Supreme Court have held that there is no reasonable expectation of privacy in garbage left for collection outside a house (*California v. Greenwood* [1988]), in greenhouses viewed from the sky (*Florida v. Riley* [1989]), in the movements of a vehicle (*United States v. Knotts* [1983]), or in bank records obtained via a subpoena from a bank (*United States v. Miller* [1976]). Firefighters do not need a warrant to enter a building to extinguish a fire or to conduct an investigation of the cause of a fire (*Michigan v. Tyler* [1978]).

HOT PURSUIT EXCEPTION

Sometimes hot pursuit is considered an exigent circumstance. Indeed, the rationale for a hot pursuit search is the same as for other exigent circumstances: to prevent harm to people or to prevent the destruction of evidence. The Supreme Court case of *Warden v. Hayden* (1967) created the hot pursuit exception to the research warrant requirement. Early one morning an armed robber entered a taxicab company, took $363, and ran. Two taxicab drivers in the area followed the man, and a dispatcher relayed the information to the police that were on their way to the scene. Within minutes, the police arrived at the house that they believed the suspect had entered. An officer knocked and announced his presence. He asked for permission to search the house, and Mrs. Hayden offered no objection. The officers found Hayden upstairs, pretending to be asleep. He was arrested. Another officer discovered a shotgun and a pistol. The pistol, a clip of ammunition for the pistol, and a cap, jacket, and pants that matched the description of the clothing worn by the perpetrator were admitted as evidence. Hayden was convicted. On appeal, the Supreme Court ruled that the police may make a warrantless search and seizure when they are in hot pursuit of a suspect. The scope of the search may be as extensive as reasonably necessary to prevent the suspect from resisting or escaping. Officers do not need to delay an arrest if doing so would endanger their lives or the lives of others, or if it would allow for the destruction of evidence. However, the warrantless entry still requires probable cause that the suspect being pursued committed a crime and is in the premises to be entered. Further, hot pursuit applies only to serious offenses, felonies, and some misdemeanors (*Welsh v. Wisconsin* [1984]).

Another case that relates to hot pursuit is *United States v. Santana* (1976). In this case, Santana was standing in the doorway of her house as the police arrived. The police had probable cause to believe that the paper bag she was holding contained heroin. The police

When Does the Vehicle Exception Apply?

Police can search for evidence in a vehicle without a warrant if there is probable cause to believe that the vehicle contains evidence. Similarly, to look inside a closed container inside the vehicle depends on probable cause to believe that evidence is contained in that container. However, closed containers may be searched in an inventory search without probable cause.

When executing a vehicle stop, the officer can order the subjects out of the vehicle, and those subjects can be searched for the purpose of discovering weapons (or searched for evidence if there is probable cause). Without probable cause to search for evidence in the vehicle, reasonable suspicion of danger to the officer is required to conduct even a brief search of the vehicle. If a search of a vehicle is conducted after an arrest is made, other rules apply (see *search incident to arrest*).

PHOTO 4.4: A search may be conducted without a search warrant if the hot pursuit exception applies. This exception exists to prevent harm to people or the destruction of evidence.

did not have a warrant to enter her house. As the police officers approached, Santana retreated into her house. The police followed her into the house and arrested her. The Supreme Court held that there is no reasonable expectation of privacy outside one's home. If a suspect enters his or her house to avoid arrest, the police may enter the house without a warrant and conduct a search accordingly.

SEARCH INCIDENT TO ARREST EXCEPTION

This exception to the search warrant requirement applies to situations in which the police conduct searches of individuals as a result of their arrest. Over the years, there have been numerous cases that have addressed this exception to the search warrant requirement. As with many of the other exceptions to the search warrant requirement, the rationale for this exception is to prevent harm to the officer and to prevent the destruction of evidence.

In the case of *Chimel v. California* (1969), police officers with an arrest warrant, but not a search warrant, were admitted into Chimel's home by his wife. On arriving home, Chimel was served with the arrest warrant. Although he denied the officers' request to "look around," they conducted a search of the entire house, including the attic,

The Bottom Line

What Places and Things Are Not Afforded a Reasonable Expectation of Privacy?

A search warrant is not required when searching certain places and things. Examples include open fields, garbage left outside on a public street or curb, tracking a vehicle with a tracking device, bank records, and entries into a building to extinguish or investigate a fire.

The Bottom Line

When Does the Hot Pursuit Exception Apply?

The hot pursuit exception applies when a suspect attempts to avoid apprehension by the police by entering a home. If the police are in pursuit of the subject and have probable cause to believe that the suspect committed a crime and is in the home, then the police may enter the home to make an arrest and to conduct a search. The scope of the search may be as extensive as reasonably necessary to prevent the suspect from resisting or escaping. Officers do not need to delay in making an arrest if doing so would endanger their lives, the life of the suspect, or the lives of others, or if it would result in the loss of evidence.

garage, and workshop. At his trial on burglary charges, items seized from Chimel's home were admitted over the objection that they had been unconstitutionally seized. The Supreme Court agreed. The Supreme Court held that the search of Chimel's home went far beyond his person and the area within which he might have harbored either a weapon or something that could have been used as evidence against him. There was no justification for extending the search beyond the area within his immediate control—the area covered by the spread of the suspect's arms and hands.

In *Maryland v. Buie* (1990), the Supreme Court ruled that a larger search was justified because of the potential for danger to officers. In this case, police officers obtained and executed arrest warrants for Buie and an accomplice in connection with an armed robbery. On arrival at the house, officers fanned out through the first and second floors. One of the officers watched the basement so that nobody could surprise the officers. This officer shouted into the basement, ordering anyone down there to come out. The officer stated that he was the police. Eventually, Buie emerged from the basement and was arrested, searched, and handcuffed. Another officer then entered the basement to determine whether anyone else was there. In plain view he noticed a red running suit similar to the one worn by a suspect in the robbery. The running suit was admitted as evidence at the trial, and Buie was convicted of robbery. On appeal, the Supreme Court held that "the Fourth Amendment permits a properly limited protective sweep in conjunction with an in-home arrest when the searching officer possesses a reasonable belief based on specific and articulable facts that the area to be swept harbors an individual posing a danger to those on the arrest scene." The officer went into the basement not to search for evidence but to look for the accomplice or anyone else who might have posed a threat to the officers. This was acceptable. However, a protective sweep by the police is not allowed every time an arrest is made, and it must be limited in scope.

If an arrest occurs outside a house, the police may not search inside a house as a search incident to lawful arrest (*Vale v. Louisiana* [1970]). However, the police may monitor the movements of a person who has been arrested. If the person who has been arrested proceeds into a private place, such as a dorm room, the police may accompany him or her. If evidence is then observed in plain view, it may be seized (*Washington v. Chrisman* [1982]). In addition, any lawful arrest justifies the police to conduct a full-scale search of that person even without officer fear for safety or belief that evidence would be found (*Gustafson v. Florida* [1973]).

If an occupant of a vehicle is arrested in or near a vehicle, the scope of the search can include a search of the passenger compartment of that automobile, including containers found within the passenger compartment, for "if the passenger compartment is within reach of the arrestee, so also will containers in it be within his reach" (*New York v. Belton* [1981]). The vehicle can be searched even if the arrestee was not in the vehicle at the time of the initial police encounter (*Thornton v. United States* [2004]).

The recent Supreme Court case of *Arizona v. Gant* (2009) further clarifies the ability of the police to search vehicles incident to arrest. In this case, Gant was arrested for driving with a suspended license and was handcuffed and placed in the back seat of a police car. It was only then that the police searched his vehicle. The search was ruled unreasonable. As explained by the Court, "The police may search a vehicle incident to a recent occupant's arrest only if the arrestee is within reaching distance of the passenger compartment at the time of the search or it is reasonable to believe the vehicle contains evidence of the offense of the arrest." In this case, Gant had no access to the vehicle when the search was conducted and there was no reason to suspect that the vehicle contained evidence relating to driving with a suspended license (also see Schott 2009 and Myers 2011).

An emerging issue is the retrieval of information from cell phones incident to arrest. Generally speaking, the courts have supported the warrantless retrieval of text messages, call histories, and stored phone numbers and addresses from cell phones upon arrest as long as that search is made soon after the time of arrest (Clark 2009).

STOP AND FRISK EXCEPTION

The police may conduct a *search* of a person even though an *arrest* of that person may not be justified. Many court decisions have clarified and defined the intricacies of this exception to the search warrant requirement. Most of the decisions note the importance of ensuring officers' safety in justifying stop and frisk or pat-down searches. The most famous of these cases was the landmark case of *Terry v. Ohio* (1968). The facts of the case are as follows: While patrolling a downtown beat that he had been patrolling for many years, Cleveland police officer McFadden observed two strangers on a street corner. It appeared to the officer that the two men were casing a store. Each of the men walked up and down the street, peering into the store window, then both returned to the corner to confer. At one point they were joined by a third man, who left abruptly. Officer McFadden followed them from a couple of blocks away to where the two men were joined by the third. He approached the men, identified himself, and asked for their identification. The men "mumbled something," whereupon McFadden frisked all three of them. Terry and one other man were carrying handguns. Both were tried and convicted of carrying concealed weapons. On appeal, the Supreme Court held that "where a police officer observes unusual conduct which leads him to reasonably conclude in light of his experience that criminal activity may be afoot and that the persons with whom he is dealing may be armed and presently dangerous" and he identifies himself as a police officer, "he is entitled for the protection of himself and others in the area to conduct a carefully limited search of the outer clothing of such persons in an attempt to discover weapons which might be used to assault him." The practice of stop and frisk is valid.

Many cases relate to the question of what constitutes "reasonable suspicion" that criminal activity is afoot—the prerequisite for a legal stop and frisk. In *Illinois v. Wardlow* (2000), reasonable suspicion was determined to have been present when the suspect fled from the police once the suspect saw the police, and because this occurred in a high narcotics trafficking area. However, in *Brown v. Texas* (1979), the Supreme Court ruled that just because an individual looked suspicious and was never seen in the area before, the police did not have reasonable suspicion that criminal activity was afoot. Vague suspicion is not enough to justify a stop and frisk of an individual or to require that the person give the police his or her name. Furthermore, a stop and frisk based on an anonymous tip is not legally permissible (*Florida v. J. L.* [2002]). Similarly, police may not stop a vehicle to check the motorist's driver's license and car registration without reasonable suspicion that the driver does not have a license, that the vehicle is not registered, or that the law is somehow being violated (*Delaware v. Prouse* [1979]), or without consideration of the totality of the circumstances that illegal actions are afoot (*United States v. Arvizu* [2002]).

When a motorist is stopped for a traffic violation, the officer may order the motorist out of the car (*Maryland v. Wilson* [1997]); however, a pat-down search for weapons requires reasonable suspicion that the person is armed (*Pennsylvania v. Mimms* [1977]).

When conducting a pat-down search under any circumstances, nonthreatening contraband, such as drugs, may be seized only if it is immediately apparent and is not found as a result of squeezing, sliding, or otherwise manipulating the contents of the defendant's pockets (*Minnesota v. Dickerson* [1993]).

The Bottom Line

When Does the Search Incident to Arrest Exception Apply?

When a suspect is arrested, the police can search the suspect for evidence and weapons, and they can also search the area within the immediate control of the suspect. When circumstances are such that a larger danger is confronted by officers (e.g., when looking for additional suspects in a house), a wider search is justified (a protective sweep).

If the person arrested is an occupant of a vehicle, the passenger compartment of that automobile can be searched if the suspect is within reaching distance of the passenger compartment at the time of the search, or if it is reasonably believed by the officer that the vehicle contains evidence of the offense at hand. Further, information from cell phones can be seized incident to arrest.

PHOTO 4.5: The police do not need a warrant to stop and frisk someone's outer clothing for weapons if they believe criminal activity is afoot.

The Bottom Line

When Does the Stop and Frisk Exception Apply?

When the police have reasonable suspicion that criminal activity is afoot, they can conduct a limited search of the outer clothing of such persons in an attempt, and in such a way, to discover weapons.

PLAIN VIEW EXCEPTION

When the police conduct a search with a warrant or when the police are legally present at a particular place and evidence is observed, that evidence may be seized under the provisions of the plain view exception to the search warrant requirement. Consider the case of *Texas v. Brown* (1983). In Fort Worth, Texas, Brown's car was stopped at a routine checkpoint at night by a police officer. The officer asked to see Brown's driver's license, shone his flashlight into the car, and saw a green opaque party balloon, knotted near the tip, fall from Brown's hand to the rear seat. Based on the officer's experience in drug offense arrests, he was aware that narcotics are often stored in these types of balloons. He then shifted his position to obtain a better view and noticed small plastic vials, loose white powder, and an open bag of party balloons in the glove compartment. After failing to produce a driver's license, Brown was asked to exit the car and was placed under arrest. At trial, Brown was convicted of narcotics offenses. The Supreme Court held that the officer's initial stop of the car was valid and that the officer shining his flashlight into the car and changing position did not violate Brown's Fourth Amendment rights. The officer had probable cause to believe that the balloon contained narcotics, so the seizure was also justified.

In the case of *Horton v. California* (1990), the police were conducting a warrant search for the proceeds of a robbery and, in the process, inadvertently discovered weapons in plain view. The Supreme Court ruled that the seizure of items not listed in the warrant was permissible as long as those items were in plain view. In other cases, however, additional actions with regard to the items found in plain view have been ruled by the Supreme Court not to be acceptable. For example, in *Arizona v. Hicks* (1987), the Supreme Court held that moving a stereo in plain view to record its serial number constituted a search and was not permissible without a warrant.

CONSENT SEARCH EXCEPTION

Of all the reasons why the police conduct searches without a warrant, by far the most frequent is because a person provides the police consent to conduct a search. One reason why consent searches are used so often is that probable cause or even reasonable suspicion are not needed in order to justify the search.

Consider *Schneckloth v. Bustamonte* (1973). A car containing six men was stopped for a traffic violation by a California police officer. The driver of the car was not able to produce a license. The officer asked the driver if he could search the car. The driver gave consent and helped the officer open the trunk and glove compartment. Under the rear seat the officer found several checks that had previously been stolen from a car wash. The checks were admitted as evidence in trial, and Bustamonte was convicted. The Supreme Court held that after validly stopping a car, an officer may ask the person in control of the car for permission to search it. Even if there is not probable cause or reasonable suspicion, the officer may conduct a search if consent is given. The voluntariness of the consent is to be determined by the totality of the circumstances. Consent need not be in writing. The police do not have to inform subjects of their Fourth Amendment rights prior to receiving valid consent; however, the burden lies on the officer to prove that the consent was valid.

In other related cases, the Supreme Court ruled that consent was valid if it was received from a third person who was believed at the time to have common authority over the premises (*Illinois v. Rodriguez* [1990]). A search of a hotel room was not valid, however, when consent was received from the hotel night clerk (*Stoner v. California* [1964]), as this person did not have common authority over that room. If two people with common authority (e.g., a husband and wife who share a home) are present and one gives the police consent to search and the other objects, then a consent search would not be justified; however, if the person who objects is not present where the search is to occur, then the search would be valid (see Benoit 2008).

In some law enforcement agencies, so-called knock and talk searches are a frequently used investigative strategy. In a knock and talk, the police approach a house, knock, talk with the occupant, and seek consent to enter and search the house. Holcomb (2006) explains that four issues need to be considered in judging the legality of a knock and talk search. First is the walk. The police should approach the premises using open and accessible areas, such as driveways, sidewalks, and front doors. Second is the encounter. Police actions should be such that a person could feel free to decline the officers' request to search. For instance, officers should not order persons to open the door, and the police should not be unreasonably persistent in attempting to gain access/consent. Third is the knock. Again, officers should not be unreasonably persistent in summonsing the occupants of the house. Holcomb cites the case of *U.S. v. Jerez* (1997), where officers simply refused to take no for an answer. They did not leave until they got a response; they repeatedly knocked on doors and windows until someone answered. Fourth is the talk. Officers should be polite and ask questions (e.g., "Can you come to the door please?") versus issuing commands (e.g., "Police, open the door!"). With these considerations in mind, a knock and talk can be a valuable and legally justified approach to obtaining consent to conduct searches.

Finally, Walker-Holcomb (2004) explains that a consent search is limited in several ways. First, it is limited by the statements and actions of officers—the officer must limit the scope of the search to that which was represented to the subject (e.g., the statement "I'm only interested in looking around in the bedroom" would preclude the officer from searching

The Bottom Line

When Does the Plain View Exception Apply?

When the police conduct a search with a warrant or when the police are legally present at a particular place and evidence is observed, that evidence may be seized under the provisions of the plain view exception to the search warrant requirement.

PHOTO 4.6: A knock and talk can be a valuable method of obtaining consent to search. In a knock and talk, police knock on a person's door, speak with that person, and seek consent to search the person's house.

other rooms). Second, the search is limited by the actions and statements of the subject—the officer may not exceed the parameters of the search as stated by the subject (e.g., "You can't search the bedroom" would prohibit an officer from searching the bedroom). Finally, the search must be reasonable. For example, consent to do a pat-down does not represent consent to do a strip search; consent to search does not allow an officer to break open things.

THE EXCLUSIONARY RULE AND ITS EXCEPTIONS

If a search is determined to be unreasonable, the evidence obtained must be excluded from trial; it is considered incompetent evidence. This basic principle is known as the *exclusionary rule*. The exclusionary rule relates specifically to unreasonable searches and seizures. As discussed later, however, evidence that is collected in violation of other constitutional rights is also excluded from trial, although not technically as a result of the exclusionary rule (del Carmen 2003). The exclusionary rule took some time to evolve. In 1914, in *Weeks v. United States*, the Supreme Court ruled that evidence obtained by federal officers in violation of the Fourth Amendment could not be used in federal prosecutions. Evidence that was collected illegally by state officers, however, could be used in federal prosecutions. It was not until 1961, in the case of *Mapp v. Ohio*, that the Supreme Court extended the exclusionary rule to the states. As a result, evidence seized in violation of the Fourth Amendment cannot be used in either federal or state prosecutions.

In the case of *Mapp v. Ohio* (1961), three Cleveland police officers arrived at the Mapp residence as a result of information that they received that "a person [was] hiding out in the home, who was wanted for questioning in connection with a recent bombing." The officers knocked on the door and demanded entrance. Mapp telephoned her attorney and refused to let the officers in without a warrant. Three hours later, additional officers arrived at the scene. Mapp's attorney also arrived, but the police would not allow him to see Mapp or enter the house. Mapp demanded to see a search warrant. A paper, claimed by the officers to be a warrant, was held up by one of the officers. She grabbed the warrant and a struggle ensued. Mapp was handcuffed, and the police searched her entire house, including dresser drawers, suitcases, and closets. In the basement, a trunk was searched and obscene material was discovered inside. Mapp was charged and convicted of possession of these materials. At the trial, no search warrant was produced. On appeal, in a 5–4 decision, the Supreme Court ruled that the exclusionary rule prohibits, in state criminal proceedings, the use of evidence that results from unreasonable searches and seizures. The evidence was not admissible.

As another example of the exclusionary rule in action, consider the case of *Davis v. Mississippi* (1969). During a rape investigation, the police collected fingerprints and palm prints from the windowsill through which the assailant entered the home. The victim, however, could not provide the police with any details regarding the assailant aside from the fact that he was an African American juvenile. The police, without obtaining warrants, took twenty-four African American juveniles to police headquarters to be questioned and fingerprinted. Davis was questioned and released. Later, without a warrant or probable cause, the police took Davis into custody and held him in jail overnight. During this time, his fingerprints were found to match those collected from the crime scene. Davis was tried and convicted of the rape. On appeal, the Supreme Court held that "fingerprint evidence is no exception to the rule that all evidence obtained by searches and seizures in violation of the Constitution is inadmissible in state court. The Fourth Amendment applies to involuntary detention occurring at the investigatory stage as well as at the accusatory stage."

There are exceptions to the exclusionary rule. The exceptions identify circumstances when something may have made the search and seizure technically illegal, but the evidence is still admissible in court. First, the courts have ruled that when the police make an unintentional error, or an honest mistake, in conducting a search with or without a warrant, the resulting evidence should not be excluded from trial. This is known as the *good faith exception,* and it is the most common and significant exception to the exclusionary rule. For example, in *Arizona v. Evans* (1995), Evans was arrested by Phoenix police during a routine traffic stop when the police computer indicated that Evans was wanted on an outstanding warrant. While being handcuffed, Evans dropped a marijuana cigarette. A subsequent search of Evans' vehicle revealed more marijuana. Later, it was determined that the warrant was no longer valid. This information had not been entered into the computer because of a clerical error. At the trial, Evans moved to suppress the marijuana as the fruit of an unlawful arrest. The Supreme Court ruled that the police acted in good faith in making the arrest and conducting the search. The error was not the fault of the police and, therefore, the police should not be punished. The marijuana was admissible. Along the same lines, when the police conduct a search with a warrant but it is later determined that probable cause for the warrant did not exist, the search and seizure is still valid (*United States v. Leon* [1984]).

A second exception to the exclusionary rule is known as the *inevitable discovery exception,* and it has usually been applied when the evidence in question is either a dead body or a weapon. This exception holds that if the police were reasonably expected to discover the evidence through lawful means and without the information produced from the illegal actions taken, then that evidence may still be admitted, despite the exclusionary rule. For

The Bottom Line

When Does the Consent Exception Apply?

The police can conduct a legally valid search without a warrant, probable cause, or even reasonable suspicion if they have consent from the person to be searched. The consent must be provided voluntarily, but it does not need to be in writing, nor do the police have to advise the person of his or her right to not give consent. Consent may be obtained from a person other than the person to be searched if that person has common authority, or is believed by the police to have common authority, over the space to be searched. Consent searches can be limited in scope by the person who provides consent. Knock and talks are a valid strategy designed to obtain consent to search.

example, in the case of *Nix v. Williams* (1984), Williams was arrested for the kidnapping of a ten-year-old girl who had disappeared from a YMCA in Des Moines, Iowa. The arrest was based on probable cause. On the instruction of Williams' attorney, the police were not to question Williams during the drive back to Des Moines. However, while on the trip, one of the officers began a conversation with Williams that led to Williams revealing where the child's body was located. The officers, knowing that Williams was deeply religious and that it was near Christmas, informed him that it would be nice to give the girl a Christian burial. They told Williams to "think it over." Williams then made statements that led to the discovery of the body. Williams' statements were admitted into trial and he was convicted of the crime. The verdict was appealed on this basis. The U.S. Supreme Court held that the evidence of the victim's body was properly admitted on the grounds that the body would inevitably have been discovered even if no constitutional violation had taken place, although the burden is on the prosecution to show inevitable discovery. Although the victim's body was admissible, the Supreme Court ruled that the suspect's statements were not (see *Brewer v. Williams* [1977] later in this chapter).

Third, the *purged taint exception* holds that the illegal actions of the police may be overcome by the voluntary actions of the suspect. In essence, the voluntary actions of the suspect can eliminate the tainted nature of the evidence and allow it to be admitted. For example, in *Wong Sun v. United States* (1963), federal agents conducted a search and arrest of Wong Sun without a warrant and without probable cause. Wong Sun was then released. Several days later, Wong Sun was interrogated. After the interrogation, the agent read back to Wong Sun the statement made by him. Wong Sun refused to sign the statement, although he admitted to the accuracy of it. A few days later, Wong Sun voluntarily went back to the police station and signed the confession. The Supreme Court ruled that Wong Sun's act manifested free will and therefore purged the taint of the illegal arrest. The act of free will broke the causal chain between the taint of the evidence and the illegal police conduct, so the evidence became admissible.

Finally, the *independent source exception* to the exclusionary rule states that evidence obtained from an independent source not directly related to an illegal search or seizure should be admissible into court. For example, consider *United States v. Crews* (1980). In the women's restroom at the Washington Monument, a woman was accosted and robbed at gunpoint by a young man. The victim immediately reported the incident to the police. Several days later a boy who matched the description of the suspect was seen by the police in the area by the monument. He was briefly taken into custody, questioned, photographed, and then released. Later, the victim identified the person in the photograph as her assailant. The suspect was then again taken into custody. During a lineup, the boy was identified by the victim. Crews was indicted for armed robbery and other offenses. The Supreme Court ruled that the initial arrest of the suspect, the identification of the suspect via the photo, and the identification of the suspect in the lineup were all illegal. However, the in-court identification of the defendant was legal. The initial illegal detention of the suspect could not deprive the prosecutors of the opportunity to prove the defendant's guilt through the introduction of evidence wholly untainted by police misconduct.

The Bottom Line

What Is the Exclusionary Rule and When Does It Apply?

The exclusionary rule holds that if the police collect evidence illegally, that evidence is to be excluded from court proceedings. However, there are several situations (exceptions) when the rule does not apply. Specifically, when the police make an unintentional error in conducting the search (the good faith exception to the exclusionary rule), when the police would have found the evidence without the illegal search (inevitable discovery), when the voluntary actions of the suspect nullify the illegal actions of the police (purged taint exception), and when evidence is obtained independent of the illegal police action (independent source exception).

THE IMPACT OF THE EXCLUSIONARY RULE ON CRIMINAL INVESTIGATIONS

The discussion of the exclusionary rule and its exceptions raises a fundamentally important question: What is the purpose of the exclusionary rule? The answer is that the exclusionary rule is supposed to deter unlawful police conduct in search and seizure cases. The reasoning is that if the police know that illegally seized evidence cannot be used in court to prove the suspect's guilt, then the police will not seize the evidence illegally—they will follow the law in collecting it. As a result, the police will not violate citizens' rights, which is the fundamental aim of the constitutional protections in the first place.

Does the exclusionary rule really deter police misconduct in conducting searches and seizures? The answer to this question is no, at least not as much as what many would hope or expect. The reason why the exclusionary rule does not necessarily deter police misconduct is that there are ways, as Paul Sutton (1986) puts it, of "getting around the Fourth Amendment." According to Sutton, the police can use several strategies to circumvent the rule. If these strategies do not break the law, they at least bend it. For example, one strategy involves the extensive use of the "consent" exception. As discussed earlier, if the police receive consent from a citizen to conduct a search, then the police can conduct a valid search. The issue becomes, however, what is "voluntary?" Consider a situation in which the police wish to conduct a search of a house where they think illegal guns may be kept, but they do not have probable cause or a warrant. The police may say to the homeowner, "If you let us come in and take a look at your guns, we won't take any of them. But if we have to go get a search warrant, we're going to come back and pack up your whole house. So . . . do you mind if we come in?" If the citizen gives consent to the police to conduct a search under these circumstances, is it voluntary? No. But if the police officer tells a judge that the citizen said, "Sure, be my guest, come on in," how is voluntariness to be determined? A judge is the final arbiter of this question, but it may be an issue of "he said, she said" between the officer and the citizen. It may be difficult to determine who is really telling the truth and, correspondingly, it may be difficult for a judge to strike down the evidence gathered from a consent search.

As a second strategy of "getting around the Fourth," the police may conduct an illegal search with full knowledge that any evidence seized would not be admissible and that the case will not be prosecuted. For instance, the police could obtain evidence illegally to pressure a particular person to provide information about a particular crime or criminal (e.g., "Tell us what you know about T-Bone and that old man getting killed or you are going to be arrested for possession of the marijuana that we found when we stopped and searched you [illegally]"). Or, the police could conduct an illegal search and seize evidence just to harass a suspect. Does this really happen? In a survey of Illinois police officers conducted by Martin (1994), it was found that 25 percent of officers stated that they witnessed at least one illegal search of a subject during the past year.

Third, Sutton (1986) reported that police officers sometimes engage in "judge-shopping," wherein "officers seek out magistrates who appear favorably disposed to warrant requests" (p. 439). Some judges may examine requests for warrants more closely than others, and some judges may be more likely to find probable cause than others. The police may use this to their advantage in requesting warrants and executing searches. Knowing this, it is interesting to note that warrant applications are rarely rejected by judges or magistrates (Uchida and Bynum 1991).

Finally, unfortunately, sometimes some police officers simply lie. For a variety of reasons, police officers may misrepresent the facts of a case to a judge or a jury and, as a result, the "fruits" of an otherwise illegal search may be admitted into trial and may be considered in determining the guilt or innocence of the accused. The fact that the police sometimes lie is well understood by other police officers, judges, and attorneys (see Dershowitz 1982). Police officers sometimes refer to testimony as "testilying" (Cunningham 1999) and to

A Question of Ethics

Do the Ends Justify the Means?

A basic and important goal of the police is to identify and apprehend criminals; this is one of the main reasons why we have the police. As a society, we expect the police to work hard to achieve this goal. A lot of money is allocated to law enforcement agencies so they can accomplish it. The question is, if the police engage in conduct that is not technically legal, but their actions result in criminals being identified and apprehended, is there really anything wrong with that? Why or why not?

reports as "lie sheets." In the research conducted by Martin (1994), it was found that 4 percent of officers knew of other officers who had provided false testimony in traffic cases, 3 percent knew of false testimony in criminal cases, and 7 percent of officers knew of arrest reports written in a false manner. Given the sensitive nature of this area of inquiry, one might expect that these illegal behaviors are greatly underreported by officers. Although deception by the police in these types of situations is certainly troubling, the issue is complicated by the fact that in other situations it is legal for the police to lie. For instance, in interrogation settings, the police can legally deceive suspects in a variety of ways. For example, the statement "Your partner in the crime just confessed, so you might as well too" would be legally acceptable even if the partner did not really confess. If the police feel that the law is simply a barrier to effective performance, deception in many situations may be understandable (but in many situations is still not acceptable). Indeed, the most common reason for police lying is that the police view it as a necessary means to achieve the desired ends (Cunningham 1999; Martin 1994). In any case, it represents a strategy of the police to get around the exclusionary rule. Clearly, the exclusionary rule does not prevent the police from engaging in any of these questionable or illegal actions.

Does the exclusionary rule result in the loss of cases? Are potentially guilty suspects freed because of search and seizure problems? Numerous studies have attempted to address these questions. When the landmark decision of *Mapp v. Ohio* (1961) was rendered, the police believed that their actions were going to be constrained in a way that was detrimental to solving crimes and obtaining convictions. The research on the issue is mixed, although the prevailing conclusion appears to be that the exclusionary rule does not result in the loss of a significant percentage of cases. A study conducted by the General Accounting Office in 1979 found that in only 0.4 percent of cases were charges dropped or not made as a result of Fourth Amendment search and seizure problems. Nardulli (1983) found that motions to suppress physical evidence were filed in less than 5 percent of all felony cases, and only .69 percent of such motions were successful. Even when the motion to suppress evidence was successful, many defendants were still convicted based on the other evidence in the case. Uchida and Bynum (1991) found that in 13 percent of cases there was a motion to suppress physical evidence, but in less than 1 percent of the cases was this motion successful. In total, 1.4 percent of all defendants in the sample of cases were allowed to "go free" because of an exclusionary rule problem. Zalman (2002) succinctly concludes that "the figures show that the exclusionary rule is not subverting law enforcement" (p. 95).

Although the prevailing wisdom is that the exclusionary rule has little impact, it is important to realize that these studies did not examine the impact of the exclusionary rule on crimes being solved. In addition, the focus on "lost cases" at the court stage during the process draws attention away from the possibility that some of the cases where the police intentionally and obviously violate the provisions of the exclusionary rule are not even brought to the attention of prosecutors for further action and, therefore, could not be "lost" at the prosecutorial stage. In these cases, the exclusionary rule did not deter police misconduct or lead to the case being lost, it simply deterred the police from formally processing the case.

THE FIFTH AND SIXTH AMENDMENTS

The Fifth Amendment to the U.S. Constitution protects citizens against self-incrimination. It reads, in part, that "no person shall be compelled in any criminal case to be a witness against himself, nor be deprived of life, liberty or property, without due process of law."

The Sixth Amendment identifies several rights. The most important for criminal investigation is the right of individuals to be represented by an attorney in legal proceedings. The Sixth Amendment states, in part, that "in all criminal prosecutions the accused shall enjoy the right to . . . have the assistance of counsel for his defense."

The protections offered in the Fifth and Sixth Amendments are relevant when determining the admissibility of incriminating statements obtained from suspects. If information is obtained from suspects illegally, then that information is inadmissible in court because it violates the due process rights of the accused. In criminal investigations, extremely valuable information can come from suspects, but this information is only useful in establishing proof in court if the police follow the legal procedures in collecting that evidence. The fundamental question is, when are incriminating statements made by a suspect admissible in court, and when are they not? Most of the remainder of this chapter is devoted to addressing this important question.

The most famous and widely applied case associated with the Fifth and Sixth Amendment protections is *Miranda v. Arizona* (1966), as described in the introduction to this chapter. The decision in Miranda requires the police to inform suspects of their Miranda rights when a suspect is in custody and prior to interrogation. The Miranda warning consists of the following:

- You have the right to remain silent.

- Anything you say can be used in a court of law against you.

- You have a right to have an attorney with you during the interrogation.

- If you are unable to afford an attorney, one will be provided for you without cost.

If these rights are waived by a suspect, the waiver is to be done voluntarily and intelligently (see Exhibit 4.4).

Exhibit 4.4 Example of a Miranda Waiver Form

Incident   Number: _____   Defendant: _____   Address: _____ Charge:_____

Constitutional Rights Miranda Warnings

_____ You have the right to remain silent. Anything you say can and will be used against you in a court of law.

_____ You have the right to talk to a lawyer and have him/her present with you while you are being questioned.

_____ You can decide at any time to exercise these rights and not answer any questions or make any statements.

_____ At this time, I, _____, wish to waive my constitutional rights and agree to voluntarily provide a written statement to the Glendale Police Department. This statement is given voluntarily of my own free will and there have been no promises or threats made to me.

Signature _____ Date _____ Time _____

Witness _____ Date _____ Time _____ Title _____ Statement:

Signature _____ Page _____ of _____

_____

To verify that Miranda warnings were given and waived, most police departments require investigators to complete a form similar to the one illustrated here prior to the interrogation of a suspect.

MYTHS & MISCONCEPTIONS 4.1

Miranda Is Not Like Houdini

It is sometimes believed that the police must inform a suspect of the Miranda rights prior to the suspect being placed in handcuffs and, if they do not, the suspect can go free. This is not true. The *Miranda v. Arizona* decision holds that the police must read or otherwise inform suspects of their Miranda rights when two conditions are met: (1) when the suspect is in custody of the police *and* (2) prior to interrogation by the police. Only when both of these conditions apply must the suspect be informed of

his or her Miranda rights. In other words, when a subject is placed under arrest, the Miranda warnings do not need to be provided. When a subject is questioned (but is not in custody of the police at the time of the questioning), the Miranda warnings do not need to be provided. However, if a suspect is in custody of the police *and* is about to be interrogated by the police, Miranda warnings do need to be provided, otherwise incriminating statements made by the suspect may not be allowed at trial.

The Miranda decision extended the earlier decisions made by the U.S. Supreme Court in *Gideon v. Wainwright* (1963) and *Escobedo v. Illinois* (1964). In *Gideon v. Wainwright*, Gideon was arrested and charged with breaking and entering—a felony. Gideon appeared in court without an attorney because he could not afford one. He asked that the court appoint counsel for him. His request was denied because the law provided a right to counsel only in capital cases. He conducted his own defense. He was convicted and sentenced to five years in prison. On appeal, the Supreme Court ruled that "the right of an indigent defendant in a criminal trial to have the assistance of counsel is a fundamental right essential to a fair trial, and petitioner's trial and conviction without the assistance of counsel violated the Fourteenth Amendment."

In the Escobedo case, Escobedo was arrested by the police, taken to police headquarters, and questioned about the fatal shooting of his brother-in-law. Escobedo was not advised by the police of his right to remain silent. During the police interrogation, Escobedo confessed to the murder. During the interrogation, he also requested to see his lawyer, who was present in the building. The police refused. His confession was admitted in trial and he was convicted. On appeal, the Supreme Court ruled that the confession was inadmissible because of the circumstances of the interrogation; namely, that Escobedo was denied the right to counsel and was not notified of his right to remain silent. The Escobedo decision extended the right to counsel to the interrogation stage. *Gideon v. Wainwright* and *Escobedo v. Illinois* set the stage for the Miranda decision that explicitly outlined the rights of the accused and required that the police explicitly inform suspects of those rights.

Several decisions of the Supreme Court relate to the technical and definitional aspects of the Miranda rights and the waiver of those rights. For example, how must the Miranda warnings be read? In *California v. Prysock* (1981), the police informed a juvenile murder suspect of his Miranda rights, but they were not read from a standard script. The suspect was told that he had "the right to talk to a lawyer before you are questioned, have him present with you while you are being questioned, and all during the questioning." He was told that he could have his parents present and then was informed that he had "the right to have a lawyer appointed to represent you at no cost to yourself." After Prysock waived these rights, he made incriminating statements that were admitted into trial. The boy was convicted of first degree murder. On appeal, the Supreme Court ruled that these warnings were adequate. The police do not have to give verbatim warnings as long as the suspect is advised of his or her rights and no limitations are placed on those rights. The order in which the warnings are read does not determine their validity. The Supreme Court ruled that the incriminating statements were admissible. In *Florida v. Powell* (2010), the Supreme Court once again affirmed that the Miranda warnings do not require precise language. Most important is that it is communicated to the defendant that he or she has the opportunity to consult an attorney prior to or during the interrogation.

In *Smith v. Illinois* (1984), the waiver of some of the Miranda rights by the suspect was clear, but the waiver of some was rather ambiguous. When asked if he understood his right to consult with a lawyer and to have a lawyer present, Smith replied, "Uh, yeah. I'd like to do that." After being read the rest of the warnings and asked if he understood them, Smith stated, "Yeah and no, uh. I don't know what's that, really." The police continued to ask Smith questions, and Smith eventually made incriminating statements. The Supreme Court ruled that the defendant's request for counsel was not ambiguous and that all questioning should have stopped at that point. The statements made by Smith were not admissible.

For what offenses and under what circumstances must the Miranda warnings be read? In *Berkemer v. McCarty* (1984), the police arrested McCarty for suspicion of intoxicated driving, and he was interrogated at the police station. At no point was he informed of his Miranda rights. During questioning, McCarty made incriminating statements including that he was "barely" under the influence of alcohol. He was later charged with, and convicted of, operating a motor vehicle under the influence of alcohol and drugs. On appeal, the Supreme Court held that the police do not have to provide Miranda warnings prior to the roadside questioning of a motorist because this does not constitute a custodial interrogation. However, any person who is subjected to custodial interrogation must be given Miranda warnings, regardless of the severity of the offense. As a result, the Supreme Court ruled that the incriminating statements made during the custodial interrogation at the police station were not admissible.

PHOTO 4.7: In a traffic stop, any incriminating information provided by a subject to a police officer as a result of questioning is admissible in court. This is the case even if the officer did not provide the subject his or her Miranda warnings.

What is an interrogation? In *Rhode Island v. Innis* (1980), the Providence, Rhode Island, police arrested Innis as a suspect in the murder of a taxicab driver based on an eyewitness identification. Innis was advised of his Miranda rights. He said that he understood his rights and wanted to speak with an attorney. He was then placed in a car and driven to the station. During the drive, one of the officers commented that there were "a lot of handicapped children in the area" because a school for such children was nearby. He further stated how horrible it would be if one of the children found the gun used in the murder and something happened. Innis then proceeded to reveal where the gun could be found. The Supreme Court ruled that the respondent was not interrogated in violation of his rights. The statements the officer made did not constitute express questioning or its functional equivalent. The officers had no reason to believe that their statements would have led to a self-incriminating response of the suspect. Subtle compulsion does not constitute an interrogation.

In the case of *Brewer v. Williams* (1977), the police explicitly sought to obtain incriminating evidence from Williams with regard to his involvement in a kidnapping/murder. Knowing that he was a former mental patient and deeply religious, the officer called Williams "Reverend" and referred to the fact that the missing girl's parents should be entitled to a Christian burial for their daughter, who was taken from them on Christmas Eve. Williams then showed the police where to find the dead body. The Supreme Court held that the "Christian burial speech" was the functional equivalent of an interrogation. The statements were not admissible as evidence, but the body of the girl was admissible under the inevitable discovery exception to the exclusionary rule (see *Nix v. Williams* [1984]).

Other decisions have been rendered that establish parameters under which Miranda warnings must be provided. In the case of *Massiah v. United States* (1964), Massiah was arrested on drug trafficking charges, retained an attorney, pled not guilty to the charges, and was released on bail. A few days later, a coconspirator of Massiah decided to cooperate with government agents in their continuing investigation of Massiah. Through the use of a radio transmitter, conversations between Massiah and his partner were recorded that were incriminating. These statements were later used in court to obtain a conviction of Massiah. The Supreme Court held that Massiah's Fifth and Sixth Amendment rights were violated in that incriminating statements were deliberately obtained from him after he had been indicted and in the absence of retained counsel. The Supreme Court ruled that once a suspect has been indicted and has engaged an attorney, the police can no longer question him.

In a related case, *Edwards v. Arizona* (1981), Edwards was arrested on charges of robbery, burglary, and first degree murder. At the police station he was informed of his Miranda rights, and he declined to talk to the police without an attorney present. The next day, Edwards was once again given his Miranda warnings and he then implicated himself in the crimes. At his trial, these statements were used, and Edwards was convicted. The Supreme Court ruled that a suspect cannot be questioned again for the same offense after invoking his or her right to remain silent unless the suspect has consulted with a lawyer or the suspect initiates further communication, exchanges, or conversations with the police. In *Arizona v. Robertson* (1988), the Edwards decision was extended to questioning about the same or different offenses and to questioning conducted by the same or different law enforcement authorities. However, interestingly enough, the Supreme Court has ruled that if a subject is out of police custody for fourteen or more days, the police can attempt to re-initiate questioning after providing new Miranda warnings (*Maryland v. Shatzer* [2010]).

Does silence on the part of a suspect constitute evidence? It depends on the meaning and form of *silence*. In *Griffin v. California* (1965), the court ruled that a prosecutor cannot comment to the jury that the defendant not testifying constitutes evidence (of guilt). However, in *South Dakota v. Neville* (1983), it was ruled that the fact that a defendant refused to submit to a blood alcohol test is admissible in court as evidence.

There are several other situations when statements made by a defendant may be admissible without the Miranda warnings having been given or having been waived. These decisions may be thought of as exceptions to the Miranda requirement. For example, in *New York v. Quarles* (1984), a woman approached two police officers who were on patrol and told them that she had just been raped. She described her assailant as a black man and told the police that he was carrying a gun and had just entered the nearby supermarket. One officer entered the store and spotted Quarles, who matched the description given by the woman. On seeing the officer, Quarles turned and ran down an aisle. Quarles was stopped and subdued. Quarles was frisked, and the officer discovered that he was wearing an empty shoulder holster. After handcuffing him, the officer asked where the gun was located. Quarles nodded in the direction of some empty cartons, where the gun was then found. Quarles was given Miranda warnings only after the gun was found. The gun was admitted as evidence and Quarles was convicted. On appeal, the Supreme Court said that the gun was admissible as evidence under a "public safety" exception. The gun posed a possible immediate danger to the public; the potential danger justified the officer's failure to provide the Miranda warnings prior to questioning. The questioning was limited and the statements were provided voluntarily (also see Benoit 2011).

When a suspect is not aware that he or she is speaking to a law enforcement officer (e.g., during undercover operations), the police are not required to provide the Miranda warnings to the suspect. Any voluntary statements made by the suspect in this circumstance are admissible (*Illinois v. Perkins* [1990]). However, as ruled in *Arizona v. Fulminante* (1991), statements obtained as a result of implied duress, and without the benefit of the Miranda warnings, are not admissible. In this case, a paid police prison informant promised Fulminante that he would protect him from the other prisoners if Fulminante would tell him the truth about the abduction/murder of a child victim. Fulminante then confessed to the crime. He was convicted of murder, partially on the basis of this confession. The Supreme Court ruled that Fulminante's confession was involuntary because it was motivated by fear of physical violence if he did not receive protection. As a result, the confession was not admissible at trial.

Voluntary statements obtained as a result of police questioning but without the full protection of Miranda may be used in court for impeachment purposes only (*Oregon v. Hass* [1975]). If a suspect testifies in a manner contrary to his or her statements that were illegally obtained by the police, those statements can be used to prove that the defendant is lying (*Harris v. New York* [1971]; also see *Kansas v. Ventris* [2009]). If the arrest is *illegal*, but Miranda warnings are provided and waived, incriminating statements may not be used against the suspect. The Miranda warnings do not purge the taint of the illegal actions of the police (*Brown v. Illinois* [1975]). However, when an arrest is legal and Miranda warnings are provided to a suspect, and the suspect invokes those rights, and the police stop questioning but the suspect subsequently provides information voluntarily, then that information is admissible at trial (*Michigan v. Mosley* [1975]).

What if a suspect remains silent after being informed of his or her Miranda rights? In the case of *Berghuis v. Thompkins* (2010), the police informed the suspect of his Miranda rights and attempted to

The Bottom Line

When Must the Police Inform Suspects of Their Miranda Rights?

A suspect must be informed of the Miranda rights when that person is in custody of the police and prior to interrogation. If the suspect states that he or she does not wish to answer the questions of the police or requests an attorney, the questioning must stop (or not begin). If a suspect neither invokes nor waives the Miranda rights, questioning can continue.

If a suspect does not wish to answer the questions of the police, the suspect is not to be questioned about that offense or a different offense, nor is the suspect to be questioned by the same or a different law enforcement agency. However, if a suspect voluntarily provides incriminating statements, even after invoking the rights to not answer questions, those statements are admissible. Further, if a suspect is out of police custody for fourteen or more days, the police can attempt to re-initiate questioning after providing new Miranda warnings.

There are several circumstances in which the police do not need to inform suspects of their Miranda rights:

- To prevent possible immediate danger to the public, the police can question suspects who are in custody in a limited manner (e.g., "Where is the gun?") without first providing the Miranda warnings.

- Police working undercover do not need to provide Miranda warnings to suspects.

- The police do not need to provide Miranda warnings during roadside questioning of motorists (e.g., questions about destination, purpose of trip), but they do in all other instances where a person is subjected to custodial interrogation.

question him. He remained silent. After three hours of questioning, a detective asked the subject if he believed in God. The subject indicated that he did. He was then asked, "Do you pray for God to forgive you for shooting down that boy?" The suspect responded, "Yes." This statement was used against the defendant at trial. The Supreme Court ruled that "after giving a Miranda warning, police may interrogate a suspect who has neither invoked nor waived his or her Miranda rights.

What if the suspect does not invoke the Miranda rights, but a third party does on his or her behalf? Are incriminating statements provided by the suspect then admissible? Consider the case of *Moran v. Burbine* (1986). In this case, Burbine was arrested for a murder and held by the police. Burbine's sister made arrangements for an attorney to represent Burbine while he was in custody, but Burbine was not aware of his sister's actions. The attorney then contacted the police and stated that she would act as his counsel. She was informed by the police that they would not question Burbine until the next day. Again, all these actions were unknown to Burbine. The police subsequently informed Burbine of his Miranda rights and he waived them. The police then questioned him about the murder. At no time did he request an attorney. Burbine confessed to the murder. The Supreme Court ruled that neither the conduct of the police nor the respondent's ignorance of the attorney's efforts taints the validity of the waiver of rights. The Supreme Court held that the confession should not be excluded.

THE IMPACT OF FIFTH AMENDMENT LEGISLATION ON CRIMINAL INVESTIGATIONS

The reaction to the Miranda decision was intense. A self-confessed and convicted rapist was given another chance at freedom because the police did not tell him about his right to remain silent and his right to have an attorney. The police were outraged. The assumption was that if suspects were told that they did not have to talk to the police and that what they said might be used against them, then suspects just wouldn't talk. Confessions, it was believed, would be a thing of the past. This was the conventional wisdom. Most of the research that has been conducted to examine the impact of Miranda on police ability to obtain confessions has shown that the Miranda decision has had minimal impact—or, at least, less of an impact than what was believed at the time of the Supreme Court decision.

To understand the impact of Miranda, at least two issues need to be considered. First, to what extent are confessions that have been obtained by the police subsequently ruled to be inadmissible? Second, to what extent are confessions not obtained by the police because of Miranda? And relatedly, what impact does the lack of confession evidence have on prosecutors' ability to obtain convictions? The second issue is more complicated than the first because it must be understood that perhaps no confession was obtained because there was no confession to give (i.e., the person who was interrogated did not commit the crime), and just because there was no confession does not mean that the case was lost; other evidence may have been available.

With regard to the first question, Nardulli (1983) examined more than 7,000 cases in Illinois, Michigan, and Pennsylvania and found that only five convictions were lost as a result of confessions being ruled as illegally obtained and therefore inadmissible. Not surprisingly, this study concluded that Miranda has had virtually no impact on police effectiveness.

With regard to the second question, Leo (1998) analyzed 182 investigations in three police departments and found that in 78 percent of the cases, suspects waived their Miranda rights and answered the questions of the police. In the remaining 22 percent of cases, suspects invoked their rights and did not talk. Cassell and Hayman (1998) examined more than 200 cases and found that of the 129 cases in which the police provided suspects with their Miranda rights, approximately 84 percent waived them and agreed to answer the questions of the police. As demonstrated in both of these studies, because a large majority of suspects still decide to speak with the police even after they are informed of their rights, it appears

Miranda Warnings Cause Suspects to Keep Quiet

Conventional wisdom and common sense hold that if suspects are told that anything they say to the police can be used against them in court and they are told that they do not have to answer the questions of the police, then suspects are not going to answer the questions of the police. Not true.

As discussed above, research has shown that the majority of suspects agree to answer the questions of the police even when they are told that they do not have to. And, as discussed in Chapter 7, many of these suspects end up confessing to the crime they are suspected of committing.

that Miranda has not kept suspects from talking with the police. Some have even suggested that the Miranda warnings may *increase* the likelihood that suspects will make incriminating statements. The Miranda warnings make it clear that the police think that the subject is guilty. It may be believed by suspects that a willingness to answer questions will help clear them of responsibility (Thomas 1998). It is interesting to note that in a study by Leo (1998a), suspects with a felony record were less likely to answer questions than suspects without a felony record, and suspects who answered the questions of the police were more likely to be convicted than those who did not answer questions. Research has also shown that innocent subjects were more likely to answer questions of the police (Kassin and Norwick 2004). These issues are discussed in more detail in Chapter 7.

MAIN POINTS

1. An arrest occurs when the police take a person into custody for the purposes of criminal prosecution and interrogation.

2. A search is a governmental infringement into a person's reasonable expectation of privacy for the purpose of discovering things that could be used as evidence in a criminal prosecution.

3. All evidence admitted into court for consideration by a judge or jury must have certain qualities. All evidence must be relevant, material, competent, and necessary. With physical evidence, a chain of custody also must be maintained.

4. The intent of the Fourth Amendment is to protect individuals' privacy and protect against arbitrary intrusions into that privacy by government officials.

5. The general rule is that the police need a search warrant to conduct a legal and valid search, and that warrant is to be based on probable cause. However, there are many exceptions to this rule. In fact, most searches conducted by the police are conducted without a warrant. These exceptions

consist of cases involving exigent circumstances, vehicles, other places/things not covered by the Fourth Amendment, hot pursuit, incident to arrest, stop and frisk, plain view, and consent.

6. The exclusionary rule holds that if the police collect evidence illegally, that evidence is to be excluded from court proceedings. However, there are several exceptions to the rule: good faith, inevitable discovery, purged taint, and independent source.

7. The purpose of the exclusionary rule is to deter police misconduct in search and seizure cases, but there are ways of "getting around" the exclusionary rule that limit its effectiveness.

8. The Fifth Amendment to the Constitution protects against self-incrimination; the Sixth Amendment provides the right of the accused to be represented by an attorney in criminal proceedings.

9. The police must inform suspects of their Miranda rights when (1) the suspect is in custody of the police and (2) prior to interrogation by the police.

10. There are several circumstances in which the police do not need to inform suspects of their Miranda rights: (1) when it is necessary to prevent possible immediate danger to the public, the police can question suspects who are in custody in a limited manner without first providing the Miranda warnings; (2) when the police work undercover they do not need to provide Miranda warnings to suspects; and (3) during roadside questioning of motorists.

11. Research shows that the impact of Miranda on police ability to obtain confessions has been minimal.

IMPORTANT TERMS

Arrest

Arrest warrant

Chain of custody

Competent evidence

Consent exception

Custodial interrogation

Daubert standard

Exceptions to the exclusionary rule

Exceptions to the Miranda requirement

Exclusionary rule

Exigent circumstances exception

Frye test

Hot pursuit exception

Material evidence

Miranda warnings

Necessary evidence

Other places exception

Plain view exception

Probable cause

Reasonable suspicion

Relevant evidence

Search

Search incident to arrest exception

Search warrant

Stop and frisk exception

Vehicle exception

QUESTIONS FOR DISCUSSION AND REVIEW

1. What qualities must evidence have in order for it to be admissible in court?

2. What is the chain of custody and why is it important?

3. What is the significance of the Fourth Amendment to the U.S. Constitution?

4. Under what circumstances is an arrest warrant necessary? When is a search warrant necessary?

5. Under what circumstances is a search warrant not required? What is the reason for each exception to the search warrant requirement?

6. What is the purpose of the exclusionary rule and what are the exceptions to it?

7. What impact does the exclusionary rule have on criminal investigations and the criminal justice process? Why?

8. What is an interrogation from the perspective of the Fifth Amendment?

9. What are the Miranda warnings? When must they be provided to suspects? When do they not need to be provided?

10. What is the impact of Miranda on criminal investigations and the criminal justice process? Why?

 ## STUDENT STUDY SITE

Visit **www.sagepub.com/brandl3e** to access additional study tools including eFlashcards, web quizzes, web resources, video resources, and SAGE journal articles.

5 Physical Evidence and the Crime Scene

Objectives

After reading this chapter you will be able to:

- Discuss the three roles or functions of physical evidence in the criminal investigation process, and describe how physical evidence can serve as direct evidence or circumstantial evidence in criminal investigations

- Discuss the scientific limitations of physical evidence

- Identify the most important guidelines that should be followed in recovering and preserving physical evidence from major crime scenes

- Evaluate the methods of searching crime scenes

- Compare and contrast class characteristic evidence with individual characteristic evidence

- Discuss the evidentiary value of different types of physical evidence

- Compare the value and contribution of DNA evidence with fingerprint evidence in criminal investigations

- Explain the Combined DNA Index System (CODIS) and how it increases the value of DNA analysis

- Discuss the precautions that are necessary when collecting and handling biological evidence

From the **CASE FILE**

The Murders of Nicole Brown Simpson and Ronald Goldman

On Sunday, June 12, 1994, just before 11:00 p.m., Steven Schwab was walking his dog in the Brentwood section of northwest Los Angeles when he was confronted by an agitated Akita. As the dog followed Steven home, he noticed what appeared to be blood on the dog's paws and belly. When Steven arrived home, the dog continued to behave in an unusual manner. Steven alerted his neighbor, Sukru Boztepe, and asked if Boztepe could keep the dog until the morning when Steven would search for its owner. Boztepe initially agreed but then decided to take the dog for a walk and see if he could find its owner himself. He proceeded to follow the dog, and it took him to the front walkway of 875 South Bundy Drive. As Boztepe looked up the dark walkway, he saw what appeared to be a lifeless human body surrounded by a massive amount of blood.

At 12:13 a.m. the first police officers arrived at the scene. Officers found the body of a woman clad in a short black dress. She was barefoot and lying face down with severe wounds to her throat and neck area, nearly to be point of being decapitated. Next to her was the body of a man. He was lying on his side and his clothes were also saturated with blood. The woman was quickly identified by the police as the owner of the house, Nicole Brown Simpson, thirty-five years old and the ex-wife of sportscaster and former pro football player O. J. Simpson. The dead body of the man next to her was identified through identification in his wallet, still in his back pants pocket, as Ronald Goldman, twenty-five, a waiter at a restaurant that Nicole and her family had visited earlier in the evening. Police also discovered the two children of Nicole and Simpson, nine and six, asleep in their beds in the house.

By 2:10 a.m. Detective Supervisor Ron Phillips and detectives Mark Fuhrman and Brad Roberts had arrived at the scene. Shortly thereafter, Phillips was notified that detectives Tom Lange and Phil Vannatter from the Homicide Special Section of the Los Angeles Police Department's (LAPD's) Robbery Homicide Division were assigned as the lead investigators in the case; these detectives were on the scene by 4:30 a.m.

In examining the area in which the bodies lay, the detectives noticed several items: a set of keys (Goldman's), a dark blue knit cap (believed to be the perpetrator's), a beeper (Goldman's), a blood-splattered white envelope (that contained the eyeglasses of Nicole's mother, who left them at the restaurant earlier that night; presumably Goldman was

PHOTO 5.1: Although the blood and bodies were the most obvious, the crime scene of the murders of Nicole Brown Simpson and Ron Goldman revealed much other evidence. That evidence associated O. J. Simpson to the crime scene and made him a suspect in the murders.

property, detectives observed a white Ford Bronco, front wheels on the curb, with the back of the vehicle sticking out into the street. It was a vehicle that was registered to Simpson. On closer examination of the vehicle, Detective Fuhrman noticed what appeared to be a blood spot on the vehicle near the door handle. Detectives called the phone number of the house to gain entry over the five-foot-high stone wall that surrounded the property, but no one responded. Fuhrman climbed the wall and let the other detectives in by unlatching the lock of the gate. The detectives knocked on the front door of the main house, but there was no answer. They proceeded to the small guest houses located on the property. When they knocked on the door of the first house, a man by the name of Kato Kaelin, a houseguest of Simpson's, answered the door. At the next house they found Arnelle Simpson, Simpson's daughter. Fuhrman stayed with Kaelin while the other detectives accompanied Arnelle to the main house to confirm that no one else

at Nicole's house to return those glasses), and a blood-soaked, left-hand leather glove (also believed to be the perpetrator's). Leading away from the bodies toward the back of the property were shoeprints transferred to the concrete surface from blood on the shoes. Alongside the shoeprint trail were drops of blood. The shoeprints and the blood drops appeared to be from the killer.

Detectives decided to try to make contact with Simpson to notify him of the murder of his ex-wife and to arrange for him to get his children, who were still at the house. It was a five-minute drive from the South Bundy address to Simpson's estate on Rockingham Avenue. It was now about 5:00 a.m. Once at Simpson's

was home or in any sort of danger. The detectives returned to Kaelin and interviewed him. He told the detectives that before Simpson caught a late flight to Chicago that previous night, he went with him to a McDonald's and then returned home. Kaelin said that when they returned, Simpson went into the house and he, Kaelin, went to his bungalow. At about 10:45 p.m. Kaelin heard several loud banging noises outside near the bungalow's air-conditioning unit. He said he thought it was an earthquake. He then went outside to investigate and saw a limousine parked at the gate to take Simpson to the airport. A few minutes later, according to Kaelin, Simpson rode off in the limousine. While talking to Arnelle, police were able to determine that Simpson was staying at the Chicago O'Hare Plaza

Hotel. While Fuhrman checked the area around the air-conditioning unit, Detective Phillips called Simpson in Chicago and notified him of the murder of his ex-wife. According to Phillips, Simpson appeared concerned about what Phillips told him, but Simpson never asked for any details about what happened, nor did he even ask which ex-wife had been killed (Simpson had two ex-wives). Simpson told Phillips that he would return to Los Angeles on the next available flight.

Shortly after this phone call, Detective Fuhrman returned to the house and told Vannatter of his discovery near the air-conditioning unit in the back of the bungalow occupied by Kaelin. There, according to Fuhrman, lying on the ground among some leaves, was a bloodstained leather glove. (The defense later argued that this glove was actually planted there by Fuhrman, who they claimed was a racist cop. Their claim was that both gloves were found at the crime scene, and Fuhrman took one of them with him to Simpson's.) It appeared to be the right-hand match of the one found at the crime scene on Bundy. Then Vannatter discovered what appeared to be blood drops in the driveway. They led to the Ford Bronco. Inside the Bronco, he saw other red spots on the driver's side door and on the console between the two front seats. He discovered more blood leading to the front door of the main house. (The defense later argued that this blood was also planted and that it actually came from the sample that was drawn from Simpson at the police department after the initial interrogation by Vannatter and Lange. Interestingly, the nurse who drew the blood from Simpson testified he drew eight cubic centimeters of blood, but the LAPD could only account for 6.5 cubic centimeters.) All this evidence was later photographed, the glove was seized, the Bronco was impounded, and the entire area was secured. Detectives then obtained a warrant to search Simpson's house and vehicle.

With search warrant in hand, the detectives returned to the Rockingham property. While they were conducting their search of the premises, Simpson arrived home. Simpson and his attorneys agreed that it would be okay for Simpson to talk with detectives Lange and Vannatter about the murders and to do so without his attorneys present. At 1:35 p.m., June 13, the interrogation of Simpson by Lange and Vannatter began. After the interrogation was over, Simpson was fingerprinted, wounds on his left hand

PHOTO 5.2: Perhaps no evidence in the investigation (and trial) of O. J. Simpson was as important and as contested as the glove found on Simpson's property. Beliefs differ over whether the glove was dropped there by Simpson or placed there by detectives.

were photographed, and a sample of his blood was drawn. The vial of blood was labeled and placed in an evidence envelope. Vannatter then took the sealed envelope back to Simpson's home and gave it to Dennis Fung, the criminalist who was responsible for collecting and recording the evidence at the Bundy and Rockingham scenes. To maintain the chain of custody, Fung checked the contents of the envelope and, according to procedure, wrote on the outside, "Received from Vannatter on 6–13–94 at 1720 hours." It was then placed in the LAPD's crime scene truck. This whole sequence of events was done in full view of the numerous media film crews who were at the scene.

Meanwhile, back at Rockingham, the search of Simpson's residence revealed additional evidence of interest, including black socks, later determined to be stained with blood, and additional blood drops inside the house (more planted evidence, according to the defense). In all, forty-one items of evidence were collected from Simpson's Bronco, his house, and the Bundy crime scene. Through scientific analysis, numerous links could be drawn from this evidence. Specifically, as outlined by Fuhrman (1997, pp. 156–164), evidence recovered from the left-hand glove found at the Bundy crime scene consisted of the following:

- One hair from Nicole
- Fibers consistent with Goldman's shirt
- Fibers consistent with Goldman's jeans
- Dog hair from the Akita

By itself, and given the evidence on it, this single glove was not that useful. One would suppose from the discovery of the glove that the murderer wore gloves while committing the homicides. However, potentially much more valuable was the right-hand glove found at Simpson's Rockingham estate. By itself, the glove connected Simpson (Simpson's property) to the crime scene. But there was more. On this glove were the following:

- Several hairs from Nicole
- Several pulled hairs from Goldman
- Fibers consistent with Goldman's shirt
- Dog hair from the Akita
- One fiber from the Bronco's carpet
- Several blue-black cotton fibers consistent with fibers found on Goldman's shirt

Given the blood and fibers found on the glove, the fact that it was found on Simpson's property, and that the identical matching glove was found at the crime scene, the glove seemed to link all the key individuals and places together: Simpson, Nicole, Goldman, and the crime scene. As such, this glove was an extremely valuable piece of evidence.

The following were present on the socks found in Simpson's bedroom at Rockingham:

- Blue-black cotton fibers
- Blood from Simpson and Nicole

If the socks were Simpson's, and if the blood was not planted on them, then the socks served as corroborative evidence that, at the least, Simpson was near Nicole when she was bleeding.

Found on Goldman's shirt were the following items:

- One hair consistent with Simpson's
- Twenty-five hairs from Nicole
- Several hairs from the Akita
- Four torn fibers from Nicole's dress
- Several fibers from the knit cap
- One fiber consistent with the lining of both gloves
- Many blue-black fibers

This evidence associated Goldman with Simpson, Nicole, the gloves and cap of the perpetrator, and probably the clothes of the perpetrator (the blue-black fibers).

On Ron Goldman's pants were found:

- Several hairs consistent with Nicole's
- Several hairs from the Akita

This hair linked Nicole with Goldman, and Goldman with the dog. This was relatively insignificant evidence in establishing who was responsible for the homicides but was perhaps useful for other purposes, such as for reconstructing the crime.

On the blue knit cap found at the Bundy crime scene were the following items:

- Several hairs from the Akita
- Twelve hairs matching Simpson's, not pulled or torn
- Several fibers consistent with Goldman's shirt
- One fiber consistent with the lining of both gloves
- One fiber consistent with the Bronco's carpet

Once again, this evidence provided additional strength to the conclusion that Simpson was at the crime scene and was wearing, at least temporarily, the cap. One might infer from this evidence alone that Simpson was the likely perpetrator. But there was even more physical evidence.

The blood evidence found at the Bundy crime scene included:

- Blood drops near the victims that matched Simpson's

- Four blood drops on the walkway that matched Simpson's

- Two shoeprints of size twelve Bruno Magli shoes in Nicole's blood

- Bloodstains from Goldman's boot that matched Goldman's and Nicole's blood

Through DNA analysis, the blood found at the crime scene that was not Nicole's or Goldman's was confirmed to be Simpson's. This evidence linked Simpson to the scene of the crime (plus Simpson had unexplained injuries to his hand). In order for Goldman's boot to leave a print in Nicole's blood, she had to be bleeding before Goldman fell. It is reasonable to conclude that Nicole was attacked first, then Goldman. The shoeprints were probably left by the perpetrator. (Later, in the civil trial against Simpson, photographs of Simpson reporting from the sidelines of a National Football League football game and wearing the shoes in question were introduced, but his lawyers argued that the photographs were altered.)

The blood evidence found in and on the Bronco included:

- Blood that matched Simpson's found on the driver's door interior and on the instrument panel

- Blood on the center console that matched Simpson's

- Blood on the steering wheel that matched Simpson's and Nicole's

- Blood on the driver's side wall that matched Simpson's

- Blood on the carpet that matched Nicole's

- Blood on the center console that matched Simpson's, Nicole's, and Goldman's

PHOTO 5.3: Detective Mark Fuhrman pointing to evidence near the body of Nicole Brown Simpson.

More evidence linked Simpson with the dead victims and the crime scene. The blood evidence at Rockingham included the following:

- Two blood drops on a sock that matched Nicole's and two that matched Simpson's

- Blood drops in the foyer that matched Simpson's

- A blood trail on the driveway that matched Simpson's

As Fuhrman (1997) explained, there was not just a mountain of evidence showing that Simpson killed his ex-wife and Ron Goldman, there was a *Mt. Everest* of evidence, but it was explained away by the defense by arguing that Simpson was framed.

In addition to the physical evidence, there were the interesting facts that Simpson had seven abrasions and several cuts to his left hand (and that the left-hand glove was found at the crime scene) and that Simpson did not have a reasonable explanation for these injuries or his whereabouts during the time the homicides occurred.

On Friday June 17, 1994, an arrest warrant for O. J. Simpson was prepared. Simpson's new attorney, Robert Shapiro, was instructed by the police to accompany Simpson to police headquarters. Simpson was to surrender at 11:00 a.m. At 11:00 a.m., Simpson was nowhere to be found. Police later discovered that he was with his friend Al Cowling driving around Orange County, near Los Angeles, in Simpson's Bronco. The police followed them, and the convoy became the famous slow-speed chase. It ended hours later at Simpson's residence at Rockingham. Simpson was arrested and taken into custody for the murders of Nicole Brown Simpson and Ronald Goldman. The investigation that led to his arrest was only the first part of the story. The jury trial began on January 23, 1995. The case took many twists and turns before Simpson was found not guilty on October 2, 1995. The jury deliberated for less than five hours.

Case Considerations and Points for Discussion ●

- As discussed here, there was a substantial amount of physical evidence that appeared to associate O. J. Simpson with the murders of Nicole Brown Simpson and Ronald Goldman. What do you think was the most powerful physical evidence that suggested that Simpson committed the murders? Why?

- According to O. J. Simpson's defense attorneys, the physical evidence that incriminated Simpson was actually planted or fabricated by the police. Explain the defense attorneys' reasoning. At the very least, detectives made several critical mistakes in conducting the crime scene investigation and collecting evidence. Identify and discuss these mistakes.

- Every investigation is a learning experience. What do you think should be the biggest lessons learned by the police as a result of this investigation?

- In the years since the murders and the trial, much attention has been devoted to the case and many have speculated whether O. J. Simpson actually committed the murders. New theories and additional mistakes made by investigators have come to light. Many people believe that O. J. Simpson got away with murder. Some believe that Simpson was at the scene when the murders occurred but that he did not actually commit them. Others believe that the police planted the physical evidence and framed a guilty man. Some people believe that he was completely innocent. What do you think? Why?

Also:

- For additional insight into other possible explanations for the crime, more details about other mistakes and oversights made by detectives, and speculation about other suspects, check out the YouTube video "BBC—OJ Simpson the Untold Story" (one hour, ten minutes long; warning: graphic photos and descriptions are contained in the video).

●●● The Role of Physical Evidence in the Criminal Investigative Process

Physical evidence, also known as *forensic evidence* or *real evidence*, can serve several important roles in the criminal investigative process. First, physical evidence can help establish the elements of a crime and thus function as corpus delicti evidence. For example, a dead body (along with the associated findings of an autopsy) may establish that a homicide occurred. Pry or tool marks on a window can help establish that a burglary occurred. Semen recovered from a victim can help establish that a rape occurred. The presence of flammable liquids or combustibles can help establish that arson occurred. Of course, a lack of a dead body, an absence of pry marks, a lack of semen, or a lack of combustibles does not necessarily indicate that a crime did *not* occur. A homicide can occur without the discovery of a dead body, a burglary can occur without evidence of forced entry, a rape can occur without semen being present (or a rape may not have occurred even if semen *is* present), and arson can be committed without flammable liquids. It is in this manner that physical evidence can *help* establish the elements of a crime or assist investigators in determining whether a crime actually occurred (see Case in Point 5.1).

A second important role of physical evidence in the criminal investigation process is that it can be used to make associations between crime scenes, offenders, victims, and instruments (e.g., tools). In fact, forensic evidence collected during criminal investigations is used most often to establish associations. Consider the case of Simpson: the glove found on Simpson's property that contained Nicole's hair and Goldman's hair and blood associated, at the least, Simpson's property with the homicide scene. Simpson's blood found at the crime scene and at his house further strengthened the association between Simpson and the homicides. As another example, in the investigation of the death of Caylee Anthony, the examination of the girl's skeletonized remains revealed that duct tape was wrapped around the skull. Investigators found duct tape of the same brand in the garage at the Anthony home. The remains of the girl were found in a wooded area and intermixed with two plastic trash bags and a Whitney Design laundry bag. Investigators also found a Whitney Design canvas laundry bag wrapped in a black plastic bag on a shelf above the washing machine in the Anthony home.

Third, in helping to establish the elements of a crime or in making associations between offenders, victims, and so forth, physical evidence can function as corroborative evidence and thereby support other evidence that establishes an issue in question. For example, physical evidence such as pry marks can support a victim's statement about a burglary having occurred, or DNA evidence such as semen can support the victim's identification of the assailant.

CASE *in* POINT 5.1 Did a Rape Occur?

Even though the presence of forensic evidence may not conclusively establish that a crime occurred, it can make establishing proof of certain crimes much less difficult. Alternatively, the lack of physical evidence can make it difficult to prove that a crime occurred. Consider the case of Mark Chmura, the former Pro Bowl tight end of the Green Bay Packers. Chmura was accused of sexually assaulting a sixteen-year-old girl (the former babysitter of his children) at an early morning after-prom party in April 1999. The assault allegedly took place in a bathroom of the house where the party was being held—the house of one of the victim's friends and a neighbor of Chmura's. According to the victim's statement to the police and the court testimony, Chmura was in the bathroom about to change his clothes after being in an outside hot tub with the victim and several of her friends when he motioned to the intoxicated victim for her to enter the bathroom. Chmura then closed the door, placed the victim on the floor, removed her pants, and penetrated her vagina in an unknown manner. Subsequent to this event, the victim underwent a sexual assault examination. The exam revealed minor injuries to the victim, but no semen was present. The defense argued that no such encounter occurred in the bathroom. There was no sexual assault. There was no semen because there was no rape. According to an expert witness for the defense, the documented injuries to the victim may have resulted from her wearing a swimsuit that did not fit well. It was argued that Chmura was set up by the victim because she did not like him and wanted to get money from him. These issues could be raised because there was no semen—no physical evidence. If semen was found, sexual intercourse would have been established and, because the victim was sixteen, consent would not have been an issue. The jury found Mark Chmura not guilty.

Finally, certain forms of physical evidence may serve an identification function. For example, as discussed in more detail later in the chapter, dental evidence such as medical records or x-rays can be used to determine the identity of an individual (usually a dead body), as can DNA evidence and fingerprints.

It is also worthwhile to note that physical evidence can act as direct *or* circumstantial evidence. In the Simpson case, for example, blood was used to conclude that Simpson was at the crime scene; Simpson's blood drops at the crime scene were direct evidence that he was at the crime scene. The fact that Simpson's blood was found at the crime scene was also used to *infer* that Simpson committed the murders.

Although physical evidence can help establish the elements of a crime; can make associations between offenders, victims, crime scenes, and so forth; and can serve a corroborative function with other evidence, physical evidence is not especially effective at identifying a culprit when one is not already known. Of course, certain forms of physical evidence can lead to a culprit being identified or the crime being solved, but in the scheme of things this is a relatively uncommon occurrence. Consider once again the case of O. J. Simpson. If Simpson had not been identified as a suspect through other means (e.g., first by being the ex-spouse of Nicole, then by having a sketchy alibi and an injured hand for which he had no clear explanation), the blood that was found at the crime scene that did not belong to either of the victims may not have been very useful in the investigation. It was only after Simpson was identified as a suspect through other means that the blood was useful for investigative purposes: the blood at the crime scene could then be compared and positively matched to Simpson via DNA analysis. As such, Simpson could be associated with the crime scene, and the blood corroborated other factors that led to Simpson being considered the culprit.

Further, consider the role of physical evidence in the following rather typical homicide cases:

- Relatives found an elderly man dead in the basement of his house with his skull crushed by a barbell that was still resting on his head. The victim's daughter told the police at the time of the discovery that a woman by the name of Jan, who was a drunken, violent prostitute, often lived with the victim. She said that her father and Jan often visited a neighborhood tavern. Investigators went to the tavern, asked about Jan, and obtained her last name and an address where she was known to sometimes sleep. In looking for Jan, they first found Jan's sister. She told police that Jan confessed to her that she killed the old man because he was going to kick her out of his house. She then told the police where Jan could be found. The police found Jan and they told her that her sister said she confessed to her. Jan then confessed to the police that she killed the old man. She was arrested and charged with the homicide.

- An individual was arrested as a "suspicious person" in Chicago. He was discovered driving a vehicle that he did not own; the vehicle was registered to a person with a Detroit address. Chicago police contacted the Detroit police about their discovery. Detroit police officers went to the address listed for the owner of the vehicle and found it locked. The police broke into the house and discovered a dead body. Through a driver's license in the victim's pocket, police identified him as the owner of the house and the vehicle. He had been stabbed to death. Chicago police were notified of the homicide. Upon checking the vehicle further, the police found many other items belonging to the victim. Upon questioning of the suspect, he confessed to the murder and theft. He was arrested and charged with murder.

- A brother and sister, both adults, were arguing about the brother moving out of the sister's house. A physical altercation resulted, and the sister was stabbed once in the leg. The police were notified of the argument and screaming by a neighbor. The police arrived and, in a dying declaration, the victim stated that her brother stabbed her. He was still at the scene. When questioned, the brother confessed to killing his sister. He was arrested and charged with the crime.

As shown here, not only did physical evidence not play a role in the identification of the perpetrator, physical evidence simply did not play any important role in the investigation or the arrest of the perpetrators. Why? In homicides, as well as in rapes, assaults, and some robberies, there is often other evidence, such as eyewitnesses, and circumstances (e.g., a relationship between the victim and the offender) that lead to the identity of the perpetrator. In a study of homicides conducted by Brandl (2004), the homicide victim and the suspect were known to each other in 69 percent of the solved cases (fifty-seven of the eighty-three cases), and an eyewitness was able to provide the name (or partial name) of the perpetrator in 66 percent of the solved cases (fifty-five of the eighty-three cases). These circumstances and the related evidence may be much more useful to investigators in identifying a perpetrator than physical evidence that may be available. Indeed, forensic evidence has the greatest impact in investigations when the chances of solving the crime are the smallest—that is, when a suspect is neither named or identified quickly after the crime.

Having said this, it is also important to understand that physical evidence is becoming much more important and influential in the criminal investigation process. This is especially true with DNA analysis, which has shown to be of tremendous benefit in some criminal investigations and still has much potential to be realized.

●●● The Crime Scene and Its Management

Physical evidence often begins its role in the criminal investigation process with its discovery and collection at the crime scene. A crime scene is the area within the immediate vicinity or location in which the criminal incident occurred or was believed to have occurred. The area where significant evidence relating to a crime is (or could be) found, but where the crime did not actually occur, is commonly referred to as a *secondary crime scene*. For example, in a homicide, several places may be related to the crime and may contain evidence associated with the crime: the place where the victim was encountered, the place where the victim was first attacked, the place where the murder occurred, the place where the body was discovered, and the place where the murder weapon was disposed of. The more sites identified by the police, the more likely the crime is to be solved (Rossmo 2000). In the O. J. Simpson case, the house of Nicole Brown Simpson was the crime scene; O. J. Simpson's house was a secondary crime scene. Depending on the crime, crime scenes commonly include residences, businesses, streets, yards, parking lots, vehicles, and hospitals. Regardless of its location, a crime scene needs to be managed and controlled in order to preserve evidence and to ensure the integrity of it.

Not all crime scenes are equal in their value to investigators. Some crime scenes may be more valuable than others because only certain people may have access to particular places. In addition, some crime scenes contain little evidence, whereas some contain a wealth of it. Accordingly, appropriate and necessary crime scene procedures vary considerably from crime to crime. In addition, resources and the policies of particular police departments may also dictate the proper course of action in crime scene investigations. Searching for and collecting physical evidence from crime scenes is not an inexpensive endeavor; it takes time. As a result, although relatively little time may be spent processing burglary crime scenes in most jurisdictions, much time may be reasonably spent on homicide scenes.

With this knowledge as a backdrop, it is important to realize that there are basic guidelines that should be followed by investigative personnel in preserving and recovering physical evidence from major crime scenes. The guidelines discussed here are typically ones that should be followed in major crime investigations such as homicides (see National Institute of Justice 2000a).[1]

---

1. Deputy Inspector William Jessup of the Milwaukee Police Department also provided valuable input on this discussion.

ARRIVING AT THE SCENE: INITIAL RESPONSE/ PRIORITIZATION OF EFFORTS

The first and one of the most important steps in a crime scene operation is securing the crime scene to minimize contamination by external factors such as bystanders or witnesses that could lead to the destruction of evidence. The initial responding officer should approach the crime scene cautiously and should be aware of any persons or vehicles in the area, or leaving the area, that may be related to the crime. The officer should make sure that it is safe to enter the crime scene to take further action. It is important that the officer remain alert and attentive when approaching and processing the scene.

Second, a determination has to be made about the legality of entering and searching the crime scene. Recall from Chapter 4 that there is *not* a crime scene exception to the search warrant requirement. A search is to be based on probable cause and/or a warrant. A crime scene can be secured and a protective sweep for suspects and/or victims can be conducted without a warrant; however, a search depends on a warrant or must be justified by an exception to the search warrant requirement (e.g., consent, plain view, exigent circumstances, hot pursuit). If an exception does not apply, a search warrant must be obtained.

Third, a top priority in and around the crime scene is officer safety. Officers should look for possible threats to their safety, including hazardous materials, chemical threats, and dangerous persons. If such threats are apparent, appropriate personnel/backup should be immediately notified.

Fourth, after neutralizing dangerous persons or other threats, the officers' next responsibility is to provide or summon necessary medical attention for injured parties. Officers should ensure that medical personnel have guided access to the scene but do not unnecessarily disturb it. If resources allow or if the victim is in grave danger of death, an officer should accompany the victim to the medical facility to document any comments made (e.g., a dying declaration) and to preserve evidence.

Fifth, the crime scene must constantly be protected from persons at or near the scene. Individuals must be prevented from entering and altering the crime scene and the physical evidence located there. Some crime scenes are emotional places where loved ones of the victim, understandably, may have little regard for the integrity and security of the crime scene. The crime scene must be protected. In addition, suspects and witnesses must be identified and separated. Critical information can be quickly compromised when witnesses are allowed to share with each other their versions of events prior to being interviewed.

Sixth, officers must establish the boundaries of the crime scene in order to protect it. Effective barriers can be established with crime scene tape and/or barricades. The boundaries should include where the crime actually occurred, paths of entry and exit of the suspects, and places where the victim/evidence may have been moved or discarded. The perimeter should be made as large as possible. No person, including citizens or media, should be allowed to enter or alter the crime scene through such actions as smoking, eating or drinking, moving any items, opening windows, or littering. Persons who are at a crime scene when boundaries are established should be removed from the scene.

Seventh, whenever appropriate, the initial responding officers should brief the investigators taking charge of the investigation. Witnesses and what they have said should be reported, physical evidence should be noted, and progress on other investigative activities should be reported. These actions provide critical continuity during the initial phases of the investigation. Communication regarding activities, responsibilities and duties, and evidence is extremely important.

Finally, all activities and observations of the responding officers should be recorded in the required reports as soon as possible. This documentation must include descriptive information about the crime and the crime scene and information obtained from witnesses, victims, suspects, and other individuals at the scene.

PHOTO 5.4: It is critical that crime scene boundaries be established and enforced. This ensures that the physical evidence contained at the scene is protected. In this case, a young woman was attacked at the apartment building and dragged to a vehicle in the road. A detective is recording license plate numbers of vehicles parked in the area (see Chapter 10 for details).

PRELIMINARY DOCUMENTATION AND EVALUATION OF THE SCENE

With investigators now in charge of the crime scene, it is their responsibility to review the activities of the initial responding officers. The first step then is once again to assess the crime scene. Safety should be reevaluated and crime scene boundaries should be confirmed. Investigators should make sure that suspects, witnesses, and victims continue to be separated and monitored. Personnel should be assigned to interview these individuals as soon as is practical. A determination should be made about the necessity of obtaining a search warrant or obtaining consent to search. A path of entry and movement for authorized personnel should be established. The need for additional investigative resources (e.g., equipment, legal consultation) should be determined and requested if necessary.

In addition to these activities, it is also important to search for and locate other witnesses who may not have been present at the immediate crime scene. This is usually performed through a neighborhood canvass. A neighborhood canvass involves the door-to-door questioning of residents who live in proximity to the crime scene. Contact should be attempted at each and every address in the designated area. Whether contact was made with residents at each address should be recorded, along with who is (and was) present in the residence. Of course, the information that was provided by the resident(s) should also be recorded. Residents may have background about the place where the crime occurred or the people involved, they may have seen or heard things that relate to the crime without knowing that they relate to the crime, or they may be the one who actually committed the crime. Because of this it is important to collect information about the activities of residents at the time the crime was believed to have occurred (alibi evidence). Other residents may not come forward with information unless they are asked by an officer or investigator. For these reasons, neighborhood canvasses can be extremely valuable in developing information. It should be understood by the personnel who conduct the neighborhood canvass that their role is to collect information, not to give it. Some information about the crime will only be known by the perpetrator, and the neighborhood canvass should not nullify this fact. A parallel activity to questioning residents is the recording of vehicle license plate numbers or vehicle identification numbers of vehicles in the area and noting where those vehicles were parked. If information arises in the investigation about vehicles that may have been involved in the incident, this information may be quite useful.

PROCESSING THE SCENE

The first step in processing the crime scene is determining who is responsible for what and establishing the composition of the investigative team. The responsibilities should be divided and the performance of activities supervised.

Second, the investigator in charge must require that all personnel follow procedures to ensure safety and the integrity of the evidence being documented and collected. Security of the evidence and the crime scene must be continually maintained.

Third, the investigator in charge must be responsible for, or supervise the taking of, photographs, video, sketches, measurements, and notes. Photographs and sketches are the primary means by which the crime scene is documented, and both serve as the official record of the condition and nature of the crime scene (see Exhibit 5.1 and Exhibit 5.2 for examples of crime scene sketches). Photographs and sketches of the scene are evidence and must be documented and treated as such. Crime scene sketches, either hand drawn or computerized, should be as detailed as possible and as close to scale as possible. Measurements of crime scenes and the placement of evidence should be included. The sketch should include the following:

- Date, time, and location
- Weather and lighting conditions
- Identification and assignment of personnel
- Dimensions of rooms, furniture, doors, and windows

- Distances between objects, persons, bodies, entrances, and exits
- Measurements showing the location of evidence
- A key, legend, compass orientation, scale, scale disclaimer ("Dimensions are not to scale"), or some combination of these features (FBI 2007)

Crime scene photographs should tell a story or should be able to be used to construct a story (see Case in Point 5.2). Also, the conditions in which the photos were taken (e.g., weather, lighting) should be recorded, as should the direction, distance, and view of each photograph. Many police departments have a report form on which photographs are to be logged. Additional specific guidelines regarding these tasks can be found in the *Handbook of Forensic Services* (FBI 2007).

Fourth, the investigator in charge should determine the order in which physical evidence is collected, focusing first on evidence that is subject to easy alteration or destruction. If appropriate and necessary, other methods of evidence collection should be considered and used, including blood pattern documentation, blood illumination techniques, and/or projectile trajectory analysis.

Fifth, the team members should ensure the proper collection, preservation, packaging, and transportation of evidence. Evidence must be collected and handled properly for it to be of use in an investigation and prosecution. The chain of custody is critical and must be maintained.

In conducting a search for evidence at a crime scene, various methods can be used. These methods include the grid, strip, and spiral search (see Exhibit 5.3).

Exhibit 5.1 Apartment Crime Scene Sketch

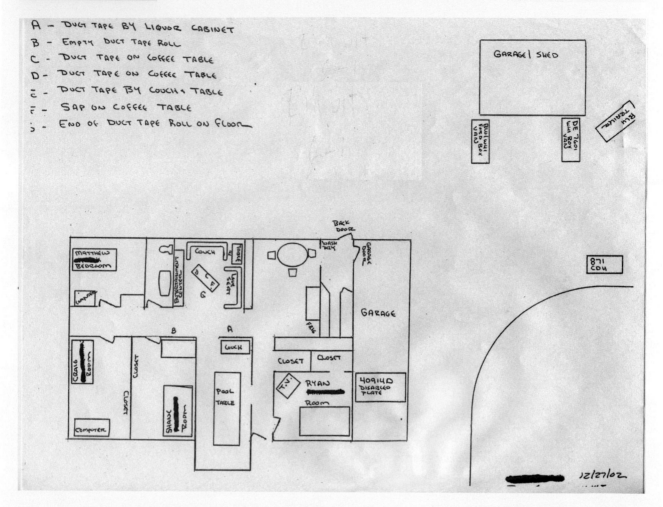

A - Duct Tape by Liquor Cabinet
B - Empty Duct Tape Roll
C - Duct Tape on Coffee Table
D - Duct Tape on Coffee Table
E - Duct Tape by Couch & Table
F - Sap on Coffee Table
G - End of Duct Tape Roll on Floor

Crime scene sketches and diagrams are useful in recording the scene and can provide a "big picture" of the place in question. The sketch relates to a home invasion robbery where the victims were bound with duct tape and robbed.

The basic idea for each of these approaches is to be thorough and systematic and not to overlook or miss any area or any item within the boundaries of the crime scene. The search should be approached with Locard's Exchange Principle in mind. This principle holds that any time a person comes into contact with a place or another person, something of that individual is left behind and something of that place is taken with the individual.

Although Locard's Exchange Principle is often valid, it is not *necessarily* valid. It is, nevertheless, a useful approach to take when conducting a search. In essence, the guiding mindset should be "Expect to find evidence." *The Handbook of Forensic Services,* published by the FBI (2007), provides the following additional guidelines for an effective crime scene search:

- Wear gloves to avoid leaving fingerprints.

- Do not excessively handle the evidence after recovery.

- Take steps to avoid inadvertently transferring evidence (e.g., carpet fibers on shoes) to a crime scene or between crime scenes.

- Make a complete evaluation of the crime scene.

Exhibit 5.2 Store Crime Scene Diagram

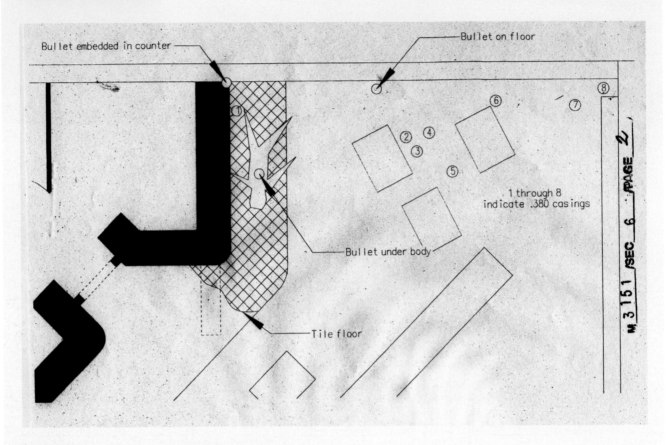

The diagram is of a store where a security guard was fatally shot.

COMPLETING AND RECORDING THE CRIME SCENE INVESTIGATION

To complete the crime scene investigation, the investigator in charge should first establish a crime scene debriefing team. This team will discuss and determine the need for any remaining activities prior to releasing the scene and will discuss immediate steps that need to be taken during the follow-up investigation. Crime scene findings can be reviewed at this time, and a summary of the evidence collected can be offered. Second, a final survey of the crime scene should be made to make sure that the crime scene investigation is complete and that no materials or evidence are left behind.

Finally, the investigator in charge should ensure that all necessary reports and other documentation are completed. This includes reports completed by the initial responding officers, emergency personnel documentation, entry/exit documentation, photographs/video, crime scene sketches and diagrams, and search warrant or other search documentation. These reports and other documentation can serve as a basis to direct further investigative activities and to provide continuity during the investigation across investigators.

An investigator usually only has one shot at a crime scene. It should be treated carefully and processed thoroughly. The value of critical evidence can be quickly destroyed through inappropriate or hasty crime scene procedures.

CASE *in* POINT 5.2 | Crime Scene Photographs Should Tell a Story[2]

As noted, photographs of crime scenes should be taken in such a way that they tell a story, as detailed in the investigation below.

On August 3, 2006, an apartment located at 7210 N. Port Washington Road was burglarized.

Entry was obtained into the apartment by prying open and removing the kitchen window screen. This happened between 12 a.m. and 4 a.m., while the elderly couple who lived in the apartment slept.

The suspect used a patio chair to climb through the window.

Partial prints were recovered from the window screen. An Automated Fingerprint Identification System (AFIS) search produced no matches.

Once inside the house, the suspect removed a wallet, purse, and a set of keys to the victims' 2004 Hyundai Santa Fe. The suspect exited the apartment via the door.

The suspect drove off in the vehicle. Two days later, the Santa Fe was recovered in a nearby parking lot. Fingerprints were recovered from the vehicle. Once again, an AFIS search did not result in a match.

2. Lieutenant Dan Herlache of the Glendale (WI) Police Department developed and contributed this example.

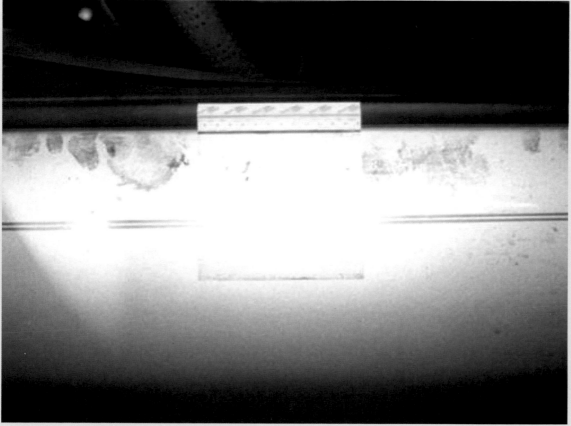

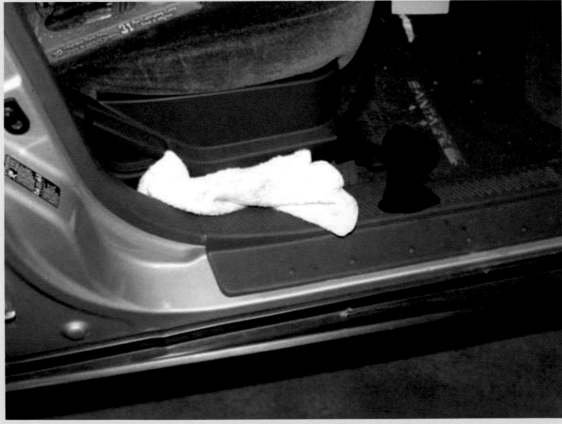

Inside the vehicle, a cigarette butt was found in the ashtray and a white hand towel that appeared to be stained with human blood was discovered on the floorboard between the seat and the door.

The cigarette butt and towel were processed for DNA, and a DNA print was developed; however, there was no match in the state's DNA data bank.

Interestingly, two years later, investigators were informed that a DNA match was obtained as a result of a new DNA database search. The match was with Tyrone Davis, who was currently in prison. With Davis's complete fingerprints now available, a comparison was made with the partial prints left on the screen and the prints obtained from the vehicle. The prints were from Davis. DNA was obtained from Davis in prison, and the resulting DNA profile was compared to the DNA left on the cigarette butt and the towel in the vehicle. They were also found to match Davis. Davis pled guilty to burglary and received a prison sentence of one year, plus three years of extended supervision.

Exhibit 5.3   Crime Scene Search Patterns

Spiral   Strip   Grid

●●● The Scientific Limitations of Physical Evidence

While physical evidence has several important functions in the criminal investigation process, it also has numerous limitations.[3] By way of introduction, some types of physical evidence are commonly referred to as having *class* characteristics, while other forms of physical evidence are said to have *individual* characteristics. As such, some physical evidence is referred to as class characteristic evidence, some as individual characteristic

---

3. Much of this discussion draws on the report titled "*Strengthening Forensic Science in the United States: A Path Forward*," published by the Committee on Identifying the Needs of the Forensic Sciences Community, National Research Council. Washington, DC: The National Academies Press, 2009. The page numbers listed refer to the page numbers of the electronic version of the report, which is available at www.nap.edu/openbook.php?record_id=12589&page=R1.

Exhibit 5.4 Identifying DNA Evidence

When processing crime scenes and collecting evidence, investigators must "think DNA." DNA could be anywhere. Listed below are a few possibilities.

EVIDENCE	POSSIBLE LOCATION OF DNA EVIDENCE	SOURCE OF DNA
Bandana, hat, mask	Anywhere (inside or outside)	Dandruff, hair, saliva, sweat
Baseball bat or similar weapon	End, handle	Blood, hair, skin, sweat, tissue
Bite mark	Clothing, skin	Saliva
Blanket, pillow, sheet	Surface area	Blood, hair, saliva, semen, sweat, urine
Bottle, can, glass	Mouthpiece, rim, sides	Saliva, sweat
Cotton swab, facial tissue	Surface area	Blood, ear wax, mucus, tissue, semen, sweat
Dirty laundry	Anywhere	Blood, semen, sweat
Envelope, stamp	Licked area	Saliva
Eyeglasses	Ear- or nose-bridge, lens	Hair, skin, sweat
Fingernail, partial fingernail	Scrapings	Blood, sweat, tissue
Ligature, tape	Inside/outside surface	Blood, skin, sweat
"Through and through" bullet	Outside surface	Blood, tissue
Toothpick	Tips	Saliva
Used cigarette	Cigarette butt	Saliva
Used condom	Inside/outside surface	Rectal or vaginal cells, semen

Source: "DNA Evidence: What Law Enforcement Officers Should Know." 2003. *National Institute of Justice Journal* 249: 1–15.

evidence. This distinction corresponds to two broad questions: (1) Can a particular piece of evidence be associated with a particular group or class of sources? and (2) Can a particular piece of evidence be identified as originating from one particular source? An example of the first question would be associating a paint chip in a hit-and-run with a particular make and model of automobile. Through an analysis of the paint, it may be possible to determine the make and model of the vehicle but not the exact car from which it came. An example of the second question would be whether a particular DNA sample came from a particular person.

According to the 2009 National Research Council report, serious problems can result when individual characteristic conclusions are drawn from evidence that has, at best, class characteristic features. Strictly speaking, only biological evidence with DNA properties (nuclear DNA) can be accurately considered individualistic evidence. With other forms of physical evidence, especially bite marks, tool marks, and writing samples, there is too little "science" associated with the interpretation and analysis of the evidence. The report states that "many forensic tests—such as those used to infer the source of tool marks or bite marks—have never been exposed to stringent scientific scrutiny" (p. 42). Even fingerprint analysis has been called into question. The report concludes that "no forensic method other than nuclear DNA analysis has been rigorously shown to have the capacity to consistently and with a high degree of certainty support conclusions about 'individualization.'" (p. 86)

As basic as it may seem, a related problem with physical evidence is how the results of the tests on the evidence are interpreted and communicated. In particular, forensic examiners often use terms such as *match* (e.g., "The hair found in the trunk matched that of the victim"), *identical, similar in all respects,* or *cannot be excluded as the source of.* These can be powerful and persuasive conclusions, yet there is no consistent agreement about the meaning of these terms. What exactly is required to conclude that one piece of evidence matches another, or that one piece of evidence is identical to another? In most areas of forensic science, these remain unresolved issues.

The National Research Council study explains that, at a minimum, laboratory reports and courtroom testimony relating to those reports should describe the "methods and materials, procedures, results, and conclusions, and they should identify, as appropriate, the sources of uncertainty in the procedures and conclusions along with estimates . . . [as to the] level of confidence in the results" (p. 186). The report also states that "courtroom testimony should be given in lay terms so that all trial participants can understand how to weigh and interpret the testimony. In order to enable this, research must be undertaken to evaluate the reliability of the steps of the various identification methods" (p. 186).

The National Research Council report provides a serious critique of the current state of forensic science. The authors highlight many problems in the field and argue that until these problems are addressed, it would be wise to consider cautiously the conclusions that related to many forensic tests.

●●● Types of Physical Evidence

The discussion offered here provides information on physical evidence, the potential usefulness of physical evidence in establishing proof, and basic guidelines for collecting and handling physical evidence. As noted, physical evidence can be broadly classified as having either class characteristics or individual characteristics. Class characteristic evidence has characteristics that are common to a group of objects or persons. A positive association or link *cannot* be made on the basis of class characteristic evidence. Individual characteristic evidence has characteristics that can be identified as originating with a particular person or source. A positive association *can* be made on the basis of individual characteristic evidence. As explained below, most biological evidence contains DNA that allows the evidence to be "individualized" to a particular person. Other forms of physical evidence, such as glass, fibers, and soil, are best considered as having class characteristics.

●●● Biological Evidence

Numerous types of biological evidence may be present and relevant in criminal investigations, including blood, semen, saliva, vaginal secretions, skins cells, hair, perspiration, urine, feces, and vomit. However, the most common types are blood, semen, saliva, and hair (National Research Council 2009). These forms of biological evidence, as well as DNA analysis, are discussed here.

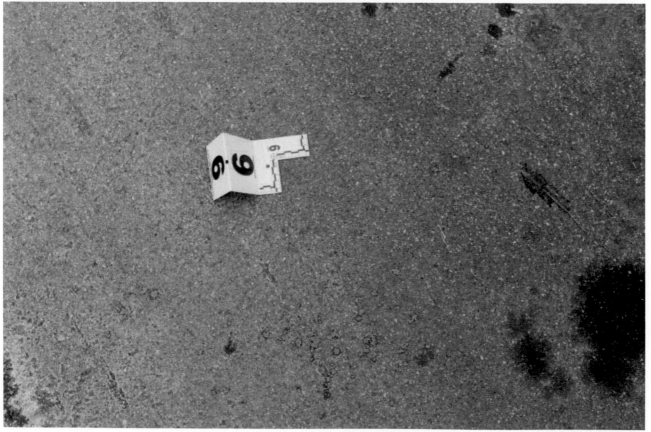

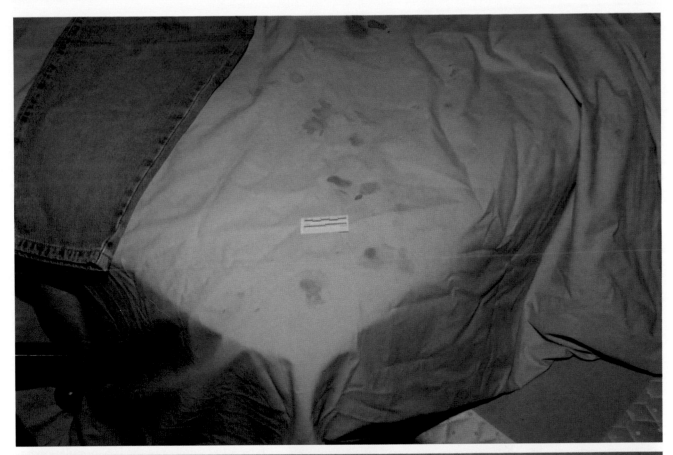

PHOTO 5.16–19: Blood is commonly encountered at scenes of violent crimes. However, it is often not found in mass quantities and sometimes may not even be obvious.

BLOOD

Blood is a common form of evidence found at scenes of serious crimes such as homicides and assaults. Blood may be found in a variety of places: on or near the victim; at entrances and especially exits of crime scenes; in or on sinks, wash basins, and towels at the crime scene; on weapons found at the crime scene; and on the victim's and perpetrator's clothing, for example. Even if attempts have been made to remove blood, it can still be located under vinyl flooring, under furniture, and in cracks and crevices.

Blood consists of red and white blood cells, which are located in plasma—a nearly clear, watery liquid. An adult body contains about ten pints of blood. In liquid form blood is red, but when dry it can take on several different colors, such as brown, black, gray, or even green, depending on the type and color of the surface on which the blood is located. Blood can be a potentially powerful type of forensic evidence. Conventional serology can reveal the blood group and blood type of an individual. There are four blood groups: type A (42 percent of the U.S. population has type A blood), type B (9 percent), type O (46 percent), and type AB (3 percent). Blood type refers to the Rhesus factor (or Rh factor). When the Rhesus antigen is present, the blood is said to be Rh positive; if it is not present, then it is said to be Rh negative. Rh positive is more common. Obviously, the ability to include or exclude an individual as the possible source of the blood depends greatly on the type and group of blood recovered. Other enzyme analyses conducted

PHOTO 5.20: Luminol, or an alternative light source, as illustrated here, can be used to locate the presence of blood that is not visible to the naked eye.

on blood can further narrow the scope of the donor pool. Further, determination of secretor status may be useful in establishing a donor pool. Secretors are people whose blood group antigens are present in other body fluids. As a result, analysis of these fluids can reveal the person's blood group. Approximately 80 percent of people are secretors.

Blood is also an excellent source of DNA and, as such, is often subjected to DNA analysis. The DNA in blood comes from the nuclei of white blood cells, as a red blood cell does not have a nucleus. DNA analysis can produce virtually certain results that two blood samples have the same donor. Blood can also be useful for evidentiary purposes through an analysis of splatters, drips, and the location in which the blood was found.

Blood is often very visible to perpetrators and investigators and, as a result, perpetrators may take precautions to minimize the presence of blood by cleaning the crime scene or cleaning or disposing of articles stained with blood. Such precautions may not be effective. Several methods are available to locate blood when it is not visible to the naked eye. An alternative light source (ALS) of 415 nanometers ("violet" light) may be used to reveal traces of blood that are not otherwise visible. In addition, application of certain chemicals, such as a Luminol solution, to surfaces that possibly at one time contained blood can reveal bloodstains via luminesces even if the blood is extremely diluted. Luminol reacts with iron contained in the blood, causing a visible blue glow. Chemicals, however, often destroy the properties of blood, so they are used primarily to detect the presence of blood that might otherwise go undetected. Other blood-illuminating chemicals, such as fluorescein, also react to other substances, such as certain cleaning products, so caution in interpretation is necessary. Finally, the procedure used to confirm that a substance is in fact blood involves mixing the substance with phenolphthalein and hydrogen peroxide. If a deep pink color is produced, the substance is blood.

Depending on the nature and condition of the blood evidence, various methods can be used to collect and package it. In liquid form, blood can be absorbed with a cotton cloth, air dried, and then packaged in a paper bag. Plastic bags or containers should not be used (FBI 2007). If blood is collected from a suspect for DNA analysis (i.e., a reference sample), it should be collected in a plastic tube by a medical professional and treated with the preservative ethylenediaminetetraacetic acid (EDTA). Blood—either in dried or liquid form—should be refrigerated (tubes of liquid blood may break if frozen) prior to submission to the forensic laboratory (FBI 2007). For long-term storage, dried blood should be refrigerated or frozen. Blood splatters should be measured, photographed, and recorded for possible later analysis (Akin 2005).

SEMEN

Semen consists of sperm suspended in seminal fluid. One milliliter of semen from a healthy adult man contains approximately 60 to 100 million sperm cells. In liquid form, semen is grayish white and has a chlorine-type odor. When dry, it is clear and starch-like. Seminal fluid is most often found as a result of sexual crimes such as rape and can be found with the victim, on the victim's clothing, on or in condoms, and in places where the assault may have taken place, such as on bed sheets or carpeting.

PHOTO 5.21: If a condom was used in a sexual assault, its discovery could be extremely useful in the investigation.

Several tests can be performed to identify the presence of semen: the microscopic identification of spermatozoa, the acid phosphatase test (which tests for the presence of the enzyme acid phosphatase that is found in seminal fluid), choline and p30 (which test for the presence of proteins in seminal fluid), and the use of ultraviolent light (White 1998). Semen and spermatozoa are a rich source of DNA and are often the subject of DNA analysis procedures.

When collecting and packaging suspected liquid semen from crime scenes, it should be absorbed onto a clean cotton cloth or swab, air dried, and then packaged in a clean paper envelope with sealed corners. Semen-stained objects should be submitted to the laboratory in whole. Suspected semen should be absorbed from immovable objects onto a clean cotton cloth or swab moistened with distilled water. All semen evidence should be packaged in paper, not plastic. For long-term storage, dried semen should be refrigerated or frozen (FBI 2007).

SALIVA

Human saliva consists of nearly all water, but it also contains mucus and certain proteins and enzymes, as well as skin cells and other substances. In a criminal investigation, saliva may be most likely to be found on cigarette butts, bite marks, bottles, cans, clothing, and envelopes and stamps. Saliva is a good source of DNA **and can be the subject of DNA analysis procedures (see Case in Point 5.3).**

Saliva can be easily overlooked as it is usually invisible to the naked eye. As with semen, there are chemical tests that can be used to identify it. In the case of saliva, such tests detect amylase, an enzyme found in high concentrations in saliva. However, the test is not definitive because other types of tissue and bodily fluid also contain amylase. Saliva may also become visible under alternative light sources.

PHOTO 5.22: Even careful perpetrators may not think before they discard a smoked cigarette at a crime scene. Of course, a cigarette butt found at a crime scene is not necessarily one that was smoked by the perpetrator.

CASE in POINT 5.3   DNA on the Duct Tape

In a recent case, an eight-year-old girl was abducted, sexually assaulted, and left for dead in a wooded area. Before leaving the victim, the perpetrator bound her hands and arms with duct tape and wrapped the tape around the girl's head, including her mouth and nose, in an attempt to suffocate her. After the perpetrator left, the girl was able to free her hands and remove the tape from her mouth and nose. She then was able to summon help from a passing motorist. Upon being interviewed, the girl provided investigators with a description of the attacker and a composite sketch was developed. The sketch was quickly released to the media. The police obtained information from several people that the person depicted in the sketch looked like a guy by the name of Robert Leven (not his real name), who worked in a prison nearby. Meanwhile, analysis was being performed on the evidence recovered with the victim. Most significant was the duct tape. Although there were no fingerprints on the tape, investigators did find saliva. It was reasoned that the perpetrator used his teeth to tear the tape and, in the process, his saliva was transferred to the tape. The saliva underwent DNA analysis and a DNA print was produced. The DNA on the duct tape matched that that of Robert Leven. Leven was arrested and convicted of sexual assault, among other offenses.

The collection and packaging of saliva (and urine) is the same as with semen. In liquid form, it should be collected via a clean cotton cloth or swab and air dried. If possible, entire saliva-stained objects should be collected. If it is not possible to collect the object that contains the saliva or to cut out the saliva sample, the saliva stain may be collected by using a cotton swab moistened with distilled water. A control sample of an area close to the saliva sample should also be collected using the same distilled water and type of swab that was used to collect the evidence. All items should be packaged in paper envelopes or bags, not plastic. The control sample should be packaged separately. Care must be taken so that metal or glass items are not frozen. **For long-term storage, dried saliva should be refrigerated or frozen (FBI 2007).**

HAIR

Hair is most likely to be found in homicides and assaults, especially when some struggle between the victim and the perpetrator took place. Hair may also be found on the victim's and perpetrator's clothing, in vehicles, and on personal items, as well as in places such as the clothes dryer lint trap, washing machines, and sinks.

Hair consists of the outer core of overlapping cells known as the cuticle, the cortex (which contains the pigment of the hair), and the medulla (an inner layer of cells). Hair also contains a root, which can be of great use in the scientific analysis of the hair. There is often significant variation in hair structure within the same individual, particularly in hair from different places on the body (e.g., head, face, pubic area). As a result, a range of samples must be analyzed when comparing the structure of the hair. Through the relatively simple microscopic examination of a hair shaft, it is possible to draw several conclusions about the hair: whether it is from a human or an animal (and if it is from an animal, what type of animal); the race of the individual; the body area from which the hair came; the method of removal; color and shaft form (e.g., straight, curly); and whether the hair was damaged or altered (e.g., dyed or bleached). Chemical examination of the hair may reveal the presence of contaminants in the hair and may identify ingested drugs and how long ago the drugs were ingested. Neutron activation analysis may be used to analyze and measure with extreme precision the presence of various trace elements in a hair sample (Owen 2000). The most powerful of all is DNA analysis performed on the root of a hair. Even DNA analysis conducted on the shaft of the hair is likely to be more useful and discriminating than analyses conducted on the features of the hair. Non-DNA analysis of hair is generally unable to

PHOTO 5.23: A hair hangs from an overhead air duct in the basement of a house where a murder occurred. Because potential evidence can be easily overlooked, the crime scene search must be focused on even the smallest details.

positively associate hair to a specific individual, but it may be useful in excluding certain persons as the source of the hair (National Research Council 2009).

Hair samples should be packaged in an envelope with sealed corners. Hair should be carefully collected with clean tweezers to prevent damage to the hair root. Hair that is mixed with bodily fluid should be air dried prior to packaging in paper, not plastic (FBI 2007). In collecting comparison samples, at least twenty-five to fifty hairs from different parts of the head (or pubic area) should be obtained. Hairs should be combed and pulled out (National Research Council 2009; FBI 2007) and collected by a trained medical professional.

●●● DNA Analysis and Its Impact on the Usefulness of Biological Evidence

The most significant advance in the technology of criminal investigation *ever* is the science of DNA. DNA, or deoxyribonucleic acid, is the genetic building block of all living organisms. It is found in virtually every cell in the human body, and its structure is the same in every cell. Except for identical twins, no two people have the same DNA. The DNA in a person's saliva is the same as the DNA in his or her hair, skin cells, blood, semen, and perspiration. Because of its absolute uniqueness and individual characteristics, human cells and the DNA contained in these cells can be a powerful form of evidence in criminal investigations.

DNA analysis (or *typing* or *printing*, as it is sometimes known) was first used in a criminal investigation in 1987 by Dr. Alec J. Jeffreys to corroborate a suspect's confession that he was responsible for two rape/murders in England. Tests proved that the suspect was not the perpetrator. Police then obtained DNA samples from several thousand men who lived in the area in order to identify the true perpetrator. Although the perpetrator attempted to avoid providing a DNA sample, he was eventually identified and charged with the crimes. DNA printing was first used in the United States in a criminal case in 1987, during which a Florida jury convicted Tommy Lee Andrews of rape (National Institute of Justice 1996).

DNA analysis may be used to associate positively and absolutely a perpetrator to a crime scene, to the victim, or to tools used in the crime. Similarly, DNA analysis can be used to eliminate positively and absolutely a person from consideration as a suspect. In each of these instances, the DNA recovered from a crime scene or victim would be compared with a DNA sample taken from a specific person. In this sense, DNA is similar to fingerprints, but fingerprints left by a perpetrator at a crime scene may be of poor quality (smudged or smeared) or may be left on surfaces from which the prints cannot be recovered (e.g., rough wood). Also, perpetrators can take relatively simple precautions such as wearing gloves to avoid leaving fingerprints at a crime scene in the first place.

DNA can also be used to confirm the identity of victims or the remains of victims when a complete body is not found. In such cases, a DNA sample may be taken from hair recovered from the victim's hairbrush or from skin cells recovered from the victim's toothbrush or clothing and then compared with the victim's remains. Another possibility is to compare the DNA from relatives with the DNA of the body or remains (National Institute of Justice 1999b). DNA analysis was used in this manner to confirm the identity of Osama bin Laden after he was shot and killed in Pakistan (McNeil and Belluck 2011).

Extraordinary caution needs to be exercised when collecting DNA-analyzable evidence for at least two reasons: first, because the biological material may contain hazardous pathogens (e.g., human immunodeficiency virus, hepatitis) that can cause lethal diseases; and second, because samples containing DNA can be easily contaminated (see Exhibit 5.5). Contamination could happen if someone sneezed or coughed over the evidence, or if one

Exhibit 5.5 Precautions When Collecting and Handling Biological Evidence

Biological material may contain hazardous pathogens such as the hepatitis A virus that can lead to potentially lethal diseases. At the same time, such material can easily become contaminated. To protect both the integrity of the evidence and the health and safety of law enforcement personnel, officers should take the following precautions:

- Wear gloves and change them often

- Use disposable instruments or clean them thoroughly before and after handling each sample

- Avoid touching any area where DNA might exist

- Avoid touching one's own nose, mouth, and face when collecting and packaging evidence

- Air dry evidence thoroughly before packaging

- Put evidence into new paper bags or envelopes. Investigators should not place evidence in plastic bags or use staples

Source: "DNA Evidence: What Law Enforcement Officers Should Know." 2003. *National Institute of Justice Journal* 249: 1–15.

simply touched the evidence without taking sterile precautions (National Institute of Justice 2003a).

When transporting or storing evidence that may contain DNA, the evidence must be kept dry. The evidence should be stored in paper bags or envelopes. Evidence that may contain DNA should never be placed or otherwise stored in plastic bags because plastic will retain moisture that may damage the DNA. Direct sunlight and warmer conditions can also damage DNA evidence. Staples should not be used to secure evidence bags as an accidental injury from the staples might lead to contamination of the evidence. Of course, the chain of custody must also be maintained. According to the National Institute of Justice (2012), the chain on custody would likely include the following individuals:

- The person who collected the particular piece of evidence and began the chain of custody
- The person who transported the evidence to the police department or crime lab
- The person who logged the evidence into the evidence room or the person who received the evidence at the lab
- The person who received the evidence from the lab for final inventory

The collection of comparison (or reference) DNA from a suspect most often involves the use of buccal (oral) swabs. Clean cotton swabs must be used for this purpose. The inside surfaces of the cheeks should be rubbed thoroughly with the swabs. The swabs should then be air dried and placed in a paper sleeve or an envelope with sealed corners. Swabs from different people should be packaged separately. The samples do not need to be refrigerated. Other, less desirable, but possible reference samples could be obtained from surgical samples, pulled teeth, an item of clothing worn only by the individual of interest, or a toothbrush used only by the person (FBI 2007).

Just like with fingerprints, elimination samples may need to be taken to eliminate from consideration those individuals who have legitimate reason to be at the crime scene or in contact with the victim. For example, when investigating a rape, it may be necessary to collect the DNA from the victim's recent consensual partner to eliminate him as a suspect in the crime. In addition, DNA should be taken from the victim to compare it with other DNA found at the crime scene. In the investigation of the murder of Nicole Brown Simpson and Ron Goldman, the analysis of the blood found at the crime scene revealed three unique DNA sequences: those of Nicole, Goldman, and someone else—that "someone else" was believed to be the perpetrator.

It would be inaccurate to consider DNA analysis only a tool of the prosecution used to convict suspects. DNA analysis is a powerful tool of justice—a tool that can be used to identify and convict the guilty *and* to free the innocent (National Institute of Justice 2012). A National Institute of Justice study published in 1996 identified and summarized twenty-eight cases in which DNA test results proved that the person convicted of a crime could not have committed that crime. These cases had numerous characteristics in common. Most of the cases occurred during the 1980s, a time when DNA analysis was available but not widely used. All of the cases involved some type of sexual assault; some involved a homicide along with a sexual assault. All of the perpetrators were male; all of the victims were female. All but one case involved a jury trial, and in most of the cases a verdict was returned in less than one day. The twenty-eight defendants served a total of 197 years in prison before their convictions were overturned on the basis of DNA evidence. Most defendants appealed their convictions at least once; many appealed more than once before being exonerated. Police knew fifteen of the defendants prior to their arrests for the crime primarily because of prior arrests. All the cases, except for the six homicides, involved the victim identifying the suspect prior to the trial and at the trial. Many cases also had other eyewitness identifications to support the conviction of the defendant. (In one case, five witnesses testified that they saw the defendant with the victim on the day of the murder.) Many of the defendants provided an alibi but, obviously, they were not believed by the juries. A majority of the cases had non-DNA physical evidence admitted into trial that supported the conviction of the defendant. Finally, eight of the cases involved allegations of police or prosecutor misconduct, including claims that officers provided perjured testimony and that prosecutors kept exculpatory evidence from the defense and intentionally and knowingly admitted erroneous laboratory results.

THE SCIENCE OF DNA

There are two types of DNA: mitochondrial (MtDNA) DNA and nuclear DNA. MtDNA is found in the mitochondrion in each cell of the body; nuclear DNA is found in the nucleus of a cell. MtDNA is more limited in function than nuclear DNA. MtDNA is inherited from one's mother only. It has limitations compared with nuclear DNA in that it cannot differentiate between individuals who have the same maternal lineage (i.e., a brother and a sister, or a mother and a daughter, will have the same MtDNA). MtDNA is analyzed when only hair shafts, bone, or teeth are available, or when other biological evidence is severely degraded (Isenberg 2002; Isenberg and Moore 1999; National Institute of Justice 2001; National Institute of Justice 2012; FBI 2007).

Nuclear DNA consists of billions of pairs (base pairs) of adenine, cytosine, guanine, and thymine (commonly referred to as A, C, G, and T) structured in the form of a double helix. Very simply, think of the double helix as a twisted ladder and the base pairs as the rungs in the ladder. About 99.9 percent of the DNA base pairs of each human are the same, but certain areas of the DNA are unique, thus making DNA unique (National Institute of Justice 2012). Of particular importance is that the sequence (or order) of the base pairs repeats, and the pattern of repeats are distinct across individuals. As such, DNA typing consists of

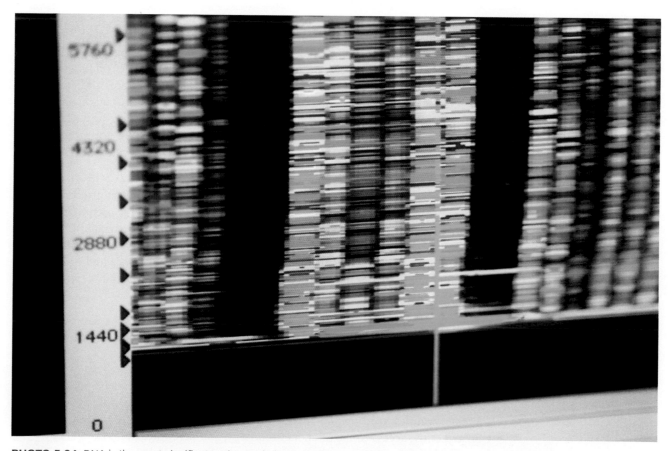

PHOTO 5.24: DNA is the most significant advance in investigative technology to date, but it still has limitations.

examining particular locations (loci) in the DNA and identifying the base pair sequence pattern. Sometimes reference is made to a *thirteen-loci DNA profile*. The FBI has chosen thirteen specific short tandem repeat (STR) loci to serve as a standard DNA comparison. The chances that two people will have the same thirteen-loci DNA profile can be as high as one chance in one billion or less (see www.nij.gov/nij/forensics/evidence/dna/basics/welcome.htm).

The general procedure in conducting DNA analysis is as follows:

- Determine whether the substance is biological evidence and whether it is from a human or animal.

- Isolate the DNA from the biological evidence.

- Analyze the DNA and obtain a DNA print (pattern) from specific regions (loci) of the DNA.

- Compare the results of the DNA analysis performed on the biological evidence with a suspect (or sample of possible suspects) to determine if the suspect is the source of the DNA.

The most common method of analyzing nuclear DNA today is known as PCR, which stands for polymerase chain reaction (again see www.nij.gov/nij/forensics/evidence/dna/basics/welcome.htm; National Institute of Justice 2003a). With the PCR technique, the DNA is copied many times (amplified). Two DNA molecules are produced from the original molecule and are repeated many times until millions of copies of the DNA sequence are produced. From these copies, a DNA print can be generated that is usually based on the examination of the thirteen core short tandem repeat (STR) loci. PCR can be used if a sample consists of a few cells or is degraded, but it is particularly susceptible to contamination.

On the basis of DNA testing, one of three conclusions may be drawn. First, the suspect may be *included* as the possible source of the evidence; however, the certainty of the inclusion will depend on the number of locations on the DNA strand that are examined and how common or rare the resulting DNA print is in the general population. Second, in the same manner that an individual can be included as a suspect, an individual can also be *excluded* as a suspect. Third, the results of the analysis may be *inconclusive*—a person cannot be included *or* excluded as the source of the evidence. Inconclusive results may occur for a variety of reasons: the poor quality of the DNA sample may not allow for interpretable results, the evidentiary sample may contain a mixture of DNA from several individuals, or the sample may have been contaminated.

While the science of DNA analysis is difficult to attack, there have been attempts to get around it (see Case in Point 5.4). More common is that the procedures used in collecting the biological evidence are called into question. For example, during the trial of O. J. Simpson, the defense attorneys did not question the scientific basis of DNA analysis; rather, they attacked the integrity by which the evidence was collected. All the science and precision of DNA analysis can be foiled if the evidence is collected incorrectly or if claims can be made about the overall integrity of the evidence.

Even though the scientific basis of DNA analysis has been established, the Supreme Court has provided for extensive discovery requirements in the admission of the results of the analysis. In *Schwartz v. State* (1989), the court stated that

> ideally, a defendant should be provided with the actual DNA sample(s) in order to reproduce the results. As a practical matter, this may not be possible because forensic samples are often so small that the entire sample is used in testing. Consequently, access to the data, methodology, and actual results is critical . . . for an independent expert review.

CASE in POINT 5.4 — A Fool's Attempt to Fool DNA

Occasionally a suspect attempts to get around the science of DNA. One such case was that of Anthony Turner, a convicted and incarcerated serial rapist. While serving time in prison for three rape convictions—convictions obtained in part through DNA analysis of semen recovered from his victims—Turner devised a plan to try to fool investigators and to make authorities question the validity of the DNA analysis results. The plan unfolded with an apparent fourth sexual assault in the same neighborhood where Turner committed his rapes years before. The victim contacted the police, told them she had been raped, and then underwent a sexual assault examination. The recovered semen was analyzed, a DNA print was created, and that print was compared with the DNA prints on file in the state's DNA bank, which contains DNA samples of all convicted felons in the state. A match was made to Anthony Turner. On hearing of this match, Turner argued that he obviously did not commit this crime since he had an iron-clad alibi—he was in prison at the time of the assault! He reasserted his claim that he did not commit any of the other rapes either. Initially, this was rather puzzling. Could two people—Anthony Turner and the real rapist—have the same DNA profile? If Anthony Turner had an identical twin, no one knew about it. As investigators began to ask questions of Turner's associates in prison and of the "victim" of the latest rape, Turner's scheme unraveled. It was discovered that about a month prior to the last "rape," Turner told his mother that she should expect an envelope in the mail from him in the next few weeks and that she should give this envelope to one of Turner's female friends who lived in the neighborhood. Investigators then learned that in this envelope was a ketchup packet that contained Anthony's own semen. Anthony smuggled his semen out of prison! Anthony's female associate used this semen to stage the rape. An ambitious and imaginative plan, but one that did not work.

Other instances have also been reported when perpetrators have left DNA evidence such as hair, fingernails, and blood from other sources at crime scenes in an attempt to foil police efforts at identifying the real culprit. Investigative personnel should be aware of this possibility in collecting such evidence.

Further, the results of laboratory examinations must be accompanied by in-person testimony of the individual who examined the evidence (*Melendez-Diaz v. Massachusetts* [2009]); a substitute witness does not satisfy the requirement (*Bullcoming v. New Mexico* [2011]).

Until relatively recently, DNA evidence was limited in the same manner that physical evidence is limited; it was generally not useful in identifying a perpetrator when one was not already known. Only when a suspect was identified through some other means could the recovered DNA evidence be compared with the DNA taken from the identified suspect. However, recent technological advances and legal provisions are making DNA much more powerful and useful in investigations. Specifically, the Combined DNA Index System (CODIS) is an electronic database that allows federal, state, and local crime laboratories to exchange and share DNA profiles electronically (FBI 2000). Today, all states participate in CODIS. As of 2010, the database contained DNA profiles of 8.6 million individuals who were convicted of certain crimes such as homicide, rape, and child abuse, as well as almost 330,000 DNA profiles collected as a result of other investigations. CODIS has assisted on nearly 120,000 investigations (see www.fbi.gov/about-us/lab/codis/codis_brochure).

In addition to CODIS, many states operate their own DNA banks. Some states require that DNA from all convicted felons be entered into the system. Some states collect DNA only from convicted sex offenders. Some states are considering collecting DNA from all individuals who are *arrested* for a felony. With such systems, investigators can enter into the system the DNA prints obtained from evidence recovered from crime scenes, and the computer will scan the stored prints for a match (See Case in Point 5.5). However, if the perpetrator's print is not in the system, a match will not be obtained. In that case, the culprit will still have to be identified through other, more traditional, means.

CASE *in* POINT 5.5 | A Textbook DNA Case

During the late evening hours of September 6, 2006, twenty-one-year-old Sara Miller (not her real name) got on a public bus for her ride home from her waitressing job at a local restaurant. She was never seen alive again. Her parents reported to the police that she did not return home that evening, and, even more concerning, they were receiving bizarre text messages from Sara—or at least from someone using her cell phone. Sara's boyfriend also received such messages. One read: "We broke both her arms and legs and cut off her feet PS put more minutes on the phone." Needless to say, everyone was extremely concerned. As police were trying to determine the whereabouts of Sara and her phone, her nude body was discovered by workers at a recycling center in the city. She had been strangled, beaten, stabbed, and sexually assaulted. Presumably, her body had been dumped in a recycling bin and then unknowingly transported to the recycling center. Investigators conducted hundreds of interviews—with bus drivers, family members, coworkers, friends, and associates—but little progress was made on finding who was responsible for killing Sara. Investigators were trying to track the location of the cell phone; whoever had it was still using it to send text messages to people listed in Sara's phone. Just as investigators were narrowing in on the location of the beacon, the phone went dead. Presumably it had been turned off and

discarded. Meanwhile, the semen recovered from the victim was analyzed for DNA, and the resulting DNA print was entered into the state's DNA bank. There was a hit: Steven Barthew (not his real name), age twenty-two. Even better, Steven was currently being held in the county jail as a result of being arrested for a hit-and-run with a car that he did not have permission to drive. His DNA profile was in the DNA bank as a result of a previous robbery conviction. Investigators went and talked to Steven. Confronted with the DNA evidence, he confessed to the murder but gave various versions of what happened. He told investigators that voices told him to kill her. Steven's apartment was searched. Among items seized was a pair of boots that were confirmed through additional DNA analysis to contain Sara's blood; the chances that it was not Sara's blood were one in eleven billion. Detectives also found a note in Steven's apartment that read "Never kill anyone you know, Never have a motive, Never follow a discernible pattern, Never carry a weapon after it has been used, Isolate yourself from random discovery, Beware of leaving physical evidence." It is pretty certain that without the DNA analysis and databank, and the DNA match, Steven would not have been apprehended quickly. There may have been many more victims. Steven was convicted of homicide and sentenced to life in prison without the possibility of parole.

●●● Other Types of Physical Evidence

FINGERPRINTS

The early foundation of forensic science rested on the principle that each person has a unique pattern on his or her fingers. This principle is still valid, and fingerprints are still potentially powerful evidence in criminal investigations. Fingerprints consist of ridges, depressions (i.e., hills and valleys), and separations (where ridge lines end or split). Fingerprints remain unchanged and consistent throughout one's lifetime. Each fingerprint on each finger is unique. Fingerprints can be useful because perpetrators can leave them on items and at crime scenes.

Fingerprints can be broadly classified on the basis of the pattern of ridges that comprise the print. As illustrated in Exhibit 5.6, these patterns are classified as loops (ulnar loop, radial loop), whorls (plain whorls, double loops, central pocket loops, accidental loops), and arches (plain arch, tented arch). The most common type of fingerprint is loops (approximately 66 percent of the population have loop prints), followed by whorls (approximately 33 percent). Only about one person in twenty has any prints that resemble arches.

Fingerprints taken as a result of the fingerprinting process (i.e., "being fingerprinted") are usually recorded on a ten-print fingerprint card, either through the use of ink or the digital capture of prints. On the card, the prints are arranged as a double row in a particular sequence (See Exhibit 5.7).

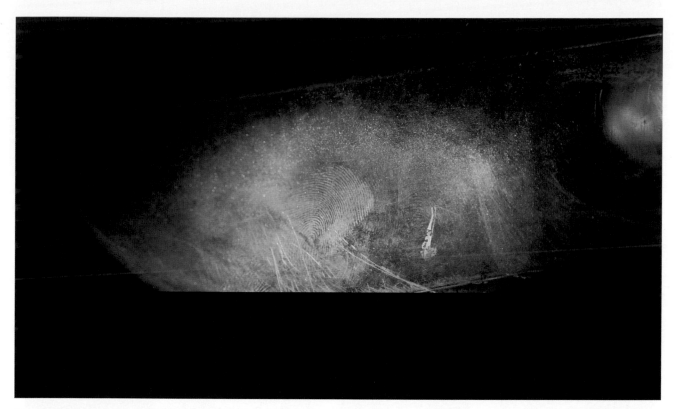

PHOTO 5.25: When searching for fingerprints, it is necessary to consider the obvious *and* not-so-obvious places. Here, fingerprints are located on the underside of a cash register drawer at the scene of a gas station robbery scene.

The analysis of fingerprints (as well as sole and palm prints) is known as friction ridge analysis, which consists of comparisons of the impressions left by the ridge structures of fingers (or hands and feet). Friction ridge analysis is a means by which individualization can be determined (National Research Council 2009). There are three conclusions that may result from a comparison of fingerprints: individualization (or identification), exclusion, or inconclusive. An identification (or individualization) is made when prints from two different sources could not have produced impressions with the same degree of agreement in ridge features. It is important to understand that in contrast to DNA matches, this is a subjective assessment as there are no statistics by which to identify the probabilities of a match based on population distributions of certain friction ridge features (National Research Council 2009). Exclusion is made when prints show observable differences in ridges. An inconclusive conclusion is appropriately drawn when similarities and differences in prints are not able to be determined.

Fingerprints recovered from a crime scene can generally be of three types: visible transferred prints, such as when ink, blood, or some other visible liquid material is transferred from the fingerprint to some other surface; visible impression prints, which occur when the print is left in a soft or sticky material such as wet paint, clay, or putty; and latent prints, the most common type, which are made when the oil and perspiration naturally present on fingertips are transferred to another surface but are invisible until developed through various techniques. The most common techniques used to recover latent prints consist of the application of powders, chemicals, and glue fumes. "Dusting" for prints involves the application of a fine powder with a fine brush to surfaces that are believed to potentially contain latent prints. The powder adheres to the oil and perspiration transferred from fingers and makes the prints visible. This technique is most likely to reveal prints when the surface is hard, smooth, and nonabsorbent, such as glass, painted wood, or metal. Powder of a different color can be applied to provide contrast with the surface being dusted. Fluorescent powder can also be used in a similar manner to enhance the visibility of latent prints.

Exhibit 5.6   Types of Fingerprint Patterns

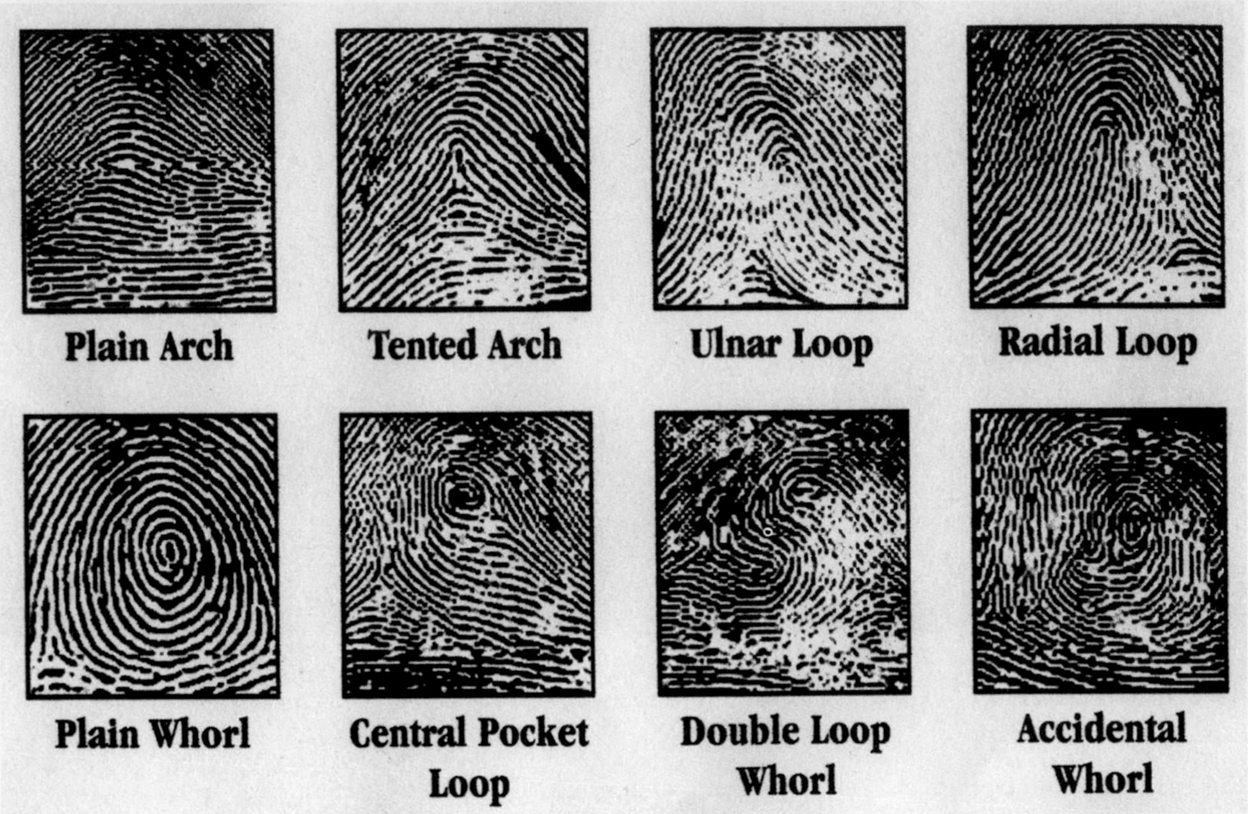

Plain Arch   Tented Arch   Ulnar Loop   Radial Loop

Plain Whorl   Central Pocket   Double Loop   Accidental
                    Loop   Whorl   Whorl

Source: Fingerprint Identification, Federal Bureau of Investigation, www.fbi.gov/about-us/cjis/fingerprints_biometrics/fingerprint-overview.

Chemical methods can be used to recover prints from soft or more porous surfaces, such as paper or clothing. Various types of chemicals can be applied either by spraying the surface, through a process of fuming, or by dipping the object containing prints into a chemical solution. Another technique involves glue (or cyanoacrylate) fuming. With this method, the object examined for prints is either placed in a sealed tank and is then exposed to the vaporized cyanoacrylate, which adheres to the print and makes it visible, or the fumes are applied via a fuming wand.

In addition to these methods, laser technology has been used for highlighting latent prints on difficult surfaces. Regardless of the method used to recover prints, the visible prints first should be photographed and then "lifted" by placing adhesive tape over the print so that the powder adheres to the tape. The tape is then placed on a card that provides contrast with the lifted print, thereby preserving the print and making it visible for further analyses and comparison.

Locating quality latent prints is not an easy task and depends on the crime scene. Obvious places such as door handles, drinking cups, and weapons, as well as less obvious places such as telephones and toilet handles, should be examined for prints. Many recovered prints are of poor quality, making them nearly worthless as evidence. Fingerprints can be smeared or can become dirty, or the fingers themselves could have been dirty, all of which would obscure the individual characteristics of the fingerprints.

If fingerprints are recovered from a crime scene, then elimination prints may need to be taken. Elimination prints are fingerprints of all persons who are known to have had legal

Exhibit 5.7 Example of Completed Ten-Print Fingerprint Card

LEAVE BLANK	CRIMINAL	(STAPLE HERE)			Mugshot File Name

STATE USAGE
NFF SECOND
SUBMISSION   APPROXIMATE CLASS   AMPUTATION   SCAR

STATE USAGE | LAST NAME, FIRST NAME, MIDDLE NAME, SUFFIX
GATSON, DANIEL LAMAR

SIGNATURE OF PERSON FINGERPRINTED | SOCIAL SECURITY NO. | LEAVE BLANK

ALIASES/MAIDEN
LAST NAME, FIRST NAME, MIDDLE NAME, SUFFIX
HUGHES, KEVIN LAMAR

FBI NO.	STATE IDENTIFICATION NO.	DATE OF BIRTH MM DD YY	SEX	RACE	HEIGHT	WEIGHT	EYES	HAIR
		01-24-1987	M	B	510	165	BRO	BLK

1. R. THUMB   2. R. INDEX   3. R. MIDDLE   4. R. RING   5. R. LITTLE

6. L. THUMB   7. L. INDEX   8. L. MIDDLE   9. L. RING   10. L. LITTLE

ID 1000 100000 20120904 14:52:03   LexT630 99208YV 20120906-10:49

LEFT FINGERS TAKEN SIMULTANEOUSLY   L. THUMB   R. THUMB   RIGHT FINGERS TAKEN SIMULTANEOUSLY

An Example of a completed ten-print fingerprint card.

access to the scene. These prints are then compared with the other recovered prints, and the ones that do not match may belong to the perpetrator.

AFIS (the Automated Fingerprint Identification System) has made fingerprints more useful in identifying perpetrators. With AFIS in place, whenever a person is fingerprinted by the police in that jurisdiction as a result of being arrested, applying for particular jobs, or for some other reason, those fingerprints are entered and stored in AFIS. Then, after a fingerprint is collected from a crime scene, it is scanned into AFIS and the computer searches the system, looking for prints with similar characteristics. The newest and most powerful systems on the market today can search hundreds of thousands of prints within minutes; older systems require hours to search the same number of prints. As a result of the computerized search, the system may identify several prints that are the most similar in their pattern and unique characteristics. The print in question must then be manually compared with the "hit" print by a fingerprint examiner. It is in this manner that fingerprints recovered from a crime scene may lead to the identity of a perpetrator.

Prior to AFIS technology, fingerprints were used in several different ways. First, when a fingerprint was recovered from a crime scene, it was simply filed away until a suspect was identified through some other means, and then a comparison of that suspect's prints and the recovered prints was made. Second, if a suspect was already identified, a comparison could be conducted immediately. Third, a manual search could be made through the fingerprints on file in that particular jurisdiction or on file with the FBI. No question, this process resembled trying to find a needle in a haystack, and rarely did it have a positive outcome.

Although AFIS provides great promise and certainly makes the processing of fingerprints much more efficient, there are several weakness and limitations to the technology. First, it must be realized that there is potentially considerable expense associated with collecting fingerprints from crime scenes and analyzing them via AFIS. Although at first glance it sounds easy—collect fingerprints from a crime scene, enter them into AFIS, get a match, and make an arrest—the process is much more complicated and time consuming. Fingerprints are most likely to be available for recovery from burglary crime scenes, stolen autos, and certain robberies. To have the most impact on solving crime then, AFIS should have the most relevance to the investigation of these crimes. However, given the sheer volume of these types of crimes in many jurisdictions, the routine collection and AFIS analysis of fingerprints may simply not be feasible. For example, in Chicago there are approximately 26,000 burglaries, 14,000 robberies, and 20,000 motor vehicle thefts annually (FBI 2012). Considering just burglaries, figure that in approximately three-fourths of these cases it would be reasonable to search for fingerprints at the crime scenes. It would take at least one hour of police time to dust or otherwise search for prints at these scenes. If fingerprints are collected from the scene, then elimination prints must be collected and analyzed, taking at least one more hour of time. Then one must consider the labor involved in entering the prints into the AFIS system. Just to this point in time, the fingerprinting process will have consumed at a minimum three additional hours of time per case. With 20,000 cases, this amounts to an additional 60,000 hours of time. Figure 60,000 hours at a minimum hourly rate of $30 and it amounts to a cost of $1.8 million. This could pay for salary and benefits of at least twenty-five officers a year. Expensive, indeed.

A second limitation is that a multimillion-dollar AFIS can be foiled by a pair of $0.59 latex gloves. That is, even if the perpetrator's prints are in the system because of a previous arrest, if the perpetrator is careful enough to not leave fingerprints, AFIS may not be of any use. AFIS may be able to compare glove prints, but the precision of these comparisons may be much less than with fingerprints.

Third, the system will only be of use if the perpetrator's prints are already contained in the system. Even if a perfectly clear fingerprint is collected from a crime scene, the perpetrator's print will not be identified if the perpetrator's prints are not in the system. Making this problem even more of an issue is that many of the larger police departments in the country own and operate their own systems. Recently, with newer and less expensive models on the market, even smaller police departments have purchased and operate such systems. Most states also operate an AFIS (operated out of the state law enforcement agencies). The downfall with this arrangement is that these systems are most often self-contained; only the fingerprints collected in that jurisdiction are contained in that system. As a result, if a perpetrator's prints are held in one AFIS but his prints are recovered by a police department in another jurisdiction, a match would not be obtained. As such, a reasonable question becomes, even if considerable resources are spent searching, collecting, and submitting fingerprints for AFIS analysis, what are the chances of obtaining a valid "hit?"

To improve the effectiveness of AFIS technology, the FBI has developed and operates the Integrated Automated Fingerprint Identification System (IAFIS) (see Case in Point 5.6). The system has been in place since 1999. According to the FBI, the IAFIS repository contains fingerprints and criminal histories on approximately 70 million subjects, including 73,000 known and suspected terrorists. The IAFIS allows federal, state, and local law enforcement agencies access to the IAFIS database and thus expands dramatically the number of fingerprints available to be searched to identify perpetrators (see www.fbi.gov/about-us/cjis/ fingerprints_biometrics/iafis).

As noted, most fingerprints from suspects are collected as a result of an arrest and are collected on ten-print fingerprint cards. Legally, in order to collect fingerprints, investigators must have either probable cause or the suspect must willingly submit to having his or her fingerprints taken (see *Hayes v. Florida* [1985]).

SHOEPRINTS, IMPRESSIONS, AND TIRE TRACKS

Shoeprints are created when material from the bottom of shoes, such as blood or mud, is transferred to another surface, leaving an outline of the bottom of the shoe. Shoe impressions and tire tracks are most often left in soft material such as mud or snow, and they reveal the outline of the shoe or tire. Shoeprints and impressions may reveal the perpetrator's entrance to, and exit from, the crime scene, as well as the movements around the crime

CASE in POINT 5.6   IAFIS in Action

On December 14, 1969, a single young mother named Diane Maxwell Jackson arrived for her shift as a Southwestern Bell telephone operator in Houston. After parking her car in the company lot, she was forced into a nearby shack by an unknown individual and brutally raped, strangled, and stabbed to death. After a thorough investigation by the Houston Police Department, no suspects were identified, and the latent prints lifted from the outside of the victim's car were filed away.

Years passed after Jackson's murder, and with no new leads, the case went cold. But in 1989, David Maxwell, the victim's brother, began reviewing the file on his sister's death. Maxwell had reconsidered his plan to become a lawyer after his sister died and instead joined the Texas State Highway Patrol and later the Texas Rangers. He asked the Houston PD to review the original evidence and witness reports for any new leads. A Houston newspaper ran an article publicizing the murder and requesting assistance from the public. At the same time, the Houston PD began a search for the latent prints lifted from the victim's car. Once located, the prints were searched against the Houston PD's local fingerprint database and the Texas Department of Public Safety's Automated Fingerprint Identification System. Neither searched yielded a positive ID.

On July 23, 2003, a Texas Department of Public Safety latent print technician prepared the prints for a search of the FBI's IAFIS. In less than five hours, the system returned a response containing twenty potential matches, and the technician determined that the latent print evidence was a match to the number one candidate—James Ray Davis. Investigators discovered that Davis had been arrested for various crimes before and after Diane Maxwell Jackson's murder—in fact, he had just finished a prison term nine days before the murder. After learning about the latent print identification of Davis, the case's lead investigator quickly located the suspect living along the Texas-Arkansas border. Investigators knew that because Davis's fingerprints were recovered from the outside of the victim's car, they would likely need a confession in order to get a conviction. After being presented with the forensic evidence and photographs of the crime scene, Davis admitted to the crimes.

Davis pled guilty in court, and on November 24, 2003, thirty-four years after the homicide, James Ray Davis was sentenced to life in prison for the rape and murder of Diane Maxwell Jackson.

Source: Adopted from "Houston Cold Case Solved," Federal Bureau of Investigation, October 14, 2011, www.fbi.gov/news/stories/2011/ october/print_101411/print_101411.

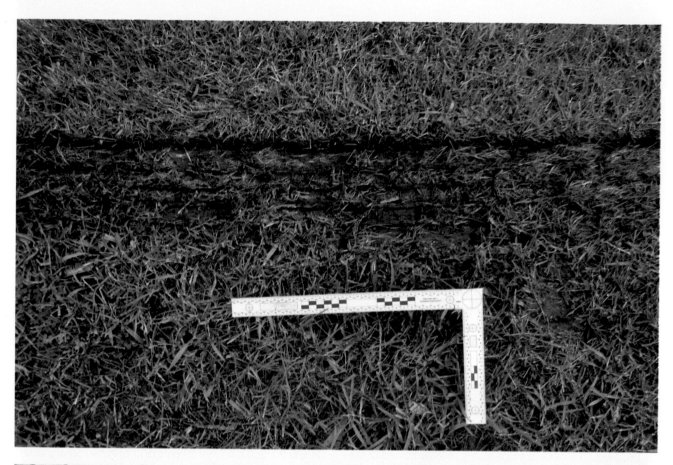

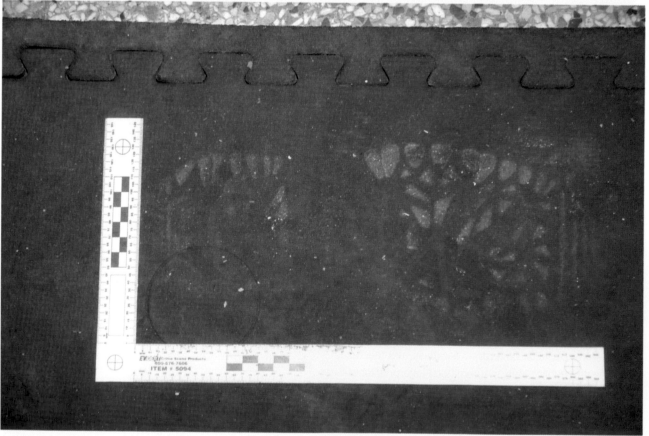

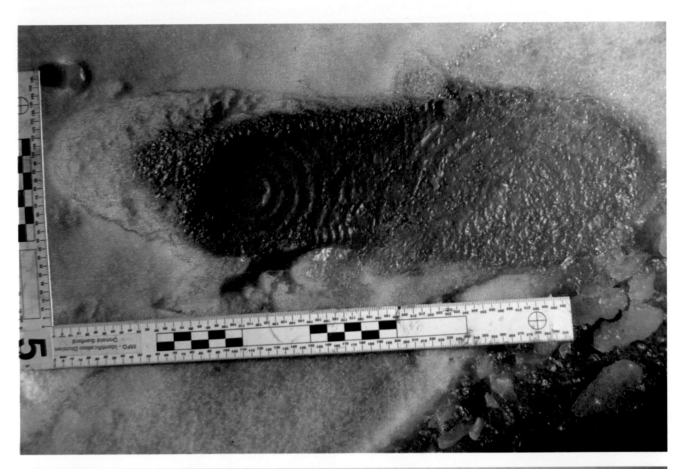

PHOTO 5.26–29: Tire tracks, a transferred shoeprint, a shoe impression in snow, and a shoeprint cast. All of these may be useful evidence in an investigation.

Exhibit 5.8   Individualistic Shoeprints

Notice how the shoeprint on the left is somehow altered and different from the shoeprint on the right. Such a pattern may make these prints and shoes individualistic evidence.

scene. It is also possible to determine from an analysis of the shoeprint or impression class characteristics such as the size of the shoe and the make and brand of the shoe, as was the case in the O. J. Simpson investigation. In some instances, shoeprints and impressions may reveal individual characteristics. Tire tracks may reveal the direction of travel, the size and manufacturer of the tires, and possibly the make and model of the vehicle. In some instances, tire tracks may be positively linked (individualized) to particular vehicles.

The scientific basis for individualization of tire or shoe tracks is that over time these items come to have features of wear that make them unique. For example, brand new shoes will have only features that allow the make and size of the shoe to be determined. Well-worn shoes, on the other hand, may show wear patterns and other wear elements that allow for individualization (see Exhibit 5.8). These wear patterns and features change as the shoes are worn, therefore making individualization dependent on time and potentially more difficult. Nevertheless, class characteristics may be identified, and with distinctive patterns of wear, individualization may be possible. However, there is no scientific agreement about the number of individual characteristics needed to make a positive identification (to say that one shoeprint matches the other) (National Research Council 2009).

Prints, impressions, and tracks should first be photographed and then, if possible, a cast of the impression or track should be made. If the impression or print is left in soil or mud, the recovery procedure involves pouring dental stone (a variant of the type of gypsum used to make dentures) into the impression. When the stone hardens, the mold reveals the outline of the impression. If the track or impression is in snow, then the snow is first sprayed with a special wax to harden the impression, and then dental stone is used to recover the impression.

TOOL MARKS

A tool mark is any mark that is created when an instrument (e.g., pry bar, screwdriver) has contact with another surface (e.g., the wood on a windowsill). The marks left by a tool may indicate the type of tool, the size of the tool, and even the skill of the perpetrator (usually, the fewer the marks/damage, the greater the skill of the perpetrator). Through microscopic examination of the marks and a tool, a tool may be linked to a tool mark. Tool marks are most commonly found around windows and doors in burglary cases. Tool marks can be photographed and casts can be made of the impressions.

BITE MARKS AND DENTAL EVIDENCE

Dental evidence can take two primary forms: dental identification and bite marks. In both instances, the fact that each individual has a unique set of teeth in terms of form, arrangement, dental work, and bite makes dental evidence a potentially powerful form of criminal evidence. The physical characteristics of bite marks and dental identification may consist of the distance between teeth, the shape of the mouth/bite, teeth alignment, teeth shape, missing teeth, and wear patterns of the teeth. A primary means of identifying decomposed dead bodies is dental identification, during which dental radiographs of the individual are compared with those of the dead body. On the basis of a comparison, a match may be made. Of course, this manner of identification is only possible if a dead body is suspected to be a particular individual and x-ray records are available from the decedent's dentist.

Bite marks can be either offensive or defensive. Offensive bite marks would be left on a victim by a perpetrator; defensive bite marks would be left on a perpetrator by the victim. Bite marks may also be an area from which DNA (saliva) can be recovered. Bite marks are seen most often in cases of homicide, sexual assault, and child abuse. There are several methods of collecting bite mark evidence from victims and suspected biters—forms of photography, dental casts, clear overlays, computer enhancement, and electron microscopy (National Research Council 2009). However, bite marks on the skin will change in appearance over time, and this may severely affect the ability to accurately link a bite to a particular suspect. The National Research Council (2009) notes the difficulties and likely errors in attempting to accurately link a suspect to a bite and therefore advises extreme caution in using bite marks as individualized evidence (p. 175).

BALLISTICS

There are various types of evidence associated with firearms, and various examinations can be done on such evidence. The gun itself can be examined to determine its general condition and whether it is functional. Alterations in the functioning of the weapon can be determined, such as if it has been altered to fire in automatic mode. The trigger pull can be tested to determine the amount of pressure necessary to fire the weapon (particularly useful if a perpetrator claims that the gun fired accidentally). Fired bullets can be examined to determine their caliber and manufacturer. Casings can be examined to determine the caliber or gauge and the manufacturer. Also, one common and useful form of evidence in crimes during which a weapon was fired is gunshot residue. Residue patterns may be found on a victim, and from this evidence the distance of the muzzle from the victim may be estimated. In addition, gunshot residue may be found on the hands or clothing of the individual who fired the weapon. Residue tests are commonly performed on individuals who were at or near a crime scene around the time of a shooting and who are believed to have possibly fired the weapon.

PHOTO 5.30–31: Tool marks may be used by investigators to determine the type of tool, the size of the tool, and, in some cases, even the skill level of the perpetrator.

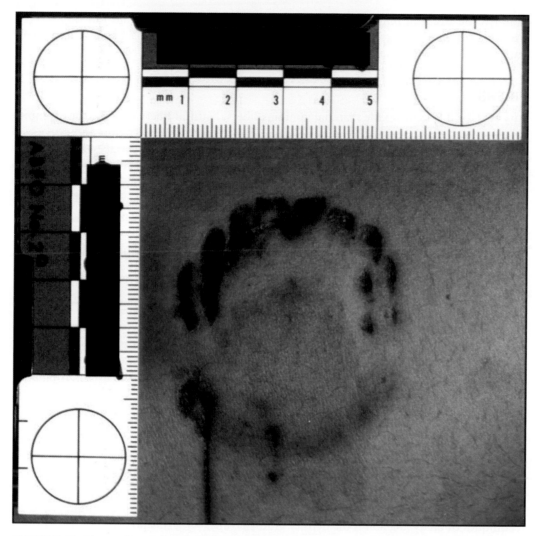

PHOTO 5.32: Bite marks can be offensive or defensive. In some cases, a bite mark left on a victim can be used to link a suspect to the crime, although this is a difficult and error-prone process.

The most sophisticated examination of firearms involves the test firing of the gun to determine whether a recovered bullet matches the test-fired bullet and, hence, if a recovered bullet was in fact fired from that gun. This examination is done through the microscopic examination of the striations on the bullet caused by the bullet moving through the barrel of the gun. Although the striations are unique for each weapon, if a recovered bullet is deformed, a valid comparison is difficult, if not impossible, to make. The Bureau of Alcohol, Tobacco, Firearms, and Explosives (ATF) operates the National Integrated Ballistic Information Network (NIBIN). This system can be thought of as being similar to IAFIS, except that instead of fingerprints being searched and compared, it is bullets that are scanned and searched. NIBIN allows for the comparison of recovered bullets and cartridge casings with images of other bullets and casings that have been entered into the system from law enforcement agencies nationwide. By comparing the striations on bullets, crimes (shootings) committed with the same gun can be identified (FBI 2007).

When collecting firearm evidence, it first should be photographed and, if possible, fingerprinted (weapons and unfired cartridges) and examined for DNA. Firearms should be handled with great care and with the use of a ring that passes through the trigger guard. The ring device prevents contact with the firearm and preserves fingerprints or other evidence on the weapon itself. Weapons, bullets, and casings should be collected and packaged separately. The firearm, bullets, casings, or other firearm evidence should not be marked. Clothing submitted for gunshot residue examination should also be packaged separately in paper envelopes.

FIBERS

Any type of fabric or textile material contains fibers. Natural fibers include, for example, wool, cotton, glass, and fur. Synthetic, or man-made, fibers include nylon and polyester, among others. Fibers from one source are easily transferred to other surfaces, such as fiber to fiber (e.g., clothing to clothing), fiber to skin, fiber to shoes, or fiber to vehicle. Examination of fiber evidence can vary in its sophistication. For example, a comparison can be made between two fibers based on a relatively simple microscopic examination of the color, diameter, and other distinguishing characteristics of the fibers. A more precise examination may be made between fibers based on color through the use of microspectrophotometry. This procedure involves essentially shining light on a fiber and recording the absorption of that light. Chromatography can also be used to identify the chemicals used to make the dye of the fiber, and comparisons can be made on this basis. In any case, even using the most sophisticated methods, fibers cannot be individualized to one particular source (National Research Council 2009).

Fiber evidence is most often found in homicides, assaults, and hit-and-run offenses, and it may be found on clothing, skin, shoes, and carpeting, among other places. Fibers should be packaged in paper envelopes with sealed corners. When possible, the entire garment or textile should be submitted for analysis (FBI 2007).

SOIL

Soil consists of organic natural materials such as rock, minerals, and decomposing plants, and it may also contain man-made materials such as brick, concrete, glass, or paint. Examination of the color, texture, and composition of soils may allow for an assessment of whether the soils share a common origin (FBI 2007). One of the most common scientific techniques of analyzing soil is the density gradient tube. With this procedure, the densities of soil samples are analyzed via chemicals that separate the particles that comprise the soil. If the pattern of separation is similar in two or more samples, it indicates soil with consistent properties (Owen 2000). Once again, despite using the best methods, soil cannot be individualized to one particular source (National Research Council 2009).

Soil evidence is most likely to be found on the bottom of shoes; places where shoes may leave soil (e.g., the floors of vehicles, hard-surface walkways); on clothing; and on the tires, fenders, and body of vehicles. It is recommended that when soil samples are to be collected that they be taken as soon as possible because soil can change quickly and dramatically. In addition, if available, soil should be collected from the immediate crime scene area, as well as from the apparent entrances and exits of the crime scene. Samples should be collected from wherever there is a noticeable change in the color or composition of the soil. It is often necessary to collect numerous soil samples from a scene. A map should be drawn showing where soil samples were taken. Investigators should not remove soil from recovered shoes, clothing, or tools. Paper bags should be used to package materials containing soil, and soil samples should be placed in plastic film-type canisters (FBI 2007).

PAINT

Paint is a pigmented polymer that is applied and adheres to various surfaces. Paint evidence may be found when paint has been transferred from one surface to another, either as wet paint or chips from dried paint. Paint may also be found on tools or on victims' or suspects' clothing. Paint is often present as evidence in hit-and-run cases, during which it may be transferred from one vehicle to another or from a vehicle to a person who has been struck. It is also sometimes present in burglaries, during which paint may be transferred from a

CASE *in* POINT 5.7 The Green River Killer

In the 1980s and 1990s, a series of murders took place in Washington State. The bodies of many women were found in and near the Green River. Gary Ridgway was arrested on charges related to prostitution, and eventually he became a suspect in the killings. DNA was obtained from Ridgway, and he was subsequently linked to four of the victims in the most curious of ways. After raping and strangling some of his victims, Ridgway put rocks in their vaginas and then put their bodies in the Green River. The rocks ended up preserving some of the semen that was in the victims. The semen was recovered, DNA was obtained from it, and it was compared and matched to Ridgway. In addition, some of the clothing that was recovered from the victims was found to have paint on it—the same type of paint that was used by Ridgway in his job as a truck painter. Based primarily on this evidence, and in order to avoid the death penalty, Ridgway plead guilty to forty-eight murders, although it is suspected that he committed many more. He was sentenced to life in prison without the possibility of parole.

building to the perpetrator or from a building to the tools used to gain entry into it. Paint chips tend to be located in pants pockets and pants cuffs.

It is possible to compare microscopically the color and shape of paint chips or other samples. It is also possible to determine through the use of gas chromatography the chemical properties of paint to determine whether samples are from the same source. When paint fragments are able to be fit back into a known source, those paint fragments may be identified as originating from that specific source; it is only in this situation that paint can be individualized as originating from one particular source (National Research Council 2009). The FBI crime laboratory maintains a database of vehicle paint samples with which the color, year, make, and model of an automobile can be determined by analyzing recovered vehicle paint samples. When paint samples are collected, it is necessary that the paint be chipped off the surface, as opposed to scraped off, in order to preserve the layer structure of the paint. With hit-and-run victims, the victim's clothing should normally be submitted for laboratory analysis, as should entire vehicle components (e.g., bumper) that contain paint evidence. Paint particles should be packaged in pillboxes or vials. Plastic bags, cotton, or envelopes should not be used (FBI 2007). Control paint chips must be collected from the suspected source of the evidentiary paint (FBI 2007).

GLASS

Like paint, glass is most often found at hit-and-run and burglary crime scenes. Through microscopic examination of glass particles and their density and refractive properties, the type of glass can be determined and can be compared to a particular (broken) source of glass. In addition, pieces of glass may be able to be fit into a broken source of glass, such as a window; thus, glass can be individualized as originating from one particular source. Glass fracture examinations can determine the direction of breaking glass. The location of broken glass may also be of evidentiary value. Glass particles should be packaged in plastic containers. Larger pieces of glass should be packaged in solid packing containers with cotton packing material (FBI 2007).

BLOOD PATTERN ANALYSIS

The interpretation of bloodstain patterns can be useful in helping investigators understand how a crime occurred. Bloodstain patterns may be present in homicides, sexual assaults, burglaries, and hit-and-run accidents. As explained by the National Research Council (2009):

> Dried blood may be found at crime scenes, deposited either through pooling or via airborne transfer (spatter). The patterns left by blood can suggest the kind of injury that was sustained, the final movements of a victim, the angle of a

shooting, and more. Bloodstains on artifacts such as clothing and weapons may be crucial to understanding how the blood was deposited, which can indicate the source of the blood. For example, a stain on a garment, such as a shirt, might indicate contact between the person who wore the shirt and a bloody object, while tiny droplets of blood might suggest proximity to a violent event, such as a beating. (p. 177)

For example, the crime scene investigation into the murders of Nicole Brown Simpson and Ron Goldman revealed that the perpetrator was bleeding and showed where the perpetrator exited the crime scene (via blood drops present along the back walkway). The fact that blood was found on O. J. Simpson's vehicle and property immediately pointed to him as a possible suspect. The fact that Goldman had Nicole's blood on the bottom of his shoes suggests that Nicole may have been attacked first. Blood splatters may also reveal the amount of force used and even the manner in which the force was delivered—factors that may be useful to know when reconstructing a crime.

DIGITAL EVIDENCE

Computers (and computer storage devices), cellular phones, and GPS devices may provide a wealth of information regarding communications, schedules, travels, and criminal behaviors, and therefore they are potentially valuable sources of evidence in criminal investigations. Through the examination of a computer's hard drive and disks, the content of e-mail, Internet activity, and other communications, useful information may be obtained. The time and sequence that files were created can be determined, files that have been deleted from the computer may be recovered, data files can be searched for a word or phrases, and passwords can be recovered and used to decrypt encoded files (FBI 2007). Examinations of electronic hardware are quite technical in nature and, if not properly performed, can result in lost evidence (FBI 2007; Chapter 14 provides a more detailed discussion of digital evidence). Cellular phone records (as well as other telephone records) can be used to establish the time and length of phone calls and the phone numbers associated with the calls. Such information is often useful in establishing the last activities of a missing or dead victim, and in examining alibis. Electronic evidence may also likely be relevant to the investigations of crimes that involved a high degree of planning, coordination, and communication with others, or that occurred as a result of, or in conjunction with, Internet activity. As noted in Chapter 1, the famous BTK Killer was apprehended in large part as a result of authorities tracing a computer disk that contained a message from the killer to a particular computer used by the killer.

The best practice for the collection of computers as a source of digital evidence is to simply disconnect the power cord and related peripherals (e.g., monitor, printer) and seize these items, along with thumb drives and CDs. The contents of the hard drive can then be determined by making a copy of the hard drive on a new, blank hard drive; this copy can then be searched, and files that have previously been deleted may be recovered. The system files can also be examined. The objective of the computer search is usually to find files of relevance to the crime at hand and to determine when and how these files came to be on the computer (National Research Council 2009)

VIDEO EVIDENCE

Video is a potentially extremely powerful form of evidence. If a crime is captured on video, there may be little doubt about who committed it. Videotape may be enhanced to maximize the clarity of the images captured on it. In addition, still photographs can be obtained from videographic images. Videotape images are most often available as evidence in robberies when surveillance is provided in a particular place, such as an automated teller machine or a convenience store. Even today there is much variation in the quality of video technology and images. This clearly has implications for the quality of the resulting evidence.

PHOTO 5.33: Bank video surveillance cameras usually provide high-quality images. Here a man dressed as a woman is demanding money from the teller. Details of the perpetrator's wig, face, purse, and other clothing are clear.

QUESTIONED DOCUMENTS/HANDWRITING ANALYSIS

Written documents can be examined in many ways. The content of the writing can be analyzed, as was the case in the Lindbergh kidnapping ransom note (Chapter 2) and the Unabomber manifesto (Chapter 1; Chapter 8 provides a more detailed discussion of psycholinguistics as applied to criminal investigations). The actual style and mechanics, as well as the penmanship of the writing contained on the written document, can be examined in order to associate a suspect with a written document or to associate written documents with each other. The paper can be analyzed as to its type, brand, and manufacturer. The ink used to write the words can be analyzed to determine the type of writing instrument used (e.g., ballpoint pen, fountain pen) and allow for a comparison of ink samples. The analysis of ink and paper is similar to other forensic chemistry work (National Research Council 2009).

Most useful may be a comparison of a written document in question with a writing example from an identified suspect, performed in order to determine if the handwriting is consistent in the two samples. In this case, several procedures are recommended (FBI 2007):

- Use the same type and size of paper, request handwriting or hand printing, and give verbal and written instructions as to what the suspect is to write.

PHOTO 5.34: Some businesses still rely on older video equipment that provides lower-quality images. Here a gas station clerk is being robbed at gunpoint by what appears to be a black male wearing a black baseball cap and carrying a black gun.

- The writer and the witness to the writing should initial and date each page of writing.

- Do not allow the writer to see the writing that is in question and being compared.

- It may be necessary to obtain several repetitions in order to obtain a natural and valid writing sample.

- Writing examples from the right and left hand should be obtained, as well as writing containing both upper- and lowercase letters.

- If possible, obtain other existing writing samples from the suspect, such as notes or letters.

The conclusion that two samples were written by the same person depends on showing that their degree of variability is more consistent with *intrapersonal* variability than with *interpersonal* variability (National Research Council 2009). The difficulty is that the handwriting of each person is not always the same. As with tool marks, fingerprints, and bite marks, it is not valid to state a percentage probability that a handwriting example was written by a particular suspect; there is no basis on which to conclude how common handwriting characteristics are in a given population.

With typewritten documents, an analysis of the typewriting may be able to identify the typewriter that produced it or the make and model of the typewriter. The same is generally true with computer printed documents. Typewriter ribbons and examples of typed words and individual letters should be obtained from the typewriter or printer that is suspected of

Exhibit 5.9 Characteristics of Drugs Most Commonly Encountered on the Street

Heroin

- Usually appears as a white to dark brown powder, sticky tar, coal-like rocks
- Highly addictive, made from morphine
- Produces euphoria, confusion, drowsiness, slowed breathing and heart rate
- Ingested via injection, snorting, smoking
- Most commonly known as dope, smack, horse

Oxycodone

- Usually appears in capsule or tablet form, or as liquid
- Highly addictive, made from codeine
- Same effects as heroin
- Ingested orally or injected
- Most commonly known as OxyContin (brand name), Oxys, OCs, killers

Cocaine

- Usually appears as white powder; "crack" cocaine as small, off-white rocks
- Highly addictive, made from coca leaves
- Euphoric and stimulating effect, rapid heartbeat
- Snorted, injected; "crack" cocaine usually smoked
- Most commonly known as blow, coke, crack, snow

Methamphetamines

- Form is varied depending on manufacturing process: tablets, powder, clear rocks
- Highly addictive
- Stimulating effect, aggression, psychotic behavior
- Snorted, smoked, ingested orally, injected
- Most commonly known as speed, meth, crystal meth, crank, poor man's cocaine
- The manufacturing process creates serious environmental hazards

Barbiturates

- Tablets or pills
- Addictive
- Euphoria, sedation, decreased blood pressure, anesthesia
- Taken orally
- Various prescription forms; downers, barbs, tranqs

Peyote and mescaline

- Small spineless cactus, gray-green or brown; powder, capsules
- Generally nonaddictive
- Altered state of awareness, elevated heart rate, perspiration, intoxicated behavior
- Chewed, swallowed
- Mescal, cactus, buttons, dry whiskey, green whiskey

LSD

- Tablets, liquid, sugar cubes, stamps, gelatin
- Generally nonaddictive
- Hallucinations, perceptual impairment, physiological changes, flashbacks
- Most often ingested orally
- Acid, fry, dose, sid, sunshine

Ecstasy

- Tablets
- Potentially highly addictive
- Simulative effects; suppresses hunger, thirst, sleep; causes jaw muscle tension (sucking on pacifiers to relieve teeth grinding)
- Most often ingested orally; may be snorted, injected, inserted as suppository
- XTC, E, Adam, hug drug, go

PCP

- White, tan, brown powder; tablets, capsules, liquid
- Generally nonaddictive
- Hallucinations, impaired coordination and speech, mood disorders, amnesia, possible psychosis
- Smoked (cigarette soaked in liquid containing PCP and dried), snorted, injected, swallowed
- Wack, dust, angel dust, DOA, juice

Marijuana

- Gray, brown, or green dried leaves
- Addictive
- Euphoria, relaxation
- Smoked, eaten
- Weed, grass, pot, blunt, joint, reefer, Mary Jane

Source: Darin D. Fredrickson and Raymond P. Siljander. 2004. *Street Drug Investigation: A Practical Guide for Plainclothes and Uniformed Personnel.* Springfield: Charles C. Thomas.

producing the document. It may also be possible to identify the make and model of a photocopier or fax machine that produced documents in question. Comparison samples from the machines are valuable in this regard. Documentary evidence must be preserved and submitted for analysis in the condition in which it was found. Photocopies should not be shipped or stored in plastic envelopes (see FBI 2007).

DRUGS

Drugs are commonly seized evidence in criminal investigations, be they in the form of pills, powders, or other forms (Exhibit 5.9). Their forensic analysis is normally quite routine; gas chromatography and mass spectrometry are usually used to identify the drug, if it is a drug. Also important is determining the weight of the drug, as criminal penalties are often based on the total weight of the drug, which is the pure drug plus what it may be mixed or "cut" with. However, there must be a "useable quantity" of the drug present in order for there to be a violation of the law. The evidence should be packaged in heat-sealed plastic bags or those that can be resealed. The drug test field kit should not be submitted with the evidence (FBI 2007).

●●● The Role of Crime Laboratories in Criminal Investigations

As discussed in this chapter, physical evidence is made most useful through scientific analysis. While most of this evidence is collected at crime scenes, most of it is analyzed in the controlled environment of crime laboratories. The fundamental role of the crime laboratory is to assist the police in conducting investigations to determine, first, whether a crime has been committed and, second, who committed it.

As of 2009, there were 411 publicly funded forensic crime laboratories in the United States. These laboratories employed over 13,000 personnel (in 2002, there were approximately 350 labs that employed 11,000 people). The average number of full-time employees employed in publicly funded crime labs in 2009 was thirty-two. The 411 crime laboratories include 217 state and regional labs, ninety county, sixty-six municipal, and thirty-eight federal labs (Bureau of Justice Statistics 2012c). In addition, numerous privately run facilities provide forensic evidence examinations. Most often the privately operated facilities are used by defense attorneys to verify the validity of the results provided by the government labs, or by public laboratories on a contractual basis. With regard to the workload of crime labs, approximately 34 percent of analysis requests were for DNA analysis of biological evidence, 33 percent related to the analysis of controlled substances, and 15 percent related to toxicology (Bureau of Justice Statistics 2012a).

Of the 411 publicly funded forensic laboratories, approximately 59 percent perform DNA analysis (Bureau of Justice Statistics 2002). Approximately 83 percent of these agencies are accredited by an official organization, most commonly the American Society of Crime Lab Directors-Laboratory Accreditation Board (ASCLD-LAB). To manage their overall workload, 28 percent of crime labs outsourced some requests for services to other private or public labs. Additional hiring of DNA analysts by laboratories is also likely to occur (see Exhibit 5.10). Still, most DNA labs report significant backlogs and delays in analyzing DNA evidence (Bureau of Justice Statistics 2012c; RAND 2001). Indeed, backlogs have been identified as the most significant problem facing DNA laboratories today. It is likely that increased demands on forensic laboratories will continue to increase at a dramatic rate in the future (Bureau of Justice Statistics 2012c; RAND 2001; also see Chapter 15).

The FBI operates the largest and most well-funded laboratory in the world; in 2009, it employed more than 500 personnel. The FBI laboratory handles requests made by the FBI as well as military, state, and local agencies across the country. All FBI laboratory services

Exhibit 5.10 Job Announcement for a Full-Time, Entry-Level Forensic Criminalist Position in a Police Department Crime Laboratory

The City of Oakland is currently recruiting to fill a Criminalist I vacancy within the Oakland Police Department, Criminalistics Division. Candidates seeking appointment to the Forensic Biology assignment must meet the FBI DNA Quality Assurance educational standards for DNA Examiner as outlined below in Minimum Requirements for Application.

Under direction in the Police Department Criminalistics Laboratory, performs professional and technical duties related to laboratory examination and physical and chemical analyses. Areas of examination may include analysis of drugs, biological evidence/ DNA typing, trace evidence, firearm and toolmark evidence, and crime scene processing; provide testimony in court regarding laboratory findings; and perform related duties as assigned.

Examples of Duties:

- Perform physical and chemical examination of evidence using quantitative and qualitative laboratory techniques; evaluate nature, origin and significance of evidence in criminal cases.

- Examine and identify controlled substances.

- Examine evidence for biological materials and conduct DNA analysis.

- Maintain laboratory equipment, instruments and work areas.

- Research, develop and/or evaluate methods and procedures for laboratory evaluation of physical evidence.

- Perform laboratory evaluation of physical evidence.

- Prepare laboratory reports of analysis; maintain records.

- Serve as custodian of evidence and maintain chain of custody on evidence under control.

- Provide expert testimony in court regarding laboratory findings.

- Provide technical assistance to Criminalists in the analysis of various other evidence materials such as physiological fluids, firearms and trace evidence.

Minimum Requirements for Application:

Any combination of education and experience that is equivalent to the following minimum qualifications is acceptable.

Education:

Graduation from an accredited college or university with a bachelor's degree in Criminalistics or a closely related physical or natural science which must include the successful completion of a minimum of seventeen (17) semester (or equivalent quarter) units of chemistry course work, including laboratory, covering general chemistry, organic chemistry and quantitative analysis.

Candidates seeking appointment to a forensic biology position must meet the FBI DNA Quality Assurance Standards educational standards for DNA Examiner, which require successful completion of nine (9) cumulative semester hours or equivalent that cover the required subject areas of biochemistry, genetics, and molecular biology; and course work and/or training in statistics and/or population genetics as it applies to forensic DNA analysis. For forensic biology candidates, biochemistry may be acceptable in lieu of quantitative analysis.

Experience:

None required.

Knowledge of:

- Theories and principles of analytical chemistry and forensic science fundamental to the practice of Criminalistics.

- Microscopy, chemical and instrumental analysis, laboratory equipment and safety.

- Report writing.

- Modern laboratory procedures, equipment and materials.

Ability to:

- Apply theories and principles of chemistry and forensic science to forensic casework situations.

- Prepare and maintain analytical and other laboratory records and technical reports.

- Communicate effectively and persuasively both orally and in writing utilizing correct English spelling, punctuation and grammar.

- Resolve analytical problems arising from casework through consultation of the scientific literature and/or applied research.

- Follow oral and written directions.

- Work effectively in a highly structured, rank organized environment.

- Establish and maintain effective work relationships with those contacted in the performance of required duties.

Salary:

$32.61 to $40.03 hourly, full-time.

LICENSE OR CERTIFICATE / OTHER REQUIREMENTS:

Individuals who are appointed to this position will be required to maintain a valid California Driver's License throughout the tenure of employment OR demonstrate the ability to travel to various locations in a timely manner as required in the performance of duties.

Must be twenty-one (21) years of age or older. Must pass a thorough background investigation.

and associated expert testimony are provided free of charge; however, the FBI will not reexamine evidence that has already been subjected to the same test, and no request will be granted from an agency that has the capability of performing the same test. In addition, the FBI laboratory only accepts evidence relating to violent crimes; it does not normally accept evidence relating to property crimes (FBI 2007). Because local agencies most often are able to submit evidence to their state crime laboratory for analysis, services are usually not requested from the FBI laboratory.

FORENSIC SCIENCE SPECIALTY AREAS

The analysis of forensic evidence relates to the field of forensic science. Forensic science broadly refers to the field of science that addresses legal questions. Specialized fields in the area of forensic science include criminalistics, forensic pathology, forensic anthropology, forensic odontology, and forensic entomology.

Criminalistics refers specifically to the science of physical evidence, which includes the scientific analysis of trace evidence (e.g., blood, semen, fibers); fingerprints; firearms; DNA analysis; and tool marks. Much of the work of crime laboratories relates to criminalistics.

Forensic pathology is the science of dead bodies and autopsies. Through the analysis of dead bodies by forensic pathologists (e.g., medical examiners), information may be obtained about identity and the nature and cause of death. In homicides in particular, an autopsy may reveal the type of weapon used, the nature of the injuries, and the time of death (see Chapter 10).

Forensic anthropology is a branch of physical anthropology that relates to the identification of skeletal remains of humans. Analysis of human remains may provide information about the gender, age, race, and height of the individual, as well as sometimes the cause of death (e.g., skull fracture). Also included in this area of study is facial reconstruction. Based on an understanding of the characteristics and variations in cranial and facial structure, faces may be developed on the basis of a skull.

Forensic odontology refers to the application of dentistry to legal matters. It involves the scientific analysis of teeth and bite marks for the purposes of identification. The specialty areas of forensic odontology and forensic anthropology provide some overlap. Analysis of teeth (of a dead body) may assist in the determination of the subject's age, facial characteristics (teeth and jaw structure), race, socioeconomic status (through dental work), and even habits or occupation.

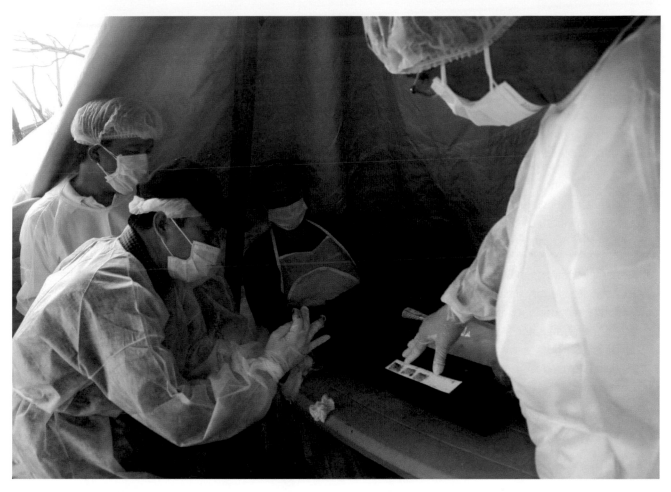

PHOTO 5.35: Forensic scientists analyze evidence to make it more meaningful to investigators and others in the criminal justice system. The work is extremely detail oriented.

TABLE 5.1	Educational Pathways to Some Forensic Science Careers
FORENSIC DISCIPLINE	**EDUCATIONAL REQUIREMENTS**
Crime scene investigation	Jobs are typically held by law enforcement personnel. Applicants must meet requirements for joining the law enforcement agency. For federal jobs, a college degree is required.
Computer crime investigation	B.S. in computer science or computer engineering
Forensic computer science	M.S. may be common
Criminalistics	B.S. in the physical sciences, with background in chemistry
Forensic pathology	Appropriate college degree, M.D. internship and pathology residency, specialized training in forensic pathology, requires state license and board certification
Forensic odontology	Appropriate college degree (D.D.S. or D.D.M.), may include additional specialized training, requires state license and board certification
Forensic entomology	Ph.D. in entomology
Forensic anthropology	M.S. or M.A. at a minimum, many have Ph.D.

Source: Adopted from R. E. Gaensslen. 2003. "How Do I Become a Forensic Scientist? Educational Pathways to Forensic Science Careers." *Analytical and Bioanalytical Chemistry* 376(8): 1,151–1,155.

Finally, forensic entomology relates to the science of insects in answering legal questions. Of particular focus is estimating the time of death based on the insect activity on the body of the deceased (see Chapter 10).

MAIN POINTS ●━━

1. Physical evidence has several important purposes in the criminal investigation process. It can help establish the elements of a crime, it can be used to make associations, it can function as corroborative evidence, and it can be used to establish the identity of a victim or offender.

2. Physical evidence can act as direct or circumstantial evidence depending on the particular evidence at hand and the conclusion trying to be established.

3. Generally speaking, physical evidence is limited in its ability to identify a suspect when one has not already been identified through other evidence. Most often a suspect is developed through other evidence, such as eyewitnesses, and then physical evidence is used to help confirm the identity of the perpetrator.

4. A crime scene is the area within the immediate vicinity where a crime is believed to have occurred. Significant evidence may also be found at a secondary crime scene.

5. Crime scenes vary in their usefulness; some crime scenes contain much evidence, some crime scenes only provide limited access to a few people.

6. There are numerous guidelines that relate to the management and processing of crime scenes. Initial priorities relate to crime scene security, officer safety, and medical attention for subjects who may be injured. Evidence collection procedures at the crime scene consist of interviews of victims and witnesses, a neighborhood canvass, documenting the crime scene (e.g., photographs, sketches), a crime scene search, and the collection of physical evidence. In completing the investigation at a crime scene, the investigators must ensure that the scene has been processed and documented thoroughly.

7. Physical evidence can have class characteristics or individual characteristics. Class characteristic evidence can be associated with a group of objects or persons; individual characteristic evidence can be identified as originating with a particular person or source. Serious errors can result when individualistic conclusions are drawn from class characteristic evidence.

8. Strictly speaking, only biological evidence with DNA properties can be accurately considered individualistic evidence.

9. The most commonly encountered forms of biological evidence are blood, semen, saliva, and hair.

10. Depending on the nature and form of evidence, various methods can be used to collect and package it. In nearly all instances, paper bags or paper envelopes should be used to package evidence. Other methods of evidence collection also apply.

11. The most significant advance in the technology of criminal investigations ever is the science of DNA.

12. DNA may be used to associate positively and absolutely a perpetrator to a crime scene, to a victim, or to tools used in the crime. DNA can also be used to eliminate a subject from consideration as the perpetrator. DNA can also be used to confirm the identity of victims or the remains of victims when there is a reference sample available.

13. Caution needs to be used when collecting and processing DNA evidence as it may contain pathogens and may be easily contaminated.

14. There are two types of DNA: mitochondrial (MtDNA) DNA and nuclear DNA. MtDNA cannot differentiate between individuals who have the same maternal lineage.

15. DNA analysis involves the examination and comparison of particular locations on the DNA. The most common method of analyzing DNA is known as PCR (polymerase chain reaction).

16. DNA data banks that electronically store and search for matching DNA prints (such as CODIS) give DNA the capability of identifying a perpetrator when one is not already known.

17. Fingerprints consist of ridges, depressions, and separations. Fingerprint patterns are unique across

individuals. Fingerprints can take the form of visible transferred prints, visible impression prints, and latent prints. Automated Fingerprint Identification Systems (AFIS) allow for the electronic search of fingerprints in order to identify a perpetrator when one is not already known; however, AFIS systems have serious limitations.

18. Other forms of physical evidence (shoeprints, tool marks, bite marks, ballistics, etc.) can play an important role in criminal investigations.

19. While physical evidence is most often collected at crime scenes, it is most often analyzed in crime laboratories. Much of the work of crime labs relates to DNA analysis, followed by the analysis of controlled substances and tests related to toxicology.

20. The FBI operates the largest and most well-funded crime lab in the world.

21. Forensic science specialty areas include criminalistics (the science of physical evidence), forensic pathology (the science of dead bodies), forensic anthropology (identification of skeletal remains), forensic odontology (application of dentistry to legal matters), and forensic entomology (the science of using insects in answering legal questions).

IMPORTANT TERMS

Associative evidence

Automated Fingerprint Identification System (AFIS)

Class characteristic evidence

Combined DNA Index System (CODIS)

Corpus delicti evidence

Corroborative evidence

Crime scene

Crime scene management

Crime scene procedures

Criminalistics

Direct and circumstantial evidence

Deoxyribonucleic acid (DNA)

DNA databank

DNA printing

Forensic anthropology

Forensic entomology

Forensic odontology

Forensic pathology

Forensic science

Friction ridge analysis

Individual characteristic evidence

Locard's Exchange Principle

Luminol

Mitochondrial DNA (mtDNA)

Neighborhood canvass

Nuclear DNA

Physical evidence

Polymerase chain reaction (PCR)

Secondary crime scene

Ten-print fingerprint card

QUESTIONS FOR DISCUSSION AND REVIEW

1. What are the three roles or functions of physical evidence in the criminal investigation process? What is the most common function of physical evidence?

2. How can physical evidence be direct evidence? How can physical evidence be circumstantial evidence?

3. What are the major limitations of physical evidence?

4. What are the most important guidelines that should be followed in recovering and preserving physical evidence from major crime scenes?

5. What does it mean to "manage" a crime scene? Why is it important that crimes scenes be managed?

6. Why might some crime scenes be more valuable to investigators than others?

7. Why are neighborhood canvasses for witnesses an important investigative activity? What are the major guidelines to keep in mind when conducting a neighborhood canvass?

8. What is Locard's Exchange Principle? Why is this principle important to consider when conducting a search of a crime scene?

9. What is the primary difference between class characteristic evidence and individual characteristic evidence?

10. What is DNA? From what types of evidence can DNA be obtained? How can DNA evidence be useful in an investigation?

11. How does DNA evidence compare with fingerprint evidence in terms of its value in criminal investigations? What are the major limitations of DNA and fingerprint evidence?

12. What precautions are necessary when collecting and handling biological evidence?

13. What is forensic science and what are the subspecialty areas of forensic science?

 STUDENT STUDY SITE

Visit **www.sagepub.com/brandl3e** to access additional study tools including eFlashcards, web quizzes, web resources, video resources, and SAGE journal articles.

6 Interviews and Eyewitness Identifications

Objectives

After reading this chapter you will be able to:

- Define interrogation and explain how it differs from an interview

- Identify and discuss the various forms of police deception in interrogations

- Discuss rationalization, projection, and minimization (RPM) in interrogations

- Differentiate between the sledgehammer and feather approach in interrogations

- Identify the nine steps in an interrogation according to Inbau et al. (2013)

- Identify the differences between emotional and non-emotional offenders, and explain the significance of the distinction

- Discuss the reasons why a person may confess to a crime that he or she did not commit

- Discuss the general theory underlying the detection of deception and identify the

non-verbal and verbal behaviors that tend to indicate deception

- Discuss the accuracy and "usefulness" of the polygraph

- Differentiate between false-positive errors and false-negative errors in polygraph examinations

- Discuss the difficulties in establishing the accuracy of the polygraph and identify the factors that may affect the accuracy of polygraph results

From the **CASE FILE**
BP Gas Station Robbery

The introduction to this chapter consists of a police report (edited for length) of the investigation of an armed robbery of a BP (British Petroleum) gas station that occurred on August 22, 2011, in Germantown, Wisconsin (a suburb of Milwaukee). The report serves as an example of a criminal investigation case report and also highlights issues

that are discussed in this chapter, including the value of eyewitness identification. Issues that are discussed in other chapters, including the important role of patrol officers in investigations, crime scene photographs, investigation of robbery and auto theft, and the value of DNA, are also discussed in this report.

Incident Report Number: 11–014277, Report of Officer Toni Olson

On Monday, August 22, 2011, I, Officer Olson, was assigned to investigate and respond to a robbery, which had just occurred at the County Line BP, located at 21962 County Line Road. Officers were advised that the clerk at the BP gas station had called the non-emergency number reporting that a younger white male came into the store and hit him over the head with an unknown object before taking money out of his cash drawer and leaving in a red SUV or truck, northbound on Bell Road. A possible registration of 583RIB was given out for the suspect vehicle. I, along with Lt. Huesemann, Officer Brian Ball, and Officer Daniel Moschea of the Germantown Police Department responded.

Upon arriving on scene, officers were advised that witnesses reported the suspect vehicle leaving the scene of the robbery northbound on Bell Road into a subdivision. The witnesses also stated that they had not seen the suspect vehicle leave the subdivision, which only has two ways to get in and out.

Upon Officer Ball's arrival, he blocked off the entrance into the subdivision at Belle Road. I blocked off the south entrance to the County Line BP directly off of County Line Road with my squad car and observed two to three vehicles at different pumps and people standing outside. I then advised Lt. Huesemann, who arrived in the area right behind me, to block off the intersection of Hollow Lane and County Line Road, which is the second point of access into the subdivision. Lt. Huesemann also requested assistance from neighboring agencies Menomonee Falls Police Department, Waukesha County Sheriff's Department, and the Washington County Sheriff's Department. Units from these agencies assisted in setting up perimeter around the subdivision.

I first made contact with a subject who stated he witnessed the clerk and suspect struggling, leaving the store, and the suspect vehicle leaving the area. This witness was identified as Daniel A. Kobcheck (w/m, 05–21–52). Kobcheck stated that he was gassing up his truck and a gas can at the County Line BP gas station and had parked his vehicle on the north set of pumps. He stated upon his arrival, he noticed a red Jeep Grand Cherokee backed up directly in front of the air pumps. Kobcheck stated he noticed the vehicle due to its engine running and an extremely loud exhaust. Kobcheck further described the suspect vehicle as an older, possibly 1984 to 1985, red Jeep Grand Cherokee.

Kobcheck informed me that while he was gassing up the gas can, his attention was brought to the front of the store when he observed the clerk chasing a white male subject out of the store. He stated the clerk was yelling at the suspect, who eventually got into the red Jeep Cherokee. Kobcheck stated the clerk had held onto the driver side door of the Jeep as the subject tried to close it and drive away, at which time Kobcheck yelled for the clerk to let it go. Kobcheck stated the Jeep then sped out of the west parking lot of the gas station, turning right or northbound onto Bell Road. Kobcheck stated he lives in the subdivision behind the gas station and knows there are only two ways to access the subdivision.

Kobcheck then told the clerk to go inside and call the police, at which time he stated he went to the south side of the parking lot parallel with County Line Road to keep an eye on the other entrance/exit to the subdivision, Hollow Lane. Kobcheck stated he did not see the suspect vehicle exit the subdivision at any point. I then asked Kobcheck if he could stay at his location and notify law enforcement if he did observe the vehicle leave the area.

I then went into the store and made contact with the complainant, who was identified as Ejaz Pasool (m/a 3–25–61). Pasool was visibly shaken up and immediately showed me his left hand and forearm, stating he was struck several times. Pasool denied any emergency treatment at that time.

Pasool informed me that the suspect had entered the store several minutes prior to the robbery. He stated that the subject immediately went to the soda cooler, taking a can of Mountain Dew or Diet Mountain Dew out of the cooler. Pasool stated the subject then asked him where the beef jerky was located in the store, at which time he pointed in the direction of the front door/main entrance. Pasool stated the suspect then walked over to the area where the beef jerky was located and stood in front of it. Pasool stated that there were approximately two other customers in the store at the same time, however, upon them leaving, the suspect walked to the area in front of the cashier counter and inquired about several different candy bars and other products, not making sense. Pasool stated that the suspect then placed the can of Mountain Dew onto the counter, at which time he asked the suspect, "What do you want?" Pasool stated that the suspect replied by stating, "I need drugs." Pasool told the suspect he was sorry but he did not have any drugs. The suspect then handed Pasool four quarters to pay for the Mountain Dew, at which time Pasool opened the cash register. Pasool stated that upon opening the cash register, the suspect asked, "Do you have that carton?" while looking at the cigarettes behind Pasool. Pasool stated that he then turned around with the cash register still open. Pasool stated that as he turned back around to ask the suspect what kind of cigarettes he wanted, the suspect was swinging a long object towards him. Pasool stated that the object was in the suspect's right hand and was approximately 12" in length and hard. Pasool could give no further description of the weapon but stated that as he was trying to defend himself by putting his arms up in front of him, the suspect hit him two to three times in the left hand and arm. Pasool stated while the suspect was swinging the object, he hit the cigarette dispenser above the counter and had been reaching across the counter with his left hand in an attempt to take cash from the cash register. Pasool stated that he believes the suspect took mostly $20 bills and possibly one or two $10 bills from the cash register drawer.

Pasool stated that while the suspect was grabbing the cash from the drawer, the two had struggled back and forth for a short time before the suspect ran out the front door. Pasool stated he ran after the suspect and observed him getting into a red Jeep, which was parked on the west side of the building in front of the air machine. Pasool stated that as the suspect got into the Jeep, he grabbed a hold of the driver side door but eventually had to let go as the suspect sped off. Pasool stated that the suspect left northbound on Bell Road and did not believe there was anyone else in the Jeep, and described the Jeep as "rusty." Pasool stated at that time, a customer who was outside of the store told him to go inside and call 911. Pasool then went inside and called the non-emergency number, reporting the incident. Pasool stated that he stayed inside the store and continued to wait on customers and spoke with officers upon their arrival. Pasool also stated he had contacted his manager, who was later identified as Waseem M. Deg (m/a 1–4–51), who arrived at the store a short time later.

Pasool described the suspect as having three to four days of facial hair growth. He also stated he believed the suspect was a white male, approximately twenty-five to thirty years of age, wearing blue jeans and a dark top. He believed the suspect was approximately 5'9," 130 lbs., and wearing a dark colored ball cap. Pasool stated the suspect did not look familiar to him. Pasool also stated that at no time did he give permission for anyone to strike him or take money or merchandise from the store.

I then made contact with a female identified as Marie E. Saunders (f/w 6–11–33), who stated she was parked outside of the gas station getting gas when she heard an argument and people yelling. She stated she witnessed two subjects struggling, followed by one of the subjects getting into a red Jeep and going northbound on Bell Road.

I also made contact with a witness identified as Michael J. Jones (m/w 7–18–57). Jones stated he was also outside of the gas station when the altercation occurred and that he assisted Kobcheck with making sure the suspect vehicle did not exit the subdivision.

I then re-contacted Kobcheck to get a better description of the suspect. Kobcheck stated that the suspect was a white male, "clean cut," approximately 6'1," 140 lbs., wearing a dark shirt. Kobcheck was certain the suspect vehicle was a Jeep Grand Cherokee, red in color. I asked Kobcheck again if he was certain the Jeep did not exit the subdivision, at which time he informed me that there was approximately a one- to two-minute time frame where he was not watching the intersection of Hollow Lane and County Line Road, when he went into the store to check on the clerk. Kobcheck state that the suspect vehicle had a registration of 583RIB.

Officers were advised by dispatch that the suspect vehicle plate information, 583RIB, was coming back "not on file" through the Department of Transportation. Officers were then later advised by dispatch that a registration plate of 583RBT was listed to a 1998 Jeep Grand Cherokee SUV, red in color, to David W. Anders (m/w 4–28–58) of 4824 N. 114th Street, Milwaukee. This vehicle matched the description of the suspect vehicle and had been entered as a stolen vehicle through the Brown Deer Police Department [a city about ten miles away from where the robbery occurred] as of the morning of Monday 8–22–11.

Dispatch later advised squads that they had received information from the Mequon Police Department [a neighboring jurisdiction] that the suspect vehicle was currently unoccupied in the Pick 'N' Save grocery store parking lot, which was located at 18273 County Line Road in the Village of Menomonee Falls [approximately three miles from the BP gas station]. Officer Ball, Lt. Huesemann, Officer Moschea, and Detective Yogerst responded to the scene.

I then made contact with the manager of the BP gas station, who was identified as Waseem Deg. Deg had Pasool close out his cash register, and it was determined that approximately $202.00 of U.S. currency had been missing from the cash register.

I took several digital photographs (flashcard inventory 28506) of the County Line BP gas station, both inside and out. I also took photographs of the refrigerator cooler from where the suspect took the can of Mountain Dew; the damaged cigarette dispenser, which was struck by an unknown blunt object; and several $1 bills, which had fallen onto the floor behind the counter during the struggle. Detective Yogerst processed the scene for other items of evidentiary value; however, nothing of value was recovered from inside the store.

I made telephone contact with the owner of the red Jeep Grand Cherokee, David W. Anders. Anders confirmed that he had filled out a vehicle theft report with the Brown Deer Police Department on 8–22–11 at approximately 11:30 a.m. Anders stated that he drove his 1998 red Jeep Grand Cherokee with registration number 583RBT to the Papa John's at the intersection of Bradley and Sherman at approximately 11 a.m. He stated when he went out to his vehicle around 11:30 a.m. to get something from inside of it, the vehicle was gone.

Supplement Report, Number: 11–014277, Report of Officer Brian Ball

Upon arrival in the area, I assisted Lt. Huesemann in canvassing the neighborhood in the area in which the vehicle was believed to have fled. Upon proceeding east on Indian Parkway, I observed, in the tall grass on the north side of the road, a black sweatshirt or shirt. I exited my patrol car and observed that the sweatshirt appeared to have been recently discarded, as it was lying on top of some tall grass. The sweatshirt itself was also in good condition and did not appear to have been weathered by rain or any other elements. That sweatshirt was later retained and placed in property inventory (28508). We continued to check the neighborhood, but we did not locate any vehicles.

At approximately 4:40 p.m. I made contact with David S. Grabowski (m/w 5–4–32) and his wife, Gloria H. Grabowski (f/w 12–30–32), at their residence on Indian Parkway, just east of Bell Road. I was advised that they observed a red older model SUV traveling eastbound on Indian Parkway. Gloria stated the vehicle had an extremely loud exhaust and it appeared to be going fast. David repeated the same. Neither Gloria nor David had ever seen the vehicle in the neighborhood before.

While traveling on Bell Road, I observed a subject in his yard, identified as Edward J. Reel (m/w 7–2–42), who advised me that he had seen a red SUV with an extremely loud exhaust traveling northbound on Bell Road past his residence. He stated that when he turned to look, he observed the red SUV traveling past. Reel stated that he did not observe the operator and said that he had no additional information.

At approximately 4:52 p.m., dispatch advised they received a call from the Mequon Police Department reporting the suspect vehicle may be parked in the parking lot of the Pick 'N' Save grocery store on County Line Road. It was later determined that the wife of a Mequon police officer was witness to the vehicle's presence, and she had received information from that Mequon officer regarding the robbery and to look out for that vehicle while she was shopping in the area.

Upon arrival at Pick 'N' Save, I drove through the lot and observed an older model Jeep Grand Cherokee, red in color, with plate 583RBT, parked in the center lot approximately 100 feet from the entrance to the store. The vehicle was identified as the suspect vehicle. A perimeter was set up at all the possible exits, and the Menomonee Falls Police Department assisted in attempting contact inside the store. At approximately 5:45 p.m., after the Menomonee Falls Police Department officers checked the inside of Pick 'N' Save, it was determined that the suspect was not present. Those officers also checked the remaining businesses located at the strip mall to determine if the suspect may have gone into one of those businesses requesting assistance or use of a phone, etc. None of the businesses checked had information regarding unusual behavior by any patron.

Prior to having the vehicle towed, Detective Yogerst photographed the vehicle and recovered a $20 bill off the floor of the driver's seat and later placed it in property inventory.

While Detective Yogerst completed the photography of the vehicle, I checked the garbage cans adjacent to the entrance/exit door at Pick 'N' Save. Upon opening the garbage lids, I noticed that the garbage had recently been emptied and there was limited trash inside the garbage. In one garbage can I observed, on top of some miscellaneous papers, a Diet Mountain Dew can. The initial report by the victim suggested that the suspect may have taken a Mountain Dew can from the store at the time of the robbery. Located in the garbage can which contained in the Mountain Dew can, I observed a black and white Nike baseball cap that appeared to be in relatively good condition. Both the can and the hat were recovered as evidence and later placed in property inventory.

The sweatshirt, baseball cap, $20 bill and Diet Mountain Dew can were photographed prior to being placed in property inventory.

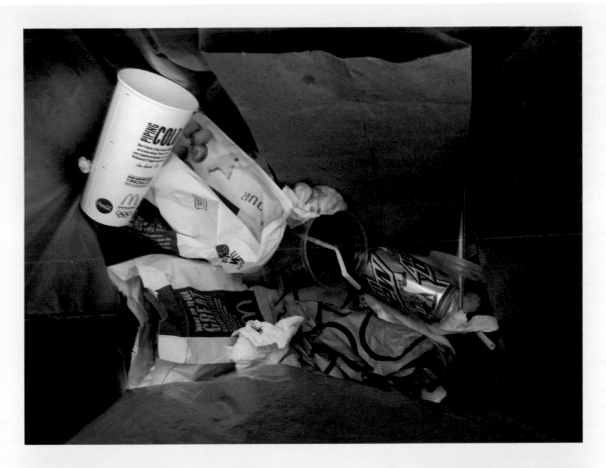

Supplement Report, Number: 11–014277, Report of Officer Jeff Stieve

On Tuesday, August 23, 2011 at 9:30 a.m., Officer Jeff Stieve and Detective Mike Yogerst inspected the red 1998 Jeep Cherokee, plate 583RBT, within the garage of the Germantown Police Department. The following items were collected from the vehicle and inventoried (PI 28512):

1. U.S. Currency—$20 bill, serial number IG93458916B, collected at 10:20 a.m. from underneath the front driver's side seat

2. U.S. Currency—$1 bill, serial number E21181706D, collected at 10:23 a.m., from underneath the front driver's side seat

3. One plastic 20 oz. Coca Cola bottle, empty, collected from the front right passenger side floor at 10:23 a.m

4. One silver key, #66, collected at 10:40 a.m. from the front driver side floor

5. Three wet DNA swabs:

   a) Swab A collected at 10:28 a.m. from the front driver side, inside the door handle

   b) Swab B collected at 10:31 a.m. from the left side of the steering wheel

   c) Swab C collected at 10:33 a.m. from the right side of the steering wheel

Supplement Report, Number: 11–014277, Report of Officer Brian Ball

On Tuesday, August 23, 2011, I conducted follow-up in the investigation of this incident. During the initial complaint, and after receiving the information regarding the suspect description, my memory recalled an incident that I investigated recently involving a male subject who was identified as Russell D. Warchol. His physical descriptors, including height, weight, and general appearance, along with facial hair, was consistent with the description provided by the witnesses to this incident. Additionally, as a result of that original investigation, I learned that the suspect's girlfriend is employed at Stein's Garden and Gifts, located on Appleton Avenue approximately two blocks north from Pick 'N' Save.

Warchol does have a lengthy criminal history, which included property crimes and drug violations. During my earlier investigation, I also learned that Warchol and his girlfriend were homeless and living out of a vehicle in a county park. Warchol is unemployed and received food stamp assistance from the state.

On August 23, 2011, I made contact with the manager at Stein's Garden and Gift's, Gwen Charowski. She stated that on Monday, August 22, 2011 (the day of the robbery), Angela Goler (believed to be Warchol's girlfriend) was working at the store, and at one point Angela asked her if she could go outside. Charowski stated that this incident occurred sometime between 1:30 p.m. and 3:00 p.m. Upon looking out into the parking lot, she observed Goler standing at the driver's side of a red, boxy-looking SUV. I presented Charowski with several black and white photographs of miscellaneous SUVs. I asked her if she recognized any of the images as the vehicle she saw in the parking lot the day before. Charowski looked at the black and white photos for approximately thirty seconds and pointed to the picture of the Jeep Grand Cherokee and she stated that she believed that was the vehicle that Angela Goler was standing by in the parking outside of Stein's on August 22, 2011. I have no further information.

Supplement Report, Number: 11–014277, Report of Detective Michael Yogerst

On 8–22–11, I responded to the area of Belle Road and County Line Road to assist in the investigation of a robbery occurring at that location. I processed the counter surface and the area adjacent to it for fingerprints, with negative results. I was advised that video surveillance equipment on the premise had not been operating at the time of the incident. I was advised by Officer Olson that the suspect had purchased a can of Mountain Dew, either regular or diet, and based on the search of the scene it appeared that the can of soda was taken by the suspect. I was also advised that the victim provided a description of the suspect wearing a black baseball type hat.

On 8–23–11, I made contact with the Brown Deer Police Department to obtain information about the stolen Jeep. At 1:15 p.m. on 8–23–11, I spoke with David Anders, the owner of the recovered vehicle. Anders stated

that before his vehicle was stolen from the parking lot at Papa John's, a male subject had come into the store and indicated that his car had broken down. According to Anders, the subject did not buy anything and left the store. According to Anders, this occurred shortly before he discovered his vehicle stolen. Mr. Anders indicated to me that there should be in-store video surveillance, which may provide a view of the subject who came into the store prior to the vehicle being stolen. Arrangements were made through the Brown Deer Police Department to obtain any video surveillance that is available.

During the course of the investigation, I received information that Officer Ball had previous contact with a subject by the name of Russell D. Warchol (m/w 12–16–72) and that this subject matches the description of the suspect of the BP gas station robbery. I contacted the Washington County Sherriff's Department for further information about this subject and was advised that Mr. Warchol was in currently in custody in the Ozaukee County jail awaiting a preliminary hearing. I was informed that Mr. Warchol had not been in continuous custody since his earlier arrest by Officer Ball.

I requested that the Ozaukee County jail provide a series of photographs to be used for a photo lineup with the victim in the robbery incident. I picked up the lineup photos from the Ozaukee County jail on 8–24–11 and met with Ejaz Pasool at the BP gas station. While at the gas station, I reviewed the photo array instructions with Mr. Pasool, explaining to him that he is not required to pick someone out and the person involved in the incident may or may not be among the images he was about to be shown. I then provided the witness, Mr. Pasool, with seven folders, six of which contained the images provided by the Ozaukee County jail.

The photos had been placed in folders number one through seven, six of which contained images. The seventh was empty and was included to aid in the random shuffling of the images prior to Mr. Pasool being presented with the folders. The folders were presented to Mr. Pasool one at a time, allowing him to look at the image and then proceeding to the next. After viewing the folders, Mr. Pasool indicated that the person depicted in folder #4 was the person who assaulted and robbed him at the gas station. Mr. Pasool indicated he was definitely certain that the individual depicted in folder #4 was the individual who had robbed him without his consent [photo #4 was of Russell Warchol].

Based on the positive identification of Mr. Warchol as being the individual who committed the robbery at the BP gas station, I contacted Warchol's probation officer, Jada Miller. I advised Ms. Miller that the Germantown Police Department would be requesting charges for robbery while armed, battery, operating a vehicle without owner's consent, and bail jumping. Ms. Miller indicated that Mr. Warchol would not be released from jail pending his appearance on any current charges. Further investigation is pending at this time.

Supplement Report, Number: 11–014277, Report of Detective Michael Yogerst

On 9–7–11, I viewed the video CD from Papa John's and observed a white male subject depicted in the video wearing a dark-colored sweatshirt and Nike hat, both of which were consistent with those recovered by the Germantown Police Department in the above investigation. Still photographs of the suspect were made and are attached to this investigation. I inventoried the CD on property inventory 28550.

On 9–8–11, I contacted Public Defender Erin Larsen, who was representing Mr. Warchol. She indicated that Russell Warchol will invoke his Miranda rights and not answer police questions about the BP robbery or the theft of the vehicle.

I advised Assistant District Attorney Peter Cannon that a request would be made for a search warrant to obtain DNA from Russell Warchol to compare with any DNA recovered from the vehicle found in the Pick 'N' Save parking lot or to other items relating to the crime.

Supplement Report, Number: 11–014277, Report of Detective Michael Yogerst

On 9–11–11, I obtained a search warrant for buccal swabs to be taken from Russell D. Warchol. I met with Mr. Warchol at the County House of Correction, where Warchol was being held on a probation hold pending revocation. I read the attached Miranda form to Mr. Warchol, which Warchol indicated he understood but did not want to answer any questions. He also refused to sign the form. I then served the warrant to Warchol and obtained two buccal swabs obtained by use of sterile cotton swabs and rubbing one on the right inner cheek and one on the inner left cheek between his teeth/gum line and the inner layer of his cheek. The swabs were then packaged according to normal procedure. The swabs were placed on PI#28571 as held as evidence in the Germantown Police Department. I returned the warrant to the Washington County Clerk of Courts Office along with a copy of the above-referenced property inventory.

On 9–20–11, I delivered the following items to the Wisconsin crime lab requesting they be examined against Warchol's known DNA:

6. Diet Mountain Dew can

7. Nike hat

8. Fender sweatshirt

9. Swab from vehicle door handle

10. Swab from left side of the vehicle steering wheel

11. Swab from the right side of the vehicle steering wheel

12. Buccal swab standard collected from Russell D. Warchol

On 12–28–11, the Germantown Police Department received a lab report dated 12–21–11. In reviewing the report, analyst Susan V. S. Noll indicated the same male STR DNA profile was obtained from the Nike hat swab, the Fender sweatshirt swabs, and the right steering wheel swabs. This STR DNA profile was compared with the STR DNA profile obtained from the buccal swab standard from Russell D. Warchol and was found to match. Ms. Noll indicated that it was her opinion that the only reasonable explanation was that the contributor of the STR DNA found on the Nike hat, the Fender sweatshirt, and the right side of the steering wheel was Russell D. Warchol, w/m dob 12–16–72. I faxed the above-referenced documents to the Washington County district attorney's office.

Postscript: Russell D. Warchol pled no contest to robbery with use of force (plea bargain). He was sentenced to five years in prison, with four years of extended supervision when released.

Note: Names of victims and witnesses have been changed.

Case Considerations and Points for Discussion

- Physical evidence and witnesses played important roles in this investigation. Discuss the value of the information that was obtained from the witnesses in the investigation, especially the information from the gas station attendant. Discuss the role and value of the Nike hat, the Fender sweatshirt, the Mountain Dew soda can, and the vehicle that was used in the robbery.

- What information from witnesses turned out to be accurate? What information was inaccurate?

- Based on your assessment and understanding of the investigation, what do you think was the most important development or discovery in the investigation? What mistake(s) did Warchol make in perpetrating the crime?

- What do you think should be the biggest lessons learned by the police as a result of the investigation?

••• Interviews Defined

An investigative interview can be defined as any questioning that is intended to produce information regarding a particular crime or regarding a person believed responsible for a crime. Interviews are usually not accusatory in nature and have the goal of developing information to move a criminal investigation forward. As seen in the BP gas station robbery investigation, the police had reason to interview numerous individuals in an attempt to develop leads in the investigation. A witness was also able to confirm the identity of the robber in a lineup. Also as seen in the BP investigation, for a variety of reasons, the information developed through interviews of witnesses may not be complete or accurate. In addition, depending on the information obtained from a subject, an interview can easily turn into an interrogation, during which accusations may be made and incriminating statements may be sought. Investigators must be aware of these possibilities throughout the process of collecting and assembling information from witnesses.

••• Types of Witnesses

Witnesses can be classified as either primary or secondary depending on the information they can provide to the police. Primary witnesses have direct knowledge of the crime in question or of the suspected perpetrator of the crime. Some primary witnesses are also eyewitnesses. Eyewitnesses are individuals who saw the crime occur or saw related events that occurred just prior to or just after the crime. Other primary witnesses may not have seen the crime occur but may have heard the crime occur or heard events just before or after the crime. There were several primary eyewitnesses at the BP gas station.

Secondary witnesses are individuals who have information about related events before or after the crime. For example, an individual who heard someone bragging about the crime, or an individual who reported seeing someone with property that was believed to be stolen would be considered a secondary witness. Crime victims—individuals who are either directly or indirectly the focus of the crime—could be primary or secondary witnesses depending on their involvement in the crime and the information they are able to provide. Confidential informants are most likely to be secondary witnesses. In the BP robbery, the woman who found the red Jeep in the grocery store parking lot and the workers at the pizza shop would best be considered secondary witnesses.

Although "secondary" may imply "less valuable," that is simply not the case. In many investigations, secondary witnesses provide critical information that leads to the crime being discovered and/or solved. For example, the perpetrator of a recent homicide was identified after a barber called the police to report that the mother of one of his clients told him about the strange behavior of her boyfriend (see Chapter 10, From the Case File). The barber was a secondary witness but provided the critical information in the investigation. In another case, a woman called her physician to get an oxytocin prescription filled. The receptionist informed the woman that in order to do so she would need to make an appointment with the physician. The woman then indicated that she was unable to come to the doctor's office because "my child died last night." The woman pleaded for the prescription to be filled without an appointment. The receptionist refused. After the phone call with the woman ended, the receptionist called the police to report this strange conversation. The police also found this to be a very odd request. The police went to the woman's home and discovered the body of a dead baby still in the home. The baby had died from severe maltreatment and abuse. The woman and her boyfriend were arrested and charged with homicide. Like the barber, the receptionist was a secondary witness who provided critical information to the police.

●●● Types of Information Obtained From Witnesses

There is a multitude of information that may be obtained from eyewitnesses and witnesses in general. Important and potentially valuable information that can be provided are the actions of the perpetrator, the description of the perpetrator, and, most useful, the identification (or name) of the perpetrator. Other useful information may include descriptions of vehicles (as in the BP gas station robbery investigation) and stolen property.

Information about the actions of the perpetrator is particularly useful in establishing his or her modus operandi (MO). In turn, this can assist the police in linking crimes to the same perpetrator and may also represent important behavioral evidence. For example, in a series of robberies that occurred recently, the robberies were linked to the same perpetrator (who wore different masks during the robberies) largely as a result of the witnesses in the robberies reporting that the robber used similar language ("This is no joke," "Do you think that this is a joke?"). In another example, in one city that experienced hundreds of robberies a year, a series of robberies was committed during which the perpetrator, after taking the victims' money, ordered the victims to remove their pants. This unique MO, which was established through the statements of victims, allowed the police to link the crimes, look for similarities in the descriptions of the perpetrator provided by victims, and develop information about the geographical area in which he was committing the crimes. When the culprit was eventually identified and arrested, the police were able to clear all the crimes that were believed to have been committed by this individual.

Seemingly small details about the perpetrator's actions and characteristics can make a big difference in an investigation. For example, in the BP gas station investigation discussed above, the witness's recollection that the perpetrator was wearing a dark hat and took with him from the store a Mountain Dew soda can turned out to be important information in the investigation.

Of course, a description may provide a basis for the development of a composite picture or sketch of the perpetrator (Mancusi 2010). A description may also provide enough information to jog the memory of police officers who may have seen the perpetrator or who may be familiar with the perpetrator. In addition, once a suspect has been located by the police, an eyewitness may identify the suspect through a show-up, a photo lineup, or a physical lineup.

●●● Methods of Eyewitness Identification

There are several methods by which an eyewitness may identify a perpetrator. These methods include (1) the witness providing information for the development of a composite picture of the perpetrator; (2) the witness viewing mug shot books (collections of photographs of previously arrested or detained persons); (3) the witness viewing the suspect in a show-up situation, during which the suspect is detained by the police at the scene of the crime or at another place; (4) the witness viewing photographs of the suspect and others in a photo lineup or photo array; and (5) the witness actually viewing the suspect and others in a physical, or live, lineup.

DEVELOPMENT OF A COMPOSITE PICTURE OF THE PERPETRATOR

Pictures of suspects can be created either through a witness providing descriptive details of the suspect's face to a police artist who then draws the portrait, or through composite software, such as FACES (see www.facesid.com). Using FACES and an interview of a witness, a technician can construct the perpetrator's face by selecting from nearly 4,000 different facial features (e.g., head shapes, eyebrows, eyes, noses, jaw shapes, facial hair, smile lines, etc.) to create a realistic-looking picture (see Exhibit 6.1). Methods of drawing a portrait of an offender differ among forensic artists (see Mancusi 2010), but essentially it involves putting a witness's description of facial features on paper (see Exhibit 6.2).

Computer-based and freestyle methods of constructing composite pictures of perpetrators each have advantages and disadvantages. A potential disadvantage of both methods is that, according to research, witnesses who provide information for the creation of a composite picture of a suspect often perform more poorly in subsequent lineup identifications than those who have not provided such information (Lindsay 1994). Basically, the composite construction exercise may influence memory in a negative way (Wells et al. 2005).

Both police artist drawings and FACES pictures score high on realism and therefore are potentially recognizable. Artists have a virtually unlimited number of features to incorporate into a sketch. FACES software is more available to the police than are capable artists. In addition, there is generally more variation in artists' pictures than in those developed through FACES. Some artists are more skilled than others, and it shows in their sketches (many examples are provided by Mancusi [2010]). Some studies (e.g., Laughery and Fowler 1980) have shown

Exhibit 6.1 Example of Composite Picture Developed with FACES Software

An example of a composite picture developed through the use of FACES software.

Exhibit 6.2 Example of Artist Composite Picture

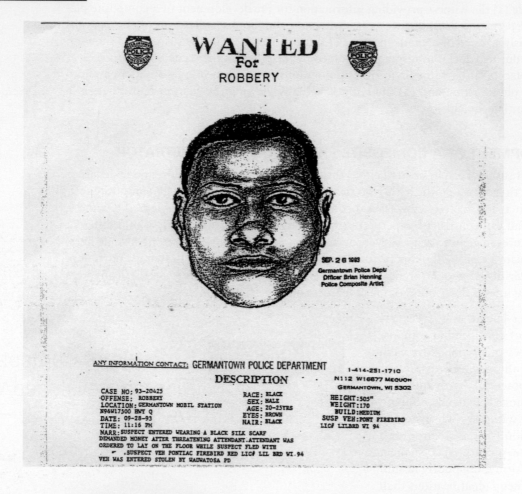

An example of a composite picture developed by a police artist and the mug shot photograph of the suspect. Do you see similarities in the picture and photo?

that sketch artists are more likely to produce more accurate facial images than composite technicians, but others show that accuracy varies little across the various methods (e.g., Ellis 1984).

Regardless of the method used to construct a facial image, the task is fundamentally difficult, especially for the witness. The witness must select or describe individual facial features and then the artist or technician must then combine these features to produce an image of a face. This particularistic approach is not congruent with the more holistic manner in which people perceive and remember faces (Wells et al. 2005). As Wells (1993) explains,

> Faces are processed not just as sets of separate features but as interactive systems of features that include interfeatural properties such as distance between features, relative sizes, and other topographical types of information. . . . The same nose on two different faces can appear to be a quite different nose; changes in the hair style can make chin lines or lips appear to change; and a simple featural change (e.g., loss of a moustache) can lead a person to notice that a face now looks different, but the person cannot necessarily specify what feature has changed. (p. 558)

Because of the likelihood that a composite picture may not accurately depict the perpetrator, some police departments are reluctant to use or disseminate composite pictures of suspects except under extraordinary circumstances. If it turns out that the composite picture does not resemble the suspect/defendant, it may work to the detriment of the police and prosecutor. The inaccurate picture may create a doubt in the minds of jurors about the responsibility of the defendant for the crime, despite other evidence in the case. Another potential problem is that pictures may generate numerous false leads and contribute to an unproductive investigation, even if they resemble the suspect.

MUG SHOT BOOKS

When the police have not yet identified a suspect and there are few other leads to pursue, the police may request that the witness view mug shot books, most often on a computer, that contain photographs of previously arrested or detained subjects in order to possibly identify the perpetrator. These photographs should be organized in ways to limit the number of photographs to be reviewed. For example, a robbery victim may be shown only photos of individuals who are believed to live or spend time in the area of the city in which the crime occurred. In addition, to minimize bias and prevent false identifications, mug shots should be organized by format (e.g., black-and-white photos, color, digital) and by general characteristics of the subjects (e.g., race, sex, age). Also, only recent photos of subjects should be included, and only one photo of each person should be included in the mug shot books viewed by witnesses (National Institute of Justice 2003b). Most often the viewing of mug shot photographs is a rather unproductive activity, akin to finding a needle in a haystack.

SHOW-UP IDENTIFICATIONS

Show-up identifications, or curbside identifications, involve bringing the suspect back to the scene or to the location of the witness, or bringing the witness to the location of the suspect to determine whether the witness can identify the suspect as the perpetrator of the crime. Show-ups are most often conducted when the suspect flees the scene but is quickly apprehended by the police. Show-up identifications are more frequently used than photo and live lineups combined (Steblay et al. 2003). Logistically, it is a simple procedure; however, show-ups are quite suggestive and, as a result, may lead to false identifications. Show-ups are suggestive because the single person available to be identified has already been detained by the police under suspicion of being a suspect in the crime. Certainly it is possible that the police could detain a wrong person as a possible suspect. As explained by Yarmey et al. (1996), research shows that "identifications from one-person line-ups are less accurate, and

Exhibit 6.3 Four Sketches of the Same Perpetrator

Four Sketches of the Same Perpetrator

A Hispanic male, described by his victims to be in his late twenties, was believed to be responsible for numerous sexual assaults in the New York metropolitan area. Four victims provided descriptions that artists used to develop composite pictures. The four sketches shown here are of the same perpetrator. Notice the considerable variation across the composite pictures.

Source: Federal Bureau of Investigation. 2006. ViCap Alert. *FBI Law Enforcement Bulletin* 75(2): 23. Washington DC: U.S. Department of Justice.

put innocent suspects at more risk, than identifications from six person line-ups" (p. 468). Not surprisingly, misidentification is most likely if the detained subject is wearing clothing similar to that worn by the culprit (Yarmey et al. 1996) or the subject generally resembles the culprit (Steblay et al. 2003).

On the other hand, show-ups may actually offer several advantages. First, with a show-up, an identification is usually made quickly after the crime has occurred, so the witness's memory may be fresh. Second, the police are probably less sure that the suspect is the culprit in a show-up situation than in a lineup, during which the police are often looking for confirmation rather than information. As a result, there may be less pressure, even subtly, placed on the witness by the police in a show-up than in a lineup. This may lessen the chances of a false identification in the show-up situation. Finally, research has shown that witnesses are more cautious in making identifications in show-ups than in lineups: "They are more reluctant to say that the person they see is the perpetrator, even when he or she is" (Gonzalez et al. 1993, p. 536). Considering these issues, the courts have generally supported the practice of show-ups and have ruled that a suspect does not have the right to counsel at a show-up.

PHOTO LINEUPS

Photo lineups are useful when investigators have a reason to believe that a particular individual is the culprit in a particular crime. As discussed in the chapter introduction, with a photo lineup, a photo of the person who investigators believe is the culprit is shown to a witness, along with usually five or six others who generally match the description provided by the witness (these other photos are referred to as foils, fillers, or distractors). Witnesses may be shown individual photographs one at a time (a sequential lineup), or the photos may be shown at the same time (a simultaneous lineup; see below for a discussion

Exhibit 6.4   Example of a Photo Lineup

An example of a six-person photo lineup.

of recommended lineup procedures). The witness is typically asked to take a good look at each of the photographs and to indicate whether any individual included in the lineup is the person who committed the crime. If a photo is selected, then the witness may be asked how confident he or she is that the person identified is actually the culprit. This process has been compared to a multiple-choice test, whereas the development of a composite picture is more like a fill-in-the-blank test (Mancusi 2010). As discussed in detail below, the procedures used in constructing and conducting a photo lineup can greatly affect the accuracy of the results. Similar to show-ups, a suspect does not have the right to counsel at a photo lineup procedure.

LIVE LINEUPS

Physical, or live, lineups involve witnesses viewing the suspect and other subjects in a controlled setting, most often at a police station or jail. Usually the witness views the individuals through one-way glass. Each individual may be asked to speak or to say a certain phrase (e.g., "Give me all your money"). Physical lineups usually consist of six people—the person the police believe is the perpetrator of the crime and five others. The foils are usually individuals who are in jail at the time the lineup is conducted. As with show-ups and photo lineups, the procedures used in conducting a physical lineup can greatly affect the accuracy of the results. As a rule, the foils should be selected on the basis of the initial description provided by the witness. At a minimum, the race and gender of the foils must be the same as the suspect. All of the participants in the lineup should be similarly dressed, especially if the suspect was described by the witness as wearing certain clothing. These and other factors are considered by the courts in determining the fairness of the procedure and the

Exhibit 6.5 Live Lineup Photo

An example of a live lineup.

potentially suggestive nature of the identification. Suspects have the right to have counsel present at a physical lineup, but suspects cannot refuse to participate, even though their participation may be incriminating.

••• Value of Eyewitness Identifications in Establishing Proof

Eyewitness identification is one of the least reliable types of evidence, yet it is extremely persuasive in establishing proof. In fact, the only evidence that is more persuasive is a confession (Wilcock et al. 2008). Nevertheless, as explained by Wells et al. (1998), "False eyewitness identification is the primary cause of the conviction of innocent people" (p. 603). Over 300 cases of false convictions are profiled on the Web site of the Innocence Project, and they reveal eyewitness error as the most common factor in wrongful convictions (see www.innocenceproject.org; also see McGough 2012, and a *60 Minutes* news segment titled "Picking Cotton" at www.cbsnews.com/video/watch/?id=4852659n). Wells et al. (1998) discuss forty cases in which people were convicted of crimes and served time in prison until DNA analysis was used to establish their innocence. These cases consisted of the twenty-eight listed in the National Institute of Justice (1996) report (see Chapter 5) and an additional twelve identified by Wells et al. Of the forty cases, thirty-six (90 percent) involved inaccurate eyewitness identification evidence. Furthermore, Wells (1993), in citing other research on the issue, explains that "analyses of what went wrong in producing more than 1,000 convictions of innocent people have revealed that the single largest factor leading to these false convictions was eyewitness error" (p. 554). Other accounts of inaccurate eyewitness identification leading to false arrests and jail time have also been reported (e.g., Ferkenhoff 2002). In nearly all of these cases, DNA evidence proved that the conviction was false. What remains unknown are the number of false convictions (for crimes such as burglaries and robberies) where there is no DNA evidence to help establish innocence. Compounding the accuracy problem is that despite the error-prone nature of the evidence, witnesses often express high confidence in their judgments and in the accuracy of their identifications. For example, in a case from Georgia, a sexual assault victim identified a photo of her attacker in a photo lineup. "From zero to 100 percent, how sure are you?" the detective asked. "I'm 120 percent sure," the woman answered. Well, she was 120 percent wrong. DNA analysis led to the exoneration of Willie "Pete" Williams for the crime. He spent nearly twenty-two years in prison for a crime that he did not commit (Jonsson 2007). Further, eyewitnesses may be confident and persuasive in their inaccurate testimony (Semmler et al. 2004), and this confidence may be quite influential on jurors and their verdicts (Rattner 1988).

MYTHS & MISCONCEPTIONS 6.1

You Never Forget a Face

There is a commonsense appeal to eyewitness identifications—we recognize many different faces many times every day. Our existence and safety depend on our ability to do so. Oftentimes we recognize a person even if we do not know their name. So, when a victim in court points a finger at the defendant and says something to the effect of "That's the person who attacked me, I'll never forget that face as long as I live," we tend to believe that person, perhaps to the detriment of the defendant. As discussed below, human memory is complicated but can be easily fooled. Many things can happen to make eyewitness identifications inaccurate.

••• The Memory Process and the Identification Task

The human memory and its associated processes have been the subject of countless theories and research studies. At the simplest level, memory consists of three phases: encoding, storage, and retrieval (Fisher and Geiselman 1992). Others have identified equivalent stages: acquisition, retention, and retrieval (Loftus et al. 1989; also see Mancusi 2010 and Wilcock et al. 2008). The encoding or acquisition stage is when the event or other stimulus is perceived and represented in the individual's mind. The storage or retention stage involves the activation of a mental record of the event and the "filing" of the information. The retrieval stage occurs when the mental record of the event or stimulus is activated and the "file" is opened. Retrieval brings about recollection. During the encoding–storage–retrieval process, many things may happen to inhibit or distort accurate memory. For example, when a crime is witnessed, it is impossible to *encode* every single detail of the incident. Rather, only certain dimensions of the situation, those deemed most significant, may be encoded (e.g., "He has a gun, a big gun, he is pointing it in my face, he is telling me to give him all my money"). If minimal attention is given to a particular dimension of the situation, it is likely that that dimension will be encoded inaccurately. During the *retention* stage, details of the event may be forgotten or may be distorted by postevent information in the form of other witness accounts or investigator statements. During the *retrieval* stage, a witness searches his or her memory and tries to recall what happened or who committed the crime. Retrieval may take the form of reporting to the police, viewing lineups, or testifying in court. At this stage, the circumstances under which the retrieval occurs may affect the accuracy of the information recalled. Errors and distortions can occur at each stage of memory; human memory is not a video recorder, and recall is not a matter of viewing the videotape (Sanders and Simmons 1983).

As discussed, in some instances, a retrieval task may involve a witness identifying the perpetrator through a lineup. According to Wells (1993), this retrieval task most often involves a relative-judgment memory process: "A relative-judgment process is one in which the eyewitness chooses the line-up member who *most resembles* the culprit *relative to the other members of the line-up*" (p. 560; emphasis added). This process is not necessarily problematic as long as the actual culprit is in the lineup. If the actual culprit is not in the lineup, a natural tendency may be for the witness to select the person who *most resembles* the mental image of the observed perpetrator. Furthermore, just because an investigator may believe that the actual culprit is included in the lineup, this is not necessarily the case. In such a situation, if a person is identified, it would be the wrong person. And, even if the wrong person is selected, the witness may still express high confidence that the person selected was actually the culprit. Eyewitness confidence does not equal eyewitness accuracy. As such, "The relative-judgment process is seductive yet dangerous" (Wells 1993, p. 560).

FACTORS THAT INFLUENCE THE ACCURACY OF EYEWITNESS EVIDENCE

Factors at each stage of the memory process—acquisition, retention, retrieval—may affect the accuracy of an eyewitness account or identification. First, during the *acquisition* stage, factors that relate to the circumstances and nature of the event, as well as the characteristics of the witness, may affect the resulting information. For instance, with regard to the circumstances of the event, it is reasonable to expect that factors such as lighting conditions, distance, and obstructed views would have an effect. The duration of the event and the amount of time spent actually observing the event may affect accuracy. Indeed, longer periods of observation are associated with better memory (Loftus et al. 1989). However, some estimates—particularly of how long certain events lasted—are frequently inaccurate regardless of the surrounding circumstances of the observation. The nature of the event may also impact the accuracy of memory. Events perceived as insignificant at the time of acquisition are less likely to be recalled accurately. Some research suggests that acts of violence are also more difficult to recall accurately. Witnesses also often experience difficulties recalling events that occurred immediately prior to their observations of violent actions (Loftus et al. 1989). Research has also shown that highly attractive, unattractive, and unusual faces are more accurately recognized than others (Mancusi 2010), that even simple disguises (e.g., wearing a cap) result in significant impairment of eyewitness identification, and that the presence of a weapon reduces the likelihood that the witnesses can identify the subject who held the weapon (known as the weapon focus effect) (Wells and Olson 2003).

Characteristics of witnesses may also have an effect on accuracy of recall. For instance, the psychological condition of the witness may be an important consideration. Research has demonstrated that fear and stress improve physical performance, including eyewitness performance, up to a certain point, but then they become counterproductive (known as the Yerkes–Dodson Law) (Goodman and Hahn 1987). Other research shows that subjects who make observations under low-stress conditions are significantly more likely to provide more accurate information than subjects in high-stress conditions (Morgan et al. 2004). In addition, people who experience chronic levels of stress or stress associated with life changes (e.g., death of a spouse, job change) show reduced memory performance, presumably because the stress causes preoccupation and distraction. Of course, the physical condition of the observer (e.g., intoxication, eyesight) may influence accuracy. A witness's expectations may also affect the ultimate accuracy of statements. That is, the way one recalls events is often the way one would expect events to occur or to be. Interestingly, in one study, subjects were asked to estimate a person's weight after being told some information about that person. Subjects' estimates of the person's weight were less when subjects were told that the person was a dancer than when they were told that the person was a truck driver (Christiaansen et al. 1983). Furthermore, the knowledge that a witness possesses regarding a particular object that is observed may also affect accuracy. For instance, an eyewitness of a robbery who knows little about guns might describe the gun held by the perpetrator as "big and shiny." An individual who is knowledgeable about guns may describe the weapon as "a blue metal .357 Glock semi-automatic." Perhaps relatedly, research has shown that people are better able to describe and recognize faces of their own race or ethnic group than others (Wells and Olson 2003; Mancusi 2010).

With regard to the demographic characteristics of witnesses and the accuracy of their memory, age has been shown to be of most importance. Research shows that young children and especially the elderly generally have the poorest perception and memory performance. Younger children have been shown to be more suggestible than older children or adults (Wells and Olson 2003) and to offer less complete descriptions (Wilcock et al. 2008). Children also tend to have difficulties with descriptions of age, height, and weight (Wilcock et al. 2008). The research on the influence of gender on perception and memory is mixed. While some research shows that females are more reliable witnesses (but males more confident in their memory) (e.g., Areh 2011), generally it has been shown that men and women focus on different aspects of events, people, and situations. Men and women tend to focus on, and remember, things of interest to them, which are often different (Wells and Olson 2003; Mancusi 2010; Areh 2011).

Second, several factors may affect the *retention* or storage of information. As noted, the most significant factor that may distort memory at this stage is misleading or inaccurate information obtained at or near the time of the event. The source of this information may be statements made by other witnesses (hence the importance of separating witnesses prior to questioning), questions asked by authorities, or information contained in newspaper accounts or even television coverage. As an example of how the questions asked of a witness may affect the information retained in memory, Loftus et al. (1989) report a study during which subjects viewed a film and then were asked questions about it. When asked, "How fast was the car going when it passed the barn?" many subjects responded as though they saw the car pass a barn, when in fact a barn was not even shown in the film. The time that has elapsed from the event to its recall also affects memory, as memory tends to deteriorate the longer it is stored (Mancusi 2010; Wilcock et al. 2008).

Third, with regard to the *retrieval* stage, several factors may serve to distort the accuracy of the eyewitness account. Of most significance is the manner in which the retrieval of information occurs. For example, the wording of questions used to elicit memory details may be influential. Loftus and Palmer (1974) conducted an experiment during which subjects viewed films of automobile accidents and then were asked questions about the events depicted in the films. When subjects were asked, "About how fast were the cars going when they *smashed* into each other?" higher estimates of speed were provided than when questions that contained the words "collided," "bumped," "contacted," or "hit" instead of "smashed" were asked. Subjects who were asked about the cars "smashing" were also more likely to state that they saw broken glass, when actually there was no broken glass. Other studies have noted differences in asking questions with more subtle wording differences such as "Did you see a gun?" versus "Was there a gun?" (the former question suggests that there may have been a gun but that it may not have been seen), or "Did you see *a* broken headlight?" versus "Did you see *the* broken headlight?" In essence, although subtle, leading questions may distort the information retrieved from a witness's memory (Loftus et al. 1989).

Finally, it is worthwhile to note that a few studies have examined the accuracy of voice identification and walk/gait identification. Although there is too little research to draw confident conclusions about these issues, the prevailing wisdom is that the identification of unfamiliar voices is often incorrect. The identification of distinct or unusual gait among strangers is more likely to be accurate; however, the accurate recognition of more typical gait even among friends is difficult (see Wilcock et al. 2008).

●●● Guidelines for the Collection of Eyewitness Evidence

Given the multitude of factors that may affect the accuracy of eyewitness statements, and given that the courts are generally concerned about quality of evidence—to the point of not allowing it to be admitted (e.g., hearsay)—one might expect that there would be a number of barriers to the admission of eyewitness evidence in court. This, however, is generally not the case, although the courts have recognized the potential problems associated with eyewitness testimony. In the case of *Neil v. Biggers* (1972), in which a rape victim identified her attacker on the basis of a show-up that took place seven months after the crime, the Supreme Court let the conviction stand but identified five criteria to be considered in determining the accuracy of an eyewitness identification of a suspect. These criteria are:

- The eyewitness's opportunity to view
- The attention paid by the eyewitness
- The accuracy of the witness's preliminary description of the culprit
- The certainty of the eyewitness
- The amount of time between the event and the attempt to identify

However, these factors have been criticized as an inadequate basis on which to judge the accuracy of eyewitness identifications. One of the criticisms is that some of the factors rely on perceptions of the eyewitness, which is exactly what is questioned in an eyewitness identification.

There are other safeguards in place that may, ideally, prevent false eyewitness identifications from leading to miscarriages of justice. For example, defendants have the right to counsel at live lineups, motions can be made by the defense to suppress eyewitness evidence, eyewitnesses may be cross-examined, and experts can be called to testify on the problems associated with accurate eyewitness identifications. In many respects, however, these safeguards are incomplete and inadequate (Wells et al. 1998). The right to counsel exists only at lineups, not photo arrays or show-ups, and most identifications of suspects are from show-ups and photos, not physical lineups. Motions to suppress eyewitness evidence are rarely successful. Cross-examination of eyewitnesses may not be helpful when witnesses are trying to be truthful but are simply mistaken. Eyewitness expert testimony may not overcome the influential nature of eyewitness evidence, it may not be allowed by the judge, and it may be prohibitively expensive (Wells et al. 1998).

Given the potential inaccuracy of eyewitness identifications and the current safeguards in place, Wells et al. (1998) identify several guidelines for the collection of eyewitness identification evidence (these guidelines are also outlined in the 1999 National Institute of Justice document *Eyewitness Evidence: A Guide for Law Enforcement;* also see *Eyewitness Evidence: A Trainer's Manual for Law Enforcement,* National Institute of Justice 2003b). These guidelines are based on theories about human memory, research findings of eyewitness identification studies, and the science of testing. The aim of the guidelines is to improve the quality of the evidence and, accordingly, to reduce the risk of mistaken identifications. The authors note that just as there are procedures and rules that must be followed in collecting and presenting physical evidence such as fingerprints and DNA, there should be rules and procedures in collecting and presenting eyewitness identification evidence through lineups and photo spreads.

First, "The person who conducts the line-up or photo-spread should not be aware of which member of the line-up or photo-spread is the suspect" (Wells et al. 1998, p. 627). This recommendation relates to the possibility that an investigator may intentionally, or unknowingly, lead a witness to select a particular lineup member. The process of identification may be one filled with anxiety and uncertainty for the witness and, as a result, the witness may be quite interested and responsive to the cues of the investigator. Wells et al. (1998) cite research that shows that subtle cues such as smiling and other nonverbal actions can call attention to a particular photograph and can lead to false identification. Previous research has shown that feedback given to the witness about the selection (e.g., "Good, you identified the right guy") can have dramatic effects on the witness's confidence about the accuracy of the selection and his or her ability to identify the suspect (Wells and Bradfield 1998). This false confidence may translate into increased but unwarranted credibility of the witness in the minds of jurors. In addition, it is not out of the realm of possibility that investigators may knowingly say something to highlight or reinforce a particular person as the suspect/culprit (see Case in Point 6.1). If the person who administers the lineup does not know who the suspect is, then that person would not be able to provide any cues or other information to influence the selection, nor would that person be able to provide any feedback to the witness that might distort the witness's certainty or confidence in the selection. This precaution should allow eyewitness identification to be based on the eyewitness's memory, not external information. It should therefore provide for a more valid lineup procedure.

Second, "Eyewitnesses should be told explicitly that the person in question might not be in the line-up or photo-spread and therefore should not feel that they must make an identification. They should also be told that the person administering the line-up does not know which person is the suspect in the case" (Wells et al. 1998, p. 629). The first part of this recommendation relates to the research that shows that eyewitnesses are less likely to identify an innocent suspect if they are told that the actual culprit may not be in the lineup. The tendency to identify the person that most resembles the culprit, even if it is not the culprit, reflects the relative-judgment process discussed earlier. Research has shown that although this warning reduces the rate of incorrect selections in lineups in which the culprit is not present, it does not reduce the rate of correct selections when the culprit is present in the lineup. Of course, if all lineups included the actual culprit, this recommendation would be

CASE in POINT 6.1 How Did That Happen?

In the case of *South Carolina v. Washington* (1997), a detective investigating a robbery believed that a person by the name of James Washington was responsible for committing the crime. The detective obtained a photograph of a person who he believed was James Washington and placed this photo, along with pictures of five other foils, in a photo lineup. He then showed it to the eyewitness and, lo and behold, the eyewitness identified "James Washington." There was only one problem: subsequent to the photo identification, it was discovered that the detective had made a mistake—the photo thought to be of James Washington was, in fact, not James Washington; it was of a person who could not have had anything to do with the robbery. In addition, the person in the picture had no resemblance to the real James Washington.

In examining the validity of this photo lineup, Wells et al. (1998) provided an actual photograph of James Washington to fifty people and asked them to select the person most similar to him from the original photo spread. Not one person identified the picture of the subject who was originally believed to be James Washington. What happened? The detective who assembled and administered the photo spread probably facilitated, in some way, the identification of the wrong suspect.

needless; however, one should not assume that this is, in fact, the case. If the investigator is so certain that the culprit is included in the lineup, what is the purpose of the lineup? According to Wells et al. (1998), the actual perpetrator was not included in the lineups for all of the forty cases of false eyewitness identifications referenced earlier.

The second part of the recommendation, that witnesses "should be told that the person administering the line-up does not know which person is the suspect in the case," is related to the first recommendation. Simply, not only should the administrator of the lineup not know who the suspect is in the case, but the witness should be *told* that the administrator does not know who the suspect is in the case. This may prevent the eyewitness from trying to look to the administrator of the lineup for cues about which person to select.

Third, "The suspect should not stand out in the line-up or photo-spread as being different from the distractors based on the eyewitness's previous description of the culprit or based on other factors that would draw attention to the suspect" (Wells et al. 1998, p. 630). If the suspect stands out in some way from the others in the lineup, it may be difficult to determine whether the selection was based on true recognition or whether it was based simply on the unique characteristic. The bottom line is that the distractors or foils included in the lineup should not necessarily look similar to the suspect, *they should be selected on the basis of the description provided to the investigators by the witness*. At the extreme, if foils are included so that they look like the suspect, one could conceivably have the suspect and his identical siblings included in the lineup. Clearly the chances of identifying and selecting the wrong person would be high in such a circumstance. On the other hand, verbal descriptions of perpetrators provided by witnesses tend to be rather general, and inclusion of individuals on this basis may allow people with different appearances to be included in the lineup. For example, in the BP gas station robbery discussed in the introduction to this chapter, the gas station attendant described the perpetrator as a white male, approximately twenty-five to thirty years of age, 5'9," 130 lbs., and having three to four days' worth of facial hair growth. The other witness described the perpetrator as a white male, "clean cut," approximately 6'1," and 140 lbs. These descriptions are quite general and allow for much variation in the characteristics of the foils to be included in the lineup.

There are several potential problems with this approach to constructing lineups. First, what if the description provided by the witness does not actually match the description of the suspect? In such a situation, it is recommended that a blend of the description of the culprit and the features of the suspect be considered when selecting foils in the lineup (Wells et al. 1998). Second, what if the suspect has a unique feature, such as a facial scar, that the eyewitness did not mention? If the witness did not mention a unique feature, then it may not be necessary to replicate that feature across the members of the lineup. If the unique feature is recognized by the witness, memory recall may be the reason. Third, what if the witness describes the perpetrator as having a unique feature, such as a particular tattoo? In this case, it may not be necessary to conduct a lineup. With a specific and unique description, there may be little doubt about the identity of the suspect. Lineups are useful when the witness's description of the perpetrator is vague and when the identity of the perpetrator is uncertain. Finally, what if there is more than one witness and they provide conflicting descriptions of the perpetrator? In this situation, it is recommended by Wells et al. (1998) that separate lineups be constructed for each witness, based on the description of the perpetrator provided by each witness.

The final recommendation offered by Wells et al. (1998) is that "a clear statement should be taken from the eyewitness at the time of the identification and prior to any feedback as to his or her confidence that the identified person is the actual culprit" (p. 635). This statement may take the form of a response to the question, "On a scale of one to ten, with ten being absolute certainty and one being absolute uncertainty, how confident are you that the person you identified is the actual culprit?" The confidence expressed by the witness at the time of the identification may be the single most important factor in judging the credibility of the eyewitness and the accuracy of the identification in further proceedings (e.g., at trial). However, as noted earlier, confidence of a witness about an identification can be affected substantially by events that occur after the identification that have nothing to do with the witness's memory. Simply stated, confidence should be based on memory, not outside forces. A clear statement from the witness, along with the administrator not knowing who the suspect is in the lineup, should help provide a valid representation of confidence in the selection.

The authors also comment on two other issues in the identification process: the use of sequential lineups and the practice of video-recording lineups. The use of sequential lineups involves the eyewitness viewing one lineup member at a time and determining whether that person is the perpetrator. Wells et al. (1998) support the use of both practices but do not consider them as significant as their four primary recommendations. The most recent and best-quality research on the issue shows that sequential lineups produce fewer identifications (Steblay et al. 2011) but also fewer mistaken identifications than simultaneous lineups (McGough 2012), especially when the culprit is not included in the lineup (Steblay et al. 2011). However, it is important to highlight that witnesses still (wrongly) identified the filler 12.2 percent of the time, as opposed to 18.1 percent of the time in simultaneous lineups (McGough 2012). Congruent with this research, sequential lineups are often recommended as the best practice. Video-recording lineups may also offer numerous benefits; however, videotaping by itself would not lessen the chance of false eyewitness identification. In addition, it is unclear how videotaping may affect the behavior of witnesses. Videotaping may raise anxiety and actually lessen the chances of accurate eyewitness identification (Wells et al. 1998). See Exhibit 6.6 for an example of a police department form with instructions for conducting a photo identification.

●●● Investigative Tools in Interviewing

HYPNOSIS

Hypnosis is most often simply viewed as an altered state of consciousness that is characterized by increased responsiveness to suggestion (Orne et al. 1984). A more elaborate definition is provided by Goldenson (1984):

Exhibit 6.6 Photo Array Identification Instruction Form

03/15/2010 12:47 FAX

☑002/005

PC-24 12/06 SUPPLEMENT REPORT MILWAUKEE POLICE DEPARTMENT	☐ INCIDENT SUPPLEMENT ☐ ACCIDENT SUPPLEMENT PAGE ____ OF ____ ☐ JUVENILE SUPPLEMENT		DATE OF REPORT	INCIDENT / ACCIDENT #
INCIDENT	DATE OF INCIDENT / ACCIDENT			
VICTIM	LOCATION OF INCIDENT / ACCIDENT (Address)			DIST
DATE OF PHOTO ARRAY TIME OF PHOTO ARRAY LOCATION OF PHOTO ARRAY				

SUPPLEMENTARY REPORT ON
Photo Array Identification Form

You have been provided with a written copy of the following instructions and you should read them as I read aloud.

The folders in front of you contain photos. In a moment, I am going to ask you to look at the photos. The person who committed the crime may or may not be included in the photos. Although an officer placed the photos into the folders, the folders have been shuffled so that right now I do not know which folder contains a particular photo.

Even if you identify someone during this procedure, I will continue to show you all folders in the series.

Keep in mind that things like hair styles, beards, and mustaches can be easily changed and that complexion colors may look slightly different in photographs.

You should not feel you have to make an identification. It is as important to exclude innocent persons as it is to identify the perpetrator.

You will look at the photos one at a time and since I have shuffled them, they are not in any particular order. When you open a folder, please open it in a manner that does not allow me to see the photo inside the folder. Take as much time as you need to look at each one. When you have finished looking at a photo, close the folder and hand it to me. I will then ask you, "Is this the person you saw [_____]?" Please circle yes or no below the respective number at the bottom of this form. Take your time answering the question. Upon conclusion of this process I will then ask you, "In your own words, can you describe how certain you are?"

Because you are involved in an ongoing investigation, in order to prevent compromising the investigation, you should avoid discussing this identification procedure or its results.

Do you understand the way the photo array procedure will be conducted and the other instructions I have given you?   Yes   No

If so please read the following paragraph and sign and date below.

I have read these instructions, or they have been read to me, and I understand the instructions. I am prepared to review the photographs, and I will follow the instructions provided on this form.

Printed Name _____   Address _____

Signature _____   Date _____

1	2	3	4	5	6	7	8
Yes	Yes	Yes	Yes	Yes	Yes	Yes	Yes
No	No	No	No	No	No	No	No

I have (identified) (not identified) a perpetrator in this offense.

The photo I identified was contained in folder _____

Signature _____   Date _____

REPORTING OFFICER	EMP. I.D. #	LOC CODE	SUPERVISOR SIGNATURE

Many police departments have incorporated lineup guidelines into departmental policy, as seen here.

[Hypnosis is] a superficial or deep trance state resembling sleep, induced by suggestions of relaxation and concentrated attention to a single object. The subject becomes highly suggestible and responsive to the hypnotist's influence, and can be induced to recall forgotten events, become insensitive to pain, control vasomotor changes and, in the hands of an experienced hypnotherapist, gain relief from tensions, anxieties and other psychological symptoms. (p. 358)

Hypnosis can be used in the therapeutic setting as well as in the criminal investigative setting. For purposes of criminal investigation, hypnosis focuses on enhancing memory recall of a witness with regard to an actual criminal event (Council on Scientific Affairs 1985; Reiser 1989). There are three approaches to obtaining hypnotically elicited testimony: free recall, during which the hypnotized witness is asked for a complete and unstructured account of everything observed; structured recall, during which the witness is asked specific questions about observations; and recognition, during which the witness is asked to recognize or identify certain aspects of a situation or event, such as the clothing worn by the perpetrator (Sanders and Simmons 1983).

The theory of hypnosis is that memory occurs at the conscious and subconscious levels. Details about observations are recorded and stored at both levels at the same time. However, a person may not know what has been encoded in the subconscious memory—or, as a defensive mechanism, conscious memories may be pushed to the subconscious level. Hypnosis is a method of retrieving subconscious observations (Reiser 1989).

Various techniques may be used to induce hypnosis. Most of these include "instructing the individual to focus attention, to concentrate on the hypnotist's voice, to relax, and eventually to close the eyes and imagine what the hypnotist is suggesting" (Orne et al. 1984, p. 175). When under hypnosis, "The subject's attention is intensely focused on the hypnotist, and there is an increased tendency to please the hypnotist and to comply with both explicit and implicit demands in the hypnotic context" (Orne et al. 1984, p. 175). As for investigative hypnosis specifically, the most widely practiced method is the television technique (Scheflin and Shapiro 1989). As described by the Council on Scientific Affairs (1985),

Once hypnotized, the subject is told to imagine a television screen in his mind and that he will soon begin to see a documentary of the to-be remembered event. As in a sporting event on television, he will be able to stop motion, go fast forward or backward, and "zoom in" in order to see any detail that might otherwise not be clear. Finally, it is explained that, while he may see himself in this documentary and accurately observe what happens, he need not experience any of the troublesome feelings of pain that may have occurred at the time, but rather will see in an objective manner the events that transpired. (p. 1919)

This technique is controversial because it encourages the hypnotized subject to imagine and fantasize (imagination inflation), which may in turn lead to the subject providing inaccurate information.

How accurate is hypnotically elicited information? Most research has come to the conclusion that hypnotically elicited testimony is deficient, especially when leading or even specific questions are asked of the subject (Sanders and Simmons 1983; Steblay and Bothwell 1994). The reason for this is that hypnotized subjects are, by definition, more susceptible to suggestion. As Orne et al. (1984) explain, "Subjects in the hypnotic situation feel relaxed and less responsible for what they say because they believe that the hypnotist is an expert and somehow in control" (p. 176). Furthermore, subjects wish to please the hypnotist and receive reassurance, so information may be provided by the subject until such feedback is received. This process can readily result in fabrications or false information, often referred to as *confabulation*. For example,

If during hypnosis, an individual is asked to "look at" an event 100 yards away using hallucinated binoculars, he or she may describe in detail the pattern on the necktie of a participant in that event, despite the fact that such a "perception" exceeds the limits of visual acuity. Needless to say, the pattern may have nothing to do with the individual's necktie unless the hypnotized person had an opportunity to see it previously. Without prior information of such details, the hypnotized subject will nonetheless respond to the suggestion to observe with binoculars by hallucinating or imagining details of the event (Orne et al. 1984, p. 177).

Steblay and Bothwell (1994) conducted a meta-analysis of sixteen studies that examined the effectiveness of hypnosis in criminal investigations. Based on their analyses, the researchers concluded the following:

- Hypnotized subjects performed better (i.e., provided more accurate information) than control subjects in free recall situations, but the difference was minimal.

- In structured recall situations during which leading questions were asked, hypnotized subjects provided less accurate information than control subjects.

- In recognition (i.e., lineup) situations, hypnotized subjects were not more likely to make accurate identifications than control subjects. In fact, several of the studies showed that hypnotized subjects were significantly less likely than control subjects to respond correctly.

- Despite the fact that hypnotized subjects usually provided more inaccurate information than control subjects, hypnotized subjects were more often more confident about the accuracy of their recall.

On the basis of their study, Steblay and Bothwell (1994) conclude that "hypnosis is not necessarily a source of inaccurate information; at worst it may be a source of inaccurate information provided with confident testimony" (p. 649).

Others are more negative on the use of hypnosis for investigative purposes. For example, consider the findings of the Council on Scientific Affairs (1985) of the American Medical Association:

When hypnosis is used to refresh recollection, one of the following outcomes occurs: (1) hypnosis produces recollections that are not substantially different from non-hypnotic recollections; (2) it yields recollections that are more inaccurate than non-hypnotic memory; or, most frequently, (3) it results in more information being reported, but these recollections contain both accurate and inaccurate details. (p. 1921)

Accordingly, the council concluded that "the use of hypnosis with witnesses and victims may have serious consequences for the legal process when testimony is based on material that is elicited from a witness who has been hypnotized for purposes of refreshing recollection" (p. 1918).

With regard to the admissibility of hypnotically elicited testimony, there is variation in how the courts treat hypnotized witnesses and the resulting evidence. The most common rule is that previously hypnotized witnesses may testify regarding their recollections prior to hypnosis, but the hypnotically elicited testimony itself, as well as testimony obtained after hypnosis, is not admissible (Wagstaff 2009). As such, it is necessary for the police to record the witness's account of the event prior to hypnosis because only this testimony is admissible. Because of the documented inaccuracies of hypnotically elicited testimony and the associated legal restrictions placed on such testimony, hypnosis is seldom used in criminal investigations today (Wagstaff 2009).

COGNITIVE INTERVIEW

Another method of enhancing witness recall is cognitive interviewing. This approach was first described by Fisher and Geiselman (1992). It is this approach that is advocated as the best practices model by the National Institute of Justice (2003b). The cognitive interview encourages the witness to reinstate the context in which the observed event took place and to search through memory systematically and methodologically for details of the event. It is the interviewer's responsibility to guide the witness through this process and to assist in the retrieval of information (for a review, see Wilcock et al. 2008).

As part of the cognitive interview approach, several techniques are used to facilitate memory recall. First, as noted, the witness is encouraged to recreate the context of the original event. The context consists not only of the event itself but also the physical and psychological characteristics of the environment in which it occurred. An interviewer can assist in the recreation of the context through instructions. For example, the interviewer can tell the witness, "Try to put yourself back into the same situation as when the crime was committed. Think about where you were standing at the time, what you were thinking about, what you were feeling, and what the room looked like" (Fisher and Geiselman 1992, p. 100). The witness may be asked to think about his or her activities prior to, during, and after the event, and even about activities that took place hours or days before or after the event. Again, the attempt is to get the witness fully immersed in the situation about which details are to be recalled.

Second, the witness is encouraged to concentrate deeply in a focused manner. Concentration is critical when searching through memory for details. As suggested by Fisher and Geiselman (1992), the following statement may serve this end:

> I realize that this is a difficult task, to remember the details of the crime. All of the details are stored in your mind, but you will have to concentrate very hard to recall them. You have all the information, so I'm going to expect you to do most of the work here. I understand that this may be difficult, but try to concentrate as hard as you can. (p. 103)

Along these lines, research has shown that deep breathing and eye closure on the part of witnesses can enhance memory (Wagstaff 2009). Another important factor that is necessary to facilitate concentration is avoiding interruptions. Interruptions on the part of the interviewer break the concentration of witnesses and inhibit recall of information. Fisher and Geiselman (1992) identify the avoidance of interruptions as the single most important skill in interviewing. Focused concentration can also be encouraged through open-ended questions and by maintaining eye contact with the witness.

Third, the witness should be encouraged to search memory thoroughly. If you lose your car keys and after a couple of minutes of searching you cannot find them, you do not just give up, right? So it is with witnesses searching for details of the crime in a cognitive interview. A thorough search of memory can be encouraged by avoiding certain behaviors such as the following, from Fisher and Geiselman 1992 (pp. 107–108):

- Opening the interview with a request for factual details, instead of a more personal introduction

- Indicating at the outset that the interview will take only a short time

- Constantly checking the time

- Leaving the radio on and interrupting frequently to listen to incoming calls

- Attending to issues related to other cases

- Fidgeting while sitting

- Standing during the interview (especially by an exit door) when it would be more appropriate to sit

- Speaking quickly

- Asking questions immediately after the [witness] stops responding

- Interrupting in the middle of the [witness's] response

Fourth, varied retrieval of the event should be encouraged. Most common and most natural is for a witness to recall the event in chronological order. However, describing an event in reverse order requires more concentration and more thought (similar to reciting the alphabet in reverse order), but additional details may be recalled. Reverse order may also reduce extraneous or even deceptive information (Bennett and Hess 1991). Another varied retrieval method is to ask the witness to slice the event into "frames"—like pictures—and then ask the witness to describe each of the frames. Yet another method is to ask the witness to provide a description of events from the perspective or location of someone else in the area in which the crime occurred. The interviewer may ask the witness to describe the event like viewing a film that was taken from an angle different from that of the witness (Bennett and Hess 1991). This technique may provide additional details about the event and may also reduce the trauma associated with the crime. However, this technique may also encourage the witness to fabricate information or to provide inaccurate information. Accordingly, the interviewer must remind the witness to report only the events and details actually observed.

Finally, during a cognitive interview, other techniques may be used to enhance the recollection of specific pieces of information such as faces, clothing, vehicles, and license plate numbers. Even though a witness may not be able to recall certain specific information, the witness may have some partial memory about it. Focused questions may be used to help retrieve this potentially useful information. For example, in recalling a license plate of a car involved in a crime, the witness may be asked about the features of the characters on the plate. These questions could include the following: Was the sequence composed mainly of digits or numbers? Were the letters consonants? Did two letters occur twice? What shape did the first or any other letter have? Was the digit pattern familiar in any way (similar to a friend's phone number)? What color were the characters and the background? (Fisher and Geiselman 1992). This sort of probing may help stimulate the witness's memory.

The cognitive interviewing approach is quite different from the approach taken during standard police interviews. Whereas cognitive interviewing encourages the witness to explore deep memory and is open ended in nature, the standard interviewing approach encourages only superficial exploration and is more closed ended in nature. Fisher et al. (1987) analyzed numerous police interviews with robbery victims and witnesses and found numerous problems that inhibited memory recall on the part of the subjects. First, interviewers frequently interrupted witnesses' descriptions and accounts of the event. This led to witnesses providing short, quick answers and encouraged witnesses to be less focused. Second, interviewers asked too many short-answer, closed-ended questions. On average, interviewers asked three open-ended questions (e.g., "Can you describe the subject's clothing?") and twenty-six short-answer questions (e.g., "What color was the subject's shirt?"). The short-answer questions may help keep the interview on track, but they require less concentration on the part of the witness and encourage short, incomplete answers. In addition, because the witness is placed in a passive role with such questions, if the interviewer does not think to ask a particular question, the witness may not provide the information. Missed information may be the likely result. The third common and significant problem with traditional police interviews is the inappropriate, arbitrary, or rigid sequencing of questions. The researchers found that interviewers often used a sequence of questions that was not congruent with the witness's memory of the event. The researchers explained that on one occasion, a witness began describing the suspect by providing an estimate of the subject's height. She was interrupted by the investigator and asked to begin instead with an estimate of the subject's age. When the researchers asked the investigator about this, the investigator responded that there was really no reason why he interrupted the witness, other than that age was asked about first on the report that he was required to complete. Again, the rigid sequencing of questions may inhibit accurate memory recall.

Numerous other problems, although less common, were also evident during the interviews. First, interviewers sometimes used negative phrasing (e.g., "You don't remember, do you, if . . . ?"), suggesting to the witness that interviewer did not believe the witness could recall or remember the details. This sort of questioning also makes it easy for the witness to respond "I don't know" and discourages a thorough search of memory. Second, investigators sometimes used non-neutral or leading questions (e.g., "Was the gun silver?"), which may suggest to the witness that the investigator's description is correct and may also bias the witness's later recollection of the event. Third, the researchers observed interviewers using inappropriate language—wording that was too formal (e.g., "Did you have occasion earlier today to witness . . ."), too stylized (e.g., "Calling your attention to the incident . . ."), or too intelligent (e.g., "So you were in a *supine* position?") (Fisher et al. 1987, p. 182). A fourth problem was the rapid rate of questioning. On average, there was one second between the end of the witness's answer and the interviewer's next question. This clearly inhibited witnesses from elaborating or clarifying previous statements. Fifth, on occasion, the researchers observed interviewers making judgmental, rude, or insensitive comments to the witnesses (e.g., "[Previous investigators] thought that it was funny that you had all of your clothes on and [the suspect] didn't have all his clothes on") (Fisher et al. 1987, p. 183). Rapport and trust can be quickly destroyed with such comments. Finally, there was at times a lack of follow-up on potential leads. For instance, on one occasion a witness stated that the suspect "looked like a librarian," but there was no follow-up questioning to explore the meaning of this descriptive statement.

As discussed by Fisher et al. (1987), the structure of a traditional police interview is conducive to note taking and report writing. Traditional police interviews also take relatively little time to complete. With cognitive interviews, on the other hand, it is more difficult for an interviewer to record the potential multitude of details provided. The difficulty in documenting an interview through notes provides a powerful rationale for video- or audio-recording interviews. Indeed, research has shown that much information is lost in verbatim contemporaneous accounts of interviews (Lamb et al. 2000). Cognitive interviews also usually take considerably more time to conduct, require more mental concentration on the part of the interviewer, and require more flexibility. However, cognitive interview techniques can be easily learned, cognitive interviewing requires little training, the method is easily administered, witnesses should have few reservations about participating in such an interview, and the method raises few legal issues compared with hypnosis.

The most significant benefit of the cognitive interviewing approach is that it has been shown to be an effective tool in enhancing memory recall (Holliday et al. 2012; Wilcock et al. 2008). In a study that examined the amount and accuracy of information obtained by detectives in standard police interviews and cognitive interviews, it was demonstrated that after being trained in the cognitive interview approach, detectives were able to obtain 47 percent more information from witnesses, and this information was deemed highly accurate—that is, it corroborated with other independent information produced in the investigation (Fisher et al. 1989). In another study, subjects viewed a film of a simulated crime and were interviewed forty-eight hours later by law enforcement personnel. Those subjects who were interviewed about the crime through the cognitive interview approach recalled 20 percent to 35 percent more (correct) information than the subjects who underwent a standard police interview (Fisher et al. 1987). In short, as stated by Geiselman and Fisher (1989), the research confirms "that cognitive interviewing reliably enhances the completeness of a witness's recollection, without increasing the number of incorrect or confabulated bits of information generated" (p. 213).

Besides the method used to elicit information from a witness, there are other principles and basic rules associated with conducting effective police interviews. First, witnesses should be separated and interviewed one at a time so that independent accounts from each witness can be received, compared, and evaluated. Reasonable precautions should be taken to prevent witnesses from sharing information with each other because witnesses can easily be influenced by the accounts of others. Indeed, misinformation from other sources can have strong and lasting effects (Zhu et al. 2012). However, in order to avoid other negative consequences, a balance is important in this regard (see Case in Point 6.2).

CASE in POINT 6.2   Witness Security versus Compassion

A thirteen-year-old boy, Darius Simmons, was shot and killed while standing in front of his residence. The shooter was the boy's seventy-three-year-old neighbor, John Spooner. Several days prior to the shooting, Spooner reported to the police that guns were stolen from his residence. Just prior to the shooting, Spooner confronted Darius on the sidewalk and demanded that he return his guns. Darius responded that he did not have his guns. Spooner then shot Darius and Darius collapsed after running a few yards. When the police arrived at 9:48 a.m., Darius's mother, Patricia Larry, who had witnessed the shooting, was standing next to him. Spooner, who was still at the scene, was arrested. Ms. Larry was placed in the back seat of a police car at approximately 10:14 a.m. Darius was transported to the hospital by medical personnel. The ambulance arrived at the hospital at 10:24 a.m.; he was pronounced dead at 11:10 a.m.

Ms. Larry sat in the back seat of the squad car for approximately fifteen to thirty minutes while medical personnel attended to Darius and while he was being transported to the hospital. At about 10:50 a.m., Ms. Larry was placed in the front seat of a detectives' car for an interview. She was interviewed for approximately thirty minutes. During this time, Ms. Larry requested to go to the hospital to see her son, but she agreed to complete the interview. At 11:36, Ms. Larry was transported to the hospital and was notified of the death of Darius when she arrived there at 11:58 a.m.

The police department and investigators in charge of the investigation were subsequently criticized for unnecessarily keeping Ms. Larry from being with her dying son at the hospital. On one hand, investigators wished to minimize the contact that the witness had with other witnesses so as to avoid contamination of memory and information. On the other hand, a more compassionate response would have been to take the witness to the hospital or even to allow her to accompany her son to the hospital in the ambulance. Departmental policy did not prohibit either of these possibilities. The official review of the investigation concluded that the investigators failed to appreciate the devastating nature of the incident on the victim's mother and that allowing the witness to have contact with her son at (and to) the hospital would not have unnecessarily jeopardized the investigation.

Second, interviews should be conducted in places that are away from distractions. The witness's work location is generally a poor place to conduct an investigative interview; the police station or even the witness's home are generally better places. Third, interviews should be conducted as soon as possible after the event except under extraordinary circumstances, such as a witness's health problem. This should allow information about the event to be more easily recalled (Geiselman and Fisher 1989). Finally, it is important for investigators to build a rapport with witnesses. Dreeke and Navarro (2009) and Sandoval and Adams (2001) suggest that interviewers engage in matching or mirroring techniques in an effort to build rapport. That is, interviewers should match or mirror the witness's kinesics (i.e., display the same sort of body language and posture as the witness), such as smiling when the witness smiles; the witness's language, such as using similar words, phrases, and expressions; and the witness's paralanguage, such as using a similar rate, volume, and pitch of speech. In addition, to build rapport, it is important for the interviewer to provide feedback to the witness that suggests an understanding of what the witness has experienced and that shows concern for the witness. Although the witness and the interviewer may have different immediate goals, emphasis should be placed on identifying common goals and team building. Research shows that rapport building leads to more accurate information being reported by witnesses, decreases inaccurate information, and reduces the influence of misinformation, especially in response to open-ended questions (Vallano and Compo 2011).

Information that comes from witnesses is potentially extremely valuable for investigators and prosecutors in proving guilt. As such, proper care and procedures need to be used to help ensure the collection of accurate information.

MAIN POINTS

1. An investigative interview refers to any questioning that is intended to produce information about a crime or regarding a person believed to have committed a crime. They are typically not accusatory in nature and are intended to develop information.

2. Witnesses can be primary or secondary depending on the information they have and provide to the police. Eyewitnesses are primary witnesses. The information provided by secondary witnesses can be as valuable as that provided by primary witnesses.

3. Eyewitnesses may be able to provide information about the MO and other actions of the offender and the description of the offender. They may also be able to identify the offender.

4. Eyewitnesses may be able to identify a perpetrator via the development of a composite picture of the perpetrator, by viewing mug shot books, or through a show-up identification, a photo lineup, or a live lineup.

5. While a composite picture of a suspect may look realistic, it may not be accurate.

6. Viewing mug shot books in an attempt to identify a perpetrator is usually rather unproductive.

7. Show-up identifications are logistically simple but may be quite suggestive to the witnesses.

8. Photo lineups consist of a photograph of the suspect along with usually five others (fillers). Photo lineups are conducted much more often than live lineups.

9. Live lineups also usually consist of six participants (the suspect and five others). They are conducted in such a way that the participants are unable to see the witness. Suspects have the right to counsel at live lineups, but they cannot refuse to participate.

10. Eyewitness identifications are extremely persuasive in establishing proof but are often among the least reliable types of evidence. The most common factor in wrongful conviction cases is false eyewitness identification.

11. Human memory consists of three phases: encoding, storage, and retrieval. During the memory process, many things may happen to inhibit or distort accurate memory. As such, many factors can influence the accuracy of eyewitness evidence.

12. The procedures used in constructing and conducting a lineup can greatly affect the accuracy of the identification. These procedures consist of the following: (1) the person who conducts the lineup should not know which photo depicts the suspect, and the witness should be told this; (2) the eyewitness should be told that the perpetrator may not be included in the lineup; (3) the suspect should not stand out in any way—as such, the foils should be selected on the basis of the witnesses description of the perpetrator; and (4) a statement about the witness's confidence that the identified person is the perpetrator should be obtained at the time of the identification. Recent research also highlights the benefits of conducting sequential lineups in which the witness views photos of subjects one at a time (versus a simultaneous lineup where the witness views all the photos at the same time).

13. Hypnosis can be used as a method of stimulating a witness's memory. However, hypnotized subjects are more susceptible to suggestion and providing inaccurate information. Because of this issue and the associated legal restrictions on such testimony, hypnosis is seldom used in criminal investigations today.

14. Cognitive interviewing is an interviewing approach that encourages concentration and has been shown to be an effective tool in enhancing memory recall. It is substantially different than the traditional or standard interview approach.

15. Regardless of the interview approach used, witnesses should be kept from sharing their observations with each other prior to the interview, interviews should be conducted in places that are away from distractions, and it is important that interviewers build rapport with witnesses.

IMPORTANT TERMS

Cognitive interview

Confabulation

Eyewitness

FACES facial identification software

Forensic sketch

Hypnosis

Imagination inflation

Investigative interview

Live lineup

Memory phases (acquisition, retention, and retrieval)

Mug shots

Photo lineup/array

Physical linup

Primary witness

Relative-judgment memory process

Secondary witness

Sequential lineup

Show-up identification

Simultaneous lineup

Weapon focus effect

Yerkes-Dodson Law

QUESTIONS FOR DISCUSSION AND REVIEW

1. What is the difference between a primary and a secondary witness? Is one more useful than the other?

2. What are the various ways by which eyewitness identifications can be made?

3. What are the advantages and disadvantages of using facial identification software and forensic sketches to create composite pictures of suspects?

4. What is the value of eyewitness identifications in establishing proof?

5. What are the three phases of human memory and how can factors at each phase affect the retrieval of information from witnesses?

6. What are the recommended procedures for conducted lineups? Why are these procedures important?

7. What is the relative judgment process and how can it be guarded against when conducting lineups?

8. What is the role of hypnosis in criminal investigation? What is confabulation? What does the research say about the accuracy of hypnotically elicited testimony?

9. How does the cognitive interviewing approach compare to the standard police interview? What does the research say about the value of the cognitive interview approach?

10. What are the recommendations regarding how and when interviews with witnesses should be conducted?

 STUDENT STUDY SITE

Visit **www.sagepub.com/brandl3e** to access additional study tools including eFlashcards, web quizzes, web resources, video resources, and SAGE journal articles.

7 Interrogations and Confessions

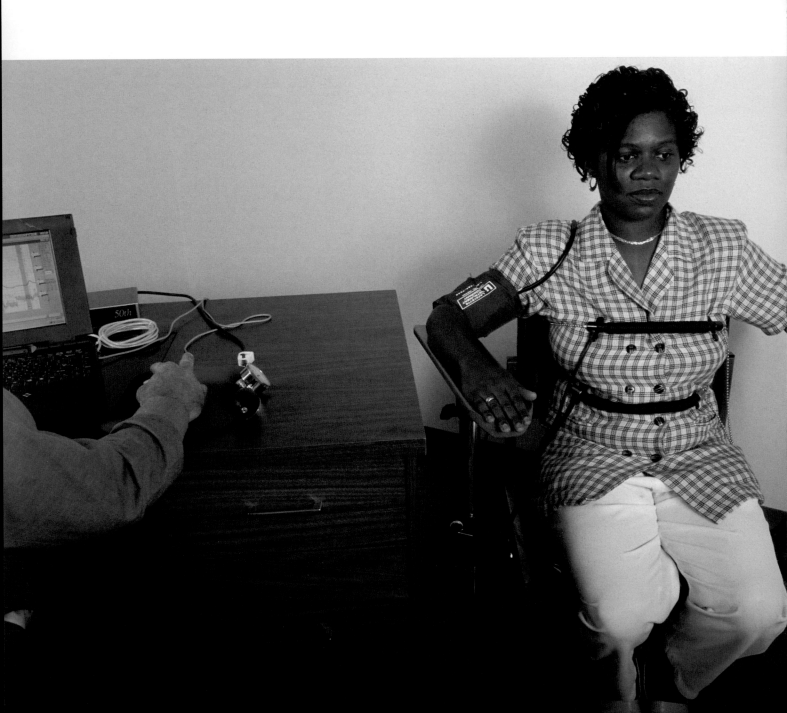

Objectives

After reading this chapter you will be able to:

- Define interrogation and explain how it differs from an interview

- Identify and discuss the various forms of police deception in interrogations

- Discuss rationalization, projection, and minimization (RPM) in interrogations

- Differentiate between the sledgehammer and feather approach in interrogations

- Identify the nine steps in an interrogation according to Inbau et al. (2013)

- Identify the differences between emotional and non-emotional offenders, and explain the significance of the distinction

- Discuss the reasons why a person may confess to a crime that he or she did not commit

- Discuss the general theory underlying the detection of deception and identify the

non-verbal and verbal behaviors that tend to indicate deception

- Discuss the accuracy and "usefulness" of the polygraph

- Differentiate between false-positive errors and false-negative errors in polygraph examinations

- Discuss the difficulties in establishing the accuracy of the polygraph and identify the factors that may affect the accuracy of polygraph results

From the CASE FILE

The "Secret" Interrogation of O. J. Simpson

The following are excerpts from the interrogation of O. J. Simpson by Los Angeles Police Department detectives Tom Lange and Philip Vannatter during the early afternoon of June 13, 1994, approximately fourteen hours after Simpson's ex-wife, Nicole Brown Simpson, and her friend Ronald Goldman were murdered outside her home in Brentwood, Los Angeles. This is the only time that detectives were able to ask questions of Simpson. Never was this interrogation brought up during the trial.

Recall from Chapter 5 (From the Case File) that as a result of the initial investigation and at the time this interrogation was conducted, there was reason to believe that Simpson may have been the perpetrator

(e.g., blood drops found at the crime scene indicated that the perpetrator was bleeding, blood was found on Simpson's Bronco and at his house, and a bloody glove that was found at the crime scene matched one found on Simpson's property). Detectives Lange and Vannatter spent thirty-two minutes questioning Simpson about his possible role in the double homicide. This transcript provides a good example of, by most accounts, a poorly conducted interrogation and is illustrative for this purpose. The transcript presented here has been edited for length. It begins after Simpson has been read his Miranda warnings and he agrees to waive them. The asterisks indicate a break in the sequencing of questions.

VANNATTER: Okay. All right, what we're gonna do is, we want to . . . We're investigating, obviously, the death of your ex-wife and another man.

*****Questions about Simpson and his relationship with Nicole Brown Simpson, their**

divorce, and their attempts at reconciliation.

*****Questions about a previous domestic violence incident between Simpson and Nicole.**

*****Questions about Nicole's maid, who lived at her house.**

LANGE: Phil, what do you think? Maybe we can just recount last night . . .

VANNATTER: Yeah. When was the last time you saw Nicole?

SIMPSON: We were leaving a dance recital. She took off and I was talking to her parents.

VANNATTER: Where was the dance recital?

SIMPSON: Paul Revere High School.

VANNATTER: And was that for one of your children?

SIMPSON: Yeah, for my daughter Sydney.

VANNATTER: And what time was that yesterday?

SIMPSON: It ended about six-thirty, quarter to seven, something like that, you know, in the ballpark, right in that area. And they took off.

VANNATTER: They?

SIMPSON: Her and her family, her mother and father, sisters, my kids, you know.

VANNATTER: And then you went your own separate way?

SIMPSON: Yeah, actually she left, and then they came back and her mother got in a car with her, and the kids all piled into her sister's car, and they . . .

VANNATTER: Was Nicole driving?

SIMPSON: Yeah.

VANNATTER: What kind of car was she driving?

SIMPSON: Her black car, a Cherokee, a Jeep Cherokee.

VANNATTER: What were you driving?

SIMPSON: My Rolls-Royce, my Bentley.

VANNATTER: Do you own that Ford Bronco that sits outside?

SIMPSON: Hertz owns it, and Hertz lets me use it.

VANNATTER: So that's your vehicle, the one that was parked there on the street?

SIMPSON: Mmm hmm.

VANNATTER: And it's actually owned by Hertz?

SIMPSON: Hertz, yeah.

VANNATTER: Who's the primary driver on that? You?

SIMPSON: I drive it, the house-keeper drives it, you know, it's kind of a . . .

VANNATTER: All-purpose type vehicle?

SIMPSON: All purpose, yeah. It's the only one that my insurance will allow me to let anyone else drive.

VANNATTER: Okay.

LANGE: When you drive it, where do you park it at home? Where it is now, it was in the street or something?

SIMPSON: I always park in the street.

LANGE: You never take it in the . . . ?

SIMPSON: Oh, rarely. I mean, I'll bring it in and switch the stuff, you know, and stuff like that. I did that yesterday, you know.

LANGE: When did you last drive it?

SIMPSON: Yesterday.

VANNATTER: What time yesterday?

SIMPSON: In the morning, in the afternoon.

VANNATTER: Okay, you left her, you're saying, about six-thirty or seven, or she left the recital?

SIMPSON: Yeah.

VANNATTER: And you spoke with her parents?

SIMPSON: Yeah.

VANNATTER: Okay, what time did you leave the recital?

SIMPSON: Right about that time. We were all leaving. We were all leaving then. Her mother said something about me joining them for dinner, and I said no thanks.

VANNATTER: Where did you go from there, O. J.?

SIMPSON: Ah, home, home for a while, got my car for a while, tried to find my girlfriend for a while, came back to the house.

VANNATTER: Who was home when you got home?

SIMPSON: Kato.

VANNATTER: Kato? Anybody else? Was your daughter there, Arnelle?

SIMPSON: Arnelle, yeah.

VANNATTER: So what time do you think you got back home, actually physically got home?

SIMPSON: Seven-something.

VANNATTER: Seven-something? And then you left, and . . .

SIMPSON: Yeah, I'm trying to think, did I leave? You know I'm always . . . I had to run and get my daughter some flowers. I was actually doing the recital, so I rushed and got her some flowers, and I came home, and then I called Paula as I was going to her house, and Paula wasn't home.

VANNATTER: Paula is your girlfriend?

SIMPSON: Girlfriend, yeah.

*****Questions about Paula, the spelling of her name, and her address.**

*****Questions about why he was supposed to be in Chicago that morning (to play in a charity golf tournament).**

VANNATTER: Oh, okay. What time did you leave last night, leave the house?

SIMPSON: To go to the airport?

VANNATTER: Mmm hmm.

SIMPSON: About . . . the limo was supposed to be there at ten forty-five. Normally, they get there a little earlier. I was rushing around, somewhere between there and eleven.

VANNATTER: So approximately ten forty-five to eleven.

SIMPSON: Eleven o'clock, yeah, somewhere in that area.

VANNATTER: And you went by limo?

SIMPSON: Yeah.

VANNATTER: Who's the limo service?

SIMPSON: Ah, you have to ask my office.

VANNATTER: Did you converse with the driver at all? Did you talk to him?

SIMPSON: No, he was a new driver. Normally, I have a regular driver I drive with and converse. No, just about rushing to the airport, about how I live my life on airplanes, and hotels, that type of thing.

*****Questions about his flight to Chicago.**

LANGE: So yesterday you did drive the white Bronco?

SIMPSON: Mmm hmm.

LANGE: And where did you park it when you brought it home?

SIMPSON: Ah, the first time probably by the mailbox. I'm trying to think, or did I bring it in the driveway? Normally, I will park it by the mailbox, sometimes . . .

LANGE: On Ashford, or Ashland?

SIMPSON: On Ashford, yeah.

LANGE: Where did you park yesterday for the last time, do you remember?

SIMPSON: Right where it is.

LANGE: Where is it now?

SIMPSON: Yeah.

LANGE: Where, on . . . ?

SIMPSON: Right on the street there.

LANGE: On Ashford?

SIMPSON: No, on Rockingham.

LANGE: You parked it there?

SIMPSON: Yes.

LANGE: About what time was that?

SIMPSON: Eight-something, seven . . . eight, nine o'clock, I don't know, right in that area.

LANGE: Did you take it to the recital?

SIMPSON: No.

LANGE: What time was the recital?

SIMPSON: Over at about six-thirty. Like I said, I came home, I got my car, I was going to see my girlfriend. I was calling her, and she wasn't around.

LANGE: So you drove the . . . you came home in the Rolls and then you got in the Bronco?

SIMPSON: In the Bronco, cause my phone was in the Bronco. And because it's a Bronco. It's a Bronco, it's what I drive, you know. I'd rather drive it than any other car. And, you know, as I was going over there, I called her a couple of times, and she wasn't there, and I left a message, and then I checked my messages, and there were no new messages. She wasn't there, and she may have to leave town. Then I came back and ended up sitting with Kato.

LANGE: Okay. What time was this again that you parked the Bronco?

SIMPSON: Eight-something, maybe. He hadn't done a Jacuzzi, we had . . . went and got a burger, and I'd come home and kind of leisurely got ready to go. I mean, we'd done a few things . . .

LANGE: You weren't in a hurry when you came back with the Bronco?

SIMPSON: No.

LANGE: The reason I ask you, the car was parked kind of at a funny angle, stuck out in the street.

SIMPSON: Well, it's parked because . . . I don't know if it's a funny angle or what. It's parked because when I was hustling at the end of the day to get all my stuff, and I was getting my phone and everything off it, when I just pulled it out of the gate there, it's like, it's a tight turn.

LANGE: So you had it inside the compound, then?

SIMPSON: Yeah.

LANGE: Oh, okay.

SIMPSON: I brought it inside the compound to get my stuff out of it, and then I put it out, and I'd run back inside the gate before the gate closes.

****Questions about the telephone number for O. J.'s office.**

VANNATTER: How did you get the injury on your hand?

SIMPSON: I don't know. The first time, when I was in Chicago and all, but at the house I was just running around.

VANNATTER: How did you do it in Chicago?

SIMPSON: I broke a glass. One of you guys had just called me, and I was in the bathroom, and I just kind of went bonkers for a little bit.

LANGE: Is that how you cut it?

SIMPSON: Mmm, it was cut before, but I think I just opened it again. I'm not sure.

LANGE: Do you recall bleeding at all in your truck, in the Bronco?

SIMPSON: I recall bleeding at my house, and then I went to the Bronco. The last thing I did before I left, when I was rushing, was went and got my phone out of the Bronco.

LANGE: Mmm hmm. Where's the phone now?

SIMPSON: In my bag.

LANGE: You have it?

SIMPSON: In that black bag.

LANGE: You brought a bag with you here?

SIMPSON: Yeah, it's . . .

LANGE: So do you recall bleeding at all?

SIMPSON: Yeah, I mean, I knew I was bleeding, but it was no big deal. I bleed all the time. I play golf and stuff, so there's always something, nicks and stuff, here and there.

LANGE: So did you do anything? When did you put the Band-Aid on it?

SIMPSON: Actually, I asked the girl this morning for it.

LANGE: And she got it?

SIMPSON: Yeah, 'cause last night with Kato, when I was leaving, he was saying something to me, and I was rushing to get my phone, and I put a little thing on it, and it stopped.

******More questions about who drives the Bronco and about Nicole.**

VANNATTER: What were you wearing last night, O. J.?

SIMPSON: What did I wear on the golf course yesterday? Some of these kind of pants—some of these kind of pants, I mean I changed different for whatever it was. I just had on some . . .

VANNATTER: Just these black pants?

SIMPSON: Just these . . . They're called Bugle Boy.

VANNATTER: These aren't the pants?

SIMPSON: No.

VANNATTER: Where are the pants that you wore?

SIMPSON: They're hanging in my closet.

***** More questions about his pants and shoes. Questions**

about the expected length of his trip to Chicago.

VANNATTER: O. J., we've got sort of a problem.

SIMPSON: Mmm hmm.

VANNATTER: We've got some blood on and in your car, we've got some blood at your house, and sort of a problem.

SIMPSON: Well, take my blood test.

LANGE: Well, we'd like to do that. We've got, of course, the cut on your finger that you aren't real clear on. Do [you] recall having that cut on your finger the last time you were at Nicole's house?

SIMPSON: A week ago?

LANGE: Yeah.

SIMPSON: No. It was last night.

LANGE: Okay, so last night you cut it?

VANNATTER: Somewhere after the recital?

SIMPSON: Somewhere when I was rushing to get out of my house.

VANNATTER: Okay, after the recital?

SIMPSON: Yeah.

VANNATTER: What do you think happened? Do you have any idea?

SIMPSON: I have no idea, man. You guys haven't told me anything. I have no idea. When you said to my daughter, who said something to me today that somebody else might have been involved, I have absolutely no idea what happened. I don't know how, why, or what. But you guys haven't told me anything. Every time I ask you guys, you say you're going to tell me in a bit.

VANNATTER: Well, we don't know a lot of the answers to these questions yet ourselves, O. J., okay?

SIMPSON: I've got a bunch of guns, guns all over the place. You can take them, they're all there,

I mean, you can see them. I keep them in my car for an incident that happened a month ago that my in-laws, my wife, and everybody knows about that.

VANNATTER: What was that?

SIMPSON: Going down to . . . And cops down there know about it because I've told two marshals about it. At a mall, I was going down for a christening, and I had just left and it was like three-thirty in the morning and I'm in a lane, and also the car in front of me is going real slow, and I'm slowing down 'cause I figure he sees a cop, 'cause we were all going pretty fast and I'm going to change lanes, but there's a car next to me, and I can't change lanes. Then that goes for a while, and I'm going to slow down and go around him, but the car butts up to me, and I'm like caught between three cars. They were Oriental guys, and they were not letting me go anywhere. And finally I went on the shoulder, and I sped up, and then I held my phone up so they could see the light part of it, you know, 'cause I have tinted windows, and they kind of scattered, and I chased one of them for a while to make him think I was chasing him before I took off.

*****Questions about this incident.**

VANNATTER: Did Nicole mention that she'd been getting any threats lately to you? Anything she was concerned about or the kids' safety?

SIMPSON: To her?

VANNATTER: Yes.

SIMPSON: From?

VANNATTER: From anybody?

SIMPSON: No, not at all.

*****Questions about security precautions taken by Nicole.**

VANNATTER: Did you ever park in the rear when you go over [to Nicole's house]?

SIMPSON: Most of the time.

VANNATTER: You do park in the rear?

SIMPSON: Most times when I'm taking the kids there, I come right into the driveway, blow the horn, and she, or a lot of times the housekeeper, either the house-keeper opens or they'll keep a garage door open up on the top of the thing, you know, but that's when I'm dropping the kids off, and I'm not going in, and sometimes I go to the front because the kids have to hit the buzzer and stuff.

***** Questions about continuing attempts at reconciliation between him and Nicole.**

VANNATTER: How long were you together?

SIMPSON: Seventeen years.

VANNATTER: Seventeen years. Did you ever hit her, O. J.?

SIMPSON: Ah, one night we had a fight. We had a fight, and she hit me. And they never took my state-ment, they never wanted to hear my side, and they never wanted to hear the housekeeper's side. Nicole was drunk. She did her thing, she started tearing up my house, you know? I didn't punch her or anything, but I . . .

VANNATTER: Slapped her a cou-ple times?

SIMPSON: No, no, I wrestled her, is what I did. I didn't slap her at all. I mean, Nicole's a strong girl. She's a . . . one of the most conditioned women. Since that period of time, she's hit me a few times, but I've never touched her after that, and I'm telling you, it's five, six years ago.

VANNATTER: What's her birth date?

SIMPSON: May 19th.

VANNATTER: Did you get together with her on her birthday?

SIMPSON: Yeah, her and I and the kids, I believe.

VANNATTER: Did you give her a gift?

SIMPSON: I gave her a gift.

***** Questions about the gift, when he gave it to her, and how she gave it back to him.**

LANGE: Did Mr. Weitzman, your attorney, talk to you anything about this polygraph we brought up before? What are your thoughts on that?

SIMPSON: Should I talk about my thoughts on that? I'm sure even-tually I'll do it, but it's like I've got some weird thoughts now. I've had weird thoughts . . . You know, when you've been with a person for sev-enteen years, you think everything. I've got to understand what this thing is. If it's true blue, I don't mind doing it.

LANGE: Well, you're not compelled at all to take this thing, number one, and number two, I don't know if Mr. Weitzman explained it to you—this goes to the exclusion of someone as much as to the inclu-sion so we can eliminate people. And just to get things straight.

SIMPSON: But does it work for elimination?

LANGE: Oh, yes. We use it for elim-ination more than anything.

SIMPSON: Well, I'll talk to him about it.

LANGE: Understand, the reason we're talking to you is because you're the ex-husband.

SIMPSON: I know I'm the number one target, and now you tell me I've got blood all over the place.

LANGE: Well, there's blood in your house and in the driveway, and we've got a search warrant, and we're going to go get the blood. We found some in your house. Is that your blood that's there?

SIMPSON: If it's dripped, it's what I dripped running around trying to leave.

LANGE: Last night?

SIMPSON: Yeah, and I wasn't aware that it was . . . I was aware that I . . . You know, I was trying to get out of the house. I didn't even pay any attention to it. I saw it when I was in the kitchen and I grabbed a napkin or something, and that was it. I didn't think about it after that.

VANNATTER: That was last night after you got home from the recital when you were rushing?

SIMPSON: That was last night when I was . . . I don't know what I was, I was in the car getting my junk out of the car. I was in the house throwing hangers and stuff in my suitcase. I was doing my little crazy what I do . . . I mean, I do it everywhere. Anybody who has ever picked me up says that O. J.'s a whirlwind. He's running, he's grabbing things, and that's what I was doing.

VANNATTER: Well, I'm going to step out and I'm going to get a photographer to come down and photograph your hand there. And then here pretty soon we're going to take you downstairs and get some blood from you. Okay? I'll be right back.

LANGE: So it was about five days ago you last saw Nicole? Was it at the house?

SIMPSON: Okay, the last time I saw Nicole, physically saw Nicole, I saw her obviously last night. The time before, I'm trying to think. I went to Washington, D.C., so I didn't see her, so I'm trying to think. I haven't seen her since I went to Wash-ington. I went to Washington . . . what's the date today?

LANGE: Today's Monday, the 13th of June.

SIMPSON: Okay, I went to Wash-ington on maybe Wednesday. Thursday I think I was in . . . Thurs-day I was in Connecticut, then Long Island Thursday afternoon and all of Friday. I got home Friday night, Friday afternoon, I played, you know . . . Paula picked me up at the airport. I played golf Saturday, and when I came home I think my son was there. So I did something with my son. I don't think I saw Nicole at all then. And then I went to a big affair with Paula Saturday night, and I got up and played golf Sunday, which pissed Paula off, and I saw Nicole at . . . it was about a week before, I saw her at the . . .

LANGE: Okay, the last time you saw Nicole, was that at her house?

SIMPSON: I don't remember. I wasn't in her house, so it couldn't have been at her house, so it was, you know, I don't even physically remember the last time I saw her. I may have seen her even jogging one day.

LANGE: Let me get this straight. You've never physically been inside the house?

SIMPSON: Not in the last week.

*****Additional questions about when he last saw Nicole and when he was last at her house.**

LANGE: We're ready to terminate this at 14:07.

Case Considerations and Points for Discussion

- How well do you think this interrogation was conducted? What were the three most important questions/issues that the detectives wanted answers to in this interrogation? Did the detectives get clear answers to these questions? Based on this transcript, how truthful do you think O. J. Simpson was in answering the critical questions of the detectives?

- Are any of the answers provided by Simpson vague, or are there any that just do not seem to make sense?

- What do you think was the most significant mistake that was made by the detectives in conducting this interrogation?

- Investigators can learn something from every investigation. What do you think should be the biggest lessons learned by the police as a result of this interrogation?

••• Interrogations Defined

An interrogation can be defined as any questioning or other action that is intended to elicit incriminating information from a suspect when this information is intended to be used in a criminal prosecution. Compared to an interview, it is more of an intimidating process during which information is extracted from a typically unwilling suspect (Schafer and Navarro 2010). Interrogations of subjects are usually conducted when the subject is in the custody of the police (i.e., custodial interrogation). *Custody* exists when the suspect is under the physical control of the police and when the suspect is not free to leave. The police may also conduct a noncustodial interrogation of a suspect. This occurs when the suspect voluntarily accompanies the police and when the suspect is told that he or she is not under arrest and is free to leave at any time (*California v. Beheler* [1983]). Although Miranda only applies to custodial interrogations, as a matter of practice, police often advise all subjects who may provide incriminating statements of their constitutional rights prior to questioning. In contrast to interviews, interrogations are usually more of a process of testing already-developed information than of actually developing information. For example, in the homicide investigation of Nicole Brown Simpson and Ron Goldman, the police had evidence that led them to believe that Simpson was possibly (or probably) responsible for the murders. In the interrogation of Simpson, the detectives attempted to test this evidence by asking him questions about when he last drove the Bronco (and where he parked it), how and when he injured his hand, and his activities the night of the murders.

The ultimate objective of an interrogation is to obtain a confession; however, the police must walk a fine line in this regard. It is possible that the individual who is believed to have committed the crime may not have actually committed it. As a result, of course, a confession would not be a desirable or appropriate outcome of the interrogation. Even if a confession is not obtained, an interrogation may be successful if the subject provides admissions to investigators (e.g., "I was at Nicole's house last night but I didn't kill her"), or even if investigators can obtain from the subject a firm and detailed account of actions that may be related to the crime (e.g., "I cut my hand on my cell phone last night"). If the alibis and explanations offered by the subject are checked and tested against other known facts of the crime, and the story is consistent with those facts and constitutes a reasonable explanation, then the subject's account may be truthful. If the subject's story is inconsistent with other facts developed in the investigation, if the subject provides contradictory or conflicting details, or if the story just does not make sense, then the subject's lies may be evidence of guilt. The attempt to deceive may suggest that the subject is hiding involvement in the crime or in some aspect of it. Further questioning may then highlight the inconsistencies of the subject's story and how it conflicts with the other facts of the investigation. This line of questioning may elicit incriminating statements from the subject. As discussed in more detail later in the chapter, it is very important to note here that statements indicative of deception may not necessarily suggest involvement in the crime in question. Subjects may attempt to deceive investigators for reasons unrelated to the crime under investigation, such as to hide other illegal or embarrassing actions. This possibility can make interrogations more complicated.

●●● The Psychology of Persuasion

Interrogation is basically a task of persuasion, of getting someone to do what he or she really does not want to do. A salesperson may persuade a man to buy a car for more money than he wants to spend, a wife may persuade her husband to go shopping when he really does not wish to, or an investigator may persuade a suspect to confess to a crime despite that fact that the confession may lead to a conviction and prison. As explained by Simon (1998), "[The detective] becomes a salesman, a huckster as thieving and silver-tongued as any man who ever moved used cars or aluminum siding—more so, in fact, when you consider that he's selling long prison terms to consumers who have no genuine need for the product" (p. 57).

So why do people get persuaded to do what they really do not want to do? Specifically, why do suspects confess? The simple answer is that the suspect comes to believe that there is some benefit in doing so. According to Gudjonsson (1992) there are basically three reasons why suspects confess. The first is to relieve feelings of guilt. One's conscience, the part of the mind that holds feelings of guilt, can make a criminal's life difficult. Confessing, often viewed as a good thing to do, may be seen as a way of making those feelings of guilt go away. A second reason why suspects confess is because of persuasive police actions. The police may wear down the suspect; they may make him or her tired. The suspect may just want the accusations to stop; he or she may just want to go home. The police may convince the suspect that confessing is the best thing, the easiest thing, or even the only thing, to do. The third reason for confessing is that the suspect *believes* that there is no point in denying the crime because the police have evidence to prove involvement in the crime. The suspect's *belief* is critical. This belief may be largely influenced by the actions and tactics of the interrogator. In most confessions, each of these three reasons may be present to some extent; a combination of factors may bring suspects to confess. In any case, the extraction of a confession is a process of persuasion.

A study that directly examined the factors that influenced whether offenders confess also highlights the important role of evidence in eliciting a confession (Deslauriers-Varin et al. 2011). The authors found that a confession was most likely when the offender was faced with strong police evidence. They also found that offender age, ethnic group, education level, and marital status had no effect on the tendency to confess. Offenders who reported guilty feelings about their crime and who did not seek legal advice were also more likely to confess. Finally, offenders who committed serious crimes were more likely to confess than those who committed less serious crimes.

••• The Role of Police Deception in Interrogations

Leo (1992) explains that the nature of interrogations in the United States has changed dramatically over the years. Although interrogations used to rely most heavily on physical violence and coercion (i.e., the "third degree"), interrogations today rely most heavily on psychological techniques of persuasion and deceit. As noted by Marx (1988), "Restrict police use of coercion, and the use of deception increases" (p. 47). Indeed, deception is central to modern interrogation methods. The irony is that the "police proclaim truth as the goal of interrogation, yet interrogators regularly rely on deception and sophisticated forms of trickery" to obtain it (Leo 2008, p. 6).

According to Simon (1998), "What occurs in an interrogation room is indeed little more than a carefully staged drama, a choreographed performance that allows a detective and his subject to find common ground where none exists" (p. 54). Similarly, Schafer and Navarro (2010) describe the interrogation process as "theater." For example, one of the fundamental objectives of an investigator conducting an interrogation is to project a sympathetic and understanding image to develop the suspect's trust. This foundation by itself may be fundamentally deceptive—the result of a carefully planned script. There is nothing legally wrong with "being nice" during an interrogation, even if this portrayal is deceptive. In fact, this is often the most effective approach in eliciting a confession. However, it is important to understand this sort of deception, combined with other forms of deceit, may also lead to problematic outcomes (see Case in Point 7.1).

CASE in POINT 7.1   "We're Going to Work Through This Together. Okay?"

Stephanie Crowe, twelve, was stabbed to death during the early morning hours of January 21, 1998, in her home while she slept in her bed. Believing the crime was committed by someone who was already in the house, San Diego County detectives immediately turned their attention to Michael Crowe, Stephanie's fourteen-year-old brother. After several hours of questioning over a period of several days, without his parents or an attorney present, Michael confessed and implicated two of his friends in the murder. The goal of the investigators who conducted the interrogation of Michael—Detective Ralph Claytor and Officer John Martin—was to obtain a confession, a goal they eventually achieved. Below are a few excerpts from the interrogation that show the interrogators' attempts to show sympathy for Michael and his predicament.

CLAYTOR: We're really trying to believe what you say. We want to believe what you say.

MARTIN: You know I'm a pretty good guy. You can obviously sense that. I mean, I'm not hitting you with a rubber hose, am I? I'm here to verify what you are saying. Okay?

MARTIN: We're going to work through this together. Okay?

MARTIN: Maybe there's something we need to understand about Michael and about your sister that we didn't understand, and maybe somebody could have helped. It's okay. It's okay to feel the way you feel.

CLAYTOR: You're a child. You're fourteen years old. Nobody's going to hold you to the same standards that they would some criminal on the street. You're gonna need some help through this.

Do you think that the investigators were really sympathetic to Michael, or were they just doing what they needed to do to getting a confession from him?

The day before the trial was to begin, charges against Michael and his two friends were dropped when it was determined that none of them had anything to do with the murder. On the basis of DNA evidence, a drifter with a long history of arrests and severe mental illness was arrested for the homicide.

See below for more details about this interrogation. Also see Leo (2008) for a more detailed discussion of the case.

In addition to the portrayal of false sympathy, police also commonly deceive suspects with regard to nature of the evidence in the case (Leo 1992). Even if there is no evidence that the suspect committed the offense, the police may legally deceive the suspect into believing that such evidence exists. This deception is limited to verbalization; it is not legally permissible to fabricate evidence even if just used in the interrogation room. Telling the suspect that his or her fingerprints were found on the murder weapon, that the suspect has been identified by eyewitnesses, or that the victim stated that the suspect was the killer in a dying declaration are common tactics.

In this regard, Schafer and Navarro (2010) recommend the use of several deceptive props for the interrogation, including a thick folder filled with papers and with the suspect's name and "EVIDENCE" written on the cover. Another ploy is for the investigator who is conducting the interrogation to receive a "well-timed" phone call during the interrogation to alert the investigator to "new evidence" in the investigation. In general, this sort of deception is legally permissible as long as it would not induce an innocent person to confess. Consider once again the Stephanie Crowe murder (Case in Point 7.1 continued).

The use of deception in the interrogation of Michael Crowe was tragic because, as noted, Michael eventually confessed, but it was determined later that he had nothing to do with the murder. A positive example of the strategic use of deception in the interrogation setting is the case of Susan Smith, the woman who, on October 25, 1994, buckled her two young children in her car and let the car roll into John D. Long Lake near Union, South Carolina. Her children drowned. Susan summoned the police and told them that a black man around forty years old, wearing a dark knit cap, a dark shirt, jeans, and a plaid shirt had carjacked her car while her kids were in the back seat. In the national media spotlight, she pleaded for the safe return of her children. Susan told the police that when her car was carjacked, she was stopped at a red light at a particular intersection and no other cars were at the intersection. Investigators found this suspicious because that particular light was set always to be green unless a car on the cross street triggered the light to switch. In order for the light to be red, another car had to be at the intersection. Additional questioning revealed other inconsistencies in her story. Susan agreed to a polygraph exam, and the results indicated deception. Additional interrogations of Susan ensued. At one point, Susan was confronted with her lie about where the carjacking actually occurred. The police told her that it could not have possibly occurred there because of the triggered light. Susan then changed her story, claiming that the carjacking actually occurred at a different intersection in a different city, fifteen miles from where she originally said that it occurred. The police then told Susan that this intersection was under police surveillance for a drug investigation at the time she said the carjacking supposedly occurred (which was not true) and that the police officers who were there did not see any carjacking. After the officer told Susan this, she reportedly began to cry and said, "You don't understand . . . My children are not all right." Susan then confessed. It was the ninth day after she reported that her children were taken.

Another deceptive tactic investigators use is one that was used in the interrogation of Michael Crowe: using technology (in this case a computer voice stress analyzer) to detect deception and then overstating the technology's capability. As discussed later in this chapter, most research has come to the conclusion that the voice stress analyzer produces unreliable and invalid results (see Case in Point 7.1 continued).

Along the same line, Simon (1998) presents a case in which Detroit detectives were said to have used a photocopy machine as a lie detector. The detectives loaded three pieces of paper in the Xerox machine. The first one read "TRUTH," the second one read "TRUTH," and the third one read "LIE." The suspect was led into the room and told to put his hand on the side of the machine. He was first asked his name. After he answered, the copy button was pushed. The paper with "TRUTH" was printed. He was asked where he lived. "TRUTH."

The following exchange took place between Michael, Detective Claytor, and Officer Martin when Michael was told that the police found his hair in Stephanie's hand and her blood in his bedroom. Neither of these claims was truthful.

MARTIN: I'm looking at you right now, okay, and inside you're about ready to burst. We can't bring her back. She's gone, okay? You're fighting it. You're, you're, you're . . .

MICHAEL: I don't know what to do anymore.

MARTIN: I understand.

MICHAEL: Now I'm being told that I'm lying and I know that I'm not.

MARTIN: Michael, I'm not saying that. Have you heard me say that? What if they come back and say to you, "Michael, we have your hair?" They say, "Michael, we have your hair in her hand." And all of a sudden you go, "Now what?" I mean what are you going to do at that point? I mean . . .

MICHAEL: At that point, I would do a complete breakdown . . . of knowing it, because I don't know.

MARTIN: Hypothetically, could this have happened?

MICHAEL: No, not that I know of.

MARTIN: Not that you know of?

MICHAEL: Like I said, I would have to be completely unaware of it.

MARTIN: Okay. Have you ever blacked out before?

MICHAEL: No, never. If I knew who did it then you would know. Everyone would know it now.

MARTIN: Okay, why?

MICHAEL: Because whoever did it, I, if I ever find out I would hate them forever. I loved her. I loved her deeply.

CLAYTOR: We found blood in your room already.

MICHAEL: God. Where did you find the blood?

CLAYTOR: I'm sure you know.

MICHAEL: (crying) Why God? No I don't know. I didn't do it. I'll swear to that.

CLAYTOR: Does that mean you can't tell me about the knife?

MICHAEL: I don't know what you are talking about.

CLAYTOR: You're fourteen?

MICHAEL: Yes.

CLAYTOR: You've got your whole life ahead of you, don't you?

MICHAEL: (crying) Yeah, God. Oh God. God why?

CLAYTOR: You tell me.

MICHAEL: Why are you doing this to me? If I did this I don't remember it. I don't remember a thing.

CLAYTOR: And you know what? That's possible.

MARTIN: I can tell you this instrument here. Okay it is what they call a computer voice stress analyzer. Now you will appreciate this, being into computers. *Its accuracy rate is phenomenal, okay?* And that's what makes it such a great tool [emphasis added].

MARTIN: What are some things we want to learn here do you think?

MICHAEL: If I know who did it, if I did it.

MARTIN: Okay, well let's do that then. Do you know who, let's say, took Stephanie's life?

MICHAEL: No.

MARTIN: Okay, would that be a good, fair question?

MICHAEL: Yes.

MARTIN: Do you know who took . . . Do you know how she died?

MICHAEL: No.

MARTIN: Are you sitting down?

MICHAEL: Yes.

MARTIN: Do you know who took Stephanie's life?

MICHAEL: No.

MARTIN: Is today Thursday?

MICHAEL: Yes.

MARTIN: Did you take Stephanie's life?

MICHAEL: No.

MARTIN: Let me go over these charts and I'll be back here in a couple of minutes, okay?

MICHAEL: Okay.

After a few minutes, Martin then returned to the interrogation room and told Michael that he failed the test and was lying when answering the critical questions.

He was asked if he shot the victim. He said "no," and the paper with "LIE" on it was printed. "You flunked," he was told, "you might as well confess." Leo (2008) provides another example. A suspect in a murder investigation was asked,

> Have you ever heard of scanning electron microscopy? It's a big old microscope, okay? And when people die, their images of what they see, like if you died right now and you saw him and I in your eyes. What happens is in the autopsy we take out the lens and we put it in the microscope and look at it, right before they die, that image is saved forever. . . . When we get those at the autopsy and pull those lenses out, we aren't going to see you pointing the gun, right? (pp. 143–144)

Another common form of deception in interrogations is misrepresentation of the seriousness of the crime. For instance, the police may tell the suspect that the murder victim is still alive, is in good condition, and doesn't want to press charges, so that the suspect can confess with few perceived implications. In a similar vein, the police may offer the suspect psychological excuses or moral justifications for his or her actions—again, in an attempt to make confessing psychologically easier (e.g., the rape was an act of love, or the victim may have come on to him). As discussed later, whatever form the deception takes, the strategic use of it by the police in interrogation settings is a powerful and oftentimes necessary, but controversial, tool in persuading suspects to confess.

A Question of Ethics

Should the Police Lie to Get Suspects to Confess?

As a society, we give the police extraordinary power and authority to investigate crimes and apprehend perpetrators. We also expect the police to abide by the law in carrying out their mandate. Indeed, we expect the police to be honorable, fair, moral, and just in their interactions with citizens. However, criminals often lie to avoid apprehension and punishment. So, the questions are as follows: Should the police be able to legally lie to suspects in order to get them to confess to their crimes? Should the police be able to lie to judges and juries in order to get suspects convicted of their crimes? Why or why not?

MYTHS & MISCONCEPTIONS *7.1*

Interrogations Involve Bright Lights and Hot Rooms

In the aftermath of September 11, 2001, and the interrogation of al-Qaeda operatives, there were many accounts of extreme interrogation methods, including "waterboarding." On other occasions, there have been news stories about American police using brutal methods and even torture to elicit confessions from unwilling suspects (see http://chicago.cbslocal.com/2012/10/16/class-action-suit-filed-on-chicago-police-torture-claims/). However, interrogation methods and approaches such as these are extraordinary and extremely uncommon. Nowadays, interrogations are usually quite friendly, albeit in a stressful sort of way. Research has shown that the "kind and gentle" approach to interrogations is much more effective than the "harsh and cruel" approach (Leo 1998). This makes sense. Think about it this way: Have you ever purchased a car?

Buying (and selling) a car is also a process of persuasion, similar to an interrogation. The investigator is trying to obtain a confession; the salesman is trying to sell a car (at the highest possible price). If you have had the experience of buying a car, chances are that the salesperson seemed pretty friendly. It is very unlikely that the salesperson hollered or threatened you. He or she might have brought you a soda, a coffee, or maybe even a candy bar. The salesperson may have talked to you about your "interesting" job, your "wonderful" family, and your "great" taste in cars—all in an effort to sell you a new one! He or she probably "worked hard" to get you a great deal from the sales manager. Just like in an interrogation, this sort of approach is much more likely to lead to the desired outcome: selling a car for more money . . . or getting a confession.

●●● The Ingredients of a Successful Interrogation

In order for an interrogation to occur, the suspect must first waive Miranda rights and be willing to answer the questions of the investigators. If the suspect invokes Miranda rights, an interrogation will not occur. Persuasion has a limited role at this stage. Legally, the police may not try to convince suspects to waive their rights. However, Leo (2008) argues that the police use various strategies to minimize the importance of Miranda to suspects, such as telling the suspect that he or she is not in custody or treating the Miranda warnings as a mere formality. In most instances, suspects agree to answer questions without a lawyer. In a study by Cassell and Hayman (1998), it was found that 84 percent of felony suspects who the police wished to question voluntarily waived their Miranda rights and submitted to questioning. In a study by Leo (1996), 75 percent of suspects waived their Miranda rights and 21 percent invoked their rights (4 percent of suspects did not receive Miranda warnings because they were not considered by the police to be in custody at the time of the interrogation). The findings of these studies are generally in line with other research that has shown that, on average, approximately 20 percent of suspects invoke their Miranda rights prior to questioning by the police (Cassell and Hayman 1998). Most suspects talk to the police because, as explained by Simon (1998), "Every last [suspect] envisions himself parrying questions with the right combination of alibi and excuse; every last one sees himself coming up with the right words, then crawling out the window to go home and sleep in his own bed" (p. 54).

According to Cassell and Hayman (1998), of those suspects who waived their Miranda rights, approximately 44 percent provided a verbal or written confession, and an additional

PHOTO 7.1: Interrogation is essentially a process of persuasion. Interrogations are usually conducted when a suspect is in the custody of the police.

24 percent of suspects provided some type of incriminating statement to investigators. As such, 68 percent of interrogations were considered successful. The bottom line is that if suspects agree to talk, they will probably say something incriminating. It is interesting to note that those individuals who invoked their Miranda warnings (i.e., who would not talk to the police) were more likely to have a previous criminal history and were slightly less likely to be convicted of the current offense. On the other hand, suspects who provided incriminating information as a result of the interrogation were more likely to be charged by prosecutors, more likely to be convicted, and more likely to receive more severe sentences following their conviction. Most often, confessions are viewed as the most powerful and persuasive form of evidence (Leo 2008)—even more powerful than eyewitness identifications or DNA matches. As discussed earlier in the book, confessions are direct evidence, and they come directly from the horse's mouth—from the perpetrators themselves.

Provided that the suspect waives his or her rights and agrees to answer the questions of the police, what are the ingredients necessary to produce a successful interrogation? The basic ingredients consist of the following:

- A plan

- Adequate time

- Control of the interrogation

- An understanding of the facts of the case

- Familiarity with the suspect's background

- A good relationship with the suspect

- Familiarity with various themes, approaches, and tactics (see Vessel 1998; Simon 1998; Napier and Adams 1998; and Leo 1996 and 1998b)

First, with regard to a plan, prior to beginning the interrogation it must be determined what information is known and what information needs to be obtained (Schafer and Navarro 2010). What dimensions of the crime and of the evidence need to be tested with the suspect? It appears from the transcript provided in the introduction to this chapter that the detectives who interrogated O. J. Simpson were not well prepared for the interrogation. The most critical questions to be asked and answered were the following: (1) When did Simpson last drive the Bronco? (2) What were his actions and activities the previous night (the night of the murders)? and (3) How did he cut his hand? These were basic but fundamentally important questions in the investigation, and, although they asked these questions, there was no concerted effort on the part of the detectives to obtain clear answers. Simpson was allowed to give confusing, vague, and contradictory answers. As one of many examples, consider this exchange:

VANNATTER: How did you get the injury on your hand?

SIMPSON: I don't know. The first time, when I was in Chicago and all, but at the house I was just running around.

Inexplicably, there was no follow-up to press for a clear answer. At the conclusion of the interrogation, the detectives had no clear explanation as to how or when Simpson cut his hand. Consider the exchange regarding when he last drove the Bronco:

LANGE: When did you last drive it?

SIMPSON: Yesterday.

VANNATTER: What time yesterday?

SIMPSON: In the morning, in the afternoon.

Later in the interrogation he stated that he last drove it "at eight-something, seven, eight, nine o'clock." Again, there was no attempt to get a clear answer on this important issue. At the conclusion of the interrogation, the detectives did not know when Simpson last drove the Bronco.

Regarding his activities the previous night, consider this exchange:

VANNATTER: That was last night after you got home from the recital when you were rushing?

SIMPSON: That was last night when I was . . . I don't know what I was, I was in the car getting my junk out of the car. I was in the house throwing hangers and stuff in my suitcase. I was doing my little crazy what I do, I mean, I do it everywhere. Anybody who has ever picked me up says that O. J.'s a whirlwind. He's running, he's grabbing things, and that's what I was doing.

Again, his answer to the question makes no sense, but little effort was made to try to pin down his activities or a timeline for those activities. In addition, it is clear that some of Simpson's answers were completely contradictory. One time he said that he "kind of leisurely got ready to go" and at another time he said that he was in a "whirlwind." This was a contradiction that Simpson was never pressed to clarify or explain.

Also, with regard to a plan, if more than one investigator is to be involved in the questioning, the respective role of each investigator must be determined beforehand. The most basic issue is deciding who is going to be in charge and lead the questioning. It appears from the Simpson transcript that neither detective was in charge. A review of the transcript shows numerous instances when one of the detectives interrupted the other or when one changed the line of questioning that the other was pursuing. Having two detectives involved in the interrogation should work to the advantage of the police, but in the interrogation of Simpson it did not.

Second, adequate time needs to be spent in an interrogation to persuade a suspect to confess or, at the least, to get the suspect to commit to a certain version of events and to get the details necessary to develop contradictions in statements. Time is also needed to allow for a relationship, for rapport, to be developed with the suspect. As such, the length of the interrogation is one of the most important factors in differentiating successful from unsuccessful interrogations. Indeed, Leo (1996) found that successful interrogations were six times more likely than unsuccessful ones to have lasted more than an hour. Nearly 30 percent of interrogations lasted for more than one hour, 35 percent lasted for less than one-half hour (including those during which the suspect immediately invoked the Miranda warnings). The interrogation of Simpson lasted just more than thirty minutes. The crime being investigated was a double homicide. Simpson was the prime suspect and he agreed to waive his Miranda rights. Given these circumstances, a thirty-minute interrogation is difficult to understand.

Third, control is fundamentally important in an interrogation setting. Investigators must control the topics of discussion during the interrogation. If investigators are determined to elicit or test certain information during an interrogation, they must direct the questioning. During the Simpson interrogation, it was sometimes difficult to determine who was questioning who. Simpson was allowed to take the questioning off course. For instance, consider this exchange:

VANNATTER: What do you think happened? Do you have any idea?

SIMPSON: I have no idea, man. You guys haven't told me anything. I have no idea. When you said to my daughter, who said something to me today that somebody else might have been involved, I have absolutely no idea what happened. I don't know how, why, or what. But you guys haven't told me anything. Every time I ask you guys, you say you're going to tell me in a bit.

VANNATTER: Well, we don't know a lot of the answers to these questions yet ourselves, O. J., okay?

Following this exchange, Simpson told the detectives about an incident during which two "Oriental guys" harassed him on the highway, and the detectives proceeded to ask questions about this completely irrelevant incident. In short, it did not appear that the detectives had control over the interrogation.

Another dimension of control in the interrogation setting is the physical environment in which the questioning takes place (Schafer and Navarro 2010). As explained by Inbau et al. (2013), the room should be quiet and have no visual distractions. There should not be a telephone in the room, nor should telephones be audible from outside the room. For safety reasons, locks should be removed from the door. The room should have proper lighting—not too dark or too bright. There should be two chairs in the room placed about four to five feet apart and they should face each other with nothing between them. The chairs should have straight backs and be of the same size so that the questioner and the suspect are at the same eye level. Ideally, the room should be equipped with an adjacent observation room, and a two-way mirror should separate these rooms. This arrangement would allow other investigators to observe the interrogation and to observe the suspect when he or she is alone in the room. The aim is to control every aspect of the interrogation session. In this sense, the suspect is placed under additional, albeit subtle, stress.

Fourth, investigators involved in the interrogation must have a good understanding of the facts of the case in order to ask the right questions and to understand when an answer is conflicting with the other facts of the case. Information about the case is also important in establishing a plan for the interrogation. During the interrogation of Simpson, the detectives knew about the blood in the Bronco, the blood at Simpson's house, and the bloody glove found at Simpson's house that matched the one at the crime scene. They asked many of the right questions but failed to get clear answers.

Fifth, interrogators should have a familiarity with the suspect's background. In the questioning of Simpson, the detectives knew that he was not an experienced criminal and certainly was not a professional killer. They knew that Simpson and Nicole had a turbulent relationship. They knew that the police were, on at least one earlier occasion, summoned to intervene in a domestic incident between Simpson and Nicole. All this knowledge could have been used by the detectives in developing a plan on how best to interrogate their prime (and only) suspect.

Sixth, investigators should build a good relationship with the suspect. The suspect has to feel like he or she can trust the investigators and that the investigators are there to help. As noted earlier, building a relationship in an interrogation setting takes time. In the Simpson case, detectives simply did not spend the time necessary to establish rapport with him. Another part of rapport building is simply treating the suspect with some degree of respect and making the suspect comfortable, which may make it easier for him or her to trust the detectives and to confess. Often, this takes the form of food, drinks, and cigarettes.

Finally, investigators should be familiar with, and comfortable using, a variety of persuasive themes, approaches, and tactics. Vessel (1998) identifies various themes, including minimizing the seriousness of the crime (e.g., "The homeowner says $1,000 was taken, but I wouldn't be surprised if it was only $100"), blaming the victim (e.g., "I agree with you. One has to ask why she was going for a walk by herself so late at night"), decreasing the shamefulness of the act (e.g., asking, "Tell me about the missing girl" without asking about the details of the suspected sexual assault of the girl), increasing guilt feelings (e.g., "If you tell me what happened, I'm sure that the guilt that is eating you alive will go away"), and appealing to the subject's hope for a positive outcome as a result of cooperation (e.g., "I'll tell the prosecutor that you were helpful"). The logic behind the use of these themes is that they lower the psychological hurdles necessary for a suspect to confess to actions for which there may be significant negative consequences.

According to Napier and Adams (1998), there are certain "magic" words and phrases that make it easier for suspects to confess. These words and phrases relate to three commonly used defense mechanisms: rationalization, projection, and minimization, or RPM.

In particular, *rationalization* "offers plausible explanations for suspects' actions that reflect favorably on them by presenting their actions in a positive light" (p. 12). It is intended that through the use of rationalizations, the suspect will believe that the investigator sees the suspect's behavior as rational in nature, thereby making it easier to confess. For example, in a child abuse case, the investigator may speak to the suspect about the importance of "discipline" to control the "misbehavior" of a child (e.g., "Discipline is necessary when a child misbehaves"). With *projection,* responsibility for the criminal behavior is given to someone else in an attempt to convince the suspect that the action was really not his or her fault. Again, as a result, it may then be easier for the suspect to confess to the criminal behavior. For example, again in a child abuse case, the investigator could state that if the *child* would have behaved, she would not have been disciplined. Or that if the *child's mother* would be more responsible for taking care of the child, this would not have happened. With *minimization,* the investigator reduces the suspect's role in the crime or the seriousness of the crime. The investigator may speak of the criminal act as an "accident" or as a "mistake," but not as a "murder" or a "beating." Soft words are chosen over harsh words. Again, the point is that this may make it easier for the suspect to acknowledge his or her role in the crime.

Along with the effective use of RPM, Napier and Adams (1998) also suggest that investigators provide the suspect with reasons to confess. These reasons may vary by individual, by motivation, and by the nature of the crime. In some cases, a good reason to confess from the perspective of the suspect might be finally to get help for the problem, to ease feelings of guilt, or to tell the other side of the story. According to Napier and Adams, to be most effective, the RPM and the reasons to confess should be delivered via a "feather" approach versus a "sledgehammer" approach. Consider the following illustrations (from Napier and Adams 1998):

SLEDGEHAMMER: Brad, you have lied to me from the beginning. You're not fooling me with the story, and I'm going to shove it down your throat. You'll be sorry.

SLEDGEHAMMER: You strangled Valerie. Why don't you just say you did it?

FEATHER: Brad, I have some problems understanding your story. I've seen this happen before and realize you are uncertain about what you can tell me. That's natural, but I'm really concerned with how you got into this mess. Let's keep it simple and honest. Let's not make this any worse than it is.

FEATHER: Brad, my experience in similar cases is that the person sitting in your chair has a lot on his mind. He is asking himself, "What is going to happen to me? Who is going to know that I did this thing? Am I better off telling the entire story and my version of how this thing started?" Let's handle these questions one at a time, keeping each concern in its proper perspective and not letting it run wild. (pp. 14–15)

The feather approach shows warmth, sincerity, and a commitment to get the truth—all of which may go a long way in persuading a suspect to do what he or she really does not want to do. As such, in most cases, the feather approach leads to a more productive interrogation. Indeed, research has shown that when interrogations are perceived as harsh and cruel by suspects, suspects are more likely to offer denials. When interrogations are perceived as more kind and friendly, suspects are more likely to provide admissions and confessions (Kassin and Gudjonsson 2004).

Leo (1996) found that some tactics were more likely than others to elicit incriminating information from suspects. In particular, the most successful interrogation tactics were to appeal to the suspect's conscience (97 percent of the time that this tactic was used it led to incriminating information being produced), identify contradictions in the suspect's story (91 percent), use praise or flattery (91 percent), and offer moral justifications and psychological excuses (90 percent). The more interrogation tactics used by investigators, the more likely the interrogation was to result in a confession or other incriminating information being produced. This factor (along with the length of the interrogation) was most important in differentiating successful from unsuccessful interrogations.

Besides the general rules that should be followed to increase the chances of a successful interrogation, Inbau et al. (2013) provide additional recommendations regarding the conduct of interrogations. These recommendations include that the investigator should not use paper or pencil in the interrogation setting, the investigator should not be dressed in a uniform nor should the investigator be armed, the investigator and suspect should remain seated throughout the questioning, language easily understood by the suspect should be used, the status of a low-status subject should be elevated (e.g., referring to the suspect as "Mr.") whereas the status of a high-status person should be lowered (e.g., referring to the subject by his first name), the suspect should be treated with respect and should not be handcuffed or shackled during the interrogation, and, finally, that reactions to the suspect's lies should be concealed. It is expected that these factors will further create an environment in which suspects will find it easier to confess.

●●● Steps in the Interrogation of Suspects

Inbau et al. (2013), the definitive source on the conduct of interrogations, outline nine steps that should be followed in conducting interrogations. These steps are outlined in this section.

The first step is to confront the suspect directly with a statement that the suspect committed the crime (e.g., "O. J., the results of our investigation tell us that you are responsible for the deaths of Nicole and Ron") and then wait for a reaction. The nature of the denial may be revealing. What would be a reasonable reaction to such an accusation? "You're wrong! You are frickin' crazy if you think I killed Nicole" or "Why do you think I did it? Honestly, I didn't do it." The second denial is certainly more curious than the first. During a recent investigation of a kidnapping/murder, the suspect's repeated denial was "As far as I'm concerned, I didn't do it." Not exactly a strong or convincing claim of innocence! Certainly, the nature of the initial denial may give additional insight into the guilt of the suspect. After the initial denial is made by the suspect, then the investigator should repeat the accusation. A statement should then be made showing the commitment to determining what really happened and who is responsible (e.g., "Okay, work with me O. J. and we're going to get this straightened out").

Second, the suspect should be classified by the investigator as either an emotional offender or a nonemotional offender. An emotional offender is one who is likely to experience considerable feelings of remorse regarding the crime. This judgment may be informed by an understanding of the crime, the suspect's background, the suspect's previous experience or involvement in similar crimes, and his or her body language. It is instructive to note that most suspects who waive their Miranda rights are best classified as emotional offenders. A nonemotional offender, on the other hand, does not experience a troubled conscience, is perhaps more sophisticated, and does not feel a need to answer the questions of the police. According to Inbau et al., this classification is important in determining which themes to use in the interrogation. The following themes are most effectively used with emotional offenders:

- Sympathize with the suspect, saying that anyone else under similar circumstances would have done the same thing. Tell the suspect that you (the interrogator) have done or have been tempted to do the same thing.

- Reduce the suspect's feelings of guilt by minimizing the seriousness of the offense (e.g., "This is really pretty normal, it happens all the time, a lot of people do this").

- Suggest to the suspect a less revolting and more acceptable motivation for the offense (e.g., "It was an accident," "It was due to having a few too many beers," "It was due to the use of drugs," "It was not planned").

- Sympathize with the suspect by condemning others (e.g., blame the victim, an accomplice, or anyone else).

- Appeal to the suspect's pride through flattery (e.g., compliment the guts and skill it took to commit the crime or

mention the good deeds the suspect has done in the past).

- Acknowledge that the accuser may have exaggerated the nature and seriousness of the crime (e.g., "I believe you had intercourse with her, but I'm not so sure it was a rape").

- Highlight the grave consequences of continued criminal behavior on the part of the suspect (e.g., "In the long run it is good that you got caught because now you can get the help that you really deserve").

Inbau et al. identify the following themes as being most effective with nonemotional offenders. It is reasonable to expect that these themes would be effective with emotional offenders as well.

- Attempt to obtain an admission about some incidental aspect of the crime (e.g., of being in the store at about the time of the robbery). Such a statement may be facilitated through the use of false evidence (e.g., "We have witnesses who saw you in the store that day"). Once this admission is made, further steps can be taken to elicit a confession.

- Point out the futility of denials. Convince the suspect that his or her guilt has been established and that there is no point in denying involvement in the crime (e.g., "The only reason I'm talking to you is so that you can explain any circumstances that may make a difference").

- When the individual's suspected partner in the crime has also been arrested, one offender can be played against the other offender (e.g., "Your buddy in the next room is blabbing away, saying you planned the whole thing. You may as well be honest with me").

The third step, according to Inbau et al., is to deal with continued denials. Denials beyond the initial one should be cut off. The suspect should not be allowed to reiterate denials. It should be pointed out, once again, that denials are pointless. Guilt has already been proved.

Fourth, a suspect who moves from denials to objections (e.g., "I couldn't have done that, I don't own a gun") is likely moving toward a confession but is not there yet. Objections may provide useful information for the development of themes. For instance, a suspect who says, "I couldn't have hurt that little girl, I love kids; I work with kids" might be susceptible to well-placed flattery or to the theme that the "thing" that happened was "an accident." In any case, the interrogator should avoid getting into an argument with the suspect. The interrogator must move forward (e.g., "You don't own a gun? That tells me that this thing was not your idea . . . that your buddy got you involved in this").

Fifth, it must be continually clear to the suspect that the interrogator is interested in getting the truth, that the interrogator is not giving up, and that the interrogator will not stop until the truth is obtained. Eye contact should be maintained. The interrogator should move his or her chair closer to the suspect.

Sixth, theme development should continue. Statements should be made to convince the suspect that confessing is the best course of action. At this point, the need for repeated questioning is minimal.

The seventh step is to present an alternative question to the suspect (e.g., "Did you plan this, or did it just happen by accident?"). The intent is to get the suspect to make a statement. Again, denials should be immediately cut off. A confession may be close at hand. A question that allows for a one-word confession should then be offered (e.g., "All you wanted to was to scare her. You didn't mean to hurt her, right?").

The eighth step is to have the suspect orally relate the details of his or her involvement in the crime. Questions should be neutral (e.g., "Then what happened?" or "What happened next?"). As the confession is in full gear, an inquiry into the details of the crime and the suspect's involvement in it should be made.

The final step is to turn the oral confession into a written one either in the form of responses to open-ended questions or a narrative written by the suspect.

CASE in POINT 7.2

"Every Time We Do Something Illegal, I'm the One Who Has to Do It."

The following is a confession statement of a suspect named Myron Edwards. Myron shot and killed a security guard at a video store in order to get the guard's gun. For background, investigators were making no progress in the investigation until the police responded to a seemingly unrelated bank robbery in which they apprehended the perpetrators as they fled the bank. Police then identified the getaway car that was to be used for the robbery. In it they found the gun taken from the security guard. The statement is verbatim, as recorded by the detective who conducted the interrogation.

Regarding the homicide of the black guard at the Blockbuster video store on E. Capital Drive about 2–3 days before New Year's. Said he had problems with his girlfriend and had no place to go. Marteze was always trying to get guns. Said the day before the shooting, Marteze and his girlfriend told Myron that they were at Blockbuster video and there was a white security guard there who was carrying a "Glock." They were talking about getting the guard's gun. Myron was asked how they were going to get the gun and he said "every time we do something illegal, I'm the one who has to do it." Stated the next night they used the white Tempo and Willie was driving and Marteze was in the front seat and Myron was in the back. They drove by Blockbuster on E. Capital and saw through the window a black security guard but they decided to get the gun anyway. Myron said he did it because he didn't want them to think he was scared. Before at the house Myron stated he smoked two marijuana cigarettes. Said Marteze gave him a silver gun with black inlay panels on the grips. Myron said he felt high as he went into Blockbuster. Once inside he was walking around and had no intention of killing anyone. Stated he was just walking around but felt "like everyone was staring at him." He said he "felt paranoid." He saw that the guard had a big gun in his holster. He said he "thought he could just run up and snatch the gun out of the guard's holster." Said the guard was talking to a black girl. He said he took out his gun and pointed it at the guard and the girl looked at him. He said he was going to yell "freeze" but the gun went off. Said he saw a lot of blood on the guard's shoulder. Said the guard was sitting on a stool or chair and once he was shot he turned around toward Myron. The guard was sliding off the chair and was also going for his gun. Said "I got real nervous, the guard was going for his gun in his right holster and I wasn't really trying to pull the trigger, it seemed like a hair trigger and it just kept going off." He said it went off "6 or 7 times." "The guard was on the ground so I reached down and pulled the gun out." "I don't know if I unsnapped the holster or not." "The gun barrel was not long and I knew it was a revolver," Myron said he walked out of the store with "the revolver in my coat pocket." Stated outside he walked then ran to the Ford Tempo. Said he either took off the hat he was wearing or he lost it. Said the car was on Humboldt Avenue. By the car he saw a white guy looking at him and Marteze said to Myron "look at that guy, you might have to shoot him." Myron said he pulled back the slide of the .380 but it was already back. He yelled at Willie "go go." He gave the .380 to Marteze and kept the .357 he got from the guard. Said he couldn't believe he did it. Later he saw the news and knew the security guard was fatally shot. Stated he hasn't had a good night's sleep since the shooting. Said "I know what I did was wrong." Said "I thought I'd always be there for my son not like other black men." Myron was cooperative with us during the entire interview.

This process is really one of guiding the suspect, step by step, to a confession. Reasons are provided to make the suspect believe that a confession is the best course of action. The reasons and rationales basically pave the way toward a confession. The suspect becomes convinced that denials and objections are pointless. Resistance is futile. A confession is the only way out.

Getting someone to confess is a good thing, unless, of course, that person is not responsible for the crime to which he or she confesses. Under deep psychological stress, it is possible that certain individuals may falsely confess. It is to this troubling issue that our attention now turns.

••• The Issue of False Confessions

A false confession is one where the individual is totally innocent but confesses to the crime, or where the individual was involved in the offense but overstates his or her involvement in the crime (Gudjonsson 1992). Why would anyone confess to a crime they did not commit? Three related explanations have been offered. The first is referred to as *stress compliant false confession*. With this type of false confession, a confession is offered "to escape the punishing experience caused by the adverse—but not legally coercive—stressors typically present in all accusatory interrogations" (Leo 1998b, p. 277). In this instance, the zealousness on the part of the police elicits the confession from the individual. The confession is an attempt on the part of the individual simply to end the misery of the interrogation.

The second explanation for false confessions is referred to as a *persuaded false confession*. In this instance, the suspect has "been persuaded (by legally non-coercive techniques) that it is more likely than not that he committed the offense despite no memory of having done so" (Leo 1998b, p. 277). In essence, the police are so convincing that the subject believes his or her guilt even though the subject has no memory of committing the crime. Numerous factors, identified in Leo and Ofshe (1998), increase the likelihood of a persuaded false confession:

- The interrogator repeatedly states his or her belief in the suspect's guilt.

- The suspect is isolated from anyone who may contradict the claims of the interrogator and is not told of other information that may lead one to believe that he or she did not commit the crime.

- The interrogation is lengthy and emotionally charged.

- The interrogator repeatedly claims that there is scientific proof of the suspect's guilt.

- The suspect is repeatedly reminded of previous instances of memory problems or blackouts. If these do not exist, then other factors are identified by the interrogator that could account for lack of memory of the incident.

- The interrogator demands that the suspect accept the interrogator's version of events and explanations for the crime.

- The interrogator induces fear in the suspect's mind about the consequences of repeated denials.

It is interesting to note that many of these factors are present in the interrogation protocol presented by Inbau et al. (2013). It is also noteworthy that *all* of these factors were apparently present in the interrogation of Michael Crowe discussed earlier. Of course, not everyone is equally susceptible to the influence of these tactics. Research has shown that the individuals most likely to provide such false confessions most often have several characteristics in common: an extraordinary trust of people in authority, a lack of self-confidence, and heightened suggestibility, which may be due to factors such as young age or mental handicap (Gudjonsson 1992). Research has shown that the one factor that both stress compliant and persuaded false confessions have in common is that they are elicited after extremely long interrogation sessions, many of which last more than ten hours. Sometimes these interrogation sessions occurred over the course of several days (Leo and Ofshe 1998).

A third explanation for false confessions is known as *voluntary false confession*. In this instance, an individual comes forward to the police and confesses to a crime that may not have even occurred (Gudjonsson 1992). There may be several reasons why an individual would take such an action: a morbid desire for fame, guilt about some other crime that was committed, mental illness (especially in cases such as schizophrenia when the individual cannot differentiate what is real from what is not), or to protect the person who actually committed the offense.

False confessions, for whatever reason they are given, are an important issue because confessions are extremely persuasive evidence in the criminal investigation and criminal justice process. In fact, confessions are *the* most powerful evidence of guilt in a criminal trial (Gudjonsson 1992; Leo and Ofshe 1998; Schafer and Navarro 2010). In addition, once a confession is made, it is extremely difficult to recant it convincingly. Indeed, taking back a confession is like trying to un-ring a bell. Accordingly, given a confession, the influence of the confession, and the defendant's possible inducements to plea bargain, one is able to understand how a (false) confession can lead to a plea bargain and, tragically then, a minimal testing of the other evidence in the case. The bottom line is that psychological methods of interrogation and persuasion may cause innocent suspects to confess. Leo and Ofshe (1998) identify sixty high-profile cases in which the police obtained, in all probability, false confessions. They identify these cases as the tip of the iceberg.

Unfortunately, the most significant legal procedure that relates to confessions, the Miranda warnings, has little impact on the issue of false confessions. As discussed in detail in Chapter 4, Miranda focuses more on the process of interrogations than on the outcomes. Did the police inform the suspect of his or her rights? Were those rights voluntarily and knowingly waived by the subject? If these questions can be answered in the affirmative, then the process requirements of Miranda are generally satisfied (Leo 1998b). Hence, Miranda is largely irrelevant to the issue of false confessions (Kassin and Gudjonsson 2004). In addition, if the methods used to elicit confessions are not deemed coercive, then false confessions are seldom deemed legally problematic (Leo 1998b).

So what can be done about the issue? First, and foremost, the police must be mindful that, for a variety of reasons, some people may falsely confess. In fact, the people who are most likely to waive their Miranda rights are the most likely to confess falsely (Malone 1998). Persuasion can simply go too far.

Second, the police must realize that a person who appears deceptive, and therefore guilty and warranting of a more pressing interrogation, may be deceptive not to cover involvement in the crime in question but to cover some other action that he or she may wish to keep secret. In addition, it is also important to note that the police are not immune from judgmental errors about suspect truthfulness and deception. Further, these initial assessments can affect how much pressure interrogators apply to get a confession from a suspect (Kassin and Gudjonsson 2004). This sequence may result in tragic consequences.

Third, the police should, as a matter of policy, videotape (or at least audiotape) the entirety of all interrogations (Leo 2008). Most states require the recording of interrogations for felony offenses (e.g., Michigan, Ohio, North Carolina), although many do not (e.g., Texas, Florida, New York, California). Some states only require that interrogations relating to homicide investigations be videotaped (e.g., Illinois). Sullivan (2004) interviewed officials from over 200 police departments in thirty-eight states who routinely record interrogations and found that the practice was uniformly supported. The benefits were multidimensional. As explained by one official, "For police, a videotaped interrogation protects against unwarranted claims that a suspect's confession was coerced or his constitutional rights violated. For prosecutors, it provides irrefutable evidence that [can be used] with a jury in the courtroom. For suspects, it ensures that their rights are protected in the interrogation process" (Sullivan 2004, p. 13). Other officials noted that video recording has led to improvements in how interrogations are conducted (e.g., investigators are better prepared for interrogations; video recordings can be used for training purposes). Research has also shown that recordings dramatically reduce the number of defense motions to suppress statements and confessions and increase the number of guilty pleas (Sullivan 2004). To be of most value, it is recommended that interrogations be recorded from the time Miranda warnings are given until the suspect leaves the room (Sullivan 2004). In addition, to avoid possible bias resulting from camera angle, it is recommended that the camera provide an equal focus on the suspect and the interrogator (e.g., a focus on the suspect alone may lead to underestimating the pressure placed on the suspect by the questioner) (Lassiter et al. 2002).

Finally, the police and prosecutors should systematically evaluate the credibility of the confessions obtained. Is there independent evidence of the suspect's guilt? Do the details of the confession correspond to the details of the investigation? Is there internal corroboration for the confession? As recommended by Leo and Ofshe (1998), until there is such evidence, an arrest should not be made. Specifically, did the confession lead to the discovery of other evidence that indicates guilt, such as the location of the murder weapon? Did the confession include detailed information that was not known to the public, such as the nature of the wounds to the victim or how the victim was clothed? These questions can allow for a judgment of the credibility of the confession and help investigators take the necessary precautions to prevent against the receipt and use of false confessions.

●●● Investigative Tools in Recognizing Deception

Given the objectives of a criminal investigation, there is much to be said for the ability to cut through the lies and deception of perpetrators; this holds true for today as well as in the past. Over time there have been many "tests" that have been used to detect deception, including the "spit a mouthful of rice" test, which was a common test in England from 800 to 1200; a truthful subject could do so, a deceptive subject could not. No question, the ability to deceive is a critical skill for criminals. For obvious reasons, offenders have a great incentive to deceive investigators. Other people, such as victims and witnesses, may also wish to deceive the police to cover their own illegal or embarrassing actions. Due to this, the ability to detect deception is important when obtaining information from people. Today, there are several methods commonly used to recognize deception. These methods can be generally classified as either nonmechanical (e.g., recognizing verbal and nonverbal cues) or mechanical (e.g., polygraph, voice stress analyzer).

The basic theory underlying each of these methods relates to the *fight-or-flight syndrome*. When confronted with a threat, such as being asked threatening questions and having to lie when answering them to avoid arrest, the human body prepares either to fight the threat or to flee from it. In preparing for this action, the body changes in physiological ways. The body increases the secretion of hormones, including adrenaline, which in turn causes an increase in blood pressure and heart rate, rapid breathing, and increased blood flow to the arms and legs, among other reactions. In an interrogation setting, physically fighting the threat (the investigator asking the questions) or fleeing the threat is not feasible or wise. As a result, the individual must try to repress the fight-or-flight response. When a person tries to repress this response, physiological changes become apparent through body movement, posture, verbal behavior, heart rate, and so forth.

VERBAL AND NONVERBAL DETECTION OF DECEPTION

At the outset, it must be realized that detecting deception from verbal and nonverbal cues is a difficult task and is subject to a high degree of error (Bartol and Bartol 2013), and yet investigators may be quite confident in their erroneous judgments (Kassin et al. 2003). Most studies show accuracy rates of judgments of deception based on such cues in the range of 45 percent to 60 percent (whereas 50 percent accuracy would be expected by chance) (Porter and Yuille 1996; Zuckerman et al. 1984; Schafer and Navarro 2010). This is at least in part because of the variation that exists among people in their behaviors. In particular, in evaluating the meaning of various nonverbal and verbal behaviors, various factors need to be considered (Schafer and Navarro 2010; Zulawski and Wicklander 1992). First, no single behavior is always indicative of deception. Second, individual differences need to be considered. Individuals may differ in their verbal and nonverbal behaviors, degree of nervousness, ability to cope with nervousness, intelligence, medical condition, and so forth. Actions that appear to signal deception for one person may not for another. Third, gender and ethnic/cultural differences need to be considered. For example, women tend to act, speak, and sit differently than men. Women tend to use "hedges" more commonly when speaking (e.g., "kind of," "sort of," "I feel"), and they tend to use more modal verbs (e.g., may, might, could, should) (Ainsworth 1998). Fourth, because verbal and nonverbal behaviors are largely situational, the situation and environment need to be considered when evaluating behaviors. For example, the amount of visible perspiration a subject might be displaying needs to be considered in relation to temperature and activities immediately preceding the questioning. Fifth, although single behaviors may not be meaningful, behavioral clusters may be. Several behavioral or verbal cues displayed at the same time are more indicative of deception than a single cue. Finally, the timing of the verbal and nonverbal cues needs to be considered. When was the cue displayed in relation to the questions asked? Timing may be an important consideration when inferring meaning from displayed behavioral cues.

KINESICS

Kinesics relates to the study of body movement and posture to convey meaning (Walters 1996). Information derived from an understanding and interpretation of body language can be useful during an investigation. Again, the fundamental theory behind the study of nonverbal behavior to recognize deception is that lying is stressful and individuals try to cope with this stress through body positioning and movement. In addition, individuals try to cope with the threat posed by the questions and the stress of the deception by engaging in self-protection-type behaviors. In this sense, the deception "leaks" from the person in the form of recognizable nonverbal behaviors. However, again, behaviors that show discomfort may be incorrectly interpreted as behaviors that indicate deception. Caution is warranted.

Some nonverbal behaviors are meant to convey direct meaning. For example, emblems are gestures that are the equivalent of words, such as shaking the head to indicate "no," shrugging the shoulders, or giving a thumbs-up. Illustrators are hand and arm displays that are used to illustrate what is being said (e.g., "The fish was this big"). Other nonverbal behaviors are more subtle. Although no single behavior is always indicative of deception, patterns exist (Zulawski and Wicklander 1992). Generally, one looks for congruence and incongruence. Congruence occurs when there is a match between truthful verbal behavior and truthful physical behavior. Incongruence occurs when the words being stated do not correspond to the nonverbal behavior (Zulawski and Wicklander 1992).

What are the most common deceptive nonverbal behaviors? With regard to facial expressions, an individual's eyes are the most revealing. In normal conversation with most people, eye contact is usually in the range of 40 percent to 60 percent, although there is significant variation across ethnic and social groups, individuals, and situations. "Any break in the normal level of eye contact, which is a timely response, is a sign of stress" and possible deception (Zulawski and Wicklander 1992, p. 91). Dry mouth, and other actions involving the mouth (e.g., biting fingernails) and nose (e.g., rubbing the nose), may also be indicative of deception (Zulawski and Wicklander 1992).

Exhibit 7.1   "The Best Way to Unsettle a Suspect . . ."

It has been suggested that the best way to unsettle a suspect is to post signs in interrogation rooms that read: "Behavior patterns that indicate deception: Uncooperative, Too Cooperative, Talks too Much, Talks too little, Gets his Story Perfectly Straight, Fucks his Story Up, Blinks too Much, Avoids Eye Contact, Doesn't Blink, Stares." (Simon 1998, pp. 63–64)

Regarding body positioning and posture, one should be most aware of protective or defensive sorts of actions taken by a subject when he or she is asked and answering threatening questions. These behaviors include moving the chair farther away from the questioner, sitting sideways in the chair, sitting in a straddle position on the chair with the back of the chair as a barrier of separation, sitting so as to protect the abdominal region (e.g., slumping, extending feet and legs to provide distance between the subject and the questioner, crossing arms, sitting with knee over leg with the knee protecting the abdomen), bouncing the legs while in a sitting position, and using the hands to cover mouth (either to muffle a deceptive answer or as an unconscious attempt to keep the mouth from making deceptive statements). A deceptive subject also tends to put his or her head back or forward out of the plane of the shoulders. The timing of these actions is critical when inferring that a subject is being deceptive.

Gestures may also be revealing of attempts to deceive. Particularly significant are the use of manipulators, or "created jobs," as an attempt to divert attention from the threatening questions being asked and the deceptive answers being provided. These created jobs are basically busywork for the hands (Walters 1996) and include such actions as checking jewelry, cleaning fingernails, and smoothing hair. As Walters (1996) explains, "Deceptive subjects generally tend to have a greater number of touches to the head than do truthful subjects," especially to the nose (p. 81) and to the neck (Schafer and Navarro 2010). Other potentially revealing gestures include coughing, yawning, throat clearing, sighing, and frequent swallowing (dry mouth and throat). Once again, the timing of these gestures in relation to the difficult and threatening questions being asked of the subject is critical and most meaningful.

VERBAL BEHAVIOR

Verbal behaviors are generally easier to control than nonverbal behaviors. As a result, extra care needs to be taken when inferring meaning from verbal behavior. Verbal behavior in the extreme is most indicative of deception.

There are numerous verbal cues of deception (Schafer and Navarro 2010; Walters 1996; Inbau et al. 2013; and Rabon 1994). In general, deceptive subjects often offer vague and confusing answers. They tend to use more generalized statements. As Rabon (1994) explains, "Some deceptive individuals will relate events vaguely, with a series of actions or blocks of time summed up in such phrases as 'messed around,' 'talked for a while,' or 'got my stuff together'" (p. 50). Truthful subjects usually provide details because it is their desire to *convey* meaning to the questioner. Deceptive subjects, however, only wish to *convince* (Schafer and Navarro 2010). For example, consider the following exchanges in the interrogation of O. J. Simpson:

PHOTO 7.2: It is helpful for an interrogator to be able to read a subject's body language. What is this subject saying with her body language?

LANGE: About what time was that [that you last parked your Bronco]?

SIMPSON: Eight-something, seven . . . eight . . . nine o'clock, I don't know, right in that area.

VANNATTER: Where did you go from there, O. J.?

SIMPSON: Ah, home, home for a while, got my car for a while, tried to find my girlfriend for a while, came back to the house.

VANNATTER: How did you get the injury on your hand?

SIMPSON: I don't know. The first time, when I was in Chicago and all, but at the house I was just running around.

Deceptive subjects also often provide conflicting statements. For example, Simpson alternated between stating that he was in a hurry when he was getting ready to leave for the airport and that he was leisurely getting ready to go:

SIMPSON: I'd come home and kind of leisurely got ready to go.

SIMPSON: I was hustling at the end of the day.

SIMPSON: I was rushing to get out of my house.

Or consider these exchanges about when he last parked the Bronco:

LANGE: When did you last drive it [the Bronco]?

SIMPSON: Yesterday.

VANNATTER: What time yesterday?

SIMPSON: In the morning, in the afternoon.

LANG: Okay. What time was this again that you parked the Bronco?

SIMPSON: Eight-something, maybe.

Deceptive subjects also have a tendency to provide explanations that do not make sense. For example, apparently Simpson had a hard time remembering how and when he cut his hand. As noted, he first stated that he cut his hand in Chicago earlier that day, and then he stated that he cut it the previous night at his house when he was running around getting ready to leave for the airport. This cut was significant enough to drip blood. One could reasonably expect that a person would remember the circumstances of such an injury, especially if it had just occurred within the last twenty-four hours. When Simpson realized that the police discovered drips of blood at his house and in his Bronco, he stated that he cut himself when he was rushing to get his cell phone.

Also with regard to the words used by subjects, deceptive individuals often use the present tense when describing a past occurrence (e.g., "He then goes to the store and buys some beer"). Deceptive subjects also tend to use modifiers in their speech (e.g., "sort of," "usually," "most of the time") more often than truthful subjects, and, as such, deceptive subjects generally lack conviction about their own assertions. Deceptive subjects tend to reduce or eliminate self-references (e.g., use of the word "I"), whereas second-person references (i.e., "you") are more likely to be used. Sentences indicative of deception are more likely to begin with verbs or with descriptions.

Deceptive subjects also often use sentences that are unusually short, unusually long, or unusually complicated. They also tend to provide incomplete sentences in answering incriminating questions. The incomplete sentences are not only a result of mental confusion about the lies and how they may overlap but also an attempt to avoid giving answers to threatening questions. The transcript of the Simpson interrogation shows repeated instances of Simpson providing incomplete sentences.

Deceptive subjects often complain (e.g., about the weather, their health, their treatment), especially early during the interrogation. This can most often be interpreted as an attempt on the part of the subject to gain the investigator's sympathy. Deceptive subjects tend to offer premature excuses or explanations. They tend to focus on irrelevant points because they are likely to be true and, as a result, easier to talk about.

There is a tendency among deceptive subjects to delay in answering even basic questions (e.g., "Did you drive to work this morning?") because subjects who intend to be deceptive must determine what they need to lie about and what they do not need to lie about. Deceptive subjects often offer verbal filler when thinking of a response to a question ("Ummmm . . ."). Deceptive subjects may have a tendency to repeat the question that has been asked or to respond to a question with another question. All these are strategies to create additional time to think about the possible incriminating nature of the question and a deceptive response to it. Consider the following exchanges in the Simpson interrogation:

VANNATTER: So what time do you think you got back home, actually physically got home?

SIMPSON: Seven-something.

VANNATTER: Seven-something? And then you left, and . . .

SIMPSON: Yeah, I'm trying to think, did I leave? You know I'm always . . . I had to run and get my daughter some flowers . . .

LANGE: Did Mr. Weitzman, your attorney, talk to you anything about this polygraph we brought up before? What are your thoughts on that?

SIMPSON: Should I talk about my thoughts on that? I'm sure eventually I'll do it, but it's like I've got some weird thoughts now. I've had weird thoughts . . .

Similarly, deceptive subjects may attempt to avoid answering the question posed. For example:

VANNATTER: What were you wearing last night, O. J.?

SIMPSON: What did I wear on the golf course yesterday? Some of these kind of pants—some of these kind of pants, I mean I changed different for whatever it was. I just had on some . . .

Deceptive subjects may also be overly helpful, excessively polite, or extremely respectful. They may talk softly, mumble, or talk through their hands. They may place extra and repeated emphasis on claims of truthfulness (e.g., "really," "honestly," "to tell you the truth") and may invoke religious statements to that affect (e.g., "honest to God," "I swear on a stack of Bibles"). These actions are usually an attempt to be extra convincing when the subject knows that he or she may not be convincing at all.

Deceptive subjects often claim to experience memory problems. They often have a selectively good memory or an extraordinary memory. It is clear from the interrogation of Simpson that he did not have a very good memory of his activities the previous evening. As Walters (1996) explains, "When discussing critical areas, deceptive subjects experience more frequent occurrences of memory failure than do truthful subjects" (p. 29). In other instances, a subject may offer an immediate response to a question that would normally require some thought, or even clarification. For example, if a subject immediately answered, "I was working on my car" to the question "What were you doing last week on Tuesday?," it would be odd and rather suspicious because the question is quite broad and the time referent is rather distant. A more reasonable response might be, "Gee, that was six days ago. Let me think. Okay. What time on Tuesday are you talking about?"

Guilty, and of course innocent, subjects typically deny their involvement in the crime in question; however, innocent subjects most often present stronger denials as the questioning continues, whereas guilty subjects most often begin with strong denials regarding their involvement in the crime (Walters 1996). Finally, deceptive subjects sometimes use "buy-out" statements (Walters 1996). These are used to try to get out of the situation without having to admit to the crime (e.g., "I didn't steal it, but I'd be willing to pay the victim for it anyway"). Truthful subjects simply are unlikely to try to engage in such a negotiation.

Schafer and Navarro (2010) present what they refer to as "a poor man's polygraph." Although not scientifically validated in any way, it offers an interesting possibility in detecting deception. It consists of four questions. According to these authors, consistent response patterns to these four questions may be indicative of deception or of truth. The first question is, "Why should I believe you?" This question would be asked of the suspect after the initial denial to the matter at hand. An honest person is likely to respond "Because I'm telling the truth," or "Because it is the truth," or some other reference to the truth. A deceptive person is more likely to say "I don't know," "You don't have to believe me if you don't want to," or some related sort of response. According to Schafer and Navarro (2010), it is reasonable for it to take up to three times of being asked "Why should I believe you?" for a truthful suspect to make reference to "I'm telling the truth." The second step of the "the poor man's polygraph" is to tell the suspect in response to his denial, "I know you are lying." A truthful response would be, "But I told you the truth." A deceptive response would more likely be "Why are you harassing me?" or some other response that does not make reference to the truth. Third, ask the question "Do you really want to get away with this?" A truthful subject will not respond either "yes" or "no," but a deceptive subject will. Finally, when asked a critical yes or no question, if the subject begins his or her response with the word "well," there is a high probability of deception. According to Schafer and Navarro (2010), verbal responses to these questions can provide a good basis upon which to form judgment about a subject's deception. While this does not provide any solid evidence as to the value of the approach, it represents an interesting line of questioning.

MECHANICAL MEANS OF DETECTING DECEPTION

The polygraph and computer voice stress analyzer are the primary mechanical methods of detecting deception.

POLYGRAPH

A polygraph is a machine that records physiological responses to psychological phenomena. Like verbal and nonverbal indicators of deception, the premise of the polygraph is that lying is stressful and that this stress can be detected in physiological ways. Specifically, the theory holds that the polygraph can detect this stress through the recording of variations in a person's respiration rate (recorded through pneumographs, which are tubes filled with air placed around the subject's chest and abdomen), blood pressure (recorded by a blood pressure cuff placed around the subject's upper arm), and galvanic skin response (a measure of sweat on the subject's fingertips recorded through the use of galvanometers attached to the fingers). However, as noted by Ney (1988) and as discussed here, "The correlations between what people feel and how they physiologically express what they feel are not at all straightforward or simple" (p. 66).

Over the years, several methods of conducting polygraph examinations have been used. The first widely used methodology was referred to as the *General Question Test* or the *Relevant–Irrelevant Test* (RIT). The RIT consisted of a series of ten to fifteen questions, some of which were relevant to the crime (e.g., "Did you kill Jake Koplin last night?") and some that were irrelevant to the crime and neutral in their content (e.g., "Are you sitting down?"). It was presumed that a guilty person would answer the relevant questions deceptively and the irrelevant questions truthfully. The physiological reactions to the truthfully answered (irrelevant) questions could then be compared with the subject's physiological reactions to the deceptively answered (relevant) questions (Raskin and Honts 2002). As such, it was expected that the deceptive subjects would react substantially more strongly to the relevant than the irrelevant questions. These expectations were shown to be naive because relevant questions proved to be arousing, and to cause a greater reaction, for truthful *and* deceptive subjects. A truthful denial can be as arousing as a deceptive denial. Research has shown this methodology to produce a substantial number of false-positive errors (identifying innocent subjects as guilty) and, as such, it is strongly biased against truthful subjects (Lykken 1981; Raskin and Honts 2002). This polygraph method is now used infrequently.

A more recent technique that is not well tested or accepted but shows interesting possibilities is the *Guilty Knowledge Technique* (GKT) or the *Concealed Information Test* (CIT). The CIT involves constructing and presenting to a suspect a series of multiple-choice questions that focus on details of the crime that only the perpetrator and police would know. For example, according to Verschuere et al. (2011), two of several such questions would be as follows:

> If you are the one who killed Glenda Fisbee, then you would know where in the house her body was found. Was it in (a) the basement, (b) the kitchen, (c) the bathroom, (d) the attic, or (e) the bedroom?

> If you committed this crime, then you would know how she was killed. Was she bludgeoned with (a) a brick, (b) a crowbar, (c) a baseball bat, (d) a pipe, or (e) a hammer? (p. 14)

The subject would be instructed to say "no" to each possibility. The expectation is that the actual culprit will have the strongest physiological reaction to the correct answer. A consistent reaction to correct answers may allow one to infer guilt. It is in this way that the test measures "guilty knowledge" as opposed to emotions or deception. Possibly the greatest advantage to this approach is that it makes countermeasures to hide deception (see later) a nonissue. Research continues to be conducted on the value of this technique (Verschuere et al. 2011; Ben-Shakhar et al. 2002).

The primary and most generally accepted methodology for conducting polygraph examinations today is known as the *Control Question Technique* (CQT). There are several variations in the CQT methodology, the most common of which is the use of "probable lie" questions (Raskin and Honts 2002). With the CQT methodology, responses to relevant questions (e.g., "Did you take the gold watch?") are compared with responses to emotionally arousing control questions (e.g., "Did you ever tell a lie?" "Did you ever take anything of value that was not yours?"). These control questions are broad, vague, and refer to behaviors any subject has likely engaged in, at least at some point in the past. It is believed that in this approach, an innocent subject who truthfully answers the relevant questions will be more concerned with and will react more strongly to the control questions than a deceptive (guilty) person (i.e., an innocent subject would not be worried about telling the truth on the relevant questions but would be more worried about the control questions). Alternatively, a subject who is deceptive on the relevant questions (a guilty subject) will be more concerned with and have a greater reaction to the relevant questions than the control questions. In essence, the control questions threaten the innocent (truthful), whereas the relevant questions threaten the guilty (deceptive) (Elaad and Kleiner 1990; Raskin and Honts 2002). An example of the questions that could comprise a CQT polygraph examination is as follows, from Raskin and Honts (2002):

> Do you live in the United States? During the first 27 years of your life, did you ever tell even one lie? Did you rob the Quickmart at Fourth and Main last night? Prior to 1987, did you ever break even one rule or regulation? Did you take the money from the cash register at the Quickmart last night? Did you participate in any way in the robbery of the Quickmart last night? Before age 27, did you ever even make one mistake? Were you born in the month of November? (p. 23)

The questions are usually presented twice in mixed order. Again, it is presumed that a person who is guilty will have the greatest physiological reaction to the relevant questions; a person who is innocent will have the greatest reaction to the control questions.

Polygraph tests normally begin with an extensive pretest interview that usually takes between forty-five to ninety minutes (Raskin and Honts 2002). During this interview, consent to administer the exam is obtained from the subject, biographical data are obtained from the subject, and the crime in question and the subject's version of events are discussed. A description of the polygraph, how it works, and how well it works are discussed. The issues under examination and the exact questions to be asked of the subject are identified and discussed by the investigator administering the exam. The transducers are then attached to the subject. After the questioning is done, an interview is usually conducted. At this time, the subject may be told that he or she was determined to be deceptive (e.g., "You flunked the test"), and this may lead to a more formal interrogation being conducted, including accusations of responsibility for the crime. The entire polygraph process usually lasts between two and three hours.

Estimates regarding the accuracy rates of the polygraph vary. Some studies estimate the CQT technique as producing accuracy rates of 80 percent to 90 percent (see Carroll 1988; Raskin and Honts 2002). Others claim the accuracy rate as closer to 60 percent to 70 percent (Lykken 1998). Leo (2008) explains that the most methodologically sound studies show accuracy rates of 60 percent to 75 percent. As stated by Raskin and Honts (2002), "The voluminous scientific literature indicates that [polygraph examinations] can be highly accurate when properly employed in appropriate circumstances, but they are also subject to abuse and misinterpretation" (p. 38). At the opposite extreme, Blinkhorn (1988) simply states that "there are no good reasons for placing credence in the results

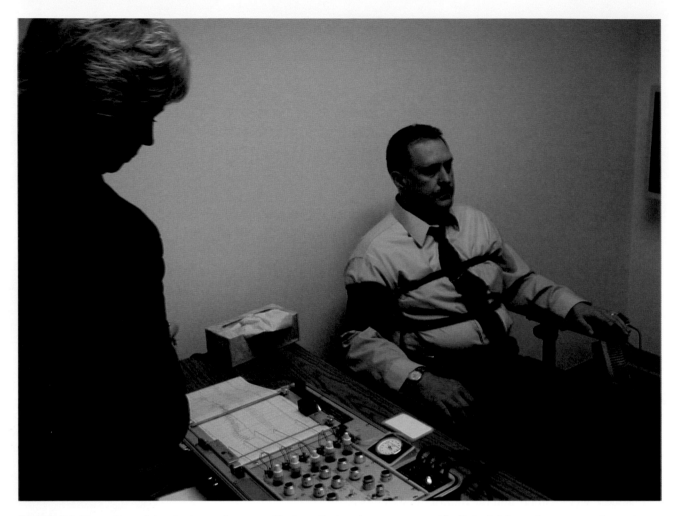

PHOTO 7.3: The polygraph is a tool sometimes used by investigators to measure a subject's truthfulness. Its accuracy depends largely on how competently it is used by its operator.

[the polygraph] produces" (p. 39). The research debate on the validity of polygraph testing is not resolved. However, the one aspect that virtually all research agrees on is that the CQT technique is more prone to false-positive errors (identifying innocent subjects as guilty) than false-negative errors (identifying guilty subjects as innocent) (Lykken 1981; Raskin and Honts 2002).

The usefulness of the polygraph may not rest entirely on its accuracy. The polygraph has proved useful in eliciting confessions regardless of its accuracy (Leo 2008). If a confession is obtained before, during, or after a polygraph test has been conducted, the confession is usually admissible (Raskin and Honts 2002). Furthermore, the polygraph may be useful as a threat by which detectives can judge the reaction of a subject when asked the feared question, "Would you be willing to take a lie detector test?" Indeed, a polygraph test is probably only administered once for every 100 times it is threatened.

Several factors have been identified that can affect the outcome of polygraph examinations. First, research has found that some personality characteristics and disorders may be related to polygraph errors. In particular, psychopaths—as well as others with a low "anxiety IQ"—may be better able to mask deception than others. These individuals may be less aroused, less worried, and generally feel less anxiety regarding the relevant questions in a polygraph examination (Lykken 1981).

Second, continuing research is examining the influence of drugs on the accuracy of polygraph results. Some research shows that subjects under the influence of alcohol or other drugs may be more likely to produce false-positive results (Raskin and Honts 2002).

Third, the skill and experience of the polygraph examiner is a factor shown to be consistently important in the accuracy of polygraph results. The equipment must be properly used, test questions must be properly worded, and the results must be properly interpreted. Examiner error is the most common and consistent problem in the administration of polygraph examinations (Elaad and Kleiner 1990; Raskin and Honts 2002). Interpretation of polygraph results can also be a difficult task. In addition, there is some debate regarding the accuracy of "friendly" polygraph examiners, which are examiners hired by the defense to perform polygraphs on defendants. Although there is no evidence that "friendly" polygraph examiners consistently identify guilty defendants as truthful (Gudjonsson 1992), this issue highlights the possibility that the test procedure may be unstructured enough so that an unethical examiner could easily bias the results.

There is much discussion and debate about whether, or to what degree, the polygraph can be "beat" (i.e., when a deceptive subject could take actions so as to be judged truthful). Gudjonsson (1992) states that "under certain circumstances, the accuracy of the polygraph in detecting deception can be seriously undermined by the use of counter measures" (p. 187). These countermeasures are meant to enhance one's reaction to the control questions so that the physiological response to the control and relevant questions are more similar. Most common are the use of physical manipulations such as inducing physical pain or muscle tension. This can include biting one's tongue, pressing toes against the floor, temporarily stopping breathing, tightening leg or buttocks muscles, and placing a thumbtack in one's sock and stepping on it when the control questions are asked (Gudjonsson 1988; Lykken 1981). Other attempted manipulations are mental countermeasures such as thinking emotionally arousing thoughts as questions are asked. Mental countermeasures are generally less effective than physical ones, but they are impossible to detect. According to Gudjonsson (1988), the use of several countermeasures at the same time appears to increase the likelihood of defeating the polygraph. If any countermeasures have an effect, they most often lead to inconclusive results (Gudjonsson 1988). If any countermeasures are discovered by the polygraph examiner, such actions would be viewed as a failure to cooperate. These actions may clearly be interpreted as attempted deception.

Polygraph results are infrequently admissible in court. The courts' primary objections to the introduction of polygraph results are that they are unreliable, that the polygraph invades the responsibility and task of the jury (to determine guilt or innocence), and that polygraph results, because of their scientific nature, may overwhelmingly influence the jury. Although each of these objections may be subject to debate, this is the prevailing wisdom of courts today. Some states have absolute bans on the introduction of polygraph evidence in court, whereas other states require a stipulation prior to admittance. In states requiring a stipulation, usually the defense and prosecution must agree to introduce the polygraph results. As one would reasonably expect, this is an infrequent occurrence. At the federal level, different circuits have different rules governing the admission of polygraph results. Without specific rules regarding what must be done for polygraph results to be admitted, the Daubert standard applies, leaving the decision to judicial discretion.

COMPUTER VOICE STRESS ANALYZER (CVSA)

The CVSA is a machine that is supposed to detect stress in one's voice. The theory is that deception causes stress, and that this stress can be detected in one's speaking voice. Similar to the polygraph, a subject's known, truthful, verbal response to a control question (e.g., "Are you sitting down?") is compared with a subject's verbal response to a relevant question (e.g., "Did you steal the gold watch?"). Differences in the voiceprint patterns in the

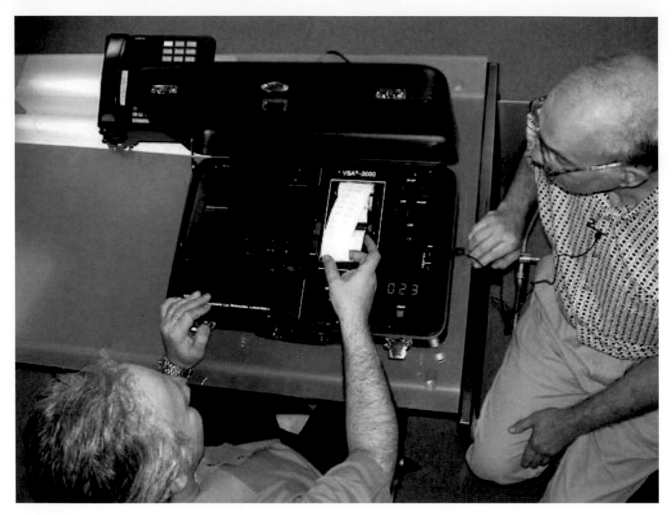

PHOTO 7.4: There is no independent methodologically sound research that indicates that the voice stress analyzer produces valid and reliable results. However, the machine might still be useful in criminal investigations if a subject can be convinced the results are valid.

questions are interpreted as a reflection of deception. The National Institute for Truth Verification markets the CVSA. It explains that, unlike the polygraph, questions are not limited to a yes-or-no response format, the machine cannot be fooled, and that results are not affected by the subject's age, medical condition, or drug use (Leo 2008).

There has been no verifiable scientific research that has demonstrated that stress in one's voice is indicative of deception, nor has any research shown that stress can be measured through voice stress analysis. A study sponsored by the National Institute of Justice found that when subjects were asked about recent drug use, voice stress analysis was able to identify deception about 50 percent of the time (the same probably as flipping a coin); however, subjects were much less likely to be deceptive when reporting recent drug use when they knew that their statements were to be analyzed for deception (Damphousse 2008). In short, the CVSA has about zero validity (Horvath 1982; Lykken 1981; Lykken 1998), but it may induce subjects to tell the truth, at least with regard to certain offenses. Further, in spite of its lack of accuracy, voice stress analysis may still be useful in eliciting confessions from subjects, as was the unfortunate case in the interrogation of Michael Crowe discussed earlier.

MAIN POINTS

1. An interrogation refers to questioning or other action that is intended to elicit incriminating information from a suspect when this information may be used in a criminal prosecution.

2. Usually interrogations are conducted when the suspect is in the custody of the police (i.e., custodial interrogations). Miranda warnings apply to custodial interrogations.

3. The ultimate goal of an interrogation is to obtain a confession; however, an admission, an unambiguous account of actions, or even a firm alibi may be a beneficial result.

4. Interrogations are basically a task of persuasion, of getting suspects to confess to crimes that they do not want to acknowledge.

5. Suspects confess to relieve feelings of guilt, because of persuasive police actions, and/or because of the belief that the police have proof and there is no point in denying the crime.

6. Besides persuasion, interrogations are also based on deceit. Common deceptive tactics used by investigators in conducting interrogations include showing false sympathy and understanding, exaggerating the evidence in the case, exaggerating or deceiving about the role and value of lie detection technology, and misrepresenting the seriousness of the crime.

7. In order for there to be an interrogation, the suspect must first wave his or her Miranda rights. In the overwhelming majority of interrogations, suspects agree to answer the questions of the police. Then, most of the time, suspects confess or say something incriminating.

8. Important ingredients in a successful interrogation are: (1) a plan, (2) adequate time, (3) control of the interrogation, (4) an understanding of the facts of the case, (5) familiarity with the suspect's background, and (6) rapport with the suspect. In addition, investigators should be comfortable using various themes, approaches, and tactics, which may vary based on the particulars of the suspect and the crime.

9. RPM is a potentially useful approach to interrogations. Rationalizations can be offered to make it appear that the suspect's actions were rational and reasonable. Projection refers to assigning responsibility for the criminal actions to someone else. With minimization, the serious of the crime or the suspect's involvement in the crime is reduced. These elements may make a confession easier to make.

10. The feather approach to interrogations is kinder and gentler than the sledgehammer approach. Research shows the feather approach to be more effective at eliciting information.

11. Inbau et al. (2013), the definitive source on the conduct of interrogations, outlines a nine-step approach to interrogations: (1) direct, positive confrontation; (2) theme development; (3) handling denials; (4) overcoming objections; (5) procurement and retention of a suspect's attention; (6) handling a suspect's passive mood; (7) presenting an alternative question; (8) having the suspect orally relate various details of the offense; and (9) converting an oral confession into a written confession.

12. False confessions are an extremely troubling issue given the persuasiveness of confessions in establishing proof.

13. There are three reasons for falsely confessing (or three types of false confessions): stress compliant false confessions, persuaded false confessions, and voluntary false confessions.

14. False confession cases have many of the same interrogation characteristics as true confession cases.

15. The Miranda requirements have little impact on, and offer little protection from, false confessions.

16. The basic theory underlying the behavioral detection of deception is that a person who is being deceptive is under increased physiological stress and that this stress can be detected and, in some cases, measured.

17. The accurate detection of deception through verbal and nonverbal behavior (kinesics) is difficult and prone to error, although there are verbal and nonverbal behaviors that tend to indicate deception.

18. A polygraph is used to detect physiological responses associated with deception. Various methods can be used to conduct a polygraph examination; the most common today is the Control Question Technique (CQT).

19. The best research shows polygraph accuracy rates of 60 percent to 70 percent. It is more common that innocent (truthful) subjects are identified as guilty than guilty (deceptive) subjects are identified as innocent. Much of the accuracy of the polygraph depends on the skill and capabilities of the polygraph examiner.

20. Most research indicates that the computer voice stress analyzer detects deception with about 50 percent accuracy, the same as flipping a coin.

IMPORTANT TERMS

Confession

Congruence and incongruence

Control Question Technique (CQT)

Created jobs

Custodial interrogation

Emblems

Emotional offender

False confession

False-positive and false-negative errors in polygraph examinations

Feather approach

Fight-or-flight syndrome

Guilty Knowledge Test

Illustrators

Interrogation plan

Interrogation themes and tactics

Kinesics

Nonemotional offenders

Persuaded false confession

Polygraph

Rationalization, projection, minimalization (RPM)

Relevant-Irrelevant Test (RIT)

Sledgehammer approach

Stress compliant false confession

Verbal behavior as an indicator of deception

Voice stress analysis

Voluntary false confession

QUESTIONS FOR DISCUSSION AND REVIEW

1. What are the differences between an interrogation and an interview? What is the ultimate goal of an interrogation? Why must an investigator be careful in pursuing this goal?

2. What are the different ways an investigator can legally use deception in an interrogation?

3. Why is spending enough time and having a plan important in an interrogation? What are the other ingredients of a successful interrogation?

4. What is the role of rationalization, projection, and minimization (RPM) in interrogations? What is the difference between the sledgehammer and feather approach in interrogations? Generally, which approach is more effective?

5. What are the nine steps in an interrogation according to Inbau et al. (2013)?

6. What are the differences between emotional and nonemotional offenders? Why is this distinction important? What themes are most effective with each of these offenders?

7. Why do people confess to crimes that they committed? Why might people confess to crimes that they did not commit?

8. Why does Miranda offer little protection from false confessions?

9. What is the theory underlying the detection of deception? How does this theory relate to the polygraph and to nonverbal behavior in particular?

10. What are the verbal and nonverbal behaviors that tend to indicate deception?

11. What is a polygraph? What are the primary methods of conducting a polygraph examination? What are false-positive errors and false-negative errors in polygraph examinations? Which is more common?

12. What are the uses of the polygraph and the results of a polygraph? Are polygraph results admissible in court? How else could they be used?

STUDENT STUDY SITE

Visit **www.sagepub.com/brandl3e** to access additional study tools including eFlashcards, web quizzes, web resources, video resources, and SAGE journal articles.

8

Behavioral Analysis and Other Related Evidence

Objectives

After reading this chapter you will be able to:

- Discuss crime scene profiling, geographical profiling, and psycholinguistics as forms of behavioral analysis

- Discuss the process of crime scene profiling, including the types of crimes for which profiling is most suitable, and the goals associated with crime scene profiling

- Differentiate between crime scene profiling, prospective offender profiling, and life history profiling

- Discuss the importance and usefulness of the distinction between organized and disorganized offenders and crime scenes

- Differentiate between MO and signature, and trophies and souvenirs

- Discuss how characteristics of the victim may reveal information about the offender

- Discuss staging, its meaning, and its drawbacks as an investigative clue

- Identify and discuss the premise and assumptions of geographical profiling, as well as its limitations

- Define psycholinguistics as an investigative tool and discuss how (and with what effect) psycholinguistics was applied to the Lindbergh baby kidnaping, the Unabomber investigation, the anthrax letter investigation, and the ransom note in the Ramsey murder investigation

From the CASE FILE
A Mutilation Murder

THE CRIME

The New York City Police Department requested the assistance of the FBI after police detectives came to an apparent dead end in their investigation of the murder and mutilation of a twenty-six-year-old woman whose body was found on the roof of a Bronx public housing apartment building where she had lived with her parents. An investigative task force of twenty-six detectives and supervisors had interviewed more than 2,000 individuals, many of whom lived or worked in the apartment building. Record checks of known sex offenders in the area were of no assistance. The police had twenty-two "good" suspects but nothing conclusive.

A fifteen-year-old boy had discovered the victim's wallet in the stairwell as he was leaving the building on his way to school. On returning home from school for lunch that afternoon, the boy gave the wallet to his father, who in turn went to the victim's apartment to return it. The victim's mother then called the day care center where the victim worked to notify her daughter

that her wallet was found. At that time, the victim's mother was told that her daughter had not shown up for work that morning. The mother, the victim's sister, and a neighbor then proceeded to search the building and discovered the body. The body was located at 3:00 p.m.; the victim had left her apartment at approximately 6:15 a.m.

The victim was found nude. She had been beaten about the face and strangled with the strap of her purse. The cause of death was determined to be strangulation—first manual and then ligature. The victim's jaw and nose were broken, and several of her teeth were loosened. She sustained several other facial fractures. Her nipples had been cut off after death and were placed on her chest. There were bite marks, which were determined to have occurred after death, on her thighs. Numerous contusions and lacerations were present on her body. "You can't stop me" was written in ink on the inside of her thigh, and "fuck you" was written on her abdomen. A necklace pendant that she usually wore was missing and presumed taken by the killer. Her underpants were placed on her head and pulled over her face. Her nylons were removed and were loosely tied around her wrists and ankles. Her earrings were removed and placed symmetrically on each side of her head. An umbrella and writing pen had been forced into her vagina, and a hair comb was placed in her pubic hair. Semen was recovered from the victim's body; it appeared that the killer stood over the victim and masturbated. Human feces were discovered on the roof landing and were covered with the victim's clothing.

KEY CRIME SCENE CHARACTERISTICS

The crime did not appear to be planned. All the instruments used to perpetrate the crime were the victim's (e.g., purse strap, umbrella, pen), except for the knife used to remove the victim's nipples. This knife was probably small enough to have been routinely carried by the killer. He probably first hit her with his fist to render her unconscious and then used his hands and the purse strap to strangle her. These are weapons of opportunity. He did not have a gun, rope, tape, or gag. If the perpetrator had such "tools," it would indicate a degree of planning. Rather, this crime appeared to have been a spontaneous event. In addition, the victim did not appear to have been threatened by the perpetrator's presence. She did not attempt to flee or scream prior to being rendered unconscious by the offender. The initial violence to the victim was sudden.

Although the crime was unplanned, it did appear to be well rehearsed and thought out. The positioning of the victim, the mutilation of the victim, the placement of the umbrella and pen, the removal and placement of the earrings, the writing on the body, and the bite marks indicated that the perpetrator was acting out something that he had seen before. The crime may have been based on sexual fantasies that may have been rooted in sadistic and violent pornography.

The offender was best classified as disorganized (see a later discussion for details on this classification and the importance of it). The crime appeared to be a spontaneous event. The victim was not stalked, but confronted. The victim appeared to have been immediately overcome with sudden violence and rendered unconscious. The victim was not moved from the general crime scene. The dead body was left in view at the location in which she was probably killed. There were sexual acts performed on the body after death. Evidence and the tools used to commit the crime were left at the scene. All of these crime scene characteristics are reflective of a disorganized offender.

The crime was high risk. It was committed in daylight. Considerable time was spent by the offender in perpetrating the crime (e.g., removing earrings, masturbating, defecating). The victim was at low risk of becoming a victim. She was a quiet woman, small in stature (4'11," 90 lbs.). She was plain looking and did not date. She lived with her parents. Her lifestyle did not expose her to much risk for victimization. The area in which the crime occurred was a low violent crime area, further reducing the likelihood of victimization.

THE RESULTING CRIME SCENE PROFILE

The profile suggested that the offender was a white man, between twenty-five and thirty-five years of age, and of average appearance. The methodical organization of the crime scene—positioning of the body, placement of earrings, etc.—would be unusual for an impulsive teenager or someone in his early twenties. It was not likely that the perpetrator was in his late thirties or forties because someone of that age would have probably committed earlier murders, and it would be difficult for a person to commit such crimes over the span of years without being apprehended. He was of average intelligence and a high school or college dropout. He was unemployed; if employed, it was in a blue-collar or unskilled job. Alcohol or drugs did not play a role in the crime. The suspect was socially inadequate and not married. He lived or worked near the crime scene. All these characteristics are typical of disorganized murderers.

The fact that the crime was a spontaneous event further increased the probability that the offender lived or worked near the scene of the crime. He had reason to be there at 6:15 a.m. If he was not planning to commit the crime at that time, he had to have some other reason for being there—probably because of employment or because he lived in the apartment building.

The sexual acts performed on the victim showed sadistic tendencies and obvious mental problems. The perpetrator likely had a collection of pornography. A rage or hatred of women was present in the crime. That he inflicted these acts on a dead or unconscious victim indicates an inability to interact with a live or conscious person and reinforced his social inadequacy.

The fact that the crime was high risk (e.g., committed in daylight, in a public place, and took considerable time) and that the victim was at a low risk for victimization suggests, once again, that the killer felt comfortable in the area. He has been there before and believed no one would interrupt the crime. He was familiar with the area and likely lived or worked there.

THE OUTCOME

After receiving the profile of the killer, the police reviewed their list of twenty-two suspects. One person seemed to match the profile more closely than the others. The suspect's father lived on the same floor of the apartment building as the victim. The suspect's father had initially told the police that his son was a patient at a local psychiatric hospital. Now, upon investigating further, the police learned that the son had been missing from the hospital the day and evening prior to the murder. Investigators discovered that he was unemployed and had dropped out of school. He was thirty years old and was never married. He had no girlfriends. He suffered from depression and was receiving treatment at the psychiatric hospital. He had attempted suicide before and after the offense. A collection of pornography was discovered during a search of the suspect's father's apartment.

The suspect was arrested, tried, and found guilty of the homicide. He never confessed to the crime, but it was proved that security was lax at the hospital in which he was staying; he could come and go as he wished. The bite marks that he inflicted on the victim were the most influential evidence against the suspect at trial. Several forensic odontologists testified that the suspect's teeth impressions matched the bite marks found on the victim's body. He was sentenced to twenty-five years to life for the crime (see Douglas et al. 1986; Geberth 1996; and Porter 1983). (Note: This crime occurred before DNA printing was available.)

Case Considerations and Points for Discussion

- What was the most important evidence that led to this extraordinarily brutal murder being solved? How valuable was the crime scene profile in the investigation? If DNA printing was available at the time of this investigation, would the conduct of the investigation have differed? How?

- Do you think investigators made any mistakes in this investigation? If not for the crime scene profile, do you think the killer would have been identified?

- What do you think should be the biggest lessons learned by the police as a result of this case?

Also:

- See the YouTube video "Former FBI Serial Killer Expert John Douglas," www.youtube.com/watch?v=OFX8_I16SUU. Douglas talks about psychological and criminal profiling (approximately twenty-five minutes).

••• Behavioral Analysis Defined

Behavioral analysis is a broad term that includes crime scene profiling, geographic profiling, and linguistic analysis. Although other activities may also be included under behavioral analysis (Bartol and Bartol 2013), these three investigative activities share several important features. First, each is designed to help identify an unknown perpetrator of a known specific crime. Second, each activity represents a means by which information on the *type* of person who committed the crime may be developed. Third, crime scene profiling, geographic profiling, and linguistic analysis are each based on an analysis of certain features and characteristics of the crimes in question. This chapter provides a discussion of these activities.

••• Crime Scene Profiling

Crime scene profiling, sometimes referred to as psychological profiling or behavioral profiling, is "a technique for identifying the major personality and behavioral characteristics of an individual based upon an analysis of the crimes he or she has committed" (Douglas et al.

1986, p. 413). In particular, as shown in the profile presented above, crime scene profiles often include information about the offender's race, age or age range, employment status, type of employment, marital status, level of education, and location of residence (Holmes and Holmes 2009). Also as shown in the introductory case example, crime scene profiles are most useful in focusing the investigation by reducing the number of suspects considered by the police. The crime scene profiling process is oriented toward answering questions about the *type* of person who committed a particular crime. Crime scene profiles are not capable of identifying a suspect when one is not already known. Never has a profile by itself solved a crime. Along with identifying the major characteristics of the offender, a profile may also provide authorities with information about items that are likely to be found in possession of the offender, such as news clippings, photos, or pornography. A profile may also include information about the interrogation tactics that would be most effective with the offender (Holmes and Holmes 2009).

MYTHS & MISCONCEPTIONS 8.1

Criminal Minds

The show *Criminal Minds* is a popular CBS television drama that first aired in 2005. The show features a team of FBI profilers and analysts who work in the FBI's Behavioral Analysis Unit. They profile crimes and then arrest those who committed them. A key character in the show is Penelope, who, with her computer, is able to provide the profilers with instantaneous information from vast databases to help develop the profiles and apprehend offenders.

Criminal Minds is to crime scene profiling what *CSI* is to scientific evidence. *Criminal Minds* presents a seriously distorted image as to the role and value of crime scene profiles in the criminal investigation process. The fact is that if the only evidence in an investigation is a crime scene profile, it is extremely unlikely that the crime will be solved. As also discussed later in this chapter, because crime scene profiles are usually performed only in cases that remain unsolved after some time due to the lack of good evidence in the case, it should not be too surprising that psychological profiles seldom lead to the identification and apprehension of offenders. In this way, psychological profiles are similar to many types of physical evidence—they are not very effective at identifying a suspect when one has not already been identified in some other way.

Crime scene profiling is different from the controversial practice often referred to as *prospective offender profiling* (Bartol and Bartol 2013). Prospective offender profiling consists of the identification of the type of person believed to be most commonly involved in a particular type of crime and the targeting of individuals by the police who match this description. Offender profiling is criticized because one of the primary descriptive features of suspected offenders is often race, hence the familiar practice of racial profiling. Crime scene profiling is also different from the profiling that occurs when psychologists and psychiatrists attempt to understand the life histories and current motivations of criminals. As an example, behavioral scientists from the FBI have interviewed suspected al-Qaeda members imprisoned at the naval base in Guantanamo Bay, Cuba, to understand better the motivations of terrorists (Newton 2002). Clearly this process is different than crime scene profiling, as illustrated in the introductory case example.

Information and details about the crimes committed represent the major input into the crime scene profiling process. Previous similar crimes for which offenders have been apprehended are used as a basis on which to identify the characteristics of the person who committed the current crime. As such, crime scene profiles are based on probabilities and inferences. For example, research has established that a serial rapist usually comes from "an average or advantaged home, and as an adult, is a well-groomed, intelligent, employed individual who is living with others in a family context" (Hazelwood and Warren 1989, p. 25; also see Rossmo 2000). Accordingly, a profile developed on an unidentified serial rapist may include this baseline description; other details may be added depending on unique features of the crimes committed.

Crime scene profiling is most appropriate "where discernible patterns are able to be deciphered from the crime scene or where the fantasy/motive of the perpetrator is readily apparent" (Holmes and Holmes 2009, p. 4). In particular, profiling is most suitable for crimes in which the perpetrator has shown indications of psychopathy, such as lust and mutilation murders, murders that involve postmortem slashing and cutting, evisceration, sexual homicide, rape, sadistic sexual assaults, pedophilia, "motiveless" fire setting, and satanic and ritualistic crime (Holmes and Holmes 2009). However, basic elements of the crime scene profiling process may be applied to other crimes as well. For example, consider a case in which a house was burglarized and an Xbox video game unit was the only property taken. Nothing else was disturbed. Based on this limited information about the crime, one may be able to take some educated guesses about the characteristics of the person who committed the crime. Since nothing else was taken or disturbed, a reasonable guess may be that the perpetrator entered the house for the specific purpose of taking the Xbox. If this is the case, this person must have known that an Xbox was in the house, perhaps because he or she was in the house previously and had seen or even played it. As such, perhaps the perpetrator is a friend (or neighbor) of the individual who owned and played the Xbox. Furthermore, it would make sense that the perpetrator is about the same age, or in the same age range, as the individual in the house who was the primary player of the Xbox. Chances are that the perpetrator is male because men/boys seem to have more of an attraction to video games (or at least to certain types of video games) and are overrepresented as burglary offenders. In sum, based on a simple analysis of a not-very-complicated crime, it would be reasonable to suggest that the perpetrator of the crime is male, probably in his teens, is a friend of the primary player of the XBox, and may live in the neighborhood, perhaps even next door. Might this profile be correct? Might certain aspects of it be wrong? Certainly. Again, a profile is a probabilistic statement based on an understanding of the current crime as well as previous similar crimes.

There are several basic assumptions to the profiling process (see Holmes and Holmes 2009). First is that the crime reflects the characteristics and personality of the offender. As stated by Douglas et al. (1986), "Behavior reflects personality, and by examining behavior the investigator may be able to determine what type of person is responsible for the offense" (p. 403). This concept is similar to the idea that one's personality is reflected, to some extent, in the clothes one wears, the car one drives, and the decorations in one's home. This is especially true if the clothing, car, or decorations are unusual or uncommon (see Exhibit 8.1). As discussed in more detail later, the manner in which the victim was killed, the amount of planning apparently involved in the crime, and how the victim was selected represent important clues about the characteristics of the offender.

A second assumption of the profiling process is that the offender's personality will not change, or at least not dramatically or quickly. One's personality is a product of biology and a lifetime of experiences. As a simple example, people have preferences for different colors and these preferences are often viewed, to some extent, as a reflection of one's personality (e.g., a person who has a color preference for black may differ in certain personality traits than a person whose favorite color is yellow). If your favorite color is pink, it is unlikely that tomorrow your favorite color will be grey. As part of the personality, people develop preferences and these preferences are unlikely to change. Even if a person wishes to change his or her personality and preferences, it is unlikely that person will be able to do so.

The third assumption is that the offender's method of operation (MO) will remain similar across crimes. MO refers to the actions taken to commit the crime. Offenders develop

Exhibit 8.1   What Does Your Car Say about You?

Men and women have different criteria for selecting a car. According to an article in *Forbes* magazine (Mitchell 2008), women tend to mention safety, reliability, and value as being most important in a vehicle, whereas men prefer performance, power, and style.

Not surprisingly then, some vehicles are more likely to be purchased and driven by men compared to women. For example, buyers of the Porsche 911 vehicle are 86.8 percent male; they have an average age of fifty-one and a median annual income of $390,000. So, what would you infer to be the characteristics of

a person that drives a Porsche 911? How about someone who drives a Lexus RX 350 SUV? Approximately 66 percent of its buyers are female, and 78 percent are married. Their median annual income is $141,000 and their average age is fifty-five.

What do you think would be some of the characteristics of a person who drives a Hummer? Or a Toyota Prius?

The point is that a person's car, just like a crime scene, says things about that person's personality and characteristics.

methods of committing crimes in which they feel comfortable, and these methods are unlikely to change dramatically. An MO may include, for example, the manner in which entry was gained into a residence, the method used to abduct the victim, or the way the victim was killed.

Fourth is that the signature of the offender will remain the same across crimes. Signature is what is done by the offender to derive emotional satisfaction from the crime. It is based in fantasy. It is a unique and personal expression of the offender (Douglas and Munn 1992). Signature may include, for example, the type and nature of injuries inflicted on the victim, or specific forms of torture inflicted on the victim (Hazelwood et al. 1992). It may include souvenir and trophy collection. Signature is less likely to change than MO (Douglas and Munn 1992).

The final but perhaps most important assumption of the profiling process is offered by Tonkin et al. (2009). It is referred to as the homology assumption. It refers to the principle that offenders with similar crime behaviors share similar characteristics. This assumption is important in that much of the profiling process is based on the belief that the unknown offender in the present offense has characteristics in common with known offenders who have committed previous similar offenses.

THE HISTORY OF CRIME SCENE/PSYCHOLOGICAL PROFILING

Psychological profiling is not a new phenomenon even though it has only become a widely known investigative technique during the past twenty-five years. One of the first written accounts of the practice of psychological profiling was in Edgar Allan Poe's 1841 classic *Murders in the Rue Morgue,* in which, based on an analysis of how the murders were committed, it was concluded that only an ape could have perpetrated the crime. Attempts were made to construct a profile of Jack the Ripper based on the mutilation murders of several women in the late 1800s in England. A crime scene profile was developed on the crimes of New York City's Mad Bomber in the 1950s and the Boston Strangler in the 1960s. It was not until the late 1970s, however, with the creation of the Behavioral Science Unit in Quantico, Virginia, that the FBI got involved in the practice of psychological profiling. In 1991, the movie *Silence of the Lambs* was the first to bring psychological profiling into popular culture. Today, psychological profiling is primarily the expertise of a select group of agents of the FBI, along with a number of other independent psychologists, psychiatrists, and behavioral scientists (Holmes and Holmes 2009).

PHOTO 8.1: *Silence of the Lambs* featured Clarice Starling (Jody Foster) as a young FBI agent who enlisted the help of serial killer Hannibal Lecter to apprehend "Buffalo Bill," another serial killer. The Academy-Award-winning movie made psychological profiling famous.

THE CONSTRUCTION OF PSYCHOLOGICAL PROFILES

The construction of psychological profiles is often seen as a mysterious process during which it is unclear how seemingly minuscule bits of information about a crime, or a series of crimes, are turned into clues about the identity of the perpetrator. The mystery is perpetuated when profilers do not explain the basis for their predictions. As a famous and often-used example, consider the profile developed for New York City's Mad Bomber in the 1950s. The profile developed by Dr. James A. Brussel, a New York psychiatrist, read simply as follows: "Look for a heavy man. Middle aged. Foreign born. Roman Catholic. Single. Lives with a brother or sister. When you find him, chances are he'll be wearing a double-breasted suit. Buttoned" (Geberth 1996, p. 708). When the man believed to be the Mad Bomber, George Metesky, was apprehended, he matched the profile exactly, including the buttoned double-breasted suit (Geberth 1996). Psychological profiling is not a mystery. It involves a process of mapping the characteristics of offenders of previously solved crimes onto offenders of currently unsolved crimes. The details about an offender that are provided in a profile are simply the result of an educated guess based on an understanding of the crime and the sort of person who would commit it.

There are several steps in the process of constructing a crime scene profile (see Bartol and Bartol 2013; Holmes and Holmes 2009; O'Toole 1999; and Pinizzotto and Finkel 1990). The first step is to develop an understanding and classification of the current crime. This involves the examination and review of police reports, the crime scene, crime scene photographs, witness statements, forensic laboratory reports, autopsy reports, autopsy photographs, and other materials that may be available. The second step is to examine the background and activities of the victim. Information about the victim's traits, marital status, lifestyle, occupation, and so forth represents important input in the profiling process. Third, the suspected motivation for the crime is considered. The fourth step is to identify the characteristics of individuals who have committed this type of offense in the past. This understanding may be based on experience or research that has examined similar previous offenders/crimes. Finally, a description of the overt characteristics of the perpetrator is provided.

In constructing a profile of a murderer, a fundamental and important classification is made between organized and disorganized crime scenes (Bartol and Bartol 2013; Holmes and Holmes 2009; Geberth 1996; Ressler and Burgess 1985) (see Table 8.1). Although this distinction was first made in 1985, it is still used today as a basis upon which to classify homicide crime scenes. An organized crime scene is likely to be orderly and reflect a high degree of control. The scene tends to be neat, even clean. There is most often little or no evidence present at the scene, nor is a weapon likely to be found there. The condition of the scene suggests that the offense was planned. The victim is likely to be a targeted stranger. Restraints are likely to have been used on the victim. Aggressive acts are likely to have occurred on the victim prior to death. The victim's body is likely to have been moved or transported and is likely to be hidden.

A disorganized crime scene, on the other hand, is likely to be sloppy and disorderly. There is most often evidence, or even a weapon, present at the scene. The weapon is likely to be something that the offender either did not carry with him or her to the crime scene (e.g., a telephone cord used to strangle the victim) or that was easily carried to the scene (e.g., a small knife). The condition of the scene suggests that the offense was not planned. The victim or the location of the murder is likely to be familiar to the offender. The victim is likely to have been overcome by a sudden and overwhelming attack. Restraints are not likely to have been used on the victim. Sexual acts are likely to have occurred with the victim after death. The victim's body is likely to be left at the death/murder scene.

This classification scheme has been developed as a result of research conducted by the FBI and has been shown to be valid (Homant and Kennedy 1998; Bartol and Bartol 2013). The value of the organized/disorganized classification is that various characteristics have been

TABLE 8.1	Crime Scene Differences between Organized and Disorganized Murderers
ORGANIZED	**DISORGANIZED**
Planned offense	Spontaneous offense
Victim a targeted stranger	Victim/location known
Personalizes victim	Depersonalizes victim
Controlled conversation	Minimal conversation
Crime scene reflects overall control	Crime scene random and sloppy
Demands submissive victim	Sudden death to victim
Restraints used	Minimal use of restraints
Aggressive acts prior to death	Sexual acts after death
Body hidden	Body left in view
Weapon/evidence absent	Evidence/weapon often present
Transports victim or body	Body left at death scene

Source: Robert K. Ressler and Ann W. Burgess. 1985. "Crime Scene and Profile Characteristics of Organized and Disorganized Murderers." *FBI Law Enforcement Bulletin* 54(8): 18–25.

associated with offenders who produce the different types of crime scenes (see Table 8.2). In particular, a typical offender who leaves a disorganized crime scene (i.e., a disorganized murderer) usually ranges in age from sixteen to late thirties. He is usually the same race as the victim, is single, and lives alone (the majority of murders are committed by men, so the pronoun *he* is used throughout the following paragraphs). The offender is usually of below-average intelligence and is often a high school dropout, or at least a marginal student. He may have a history of mental illness. Geberth (1996) adds that a disorganized murderer usually has a thin build and has some form of physical or verbal impediment. He tends to live or work near the crime scene and may not own a vehicle. If a vehicle is owned, it is often an older model that is "junky" in appearance. If the offender is employed, it is usually in unskilled work (e.g., dishwasher, maintenance, etc.).

Disorganized murderers usually do not have any prior military history. Previous arrests for offenses such as voyeurism, burglary, or exhibitionism are common. The disorganized murderer is often a loner and might be considered by others as "weird" or "odd" (Geberth 1996). He is sexually incompetent and may never have had a sexual experience with someone of the opposite sex. Interpersonal relationships are difficult for the disorganized offender.

A typical organized murder offender is usually approximately the same age as the victim. The mean age for this type of offender is younger than thirty-five years. He is usually the same race as the victim. He is usually married or living with a partner. He is usually of average or above-average intelligence and may have attended or graduated college. He is not likely to have a history of mental illness. He is likely to be well built, even athletic (Geberth 1996). He most often lives away from the crime scene and has a clean and well-maintained car. He is likely to be employed in a skilled profession. He may have a military history. He may have previous arrests for offenses such as driving while intoxicated, interpersonal violence, or sex

TABLE 8.2 Profile Characteristics of Organized and Disorganized Murderers

ORGANIZED	DISORGANIZED
Average to above average intelligence	Below average intelligence
Socially competent	Socially inadequate
Skilled work preferred	Unskilled work
Sexually competent	Sexually incompetent
High birth order	Low birth order
Father's work stable	Father's work unstable
Inconsistent childhood discipline	Harsh discipline as a child
Controlled mood during the crime	Anxious mood during crime
Use of alcohol with the crime	Minimal use of alcohol
Precipitating situational stress	Minimal situational stress
Living with partner	Living alone
Mobility with car in good condition	Lives/works near the crime scene
Follows crime in news media	Minimal interest in news media
May change jobs or leave town	Significant behavior change (drug/alchohol abuse, religion, etc.)

Source: Robert K. Ressler and Ann W. Burgess. 1985. "Crime Scene and Profile Characteristics of Organized and Disorganized Murderers." *FBI Law Enforcement Bulletin* 54(8): 18–25.

offenses (Geberth 1996). He is usually an outgoing, socially competent person. He may be described as a "good talker" and a "lady's man" (Geberth 1996). In short, as explained by Douglas et al. (1986):

> Motivation is more easily determined in the organized offender who premeditates, plans, and has the ability to carry out a plan of action that is logical and complete. On the other hand, the disorganized offender carries out his crimes by motivations that frequently are derived from mental illness and accompanied distorted thinking. (p. 414)

The organized/disorganized classification and corresponding characteristics are ideal types. In the real world, "pure" organized crime scenes and offenders and "pure" disorganized crime scenes and offenders may not be frequently encountered. Such cases fall into a mixed category where the most important dimensions of the crime must be determined and analyzed. Exactly what is most important is yet to be clearly articulated (Homant and Kennedy 1998). In other cases that reflect a mix of organization and disorganization, this may be because more than one offender was involved in the crime (e.g., one offender was disorganized, one was organized). Note that the crime scene described in the introduction to this chapter fits well into the disorganized category, as did the offender.

THE MEANING OF PERPETRATOR ACTIONS AND CRIME CHARACTERISTICS

Beyond the primary classification of a crime scene as being organized or disorganized, and the associated link to offender characteristics, there are other inputs to the crime scene profiling process. First, for example, the crime may reveal whether the offender has likely struck before or may strike again. For a murder, such evidence consists of postmortem mutilation or cannibalism, particular positioning of the corpse, sexual assault, overkill, torture, souvenir and trophy collection, and necrophilia (Kocsis and Irwin 1998). Souvenirs provide the culprit with a memory of the victim and the crime (e.g., an earring taken from the victim). Trophies are something of intrinsic value to the offender, a reward for committing the crime (e.g., a body part) (Holmes and Holmes 2009). In a rape, evidence that the perpetrator committed previous crimes or will likely commit future crimes consists of the manifestation of sadistic or violent behavior, verbal scripts demanded from the victim, the offender's inability to penetrate the victim or to climax, and souvenir or trophy collection (Kocsis and Irwin 1998). With arson, such evidence consists of sexual activity at the crime scene, the presence of signature (e.g., graffiti, described later), destruction of property in addition to the fire damage, and particular behaviors used in the setting of the fire (Kocsis and Irwin 1998).

Second, crimes may reveal if they were committed by the same person, and this information may be included in a profile. As discussed earlier, individuals' preferences tend to remain relatively stable. Personalities do not change or, if they do, they change gradually. Human beings are creatures of habit. As such, an offender's behavior at a crime scene may indicate whether the offender has committed other crimes as well. An understanding of the offender's MO and signature are significant in this regard. As noted, MO refers to the actions taken to commit the crime. Signature is what is done by the offender to derive emotional satisfaction from the crime.

Although the distinction between MO and signature may initially appear clear, there are problems. First, signature may also change. It may evolve; it may become more developed and clearer over time. Second, signature may not be present at every crime scene. The offender may be interrupted or may not have received the expected or desired victim response. Third, signature may not be obvious or even identifiable because of its subtle nature or even because of factors such as decomposition of the body. Finally, it may not be discernible as to what is MO and what is signature. For example, it is possible that a particular method used by an offender to abduct a victim may actually be emotionally satisfying to the offender, to be signature and not just MO. Or, as an example discussed earlier in the book, consider the robber who demanded that victims remove their pants after they gave him their money. Was this action part of his MO or was it signature? It is difficult to determine. In any case, even if MO is not differentiated from signature, behavioral patterns evident in a crime or crime scene may serve to establish a link between crimes, and this may be determined through the process of psychological profiling.

Third, information about the victim may reveal characteristics of the offender. As noted by Rossmo (2000), "Victim choice may provide insights to the nature of the offender, and detailed victimology is one of the key information requirements in the criminal profiling process" (p. 27). Particularly informative is an assessment of how prone the victim was to criminal attack. According to Hazelwood (1995), a low-risk victim is one whose activities would not normally expose the victim to risk of criminal victimization. A murderer or rapist who victimizes this type of individual is likely to know the victim and to seek out the victim (O'Toole 1999). A moderate-risk victim is one whose victimization risk is elevated because of employment (e.g., nature of employment, working hours), lifestyle (e.g., dating), or personal habits (e.g., going for long walks at night). A high-risk victim is one whose lifestyle (e.g., drug dealing) or employment (e.g., prostitution) consistently exposes him or her to the risk of victimization. The probability of constructing an accurate profile with high-risk victims is small, simply because the number of potential offenders is large (O'Toole 1999). Information about the victim may also be helpful for other investigative purposes. In particular, information about the victim's lifestyle, occupation, last known activities, and so forth may bring to light the victim's associates, friends, enemies, and other possible suspects (Holmes and Holmes 2009).

Fourth, an assessment of the risk associated with the crime itself is an important input in the profiling process. The risk associated with a crime is determined by the circumstances of that crime, such as the place that it occurred, the time of day at which it occurred, and the type of victim involved. Crimes that are high risk to the offender usually indicate either that the offender targeted that particular victim (and that there was a relationship between the victim and the offender), or that the offender needed an element of high risk or thrill to be satisfied by the crime (i.e., signature) (O'Toole 1999).

Fifth, the offender's method of approach or attack may provide clues regarding his characteristics. A surprise or blitz-style attack during which the victim was immediately rendered unconscious may indicate a lack of social abilities on the part of the offender. Low self-esteem or a verbal or physical impediment of some sort may prevent a conversation to be used to lure the victim away (Geberth 1996). In addition, a blitz-style attack often indicates a younger killer and, as noted, a disorganized offender. A victim who was killed slowly and methodically indicates a more sadistic personality and an offender in his twenties or thirties. Defensive injuries, such as knife wounds to hands, are an indication that the attack was not blitz style. The presence of defensive injuries on the victim often indicates that the interaction began as a verbal exchange or altercation and was followed by physical assault, during which the victim had time and warning to react (O'Toole 1999).

Sixth, evidence of depersonalization may be indicative of the characteristics of the offender. For example, trauma to the face usually indicates a relationship between a victim and an offender; the more severe the attack, the closer the relationship. The use of blindfolds on the victim and covering the victim's face may or may not be indicative of a relationship between the offender and the victim (Holmes and Holmes 2009). Holmes and Holmes note that forced oral sex with a blindfold on the victim usually indicates a stranger-perpetrated crime; no blindfold usually indicates an acquaintance-perpetrated crime. In general, acts of depersonalization are often associated with disorganized murderers.

Seventh, interestingly, Holmes and Holmes (2009) explain that the use of duct tape in the crime can reveal information about the background of the offender. In particular, "When duct tape is used on a murder victim, it may be an indication that the perpetrator has been in prison at some time or is a past or present member of a special services branch of the military" (p. 143).

Finally, the presence of staging may reveal information about the identity of the culprit. Staging "occurs when someone purposely alters the crime scene prior to the arrival of the police" (Douglas and Munn 1992, p. 7). Staging consists of the introduction of false clues designed to throw the police investigation off course. For example, it may appear that a door was broken down in order to gain entry into the house when in fact a key was used to the door and the door was damaged simply as staging. A crime scene is usually staged by an offender who knows or is familiar with the victim. The staging is done in an attempt to distract the police from discovering such a relationship. In this situation, staging is most often done by an organized offender. Another reason why scenes may be staged is to protect the victim or the victim's family from embarrassment. For example, in rape/murder cases or autoerotic deaths, the family member who discovers the body may dress the victim or make it look like a suicide, sometimes even writing a suicide note (Douglas and Munn 1992). Although the presence of staging may allow one to infer information about the identity of the perpetrator, the difficulty is that it may be hard to determine whether a particular crime scene dimension is staged or whether it is legitimate. In short, the recognition of staging at the crime scene may provide useful clues, but staging is not always easily identifiable.

As a side note, it is worthwhile to highlight that research, although quite limited, has examined how and in what way various types of crime scene evidence may reveal the perpetrator's characteristics. As an example of such a study is Tonkin et al. (2009). These researchers studied the possible relationships between an offender's shoes (as determined by footwear impressions and prints left at crime scenes) and the offender's characteristics. They found that unemployed offenders who lived in economically disadvantaged areas were more likely to wear expensive shoes to the crimes they committed. Apparently, not only does your car reflect your characteristics (Exhibit 8.1), so do your shoes. While there were many limitations to this study, it represents an interesting avenue for further research on the information inputs to behavioral profiles.

THE EFFECTIVENESS OF CRIME SCENE PROFILES

Psychological profiles are most often used when all leads have been exhausted in an investigation, which may happen relatively quickly in some crimes, particularly those without an apparent "normal" motive such as passion, hatred, revenge, jealousy, or fear (Douglas 1996). Motive often casts light on the relationship between the victim and the perpetrator and, hence, on possible suspects. For example, investigators attempt to determine who was jealous of the victim, who hated the victim, and so forth, because people who hate each other or are jealous of each other are also often known to each other. Motive links victims and perpetrators together. Because psychological profiles are often used in cases without a typical motive, they are often used in the most difficult of investigations. As a result, it may not be surprising if the effectiveness of profiles is limited.

Few studies have empirically examined the overall usefulness of behavioral profiles in the criminal investigative process. In 1981, the FBI conducted an internal study on the value of psychological profiles to the agencies that requested them (reported in Pinizzotto 1984). Of the 192 total requests for a profile, a suspect was identified in eighty-eight cases (46 percent). Of these solved cases, it was reported that in fifteen of them (17 percent), the profile helped in the identification of the suspect. In another fifteen cases (17 percent), the profile was deemed by investigators to be of no assistance. In the remaining solved cases, the most commonly cited benefit of the profile was that it helped focus the investigation (see also Homant and Kennedy 1998).

In a study by Trager and Brewster (2001), representatives from primarily large police departments in the United States were surveyed and asked about their experiences with psychological profiles in criminal investigations. Twenty-five departments (63 percent) stated that they had used psychological profiles in the past. Of these departments, ten

(38 percent) indicated that psychological profiles had helped identify a suspect, but six (25 percent) indicated that psychological profiles actually hindered the identification of a suspect. Few methodological details or other findings were provided in the study.

A few studies have examined the accuracy of psychological profiles. Kocsis et al. (2008) provided an overview of the research on the performance of profilers in identifying accurate details of the offender. They concluded that expert profilers can more accurately predict the characteristics of an unknown offender than nonprofilers. However, the expert profiles may still not be very accurate. For example, in another study, experienced profilers reviewed case documentation on two actual cases, a murder and a rape. Profilers then constructed profiles of the perpetrators based on this information. It was determined that approximately half the information provided by the experienced profilers was correct, although there was considerable variation among it. For the nonprofilers—university students who reviewed the case materials and constructed the profiles—it was found that approximately 40 percent of the resulting details were correct (Pinizzotto and Finkel 1990). Other literature that makes claims about the accuracy of profiles provides primarily anecdotal accounts of profiles that have been "right on the mark."

Given that not much research has been conducted on the topic, it is hazardous to draw conclusions about the impact and accuracy of behavioral profiles in criminal investigations. According to Homant and Kennedy (1998),

> Our take on the evidence at this point is that it is important to expect that a significant number of mistakes will occur with profiling. Where the mistakes can be guarded against, there is no reason not to use it. For example, in the area of criminal investigation, certainly no significant leads should be overlooked simply because someone does not fit a profile, and no particular suspect should be focused on without supporting evidence. (p. 339)

Devery (2010) is more skeptical. He argues that criminal profiling "is based on a compendium of common scene intuitions and faulty theoretical assumptions, and in practice appears to consist of little more than educated guesses and wishful thinking" (p. 393). As a result, he states, "Police agencies should carefully consider whether [criminal profiling] is justified" (p. 393). Similarly, Snook et al. (2008) simply state that the belief in criminal profiling may be "an illusion" and that "criminal profiling should not be used as an investigative tool because it lacks scientific support" (p. 1257). Indeed, although few in number, empirical research studies have not even been able to consistently support a fundamental assumption of profiling: that criminals who exhibit similar crime scene actions have similar background characteristics—i.e., the homology assumption (Tonkin et al. 2009; Doan and Snook 2008). As such, and at a minimum, to be more confident and certain about the utility and accuracy of psychological profiles in criminal investigations, more research is clearly needed (Dowden et al. 2007). In particular, the research needs to be conducted by neutral researchers who do not have a vested interest in the success of psychological profiles. In addition, the studies should not be published for only a limited (e.g., agency-based) audience. Finally, the studies need to include a representative sample and provide systematic analyses of the data. Each of the studies reported here that has examined the utility of psychological profiles has at least one or more of these deficiencies. Although there is clearly room for improvement, it should also be noted that it may be difficult to assess empirically the accuracy of psychological profiles if the suspect is never apprehended. "It is possible that accurate profiles may be more likely to result in solved cases; thus inaccurate profiles may be less likely to come to light" (Homant and Kennedy 1998, p. 340).

●●● Geographical Profiling

Geographical profiling "is an investigative methodology that uses locations of a connected series of crimes to determine the most probable area of offender residence" (Rossmo 2000,

p. 1). This methodology is useful in serial crimes as well as "single crimes that involve multiple scenes or other significant geographic characteristics" (Rossmo 2000, p. 1). As defined by Bartol and Bartol (2013),

> Geographic profiling is a technique or process that can help locate the area where an offender resides, or other place that serves as an anchor point or base of operations. . . . It can be a powerful tool that provides police with a better starting place for following up on leads and narrowing their searches." (p. 98)

While there are several methods by which to construct a geographic profile, the most sophisticated methods involve the use of computer programs (Bartol and Bartol 2013).

The fundamental premise of geographical profiling is that human beings do not move randomly throughout their environment. People spend time in areas in which they are most familiar: they spend most of their time in their "comfort zone." So it is with offenders: "The typical criminal is unlikely to commit crimes that take him or her too far away from familiar surroundings" (Bartol and Bartol 2013, p. 101). Within this area of familiarity, there are anchor points and familiar routes to and from these points. Anchor points consist of the most important places in the zone and most often include an individual's residence as well as work site, friends' homes, places of entertainment, and so forth. The familiar routes to and from these places comprise an individual's cognitive map of an area. This understanding may be helpful in trying to predict where an offender may commit a crime (or, where a person goes grocery shopping for that matter; see Exhibit 8.2). The fewer the anchor points and familiar routes, the smaller and less detailed is the cognitive map. So, for instance, a person who does not have or drive an automobile, but instead walks wherever he or she needs to go, is likely to have a smaller cognitive map compared to a person who drives. A person who drives 3,000 miles a year is likely to have a smaller cognitive map than someone who drives 30,000 miles a year.

Exhibit 8.2   Where Do You Go Grocery Shopping?

The concepts of geographical profiling can help identify the area where an offender lives in relation to where he or she commits crimes, just as it can predict where a person does other things, such as grocery shopping. Chances are that when you go grocery shopping, you shop at a particular store more often than you shop at any other, even though there may be numerous stores at which you could choose to do your shopping. Correct? This store is likely to be in relatively close proximity to where you live or on a street that you travel regularly (e.g., the route that you take from your home to where you work or go to school). Right? The fact that this store is located in a familiar area and that you visit this particular store more often than any other store provides a certain comfort level that encompasses everything from how to get to the store, where to park when at the store, the layout of the store, and the things sold at the store. This familiarity makes the task of shopping relatively easy. Have you ever, just for the fun of it, randomly picked a store on the other side of town, or in a different city, in which to go grocery shopping? Probably not. It would be more difficult to shop at this place. You might need your GPS to get there, you might feel uncomfortable there, and you might just feel lost. The desire to exist and live in familiar areas is a powerful force on human behavior. The same logic can be applied to criminal behavior. For example, in investigating a murder, it is important to ask why the killer decided to search that particular area for a victim, chose a particular area to dump the body, and pick that particular travel route. What were the geographic characteristics that made the victim selection area, body disposal location, and route of travel so attractive? These choices of the particular offender should not be considered to be mere accident (Holmes and Holmes 2009).

The assumptions of geographical profiling—namely, that most activity occurs in one's comfort zone and that travel is nonrandom—is well supported by the research that has examined spacial issues in the distribution of criminal behaviors. One of the most significant and consistent findings is that "as the distance from an offender's home increases, the probability of his or her committing a crime decreases" (Bartol and Bartol 2013, p. 106). This concept is often referred to as distance decay. In other words, offenders most often commit crimes relatively close to their homes. This is especially true for juvenile offenders, for those who commit violent crimes, and for the initial crimes of serial offenders (Holmes and Holmes 2009; Bartol and Bartol 2013). While offenders tend to commit crimes in relative proximity to their homes, they tend to not commit crimes *too* close to their homes. The area around the offender's residence where he or she has a strong inclination to *not* commit crime is known as the buffer zone. Bank robbers typically have a five-mile buffer zone, and car thieves have about a one-mile zone (Bartol and Bartol 2013). The size of the buffer zone has much to do with the offender's perception of crime opportunities and risks and their individual preferences.

One important consideration that complicates the fundamental premise of geographical profiling is that offenders may not operate from a home base. They may operate out of the home of a friend and/or relatives, or they may live out of a car (as was the case with the Beltway snipers; see From the Case File in Chapter 9). Obviously, if the objective is to identify the area in which the offender lives, but that offender lives in several places, the task becomes much more complicated and prone to error.

As is the case with the construction of psychological profiles of offenders, certain actions of the perpetrator may provide probabilistic clues regarding the characteristics of the perpetrator. For example, a crime scene (e.g., a place where the victim's body was disposed of) on or close to a major road may indicate that the murderer is not from the area or is not intimately familiar with the area. A crime scene a mile or more from a major road suggests the killer is from the area (Rossmo 2000). The more remote the area of the crime scene (e.g., location of the encounter, attack, crime, body disposal, etc.), the more likely the culprit is well acquainted with the area.

The ultimate objective of geographical profiling is to identify the area in which a suspect lives. Indeed, although stated with few supporting details and little empirical support, Rossmo (2000) claims that "geographic profiling determines the location of offender residence within 5% of the total hunting area" (p. 242).

••• Psycholinguistics

Psycholinguistics involves the analysis of spoken or written words to (1) develop information about the person responsible for the statement, (2) associate crimes based on the similarities of communication, and (3) identify deception and other hidden meanings of the statement (Adams 1996; Gudjonsson 1992; Miron and Douglas 1979). The theory that underlies the methodology of psycholinguistics is that the words and patterns evident in written statements are potentially unique to the writer and may reveal the characteristics of the writer.

Psycholinguistics is also often referred to as *statement analysis* or *stylometry*—the branch of psycholinguistics that attempts to identify the ways in which the writings or spoken words of one individual differ from those of others (Adams 1996; Gudjonsson 1992). In each approach, the language structure of the statement or document is analyzed for clues about the individual who wrote or spoke the words. This analysis may include an examination of grammar, the use of certain words, syntax, spelling, word frequency, sentence length, sentence structure, number of syllables used per 100 words, and other linguistic characteristics (Gudjonsson 1992; Miron and Douglas 1979).

Specifically, the analysis of language may reveal an individual's geographic origins, ethnicity or race, gender, and age, along with other characteristics. For instance, people who live (or once lived) in certain areas of the country (or world) may be more likely to speak with a certain dialect (e.g., many southerners commonly use words such as "fixin'" and "y'all"). People from different regions of the country may also speak with unique and identifiable accents. With regard to age, older and younger people are likely to use different identifiable words (e.g., "dude" or "sketch," versus "a young man" or "of questionable character"). Regarding gender, as discussed in Chapter 7, women are more likely to use certain words and qualifiers compared to men (e.g., "seems," "suppose," "I'm sorry"). Grammatical skills and word choice may indicate educational level and occupation (Smith and Shuy 2002). Language patterns have also been associated with certain personality traits (Smith and Shuy 2002).

As an example of how psycholinguistics may be used to develop information about a culprit, consider the investigation of the anthrax letters sent to the editor of the *New York Post,* Senate Majority Leader Tom Daschle, and NBC news anchor Tom Brokaw in September and October 2001 (Kovaleski and Horwitz 2002) (see Exhibit 8.2). Each letter contained deadly anthrax. The letters contaminated several U.S. Post Office facilities and other places, led to the deaths of five people, injured eighteen other people, and required 35,000 people to take antibiotics as a precautionary measure. A week after he committed suicide in 2008, a government scientist named Bruce Edwards Ivins was identified by the FBI as the person responsible for the letters (although with limited evidence and Ivins unable to defend himself, the clearance remains controversial).

The first determination made by linguistic experts was that the three letters were written by the same individual. As noted by Gideon Epstein, former chief forensic document examiner for the U.S. Army and the INS, the letters sent to the *Post* and to Tom Brokaw were identical in form and content. The letter to Daschle was similar to the other two in content, although it was more threatening (e.g., "You die now"). The spacing between words, letters, and lines was consistent across the notes, as were the margins. Each note contained letters that were very similar in structure (e.g., Gs that looked like 6s) (Peterson and Jackson 2001). As for clues about the writer, the phrase "Allah is great" was potentially most revealing. This simplistic and obvious stereotypical slogan might point to someone who was a theologically conservative Muslim or, more likely, someone who was trying to disguise the letters as being written by a Muslim terrorist. A more common Arabic phrase, "Allahu Akbar," would more likely be used by Muslims in such a context (Peterson and Jackson 2001). In addition, all of the notes had childlike, simple letters, which might indicate that the writer was someone unfamiliar with the English language or, perhaps more likely, was trying to disguise his handwriting deliberately. The misspelling of "penicillin" might also be meaningful. It could suggest a foreigner or, more likely, someone who was trying to make the notes look like the work of a foreigner. In addition, the advice provided in the two letters to "take penicillin now" is curious because penicillin is the wrong antibiotic to take. Whoever was dealing with this sophisticated form of anthrax probably knew that penicillin was not the medication to take; this was probably an attempt to throw off investigators.

As with psychological profiling and geographical profiling, statement analysis may be most useful in focusing an investigation; although, as noted in this case, little solid information that actually points to the identity of the perpetrator can be derived from the notes. As another example of the application of psycholinguistics, consider the investigation into the murder of six-year-old JonBenet Ramsey (Case in Point 8.1).

As additional examples, consider the Lindbergh baby kidnapping discussed in the introduction to Chapter 2. Several of the words used, and the spelling of those words (e.g., "mony," "anyding," "gut"), suggested that the author was German speaking with a German accent. In the Unabomber investigation, discussed in Chapter 1, consider the significance of the phrase "You can't eat your cake and have it too." Recall, this phrase was included in the

Exhibit 8.3 Anthrax Letters

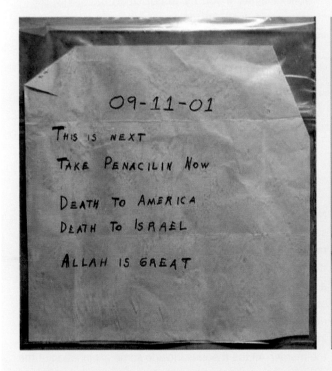

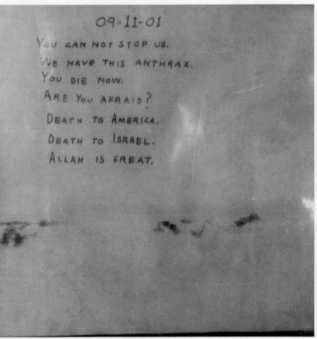

PHOTO 8.3: These letters, which contained deadly anthrax, were sent to three addresses in September and October of 2001. Linguistics experts examined them for clues about the perpetrator.

Unabomber's manifesto, which was published in *The Washington Post* and recognized by David Kaczynski, Ted Kaczynski's brother, as a unique phrase used by Ted. These signature words, and later a more thorough comparison of the manifesto with other writings of Ted, led to the identification of Ted Kaczynski as the Unabomber.

The analysis of language, especially the identification of particular pronouns, nouns, and verbs, and how they are used in statements, may also provide a basis on which to identify deception. For example, with regard to the use of pronouns, most people use "I" to refer to their own behaviors and actions. If another pronoun (or no pronoun) is used, it may signal an attempt to hide or minimize involvement in some action. Consider this statement:

CASE *in* POINT 8.1   The Murder of JonBenet Ramsey

At approximately 5:00 a.m. on December 26, 1996, Patsy Ramsey, the mother of JonBenet, woke and proceeded down the steps of their exclusive home in Boulder, Colorado. At the foot of the staircase, she found a two-and-a-half page ransom note that stated that JonBenet had been kidnapped. She then went to JonBenet's bedroom, opened the door, and found that her daughter was not in her bed. The police were notified and arrived minutes later. After searching the home several times, John Ramsey, JonBenet's father, discovered JonBenet's dead body in a closet in the basement of the house. It was determined that she had died as a result of a blow to the head and was strangled via ligature. Investigative attention immediately focused on the ransom note.

The note was handwritten with a pen and written on a tablet of paper from the house. It read as follows:

Mr. Ramsey:

Listen carefully! We are a group of individuals that represent a small foreign faction. We [crossed-out] respect your business but not the country that it serves. At this time we have your daughter in our possession. She is safe and unharmed and if you want her to see 1997, you must follow our instructions to the letter.

You will withdraw $118,000.00 from your account. $100,000 will be in $100 bills and the remaining $18,000 in $20 bills. Make sure that you bring an adequate size attache to the bank. When you get home you will put the money in a brown paper bag. I will call you between 8 and 10 am tomorrow to instruct you on delivery. The delivery will be exhausting so I advise you to be rested. If we monitor you getting the money early, we might call you early to arrange an earlier delivery of the [page 2] money and hence a earlier [delivery crossed-out] pick-up of your daughter.

Any deviation of my instructions will result in the immediate execution of your daughter. You will also be denied her remains for proper burial. The two gentlemen watching over your daughter do not particularly like you so I advise you not to provoke them. Speaking to anyone about your situation, such as Police, F.B.I., etc., will result in your daughter being beheaded. If we catch you talking to a stray dog, she dies. If you alert bank authorities, she dies. If the money is in any way marked or tampered with, she dies. You will be scanned for electronic devices and if any are found, she dies. You can try to deceive us but be warned that we are familiar with Law enforcement countermeasures and tactics. You stand a 99% chance of killing your daughter if you try to out smart us. Follow our instructions [page 3] and you stand a 100% chance of getting her back. You and your family are under constant scrutiny as well as the authorities. Don't try to grow a brain John. You are not the only fat cat around so don't think that killing will be difficult. Don't underestimate us John. Use that good southern common sense of yours. It is up to you now John!

Victory!

S.B.T.C. (Douglas 2000)

No doubt, much was made of the ransom note. It was odd for several reasons, not the least of which was that JonBenet was not taken from her house. When a ransom note is present, there is rarely a body; when a body is present, there is rarely a ransom note. The note did not seem to fit. But was the note staging? Over the years, a multitude of theories have been developed to explain the still-unsolved homicide. Many include John or Patsy as being responsible for the note and the murder. All the theories include some explanation of the ransom note. John Douglas, the famed and now retired FBI profiler, was hired by the Ramseys to assist in the investigation. In his book *The Cases That Haunt Us* (2000), he provides his thoughts on the ransom note and who was responsible for writing it. Among his conclusions are the following:

- The note was written with block letters, not a common style of printing. This suggested someone who was either very nervous or someone who was trying to disguise his or her handwriting.

- Given the length and the rambling nature of the note, it had to have been written prior to the murder. No one would have the ability to compose such a letter after killing the little girl and with her body lying in the basement. As such, it could not have been part of a staged crime scene. "Anyone trying to make up a ransom note as staging would write something as short and to the point as possible. You'd be careful not to give any unnecessary clues." (p. 322)

- Except for a few instances, the spelling is correct and syntax is proper, indicating that an educated individual wrote the note.

- The ransom amount is curious. It is a small amount, given the wealth of the Ramsey's, and it is specific—$118,000. This amount of money had been recently deposited into John Ramsey's bank account. The writer was not a sophisticated or professional criminal (or the amount would have been much larger). The writer of the note was likely in the house before and had seen some documentation regarding this amount of money. This "inside" information is more reason that the Ramseys were not responsible than it is that they were responsible. Why would they point the finger at themselves with this information?

- Some sentences are awkward and rather silly (e.g., "Listen carefully!" and "We are a group of individuals that represent a small foreign faction.") This is the sort of line one might expect to hear in a Hollywood movie. These sorts of phrases may indicate a teenager or young adult who is familiar with movies. Other phrases in the note also parallel movie lines (e.g., "Don't try to grow a brain") (see Douglas 2000, p. 323 for other examples).

- The references to "execution" and "beheaded" are also unusual, especially from parents who may have been involved in the death of their child. The thought of being "denied her remains for proper burial" is also unheard of coming from parents of a dead child.

Douglas concludes: "I can't be certain from the note who wrote it and who killed JonBenet, but from the psycholinguistic analysis, it does not appear to have been written by a 40 year-old woman panic-stricken over having just accidentally killed her daughter" (p. 324).

PHOTO 8.3: Here is a photograph of the first page of the handwritten ransom note left at the Ramsey home.

Other experts have also analyzed the note and have come to a different conclusion. Of particular significance include the following: (1) the note does not make sense as a true ransom note, (2) the peculiar use of the word "hence" and the corresponding sentence structure, and (3) the odd use of several other words. For example, the word "hence" is unusual, and the sentence in which it is used is noteworthy: "We might call you early to arrange an earlier delivery of the money and hence a earlier [delivery crossed-out] pick-up of your daughter." The word "delivery" was used before and after the word "hence" (although the second "delivery" was crossed out), and the word "and" was placed before "hence," which is not necessary or usual. In December 1997, almost a year after the murder, a church service was held in Boulder for JonBenet. In the program there was a written message from the Ramseys. It read, "Had there been no birth of Christ, there would be no hope of eternal life, and hence, no hope of ever being with our loved ones again." Does the sentence structure look familiar? A coincidence? The case remains unsolved.

> *I* got up at 7:00 when my alarm clock went off. *I* took a shower and got dressed. *I* decided to go out for breakfast. *I* went to the McDonald's on the corner. Met a man who lives nearby. Talked to him for a few minutes. *I* finished breakfast and drove to work. (Adams 1996, p. 14)

The first four sentences show normal use of the pronoun "I," but the next two statements are odd in that "I" is not included. On the face of it, it is not clear why the speaker changed his pattern of speech; however, it is potentially significant and worthy of additional exploration. Perhaps meeting this man was incriminating in some way and the speaker wished to minimize his involvement with this individual.

Along the same line, most people use the pronoun "we" to indicate more than one person and to show a togetherness or relationship of some sort between people. The use of "we" is appropriate and normal in some instances but not in others. Consider a statement from a rape victim that "We then went into the woods." It is unusual that a rape victim, or any victim for that matter, would use the word "we" to indicate herself and the perpetrator. More likely would be a statement such as "*He* forced *me* into the woods." At the least, the use of the pronoun "we" indicates a relationship between the victim and the offender, and this possibility should be explored during the investigation (Adams 1996).

The use of possessive pronouns (e.g., "my," "his," "their") may also be revealing. Possessive pronouns indicate attachment toward a person or object. Changes in the use of possessive pronouns may be an attempt to hide attachment. Consider this statement from a person whose home burned to the ground (Adams 1996):

> I left *my* house right after breakfast to join my friends at the track for the day. . . . I drove back to *my* house, made a few phone calls, then went out to dinner with Stan Thompson. . . . Stan dropped me off at *my* house around 10:00. After I changed my clothes I left *the* house to spend the night at my cousin Tom's. Around midnight we heard fire engines and got up to see what was going on. (p. 16)

What is most curious about the statement is the last reference to his house as "*the* house." Prior to the mention of "*the* house," "*my* house" was used consistently. Was that because he gave up possession of the house before it was set on fire? Again, this unusual word usage may be worthy of further exploration and questioning by investigators.

Another potentially important dimension of statement analysis is an examination of the use of nouns (words used to indicate persons, places, or things). Once again, changes in the use of nouns in a statement may be a red flag and worthy of additional attention. For example, a husband was a suspect in the fatal shooting of his wife. The statement that he provided to the police made consistent reference to "my wife" seven times, and then the noun use changed abruptly as he described the actual shooting:

> I lost control of the gun. I sensed that the barrel was pointing in *Louise's* direction and I reacted by grabbing at the gun to get it back under control. When I did this the gun discharged. It went off once and I looked over and saw blood on *Louise's* face. (Adams 1996, p. 16)

Why did the noun referent change? Perhaps it would have been more difficult to admit to killing his "wife" than it was to shoot this person named "Louise" accidentally. Perhaps even more significant and revealing would have been if he had simply used the pronoun "her" instead of "Louise."

Finally, the verbs one uses in expressing meaning may be revealing. Verbs are action words and can be expressed in the past, present, or future tense. The norm is past tense because when the event is recalled, it has already occurred. Although past tense is normal in recounting past events, use of the present tense is normal in referring to missing persons. For example, one of the statements made by Susan Smith to the media in speaking about her missing children was "They *needed* me" (Adams 1996). This was an unusual statement because at the time it was reasonable to believe, especially from the children's mother, that the children were alive and that they were still in *need* of her. As it was later revealed, they did not need her at the time she made the statement because they were already dead, and she knew it.

In sum, behavioral evidence, analyzed through the methods of psychological profiling, geographical profiling, or psycholinguistics, is potentially useful evidence in the criminal investigative process. It is by its nature, however, probabilistic and subject to error, as are many other types of evidence available to investigators.

MAIN POINTS

1. Behavioral analysis includes crime scene profiling, geographic profiling, and linguistic analysis. The goal of each of these activities is to help identify an unknown perpetrator of a specific known crime, each is intended to develop information on the type of person who committed the crime, and each method is based on an analysis of certain features of the crime in question.

2. Crime scene profiling (or psychological profiling or behavioral profiling) involves identifying the personal characteristics of an offender based on an analysis of the crimes he or she committed.

3. Crime scene profiles are intended to help focus an investigation when there are several suspects. They are not capable of identifying a suspect when one is not already known. Crime scene profiles may also provide information about the items that may be found in possession of the offender and provide suggestions as to interrogation strategies to be used with the offender.

4. With crime scene profiling, previous similar crimes for which there are known offenders are used as a basis on which to identify the characteristics of the person who committed the present crime. They are most appropriately conducted on crimes that display indications of psychopathy. Crime scene profiles are based on probabilities and inferences.

5. There are several basic assumptions to the profiling process: (1) the crime reflects the personality of the offender, (2) personality does not change, (3) the offender's MO remains similar across crimes, (4) signature remains the same, and (5) offenders with similar crime behaviors share similar characteristics (known as the homology assumption).

6. Crime scene profiling is not new, although it has become widely known in the past twenty-five years.

7. A fundamental distinction in profiling is between organized and disorganized offenders (murderers) and organized and disorganized crime scenes.

8. Many other crime scene behaviors and other actions can reveal information about the offender's characteristics, including, among others, whether the offender has struck before, whether crimes were committed by the same person, and the relationship between the victim and the offender.

9. Several studies have examined the effectiveness and accuracy of behavioral profiles. Conclusions vary as to the value of behavioral profiles in criminal investigations.

10. The goal of geographical profiling is to identify the area where the offender lives or his or her base of operations. To do so, the location(s) at which the offender committed crimes (and related areas) is considered.

11. The premise of geographical profiling is that people spend time and engage in activities (including criminal activities) in areas in which they are most familiar—in their "comfort zone."

12. Offenders tend to commit crimes relatively close to their homes, but not too close. This principle relates to the concepts of distance decay and buffer zone.

13. Psycholinguistics (or statement analysis or stylometry) involves the analysis of spoken or written words in order to develop information about the type of person responsible for the statement, associate crimes based on similarities of communication, and identify deception or hidden meanings in the communication.

14. Examples of how psycholinguistics may be used include the analysis of the anthrax letters, the ransom note in the JonBenet Ramsey murder investigation, the Lindbergh baby kidnapping note, and the Unabomber's manifesto.

15. The analysis of pronoun, noun, and verb usage in language may be a basis on which to identify deception.

16. Regardless of its specific form, behavioral evidence is probabilistic and subject to error, not unlike many other forms of evidence available to investigators.

IMPORTANT TERMS

Anchor points

Behavioral analysis

Buffer zone

Cognitive map

Comfort zone

Crime scene profiling

Distance decay

Geographical profiling

Homology assumption

Life history profiling/analysis

Modus operandi (MO)

Organized and disorganized crime scenes

Organized and disorganized offenders

Prospective offender profiling

Psycholinguistics

Psychological profiling

Signature

Souvenirs

Staging

Statement analysis

Stylometry

Trophies

QUESTIONS FOR DISCUSSION AND REVIEW

1. What is the process of crime scene/psychological profiling? For what types of crimes is profiling most suitable? What are the goals of crime scene profiling?

2. What are the basic theory and assumptions of crime scene profiling? What is the homology assumption?

3. What is the importance and usefulness of the distinction between organized and disorganized crime scenes? What are the personal characterizes of organized and disorganized offenders? What are the crime scene characteristics of organized and disorganized offenders?

4. What is the meaning of other perpetrator actions and crime characteristics?

5. What is the difference between MO and signature, and between trophies and souvenirs?

6. How useful, accurate, and effective is crime scene profiling? What are the limitations of crime scene profiling as an investigative tool?

7. What are the premise and assumptions of geographical profiling? What is the goal of geographical profiling? What are the limitations of geographical profiling as an investigative tool?

8. What are anchor points, comfort zone, cognitive map, distance decay, and buffer zone?

9. What is psycholinguistics as an investigative tool? What is involved in the linguistic analysis of statements? What are the goals associated with the method? What are the limitations of psycholinguistics as an investigative tool?

STUDENT STUDY SITE

Visit **www.sagepub.com/brandl3e** to access additional study tools including eFlashcards, web quizzes, web resources, video resources, and SAGE journal articles.

WANTED BY THE FBI

UNLAWFUL FLIGHT TO AVOID PROSECUTION - MURDER SECOND DEGREE

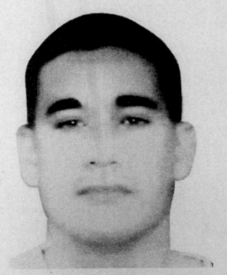

Photo taken about 4/97

Date of Photo Unknown

ANDREW PHILLIP CUNANAN

Alias: Andrew Phillip DeSilva

DESCRIPTION

Date of Birth: August 31, 1969; Place of Birth: San Diego, California;

Objectives

After reading this chapter you will be able to:

- Discuss tip lines in their various forms and some of their benefits and limitations

- Identify some of the television shows that are designed to assist investigations and evaluate their usefulness

- Discuss AMBER Alerts, what they are, how they are supposed to work, and their benefits and limitations

- Discuss the role of confidential informants in criminal

investigations and their various motivations for providing information to the police

- Explain why the collection of gang intelligence is useful for criminal investigations

- Discuss the basics of gang graffiti

- Describe the various forms of crime analysis and how they can be used as tools in criminal investigations

- Discuss the purpose of ViCAP; explain how it works and its major limitations

- Discuss the role of computer databases and information networks including NCIC and NLETS

- Discuss the role of social networking and other Internet sites in proving criminal intelligence to investigators

From the CASE FILE

The Investigation of the Washington, D.C., Beltway Snipers

The manhunt began the night of October 2, 2002, when James Martin, fifty-five, was shot dead in a parking lot of a grocery store in Wheaton, Maryland. It ended twelve victims and twenty-one days later when two suspects, John Allen Muhammad, forty-one, and John Lee Malvo, seventeen, were arrested while they slept in their car at a rest stop off Interstate 70, approximately fifty miles northwest of Washington, D.C. During the course of the deadly rampage, thirteen people were shot, each with a single bullet fired from a distance with a high-powered rifle; ten of the victims were killed, three were critically injured. The deadliest day was October 3, when five people were shot. All the victims were going about their usual activities at the time they were gunned down—mowing the grass, cleaning the car, leaving a restaurant, getting off a bus, going to school, shopping. The victims varied in age; the youngest was thirteen, the oldest was fifty-five. The victims were white, African American, and Latino. The shootings occurred at night, during the day, on weekdays, and on weekends. Seven of the shootings took place in Maryland, five in Virginia, and one in

Washington, D.C. The millions of people who lived and worked in the area were in the firm grip of fear. A sniper was on the loose.

For the first seven shootings, which occurred October 2 through 4, the police had few clues—few good leads. What seemed to be most significant was that the police had witnesses. No one actually saw the shooter, but witnesses reported seeing a white van in the area after several of the shootings. In other incidents, witnesses reported seeing a white box truck in the vicinity. In one incident, a witness told the police that he saw a dark-colored Chevrolet Caprice driving away from the scene with its lights off. The importance of the Caprice, however, was drowned out by the continued sightings of the white van and white truck. By October 12, the police and FBI had obtained enough information from witnesses to develop a composite picture of the van and the truck believed to be involved in the shootings. The pictures of these vehicles were then released to the public through the media. The police checked and searched hundreds of white vans and trucks, looking for anything suspicious or anything that was linked to the shootings. They found nothing.

Along with the witness reports of the white van and truck, the police also had some idea regarding the sniper's MO. In particular, all the victims were shot with the same ammunition—a .223-caliber bullet, popular with hunters, competitive shooters, and the military. Given the distance at which many of the victims were believed to have been shot, the police also suspected that the sniper had some skill and training as a marksman, maybe from a military background. Most of the shootings were concentrated in the Montgomery County area, suggesting that the killer lived in that area. There was also a hint that the killer was watching developments in the investigation on television and altering his activities based on investigative developments. For example, when officials appeared on television and discussed how geographical profiling was going to be used in the investigation and what it could reveal about the killer, the shootings moved to Virginia. When Montgomery County police chief Charles Moose appeared on television and reassured parents that their children were safe, the sniper's next victim was a thirteen-year-old boy who was critically wounded after arriving at school. It was after this shooting on October 7 that the police searched the area around the school where the shooting occurred and found a tarot "death" card and a spent shell casing in some matted grass. On the back of the card was a message that read, "Dear Policeman, I am God." Along with the card was a note that stated that the police should not reveal the message to the media. Nevertheless, the discovery of the card and its message was "leaked" to the media and, for reasons that became clear later, this eventually helped the investigation.

In the event any additional shootings occurred, the police devised a plan to shut down Interstate 95, the shooter's suspected escape route after previous shootings, and set up roadblocks and checkpoints. It was hoped that after a shooting, the sniper would get ensnared in the roadblock on his way back to his home territory of Montgomery County. The police had to wait about a week to put their plan into action. On October 14, a woman was gunned down in the parking lot of a Home Depot store in Falls Church, Virginia. The police immediately obtained information from several witnesses that, again, a white van was seen driving away from the scene after the gunshots were heard. One witness in particular provided what seemed to

be a good lead and the most specific information yet: the shooter was driving a cream-colored Chevrolet Astro van with a burned-out left taillight and a chrome ladder rack on its roof. Better yet, the witness also told the police that he saw the shooter and his gun. The gun was described as an AK-47, and the witness said the shooter had dark skin. Another witness reported seeing a dark-colored Chevy or Chrysler leaving the store parking lot after the shooting. The police focused on the more specific white van. The plan to shut down traffic was quickly implemented. Traffic around the Washington, D.C., area was backed up for miles as the police searched dozens upon dozens of white vans as they moved through the roadblocks. Again, the police found nothing. The roadblock tactic was used two more times, after two more shootings. None of the roadblocks were helpful in the investigation. At the time, the police reasoned that the shooter was familiar enough with the area to evade the police by using side roads. After additional questioning of the witness who provided the information about the van and the shooter, the police concluded that it was impossible for him to have seen what he said he saw. Security surveillance video from inside the Home Depot store showed that he was actually inside the store when the shooting occurred. The "witness" just made up the information. He was subsequently charged with providing false information to the police. More frustration for police, and they were still not even close to identifying the killer.

On October 17, an operator at the police tip line that was established to receive tips from the public about the shootings received a telephone call from an individual who stated that he was the sniper. The caller said he was angry because he was unable to get through to the police earlier and was hung up on. Reportedly, the police tip line received hundreds of apparently bogus calls during which the caller claimed to be God. In this call, the man said,

> Good morning. Don't say anything, just listen. We're the people that are causing the killing in your area. Look on the Tarot card. It says "Call me God. Do not release to the press." We have called you three times before, trying to cut a negotiation. We've gotten no response. People have died.

Now, in an effort to get the police to take him seriously, the sniper provided a clue, a big clue, to the operator of the tip line. The caller told the operator that the police should "look to Montgomery" and that they would realize then that he was not joking. The operator reported the phone call to her supervisors. The police were initially unsure as to what the message meant, or its validity. What was this about "Montgomery?" The only thing that was clear was that the caller spoke broken English and had a strong but unidentifiable accent.

The next day, October 18, the sniper was back at work in Ashland, Virginia. At 8:00 p.m. a man was fatally shot in a Ponderosa restaurant parking lot. In searching the area around the restaurant after the shooting, the police found a note tacked to a tree in nearby woods. It was handwritten and was four pages long, including a cover page on which five stars were neatly drawn. The letter contained threats and made demands. In the note, the sniper railed about his previous attempts to communicate unsuccessfully with the police. It identified the phone numbers that he called and the names of the persons with whom he spoke on the six previous calls to the police. It also made reference to a phone call he made to a "Priest in ashland." As reported in Kovaleski and Horwitz (2002), the note read, in part:

> These people took our calls for a Hoax or Joke, so your failure to respond has cost you five lives. If stopping the killing is more important than catching us now, then you will accept our demand which are non-negotiable.

> You will place ten million dollar in Bank of America account no. xxx, Pin no. xxx, Activation date xxx, Exp date xxx, Name xxx, member since xxx, Platinum Visa Account.

> We will have unlimited withdrawl at any atm worldwide. You will activate the bank account, credit card, and Pin number. You have until 9:00 am Monday morning to complete transaction. Try to catch us withdrawing at least you will have less body bags. . . . If we give you our word that is what takes place. "Word is Bond."

> P.S. Your children are not safe anywhere at any time.

The note contained a wealth of clues. First was the Bank of America bank information. When police traced the credit card identified in the note, it was discovered that it had been reported stolen in Arizona on March 25, 2002. The victim did not realize that it was taken from her until April 11, when the bank contacted her about a gasoline purchase in Tacoma, Washington. That purchase was determined by the bank to be fraudulent and the account was closed.

The writing style of the note was also of significance. It appeared to match the speaking style of the individual who made the earlier phone call to the police. The reference to the phone call that was made to the "Priest in ashland" was also intriguing. Further investigation into this phone call led investigators to the Reverend William Sullivan, a priest at St. Ann's Church in Ashland, Virginia. When questioned by investigators, he told them that on the prior day, October 18, he received a phone call from someone who stated that he was God and that he was the sniper. The caller said that he was calling because he was not able to get through to the police. The priest also told the police that the caller made reference to a crime that occurred recently in Montgomery, Alabama. The priest said that he dismissed the call as a hoax and therefore did not report it earlier to authorities. With this information, particularly the reference to the shooting in Montgomery, Alabama, the earlier phone call reference to "Montgomery" made sense. The FBI immediately contacted the police department in Montgomery and learned about a robbery/homicide that had occurred there on September 21. The police in Montgomery explained to the FBI agents that two clerks who worked at the ABC Liquor Store were shot by a black man who was approximately twenty years old. One of the clerks was killed; the other injured. The suspect fled the scene on foot and was chased by responding officers. Although the killer was not apprehended, a composite sketch of the suspect was developed, and a fingerprint was recovered from a gun catalog that the suspect was believed to have been looking at just prior to the robbery. The Montgomery police explained that they ran the print through their AFIS but were unable to match the print to a suspect.

On October 20, the fingerprint recovered from the crime scene in Montgomery, Alabama, was examined through the use of the FBI's IAFIS, which also includes fingerprints obtained from the Bureau of U.S. Citizenship and Immigration Services (USCIS). This time there was a hit—the fingerprint was that of an individual by the name of John Lee Malvo. His fingerprint was in the file because he was known to be a Jamaican citizen who was in the United States illegally. The pieces were beginning to come together. Investigators speculated that the five stars drawn on the cover page of the note left at the Ponderosa shooting scene were related to the Jamaican band Five Stars. "Word is bond" were lyrics to a song sung by the band. The possible Jamaican connection also fit with the heavy accent noted in the previous October 17 phone call to the police and with the poor English used in the note. The information on John Lee Malvo that was contained in the fingerprint file led investigators to Washington State, the same place where the stolen credit card identified in the note was used to purchase gasoline. At about this same time, the police tip line received a telephone call from a resident of Tacoma who reported that a person named Muhammad and another person with the nickname "Sniper" used to live at a specified address in Tacoma and had, on occasion, used a tree stump in their backyard for shooting practice. Once investigators were in Tacoma, the link between John Malvo and an individual by the name of John Muhammad was confirmed, and information was received that Muhammad was possibly Malvo's stepfather. It was also learned that Muhammad was previously in the military and was a Gulf War veteran.

On the morning of Monday, October 21, the sniper called the police to reiterate his demands. The police were ready, or so they thought. The phone call made by the suspect was traced to a public telephone at a gas station near Richmond, Virginia. Shortly after the call was received by the police, they converged on the telephone and found a white van parked next to it. Two Hispanic men were pulled from the van and arrested. Headlines immediately followed: "Two Men in Custody in Sniper Hunt" (Breed 2002). There was only one problem: they were not Malvo and Muhammad. The two individuals in the van happened to be in the wrong place at the wrong time. They had nothing to do with the shootings. And, as coincidence would have it, they were driving a *white* van. If the snipers had used that phone to contact the police, they got away before the police arrived. That afternoon Chief Moose provided a message to the sniper through the media: "The person you called could not hear everything you said. The audio was unclear and we want to get it right. Call us back so that we can clearly understand."

In the images on television, the police were looking silly. On the morning of October 22, the snipers claimed their thirteenth victim. Conrad Johnson, thirty-five, a city bus driver, had parked his bus on the side of a street in Silver Spring, Maryland. As he stood up and began to walk down the steps of his bus, he was shot once in the abdomen. He died hours later. A note found in a nearby park reiterated the demand for $10 million.

As the police were investigating this latest shooting, investigators were busy developing information

in Washington State. Additional information was received by investigators that confirmed Malvo and Muhammad used to live in the same house in Tacoma and that on several occasions while they lived there, gunshots were heard from the house. It was reported by a neighbor that a tree stump in the backyard served as a target stop for what sounded like a high-powered rifle. Police conducted a search of the home and cut and carried away a large stump that reportedly contained bullet fragments. The search of the outside of the house and the removal of the tree stump by investigators was broadcast live on national television. Investigators also visited Bellingham High School seeking information on John Malvo, who used to attend the school. Handwriting samples of Malvo were collected.

Reasonably certain now that Malvo and Muhammad were connected to the sniper shootings, investigators requested that police from area departments query their databases for any noted police contact with either of these suspects. It was discovered that on the night of October 8, the day after the thirteen-year-old boy was shot outside his school, Baltimore police had contact with John Muhammad when they found him asleep in his car in a parking lot outside a Subway sandwich shop. The police woke him and told him to be on his way. It was noted in the police computer that he was driving a blue 1990 Chevrolet Caprice with a New Jersey license plate, number NDA21Z. After the license plate number was discovered, police from area departments were asked once again to query their databases for any recorded check of the plates. It was found that between October 2 and October 23, the police had seen the Caprice and checked the license plate number at least twelve times. After finding that the car was not stolen and the occupants were not known to be wanted for any crimes, no additional investigations of the vehicle or its occupants were conducted.

With this information in hand, at approximately 9:00 p.m. Wednesday, October 23, Chief Moose revealed on national television that one John Muhammad, age forty-one, and John Malvo, age seventeen, were wanted in connection with the sniper shootings. He stated that these individuals were last seen driving a blue 1990 Chevrolet Caprice and provided the license plate number. Approximately four hours later, the police received a telephone call from a truck driver who said that he was currently at a rest stop off Interstate 70 near Frederick, Maryland, and that the car they were looking for was parked there. The police

PHOTO 9.1: Witnesses to the early shootings in the D.C. sniper case told the police that they thought the shooter was in a white van. The police alerted the public to this information, and witnesses at subsequent sniper shootings also reported seeing a white van. The search was on for a white van. But the snipers never used such a vehicle. They were driving a blue four-door 1990 Chevrolet Caprice, pictured here.

PHOTO 9.2: Notice how the trunk of the snipers' vehicle was configured so that a person could lie in it. Also observe the notch cut out of the trim to accommodate the barrel of a rifle.

instructed him to block the exit with his truck and for him and the others in the area to stay in their vehicles with their doors locked. A police tactical unit arrived shortly thereafter and found Malvo and Muhammad asleep in the car. They were arrested without incident. Reportedly, a Bushmaster XM15 rifle was found in the car, along with a global positioning satellite system, a pair of two-way radios, two handguns, two shooting mittens, a Sony laptop computer, a single .223-caliber cartridge, a pair of bolt cutters, and a wallet containing several driver's licenses with Muhammad's photograph but with different names. It was also reported that there was a hole cut in the back of the trunk of the car, from which the shots were probably fired. The police had the snipers. Malvo and Muhammad appeared to have been living out of their vehicle.

Further investigation has revealed that Malvo and Muhammad are also believed to be responsible for at least seven other shootings in the Washington, D.C., area; Washington State; Arizona; and Louisiana. From 2003 to 2006, Muhammad and Malvo were tried and convicted of their crimes in Virginia and Maryland. Muhammad was sentenced to death, Malvo to multiple life without parole sentences. Muhammad was executed in Virginia by lethal injection on November 10, 2009.

Case Considerations and Points for Discussion

- As discussed, in the investigation of the Beltway sniper case, one piece of evidence led to another until investigators identified and apprehended the killers. In your assessment, what was the most important development in the investigation? Specifically, what was the role of the media and the public in the investigation?

- In just about any criminal investigation there are difficulties in the investigation and problems with the evidence. This investigation was no different. What was the most significant mistake made by investigators in this case? If this mistake had been avoided, how might the investigation have been different? What was the most significant mistake made by the perpetrators?

- What do you think were the biggest lessons learned by investigators as a result of this investigation?

Also:

- Watch the four-part YouTube video "Final Report— the DC Sniper" for an excellent discussion of the investigation and the difficulties encountered by investigators.

●●● The Role of the Public and Media in Criminal Investigations

People may have knowledge about a crime simply because they saw or heard something during the course of their normal activities, even though they may not realize that their observations actually relate to a crime. Some of these people may be identified as witnesses through traditional methods, such as neighborhood canvasses. At other times, however, the task for the police is to get these people to realize that they may have information that relates to a crime and to report the information that they possess. Sometimes, citizens realize that they possess information that relates to a crime and need only minimal encouragement to report the information. To identify these people and to obtain information from them, the police have several strategies at their disposal. These include the use of tip lines, television shows, and special alerts, along with other public information strategies. Each of these strategies is discussed here.

TIP LINES

Tip lines are designed to be an easy and convenient method for citizens to provide information to the police via a telephone. Tip lines can be created for, and dedicated to, specific crimes, such as the one set up during the sniper investigation, or they can be oriented toward any crime on which a citizen may wish to report information, such as Crime Stoppers.

Crime Solvers, WeTip, and Crime Stoppers are examples of well-established and continuously operating tip lines. Crime Stoppers is a nonprofit corporation established in 1976 (see www.c-s-i.org). Crime Stoppers offers cash rewards up to $1,000 to anonymous persons who contact the tip line and provide information that leads to the arrest of persons

Exhibit 9.1　Tip Line Billboard

One method of developing information in an investigation is through a tip line. Here the police are seeking information about Michael A. Mitchell. A telephone number for the police department is provided.

responsible for any crimes. Law enforcement personnel staff the phone lines, which are most often located in police dispatch centers, and draft press releases on crimes in the community.

According to the Crime Stoppers Web site, information provided to Crime Stoppers programs has led to nearly a half million crimes being solved, more than $6 billion worth of stolen property and narcotics being recovered, and $17 million of rewards being paid. Although these are impressive statistics, it may actually be quite difficult to determine precisely the role and value of the information received through the tip line in solving crimes. Of course, information in an investigation may come from various sources (e.g., physical evidence, other witness statements) beside the tip line, and each of these sources of information/evidence may contribute to the crime being solved. There is no research that has examined the actual impact of tip line information on the likelihood of crimes being solved (Rosenbaum et al. 1989), nor is there research that has examined what proportion of tips are detailed and credible enough to warrant any police action.

In some instances, tip lines have been established on the Internet. For example, in the wake of September 11, 2001, the FBI established an online tip line as a way of receiving information from the public concerning suspected terrorist activity. After the Boston Marathon bombing, the FBI established an Internet tip line (bostonmarathontips.fbi.gov) and a phone tip line (1–800–CALL–FBI). The National Center for Missing and Exploited Children (NCMEC) has in place a cyber tip line to receive information about child pornography, sex offenders, and children who are at risk of sexual abuse.

As discussed in the introduction to this chapter, several members of the public provided critical information to investigators during the sniper investigation—in particular, the priest, the resident in Tacoma, and the truck driver. Most of this information was provided to the police through the tip line that was established especially for the investigation. The most important information in the investigation may have been provided by John Malvo, one of the snipers, also through the tip line. Citizen tips were also key in the identification and apprehension of the Boston Marathon bombers. The images of the suspects shortly before and after the bombs were detonated were broadcast by the FBI nonstop nationwide. Immediately, information about the identity of these two individuals was provided to authorities. While Tamerlan Tsarnaev was killed by the police, his younger brother, Dzhokhar, was able to escape. Later, a citizen called the police to report that he saw blood on the ground near his boat, which was dry docked in his back yard. He told police that he looked in the boat and saw who he thought might be Dzhokhar Tsarnaev. The police responded and the suspect eventually surrendered. No doubt, tip lines allow for the easy transmission of potentially important information to the police.

TELEVISION SHOWS

Television shows such as *America's Most Wanted* are also used to disseminate information about unsolved crimes and to encourage citizens to contact authorities with related information. *America's Most Wanted* has been described as a "nationwide neighborhood watch" and an extension of the FBI's Ten Most Wanted List. (This list was first used in the 1950s to enlist the assistance of the public in solving crimes [Nelson 1989].) *American's Most Wanted* premiered in 1988 and is hosted by John Walsh, whose own son was abducted and murdered by a serial killer in 1981. According to the show's Web site, www.amw.com, as of 2013, more than 1,200 persons have been captured as a result of the show. The show

PHOTO 9.3: Authorities conducted a massive search for Dzhokhar Tsarnaev, one of the suspects in the Boston Marathon bombings. He evaded capture until a citizen discovered him hiding in his boat and called the police.

consists of reenacted crimes with actors playing the victims and offenders. After the case is presented, viewers who believe they have information about the perpetrator are asked to contact authorities through the show's toll-free telephone tip line, 1–800–CRIME–TV. The tip line center is staffed by investigators from the agencies responsible for the cases profiled. Nearly all the cases profiled on the show involve serious violent crimes for which the police have a good idea about the identity of the perpetrator. The suspect's name is often known, a photograph is often shown, and details about the person are often provided (e.g., she likes to drink Pepsi, he is a soccer fan, he is a skilled carpenter) (see Case in Point 9.1).

Throughout the years, other "crime-time" television shows (Nelson 1989) have also aired that focus on particular unsolved crimes, including the 1988 special *Manhunt Live!*, a show about the Green River, Washington, serial homicide case, and *Unsolved Mysteries*, a television series that premiered in 1987 and that includes unsolved crime stories as well as other "mysteries," including UFO sightings and ghost encounters.

CASE *in* POINT 9.1

America's Most Wanted: Oscar Antonio Menjivar-Herrara

Wanted For:

- First Degree Sexual Assault of a Child

- Sarpy County, NE

Possible Location(s):

- Chicago, IL

- Ft. Myers, FL

- Nebraska

- New York

- California

- Denver, CO

Oscar Menjivar-Herrera is wanted for sexually assaulting a fourteen-year-old girl. He was arrested by the U.S. Marshals in Florida but escaped custody while being extradited back to Omaha, NE. Authorities tell AMW that Menjivar-Herrera has most likely fled back to El Salvador and has re-established himself with his family.

Sex: Male

Race: Hispanic

Current Age: 31

Height: 5'5"

Weight: 140 lbs.

Hair: Black

Eyes: Brown

Traits and Habits:

- Uses social media as a means to target victims

- Dress and acts much younger than actuality in order to appeal to younger victims

- Very confident

- May have gang ties—specifically with MS-13

- Works construction

Vehicle to Look For:

- Menjivar-Herrera might be driving a 2001 gold Honda Civic or possibly a white SUV, possibly a Chevrolet Trailblazer.

Source: Information adapted from the *America's Most Wanted* Web site, www.amw.com, November 9, 2013.

AMBER ALERTS

Another method of mobilizing the public to provide crime information to the police is the AMBER Alert. Some states have similar programs with different names. The AMBER Alert (America's Missing: Broadcast Emergency Response) was created in 1996 after nine-year-old Amber Hagerman was abducted and murdered while riding her bicycle in Arlington, Texas. With the AMBER plan, when a law enforcement agency is notified that a child abduction has taken place or is suspected of having taken place, an alert that includes a description and picture of the missing child, the suspected perpetrator, the suspected vehicle, a tip line phone number, and any other information that may assist in locating the child is transmitted to area radio and television stations for immediate broadcast. In some situations, information relating to the abduction is placed on electronic freeway emergency signs. The AMBER plan and alert system is modeled after the alerts that are used to notify people of impending severe weather. Prior to an alert being activated, it has been suggested that three criteria be satisfied (see www.ncmec.org):

- Law enforcement officials confirm a child has been abducted.

- Law enforcement officials believe that the circumstances surrounding the abduction indicate that the child is in danger of harm or death.

- There is enough reliable information about the child, the suspect, or the suspect's vehicle to believe that an immediate alert will be of help.

The logic behind AMBER Alerts is that when children are abducted by strangers, harm to them comes quickly; thus, a quick law enforcement response is needed. For example, it is known that if a child is abducted by a stranger, the victim is killed within the first hour in 44 percent of cases, within three hours in 74 percent of cases, and within twenty-four hours in 91 percent percent of cases (Rossmo 2000).

According to the NCMEC, as of 2013, there have been over 600 successful recoveries of children as a result of AMBER Alerts (see Case in Point 9.2 and Case in Point 9.3 for a summary of a few of them). However, research that has examined the impact of AMBER Alerts highlights some of the particulars of the strategy, as well as some of its limitations (Griffin et al. 2007). First, AMBER Alerts are relatively infrequent in stranger abduction cases (at least in part because stranger abduction cases are relatively infrequent). When examining 275 AMBER Alerts, Griffin et al. (2007) found that 45 percent of the alerts involved abductions involving parents (cases where the child is significantly less likely to be harmed), 35 percent involved other relatives or acquaintances, and 20 percent involved strangers (the stereotypical child abduction case).

Second, in nearly all instances when an AMBER Alert is issued, the child is recovered; however, in most cases the AMBER Alert itself had nothing to do with the recovery. Specifically, in 95 percent of the cases where an AMBER Alert was issued, the child was recovered (in 5 percent of the cases the child was murdered or never recovered), but the AMBER Alert had a direct effect on the recovery in "only" 33 percent of these cases. The authors discuss the abduction of Tamara Brooks and Jacqueline Maris as an example of where the AMBER Alert actually was credited with a positive outcome, but other factors were also important in this regard (see Case in Point 9.3).

Third, and perhaps most important, the researchers found that AMBER Alerts that involved a stranger abducting a child were much less likely to result in a recovery of the child. In these cases, harm was also more likely to have been done to the child prior to recovery. Finally, the researchers found that in cases where the child was recovered, in only 17 percent was the recovery within six hours of the abduction. This is significant given the research finding that if harm is to be done to a child in an abduction case, it is usually done within the first three hours (see Case in Point 9.4). Overall, while the AMBER Alert does have benefits, it is important to keep those benefits in perspective.

CASE *in* POINT 9.2   A Few AMBER Alert Success Stories

October 30, 2012

Barrio Oberero, PR

A six-year-old boy was abducted when he and his father were confronted by four armed men in black ski masks. The men took the child and fled. Later, the child was dropped off at a shopping center where a guard recognized the child from the AMBER Alert broadcast. The guard contacted law enforcement and the child was safely rescued.

October 24, 2012

Poplar Bluff, MO

An AMBER Alert was issued when a five-year-old girl was abducted from her yard by a registered sex offender. The child's mother noticed the child was missing and saw the vehicle driving away. The abductor became aware of the AMBER Alert and contacted law enforcement to turn himself in and surrender the child. The child was safely rescued.

October 16, 2012

Lithonia, GA

A two-year-old girl was left in a car by her caregiver. When the caregiver returned, she found the vehicle had been stolen with the child inside, and an AMBER Alert was issued. Later, a citizen recognized the vehicle from the AMBER Alert in a parking lot and discovered the child was inside the vehicle

alone. Law enforcement was notified and the child was safely rescued.

October 11, 2012

Niles, OH

A three-year-old child was left sleeping in his father's car while his father went inside a house to pick up another child. When the father came back outside a couple of minutes later, he saw someone driving away in the vehicle with the child inside. An off-duty police officer heard the AMBER Alert issued for the child and looked for the vehicle. He located the car, the child was safely rescued, and the suspect surrendered without incident.

June 22, 2012

Selma, TX

A six-year-old boy was abducted by his noncustodial mother when she and several masked associates stormed the home of the child's grandmother. They also took multiple weapons, and the abductor was a known drug user. Law enforcement issued an AMBER Alert, fearing for the child's safety. They subsequently received a tip that someone had recognized the child in a hotel swimming pool, resulting in the safe recovery of the child.

November 9, 2012.

Source: Adapted from The National Center for missing and Exploited Children's Web site, www.ncmec.org/missingkids/servlet/PageServlet?LanguageCountry=en_US&PageId=2248.

OTHER INFORMATION DISSEMINATION STRATEGIES

Along with tip lines, television shows, and special alerts, other methods have also been used to obtain information from the public. For example, NCMEC regularly sends "Have you seen me?" mailings via the U.S. Postal Service. As explained on the NCMEC Web site,

> As a direct result of leads generated by the "Have You Seen Me?" program, 144 missing children to date have been safely recovered. According to NCMEC, photos are the number one tool parents and law enforcement officials have in their search for missing children. By featuring recent or age-progressed photos of missing children and their alleged abductors, the program empowers the American public to help safely recover missing children.

PHOTO 9.4: AMBER Alerts are designed to get information about child abductions to the public in a timely manner.

CASE *in* POINT 9.3   Another AMBER Alert Success Story

A spectacular AMBER Alert case involved two teenagers, Tamara Brooks and Jacqueline Maris. An armed man kidnapped the two young women from a remote location in Los Angeles County, California, and kept them for approximately twelve hours while traveling in a vehicle stolen from one of the victims' male companions. Based on a citizen tip solicited by the AMBER Alert, the perpetrator was cornered and shot to death by sheriff's deputies and the young victims were rescued.

As stated in Griffin et al. (2007),

> The case was touted as an example of AMBER Alert rescuing victims from imminent harm, and was coded as such in this data set. However, part of the success must also be attributed to the ineptitude and hesitancy of the assailant, who, if he had murderous intentions, committed several stunning blunders. He left living witnesses (the girls' male companions) who could report the crime and describe the vehicle, he remained in said vehicle with the young women for 12 hours after the abduction, he stopped at one point to buy the victims refreshments at a convenience store, and later drank himself unconscious. Even when he subdued the girls after they failed in a bid to attack him, he did not murder them. Thus in this case the AMBER Alert was "effective" largely because the abductor was fortuitously incompetent and indecisive. This is certainly not to say that the alert deserves no credit, or that law enforcement officials did not act appropriately and heroically in this case. The point is simply that the "success" resulted in large measure from astonishing good luck, and that it is unreasonable to expect that such luck will typically prevail in stereotypical abduction cases where AMBER Alerts are issued. (p. 388)

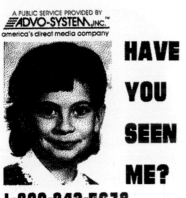

A PUBLIC SERVICE PROVIDED BY
ADVO-SYSTEM₁INC.™
america's direct media company

HAVE
YOU
SEEN
ME?
1-800-843-5678
National Center for Missing and Exploited Children.
NAME: CHERRIE ANN MAHAM   DOB: 08/14/76   AGE: 9
HT.: 4'2"   EYES: Hazel   HAIR: Brown   WT.: 68 lbs.
DATE MISSING: 02/22/85 FROM: Pittsburgh, Pennsylvania

239 Service Road
Hartford, CT 06120

CAR RT SORT
Bulk Rate
US Postage
PAID
Advo-System, Inc.

Postal Service Regulations require that this address card be delivered together with its accompanying postage paid mail advertisements. If you should receive this card without its accompanying mail, please notify your local postmaster.

PHOTO 9.6: One challenge for the police in developing information in an investigation is to get the word out to people who know about the crime in question and prompt them to contact the police with that information. The National Center for Missing and Exploited Children has developed the "Have you seen me?" fliers for home delivery by the U.S. Post Office.

Along the same line, in partnership with the NCMEC, more than 4,000 Walmart and Sam's Club stores post photographs of missing children in the stores, alerting shoppers to be on the lookout for the children. According to the NCMEC, these flyers have led to the recovery of more than 164 children since 1996.

Some agencies have assembled their own "most wanted" lists and have publicized them in newspapers and on the Internet. Some police departments regularly disseminate crime alerts to notify citizens of particular criminal incidents and to put them on the lookout for related suspicious activity. One commonly cited limitation to newspaper and news alerts is that the people who may most likely know about crimes and criminals may not regularly read the newspaper or watch the television news. In recognition of this, many police departments, through the media, place crime stories and calls for information on YouTube. Police in Seattle, Washington, are experimenting with billboards and bus ads that feature photos of homicide victims in cases where the perpetrators have not yet been identified (Green 2012). Placed above the photos is the simple question, "Who Killed Me?"

Other cities have experimented with making standardized forms available in churches and other public places that citizens can use to anonymously inform on drug dealers and other criminals. The Bergen County Sheriff's Department in New Jersey developed FaceCrook (www.facecrook.net), a computer application available to jail inmates that allows them to anonymously provide information to implicate others involved in crimes (TechBeat 2013).

In one way or another, each of these strategies is designed to elicit information from members of the public (or inmates, in the case of FaceCrook). While these methods can assist in investigations, they are not without limitations. First, with regard to tip lines in particular, the police can get easily overwhelmed with "leads," most of which are likely irrelevant in the investigation. Members of the public may think that their information may relate to the crime in question when actually it does not, but at the time the information is received, the police may not be able to recognize the information as false or irrelevant. For example, during the Washington, D.C., sniper investigation, residents called the police to report sightings of hundreds upon hundreds of white vans and white box trucks. As it turned out, none of this information was useful or relevant. In the Unabomber investigation (Chapter 1), the

PHOTO 9.7: Another way to get the word out about missing persons is by putting requests for information on semi-truck trailers.

police received more than 20,000 calls to their tip line, but none of them turned out to be useful in the investigation. Within a month after the September 11, 2001, terrorist acts in New York and Washington, D.C., authorities had received nearly 500,000 tips on suspected terrorists and terrorist activity (Davis et al. 2002). After the anthrax letters case was profiled on *America's Most Wanted*, more than 700 tips were received by authorities.

Second, the false information received through tip lines and other sources may bring to police attention innocent "suspects." Accordingly, questions may be raised about how subjects may be affected when the police take action against them as a result of anonymous information. It is certainly possible that in some instances individuals may call to falsely report the conduct of friends, associates, ex-husbands, or ex-wives as a way of getting revenge. The police can be used by citizens in this regard, and the consequences may be unpleasant for everyone.

Another potential problem is determining how reward money should be fairly allocated among the people who provided useful information. In the Beltway sniper case, for example, the reward fund was $500,000 and would have likely been more if it had not been not capped (Schulte and Moreno 2002). Who should get the money and how should this decision be made? Should the priest have gotten it? The caller from Washington State who reported that Malvo and Muhammad used a high-powered gun in their backyard? The individual who noticed the suspects' car at the rest stop? These are difficult decisions, and there is no precise way of making them. It has not been reported how the reward money was allocated (Potter 2002).

Other potential problems associated with the use of the public as a source of information include questions about (1) the credibility and motivation of citizens who inform for purposes of money, especially when they remain anonymous; (2) how the publicity on the case may affect the perceptions of others with information on the case (e.g., the repeated sightings of a white van in the sniper investigation); (3) how publicity may affect other dimensions of the case (e.g., pretrial publicity and the ability to receive a fair trial); and (4) whether money should be paid for actions that are arguably one's civic responsibility.

PHOTO 9.8: A street billboard is used to seek information about a murder investigation.

These are difficult questions to address, but investigators should at least be aware of them when considering information from the public.

●●● Confidential Informants

While members of the public who provide information to the police on usually a one-time basis may be best considered *informers,* those who assist law enforcement in a more active and ongoing capacity are best considered *confidential informants* (Miller 2011). Confidential informants, also referred to as CIs or "street sources," are most often used by the police in ongoing undercover investigations, especially those that are drug related. Informants are often associated with the criminal underworld; they are in a position to have the information that the police need to make cases and the knowledge about the inner workings of criminal groups (i.e., who, what, where, when, and why).

Obviously, the police and investigators have regular contact with criminals and with other people who are familiar with criminals and their activities. It is from these contacts that informants can be found or recruited. In particular, suspects who were recently arrested or those who are about to be arrested are particularly good candidates for being "turned" as informants (Botsch 2008). An investigator may say something like, "You're on paper (parole)? And you got weed? You are going to jail unless you tell me about who is dealing drugs in the neighborhood." If this sounds like a controversial practice, that is because it

CASE *in* POINT *9.4*   The Murder of Carli Brucia

The well-publicized Carlie Brucia case provides a grim example in which fortune did not favor the victim for whom an AMBER Alert was issued. Carlie Brucia was abducted by a stranger on the evening of February 1, 2004, near a car wash in Manatee County, Florida. By chance, the abduction was recorded by a surveillance camera examined the next evening, leading to an immediate nationwide AMBER Alert. NASA technology was used to improve the surveillance video's accuracy, and with tips from citizens, investigators identified, captured, and elicited a confession from Carlie's abductor by February 5. It is difficult to see how authorities could have acted more swiftly or professionally. Yet, tragically, Carlie was already dead when the alert was issued on February 2 (quoted from Griffin et al. 2007, p. 388).

PHOTO 9.5: Within approximately twenty-four hours of Carlie Brucia's abduction, an AMBER Alert was issued. The alert led to information about who abducted her (the man seen in this still video photograph). Unfortunately, Carlie was murdered prior to the issuance of the alert.

is. The use of informants is often viewed as a necessary evil. Perhaps lessening the controversy a bit is that not all informants are turned as a result of coercion. When coercion is not a factor, officers need to build relationships with people who are familiar with the criminal culture. Like any relationship, these relationships need to be nurtured and built on trust and respect (Botsch 2008). The relationship is not necessarily with the police agency, it is with individual police officers or detectives; as such, street sources should be encouraged to contact officers directly when they have information to share (Botsch 2008).

Miller (2011) explains that there are four different types of informants, each with a different motivation for cooperating with the police. First, the "hammered" informant, the most common, is coerced by the police to provide information. As noted above, these individuals are "squeezed" for information. These subjects cut a deal with the police to avoid arrest or to obtain lenient treatment (e.g., "Tell me what you know about T-Bone or you're going to jail"). Miller (2011) quotes an informant who expressed this motivation: "I wasn't very cool and acted desperate because I thought I was headed to jail. I offered to do what they wanted and just kept saying I didn't want to go to jail" (p. 211). The next most common type is the "mercenary" informant. This person is motivated by money. He or she is interested in basically selling information to the police. Third is the "vengeful" informant. This person is motivated by revenge against others, such as a competing drug dealer, a competing gang, or nuisance neighbors. Finally, the least commonly encountered informant is the "police buff" informer. This person is a fan of the police—a police wannabe. Unlike the others, this person may not be immersed in the criminal culture, so often their access to critical and accurate information is limited. Understand that any combination of these motivations may be at play with any particular informant and that people may initially provide information to the police for one reason (e.g., coercion) and then continue their relationship with the police for another (e.g., money).

Exhibit 9.2   Tips for Handling Informants

- Maintain control of the informant and the case; the investigator is in charge, not the informant.

- Limit the informant's exposure to other undercover officers and share only necessary information with the informant. The informant may be the subject of an investigation in the future, so he or she should not know too much.

- Maintain the informant's confidentiality when promised; the success of the case and the informant's safety may depend on it.

- Only make promises to the informant that can be kept.

- Informants should be treated with respect, but the relationship should remain professional.

- Meetings with informants should be with two officers, for safety reasons as well as to guard against allegations of officer misconduct.

- If the informant is to be paid, he or she should receive payment as soon as the agreement has been fulfilled. Payment should be documented and managed.

- Informants should be used and managed in accordance with agency policy.

Source: Adapted and modified from Darin D. Fredrickson and Raymond P. Siljander. 2004. *Street Drug Investigation: A Practical Guide for Plainclothes and Uniformed Personnel.* Springfield: Charles C. Thomas, pp. 133–135.

Although the use of informants is often necessary during certain investigations, the practice is clearly not without controversy. In particular, is it okay to forgo criminal penalties in exchange for information? Is it ethical for the police to pay criminals for information? Other controversies arise from the sometimes close working relationship between the police and informants. In any case, it is certainly an area that needs to be managed closely (Mount 1990; Fredrickson and Siljander 2004). According to Marx (1988), "The problems created by informers can be lessened by awareness and constant vigilance and by appropriate policies and procedures, which include written guidelines, criteria for selection and evaluation, centralized informant records, and explicit instructions" (p. 158) (See Exhibit 9.2).

●●● Gang Intelligence

A relatively small proportion of the population is responsible for a relatively high proportion of all crime, especially violent crime. In particular, gang members are disproportionately involved in all serious violent crime, especially murder, other nonfatal shootings (especially drive-by shootings), and robbery. The 2011 National Gang Threat Assessment released by the National Gang Intelligence Center (NGIC) found that gangs are responsible for an average of 48 percent of violent crime in most jurisdictions and up to 90 percent in several others. Gangs are also heavily involved in drug trafficking and dealing, as well as other nontraditional gang-related crimes such as alien smuggling, human trafficking, and prostitution. Gangs are also engaging in white-collar crimes such as counterfeiting, identity theft, and mortgage fraud (National Gang Intelligence Center 2011). As a result, in urban areas, and in some not-so-urban areas, the police have frequent dealings with gang members.

Given the involvement of gangs in crime, it is necessary for investigators to understand the operations and workings of gangs in their communities. Some police departments have a specialized gang unit designed to collect and act upon gang information. This information (or, as it is often called, intelligence) can be obtained from a variety of sources, including citizens, informants, the offenders themselves, and officers on the street. In many instances, the information can be stored electronically and can be a useful source of potential leads in investigations. As explained by the NGIC:

> Gang units and task forces are a vital component in targeting gangs and have played a substantial role in mitigating gang activity in a number of US communities. The majority of NGIC law enforcement partners report that their agency has or participates in a gang task force, and most utilize a gang database to track and monitor gang members in their jurisdictions (see www.fbi.gov/stats-services/publications/2011-national-gang-threat-assessment).

One such database is GRIP (Gang/Narcotics Relational Intelligence Program). GRIP provides a way to compile, store, categorize, and retrieve information on suspected gang members. The database can store various types of information on subjects, including demographic data, physical characteristics, gang affiliation, criminal history, aliases, vehicles, and addresses and phone numbers associated with subjects. Pictures of subjects can also be included in the database. Searches of the database can be made on any of these dimensions. Along the same lines, Tattoo-ID is a computer software program that allows for the identification of persons (offenders and/or victims) based on images of tattoos that are maintained in the database. Suspect's tattoos can be photographed and these images stored in the database. The database can be searched using descriptions of the tattoos or actual images of the tattoos (White 2008).

WHAT IS A GANG AND HOW PREVALENT ARE THEY?

There is no single agreed-upon definition of a gang. However, there are several criteria that show up repeatedly in definitions of gangs (see www.nationalgangcenter.gov/About/FAQ#q1):

- The group has three or more members, generally aged twelve to twenty-four.
- Members share an identity, typically linked to a name, and often other symbols.
- Members view themselves as a gang, and they are recognized by others as a gang.
- The group has some permanence and a degree of organization.
- The group is involved in an elevated level of criminal activity.

Gangs vary by city (e.g., the gangs in Chicago are not the same as the ones in Los Angeles), state (e.g., the gangs in northern California are not the same as the ones in southern California), and geographical region (e.g., gangs on the east coast are not the same as the ones on the west coast). Gangs are also most often differentiated by race or members' country of origin. For example, Gangster Disciples, Bloods, and Crips are primarily African American gangs, Mexican Posse is a Hispanic gang, Asian Boyz is an Asian gang, the Trinitarios is a Dominican Gang, and the Juggalos is a primarily Caucasian gang. Law enforcement experiences with gangs will also vary considerably across communities.

According to the NGIC, there were approximately 33,000 gangs criminally active in the United States in 2011. Certainly, major, large gangs are far fewer in number. Approximately 1.4 million members belonged to these gangs, although what constitutes being a "member" of a gang is subject to some debate. Arizona, California, and Illinois have the greatest number of gang members. California alone has over 300 different identifiable street gangs.

GANG MEMBER IDENTIFICATION

Although gangs are heavily involved in criminal behavior, their orientation, structure, and operations vary. Some gangs are very tightly organized with a clear chain of command; some are loosely organized. Some gangs are oriented exclusively to drug sales; others are involved in not only drug sales but a wide range of illegal activity such as human trafficking, immigrant smuggling, and prostitution. Some gangs are oriented toward turf; others are oriented more toward profit.

As an identified group or organization, gangs have identifiers, primarily colors and symbols. This is not unlike your college or university that also has colors and symbols. (My university, The University of Wisconsin-Milwaukee, has gold and black colors, a panther is the school mascot, and it is known as UWM.) Gang colors are often worn, and symbols often show up in graffiti, tattoos, and hand signs (e.g., "throwing" a sign). The recognition of colors, tattoos, and gang signs, and the comprehension of graffiti, can be valuable in the identification of gang members and activities (Exhibit 9.3).

Exhibit 9.3 The Basics of Gang Graffiti

Graffiti is a method of communicating in the world of gangs. Some people post an ad in the newspaper or post status updates on Facebook; gangs more often write graffiti on walls, street signs, and buildings. Graffiti is most often used to mark the territory of gangs and to communicate with other gangs—or even the police. Graffiti is an indicator of disorder in an area and, as such, can have many negative effects on a neighborhood and its residents. Graffiti should be removed as quickly as possible or more is sure to appear. Not all graffiti is the work of gangs. "Tagging" appears more as colorful art in the form of words or names, and most often consists of "bubble" letters. This graffiti is not likely to be gang related. Gang graffiti is generally less artistic. It is more likely to be in the form of code, such as a series of letters that do not form a word; more likely to be in only one color of paint; more likely to be written with "stick" letters and numbers; and more likely to include other symbols (e.g., pitchforks, stars, etc).

There is much variety and meaning to gang graffiti. Entire books and training seminars are devoted to the topic. Discussed here are a few of the basics. Two-digit numbers most often indicate a Hispanic gang, especially 13 and 14. Other gangs are most often represented with letters or abbreviations (e.g., GD for Gangster Disciples, VL for Vice Lords, B for Bloods, C for Crips). *F* most often indicates "folks," and *P* indicates "people" (most street gangs are affiliated with one or the other larger groups). Three-digit numbers most often refer to an area code in which the gang operates, although it can have other meanings as well. The letter *K* stands for "kill" and is a threat to what comes before or after it. Similarly, crossed-out letters also indicate a threat to kill. The letters *N, S, E,* and *W* most often refer to directions and indicators as to the territory of the gang. *A* usually stands for "almighty," *N* for "nation"—standard add-ons without too much meaning. Of course, the specific types of graffiti present in a particular community will depend on the gangs that are active in that community.

PHOTO 9.9: Citizens often confuse tagger graffiti with gang graffiti. If it looks artistic, as in the photo above, it is most likely not gang graffiti.

Because gang members can be identified on the basis of their colors, tattoos, and hand signs, some gangs have stopped using these indicators. Some gang members have formed hybrid gangs (gangs with multiple affiliations, a loose structure, members with multiple ethnicities) to avoid police scrutiny and to make it more difficult to identify and monitor their activities. Many gangs are becoming involved in more sophisticated crimes, including identity theft, computer hacking, and currency counterfeiting (National Gang Intelligence Center 2011). They are also becoming increasingly technology savvy, using discreet electronic methods for communication and using the Internet for recruitment, gang promotion, and witness intimidation (National Gang Intelligence Center 2011). These facts clearly underscore the need for investigations to include social networking and other Internet sites as a source of information in gang investigations (see below for additional related discussion).

Exhibit 9.4

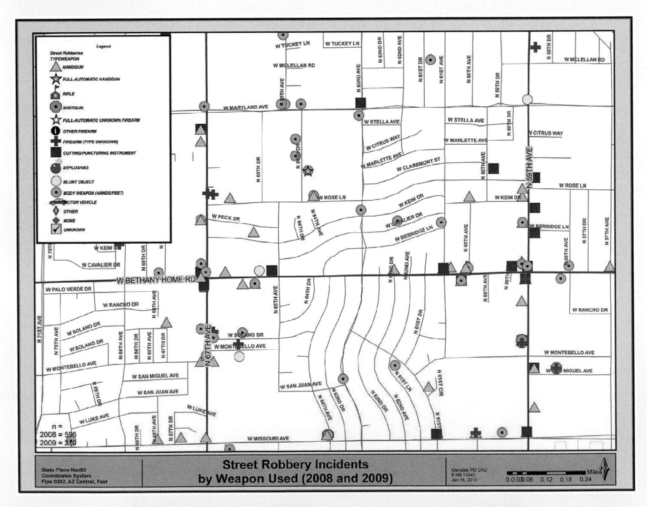

Crime maps are frequently used in crime analysis and provide an easy way by which to visualize how crime is distributed in a community.

Source: Khadija M. Monk, Justin A. Heinonen, and John E. Eck. 2010. *Street Robbery*. Problem-Oriented Guides for Police Series: Problem-Specific Guide No. 59. Washington, DC: U.S. Department of Justice

CRIME MAPPING AND ANALYSIS, AND GEO-SPATIAL ANALYSIS

Broadly defined, "Crime analysis involves the collection and analysis of data pertaining to a criminal incident, offender, and target" (Canter 2000, p. 4). Crime analysis often serves as a basis on which police managers develop strategies to confront and investigate particular crimes or patterns of crimes. Crime analysis can provide the necessary information to make informed patrol allocation decisions, to make predictions about when and where crime will occur, to identify future targets of offenders, and to track offender movements. Because crime analysis is often geographically based (geospatial), maps are a commonly used and useful tool in the task of crime analysis.

Methods of geographic-based crime analysis vary considerably in their sophistication. At the most basic level are maps with color-coded pins that are used to illustrate visually where various crimes have occurred in a particular jurisdiction over a particular period of time. Through a quick inspection of such a map, a basic understanding of the distribution of crime across space can be developed. More elaborate crime analysis methodologies include the use of geographical information systems (GIS) that allow for the automated recording and plotting of criminal incidents on detailed computerized maps. Many of these systems also allow for the manipulation of the corresponding crime data to reveal patterns of crime, or certain types of crime, across time (time of day, week, month, year) and space (e.g., crime that occurs in and around schools, public transportation stops and stations, etc.). One of the primary objectives of geospatial crime analysis is to predict where and when future crimes will occur and to allocate resources to these places and times in order to either prevent the crime from occurring or to apprehend perpetrators as crimes occur. That crime is a *non*random phenomenon provides a theoretical rationale for geospatial crime analysis and the goals associated with it (see Myths and Misconceptions 9.1).

MYTHS & MISCONCEPTIONS 9.1

Crime Is a Random Phenomenon

If we are to believe the media, crime is substantially a random and unpredictable phenomenon. Headline stories such as "Acid Attacks on Mall Shoppers under Investigation," "University Student Gunned Down on Way to Class," and "Random Shooting on City Beach" clearly create and reinforce this view. The fact is that while some crime is random, the majority of it is not. In particular, predatory street crime (murder, rape, robbery, shootings, etc.) is not distributed evenly across time or space. In other words, some *times* are more likely to experience crimes than other times (e.g., there is more crime at night than during the day, there is more crime on Saturdays than Mondays) and some *places* are more likely to experience more crime than other places (e.g., taverns have more crime than churches) (Sherman et al. 1989).

The so-called cockroach theory of crime suggests that places (and times) that have experienced a lot of crime in the past will likely experience more crime in the future (i.e., if a place has fifty cockroaches, chances are that another will show up soon). However, a place that has not experienced any crime in the past will likely not experience crime in the future (i.e., if a place has no cockroaches, chances are there won't be any in the near future either). At the very least, one would be confident in the prediction that if there is going to be another crime in the future, it is more likely to occur at the place that has had more crime in the past, not at the place that has not had any crime in the past. Crime does not just happen randomly. This basic understanding allows for predictions about where and when it will occur and the corresponding introduction of appropriate interventions to prevent it.

Some crime analysis systems operated by police departments include automated crime report information. These systems allow investigators to extract specific subsets of data records (e.g., all robberies that occurred between 1 a.m. and 3 a.m. on Fridays in which the perpetrator was described as a white man approximately twenty years of age) to identify more clearly patterns of crimes (Maltz et al. 1991). Some police departments have made the crime analysis function central to the management of the organization. Such is the case with COMPSTAT in the New York City Police Department and other departments. This system has been used to identify crime patterns and to manage, monitor, and assess the impact of various crime control strategies. Critical to the COMPSTAT system are the meetings that take place during which precinct commanders brief department executives on the results of crime control initiatives that have been undertaken to deal with the identified crime problems (McGuire 2000). Rightfully or not, the dramatic crime decline in crime in New York City during the 1990s was largely attributed to the use of COMPSTAT (McGuire 2000).

VIOLENT CRIMINAL APPREHENSION PROGRAM (ViCAP)

Another example of a sophisticated crime analysis system is ViCAP. ViCAP is a nationwide computerized database system maintained and operated by the FBI as part of the National Center for the Analysis of Violent Crime (NCAVC). It has been in operation since 1985. The system is designed to collect, collate, and analyze specific crimes of violence to identify similar MO or signature aspects of the crime. The goal is to identify crimes that have been committed by the same person. ViCAP is focused on three primary types of crimes: (1) solved or unsolved homicides or homicide attempts (especially those that involve an abduction, appear sexually motivated, or are suspected of being part of a series), (2) missing persons cases in which foul play is suspected, and (3) unidentified dead bodies in which the cause of death is believed to be as the result of a homicide. If crimes can be linked—if the crimes were committed by the same offender—then representatives from the various agencies can come together and work cooperatively in investigating the crimes. Along with the operation of the ViCAP computer system, ViCAP also issues alerts for law enforcement in an attempt to identify associated cases and offenders. An example of a ViCAP alert on a crime that was eventually solved is provided in Case in Point 9.5.

ViCAP is a tool that can be used to overcome what has been referred to as *linkage blindness*—the tendency of law enforcement agencies to be unable to identify serial crimes that occur across jurisdictional boundaries (Egger 1998). Similar crime databases are operated in several states and are integrated with the ViCAP system. Examples of this are the Homicide Investigation and Tracking System, or HITS, in Washington State, and the New Jersey Homicide Evaluation and Assessment Tracking, or HEAT (Keppel and Weis 1993; Rossmo 2000).

In 1996, an audit of the ViCAP system showed that it was being dramatically underutilized: relatively few homicides were contained in the nationwide database, homicides from large cities were rarely included, and analyses were not performed on a timely basis (Witzig 2003). As a result, ViCAP was redesigned to be more user-friendly. Along with still offering centralized case submissions and analysis at the FBI academy, the new VICAP now provides for networked computer terminals and software in police departments so investigators can have direct access to cases in the ViCAP system nationwide. Police departments can also use ViCAP to store information about cases in their own jurisdictions. In addition, the original 189-question ViCAP form that was used to capture case information (e.g., victim information, offense MO, condition of victim, cause of death) was redesigned to ninety-five questions (Witzig 2003). There are many success stories associated with the operation of the ViCAP system (see Case in Point 9.6).

Clearly, ViCAP has the potential to be a powerful tool in linking the crimes of serial offenders; however, it also has limitations. Most importantly, if the MO used by the offender

CASE in POINT 9.5   ViCAP Alert

On May 21, 2002, Stephanie Renee Bennett, a twenty-three-year-old white female with brown hair and brown eyes who stood 5' 5" and weighed 125 pounds, was found dead in her apartment, which was located in northwest Raleigh, North Carolina. She had been sexually assaulted and murdered. Stephanie recently had graduated from college and had lived in the apartment for about ten months with two female roommates, one of whom was her stepsister. At about 3:30 p.m. on May 21, 2002, Stephanie's stepsister authorized apartment management personnel to enter the apartment for a welfare check after she could not contact Stephanie at the apartment. Stephanie was discovered deceased.

Stephanie and her two roommates lived on the first floor of a three-bedroom corner apartment in a building centrally located within the complex. Evidence suggests that the offender's initial contact with Stephanie was in her bedroom. Egress into the apartment appears to have been made by removing the screen to an unlocked window in one of the unoccupied bedrooms. Even though there was very little disturbance within the apartment, including no signs of a struggle, some articles (pictures and stuffed animals) deliberately had been moved from one location to another. Additionally, a cordless telephone unit, consisting of the base and handset, was disconnected from the cord in the bedroom and placed in the bedroom closet. The offender took the victim's nightwear and an old stereo when he left the apartment.

Stephanie was found completely nude, lying on her back, with her legs spread open and her head tilted to one side. In her mouth was a gag (a pair of unused panties that belonged to one of her roommates). Visual marks were on Stephanie's wrist and ankles and attributed to a form of restraint used by the offender to immobilize her. These marks were similar to those left by handcuffs or a narrow type of restraint, such as a telephone cord or electrical ties. A well-defined ligature injury mark encompassed Stephanie's neck, and several marks at the rear base of her neck gave the appearance that a garrote-type device was used in conjunction with the ligature. The restraints and ligature were removed by the offender and taken with him when he left the crime scene. An autopsy report disclosed that Stephanie was sexually assaulted orally, anally, and vaginally. DNA from the unidentified offender has been profiled and is maintained in the FBI's Combined DNA Index System (CODIS) and the North Carolina State Bureau of Investigation Laboratory.

Law enforcement agencies should bring this information to the attention of all crime analysis and sexual assault units, as well as officers investigating crimes against persons. Also, the offender's DNA profile should be provided to local and state laboratories for comparison purposes. Any agency with similar crimes should contact Crime Analyst Glen W. Wildey Jr., VICAP, Quantico, Virginia, at 703–632–4166.

Update: In October 2005, Drew Planten, thirty-five, was arrested in connection with the sexual assault and murder of Stephanie Bennett. At the time of the crime, Planten lived in the apartment complex located next to Stephanie. In the spring of 2004, residents reported to the police that Planten possibly matched the description of a Peeping Tom seen near Stephanie's apartment weeks before her death. But Planten was just one of many suspects, one of many names that came up in the investigation. In an attempt to identify the perpetrator, or at least develop leads on the cold case, investigators set up a Web site, www.StephanieBennett.com, and monitored who visited the site. One of the computers that accessed the site was located at the North Carolina Department of Agriculture. This computer was used by Drew Planten, a chemist who worked there. Authorities already knew of Planten from the earlier identification. Authorities obtained a pair of gloves that he used at work (taken by a coworker and given to the police), and from the gloves a DNA profile was obtained. It matched the DNA profile taken from Stephanie. Investigators obtained a search warrant of Planten's premises and recovered numerous items, including property taken from Stephanie's apartment (e.g., her bank statements, college loan papers) and a large collection of guns and pornography. One of the guns seized from his apartment was linked to an unsolved homicide of a young woman in Michigan several years prior. While awaiting trial, Drew Planten committed suicide in jail on January 3, 2006.

Source: Adapted from Federal Bureau of Investigation. 2004. ViCap Alert. FBI Law Enforcement Bulletin 73(10): 13. Washington DC: U.S. Department of Justice.

CASE *in* POINT 9.6   ViCAP Success Stories

ViCAP became involved in the investigation of [Rafael] Ramirez, who would eventually be the suspect in various crimes in Texas and Kentucky. When Texas authorities first learned that two Texas cases were possibly linked by a common offender, ViCAP was contacted. Based on certain behaviors and methodology of the offender in their two cases, ViCAP was able to tell them of a similar case in Kentucky that had occurred two years before. Investigators followed up with a DNA analysis, which matched the cases, and this became the catalyst for authorities to realize that they had a national serial offender on the loose. ViCAP assisted the investigation by providing the Texas authorities

with other possibly related cases occurring elsewhere in the United States.

ViCAP continues to be used to solve crimes from the past. In 1989, investigators from Pennsylvania entered a case from 1951 into the ViCAP database. In this case a man was found guilty of murdering a young girl. Not long after, investigators from Illinois entered an unsolved case from 1957 in which an approximately eight-year-old girl was murdered. Analysis in ViCAP noticed similarities in the two cases. Due to these similarities and other related evidence, detectives in Illinois were able to solve a crime that occurred almost forty years ago.

across crimes is not similar, or if signature aspects of the crime are missing, not recognized, or change across crimes, the ViCAP system may be of limited use. In addition, by its design, ViCAP may do little in actually solving crimes—that is, identifying and apprehending perpetrators. As noted, the system is designed to identify crimes committed by the same offender, not necessarily to identify that offender. As illustrated in the second example provided earlier, only in select instances may VICAP *directly* contribute to the solving of crimes. Finally, to link crimes, crimes have to be contained in the database. Investigators must voluntarily submit their case data to the FBI ViCAP or enter case data on their own, and this involves additional work on the part of investigators. Up until the last few years, the system contained information on only 15,000 cases. ViCAP now reportedly contains more than 84,000 cases (see www.fbi.gov/about-us/cirg/investigations-and-operations).

EMPIRICAL CRIME ANALYSIS

A different but somewhat related form of crime analysis involves the empirical analysis of previous crimes in an effort to respond more effectively to such crimes in the future. As noted earlier in this chapter, research on abduction cases has shown that if a child is abducted by a stranger, the child is killed within the first hour in nearly half the cases, within three hours in nearly three-quarters of the cases, and within twenty-four hours in 91 percent of cases (Rossmo 2000). In cases in which a victim was killed and was not believed to have been transported by vehicle, 98 percent of the bodies were found within fifty yards of a footpath. In cases that involved victim transportation, 88 percent of bodies were located within fifty yards of a road or vehicular path (Rossmo 2000). This type of information may be useful in directing search efforts for missing (abducted) persons. Other analyses conducted on offender characteristics may provide assistance in the construction of psychological profiles.

●●● Electronic Databases and Information Networks

A multitude of electronic databases exist that investigators may use to obtain critical information needed during a criminal investigation. These databases can be classified as either intradepartmental or interdepartmental.

INTRADEPARTMENTAL DATABASES

Intradepartmental databases are ones that are operated and maintained by individual law enforcement agencies. Depending on the resources available and the size of the agency, there may be many such systems available to investigators. For example, investigators may have access to pawnshop records. In many jurisdictions, pawnshop operators (and/or second-hand dealers) are required to submit to their local police department a record of all merchandise received and information about from whom the merchandise was purchased. Depending on the organization of the system and how current the information is kept, such records could be particularly useful in burglary and robbery investigations. As another example, some police departments keep computerized files on all individuals with whom the police have had contact (e.g., as victims, complainants, witnesses, suspects, etc.). This information may be useful in developing a police contact history of individuals.

INTERDEPARTMENTAL DATABASES

The two largest and most used interdepartmental databases are the NCIC and the NLETS. These and several other databases are discussed below.

NATIONAL CRIME INFORMATION CENTER (NCIC)

The NCIC is the largest and most well-known crime information network system in the United States. It is maintained by the FBI at its headquarters in Washington, D.C. The NCIC began operations in 1967; by 1971, police agencies in all fifty states were linked to the system. Today, more than 80,000 law enforcement and criminal justice agencies have access to the NCIC database. The system contains more than 34 million records (including criminal history records contained in the Interstate Identification Index). Nearly two million queries are made of the system daily.

The NCIC consists of a centralized database and a network of connecting computer terminals located in criminal justice agencies throughout the country. Representatives of agencies may enter information into the database and make queries of the database. The originating agency also has the responsibility for removing records once the record is no longer valid (e.g., when a missing person is found). The system contains information in various files, including the following (from www.fas.org/irp/agency/doj/fbi/is/ncic.htm):

- Wanted persons (for either questioning or arrest; including name, DOB, offense, date of warrant, whether armed, number of companions, and whether the person is considered dangerous)

- Missing persons (divisions within this file consist of missing disabled persons, endangered missing persons, involuntary missing persons, and missing juvenile persons)

- Unidentified persons (descriptions of unidentified dead persons)

- Criminal history and fingerprint classification (details on individuals who have been arrested for felony, murder, and other serious crimes, as well as a description of their fingerprint patterns)

- Stolen and felony vehicles (contains information on vehicles that have been reported stolen as well as those vehicles known to have been used in the commission of a crime)

- Recovered vehicles (contains information on vehicles that have been recovered by law enforcement authorities)

- Stolen and recovered firearms (includes information on the type and description of the firearm, serial number, date of theft/recovery, and persons apprehended during the course of recovering the firearm)

- Stolen and recovered heavy equipment (contains information on stolen farm and construction equipment)

- Stolen and recovered boats and marine equipment (includes date of theft/recovery, description of boat, type of boat, registration number, and hull identification number)

- Stolen license plates (includes date of theft, license number, state, year, and number of plates stolen)

- Stolen and recovered securities (includes serial numbers and other details about stolen U.S. Treasury notes, bonds, and bills; municipal and corporate bonds; and stocks)

- Stolen and recovered identifiable articles (includes identifying details about stolen and recovered auto parts, avionic equipment, computers, cameras, tools, musical instruments, and office equipment)

- Canadian warrants (includes information on individuals that are wanted on warrants issued by the Royal Canadian Mounted Police and who may be in the United States)

- U.S. Secret Service protective file (a classified data file that contains information on individuals considered a danger to the president, former presidents, high officials, and visiting heads of state)

- Interstate identification index (provides criminal history information on individuals who are either wanted or missing)

- Foreign fugitive file (provides information on foreign individuals who are wanted on warrants)

- Violent gang/terrorist file (provides information on individuals believed to be terrorists or members of violent gangs)

The NCIC has the capability of quickly putting vast and critical information in the hands of police and investigators. As such, the NCIC can be a powerful investigative tool. The list of instances when NCIC information led to the apprehension of offenders, the discovery of missing persons, and the recovery of property is a long one. As just one example, consider the apprehension of Timothy McVeigh, who was responsible for the bombing of the federal building in Oklahoma City. Once investigators had developed McVeigh as a suspect in the bombing, they entered his name in the NCIC database and learned that an Oklahoma state trooper had just run an NCIC search on him. A telephone call to this agency revealed that McVeigh was stopped on the highway and was currently in custody of the police. Only as a result of the NCIC was such a quick apprehension possible.

NATIONAL LAW ENFORCEMENT TELECOMMUNICATIONS SYSTEM (NLETS)

The NLETS is a network that links law enforcement agencies, other criminal justice agencies in the United States, and motor vehicle and licensing departments. The information available through the system includes:

- Vehicle registrations by license or VIN

- Driver's license and driving record by name and birth date or driver's license number

- Criminal history records by name and birth date

- Boat registration information

- Snowmobile registration information

- Hazardous material file data

- Private aircraft data, including registration information

- Index to parole/probation and corrections information

- Sex offender registration information

INTERPOL CASE TRACKING SYSTEM (ICTS)

The ICTS contains information about persons, property, and organizations involved in international criminal activity.

CENTRAL INDEX SYSTEM (CIS) AND RELATED DATABASES

The CIS is operated and maintained by the Bureau of U.S. Citizenship and Immigration Services (USCIS). It contains information on legal immigrants, naturalized citizens, and aliens who have been formally deported or excluded from the United States. The Nonimmigrant Information System of the USCIS contains information on the entry and departure of nonimmigrants (aliens) in the United States for a temporary stay. The Law Enforcement Support Center is also operated by the USCIS and provides information to local, state, and federal law enforcement agencies about aliens who have been arrested. The National Alien Information Lookout System consists of a USCIS index of names of individuals who may be excludable from the United States. The Consular Lookout and Support System is a related database operated by the U.S. Department of State. It contains information on several million individuals who have been determined to be ineligible for visas, those who need additional investigation prior to issuance of a visa, and those who would be ineligible for visas should they apply for one.

NATIONAL INTEGRATED BALLISTIC INFORMATION NETWORK (NIBIN)

As discussed in Chapter 5, the NIBIN is operated by the ATF. It is a computerized database that is similar in concept to AFIS, except that the NIBIN contains digital images of markings made by firearms on bullets and cartridge casings. Images of recovered bullets and casings are entered into the system, and a comparison search is made. In this way, gun crimes, and guns and offenders, may be linked together based on bullets/casings left at crime scenes and guns recovered from suspects.

EL PASO INTELLIGENCE CENTER (EPIC)

EPIC is designed to collect, process, and disseminate information concerning illegal drug use, alien smuggling, weapons trafficking, and related criminal activity. EPIC was established to facilitate the exchange of information across agencies that are responsible for the enforcement of drug and related laws.

SENTRY

Sentry is operated by the Federal Bureau of Prisons and contains information on all federal prisoners incarcerated since 1980. The available information includes the inmate's physical description, location, release information, custody classification, and sentencing information, among other items.

EQUIFAX

Equifax is a company that provides credit information on individuals. Databases within its operation may be used to collect various information on people, including recent addresses and demographic information. TransUnion is another consumer credit information company that offers background information, spending activity, and employment information on individuals.

OTHER DATABASES

In addition to these databases, numerous other sources of public information may be useful to investigators in investigating crimes. These sources are diverse, and their particular usefulness depends heavily on the issue at hand. These sources include motor vehicle registrations (e.g., useful when constructing a list of all vehicles registered in a particular area that match a particular description), credit card receipts and information (e.g., to document purchases and travel), bank records (e.g., to verify unusual deposits and withdrawals), attendance records at school or work (e.g., to verify a suspect's alibi or to help verify when a victim was last seen), reverse telephone directories (e.g., to determine a phone number from a known address), other telephone records (e.g., to verify phone calls made and received and the timing of those calls), and sex offender registries and related Department of Corrections information (e.g., to determine the whereabouts of particular offenders or to identify offenders who live in a particular area) (see www.nsopw.gov/ for a listing of state's sex offender registry Web sites).

LIMITATIONS

The primary limitation of information databases is that the database is only as good as the information that it contains. Of course, if information is not entered into the system—for example, in the case of the NCIC, if a gun is not reported as stolen or a missing person is not entered as missing—the database will be of little use to the police in this regard. Similarly, if a person has not been identified as "wanted" in a particular crime, the information contained in the database will not provide the information necessary to make an apprehension. Consider the Washington, D.C., sniper case discussed in the introduction to this chapter. As noted, at various times during the course of the shootings, police in the D.C. area performed numerous NCIC and NLETS queries on the vehicle that was eventually linked to the shooters. On at least one occasion, the name of the driver of the vehicle—John Muhammad—was run through the system. None of the checks revealed that the vehicle or the driver was wanted or connected to any crime. Indeed, the vehicle was not stolen, nor was the driver wanted for previous offenses. It was only after the suspects were identified by name through other means that the NCIC and the NLETS were useful in identifying the make and model of the car that the suspects were believed to be driving. Similarly, it has been reported that Tamerlan Tsarnaev, the mastermind of the Boston Marathon bombing in 2013, was on a national terrorism database watch list. This information was of no use in the prevention of the bombings or in his identification.

••• Social Networking and Other Internet Sites

For many people, social networking means Facebook and Twitter, although there are numerous other social networking (or entertainment) sites available on the Internet, including Instagram, Vine, and MySpace. Facebook was created in 2004 and today has over one billion users worldwide. The rules of Facebook state that a member must be at least thirteen years old to join. There are no user fees associated with registering or using Facebook; Facebook revenue is derived primarily from advertising. Members register on the site and add other members as "friends." Friends can communicate with each other in various ways, including through the sharing of messages and photos. According to Facebook, approximately 250 million photos are uploaded on Facebook every day; currently the site holds more than 90 billion photos. One of the primary concerns associated with Facebook is user privacy. Because it is possible for members to see content posted by other members, Facebook provides various privacy settings, which can limit the amount of information available to members who are not on a member's friends list.

Facebook holds a wealth of information (intelligence) for investigators. It is possible for an investigator to become a member of Facebook and anonymously search (stalk) by name people who he or she is interested in learning about. Without restricted privacy settings on the part of the subject in question, investigators may be able to identify the subject's friends, see written conversations between the subject and his or her friends, learn of the subject's recent activities and whereabouts, and view photographs on the subject's page. In a recent case, investigators searched for a particular subject on Facebook, and on his page they saw a photograph of him posing with his girlfriend and holding a shotgun. One problem . . . he was a convicted felon. Convicted felons are not allowed to possess firearms. On the basis of this photo, the subject was arrested and his parole was revoked.

If members have restricted privacy settings on their page, investigators may register and then request to be added as a friend. To do so, the investigator may need to "go undercover" and register as a fictitious person, perhaps with a fictitious profile photo. Many members, especially many young adults, have hundreds or even thousands of friends on Facebook, many of whom the member may never have even met. This provides an opportunity for the undercover investigator to get "friended" by the subject and then gain access to all the information available on the subject's page. Again, photographs may be most useful, including those of subjects posing with stolen merchandise or subjects seen doing illegal things (even drinking or using drugs). These photographs are evidence—corpus delicti evidence. Members can also affiliate themselves with others by joining or "liking" groups and interests on Facebook. Groups and interests may include everything from street gangs to terrorist groups.

Similar to Facebook, Twitter has the potential to be a useful source of information in investigations. Users post comments and information on their activities; "followers" receive this information, which can be incriminating. Reportedly, Dzhokhar Tsarnaev, one of the Boston Marathon bombers, "tweeted" shortly before the bombings, "Ain't no love in the heart of the city. Be careful people."

Many police departments also use Facebook and Twitter to disseminate information, to alert citizens to incidents, and to request information. As noted earlier, one of the limitations of traditional media as a way of prompting citizens to provide crime tips is that the people who may be most likely to have such information may be the least likely to use traditional media. Social network sites represent a potential remedy to this problem.

Craigslist, an Internet-based marketplace, also offers opportunities for the police to detect criminal behavior, especially prostitution. Although the site does not officially allow illegal activity to be posted, many have criticized it for not doing enough in keeping such listings off the site. Indeed, ads abound on Craigslist for sex without explicitly acknowledging that it is sex for pay. Similar to the enforcement of such crimes on the street, investigators go undercover, respond to the ads, set the terms of the transaction, and then make arrests.

Finally, YouTube is another potential source of information on crimes and criminals. YouTube is an Internet site that contains videos that are uploaded by people, as well as by television networks and other sources. Police departments also use YouTube to disseminate information. There is a video on just about everything on YouTube. For some reason, some people post videos that show illegal activity. In one case, a subject stole a Taser from a police vehicle, went home, and video recorded himself and his father "tasing" each other. The subject then uploaded the video to YouTube. Further investigation by the police led to the subjects and to the YouTube video. There are many other stories where subjects video-recorded various criminal acts as they occurred and then posted them on YouTube for later discovery by the police. No question, as technology evolves, other avenues will present themselves as sources of intelligence for criminal investigations.

●●● Psychics

When all else fails, when there is nowhere else to turn, when the police are at a loss regarding what to do next, the police may turn to a psychic for assistance in an investigation. In such a situation, investigators may be trapped between the embarrassment of an unsolved high-profile case and the embarrassment of enlisting the help of a psychic.

Psychic phenomena are related to the science of parapsychology, or extrasensory perception (ESP). There are several forms of ESP, including telepathy (the ability to read minds and transmit thoughts, or *thought transference*); clairvoyance (the ability to see objects and events beyond the range of physical vision); precognition (the ability to perceive future events); and retrocognition (the ability to see into the past). These phenomena have been studied at length; in fact, there is even a scholarly journal devoted to the study of such phenomena, the *Journal of Parapsychology*. Although there is a paucity of scientific research that documents and verifies the existence of ESP, there is much anecdotal evidence that some people have such abilities. Indeed, you may believe that you have experienced ESP at some time (or perhaps all the time). If this is the case, you are not alone. Sixty-seven percent of adult Americans have said that they have experienced ESP on at least one occasion (Constable 1987).

During the past several decades, there have been a number of stories about psychics assisting in criminal investigations; even today there is occasional reference to "psychic detectives." However, no empirical studies have demonstrated the usefulness or validity of psychic information in criminal investigations.

Although it is possible that certain people may have psychic abilities at certain times and under certain circumstances, there are undoubtedly a nearly countless number of pretenders. With regard to the value of psychics in criminal investigations in particular, one must consider the number of details provided by the psychic in relation to the number of accurate details *and* the usefulness of those details in advancing the investigation. The problem is that numerous details may be provided and, at best, only a few (if any) may be accurate. Even the information that is accurate may not provide leads for the police to pursue (e.g., the victim is female).

MAIN POINTS

1. The police have several strategies by which to find witnesses. These include the use of tip lines, television shows, special alerts, and other public information strategies, including the use of billboards, YouTube, and other advertising campaigns.

2. Crime Solvers, WeTip, and Crime Stoppers are examples of tip line programs. Each of these provides cash rewards for information that leads to the arrest of persons responsible for crimes. Tip lines have also been established for particular crimes, and on the Internet.

3. Another method of mobilizing the public in providing crime information to the police is the AMBER Alert. With an AMBER Alert, when a law enforcement agency is notified that a child abduction has taken place or is suspected of having taken place, an alert that includes information about the child, the suspected perpetrator, the vehicle involved, a tip line phone number, and any other information that may assist in locating the child is transmitted to the media for immediate broadcast. The AMBER plan and alert system is modeled after the alerts that are used to notify people of impending severe weather. Research on the use of AMBER Alerts questions the actual impact and effectiveness of the strategy.

4. While tip lines, television shows, and alerts can assist in investigations, they are not without limitations. These include that the information provided may be irrelevant or false and the difficulties in allocating reward money in an equitable sort of way, among other issues.

5. Confidential informants most often have some connection to, or knowledge of, the criminal underworld. They often assist law enforcement in an active and ongoing capacity by providing information to them. They are most often used by the police in ongoing undercover investigations, especially those that are drug related. Although the use of informants is often viewed as necessary during certain investigations, the practice is not without controversy.

6. Gang members are disproportionately involved in all serious violent crime, especially murder, other nonfatal shootings (especially drive-by shootings), and robbery. It is necessary for investigators to understand the operations and workings of gangs in their communities. Some police departments have a specialized gang unit designed to collect and act upon gang information. This information (or intelligence) can be obtained from a variety of sources, including citizens, informants, the offenders themselves, and officers on the street.

7. An interpretation of gang graffiti can help understand gang activities in the community.

8. Crime analysis can provide the necessary information to make informed patrol allocation decisions, to make predictions about when and where crime will occur, to identify future targets of offenders, and to track offender movements. Maps are a commonly used and useful tool in the task of crime analysis. The fact that predatory crime is typically nonrandom provides a basis for the prediction of crime.

9. The Violent Criminal Apprehension Program (ViCAP) is an example of a sophisticated crime analysis computer system. Operated by the FBI, it is designed to collect, collate, and analyze specific crimes of violence to identify similar MO or signature aspects of the crime. The goal is to identify crimes that have been committed by the same person.

10. A multitude of electronic databases exist that investigators may use to obtain critical information needed during a criminal investigation. These databases are intradepartmental (e.g., gang intelligence records) and interdepartmental (e.g., the NCIC). Of course, the primary limitation of information databases is that the database is only as good as the information that it contains.

11. Social networking sites such as Facebook hold a wealth of information (intelligence) for investigators, as do other Internet sites such as YouTube. These sites are also used by police departments in disseminating information.

12. Psychic phenomena are related to the science of parapsychology, or extrasensory perception (ESP). Although there are stories about the successful use of psychics in criminal investigations, the limited research on the topic does not show psychics to be of use in solving crimes.

IMPORTANT TERMS ●━━━━━━━━━━━━━━━━

AMBER Alert

America's Most Wanted television show

Cockroach theory

COMPSTAT

Confidential informants (CIs or "street sources")

Crime analysis, crime mapping, geospatial analysis

Gang identity

Gang intelligence

Graffiti

Hammered informant

Mercenary informants

National Crime Information Center (NCIC)

National Law Enforcement Telecommunications System (NLETS)

Parapsychology

Police buff informant

Psychics

Social networking sites (Facebook, Craigslist, YouTube)

Tagging

Tip line (Crime Stoppers, Crime Solvers, WeTip)

Vengeful informant

QUESTIONS FOR DISCUSSION AND REVIEW

1. What are tip lines? What are their major benefits and limitations?

2. What are AMBER Alerts? How are they supposed to work? What are their benefits and limitations?

3. What is the role of confidential informants in criminal investigations? Why is the use of CIs sometimes controversial? What are the common motivations of informants?

4. What dimensions represent the identity of a gang? What some of the basic interpretations of gang graffiti?

5. How can crime analysis be used as a tool in criminal investigations? What is the cockroach theory?

6. What is ViCAP? What are its major limitations?

7. How are computer databases and information networks useful in criminal investigations?

8. In what ways can social networking sites be useful in criminal investigations?

9. What are psychics? What value can they add to criminal investigations?

 STUDENT STUDY SITE

Visit **www.sagepub.com/brandl3e** to access additional study tools including eFlashcards, web quizzes, web resources, video resources, and SAGE journal articles.

UNLAWFUL FLIGHT TO AVOID PROSECUTION - MURDER SECOND DEGREE

Photo taken about 4/97

Date of Photo Unknown

ANDREW PHILLIP CUNANAN

Alias: Andrew Phillip DeSilva

DESCRIPTION

Date of Birth: August 31, 1969; Place of Birth: San Diego, California;
Race: White; Sex: Male; Height: 5' 9"– 5' 10"; Weight: 160 – 180 pounds;
Eyes: Brown; Hair: Dark Brown.
Remarks: Cunanan may wear prescription eyeglasses. He has been known to change his hairstyle and weight. He allegedly has ties to the gay community. He has portrayed himself as being wealthy.

CAUTION

CUNANAN IS BEING SOUGHT FOR AN APRIL, 1997 MURDER, WHICH OCCURRED IN CHISAGO COUNTY, MINNESOTA. ALSO, HE IS WANTED FOR QUESTIONING IN CONNECTION WITH ADDITIONAL MURDERS, WHICH OCCURRED IN CHISAGO COUNTY, MINNESOTA; CHICAGO, ILLINOIS; AND PENNSVILLE, NEW JERSEY. CUNANAN MAY BE IN POSSESSION OF A HANDGUN.

ARMED AND EXTREMELY DANGEROUS

10 Death Investigation

The purpose of Chapters 10 through 14 is to familiarize you with the major types of crimes investigated by the police, examine the motivations and tactics of perpetrators in committing these crimes, and discuss the evidence and challenges most likely to be present in these investigations. The discussion in these chapters calls attention to the importance of various tasks in investigating particular crimes. Details provided in other chapters that relate to other principles of evidence and investigation (e.g., legal issues, evidence collection, crime scene searches, physical evidence, interviews, interrogations, etc.) are not repeated here.

Objectives

After reading this chapter you will be able to:

- Identify the four ways by which people may die (manner of death) and their relative frequency

- Identify three factors that must be considered in determining manner of death

- Identify the major patterns and characteristics of homicides

- Describe the fundamental questions that guide a homicide investigation

- Discuss the importance of motive in identifying a homicide perpetrator

- Identify and discuss various methods of determining post mortem interval (PMI) and explain why establishing PMI may be of importance in a homicide investigation

- Identify the typical decomposition pattern and discuss factors that may lead to deviations from this pattern

- Discuss why serial homicides present major challenges to investigators

- Discuss task forces as an investigative response to serial homicides (and certain other crimes)

- Evaluate the effectiveness of cold case squads and the difficulties in investigating "cold" homicides

From the CASE FILE

He Hit Her Until She Fell . . . and That Was Just the Beginning

It was a cold January 26, 2003, in Milwaukee, Wisconsin, on Super Bowl Sunday. Jackie Lawer and her friends were having a party. (Note: the name of the witness and other innocent parties in this story have been changed.) Jackie was twenty-four years old and worked as a bartender at a popular restaurant and tavern in Milwaukee. She had a lot of friends and knew a lot of people. She was typically happy and enjoyed life, and this particular Sunday was no different. The usual crowd was at the party—mostly people who worked together at the restaurant. As the game ended and the party came to end, one of Jackie's friends, Patrick Hubbart, twenty-two, agreed to give Jackie a ride home. Patrick wasn't her boyfriend; they were just good friends. They joked and laughed as they rode to Jackie's apartment building on the trendy east side of the city. It was about 2:30 a.m. when the two of them pulled up in front of the building. Jackie and Patrick said goodnight, and Jackie hurried to the front door of the apartment building. Patrick watched as Jackie walked up the front sidewalk of the building toward the front door. As he drove off, he saw Jackie

approach the door. He then did a U-turn and again drove past the front door of the building. He could no longer see Jackie, so he assumed she made it safely into the building. Patrick then headed home to get a little sleep. He had to take his parents to the airport in just a few hours.

Just before 8:00 a.m. on January 27, the Milwaukee Police Department received a phone call from a citizen who reported that there was a body lying in his backyard. Officer Sanchez responded to the location, as did Detective Olson. As written in Detective Olson's report:

> The human body was face down just off of and east of the alley pavement at the rear of 2471 N. Palmer. The body was located just south of a foundation wall that runs west to east from the alley along the probable north property line of 2471 N. Palmer for almost 20 feet. The victim's head was in a northeast direction just south of the wall and at the base of a tree six feet east of the alley pavement. The victim's feet extended

in a southwest direction toward the alley. It could not be immediately determined if the person was male or female, as the upper torso had a bloody yellow jacket pulled up the body and over the head. The lower torso of the body was nude except for a sock that was on one of the feet.

Milwaukee Fire Department arrived and began resuscitation efforts on the body just after PO Sanchez arrived. While this was done, PO Sanchez taped off the scene to prevent scene contamination. PO Sanchez indicated that as the Fire Department personnel attended to the victim, they removed the bloody yellow jacket from the victim's body and moved it to the south of the body. Firefighter Irrizary found a driver's license in the lower, left front coat pocket of the bloody yellow jacket and gave the ID to PO Sanchez. The victim's body was then conveyed from the scene by the MFD to St. Mary's Hospital.

The driver's license belonged to Jackie Lawer. She had a faint pulse and a core temperature of eighty-one degrees. The outside temperature was four degrees Fahrenheit. At the hospital, doctors reported to the attending detectives that Jackie had severe injuries and lacerations to the back of her head. Jackie died on January 27, 2003, at 3:45 p.m.

Investigators collected numerous items of possible evidence in the area where the body was found. There was so much trash in the area that investigators were uncertain if any or all the items actually related to the crime. Investigators collected the clothing that was removed from the body by the fire department. They also found and collected from the immediate vicinity what appeared to be a towel with blood on it, three used condoms, five keys on a key ring, an unopened pack of Marlboro Ultra Light cigarettes (from the pocket of the victim's yellow jacket), blood from the grass where the victim was found, a partial wrapper for fudge chocolate chip cookies, an ATM slip, an envelope, a broken flashlight, and the victim's ID.

PHOTO 10.1: The area in which the victim was found. Notice her yellow jacket and numerous other items at the scene.

PHOTO 10.2: A close-up of the victim's bloody jacket and other items.

While investigators were collecting the evidence where the body was discovered, other detectives went to the address listed on the victim's ID with hopes of contacting and notifying friends or relatives. As these detectives approached the apartment building where Jackie lived, they found a large amount of blood near the door of the building, with a blood trail leading to and ending in the street in front of the building. Also near the door was a hamburger still in its wrapper.

The area in front of the building and the street were secured, and a neighborhood canvass was conducted by officers. None of the twenty-four people who lived in and around the apartment building had seen or heard anything the night before. When one of Jackie's neighbors was asked by the police if she saw the blood on the front stoop of the building, she said she saw it as she left the building in the morning but thought someone had dropped a red slushy on the steps. The attendant who was working the previous night at a nearby gas station was also questioned. He reported that someone matching Jackie's description came into the store at about 3:45 a.m. Upon checking

the cash register receipts and the video surveillance, it was indeed Jackie, and she had purchased a pack of cigarettes and a hamburger. The surveillance video showed several people entering the store before Jackie, and several entered after she left; investigators wondered if any of these people were responsible for her murder.

While the police were inside Jackie's apartment, the phone rang. An officer answered it, and the caller was Patrick. Investigators told Patrick that Jackie was in the hospital and that they needed to talk to him. Upon being questioned, Patrick told the police about the party and that he had given Jackie a ride home and dropped her off at about 2:30 a.m. He denied doing any harm to Jackie. He stated that he did not have a romantic or intimate relationship with Jackie. He said that he had no reason to do any harm to her. Patrick told the police who else was at the party. After interviewing Patrick, investigators contacted Jackie's other friends who were at the party. Patrick was of special interest to the police because he was apparently the last one to see Jackie alive. He

PHOTO 10.3: A close-up of blood splatter on the tile and concrete near the front door of the victim's apartment building.

PHOTO 10.4: The front entrance of the victim's apartment building. Notice the blood at the approach to the front door. Marker #8 indicates the hamburger still in its wrapper. The other markers indicate bloodstains.

PHOTO 10.5: A wide view of the front of Jackie Lawer's apartment building secured with crime scene tape.

PHOTO 10.6: The front of the victim's apartment building with crime scene markers indicating blood stains.

also had what appeared to be some scratches on his body and a cigarette burn on his face. In Jackie's apartment, investigators found pieces of paper with boys' names and phone numbers. They also heard from Jackie's friends that Jackie was recently concerned that someone had entered her apartment and put pennies in her bathtub. On another occasion she told her friends that she thought someone was in her apartment while she was taking a shower. Investigators were still most interested in Patrick. He was the prime suspect—really the only suspect. At the very least, they figured that the perpetrator was most likely someone that Jackie knew. Patrick agreed to a physical forensic exam and the collection of DNA, to have his apartment and vehicle searched, and to have his parents' house searched. Investigators found nothing that linked him to Jackie's murder.

On January 28, an autopsy was conducted on the victim by Dr. Mainland. The autopsy was witnessed by Detective Valuch. As stated in Detective Valuch's report:

> Dr. Mainland examined the victim prior to the autopsy and observed the following injuries. Victim had a 7/8" long laceration behind her left ear. There was a laceration to her right ear lobe. There were abrasions to her right buttocks and the back of her right leg and also on the back of the victim's right bicep. Dr. Mainland believes that these abrasions were what she described as drag marks. Dr. Mainland observed blunt force trauma to the victim's head, specifically there was a contusion and laceration to the back of the victim's head. There were two contusions and lacerations to the back of the victim's right side of her head and one to the top of the head. At the conclusion of the autopsy, Dr. Mainland stated that the cause of death was due to blunt force trauma, specifically head injuries. Dr. Mainland stated the victim was struck in the head at least six times and probably more like eight or nine times.

On Wednesday January 29, Dr. Mainland again examined the victim for any bruising, which may have shown itself overnight. Dr. Mainland noticed what she described as extensive bruising to both of the victim's hands, specifically the back of the hands. Dr. Mainland noted extensive bruising on the victim's right palm and on both of the victim's forearms. Dr. Mainland described this bruising as being defensive wounds. Dr. Mainland also noticed what appeared to be a bite mark

at the victim's right breast, specifically at the nipple area. Dr. Johnson, a forensic odontologist, confirmed what he believed to be a human bite mark to the victim's right nipple area.

In putting the pieces of the incident together, police reasoned that Jackie was dropped off at her apartment and went into the building. About an hour later she left her apartment building to go to the corner gas station to get cigarettes and a hamburger. As she made her way back to her building and approached the front door, someone hit her over the head with a blunt object. Her body was then taken to the street (which would account for the blood found on the street) and placed in a vehicle that then was used to transport her to where she was eventually found. Although investigators believed they knew what happened, they had no idea who did it or why. Little did they know that by the end of the next day, Friday, January 31, they would have the killer and a confession.

On the morning of January 31, five days after the homicide occurred, the police received another phone call. The man identified himself as Tyrone Harris and said he was a friend of a woman named Jennifer Mohammed. Harris explained that he was a barber and that about a month ago, Jennifer came into the barbershop with her son, "Mike," to get a haircut. After this visit, he and Jennifer became friends. Harris said that on January 28, Jennifer called him at the barbershop and asked him if he heard about that girl getting killed. Harris told her that he did hear about it but did not know any of the details. Jennifer then told Harris that her boyfriend did it. According to Harris, Jennifer said that he did not mean to do it, that he was under the influence of alcohol at the time. Jennifer continued to tell Harris about the details of the incident. According to the police report, she stated that "he took her clothes off to get rid of some of the blood and that he was partially nude because he took off his clothes because of the blood." Jennifer also told Harris that her boyfriend said he was going to take the victim to the hospital because of her injuries, but that he never did. She also said that her boyfriend got $11 from the victim because he robbed her.

To the detectives, this sounded like specific, credible, and believable information. With the information in hand, the next step was to talk to Jennifer Mohammad. Later in the morning on Friday, January 31, the police located Jennifer at her home, interviewed her briefly, and transported her to the police department for a more detailed interview. On the way to the police station, Jennifer led detectives to where her boyfriend's vehicle, a blue 1987 Dodge Ram pickup truck, was located. Arrangements were then made to tow the vehicle so that a search of it could be conducted by crime lab personnel.

During the interviews, Jennifer told detectives her boyfriend, Kimani Ward, slept in the basement of her house. She explained that on January 26, Super Bowl Sunday, Ward left the residence at about 3:00 p.m. and stated that he was going to "take care of some business and sit with his friends in the bar." He left in his blue pickup truck. The next day at about 5:30 a.m., she went into the basement and Ward was not there. She left the house and returned about 9:00 a.m. and Ward was then home. She asked him why he got home so late and he replied that "I was on the east side." She told the police that this led to an argument between her and Ward, and then Ward left the house. Later on Monday, at about 4:00 p.m., Ward came back home and told Jennifer that he needed a stiff drink and that he needed to change his life. She noticed that something seemed to be the matter with him because he was shaking and was sad. Ward asked Jennifer, "Are you ready for this?" He explained that he saw this girl on the east side. He thought she had some money. He told Jennifer that he was in his truck and snuck up behind the girl and hit her in the head with a

crowbar. Jennifer also said that Ward told her that he didn't mean to use a lot of force. Jennifer asked him how much he got from her and he responded that he got $11. He told Jennifer that he used the money to put gas in his truck. He said that after he hit the girl, she fell down, so he picked her up and carried her to his truck and put her in its flatbed. Jennifer told detectives that Ward said that he was going to take her to a hospital, but he thought if he did that he'd get in trouble. He said that he took her clothes off because there was a lot of blood on them. Jennifer asked why he took her clothes off, and he stated that he didn't want his fingerprints or DNA on anything. Jennifer also told the police that Ward bought a newspaper because he said that he wanted to know if the police had a suspect; she thought that was also strange because he never read the newspaper. He also told her that he put bleach in the back of his truck and washed it. He had blood on his shoes and he put bleach on those as well.

Shortly after Jennifer Mohammad was conveyed to the police station for questioning, other detectives located Ward at his residence and transported him to the police department for questioning as well. The following is the detailed statement provided by Ward, as written by Detective Gary Temp in police supplemental report 2–15:

On Friday January 31, 2003, at 11:30 a.m. in room 414 of the Criminal Investigation Bureau, I advised Kimani K. Ward of his Miranda rights in the presence of Detective Randy Olson. Ward states he understands his rights, is willing to waive them, answer questions, and make a statement.

Regarding the homicide of Jackie Lawer on 1–27–03 at 2423 E. Bellview Place, Ward states that he is responsible for Jackie's death. Ward states he struck Jackie in the head with a tire iron while robbing her.

Ward states that on Sunday 1–26–03 he went to the Shortstop Inn on S. 19th and W. Lincoln Ave. Ward states he can't remember what time he got there. Ward states that while at the tavern he had eight shots of vodka and five beers. Ward states he has friends at this tavern and is friends with the owner's son. Ward states he left the tavern about 3:00 a.m. on Monday 1–27–03.

Ward states that when he left the tavern he drove his 1987 Dodge Ram pickup truck light blue/dark blue with Minnesota license plates to the east side of Milwaukee. Ward states that the reason he did this was that he was going to break into some cars because he needed some money.

Ward states that he first saw the victim (Jackie) walking away from the Citgo Gas station at Maryland and Farwell. Ward states he did not know the victim. Ward states the victim was walking alone. Ward states he then thought about robbing the victim because she probably had money on her because she just left the gas station. Ward states he figured the victim would have at least $40 on her. Ward states the victim was wearing a yellow coat with a hood and blue pants.

Ward states the victim walked north on N. Farwell to E. Bradford. Ward states he then drove his truck north on N. Maryland and turned and proceeded east on E. Bradford. Ward states he then turned south onto N. Downer

Ave and parked his truck facing south in front of 2475 N. Downer Ave. Ward states he lost sight of the victim when he parked his truck.

Ward states that when he got out of his truck he took a "crow bar." Ward described this crowbar as a star type tire wrench. Ward states the tire wrench has three sockets and one flat end. Ward states he walked west on the north side of E. Bradford. Ward states he then walked north in the 2500 block of N. Stowell. Ward states as he was walking he was looking into cars for something to steal.

Ward states that he was about mid-block when he saw the same white female walking by herself north in the 2600 block of N. Stowell. Ward states he ducked behind a car so the victim would not see him.

Ward states he started following the victim north on N. Stowell. Ward states he was about 15 feet behind the victim. Ward states he was deciding if he should rob the victim as he followed her. Ward states the victim turned and went west on E. Bellview Place. Ward states the victim walked up to the front door of an apartment building at 2423 E. Bellview Place.

Ward states he suddenly made up his mind that he would rob the victim. Ward states the victim was by the front door and he ran up on her. Ward states he ran up on the victim and began hitting her in the head with the "crow bar." Ward states he was swinging the "crow bar" in an overhead motion downward toward the victim's head. Ward stated he hit Jackie three or four times but it could have been more. Ward states Jackie never fought back. Ward states he hit the victim until she fell down.

Ward states that after the victim fell he saw she wasn't moving. Ward states he then ran back to his truck. Ward states he saw blood on the victim's hood at first. Ward states he ran the two or three blocks back to his truck.

Ward states he got in his truck, made a U-turn on N. Downer and drove back to 2423 E. Bellview Place. Ward states he parked his truck in the middle of the street facing west. Ward states he then got out of his truck and ran over to the victim who was lying in front of the front door of the apartment. Ward states there was a lot of blood by the victim and she wasn't moving. Ward remembers her eyes being open.

Ward states he then dragged the victim to his truck. Ward states he grabbed the victim under the arms and dragged her to his truck. Ward states he lowered the tailgate of his truck and lifted the victim onto the truck-bed. Ward states he lifted the victim's upper body onto the truck first and then swung her legs up onto the truck-bed. Ward states he then got up onto the truck-bed and pulled her the rest of the way in.

Ward then described to detectives where he drove with the victim in the bed of the truck. He stated that he stopped and pulled his truck over on the side of the road five different times, got out, and got into the truck bed to look at the victim. He stated that each time her eyes were open and she did not appear to be breathing. He stated that one of the times he stopped his truck it was near a hospital, and he looked at the emergency room and thought about dropping the victim off there. The report continues:

Ward states he eventually stopped his truck in an alley at the rear of 2471 N. Palmer St. He stated his truck was facing south in the alley. Ward states he got out of the truck and pulled the victim's body off the bed of his truck. Ward states as he pulled the victim's body off of the truck her pants and underwear got snagged and were pulled off. Ward states he then left the victim's body behind 2471 N. Palmer St.

Ward then states that at this time he could see her vaginal area. Ward states the victim's coat was pulled up and he could see her breasts. Ward states he thought to himself he had come this far he might as well have sex with her.

Ward states he put a rubber (condom) on. Ward states he then tried to place his penis into the victim's vagina. Ward states that the victim was unconscious. Ward states he tried to have sex with the victim for about one minute but could not stay hard. Ward states during the sex act he may have bitten the victim's breast. Ward remembers he was hard enough to "get in" penetrate the victim, but was having trouble staying hard so he stopped. Ward states he had sex with the victim because he remembers thinking that she died for nothing. Ward states he can't remember what he did with the condom he used during the sex act.

Ward states he took the victim's pants into the cab of the truck with him. Ward states he drove out of the alley and went back to North Ave. Ward states he began driving west. Ward states that when he was stopped at a traffic light he searched through the victim's pants.

Ward states he took $11 out of one of the pants pockets. Ward states it was either two fives and a single or one five and six singles. Ward states he later used this money to put gas in his truck.

In the interrogation, Ward then stated the various places he drove and where he got rid of the "crow bar," the victim's pants, and his K-Swiss shoes, coat, long underwear, and jogging pants. Ward stated that he then went home and that he was naked when he went into the house. He stated that later in the day he poured some bleach into the bed of his truck and then took the truck through a car wash in order to get the blood out of the bed of the truck. He said that he then found a trash dumpster and threw out some old tires and other things what were in the truck bed. The report continues:

Ward states he did tell his girlfriend Jennifer about this incident. Ward states that he told Jennifer about the robbery and homicide. Ward states he didn't tell Jennifer about the sex act. Ward states he didn't tell Jennifer as many details as he told us.

Ward states he did agree to ride with us in a squad car and point out where everything occurred. Ward states he did show us where he got rid of the victim's shoes, had sex with her and dumped her body. Ward states he also pointed out locations where he disposed of the crow bar, victim's pants, and his own clothing.

Ward states he wants to tell the victim's family he is sorry and he didn't mean to hurt their daughter like that.

Ward states that the bag of women's underwear found at his house he got when he has broken into cars. Ward states he has no idea why he kept the underwear.

Ward states he has never done anything like this before in his life. Ward states he still doesn't know why he did this.

From 2:30 p.m. to 5:15 p.m. Ward was with us in squad 124 A driving around various locations in the city. At 3:40 p.m. Ward used the restroom at District 5 police station. At 4:30 p.m. at 4912 N. 108th St. (his residence) Ward used the restroom, brushed his teeth, and got a pair of shoes. Ward also changed into a sweater and left his coat and t-shirt at 4912 N. 108th St. Ward also said to his family members at that time "I fucked up, I'm sorry for bringing this to all of you."

In room 414, Ward smoked freely, was given water, Coca Cola, two cheeseburgers and french fries. Ward also had a Sprite from McDonalds on E. North Ave, while with us in the squad car. In the squad car, Wards hands were handcuffed in the front of him. In room 414 Ward was not handcuffed. One break 5:50 p.m. to 6:30 p.m.

The entire statement was read to me by Detective Temp and is true and correct. (signed Kimani Ward)

Ended 10:00 p.m.

As a result of the information provided by Ward as to the disposal of clothing and other evidence in the crime, the following items were found, photographed, and collected:

- Two black slip-on shoes and one black fur-lined glove, believed to have belonged to the victim. One of the shoes had a visible blood smear.

- Two black leather K-Swiss shoes, which belonged to Kimani Ward

- A black jacket and blue pants, which belonged to Ward. The pants contained a visible blood splatter on the right thigh area.

The search of the Ward's truck revealed three areas in the truck bed near the tailgate where blood and

PHOTO 10.7: The perpetrator's pants, which he discarded before returning home. Notice the blood splatter on one of the pant legs; this blood was matched to the victim through DNA analysis.

PHOTO 10.8: The perpetrator's truck, which was used to transport the victim after she had been attacked. The photo was taken after the truck had been impounded by the police.

PHOTO 10.9: A close-up photograph of the bed of the perpetrator's truck. Notice the bloodstain that was found in the crack of the bed and tailgate. The blood was the victim's.

hair evidence was located. Analyses conducted by the crime lab revealed that the DNA obtained from the blood on Kimani Ward's pants and from the blood found in his truck matched that of Jackie Lawer. Another bloodstain in the truck came from an unknown male subject. Semen was not identified from any samples taken from the victim. The DNA obtained from the bite mark area on the victim contained DNA from at least three sources (possibly from the medical personnel who attended to the victim) and could not be matched to Ward.

Kimani Ward was sentenced to life in prison without the possibility of parole for the crimes he committed against Jackie Lawer.

Case Considerations and Points for Discussion

- How was Kimani Ward first identified as a suspect in the murder of Jackie Lawer? What value did DNA analysis, and physical evidence more generally, provide in this investigation?

- The investigation appeared to be at a standstill until what happened? Did the police do anything to make this happen? What was the role of the media in the investigation?

- From the description of the investigation provided above, does it appear that the police made any mistakes in the investigation? Perpetrators are often identified as a result of mistakes that they made in committing the crime. What do you think was the biggest mistake that Kimani Ward made in committing these crimes?

- Investigators learn something from every investigation. What do you think were the biggest lessons learned by the police as a result of this investigation?

••• Issues in the Investigation of Death

All deaths can be explained in one of four ways: deaths are the result of natural causes (e.g., heart attack or illness), accident (e.g., vehicle crash), suicide (e.g., willfully jumping from a tall building), or homicide. According to annual mortality statistics provided by the Centers for Disease Control and Prevention, the overwhelming number of deaths are as a result of natural causes (approximately 93 percent), followed in frequency by accidents (approximately 5 percent; approximately 28 percent of which are traffic accidents), suicides (1.5 percent of all deaths), and homicide (approximately .5 percent of all deaths; see Exhibit 10.1).

Typically, only suspected homicides, suicides, and other sudden deaths (natural and accidental) come to the attention of the police. In other cases, there is little or no question that the death was of natural causes. Even among most homicides, suicides, and other sudden deaths, the manner of death is not a difficult determination. However, this is not always the case. When investigators are called to death scenes, the manner of death should be assumed to be homicide until homicide is ruled out. It is also important for investigators to remember that, in rare instances, deliberate efforts may be made by others to disguise the true

Exhibit 10.1 Quick Facts about Death

With regard to all deaths:

- In recent years in the United States, there were approximately 2.5 million deaths a year.

- Most people who die are eighty-five years old or older.

- The most common cause of death is cardiovascular disease.

With regard to accidental (unintentional) deaths:

- In recent years in the United States, there were approximately 120,000 accidental deaths a year.

- Approximately 28 percent of these deaths were a result of vehicle traffic accidents, 27 percent were a result of accidental poisoning, and 22 percent were a result of unintentional falls.

- .5 percent of unintentional deaths were a result of an accidental discharge of a weapon.

With regard to suicides:

- There are approximately 38,000 suicides a year in the United States.

- Suicides among males is four times higher than among females and represents 79 percent of all U.S. suicides.

- Firearms are the most common method of suicide among males (56 percent); poisoning is the most common method among females (37 percent).

- Suicide is the third leading cause of death among persons fifteen to twenty-four years old, the second among persons aged twenty-five to thirty-four, the fourth among persons aged thirty-five to fifty-four, and the eighth among persons aged fifty-five to sixty-four.

With regard to homicides:

- In recent years in the United States, there were approximately 13,000 homicides a year.

- Approximately 50 percent of victims and 52 percent of offenders are black.

- Approximately 78 percent of victims and 89 percent of offenders are male.

- Approximately 61 percent of victims and 51 percent of offenders are aged seventeen to thirty-nine.

- Firearms are used in approximately 68 percent of homicides.

Source: Centers for Disease Control and Prevention.

manner of death through the process of staging. When staging occurs, it is most common that a murder is made to look like an accident or a suicide. Other instances of staging may involve making a suicide look like an accident or making a murder that occurred between intimate partners appear as one that occurred between strangers (and having a sexual motive) (Geberth 1996).

To determine manner of death, at least three considerations are paramount: (1) the nature of the injuries sustained by the decedent (the cause of death), (2) the characteristics of the decedent, and (3) the circumstances of the death. This information may come from an examination and/or autopsy of the body, an examination of the scene, and/or from witnesses. In particular, information from witnesses may be of great assistance in determining manner of death. The person(s) who last saw the decedent alive may have particularly important information about the manner of death. This information may include the decedent's state of mind (e.g., "He seemed very depressed"), last activities (e.g., "He was arguing with another person"), or state of physical well-being (e.g., "He was complaining of chest pain").

Some determinations of manner of death depend heavily or even entirely on medical findings of fact; some do not. For example, a ninety-two-year-old female was found dead at her home in bed. There were no visible injuries to the body. There were no signs of forced entry into the home. Relatives reported that the woman lived alone and that she had a history of poor health. In such a case, death by natural causes would be a reasonable inference. If a woman was discovered partially nude in an alley in freezing temperatures, with her clothing missing, and it was determined that she had been beaten about the head, that blood was located on the stoop of her apartment building several miles away, and that a friend reported dropping her off at her apartment several hours prior to the discovery of her body (as with the case described in the chapter introduction), a homicide would be a most logical conclusion. Or, consider the case where a young man with traumatic head injuries was found dead at home, sitting in a chair, and holding onto a handgun. A note was found near his body explaining why he shot himself. Family members reported that at the time of his death he was home alone and that he had been depressed over a failed relationship and fired from his job. In such a case, a suicide would be a logical initial conclusion.

In some cases though, establishing the manner of death is not always quite so straightforward. When there is uncertainty regarding the manner of death, it usually involves differentiating between suicide and homicide, or between suicide and accident. In some cases, the differentiation between a suicide and an accident depends on the deceased's state of mind at the time of death. As such, the manner of death remains a judgment call; the only person who knows for sure is dead. A death by drug overdose provides a good example. Did the victim ingest a lethal amount or combination of drugs on purpose (suicide) or unintentionally (accidental death)? This is often a difficult determination to make as it depends on knowing the victim's state of mind just prior to the consumption of the drugs. This determination would ultimately be the responsibility of a medical examiner or coroner.

Autoerotic deaths (or sexual asphyxia) pose a similar challenge for investigators. Autoerotic deaths usually involve solo sex-related activity gone wrong, in which the participant dies as a result of asphyxia of some form (suffocation, strangulation, or chemical asphyxia). These very uncommon occurrences present an unusual scene where the (typically male) decedent may be dressed in women's clothing, be nude, and/or be in various restraints. What first appears to be a homicide or perhaps a suicide is actually most likely an accident. Geberth (1996) identifies five indicators of such deaths: (1) an arrangement or contraption whereby the victim may self-rescue, (2) evidence of solo sexual activity, (3) evidence of sexual fantasy aids, (4) evidence of prior autoerotic practice, and (5) no apparent suicidal intent. Basically, an autopsy could determine the cause of death (asphyxia), but the circumstances of the death and the scene would lead to the correct conclusion about the manner of death.

If suicides can first be ruled in (or out) as the manner of death, then the manner of death may be more easily determined since homicides and accidents seldom look similar. As such, indicators of suicide as a manner of death include the following:

- A weapon or other means of death is present at the scene.

- Wounds are present that were, or could have been, self-inflicted (of course, multiple gunshot wounds to the head, multiple stab wounds, and gunshot wounds from a gun fired at a distance are indicative of a homicide not a suicide). Suicide by firearm deaths almost always show contact wounds (see Exhibit 10.2).

- The body shows a lack of defense wounds (i.e., injuries that appeared to have been sustained by the deceased

in an attempt to protect himself or herself, such as cuts to the hands from grabbing the blade of a knife, are not indicative of a suicide, but rather a homicide).

- A suicidal motive is often accompanied by indications of mental health issues, distress, depression, and/or behavioral changes, which are established through family, friends, or other relatives.

- A suicide note may or may not be present; suicide notes should be examined to determine whether the note was written by the deceased.

Exhibit 10.2 Location of Gunshot Entrance Wounds in Suicides

Kohlmeier et al. (2001) analyzed over 1,700 firearm suicides and documented the characteristics of the associated injuries. They found that most firearm suicides (approximately 70 percent) were committed with handguns, and 98 percent revealed contact wounds from the firearm. With regard to entrance wounds, the following patterns were found:

Suicidal Firearms Deaths

SITE	HANDGUN (%)	RIFLE (%)	SHOTGUN (%)
Right temple	50.0	22.9	9.3
Left temple	5.8	3.3	3.7
Mouth	14.5	24.3	31.7
Forehead	5.9	15.7	8.1
Under chin	2.4	9.1	10.6
Back of head	3.6	3.8	1.2
Chest	13.2	15.7	19.9
Abdomen	1.4	1.9	5.6
Other	3.2	3.3	9.9
Total	100.0	100.0	100.0

Clearly, the most common entrance wound in a firearm suicide occurs when the subject uses a handgun to make contact with his or her right temple. Notice that it is not unheard of that entrance wounds in firearm suicides are in the back of the head. When rifles and shotguns are used, most often entrance wounds are in the mouth.

●●● Patterns and Characteristics of Homicide

Murder, as defined by the FBI's *Uniform Crime Report,* refers to the "willful (non-negligent) killing of one human being by another" (FBI 2012). To establish that a murder has occurred, there must be evidence of a dead body (or that death has occurred if a dead body is not recovered) and that another person willfully caused that person's death. As discussed, a basic task of investigators is to determine whether the death was a result of foul play or whether it resulted from natural causes, accident, or suicide. In this respect, a murder investigation is similar to an arson investigation, in which it must be determined whether the fire was caused by arson, accident, or other means. Fortunately, there is often much evidence available in homicide incidents that assists in accurately determining the manner of death as a homicide.

Murder is a relatively infrequent crime. In 2011, 12,664 persons were murdered in the United States (FBI 2012). There are typically more murders and a higher murder rate (i.e., the number of murders per 100,000 persons) in large, urban areas than in smaller cities, suburbs, or rural areas. Given the extraordinarily serious nature of the crime, police departments that regularly investigate murders devote a large proportion of resources to these investigations. In addition, unlike other most other crimes, homicide cases are likely to be assigned to numerous investigators.

With regard to the characteristics of homicide victims, the largest proportion of victims (18 percent) are between the ages of twenty and twenty-four. Approximately 61 percent of victims are between seventeen and thirty-nine. More than 78 percent of homicide victims are male; just under 22 percent are female (FBI 2012). As for offenders, 89 percent of known offenders are male, and the largest proportion (16 percent) are between the ages of twenty and twenty-four.

Homicide is very much an intra-racial crime; when the victim is black, 91 percent of the time the offender is also black. When the victim is white, 83 percent of the time the offender is white. Homicide is also very much a male crime. When the victim is male, 87 percent of the time the offender is also male; when the victim is female, 91 percent of the time the offender is male. Females are very unlikely to kill other females. In the uncommon instance that a female commits a murder, it is usually of an intimate partner who is male.

The most common circumstance in which homicides occur is during an argument between the victim and the offender (30 percent). The second most common circumstance in which homicides occur is in conjunction with other felonies, particularly robberies (7 percent) and drug transactions (4 percent). These homicides are often referred to as *felony murders.* Juvenile gang killings account for just less than 6 percent of homicides. In just more than 35 percent of homicides, the circumstances associated with the incident are unknown because the case is unsolved (FBI 2012).

With regard to the relationship between the victim and the offender, approximately 44 percent of victims know their assailant (approximately 30 percent are acquainted with the killer; 14 percent are related to the assailant). Twelve percent of murder victims are known to have been murdered by a stranger. In the remainder of cases, the relationship between the victim and offender is unknown. The most striking pattern concerning relationships between victims and offenders is that, in 2011, approximately 33 percent of *female* homicide victims were killed by a husband or boyfriend. In contrast, of all *male* homicide victims, less than 3 percent were killed by a wife or girlfriend (FBI 2012).

Several methods are used most commonly to kill others (see Myths and Misconceptions 10.1). Without question, firearms are the most common means by which homicides are committed. In 2011, 68 percent of all homicides involved the use of a firearm, and most of these firearms were handguns. Other weapons used in homicides were knives, personal weapons (e.g., hands, fists, feet), and blunt objects (e.g., clubs, hammers, etc.). Very seldom are people killed in other ways (FBI 2012).

MYTHS & MISCONCEPTIONS 10.1

The Methods of Murder

The reality of how people kill each other is very different than how murder is portrayed in the media. Even in the news media, most often the most unusual murders receive the greatest amount of attention. In the entertainment media, such as on *CSI,* an unusual murder makes for a more interesting episode. In reality, firearms are by far the most common means of murder—no other method or weapon even comes close in frequency. Murders committed by means other a firearm are relatively uncommon, even for the seasoned homicide investigator.

In 2011, there were 12,664 murders in the United States (FBI 2012). Of these:

- 8,583 (68 percent) were committed with a firearm (72 percent of these involved handguns).

- 1,694 (13 percent) were committed with a knife.

- 496 (4 percent) were committed with a blunt object (e.g., club, hammer).

- 728 (6 percent) were committed with personal weapons (e.g., hands, fists, feet).

- 853 (7 percent) were committed with other weapons.

All other means *combined* accounted for less than 2.5 percent of all homicides:

- Five were committed with poison.

- Twelve were committed with explosives.

- Seventy-five were committed with fire.

- Twenty-nine were committed with narcotics.

- Fifteen were committed by drowning.

- Eighty-five were committed by strangulation.

- Eighty-nine were committed by asphyxiation.

Source: FBI Uniform Crime Report (2012).

The circumstances in which the homicide took place, the relationship between the victim and the offender, and the nature of the weapon used in the offense may represent important and useful information during an investigation. Partly because of the circumstances of the crime, and the fact that most victims know or are related to the perpetrator, murder has the highest clearance rate of any index offense at approximately 65 percent (FBI 2012). There is, however, considerable variation in homicide clearance rates across police departments. In general, as in many other crimes, smaller departments tend to have higher clearance rates for murder than larger departments. Even among large agencies, however, there may be considerable variation. For instance, in recent years, Baltimore, Maryland, has experienced about 250 homicides a year and has a clearance rate of approximately 75 percent for these crimes. Detroit, Michigan, on the other hand, usually has about 450 homicides a year and has a clearance rate of just over 40 percent. These differences are probably best explained by the nature and circumstances of homicides in each jurisdiction and the investigative response of each agency (Wellford and Cronin 1999).

●●● Investigative Considerations With Death and Homicide

Death investigations—homicides in particular—usually begin with a focus on the dead body and the place where the body was found. In the case of a homicide, the place where the body was found is usually, though not always, where the crime occurred. As noted earlier in the text, crime scenes are potentially valuable because of the evidence (e.g., physical evidence, witnesses) that may be found there. They may also be valuable because of who had access to the scene. Never is this truer than with homicides. The procedures for processing, searching, and documenting crime scenes, outlined in Chapter 5, are most relevant in homicide investigations.

Several basic questions are relevant in death investigations:

- Who is the decedent?

- What was the cause of the death?

- And, if the death is as a result of a homicide, who is the offender?

Each question is discussed in turn.

WHO IS THE DECEDENT?

Usually it is not a major investigative challenge to determine the identity of the decedent. Witnesses, friends, neighbors, or family members may be at the scene and may be able to provide this information to the police. In other instances, the police may be able to make a tentative identification through items in the possession of the person (such as an identification card, as was the case in the identification of the victim in the chapter introduction), and then a positive identification may be made by a family member or friend at the hospital or the medical examiner's office. In some instances, because of injuries or decomposition, the body may not be recognizable. In these cases, identification may be made through scientific methods such as fingerprints, dental records, or DNA comparisons, or a tentative identification can be made through personal affects or other means, such as physical characteristics or a unique tattoo. With the discovery of a unidentified and unknown dead body, it may first be necessary to compare the circumstances of the discovery and characteristics of the found body with missing persons reports and the reported circumstances of those disappearances. In rare instances, there may be a need for anthropological facial reconstruction to recreate the face of the decedent for recognition purposes. In such cases, media coverage may assist investigators in developing necessary information to determine the identity of the decedent.

WHAT WAS THE CAUSE OF DEATH?

Just as when determining the manner of death, it is necessary to consider directly and carefully the nature of the injuries sustained when determining the cause of death. Cause of death is an especially important element in the understanding of the circumstances of a murder. Of course, deaths that are caused by different actions will leave different wounds and/or indicators on the body (Geberth 1996; Castleman 2000).

GUNSHOT WOUNDS

As discussed, most homicides are the result of firearms. Of course, shell casings in the vicinity of the body are an immediate and good indicator of a firearm homicide. Gunshot wounds to a body have different characteristics depending on the type and caliber of the gun used, the size and type of bullet, the area of the body that sustained the gunshot wound, the distance of the gun from the body at the time of the shooting, and whether the bullet first passed through clothing. Also, with every gunshot entrance wound there may or may not be an exit wound.

The identification of entrance and exit wounds is important for several reasons, not the least of which is to gain an understanding of the basic circumstances of the shooting (e.g., to determine whether the victim was shot from the back or front). Generally speaking, entrance wounds are smaller than exit wounds, although this is not necessarily always the case. Entrance wounds are typically round with a gray or black ring around the wound, while exit wounds often show torn or ragged tissue. Entrance wounds may reveal relatively

PHOTO 10.10: An immediate clue as to cause of death (or injury) is the presence of shell casings at the scene. Shell casings are a frequently retrieved form of physical evidence.

PHOTO 10.11: The subject in this photo sustained a single gunshot wound to the head at close range with a large-caliber handgun. The result was catastrophic and massive head trauma.

little blood compared to exit wounds. In the case of multiple gunshots to the same area of the body, it may not be possible for investigators to determine which exit wound corresponds to which entrance wound. This is because bullets do not necessarily travel in a straight line through the body. As seen in Case in Point 10.1, an autopsy can provide information on the track of the bullet.

The distance of the gun from the body at the time of the shooting is an important, but difficult, determination. Like the identification of entrance and exit wounds, it can also assist in identifying the shooting as a homicide or a suicide, as well as shed light on the particular circumstances of the incident. A distinction is often made between a contact, close, and distant gunshot (Geberth 1996). A contact wound is one that is made when the muzzle of the gun is touching the body when the gun is fired. When a gun is in contact with flesh when fired, residue from the gun, bullet, and shell casing, along with the bullet itself, enters the body. These particulates can be found during the autopsy. A larger, irregular-shaped entrance wound is likely to be present, as is charring of the skin around the entrance wound. A close shot, in which the muzzle is less than eighteen inches from the body at the time the gun is discharged, typically produces a smaller entrance wound (compared to a contact shot) and evidence of gunshot residue and/or burned powder and fragments on clothing or on the skin ("tattooing" or "stippling"). A distant shot, in which the muzzle is more than eighteen inches from the body, usually produces a wound that is smaller than the diameter of the bullet as a result of the skin stretching when contact is made with the bullet and then contracting after the bullet enters the body. This type of shot may not reveal any blackened area around the wound or any other effects of residue from the firearm, only a contusion ring caused by the projectile entering the tissue.

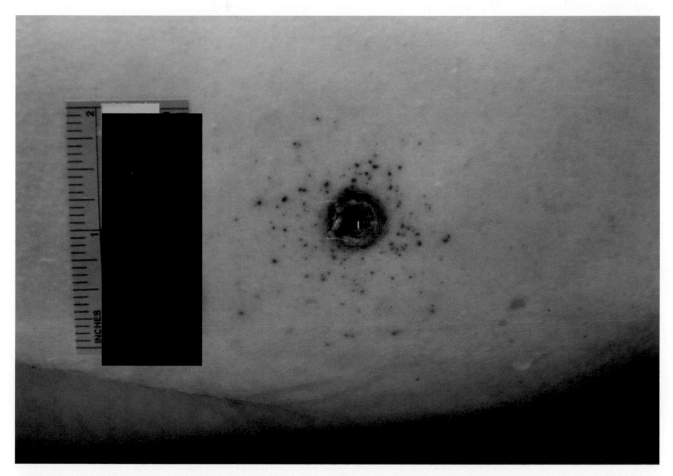

PHOTO 10.12a: An intermediate gunshot wound to a victim's shoulder. Notice the powder "tattooing."

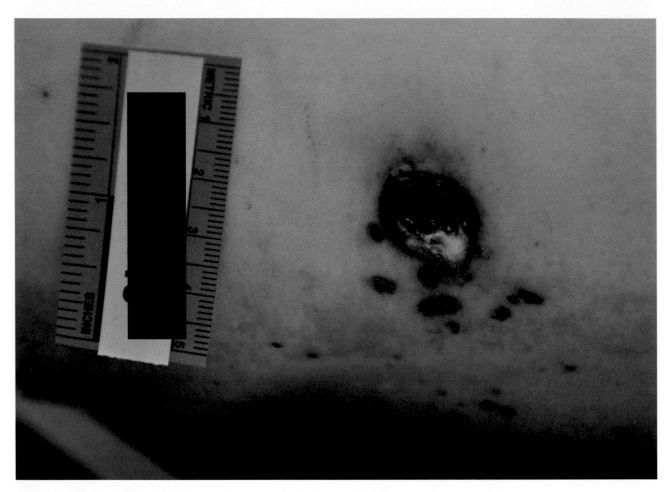

PHOTO 10.12b: A gunshot wound that appears to have occurred in closer proximity to the victim than the one in the photo above. Notice the blackish discoloration around the wound, along with the powder tattooing.

Generally speaking, the larger the caliber of the gun used, the more trauma sustained as a result of being stuck by its ammunition. This is particularly true with regard to rifle and shotgun gunshot wounds, which cause massive tissue damage.

Finally, there may be considerable variation in the characteristics of gunshot wounds to various areas of the body. Gunshots to soft tissue, such as the abdomen, generally produce wounds that are smaller and may produce less tissue destruction than gunshots to areas of bone, especially the head.

Gunshot residue (GSR) may be important evidence in a shooting. When a gun is fired, soot and other particles (residue) are discharged from the gun. As noted, depending on the distance of the gun from the victim, some of this residue may fall upon the victim around the area of the wound. Some of the residue may be present and detectable on the person who fired the gun and on other people who were near the gun when it was fired. Gunshot residue collection kits are often used to collect GSR. The primary method of collecting GSR is through adhesive lifters often referred to as dabs or stubs. Because gunshot residue can dissipate quickly, it is imperative that the collection be conducted as soon as possible. Typically, gunshot residue is collected from a subject's hands and face. There can be no particular significance to finding GSR on one of the hands of a suspect, but not the other. For example, if GSR is collected from the left hand of a suspect, it does not necessarily mean that the suspect held the gun in his or her left hand. It must also be understood that lack of gunshot residue on a suspect does not mean that the suspect did not fire a gun. Washing hands may quickly eliminate GSR residue from hands. Even activities such as touching other items, putting

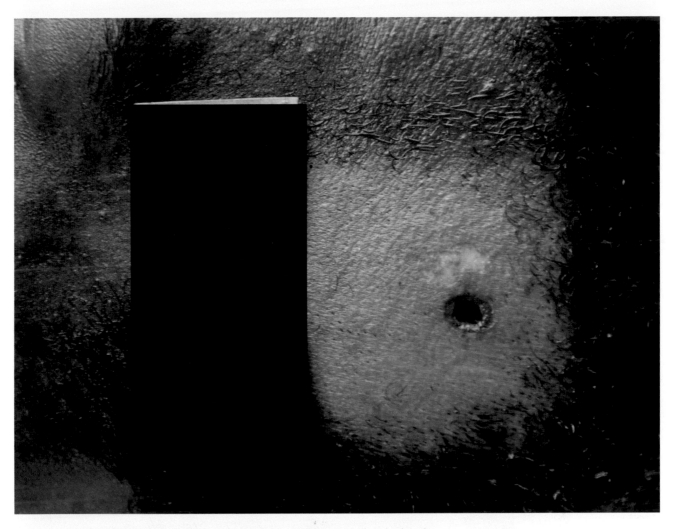

PHOTO 10.13: A gun fired from a distance caused this entrance wound to the head.

hands in pockets, and rubbing hands together may lead to the dissipation of GSR. Normally, particles will not be detectable four or five hours after the shooting (Trimpe 2011). Similarly, the presence of gunshot residue does not necessary mean that person actually fired the gun, as gunshot residue can be present on individuals who were in the vicinity of the fired gun. People standing within three feet of the fired gun may have GSR on their hands and clothing, although this may depend on the type of gun, the number of shots fired, and the environmental conditions of where the shooting occurred (Trimpe 2011). A positive test for GSR residue may also occur if a person handled an item with residue on it. In short, GSR examinations cannot conclusive prove that a particular person shot a gun or did not shoot a gun.

CUTTING AND STAB WOUNDS

Cutting wounds, such as those from a knife, will most often show a slicing of tissue with smooth edges. Stab and puncture wounds (e.g., from knives or screwdrivers) will present as holes in the tissue. Depending on the instrument used, they may initially appear similar to gunshot wounds. Cutting wounds are most often found on the arms, face, and legs; stab wounds are more likely to be found on the back, chest, and neck. Cutting and stab wounds are most likely to be lethal when in the chest, neck, head, or back. The magnitude and seriousness of the wound largely depends on the size and sharpness of the weapon, the body area affected, and the force used in causing the wound. A small but sharp blade directed with force to a vital area of the body can be extraordinarily lethal. It is extremely difficult

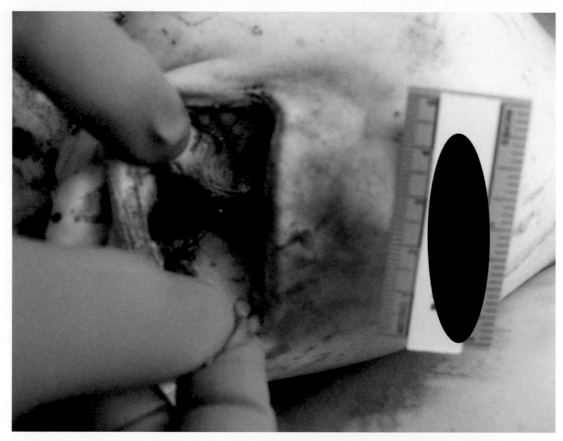

PHOTO 10.14a: This photo is of an entrance wound sustained by a victim who was shot in the mouth.

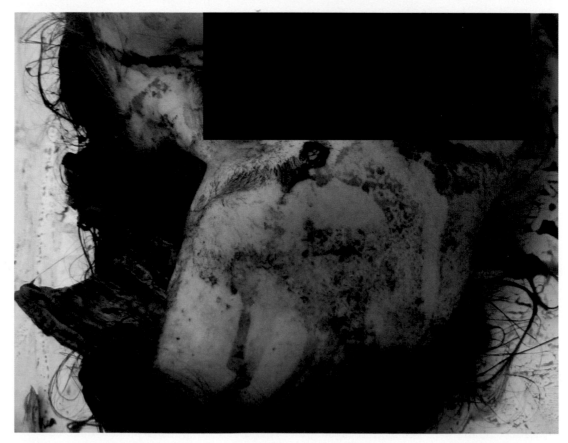

PHOTO 10.14b: The exit of the bullet through this victim's skull caused massive injuries and deformed the shape of the skull that remained intact.

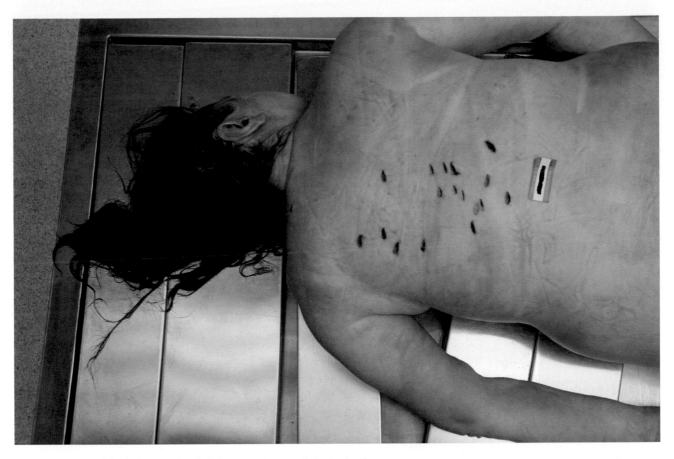

PHOTO 10.15a: This victim sustained eighteen stab wounds to the back.

to determine the type or size of instrument used when cuts are made to the tissue; however, the size (width and length) of the blade that caused stab and puncture wounds can be estimated via an autopsy of the victim. Externally visible stab wounds inflicted by the same weapon can vary in their shape and size depending on the area of the body where the wound was sustained and the angle and force of the thrust. As a result, what may initially appear to be injuries caused by multiple weapons may, in fact, be only from one weapon. Cuts to the victim's hands, fingers, and forearms are likely to be defense wounds. Such wounds result when a person instinctively attempts to prevent a stabbing by grabbing at the weapon or blocking an attack with a knife.

When death results from stabbing, it is typically a result of catastrophic damage to a vital organ, internal bleeding, shock, and/or infection. The cutting (or stabbing) of human tissue very often produces much bleeding depending on the area of the body affected. In many instances, death may result from blood loss. The bloodiest crime scenes usually result from stabbings or cuttings (or gunshot wounds to the head).

BLUNT FORCE INJURIES

Blunt force injuries are evidenced by irregular or rough-edged lacerations, bruising, and possibly broken bones in the area of impact. Most often, blunt force is directed at the victim's

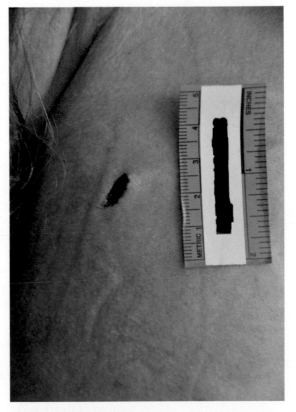

PHOTO 10.15b: A close-up of the wound in the area of the victim's shoulder.

head; injuries to the back of the head are most likely to be fatal (Geberth 1996). Skull fractures may be indicated by hemorrhaging of the upper eyelids (sometimes referred to as "raccoon eyes"; this symptom is also likely be present when there are gunshot wounds to the head). Blunt force injuries are often caused by hammers, pipes, crowbars, and clubs. Blunt force injuries may also be inflicted when a person is stuck by the grip of a firearm ("pistol whipping"). Depending on the area of the body affected, internal injuries as a result of blunt force may be much more significant than the external injuries. In particular, blunt force to the head, chest, or abdomen may be fatal without significant externally visible wounds. Internal injuries can be documented through an autopsy of the victim. Note that it is not uncommon that in the case of an attack with a blunt or other object, defense wounds may present in the form of bruising to the hands and forearms. Recall that the cause of death in the murder described in the introduction to this chapter was blunt force to the victim's skull.

ASPHYXIA

Any action or use of material that prevents a person from breathing is considered asphyxia (Geberth 1996). Death by asphyxiation can occur in several ways, including strangulation, hanging, suffocation, or drowning (Geberth 1996). Asphyxia may also occur as a result of chest compression, which prevents air from entering the lungs.

Most often, strangulation (effectively choking the victim) occurs manually (with hands) or with a ligature (such as a rope, purse strap, or wire). Ligature strangulation will leave an imprint of the ligature on the victim's neck; at the time of the discovery of the victim's body, the ligature may still be around the victim's neck. There may also be scratch marks on the victim's neck around the area of the ligature. These marks may be from the perpetrator's or victim's fingernails. If from the victim, the marks are likely a result of the victim's attempt to loosen the ligature. Manual strangulation will most likely leave bruising and hand or finger marks on the victim's neck. Two other indicators of strangulation/asphyxia-type death include petechial hemorrhages (small red dots in the inner surface of the eyelids, the whites of the eyes, or other skin surfaces) and trauma to the victim's tongue (as asphyxiation often leads to a victim biting his or her tongue) (Geberth 1996).

Rarely do homicides occur as a result of hanging. Most often, hangings are the result of suicides, or sometimes accidents, as in the case of autoerotic deaths (see above). Death by hanging occurs when the air supply is obstructed at the neck by some instrument or material, such as a rope. Rarely does death occur as a result of a fractured neck. In hanging deaths, the decedent is most likely to be found in a hanging position; however, a body need not be completely suspended to cause death. Often portions of the descendant's body (e.g., feet, legs) will be in contact with the floor. Investigators must be aware that in instances of hanging, staging may be present. In the case of a hanging by suicide, a family member may alter the scene to make it appear that the death resulted in some other way, or a murder that occurred in some other way may be staged to make it appear as a hanging. A death by hanging may be indicated by a mark across the neck (depending on the material used to obstruct the airway). If there is a groove line on the neck, there will likely be small black and blue marks in the area of the line. Additionally, persons who die as a result of asphyxia may expel urine/feces upon death, and the pattern of livor mortis (settling of the blood upon death; see below) will be consistent with the position of the suspended body.

Suffocation occurs when a person is unable to breathe due to a blocked mouth and nose. In a homicide, this could be accomplished via hands over the victim's mouth/nose, a pillow compressed over the victim's face, a plastic bag over the victim's head, or any other means by which the victim's air supply may be cut off or obstructed. Suffocation and smothering as a cause of death is determined as a result of an autopsy on the decedent.

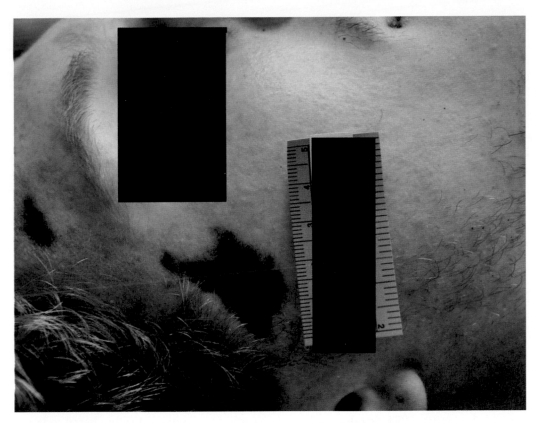

PHOTO 10.16a: Blunt force trauma to the head. Blunt force trauma injuries often cause more serious internal injuries than external.

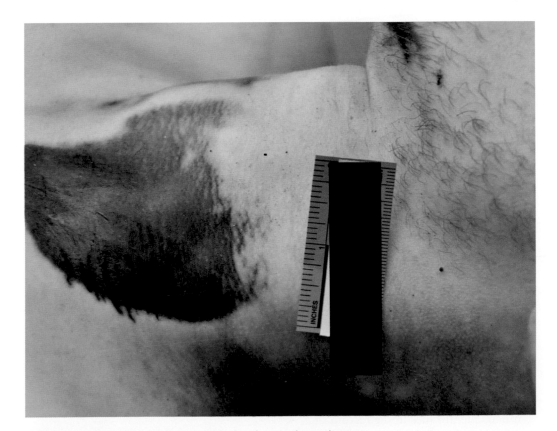

PHOTO 10.16b: Blunt force trauma with abrasions to the neck area.

Drowning occurs when fluid prevents intake of air into the lungs. By far, most drowning deaths are accidental; some are as a result of suicide. Seldom are drowning deaths the result of homicide. Of course, most bodies of drowning victims are located in water, but homicide victims who died in a way other than drowning are also sometimes found in water. The primary external indicator of a drowning death is white foam in the area of the mouth and nose. The foam forms when mucus of the body mixes with water. However, the external visible foam usually dissipates soon after death. Additional autopsy findings that support drowning as a cause of death include hemorrhage into the middle ears and water in the stomach or lungs (Clark et al. 1996).

Bodies that have been in water for long periods of time (whether as the result of drowning or some other cause of death) are affected by the water in severe ways.

The body of a person that drowns in a body of water such as a river or a lake will initially sink and then will rise later as a result of the buildup of gases from decomposition of the body. The amount of time from sinking to floating depends on many conditions, including the water temperature, the size of the body, and other water conditions. An autopsy may reveal whether the cause of death was drowning or whether the person was deceased before entering the water.

POISONING

Most poisonings are either accidental or as a result of a suicide. However, in rare instances, a homicide will occur as a result of poisoning. Death by poison may not produce any obvious indicators, but this depends on the type of the poison ingested. For example, carbon monoxide deaths will be evidenced by the victim's skin having a bright cherry-tone red color. The oral ingestion of other types of poisons characteristically produces vomit of different colors. Toxicology tests on the body conducted during an autopsy may confirm the presence of poison in the body.

DRUG OVERDOSE DEATHS

As with poisoning in general, seldom are homicides the result of drug overdoses. However, it is a serious crime to distribute or supply drugs that lead to a death or serious bodily injury. (The law governing this is the Anti-Drug Abuse Act of 1986, sometimes informally known as the Len Bias Law. Len Bias was an NBA first-round draft choice who died of a drug overdose [Prough 2009].) As such, overdose investigations are often about determining who supplied the lethal drugs to the victim. The scene should be treated as if it was the site of a homicide.

At the time of the discovery of a death via drugs, the manner and cause of death is likely to be unknown. As such, a working knowledge of pharmacology and drugs is useful for criminal investigators. Drugs can be introduced to the body in many ways (Clark et al. 1996):

- Intravenous: injected into a vein or artery (e.g., heroin)
- Intramuscular: injected into muscle mass (e.g., antibiotics)
- Oral: taken by mouth (e.g., aspirin)
- Cutaneous: absorbed through the skin (e.g., nitroglycerin)
- Rectal/vaginal: absorbed through the mucus membranes in the rectum or vagina (e.g., suppository)
- Inhalation: absorbed through the lungs, snorted (e.g., cocaine, nitric oxide)
- Subcutaneous: injected directly under the dermis
- Sublingual: placed under the tongue for absorption

Clearly, given the number of ways drugs can be ingested, investigators should be aware of items around the body that may indicate drug overdose. These items might include pills, pill bottles, syringes, needles, powder, aerosol cans, rolled paper, and/or spoons and lighters. Most drugs, ingested at a high enough level, can be fatal, including aspirin and acetaminophen (i.e., Tylenol). Combinations of drugs can be especially toxic. Drugs can lead to death through several processes, including oxygen deprivation, seizures, arrhythmia, or poisoning. Except for intravenous injection of drugs and the corresponding physical signs of it (e.g., track marks on arms, or even legs, eyelids, or toes), drug overdose deaths may not present clear externally visible evidence. One exception is with opiate overdoses (e.g., morphine, heroin, and oxycodone) where the presence of foam, many times tinged orange or red, is often present around the victim's nostrils and mouth (Prough 2009). The drugs cause a decrease in heart rate and breathing that leads to fluid buildup in the lungs, which may be expelled with gas bubbles forming a foam "cone" near the mouth and nose. As with suspected poisoning

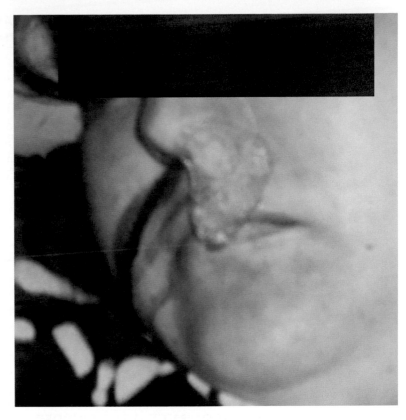

PHOTO 10.17: A foam "cone" that appeared around the nose and mouth of an opiate overdose victim. Depending on the time of discovery in relation to the time of death, a foam cone may not be present or obvious.

deaths in general, toxicology tests need to be conducted on the body during an autopsy in order to confirm drug overdose as the cause of death. Other evidence at the scene, such as cell phones, may be useful in determining contact between the victim and a drug supplier, as well as the identity of the supplier.

DEATH VIA FIRE

A dead body at a fire scene presents challenges to an investigator. Was the fire a result of arson, was it an accident, or did it have some other cause? Did the fire cause the victim's death, or was the fire set after the victim was already dead? Did the decedent die as a result of a homicide? Because of burns to the body, there may be additional challenges in identifying the decedent. The results of an autopsy are of great assistance in answering several of these questions.

Most deaths associated with fire are as a result of smoke inhalation, not the actual burning of the body. If there is burning to the flesh, it typically occurs after death. Indications that the victim was alive at the time of the fire include smoke/ash stains around the nostrils and in the nose and air passages, carbon monoxide in the blood, and blistering and reddening of the skin (Geberth 1996). Regardless if dead or alive at the time of burning, a body exposed to the heat of a fire will take a position of "pugilistic attitude" where arms and legs are drawn in and up to the body. This is as a result of the dehydrating effect of the heat on the body. Other apparent injuries to the body may also be present as a result of the heat and charring effects of the fire, such as skull fractures, broken bones, or the splitting of skin. Investigators must be careful to avoid premature conclusions about cause and manner of death in fire situations and rely on the expertise of the medical examiner who conducts the autopsy of the body.

THE VALUE OF AN AUTOPSY IN ESTABLISHING THE CAUSE AND MANNER OF DEATH

As discussed above, information developed from the autopsy of the victim is likely to be extremely useful in the determination of the manner and cause of death. Indeed, the autopsy is the definitive word on the cause and manner of death. The conduct of the autopsy may vary given the condition of the body and the circumstances of the death. Briefly, the process begins with the transportation of the body to the medical examiner's facility in a body bag or evidence sheet. This also begins the chain of custody of the body. If it is possible that there is evidence on the hands, fingers, or fingernails of the decedent, the hands should be protected by paper bags. The autopsy itself consists of two parts: the external examination and the internal examination. Briefly, the external examination consists of photographing the body, noting the clothing on the body, and an examination of the body for evidence. Samples of body tissue are collected for toxicology and other tests. The body is then removed from the bag, undressed, examined for additional evidence, cleaned, weighed, measured, and prepared for the internal examination. The internal examination involves opening the chest, abdominal, and pelvic cavity in order to remove and inspect internal organs. The skull is then opened and the brain removed and inspected. In the process, trauma to internal organs and other evidence is noted in an effort to reach conclusions about the manner and cause of death and about other injuries sustained by the victim. After the autopsy is complete, the body is reconstructed. Case in Point 10.16 provides an example of an autopsy report completed as a result of a murder investigation (also see www.autopsy. org for other examples of autopsy reports).

WHO COMMITTED THE MURDER?

As discussed earlier in this book, physical evidence, witnesses, suspects, and other evidence are likely to play important roles in answering this question. Some additional considerations are discussed here.

CIRCUMSTANCES

Information about the circumstances of the incident and the characteristics of the victim are critical in determining the identity of the perpetrator. For example, if the murder occurred in a private place (e.g., a residence), it is very likely that not only did the victim and offender know each other but there is a good chance there was some sort of relationship between them, thereby reducing the pool of suspects for investigators to consider. In other instances, information may come from witnesses or other individuals with relevant information. In some cases, these witnesses will be able to identify the offender. Often, the most critical and difficult task for investigators is locating witnesses who have this information. Neighborhood canvasses, media publicity, and tip lines may serve important purposes in this regard.

It is interesting to note that a study of nearly 800 homicide investigations in four jurisdictions—Detroit, Baltimore, Los Angeles, and Milwaukee—found that the circumstances of the incidents made a big difference in whether cases were solved (Wellford and Cronin 1999). In particular, it was found that a homicide was more likely to be solved if drugs were not involved in the crime, if a witness at the crime scene provided valuable information, and if the crime occurred in a private place. The authors also found that cases were more likely to be solved if three or more detectives were assigned to the case and if detectives and evidence technicians responded quickly to the crime scene.

Based on the typical characteristics of homicide victims and offenders, investigators may also consider statistical probabilities when considering possible perpetrators. For example, in any homicide, it is more likely than not that the offender is male, between the ages of seventeen and thirty-nine, and knew the victim. If the victim is black, chances are the perpetrator is also black. If the victim is white, chances are the perpetrator is white. Regardless

CASE *in* POINT 10.1   Autopsy Protocol of Anthony Porter, Homicide Victim

Anthony Porter was working as an armed security guard at a store when a subject entered the store, approached Anthony, shot him several times, and took his gun from his holster. The subject then fled the store (see Case in Point 10.3 for additional details about this incident). What follows here is the verbatim report from the autopsy of Anthony Porter. It shows the detail in documenting the exact injuries sustained by the victim and the corresponding cause of death.

Final Anatomic Findings: Cause of Death

1. Exsanguination, secondary to multiple gunshot wounds to the chest and abdomen.

    a. Lacerations of the left subclavian and left internal jugular veins.

    b. Lacerations to bilateral lungs, liver, and ascending colon.

    c. Bilateral hemothorax.

    d. Seven entrance wounds to chest and upper extremities.

    e. Two exit wounds to right and left upper extremities.

2. Laceration of trachea with aspiration of blood to distal airways.

Evidence of Internal Injury

The bullet entering through WOUND #1 passed through the right apex of the chest cavity and ended in the musculature just anterior to the scapula. There was a fracture in the scapula near where the bullet was recovered. This bullet is a deformed 5.7 gm copper jacketed projectile with visible lateral rifling. The angle of the bullet was mostly left to right at 45 degrees off of horizontal, anterior to posterior very slightly and downward at 60 degrees off of sagittal. The left internal jugular vein was also lacerated by this bullet.

The bullet entering through WOUND #2 passed between the left first and second ribs, then through soft tissue surrounding the thoracic aorta to lodge posterior to T4. The bullet recovered from this site was a mushroomed 5.7 gm copper jacketed projectile with visible lateral rifling. This bullet was angled from left to right at 60 degrees off of horizontal, from anterior to posterior very slightly off of the coronal plane, and

downward at 45 degrees off of the sagittal plane. The left subclavant vein was lacerated by this bullet.

The bullet that entered through WOUND #3 passed through the soft tissues in the right anterior shoulder to exit though WOUND #11. This bullet angled from left to right at approximately 5 degrees off of horizontal from anterior to posterior at 5 degrees off of the coronal plane, and downward at 5 degrees off of horizontal.

The bullet that entered through WOUND #4 passed between the right first and second ribs laterally and then between the first and second ribs medially to be embedded in T2. The bullet recovered from this site was a 5.7 gm mushroomed copper jacketed projectile with visible lateral rifling. The bullet angled anterior to posterior at 5 degrees off of coronal, right to left at 5 degrees off of coronal, and upward at 5 degrees off of horizontal.

The bullet that entered through WOUND #5 passed between the left fifth and sixth ribs then through the left upper lobe and the apex of the left lower lobe, through the inferior pericardium and then through the left diaphragm, through the left and caudate lobes of the liver, through the ascending colon, and then through the lateral aspect of the right lobe of the liver to come to rest in the peritoneal cavity just deep to the liver. The bullet causing WOUND #10 first passed through the clothing (an intermediate target) in the left lateral seam of the outer shirt and causing WOUND #10, passing through the soft tissue of the abdomen at WOUND #6 where it lay embedded in the subcutaneous tissue just deep to the skin. This bullet was a 5.7 gm mushroomed copper jacketed projectile with visible lateral rifling. This bullet had moved from left to right at a 45 degree angulation off the coronal plane. It moved in a downward direction at 5 degrees off of horizontal and from posterior to anterior at 60 degrees off of sagittal.

The bullet that passed though WOUND #7 exited the left arm at WOUND #8 and then impacted the skin of the left lateral chest at WOUND #9, causing an abrasion. From here, it bounced off of the body. The regulation of this bullet was mostly left to right with a 30 degree angulation off of horizontal, slightly posterior to anterior at 5 degrees off of coronal, and downward at approximately 30 degrees off of horizontal. The left pleural cavity contained 650 cc of blood and the right pleural cavity contained 400 cc of blood.

if the victim is male or female, there is a high probability that the perpetrator is male and knew the victim. Along these same lines, crime scene profiling may assist in focusing the investigation. Investigators must be aware, however, that statistical probabilities and profiles may be wrong.

MOTIVE

Another consideration is the motive for committing the crime. Who would have wanted the victim dead? Who would benefit from this person being dead? Establishing a motive, or considering various motives, is often useful in reducing the scope of suspects. Sometimes motive first appears to be one thing but actuality turns out to be another. Investigators must be cautious and guard against drawing conclusions too quickly in spite of the most obvious evidence (see Case in Point 10.2).

CASE in POINT 10.2   Things Are Not Always as They Seem

On the night of October 23, 1989, Charles Stuart and his pregnant wife, Carol, both thirty years old, left childbirth class at Boston's Brigham and Women's Hospital. Minutes later, Charles called 911 on his cell phone from his car to report that he and his wife had just been robbed and shot. Charles, seriously injured and bleeding from a gunshot wound to his abdomen, was unable to tell the police his location. Charles assisted the police in locating him and his wife by listening for the police sirens, judging the proximity of the police from the sirens, and then directing the police to where they were. After thirteen minutes, with Carol still clinging to life, the police located them. Charles immediately described the assailant as a young black man wearing a jogging suit. The search was on.

Carol died that night of a single gunshot wound to the head, shortly after giving birth to her son by cesarean section; the baby died seventeen days later. Charles spent six weeks in the hospital, including ten days in intensive care. During this time, the police launched a massive manhunt for the killer in the largely black Roxbury/Boston neighborhood. Police believed they found their killer when Charles identified William Bennett, thirty-nine, as the man who looked "most like" his attacker in a police lineup. Bennett originally became a suspect when the police obtained information from some of his acquaintances that he bragged about the murder and that he said he saw Charles look at him in his rearview mirror during the robbery (Charles earlier told a similar story to the police). In addition, Charles recognized Bennett in a photo that was shown to him by the police while he was still in the hospital. On top of all this information, Bennett had a long criminal record.

With Bennett in police custody, and most of Boston relieved that the killer was caught, the investigation took a wild and dramatic twist. Matthew Stuart, Charles's younger brother, came forward and told the police that on the night of the murder, he met Charles, as planned, and that Charles, while still seated in his car, threw Carol's purse to him. Matthew stated that inside the purse he found Carol's engagement ring, other items reported stolen, and a revolver. He told police that he threw most of the items into a river—except for the ring, which he kept. He gave the ring to the police. It became clear to the police that Charles was, in fact, responsible for the murder of his wife. On January 4, 1990, Charles drove to the Tobin Bridge in Boston, stopped his car, got out, and jumped. The police later recovered his body, along with a suicide note that read, in part, "I love my family . . . the last four months have been hell."

Upon further investigation, the police learned that Charles was having an affair and had significant financial problems. They also learned that Carol had a large life insurance policy. It was also later determined that the police may have "coached" Charles for the statement that he looked at the shooter in the rearview mirror (the same statement that the shooter allegedly made) and that Charles may have recognized Bennett in the lineup because the police earlier showed a photo of Bennett to Charles in the hospital. In addition, after Bennett's arrest, acquaintances of Bennett who had reported that he was bragging about the crime recanted their statements (Alter and Starr 1990; Baker 1990). Clearly, investigators need to be mindful that crimes are not always as they first appear.

When trying to establish motive, diaries, letters, e-mail, appointment books, recent telephone calls of the victim, and friends and associates of the victim may cast light on persons who may have wished the victim harm and provide clues about the identity of the killer. When it is difficult to establish a motive, when the homicide does not have a "rational" motive, or is "random," homicides may be much more difficult to solve. Consider the case discussed in the chapter introduction. The primary suspect in the murder of Jackie was the friend who dropped her off at her apartment the morning she was killed. Given Jackie's characteristics and lifestyle, she was at low risk of becoming a homicide victim. As such, chances were that she was targeted, targeted by someone she knew, and targeted for some reason relating to their relationship, but that was not the case. As another example, see Case in Point 10.3.

PHYSICAL EVIDENCE

Working the crime scene and other associated investigative procedures are perhaps more important in homicide investigations than any other criminal investigation. Of course, no crime is more serious, and in no crime are investigative errors more critical. As such, the procedures outlined in Chapter 5 are most relevant in homicide investigations. Physical evidence on the victim's body or at the crime scene may hold the key to the identity of the killer.

Crime scene procedures are extremely important in locating and preserving physical evidence. The crime scene may contain the perpetrator's blood or other biological evidence, other physical evidence (e.g., shoeprints, fingerprints, cigarette butts), or discarded or forgotten personal items (e.g., clothing, billfold). Investigators should consider everything as evidence and should expect to find physical evidence at homicide crime scenes.

Clearly, the victim represents critical evidence in a murder investigation. On the victim there may be evidence that could lead to the identification of the perpetrator (e.g., semen, saliva, fingernail scrapings, other DNA). Again, the autopsy may reveal information not only about the manner and cause of death but also the circumstances of the murder, including the time of death.

In spite of the *potential* value of DNA and other physical evidence in homicide investigations, studies suggest that such evidence may not have a significant impact on whether suspects are identified. In particular, Baskin and Sommers (2010) analyzed homicide investigations and found that forensic evidence did not have any appreciable effect on whether the case was solved (the perpetrator identified). They found that homicides with witnesses were more likely to be solved, and homicides committed with a firearm were less likely to be solved. Schroeder and White (2009) found that DNA evidence was seldom used by homicide detectives in first identifying the perpetrator and, like Baskin and Sommers (2010), found that it was not significantly related to case clearance. As discussed in Chapter 5, physical and DNA evidence may be of most value *after* the perpetrator has been identified and in confirming that the defendant committed the murder.

ESTIMATING THE TIME OF DEATH

In some homicide investigations, the time at which the victim died is unknown, but it may be a critical piece of the evidence puzzle, particularly as it relates to the alibi of the suspect. Approximate time of death, or the approximate time the crime occurred, may be estimated by the circumstances of the crime as established by witnesses or by the condition of the dead body. As an example of the former, with regard to the murders of Nicole Brown Simpson and Ron Goldman, the time at which the crimes occurred was critical. O. J. Simpson was known to be on his way to the Los Angeles airport shortly after 11:00 p.m. the night of the murders. As a result, the closer the murders occurred to 11:00, the less likely that Simpson could have been the killer. The approximate time at which the crime occurred, approximately 10:00 p.m., was established through various witness statements about related events the night of the crime (e.g., witnesses hearing a barking dog that was later determined to belong to Nicole, another witness discovering the dog outside Nicole's property).

CASE *in* POINT 10.3   Why Was Anthony Porter Murdered?

Earlier in the chapter, the autopsy report of Anthony Porter was provided. Here are some the details about the circumstances of his murder and the ensuing investigation. As noted, Anthony was working as an armed security guard at a store when someone entered the store, approached him, shot him seven times, took his gun, and fled the store. The gun used was a Smith and Wesson .357 magnum.

Upon arrival at the scene, the police officers and detectives interviewed twenty-two people who were in or near the store at the time of the shooting. No one was able to provide any details except for two witnesses who reported that after the shooting they saw a black man run out of the store and toward the adjacent parking lot of a large grocery store. Appropriately, police then focused much attention on the people who were in the grocery store. Did any of them know the victim or have a link to the victim or to any associates or friends of the victim?

Initially, the biggest question was motive. Why would someone enter a crowded store, shoot and kill the security guard, and then take his gun? It did not seem to make much sense. The perpetrator made no attempt to rob the store. The victim appeared to be targeted and, since he was shot seven times, it appeared that the perpetrator definitely wanted him dead. Why?

By its second day, the investigation was going in several different directions. In addition to the people who were in the grocery store, extensive investigation was being conducted on the victim and his background. Who were his friends? Who were his enemies? Who could have wanted him dead? The police talked to Porter's family members; they talked to his supervisor and to his coworkers. They interviewed numerous friends of Porter, including his current girlfriend and an ex-girlfriend. The police talked to the current boyfriend of the victim's ex-girlfriend. From these interviews it was learned that Porter was an honest and hardworking guy. He had a good relationship with his girlfriend, and the two were planning a not-too-distant wedding. Porter was not a gang member, he did not use drugs, and he did not sell drugs. Porter's girlfriend said that she did not have any jealous previous boyfriends.

Porter's previous girlfriend had had no contact with him for years. No good leads.

Tips were provided to the police by other citizens who came forward during the investigation. One of the potentially most valuable bits of information came from a witness who told the police that while she was in the parking lot of the grocery store on the night of the homicide, a black man asked for a ride, but she did not give him one. Another citizen told the police the name of an individual who she thought might have committed the murder. On a previous occasion, she told the police, the victim flirted with the girlfriend of the cousin of this named person. She thought that he might have gotten back at Porter by killing him. The police checked out these leads. More dead ends.

The police also wanted to find Porter's gun, which was taken from him after he was shot. The serial number of the gun, along with its description, was entered into the NCIC database and officers in the department were made aware of the significance of this gun. Investigators figured that if they could find the gun, they might find the killer.

Three days later, a bank in the city was robbed. As the two perpetrators were fleeing the bank, dye packs in one of the bags of money taken from the bank exploded. The suspect carrying the bag dropped it, and paper bills began blowing around in the wind. One of the robbers continued to run, but the other stopped and attempted to pick up the money. As he was doing this, the police arrived at the scene and took him into custody. In searching the area around the bank, the police located a vehicle with one person sitting in it. It was the getaway car. This person was also taken into custody. On searching the car, the police discovered a gun. It was a Smith and Wesson .357 magnum handgun registered to Anthony Porter.

On interrogating the would-be driver of the getaway car, he confessed to his involvement in many prior robberies and the homicide of Anthony Porter. He also implicated his two friends, Willie Dortch and Myron Edwards, in these crimes and identified Edwards as the shooter of the security guard.

With regard to estimating time of death from the condition of the dead body, it is necessary to consider what happens to a body upon death. When a person dies and the heart stops beating, a series of relatively predictable changes begin to occur in the body. These changes may provide a basis on which to make an *estimate* regarding the time of death or, as it is sometimes called, the postmortem interval (or PMI). Many factors can influence the changes and the rate of the changes that occur in the body after death. As a result, it is important to realize that the estimates are, at best, approximations of PMI.

The first indicator of PMI is the temperature of the body. The cooling of the body upon death is referred to as algor mortis. Normal body temperature is 98.6 degrees Fahrenheit. Upon death, at an environmental (ambient) temperature of 70 to 75 degrees Fahrenheit, the internal body temperature normally falls at a rate of approximately one and one-half to two degrees per hour depending on the build of the victim, other victim characteristics, and amount of clothing on the body (Owen 2000; Dix and Graham 2000). Because of variable environmental temperatures and other considerations, determining PMI via body temperature may be quite prone to error. In apparent recent deaths, investigators should make an assessment of body temperature at the time of the discovery of the body, noting whether the body was cold, cool, warm, or hot, and record that information in the written report (Clark et al. 1996). It is also necessary to document environmental conditions, especially the temperature. In other instances, the condition of the body should be noted. The body should not be unnecessarily moved prior to these observations (Dix and Graham 2000).

Within one to two hours of death, livor mortis usually becomes evident. When the heart stops beating, blood begins to pool in the body in accordance with gravity. The blood settles and shows as a bruising purplish type of discoloration on the body. After eight to twelve hours, depending on the ambient temperature, the blood becomes fixed and the areas of discoloration will not move, even if pressure is applied or the body is moved. Accordingly, if there is a question about whether the body has been moved after death (e.g., because of an attempt to stage the scene or for some other reason) and if full livor mortis is present, an examination of the pattern of livor mortis may reveal the answer. However, pale areas within the area of livor mortis may be caused by tight clothing or pressure from objects pressing against the skin. A person who incurred substantial blood loss may not show livor mortis; neither would an individual with dark pigmented skin (Dix and Graham 2000). Livor mortis is visible until further discoloration occurs due to decomposition.

Shortly after death, as a result of chemical changes in the dead body, the muscles of the body begin to become stiff. This process is referred to as rigor mortis. It is first most apparent in the smaller muscles of the body and then extends to the arms (elbows) and then the legs (knees). It is usually begins two to four hours after death and is fully established after eight to twelve hours of death. It will be fully present for at least twelve more hours. It will begin to disappear after another twelve hours and usually will be gone within sixty hours of death (Castleman 2000). Again, this process is greatly affected by individual (e.g., weight) and environmental (e.g., temperature) factors. The rate of onset and dissipation is faster with children than with adults (Clark et al. 1996) and is more apparent in adults than children. Variation in the rate of rigor mortis also depends on environmental temperature, muscle mass, internal temperature, and the decedent's activity prior to death (Dix and Graham 2000). Freezing of the body due to cold weather must not be confused with rigor mortis.

Another method of determining PMI involves the measurement of potassium levels in the vitreous humor, the fluid that fills the inside of the eyeball. As blood cells break down through the process of livor mortis, potassium is released. Measurement of the potassium may provide an estimate regarding the time of death (Owen 2000), although much variation across individuals has been noted, making its use as a determinant of PMI questionable (Dix and Graham 2000). Relatedly, it is useful to note that the cornea (the area of the eye that covers the iris and pupil) will become cloudy one to two hours after death.

Another method of estimating time of death involves an analysis of the contents of the victim's stomach or gastrointestinal tract. If the time of the last meal is known, and the body is not in a state of advanced decomposition, it may be possible to estimate the time of death based on the degree to which food has been digested. Generally, the stomach empties in two to six hours after consumption of food (Castleman 2000; Dix and Graham 2000).

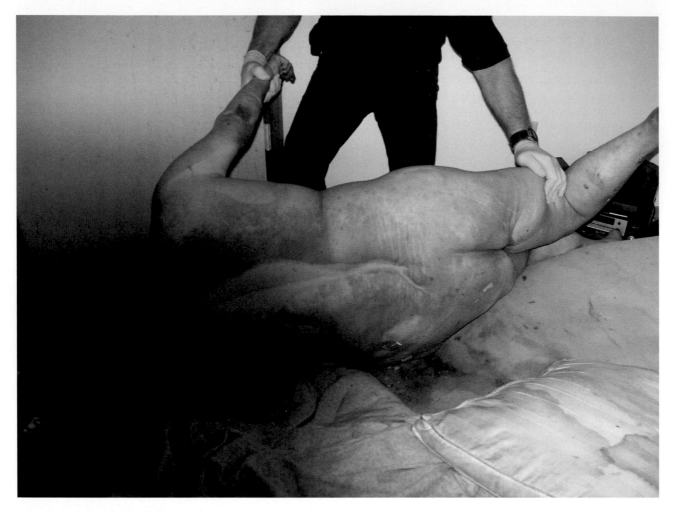

PHOTO 10.18: An example of livor mortis, which is the settling of the blood upon death. Approximately how long would you estimate this subject has been deceased?

The degree of decomposition of the body can also serve as an indicator of the time of death; although, once again, decomposition is greatly affected by environmental conditions, especially temperature. In particular, buried bodies, bodies in water, and bodies in the hot sun will vary substantially from the "typical" decomposition pattern, as will bodies exposed to widely fluctuating temperatures. A typical decomposition pattern follows a general, but not necessarily uniform, pattern (adapted from Clark et al. 1996, p. 48; also see Castleman 2000; Goff 2000; Owen 2000):

- Within 24 hours: likely greenish discoloration of the lower right abdomen

- Within 24–36 hours: greenish discoloration of the abdomen

- Within 36–48 hours: marbling (purplish lines) of the body, bloating of the face

- Within 48–60 hours: desiccation (drying) of the fingertips

- Within 60–72 hours: bloating of the body

- Within 4–7 days: skins blebs (blisters), fluid seepage, hair sloughing (falling off), skin slippage, putrid odor

- Within days–weeks: dehydration of body tissues

- Within weeks–months: adipocere (transformation of fat into a waxy type substance), mummification, skeletonization

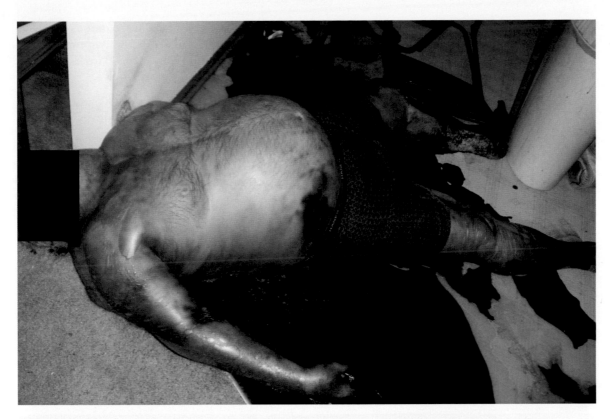

PHOTO 10.19a: An example of advanced decomposition. Approximately how long would you estimate this subject has been deceased?

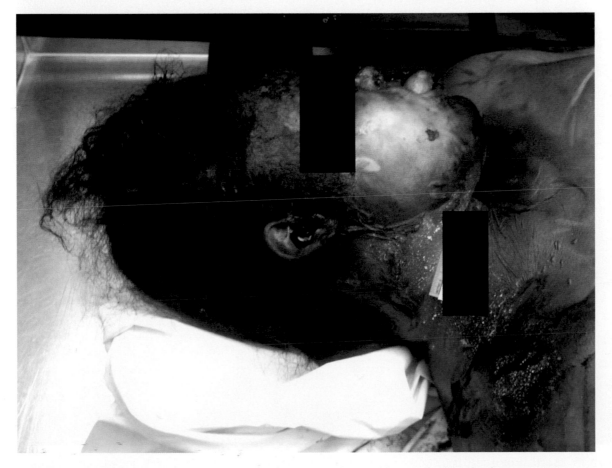

PHOTO 10.19b: Another example of advanced decomposition. What would you estimate to be the postmortem interval of this subject?

If the state of decomposition is not congruent with the environmental conditions in which the body was located, then an investigator might suspect that the body was moved after death from one environment to another (see "Secrets of the Body Farm" parts 1, 2, and 3 on YouTube for additional discussion).

Depending on the environment, during the process of decomposition visible insect and/or animal activity may also to be present. Insects are most likely first to invade open wounds and areas of bleeding. After these areas are attacked, then the eyes, mouth, nose, and ears are attacked. Next to be invaded are the genitals and anus, if exposed. Usually the pelvic area is not attacked by insects for as long as twelve to thirty-six hours after death, unless there was trauma and bleeding in those areas (Haskell and Haskell 2002). With bleeding, insects will be present much sooner. Accordingly, if insects (larva) found on the face are at the same stage of development as those in the pelvic region, it may be concluded that these areas were invaded at about the same time and, hence, that there was pelvic trauma (Haskell and Haskell 2002). In addition, wounds inflicted after death (postmortem) are generally less attractive to insects than wounds inflicted before death (antemortem) or at the time of death (perimortem) because of the lack of blood at the site of the wound. It is also interesting to note that it is possible to detect chemicals or poisons that are in a decomposing body through an analysis of the contents of the guts of maggots recovered from the body. In addition, if there is a question about whether the recovered maggots were actually feeding on a particular corpse, it is possible to extract human DNA from the maggot and associate it with a particular body (Wells et al. 2001).

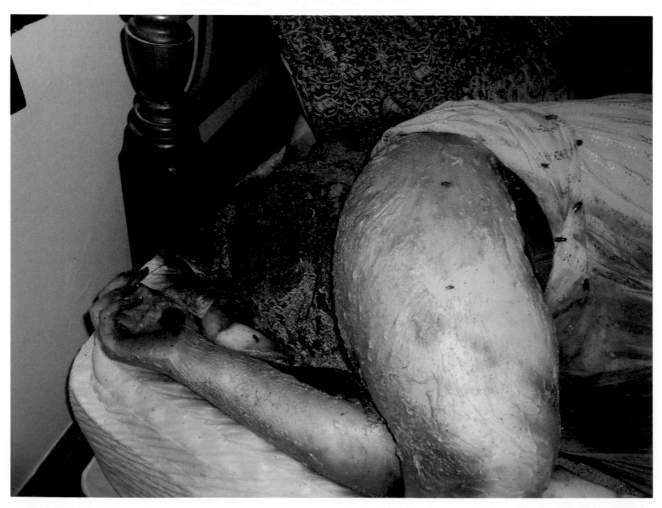

PHOTO 10.20: Insect activity on a dead body. Notice the increased activity at the eyes, ears, nose, mouth, and ears. There appear to be adult green bottle flies on the subject's clothing.

The types of insects that are present on the body can also be informative. Certain insects are most likely to be the first to lay eggs on the body; others are more likely to be present later. Blow flies (green bottle and blue bottle flies) are generally the first to arrive and may lay eggs on a dead body within minutes of death. Eggs hatch between eight and fourteen hours later depending on environmental (temperature and humidity) conditions. Maggots then develop and proceed through three developmental stages, reaching maturity ten to twelve days after the eggs were laid (Owen 2000). Dump flies (a relative of the housefly) may be present on the body several days to several weeks after the time of death. False stable flies (another relative of the housefly) usually appear after the dump flies (Haskell and Haskell 2002). By this time, beetle activity is most prominent on the body. After all insect activity has stopped, only bones and hair remain.

Animals may also feed on dead bodies. Pet dogs and cats, if hungry enough, will consume human remains. Other animals, including mice, rats, raccoons, and possums, will also consume human flesh. Evidence of animal activity can be interpreted by a pathologist through an autopsy. Animals may also scatter human remains; what may first appear as dismemberment by a killer may be the result of animal activity.

●●● Major Challenges in Homicide Investigations: Serial Homicide

Homicide investigations in which there is no apparent relationship between the victim and the offender pose a unique challenge to the police. The ultimate investigative challenge, however, is investigating homicides that are suspected of being part of a series—homicides that are suspected of being the responsibility of a serial killer. These crimes often appear as random and without a traditional motive. Serial murders may be mobile, further complicating the task of identifying the perpetrator. These crimes are often well planned and lack witnesses and other evidence. There may not be a crime scene, or even a body. The difficulty in investigating such crimes is apparent in the nature of the crime. The killer is able to be a *serial* killer because he or she is not caught. If caught after the first homicide, the killer would not have a chance to continue the crimes. Fortunately, serial homicides are relatively uncommon. Given the lack of favorable investigative circumstances in investigating homicides suspected of being part of a series, investigators often have to rely on nontraditional investigative techniques in such cases. Primary among them, as discussed in previous chapters, are psychological profiling, crime analysis networks (e.g., ViCAP), and media alerts (e.g., AMBER Alerts).

A single homicide creates much work for investigators. A series of homicides translates into a lot of work, to say the least. Complicating matters even further is that several law enforcement agencies may be involved. In response, investigative agencies may form task forces. Task forces are usually temporary in nature and bring together representatives of agencies to deal with a particular crime or crime problem. A task force is a high-profile investigative response. Task forces are common in investigating serial crimes, especially serial homicides and rapes, as well as drug trafficking. By bringing together representatives from various agencies, task forces can enhance cooperation, communication, evidence sharing, and person-power in an attempt to solve the crimes in question (Hayeslip and Russell-Einhorn 2003).

●●● Major Challenges in Homicide Investigations: Cold Cases

In most solved homicides, a suspect is taken into custody within twenty-four hours. If a case is not solved within this time frame, then the chances of it ever being solved fall drastically

(Keppel and Weis, 1994). While this is true, it is also important to understand that the time that elapses may not, by itself, determine whether the crime is solved. Rather, homicides that are solved within twenty-four hours are likely to have certain characteristics—namely, considerable evidence, such as an eyewitness who provides investigators with the name of the perpetrator. Therefore, homicides *with certain characteristics* are most likely to be solved within twenty-four hours; homicides without those characteristics may not be solved within that time frame.

Regardless, caseload and corresponding time pressures often lead to old cases being set aside so that new cases with fresh leads can be investigated. Given the seriousness of some cases, however, it may not be appropriate or wise to suspend or terminate investigative activities on them. Cold case investigations address this dilemma. They allow for new eyes to be put on old cases.

According to Davis et al. (2011), there are three types of cold cases: (1) cases where the investigation is reopened due to family pressure, media inquiries, or standard police department procedures that required review of unsolved cases after a specified period of time; (2) cases that are reopened due to the availability of previously untested DNA evidence; and (3) cases that are reopened when a person (e.g., a prisoner) confesses to an unsolved crime or a new witness comes forward with information about a crime. The authors found that 90 percent of cold cases were reopened due to the availability of DNA evidence or because of new witnesses. Indeed, in the decades prior to the 1990s and the common usage of DNA analysis, the biological evidence that was recovered from crime scenes was sometimes kept in storage, even long after the investigation concluded. Now, DNA analysis may be performed on this evidence and perpetrators may be identified as a result. See Case in Point 10.4.

The authors also found that there were substantial difficulties, and limited success, in making arrests in cold case crimes; only one case in twenty resulted in an arrest and one case in 100 resulted in a conviction. The difficulties involved included uncooperative witnesses, the inability to locate key witnesses, the suspect being deceased or immune from additional charges (due to a prior plea bargain deal), and/or DNA results that did not identify a perpetrator or were otherwise inconclusive. Finally, the authors found a cold case was more

CASE in POINT 10.4 Cold Case Cleared

Five-year-old Alie Berrelez was kidnapped while playing with friends outside of her apartment building in Englewood, Colorado, on May 18, 1993. A massive search for the girl ended four days later when her body was found in a canvas bag near a creek approximately fourteen miles from her home. Nicholas Stofer, forty-one, was immediately identified as a suspect in the girl's disappearance, but he was never arrested due to lack of evidence. The best evidence available came from Alie's three-year-old brother, who witnessed the abduction. He told police that "the old man" took Alie. He then led the police to a neighboring apartment where Stofer lived. Although blood and hair samples were taken from Stofer and compared to evidence on the girl's body, the analyses were inconclusive (DNA analysis was not used at the time). In addition, the scent dogs that assisted the police in locating the body then followed the scent back to the apartment complex, further casting suspicion on Stofer.

Fast-forward eighteen years. As the result of a cold case review, the girl's underwear were again examined and DNA was recovered. The DNA matched Nicholas Stofer. Although the crime was finally solved, Stofer did not face charges. He died of natural causes in 2001.

likely to be solved if certain circumstances were present. These circumstances include the following:

- The crime occurring recently
- The crime not involving a drug user
- The victim being found in a private residence
- The victim being younger or male
- There being a known motivation for the crime
- A prime suspect having been earlier identified

As an example of a cold case squad, the Washington, D.C., Metropolitan Police Department (MPD) cold case unit consists of twelve homicide investigators and a supervisor. When a case remains unsolved for thirty-six months, it is considered "cold." At this time, the case is reviewed by investigators. If there are no additional leads, the case is closed. If there are leads, the case is assigned for additional follow-up. The unit reviews sixty to seventy cases a year and clears approximately ten a year (Davis et al. 2011).

MAIN POINTS

1. All deaths can be explained in one of four ways (manner of death): deaths are the result of natural causes, accident, suicide, or homicide. Most frequent is natural causes, followed by accidents, suicides, and homicide.

2. To determine manner of death, at least three considerations are paramount: (1) the nature of the injuries sustained by the decedent (the cause of death), (2) the characteristics of the decedent, and (3) the circumstances of the death. This information may come from an examination and/or autopsy of the body, an examination of the scene, and from witnesses or family/friends.

3. Most often, determining manner of death is straightforward. When there is uncertainty regarding the manner of death, it usually involves differentiating between suicide and homicide, and between suicide and accident.

4. Most homicides involve victims and offenders who are young males and who know each other. In most instances a firearm was used to commit the murder, and the murder resulted from an argument. Murders caused by poisoning, drowning, strangulation, or asphyxiation are very uncommon.

5. Three basic questions guide a homicide investigation: (1) Who is the decedent?, (2) What was the cause of the death?, and (3) Who is the offender? Usually it is not a major investigative challenge to determine the identity of the decedent. There are many potential causes of death in a homicide, including gunshot wounds, knife wounds, blunt force, asphyxiation, drowning, poisoning, and fire. The circumstances of the incident, physical and DNA evidence, the possible motive of the offender, and time of death may help in identifying the perpetrator.

6. The particular characteristics of injuries to a homicide victim provide indications and clues about cause and circumstances of death. For example, much can be learned about how the homicide occurred as a result of an analysis of gunshot wounds.

7. Considering various motives for a homicide may help narrow the pool of suspects.

8. Things are not always as they first appear to be in criminal investigations.

9. An autopsy consists of an external and internal examination of the body. Information developed from the autopsy of the victim is likely to be

extremely useful in the determination of the manner and cause of death. The autopsy is the definitive word on the cause and manner of death.

10. In some homicide investigations, the time at which the victim died is unknown, but it may be a critical piece of the evidence puzzle, particularly as it relates to the alibi of the suspect. Approximate time of death may be estimated by the circumstances of the crime, established by witnesses, or gauged by the condition of the dead body.

11. When a person dies, a series of relatively predictable changes begin to occur in the body. These changes may provide a basis on which to make an *estimate* regarding the time of death, or postmortem interval (PMI). Many factors can influence the changes and the rate of the changes that occur in the body after death. As a result, it is important to realize that the estimates are, at best, approximations of PMI.

12. PMI may be estimated by the temperature of the body, livor mortis (pooling of blood), rigor mortis (stiffening of muscles), stomach contents, and/or the degree of decomposition. Decomposition also follows a general pattern: discoloration, marbling, bloating, desiccation of the fingertips, skins

blebs, fluid seepage, hair sloughing, dehydration of body tissues, adipocere, mummification, and skeletonization.

13. When insects are found on a body, their stage of development and the contents of their gut may reveal information about the circumstances and cause of death, as can the types of insects present.

14. Serial homicides present a major investigative challenge. These crimes often appear random and without a traditional motive. Serial murders may be mobile, further complicating the task of identifying the perpetrator. These crimes are often well planned and lack witnesses and other evidence. There may not be a crime scene, or even a body. In such investigations, task forces are often formed to deal with the workload associated with such crimes.

15. Cold cases, which are homicides that have not been solved after some time, pose another challenge to investigators. Most cold cases are reopened due to the availability of DNA evidence or because of new witnesses. Although many cold case homicides have been solved, studies show that there are substantial difficulties and limited success in making arrests in such cases.

IMPORTANT TERMS

Algor mortis

Antemortem

Asphyxia

Autoerotic death (sexual asphyxia)

Autopsy

Cause of death

Cold case investigations

Contact, close, and distant gunshot wounds

Cutting and stab wounds

Decedent

Decomposition process

Defense wounds

Drowning

Felony murder

Gunshot residue (GSR)

Gunshot wounds

Hanging

Ligature strangulation

Livor mortis

Manner of death

Manual strangulation

Murder

Perimortem

Petechial hemorrhages

Poisoning

Postmortem

Postmortem interval (PMI)

Pugilistic attitude

"Raccoon eyes"

Rigor mortis

Serial homicide

Staging

Suffocation/smothering

Task force

QUESTIONS FOR DISCUSSION AND REVIEW

1. What are the four ways by which people may die (manner of death)? What is most common? What is least common?

2. What are three factors that must be considered in determining manner of death?

3. What are the major patterns and characteristics of homicides?

4. How might the circumstances of a murder reveal information about the perpetrator?

5. What is the importance of motive in identifying a homicide perpetrator?

6. What are the major characteristics of gunshot wounds, stabbings, blunt force trauma, and other injuries?

7. What are the various ways of determining postmortem interval (PMI)? Why might PMI be of importance in a homicide investigation?

8. What is the typical decomposition pattern of a human body? What factors may lead to deviations from this pattern?

9. What may be determined through an analysis of insect activity on a dead body?

10. Why do serial homicides present major challenges to investigators?

11. What is a task force and why might a task force be useful in an investigation?

12. What is a cold case squad? What are the difficulties in investigating cold homicides?

 STUDENT STUDY SITE

Visit **www.sagepub.com/brandl3e** to access additional study tools including eFlashcards, web quizzes, web resources, video resources, and SAGE journal articles.

11

The Investigation of Sex Crimes, Assault, Child Abuse, and Related Offenses

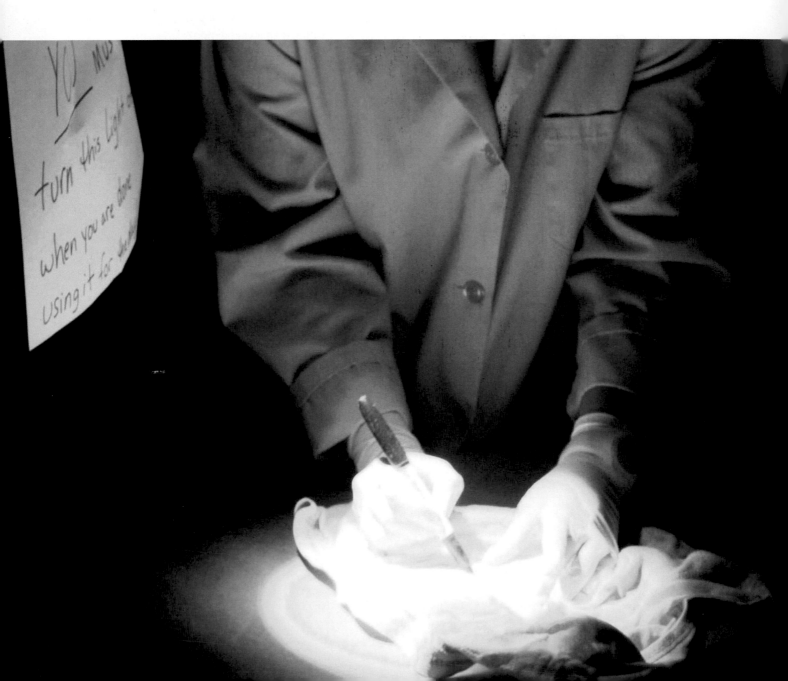

Objectives

After reading this chapter you will be able to:

- Identify the varieties and characteristics of rape and other sexual assaults

- Discuss how investigators should respond to victims of sexual assault and identify the recommendations that investigators should follow when conducting interviews of sexual assault victims

- Explain the potential value of physical evidence in sexual assault investigations, and discuss how the MO and signature of the perpetrator can be established and what value this information may have in a sexual assault investigation

- Identify possible crime scenes in a sexual assault investigation and discuss the types of evidence that may be located at these places

- Discuss the procedures associated with collecting physical evidence from sexual assault perpetrators

- Discuss how an interrogation of a sexual assault suspect may be assisted by an understanding of his motive in committing the crime

- Discuss the frequency, indicators, and possible motives of false reports and allegations of sexual assaults

- Discuss the characteristics of domestic violence or IPV, and identify the most challenging and least challenging aspects of domestic violence investigations

- Discuss the characteristics and types of child abuse, and identify the most challenging and least challenging aspects of child abuse investigations

- Discuss why interviewing procedures are so important in conducting child abuse investigations

From the CASE FILE
"Since You Don't Have Any Money . . ."

On September 30, 2011, Latasha Wray (not her real name), a twenty-one-year-old mother of two children, called the police to report that she had been sexually assaulted by a man she did not know. What follows here is the verbatim police report that was written as a result of investigators' interview of Latasha. (Except for the perpetrator and detectives, all names and addresses have been changed.)

The victim states that on the evening of Saturday, September 24, 2011, around 9:30/9:45 p.m., she was walking eastbound on N. 14th Street when she was approached by the subject from behind. Ms. Wray states that originally she felt someone walking close behind her. Once she looked back over her right shoulder, she was about to say "You scared me." She states that it was at this time she saw the suspect who she described as a black male, 20–25 years of age, 5'6," 150 lbs., a smaller build, a low haircut, medium competition, deep voice, wearing a black hooded sweatshirt with a zipper (hood half way on his head), dark blue jeans, and navy blue "Dukies," which she stated are Nike Force Once brand gym shoes.

The victim states that the suspect then showed her a black medium size handgun by lifting his shirt that he had inside his right front pocket. The victim states that the suspect then asked her, "Where's the money at?" The victim states that she told the suspect that she didn't have any money. She then attempted to show him that she was wearing black stretch pants (leggings), so she didn't have pockets, but by that time the suspect grabbed her by the back of both her shoulders and began pushing her.

The victim stated that the suspect then told her to walk forward. The victim states that she and the suspect went up two steps along the side of a church which she believes is St. Paul's on Oak Street. The victim states that then they cut across a field and went into an alley, then to the back of a house by a garage. The victim states that they were on concrete and she remembers there was a red newer model bigger sized pickup truck that was parked close by. The victim states that next door to where they were located she remembers there was a white garage.

The victim states that the suspect then took out his black handgun from his right pocket and sat it on the rear tire of this newer red truck. The victim states that the suspect then told her, "Since you don't have any money, you're going to give me some pussy." The victim stated that she told the suspect, "No, my mom's waiting on me, she has my kids." Victim states that she repeated this to the suspect over and over because she just wanted him to allow her to leave. Victim states that her phone was ringing and she knew it was her mother calling. The victim states that the suspect told her, "Don't worry, it will be really quick."

The victim states that the suspect then pulled her black leggings and also her panties down. The victim stated that the suspect then licked her "private part." She then stated that she was referring to her vagina. The victim states that the suspect then pulled his pants down as she told him at least two times "I got to go." The victim stated that the suspect told her, "Shut up or I'll smack you with the gun." The victim states that she did shut up and she began crying, but she never said anything else. Victim states that the suspect, while still standing behind her, told her to bend over. The victim stated that she then, while in a standing position, bent forward at the waist and the suspect stuck his "private part" which she then stated, "his penis," into her vagina. The victim states that the suspect did not use a condom and she is not sure if he ejaculated inside or outside of her. The victim states that this nonconsensual sex act occurred for two to three minutes. The victim states that she then pulled her clothes up because the suspect had finished. Victim states that she was starting to walk back in the same direction that they originally had walked from and the suspect told her, "No, go the other way."

The victim states that she then went straight through the alley, at which time she ended up at her mother's house. The victim then stated that her mother lives at the location of 4512 N. Pine Street. The victim informed me that her mother's name is Gloria Jones and has a home phone number of 412–229–7698. The victim states that after this happened, she was in shock, so she didn't think that she would tell anyone. The victim states that on the evening that this occurred, she was wearing a black and white longer striped halter shirt, black stretch pants (leggings), black and gold panties, a black hooded coat, and red croc style shoes.

Victim states on Thursday, September 29, 2011, she was walking to the #29 bus stop going to pick up her son from school. The victim states that it was at this time she again saw the suspect. The victim states that the suspect looked at her and watched her as she was walking. The victim states that the suspect was wearing a beige and brown hooded stripe sweatshirt, green pants, and the same navy blue Dukie gym shoes that she remembered him wearing the previous Saturday when he sexually assaulted her. The victim states that as she kept walking, she observed the suspect approach a house. Victim states that the suspect walked up three or four steps that led him to a front door at this residence. Victim states that this house was brown and white in color (aluminum sided). Victim states that this house also had a chain link fence around the front and a white security door. Victim states that the suspect knocked on the door and an unknown person let him inside.

The victim states that she originally wanted to forget that the sexual assault had occurred because of the humiliation that she felt about it, but once she saw the suspect and also saw that he lived so close by her residence, she knew that this was something that she wouldn't forget and needed to be reported. At this time, I informed Detective Timothy Wallich, Squad 3825 that I needed to take the victim to the area of the #29 bus stop to have her point out the residence that the suspect walked into on Thursday, September 29, 2011. Squad 3825 also conveyed the victim to the area of Oak Street to point out the scene where the sexual assault occurred.

The victim also informed me that she has not had sexual intercourse with her boyfriend in the past two weeks and has had no other sexual partners in the past four years.

—Report written by Detective Carmen Rodgers

After this interview, detectives got busy. First, the clothing (pants and undergarments) that the victim wore at the time of the assault were collected and submitted to the crime lab for DNA testing. A request was made to check the DNA print with the DNA prints contained in the state's DNA data bank. That search eventually came back without a match. Investigators retraced the route from where the victim was first approached to the area where the assault took place, looking for possible evidence and possible video surveillance cameras in the area that may have captured images of the suspect and victim. No such luck. During a neighborhood canvass of the area, they spoke with twenty-one residents who lived along the path traveled by the suspect and victim and who lived in the area where the assault took place. No one had seen or heard anything.

Using the information from the victim, investigators identified the house where the victim saw the suspect enter. They checked the department address database and discovered that a subject, Laron D. Ferguson (b/m 2–25–93), who was arrested in 2009 and 2010, listed this residence as his home. Ferguson matched the description of the perpetrator provided by the victim. A photo lineup was then conducted for the victim with Ferguson included; Latasha identified Ferguson as the person who sexually assaulted her. Consequently, a felony warrant was issued for Laron D. Ferguson and officers went to his home. He was there and was arrested without incident. A consent search of the residence was conducted and officers discovered a black P23 pellet/BB gun, blue Nikes, a black sweatshirt, a pair of woman's pink/white underwear, a woman's black purse, a woman's brown wallet, a pink Baby Phat credit card, men's black jean pants, and numerous miscellaneous papers, credit cards, and photos. Due to the discovery of this material, investigators figured that there were more victims. They had more work to do.

Meanwhile, Laron Ferguson was questioned by investigators. As written in the police report, this is what he said:

Ferguson stated that last weekend at about 11:00 p.m. he left his friend Terrell's house on N. 12th Street and walked home. He stated that he found a BB gun in the street as he was walking home. Ferguson stated that he picked up this BB gun and stuck it in his waistband. He continued walking home. Ferguson stated that he lives at 3480 North 14th Street. Ferguson came home and then left to go back out. Ferguson stated that he has not had a job in a couple of months and needed money. He stated that he went out to look for people to rob and make some money.

Ferguson stated that he walked on N. 14th Street where he observed a girl that was wearing all black. She was wearing "leggings" according to Ferguson. Ferguson stated that he does not know this girl and has never seen her before, but believed she was a prostitute. As he was approaching this girl, Ferguson stated that she noticed that he had a gun in his waistband (the BB gun). Ferguson stated that he did not have to "force force" this girl into the alley with him, but that he told her to go into the alley. He stated that she told him her boyfriend was around and that he could see them. Ferguson stated he walked to an area behind a church with this girl and they stood behind a parked truck. Ferguson stated he was "feeling" on this girl and that she bent over and took her pants and underwear off. Ferguson stated that he placed the BB gun on top of the tire of the truck that they were next to. He stated that the girl saw the gun at this time. Ferguson stated that he did not take her clothes off. Ferguson stated he licked his fingers and got the girl's vagina wet with his saliva. He then performed penis to vagina sexual intercourse on this girl without a condom. Ferguson stated that he ejaculated in the girl's vagina. The two of them got dressed and walked away in separate directions. Ferguson stated that the girl did not say anything to him and that he did not say anything to her as they were walking away. Ferguson stated that he did not ask for anything from this girl and that he did not obtain anything from her. He took the BB gun with him.

When asked about any other incidents that he might have been involved in, including other robbery incidents, Ferguson proceeded to tell detectives about an incident in the same area near the same date where he approached two women, pointed his handgun at them, and demanded money. One of the ladies gave him her small brown wallet, which contained a Baby Phat credit card but no cash. Ferguson stated that once he got home he just threw the purse in a drawer. At the conclusion of the interview, Ferguson consented to the collection of his DNA. The detective then collected a sample of his DNA with two buccal swabs.

PHOTO 11.1–11.3: When the suspect in the sexual assault of Latasha Wray was apprehended and a search of his house was conducted, investigators found a black gun, blue Nikes, and a black sweatshirt, just as described by Wray.

Detectives checked for previous reports of robberies that had occurred in that area but found none. The police then located and talked to the woman whose name was on the recovered credit card. She stated that yes, she and her friend had been robbed at gunpoint, but they did not report it to the police. A photo array that included Ferguson was constructed and shown separately to each of the two robbery victims. One of the victims identified Ferguson as the perpetrator; the other could not.

Meanwhile, the DNA from Ferguson was submitted to the crime lab to be compared with the DNA obtained from the sexual assault victim's clothing. It matched. Ferguson was eventually found guilty of second degree sexual assault and two counts of armed robbery. The charges of attempted armed robbery and kidnapping of the sexual assault victim were dropped in exchange for a guilty plea. Ferguson was sentenced to ten years in prison for his crimes.

Case Considerations and Points for Discussion ●━━━━━━━━━━━━━━━━━━

- Although there were several dead ends in this investigation (e.g., no witnesses found as a result of the neighborhood canvass, no surveillance video, no DNA match to the perpetrator in the DNA database), there was excellent evidence that led to the perpetrator being identified. What was this critical evidence? From whom did it come? How did investigators use this evidence to identify the perpetrator?

- The sexual assault victim's statement and the perpetrator's confession differed on several dimensions. On what points did they differ? On what points were they similar? To what extent did these discrepancies matter?

- What mistakes did the perpetrator make in committing these crimes that led to his identification? Did the police make any mistakes in this investigation?

●●● Varieties and Characteristics of Rape and Other Sexual Assaults

As defined by the FBI's *Uniform Crime Report,* forcible rape refers to "the penetration, no matter how slight, of the vagina or anus with any body part or object, or oral penetration by a sex organ of another person, without the consent of the victim." Unlike the FBI's earlier definition of rape, the new definition includes crimes against males and females, and acts other than sexual intercourse. Most states also further classify sexual assaults by their seriousness (or degrees) to include other forms of sexual contact. Some states also define and consider separately the behaviors of indecent assault or sexual assault of a child. The degree of the crime may depend on many factors, including whether or not a weapon was used in the crime, the age of the victim, the extent of the victim's injuries, if multiple offenders were involved, or if the victim was unconscious, among other factors.

According to the FBI, the crime of rape is relatively infrequent; only murder occurs less often. Although these statistics are based on the previous, less inclusive, definition of rape, in 2011 there were 83,425 rapes reported to the police (FBI 2012). Based on FBI statistics, 52.7 of every 100,000 females were victims of forcible rape in 2011 (FBI 2012). Understand however, that *rape* is narrowly defined; when considering all possible forms of sex offenses, these crimes occur much more frequently and are often encountered by investigators. Given the serious nature of these crimes, police departments that regularly investigate rape and other sexual assaults devote a large proportion of investigative resources to these investigations. Additional demands are also placed on investigators because of the sensitive nature of the crimes. In fact, in many larger departments, these crimes are handled by investigators who are assigned to a sensitive crimes unit.

Most sexual assault victims are young and female. The highest victimization rate is for females between the ages of sixteen and twenty (Bureau of Justice Statistics 2010). Approximately 8 percent of rape and sexual assault victims are male—again, most often young males. Most rapes and sexual assaults result in some physical injuries to the victim; approximately 58 percent of victims reported injuries such as bruises, internal injuries, broken bones, and gunshot wounds, among others (Bureau of Justice Statistics 2013). Of victims who were injured, approximately 65 percent did not seek medical attention for their injuries (Bureau of Justice Statistics 2013).

With regard to the relationship between the victim and the offender, of all rapes and other sexual assaults, approximately 78 percent involved an offender who was a family member, intimate partner, friend, or acquaintance (Bureau of Justice Statistics 2013). However, in those crimes reported to the police, a smaller proportion of cases involve victims and offenders who know each other. The closer the relationship between the victim and the offender, the less likely the crime was reported to the police (Bureau of Justice Statistics 2002b). Rapes/sexual assaults are usually committed by an offender without a weapon. In the 11 percent of cases during which a weapon was present, most commonly it was a firearm (Bureau of Justice Statistics 2013). The use of a weapon was more common when the victim and offender were strangers (Bureau of Justice Statistics 2012b). Approximately 55 percent of incidents occurred at or near the victim's home, and 90 percent of the incidents were committed by a lone offender (see Myths and Misconceptions 11.1).

Favorable evidentiary circumstances, such as face-to-face contact between the victim and the offender or the presence of a relationship between the victim and the offender, may lead to the identification of the offender. Nationally, according to the FBI, just more than 41 percent of rapes were cleared in 2011 (FBI 2012). Of the rapes that were cleared, approximately 84 percent of individuals arrested were adult, and 99 percent were male. Only homicides involved juveniles as arrestees to a lesser extent than rapes (FBI 2012). By race, 66 percent of those individuals who were arrested were white, 32 percent were black, and the remaining arrestees were of other races (FBI 2012). The race of offenders (and victims) depends much on the demographics of the jurisdictions where the crime occurred.

MYTHS & MISCONCEPTIONS 11.1

The Circumstances of Rape

If we were to believe the movies and the media about the circumstances in which most rapes occur, we would have a severely distorted understanding of the crime. Most rapes do not involve strangers. In most rapes a weapon is not used. Most rapes do not occur in dark alleys, or even outside at all. In reality, most rape incidents are more like the one described in Case in Point 11.1 than they are like the ones described in Case in Point 11.2 or in the introduction to this chapter. The fact of the matter is that the overwhelming majority of rapes (1) are committed by someone who is known to the victim, (2) occur in the victim's home, and (3) do not involve the use of a weapon in committing the act. One should also understand that rapes (which involve sexual intercourse or other penetration) are only the tip of the sex crimes iceberg. The overwhelming majority of sexual offenses that are known and investigated by the police do not involve sexual intercourse; rather they involve other nonconsensual sexual contact or touching. Usually these incidents are also committed by someone who is known to the victim.

●●● Investigative Considerations with Rape and Other Sexual Assaults

The most important source of information in a sexual assault investigation is usually the victim. In particular, critical information about the crime is often obtained from the investigator's interview of the victim and from a forensic medical examination of the victim. These and other related issues are discussed here.

●●● The Experience and Perspective of the Victim

Sexual assault is one of the most traumatic types of criminal victimization. In most instances, the emotional trauma caused by the crime is greater than the physical trauma. As a result, it is critical that investigators be mindful of victims' experiences and be sensitive to their needs. Investigators who are compassionate, sincere, and comforting in their interactions with victims may create a positive atmosphere in which victims may regain a sense of control and seek to be of assistance in the investigation. This is true in all investigations, but especially in sexual assaults. To provide a more compassionate investigation, it is important that police officers and investigators understand the psychological and physical responses experienced by sexual assault victims.

Upon first contact and interview with investigators, different victims may have different emotional dispositions. It is a myth that victims are always hysterical and crying after a rape. Some victims are; some are not. Most common is that victims are in a state of shock and disbelief (Burgess and Hazelwood 1995). Victims may be expressive of their emotions or more guarded. Expressive victims show their emotions, which are typically fear, anger, and anxiety. Each of these emotions may be expressed in awkward ways, such as smiling as an expression of anxiety. If victims are more guarded in their emotions, they may appear more composed only because of shock or physical exhaustion, or because feelings are masked. What may first appear as odd or even deceptive behavior may actually be as a result of complex psychological processes caused by trauma and stress (Burgess and Hazelwood 1995). It is also not uncommon that victims display different demeanors in different investigative interviews. Victims' demeanor may be a function of many factors, including their psychological adaptions, the setting of the interview, and the approach and characteristics of the interviewer.

Physically, depending on the nature of the attack, sexual assault victims are likely to experience soreness for days, weeks, or even months after the assault, particularly in areas of the body that were attacked by the perpetrator (e.g., face, arms, legs). Difficulty sleeping and eating disturbances (eating more or less than normal) are commonly experienced by victims. Psychologically, the prevailing emotion in the aftermath of a sexual assault is fear: most victims consider the sexual assault as a near-death, or "nearly killed," experience. It is this belief that causes such emotional trauma. A long and varied list of other emotions can combine with fear, such as humiliation, degradation, guilt, shame, embarrassment, anger, revenge, and so on. Victims may also show displaced anger and dramatic mood swings (Burgess and Hazelwood 1995). Victims may continuously or often think about the incident. Some victims describe it as being "haunted" by the incident. At the least, these troubling thoughts may often lurk just below the victim's consciousness.

The emotional, and perhaps physical, trauma of the sexual assault may last for weeks, months, years, or even a lifetime. The time it takes for victims to reorganize their lives, or to move on psychologically, may depend on many factors, including the victim's personality, the social supports available, the degree of disruption in relationships after the assault, and the outcome of the investigation and prosecution. As they heal physically, victims may continue to experience sleep disruptions, particularly in the form of nightmares. Even victims of burglary and theft sometimes experience nightmares about the incident; that emotional trauma is miniscule compared that of a rape victim. Lingering feelings of fear may also be disruptive to the victim's normal lifestyle (e.g., fear of being home alone, fear of being outside, fear of sexual relations). There may be a strong desire to leave town and/or permanently relocate. Of course, this desire may have implications for the investigation and prosecution of the offense. Another major challenge for many sexual assault victims is resuming a normal relationship with a partner, and not just in a sexual sort of way. The feelings and behaviors of the victim's partner toward the victim and the assault can also make a major difference in the reorganization of the victim's life (Burgess and Hazelwood 1995). Counseling and crisis intervention may be appropriate and necessary for the victim to resume a normal lifestyle.

An understanding of the emotional consequences of sexual assaults may assist investigators in appreciating the very difficult situation of sexual assault victims. In turn, this may allow for a more competent and compassionate investigation of sexual assault offenses.

••• The Police Response and the Interview of the Victim

Considerable attention has been devoted to how the police and other criminal justice personnel can best respond to crime victims in their time of need. A U.S. Department of Justice (2001) report titled *First Response to Victims of Crime* offers several suggestions for investigators about how they should respond to victims of sexual assault. These include the following:

- Be unconditionally supportive and permit victims to express their emotions.

- Approach victims calmly. Showing your outrage at the crime may cause victims even more trauma.

- Interview victims with extreme sensitivity.

- Minimize the number of times victims must recount details of the crime to strangers.

- Ask the victims whether they would prefer talking with a male or a female officer.

- If possible, only one investigator should be assigned to the initial and subsequent interviews.

- Remember that it is normal for victims to want to forget, or actually *to* forget, details of the crime that are difficult for them to accept.

- Encourage victims to get medical attention. Explain to the victim why medical attention and a forensic examination are important.

- Encourage victims to obtain counseling. Identify and refer them to support services for assistance. (p. 1)

In addition, several specific recommendations should be followed when conducting the interview of the victim (Burgess and Hazelwood 1995):

- While there may be a valid need to interview the victim more than once, the number of interviews should be limited to no more than what is absolutely necessary. An initial interview may be conducted to obtain details about the elements of the crime and the nature of the criminal acts, information about possible suspects and witnesses, and information about the crime scene(s). Subsequent interview(s) of the victim may provide additional details about the incident.

- Ideally the same investigator should conduct the initial and subsequent interviews. The interviews should be conducted at the police department or another private place in order to avoid distractions and to offer privacy to the victim. Often, victims proceed to a hospital before the police are even contacted. In such cases, police interviews with victims may be best conducted in a private room at a hospital.

- Investigators must realize that the interview of the victim is not an interrogation. The primary purpose of the interview is to obtain information that may advance the investigation, not to test or question the veracity of the information provided by the victim.

- The victim should be involved in the interview process. The procedures of the investigation should be explained to the victim. The investigators' contact information should be provided to the victim.

- To the extent practical, allow the victim some control in the process. For example, ask if the setting for the interview is okay. Ask how she would like to be addressed; ask permission to use her first name. Ask if she would like to tell about what happened in her own words or if she would like to be asked questions. Encourage the victim to tell what happened in her own words. Allow the victim time and allow her to concentrate. Avoid interruptions.

- Be receptive and respond to her requests.

- Listen to what the victim says and be aware of her feelings. Be reassuring.

- Balance difficult questions (e.g., about the acts that were committed against her) with questions that show an understanding of her feelings (e.g., "Would you like to take a break?").

- Use professional language and ask for clarification when necessary. Be sensitive in the language used. Do not use judgmental or threatening language. For example, say "Please describe the assault," not "Tell me about your rape."

- It should be clear from the words and actions of the investigator that the sexuality of the assault is not the focus of the interview, of the investigation, or even of the assault, for that matter. The focus is on the violence, bringing the perpetrator to justice, and assisting the victim.

- Given the traumatic nature of the crime, investigators must show sensitivity in obtaining detailed information from the victim. Insensitivity may lead to important details not being provided by the victim and to an uncooperative victim, two factors that will undoubtedly have negative effects on the investigation and prosecution.

- At the conclusion of the interview, the victim should be told what to expect next from the police. She should be provided information about counseling and victim advocate services. The investigator should make sure that the victim has the phone number of the investigator and knows how to contact him or her. The victim should be asked if she has any questions. The investigator should thank the victim for helping in the investigation and tell her that the police will do everything they can to find the person who committed the crime. At the conclusion of the interview, the victim should feel good that she did the right thing in reporting the crime to the police.

PHOTO 11.4: The approach used in the investigative interview of a sexual assault victim can have major implications for the amount and quality of information provided by the victim.

CASE *in* POINT 11.1 "My Stepbrother Assaulted Me"

In 2011, police received information from a school counselor that a fourteen-year-old girl disclosed to her that her step-brother had touched her inappropriately several times over the past several years. Investigators went to the girl's school and interviewed her. As documented by the investigator in the report:

> Sema was emotional when talking about the incident. She related the first time anything happened was when she was eleven. She stated that Francisco is her half-brother, at that time he was about 15 years. She stated she has the same mother but different father than Francisco. Stated he had come from Mexico to live with them when they were staying on Lloyd Street. Stated they had the bedrooms in the attic. She recalled waking up to Francisco feeling on her, fondling her bare vagina. Stated she immediately got up and went downstairs. Stated it was late at night and everyone was sleeping. Stated after waiting a while she went back upstairs and Francisco was not in her room. Stated she then went back to bed. Stated that when she woke up the next morning she told her mother right away and she confronted him. Stated her mother slapped him and yelled at him to keep his hands to himself. Francisco told her that he probably touched her with his foot by mistake. Stated nothing happened until 2009 when she was 13 and living in her present home. Stated she and her sister had bunk beds in the same room. Stated she was sleeping and woke to Francisco's hand in her underwear. Stated he was moving it around. Stated she was afraid to move. Stated that she heard him open something and thought it was a condom. Stated he tried to put his penis "in the place where it goes." I asked her to explain this. She then stated "my vagina." Stated it felt hard and it was poking her as he tried to get it in. Stated she was scared and got up and went to the bathroom. Stated Francisco was acting like he was sleeping. At this point she became very emotional

saying she felt traumatized and scared by what has happened to her. She asked me if she was doing the right thing by reporting this. I assured her that she was doing the right thing. She stated the last time anything happened was about two or three weeks ago. Stated he tried to do the same thing as last time. I asked her to tell me. Stated she was in her room sleeping and he tried to have sex with her and she wouldn't let him. She stated that "he tried to put it in like last time." She was not able to provide any more details. Stated that she wanted him to answer for what he has done to her and blames him for her emotional state of mind. She was crying as she told me this.

The investigator then spoke with the school counselor and the victim's mother. A felony warrant was issued for Francisco Javier Pacheco. Francisco was arrested on the warrant five days later as a result of a traffic stop. Francisco was arrested and transported to the police station for questioning. After being informed of, and waiving, his Miranda rights, Francisco told the investigators that in December 2009 he and his sisters Sema and Sara were smoking marijuana and hanging out. Francisco then stated that they all fell asleep around 1:00 a.m. Francisco and Sema fell asleep in the same bed. He stated that he woke and started to fondle Sema's breasts. He then stated that he got a condom from his wallet and put it on. He stated that he did not remove the shorts that Sema was wearing but just moved them. He then attempted to insert his penis in her vagina. He stated that he touched her vagina with his penis but was not able to insert it. He then got nervous and stopped. He stated that he then went to the bathroom to masturbate. Francisco stated that was the only time he had done this and that the time before was an accident (when he touched her vagina with his foot as they were sleeping in the same bed).

Francisco Pacheco pled guilty (plea bargain) to second degree sexual assault of a child and was sentenced to three years in prison.

From an evidentiary perspective, the interview of the victim is extremely important because the victim is usually the only witness to the crime. If information is to be produced about the offender, it is most likely to come from the victim. As noted, in many instances the perpetrator is known to the victim by name. In these types of cases, the perpetrator's most likely defense is either that the sex acts were consensual or that they just did not happen.

As such, an important investigative issue is to establish the victim's lack of consent for the act. The issue of consent is rather unique in rape cases; it rarely, if ever, emerges as a problematic element to be proved in other type of crimes. The victim's statement that the sexual acts were not consensual, along with other factors such as documentation of injuries to the victim, the use of a weapon, and other circumstances of the crime (e.g., the age of the victim) can establish lack of consent. Physical evidence (e.g., semen) can be used to establish sexual contact/intercourse. That the acts actually occurred can also be established by the victim's detailed statement of what transpired and/or a confession from the perpetrator (see Case in Point 11.1).

In other instances, as with the case discussed in the introduction to this chapter, the victim and perpetrator do not know each other by name, but the victim is able to recognize and identify the perpetrator. In these types of cases, the perpetrator's primary defense is likely to be either that the sex acts did not happen or the victim/police identified the wrong guy. Again, the victim's detailed description and identification of the perpetrator, physical evidence, and the interrogation (confession) are critical in confirming that the person identified actually committed the assault. Physical evidence may also be used to establish that sexual contact/intercourse occurred.

If the assault was not committed by someone the victim knew or was acquainted with, and/or the victim is not able to provide a name of the suspect, then the task of identifying the perpetrator is likely to be more challenging. In these cases, details from the victim regarding the characteristics of the perpetrator may be especially useful. Besides descriptive information about the offender (e.g., approximate height, weight, hair color, build), information may be obtained for the development of a composite picture of the perpetrator and/or later identification of the perpetrator. Other descriptive details may also be of value. For instance, given the close contact between the offender and the victim during the assault, the victim may have noticed tattoos, unusual or distinctive body marks (e.g., moles), a unique smell of the perpetrator, or other distinctive characteristics or mannerisms (e.g., style of walking, speech impediments). No detail about the incident from the victim (or from witnesses) should be considered insignificant. For example, Case in Point 11.2 highlights the value of the victim's description of a vehicle in eventually leading to the identification and apprehension of the perpetrators.

In these types of cases, if the perpetrator provides a defense, it is most likely that the victim/police identified the wrong guy. Again, the victim's detailed description and identification of the perpetrator, physical evidence, and the interrogation (confession) are critical in confirming that the person identified actually committed the assault. Of course, physical evidence (DNA) may also play a role in identifying the perpetrator in the first place and establishing sexual contact/intercourse.

Along with getting descriptive information about the offender from the victim, it is important that investigators ask other questions as well. Answers to questions about the nature and circumstances of the attack may provide investigators with insight into the type of person who committed the crime, his method of operation (MO) and signature, other clues about his identity, and which strategies may be most effective when the perpetrator is apprehended and interrogated.

With regard to a rapist's MO and signature, MO typically serves one or more purposes for the perpetrator:

- It protects his identity (e.g., wearing a mask, wearing a condom).

- It helps him complete the rape (e.g., using a gag to silence the victim, using a weapon to control the victim).

- It facilitates his escape (e.g., use of a vehicle, rendering victim unconscious to delay reporting).

One Thing Leads to Another and a Brutal Rape Is Solved

At about midnight, a man discovered a woman covered in blood on the sidewalk. He flagged down a bus and the bus driver called 911. The police responded to the scene but, given the condition of the victim, they were unable to interview her at that time. She was transported to the hospital by fire and rescue personnel and immediately underwent surgery. Her injuries consisted of severe lacerations to the left side of her head, a one-inch laceration to each of her inner thighs, a deep laceration to each of the labia majora, and a laceration around her anus and vaginal wall. She was near death.

While searching the victim's clothes at the scene, police recovered cash from her pants pocket. These bills were photographed and fingerprinted. The police searched where she was found and discovered blood on the sidewalk and in a nearby alley. The blood was photographed and samples were collected. Garbage cans in the alley were searched. A utility knife and two white paper towels with bloodstains on them were found in one of the cans. These items were also photographed and seized. A neighborhood canvass of houses in the area was initiated. No one saw or heard anything . . . except for two people. One witness stated that when he came home from his job at about 11:20 p.m. that night and was pulling into the alley at the rear of his home, he saw a smaller, white, model two-door car with the letters GT on the side parked in a gravel parking spot near the rear of his residence. He stated the car was running. He said the back windows of the vehicle were tinted, both front seats were tilted forward, and there did not appear to be anyone in the front seat. He further stated that the cover on the flip-up headlight on the driver's side was missing. After parking his car, he went into the house but continued to wonder why the car was running with no one in it. He then saw a man approximately 6'0" exit the passenger door of the car and get into the front driver's side. The auto left going northbound out of the alley.

The other witness reported that she was sitting on the front porch of her house at about 11:30 p.m. and heard a car running in the alley located behind her house. She walked back to the alley to investigate and observed a white two-door Ford Probe parked with its engine running. The driver briefly looked at her and then pulled into a parking space between two other vehicles. The driver then exited the vehicle. He was described as a Hispanic male, mid twenties, 5'4," 130 lbs. with black, shoulder-length hair that was combed back. The car was a 1993 Ford Probe GT two-door and had tinted windows. She told police she was sure of the year, make, and model of the car because her husband owns a 1993 Ford Probe. She said that after seeing the vehicle, she went back to her porch. About ten minutes later she saw the vehicle leaving. Investigators wondered, might this car have something to do with the rape?

Meanwhile, another investigator interviewed the victim after her surgery and while she was still in the intensive care unit at the hospital. The victim told the investigator that she was a prostitute and that at approximately 11 p.m. the previous night, a white, older model, two-door vehicle with pop-up headlights pulled up to the curb in front of where she was standing, near the 7–11 store on 60th Street and North Avenue. In the car were two Hispanic males. The driver was about twenty-eight years old; 170 lbs.; had black, shoulder-length, straight hair; and was wearing a blue and white shirt. The passenger was about twenty-two years old; 160 lbs.; thin in build; had black, straight hair; and was wearing a dark shirt and tan shorts. She said that they spoke broken English. They told her they wanted sex and asked how much. She said $25, they agreed, and she proceeded to get into the back seat of the car.

The driver then drove into a nearby alley and stopped the car. The driver got out and got into the back seat of the car with her. She told the investigator that she then pulled her pants down and removed her left leg from her pants. She said that the driver then removed his pants and got on top of her and they proceeded to have penis to vagina sexual intercourse. She told the suspect that it was taking too long and that he should hurry up. He said, "Ten more minutes," but she said no and pushed him off of her. She then told the passenger to get in the back seat with her. She and the passenger then had penis to vagina sexual intercourse. The driver then told her to perform oral sex on him while the other suspect (the passenger) was on top of her. She again told him that it was taking too long. The passenger and driver then switched positions. The passenger climaxed in her mouth and she spit it out. The passenger then put his hand over her mouth and had his arm around her neck and began to choke her. She stated that this caused her to pass out. She stated that at some point she recalled the passenger punching her in the head. The next thing she recalled was waking up in an alley with her pants around her ankle and her shoe next to her. She stated that she sat up for a few minutes and then realized that she was bleeding from her head and vagina. She put her pants on and stumbled out of the alley, at which point a man flagged down the bus driver who called 911. She added that the suspects were drinking Corona from a bottle. She did not see any type of weapon. She thought that she was in the vehicle for about forty-five minutes.

With the information from the witnesses and the victim, the search was on for the suspects' vehicle. Many such vehicles were located and checked. Two days after the incident, an officer on routine patrol came across what they were looking for. Parked on the street was a white, two-door Ford Probe with pop-up headlamps and the left headlight cover missing. The vehicle had very dark tinted windows and a GT sticker on the right front door. The officer looked through a section of the window where the tint had peeled away and saw various stains on the rear seat and a package of hand wipes in the right side door pocket. The officer also saw a partial handprint in blood on the right side of the hatchback of the auto. The officer called for backup.

The officers then approached the residence to which the vehicle was registered. The woman who answered the door told police that an Oscar Morales operated the vehicle but was not at home. The woman allowed the officers to come in the house. The officers then heard noise in a bathroom and a shower being turned on. One of the officers went into the bathroom. The subject in the bathroom identified himself as Oscar Morales. He was led out of the bathroom and told to sit on a dining room chair. Morales asked for a pair of shoes to wear. The officer saw a pair of white gym shoes under the table and asked Morales if those were his. He indicated that they were. The officer inspected the shoes and noticed what appeared to be blood on them. The officers believed that Oscar Morales had something to do with the assault, so he was arrested and transported to police headquarters for questioning. The Ford Probe was impounded for evidence collection.

Upon being interviewed, Morales confessed to the crime and implicated his friend Jose Lorenzo-Severiano. He agreed to show detectives where the assault took place and where the victim was dumped from the vehicle. As a result, more blood and hair evidence was recovered from the alley. The vehicle was processed, and additional evidence was recovered from it, including bloody palm prints and fingerprints, other blood stains, pubic hair, and long strands of hair. The hair and blood were matched to the victim through DNA analysis. DNA from Morales and Lorenzo-Severiano was also recovered from the vehicle.

Two photo lineups were prepared for the victim; one contained a photo of Morales, and the other contained a photo of Lorenzo-Severiano. The victim identified each of the perpetrators—Morales as the driver, Lorenzo-Severiano as the passenger.

Due to the evidence from the vehicle and crime scene, the identification of the perpetrators by the victim, and the confessions provided by the perpetrators, Morales was found guilty and sentenced to forty-five years in prison. Lorenzo-Severiano was also found guilty of numerous crimes in this incident and sentenced to fifty-five years in prison.

The signature aspects of rape—actions that are not necessary to complete the act but are taken to express emotion or fantasy in a rape—can serve similar investigative purposes as MO. Signature aspects of the crime most often relate to the verbal, physical, and especially the sexual acts committed. These can include the use of particular words or vulgarities, the amount and type of injury inflicted on the victim, the methods used to inflict pain on the victim, the taking of items from the victim, and the manner in which the victim's clothing was removed (Turvey 2005). Details about MO and signature can be valuable in an investigation. This information can be used to help identify crimes as being committed by the same person, can provide clues as to the traits and characteristics of the perpetrator, can be used to eliminate persons as suspects, and can assist in clearing cases when a perpetrator is identified (Turvey 2005).

To obtain information about the offender's MO and signature from the victim, Hazelwood and Burgess (1995) recommend that "behavioral-oriented" interviews be conducted and that the following information be collected either through the victim's own account of the crime or through direct questioning:

- What method of approach was used by the offender? Did he "con" or trick the victim into gaining his trust? Did he use immediate and overwhelming physical force? Did he surprise the victim with his attack?

- How did the offender maintain control during the incident? Did he use verbal threats, display a weapon, use a weapon, or use other force?

- What amount of physical force was used by the attacker?

- Did the victim resist and, if so, how? Did the victim's actions cause injury to the attacker? If the perpetrator is identified, would one be able to see these injuries?

- If resistance occurred, what was the offender's reaction? Did he change his demand, compromise, use threats, or use force?

- During the attack, did the assailant experience a sexual dysfunction such as erectile insufficiency, premature ejaculation, retarded ejaculation, or conditional ejaculation? It is worthwhile to note that these conditions may also be experienced by the offender when he is with his consensual partner. If a suspect is identified, this information may be verified.

- What type and sequence of sexual acts occurred during the assault? This information may provide insight into the motivation, preferences, and experiences of the offender.

- What was the exact verbal activity of the attacker? Did he use particularly unusual words or phrases? An understanding of the language used by the offender may help establish MO and the motivation for the attack. Verbal activity of the attacker may also reveal clues about his identity.

- Was the victim forced to say anything? What were these words or phrases? Again, this information may reveal motivation and signature aspects of the crime.

- Was there a sudden change in the offender's attitude/behavior during the attack? If so, is there any speculation on the part of the victim about what may have prompted this change?

- What precautionary actions were taken by the offender? For example, did he wear a mask? Disguise his voice? Order the victim to shower? The degree of sophistication in the precautionary actions of the offender may serve as an indicator of his experience level.

- Was anything taken by the offender? Were these items of evidentiary value (e.g., clothing with biological stains on them), personal value (e.g., photographs of the victim), or monetary value (e.g., jewelry)?

- Does the victim have any reason to believe that she was targeted as a victim? For example, does she have any knowledge of Peeping Tom activity or prowlers at her house or in her neighborhood? Did she recently receive any unusual phone calls or notes? If the victim was targeted, there is a good chance that the perpetrator may have previous arrests for burglary, prowling, or voyeurism.

Effectively interviewing adult sexual assault victims may be a challenge for investigators but, no question, interviewing child sexual assault victims poses even greater challenges (see discussion later in this chapter). Successfully interviewing child victims requires investigators to have special communication skills, knowledge of child psychology, and training in the use of various supplementary interviewing methodologies, such as the use of artwork and sketches, and anatomically correct dolls. Regardless of the age or other characteristics of victims, compassion and understanding on the part of investigators during the interview are absolutely necessary.

●●● Physical Evidence

In perhaps no other type of criminal investigation does physical evidence play such a potentially large role as it does in the crime of rape. Physical evidence may lead to the identity of the perpetrator if not already known, confirm the identity of the perpetrator if he has already been identified, and help establish the elements of the crime (e.g., the presence of semen to establish sexual intercourse). As discussed earlier in this book, care must be taken when interpreting physical evidence, or the lack of it. For instance, of course, a lack of semen does not necessarily indicate that sexual intercourse did not occur.

With rape, the victim's body is a crime scene. It is important for investigators to keep perspective and to remember that the victim has undergone a traumatic experience. Sensitivity is as critical when seeking physical evidence as it is when conducting an interview. Forensic examinations of victims are conducted at hospitals and are performed by either a physician or a nurse who has received special training in forensic matters. Nurses with such training are referred to as sexual assault nurse examiners (or SANEs). The primary objectives of forensic examinations of sexual assault victims are to document injuries caused by the assault, recover biological evidence present as a result of the assault, and to provide treatment for injuries sustained as a result of the assault (see Crowley 1999 for an excellent and detailed discussion of forensic issues in sexual assault cases).

Although it depends on the nature and circumstances of the assault, the victim's physical examination usually involves a number of procedures, including the collection of (1) oral, nasal mucous, vaginal, and rectal specimen samples; (2) the victim's clothing that was worn at the time of the assault; (3) fingernail scrapings from the victim; (4) any foreign material or debris on the victim's body (e.g., dirt); (5) other substances that may be in the form of stains on the victim's body; (6) pubic hair combings (which may include hair from the attacker); (7) swabs and photographs of bite marks (for documentation purposes and possible traces of saliva); and (8) blood and urine samples for toxicology screening. Toxicology screens may be conducted to test for the presence of alcohol, drugs, and, if suspected, Rohypnol or GHP, two of the more common so-called date rape drugs (see below). Tests may also be conducted for pregnancy and sexually transmitted diseases.

In addition, reference standards may be collected from victims and their recent consensual partners. Reference standards are specimens collected to determine whether other recovered evidence (e.g., evidence collected from the victim's body, clothing, or actual crime scene) is from the victim, the victim's consensual partner(s), or from someone else, such as the perpetrator. Reference samples typically include blood, pulled head hairs, pulled pubic hairs, a saliva sample, and other body hair samples (if the victim is male). The collection of specimen samples and reference standards may be facilitated through the use of a sexual assault evidence kit, which is a preassembled package of pre-labeled containers that are used to collect and store the physical evidence collected from a particular victim. A sexual assault evidence kit should not be confused with a rape kit, which more often refers to a collection of tools (e.g., rope, gloves, tape) that may be used by a rapist to facilitate an attack and that may be found in possession of the perpetrator.

On occasion, rapists use condoms in an attempt either to limit the biological evidence available for recovery and analysis or to protect against sexually transmitted diseases. When perpetrators use condoms, other valuable evidence may be left behind (Blackledge 1996). For instance, trace amounts of particulates (e.g., the powder in condoms that prevents them from sticking to themselves), lubricants, and spermicide may be recovered during the forensic examination of the victim. If such evidence is recovered, it may be possible to link the

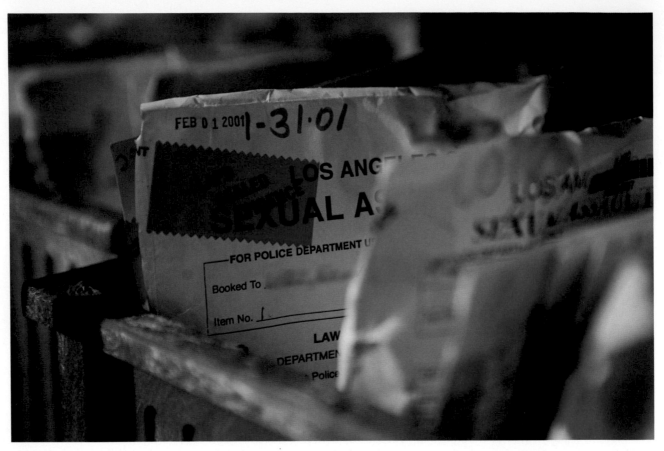

PHOTO 11.5: The sexual assault evidence kit is used by medical personnel to collect and preserve physical evidence of a sexual assault.

condom to its manufacturer and to determine the brand. In addition, such evidence may help establish corpus delicti of the crime, link crimes of a serial rapist, be a source of other physical evidence (e.g., fingerprints on the condom package found at the scene), or be of other value (e.g., condoms of a particular brand may be subsequently found in possession of the perpetrator during the execution of a search warrant).

It is important for investigators also to search for and collect evidence from crime scenes in sexual assaults. It is around crime scenes that physical evidence and witnesses may be located. Victims play a critical role in identifying crime scenes. As discussed in Case in Point 11.2, the victim described the vehicle and the area in which the attack took place (two crime scenes), and the police then identified witnesses who lived in the area where the attack took place that were able to provide additional critical information about the vehicle. This information eventually led to the identification of the persons who committed the crime. In a rape, there may be many crime scenes, both primary and secondary. These could include the place where the victim was approached (e.g., on the street), the place(s) where the victim was attacked (e.g., in a car in an alley), the place where the victim was disposed of (e.g., in the alley), and the place the perpetrator fled after the crime (e.g., possibly his home). Evidence of the victim and offender may be found at each of these places. It is in searches of these places that the procedures outlined in Chapter 5 are of most relevance.

As noted, the objectives in processing crime scenes are to protect, document, preserve, and collect evidence (Savino and Turvey 2005b). There is no such thing as a crime scene that has been over-protected or over-documented (Savino and Turvey 2005b). Since it is not likely

PHOTO 11.6–11.8: Used condoms and condom wrappers at a crime scene can provide investigators with valuable evidence if a suspect is identified.

to be clear what is evidence and what is not, the rules should be, "When in doubt, collect" and "Overlook nothing." The evidentiary possibilities are nearly limitless: weapons, biological material from the victim and perpetrator, footwear impressions and prints, tire marks, tool marks, and everything and anything that may contain fingerprints or DNA (e.g., victim and offender clothing, pillows, sheets and blankets, condoms and condom wrappers, cell phones, food wrappers, remote controls, towels, and door handles, just to name a few possibilities). Of course, evidence must be properly documented and collected in accord with the best collection methods, as discussed in Chapter 5.

DATE RAPE DRUGS

Rohypnol and GHB are the two most common so-called date rape drugs. They are called date rape drugs simply because when these drugs are used to facilitate a rape, the perpetrator is typically someone the victim knows. Because the drugs are most often slipped into a drink or otherwise unknowingly given to the victim, this may happen in the context of a date.

Rohypnol is a tranquilizer. It is not FDA approved in the United States, so it is not prescribed by physicians or otherwise legal in the United States. It is, however, legal and prescribed as a sedative in other parts of the world, commonly as a treatment for insomnia. Rohypnol comes in the form of small white tablets or hard green oval tablets with a coating that makes them more difficult to dissolve. Both forms are tasteless and odorless; the green tablet contains a blue dye that is designed to add color to any liquid in which it is placed.

It is most often ingested orally, but illicitly it can be snorted, smoked, or injected. Street names for Rohypnol include "forget-me pill," "roofies," "Mexican Valium," "roaches," and "ruffies," among others. Once the drug is ingested, most users fall asleep within two hours, although some people experience a blackout period during which they remain awake, although impaired, in a "zombie-like" state. Memory is severely affected, thereby limiting the ability of the victim to provide an account of exactly what transpired before, during, and after the assault. The drug can be detected in urine samples for five days or longer (Pittel and Spina 2005).

Gamma-hydroxybutyrate (GHB) is a powerful central nervous system depressant. It was sometimes used in the United States as a general anesthetic in the 1960s and 1970s. GHB has also been used by bodybuilders as a method of stimulating growth hormone, but it was banned by the FDA in 1990. Illicit GHB is a chemical mix that consists of GBL (gamma-butyrolactone) and lye. Muriatic acid or vinegar is also used in the manufacturing process. Common names for GHB include "liquid ecstasy," "liquid X," "goop," "G," and "aminos," among others. GHB is a clear liquid. The drug is sometimes voluntarily used to cause a euphoric feeling without any hangover effects. When used to facilitate a sexual assault, the drug is most often mixed into a strong alcoholic drink in an attempt to mask the unpleasant taste of the drug. Full effect of the drug is usually present twenty to sixty minutes after ingestion. Effects of the drug depend on dosage and can range from low-level intoxication-type symptoms to unconsciousness. The effects of GHB on memory are

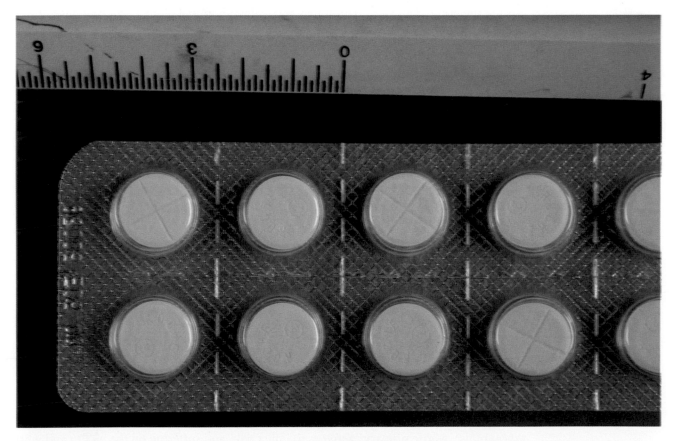

PHOTO 11.9: Rapes facilitated with "date rape" drugs present additional difficulties for investigators, one of which is that the drug typically affects a victim's memory of the assault.

similar to those of Rohypnol. GHB can be detected in urine for seventy-two to ninety-six hours (Pittel and Spina 2005).

●●● Information From Perpetrators: Physical Evidence and Confessions

If a suspect can be named by the victim, then the physical evidence recovered from the victim or from the crime scene may be immediately used for comparison purposes. In addition, when a suspect is identified, a search of the suspect's home or automobile may be conducted (based on probable cause or consent) to seize evidence related to the crime. Furthermore, based on a search warrant or consent, the suspect may be required or asked to undergo a forensic physical examination. Depending on the nature of the assault, the acts committed, and the time that elapsed from the time of the crime to the time of the examination, the examination of the suspect may involve the documentation of the wounds inflicted by the victim (e.g., bite marks, scratches); the collection of saliva, blood, and hair (e.g., head, facial, body, pubic) specimens; the seizure of the suspect's clothing worn at the time of the attack or that may contain suspected evidence; and the collection of penile swabs for evidence that may link the suspect to the victim.

Interrogation of the suspect may produce information that confirms that the suspect is the perpetrator. As discussed in Chapter 7, identification of the most productive tactics to be used during an interrogation of a suspected rapist, or a suspect in any type of crime for that matter, often depends on an understanding of the motivations of that individual for committing the crime. This information may relate directly to the motivations and MO of the offender. For instance, Merrill (1995) makes the distinction between "contact" rapists and "sexual aggressor" rapists. Contact rapists are those perpetrators whose primary motivation is sexual pleasure, and their victims are most often their "friends" or acquaintances. Contact rapists are most likely to respond to emotional themes during the interrogation when the investigator blames the victim or reduces the moral seriousness of the offense. As explained by Merrill, investigators "should emphasize that the suspect, a healthy man with normal needs and desires, simply allowed the situation to escalate beyond his control" (p. 10). Ideally, this will allow the suspect to confess without embarrassment and to place some of the blame for what happened on the victim.

Sexual aggressor rapists, on the other hand, usually do not know their victims. The act of rape is an expression of anger or control. Merrill draws on the work of Hazelwood and Burgess (1995) in further differentiating different types of sexual aggressor rapists. Briefly, for the *power reassurance* type of rapist, rape is an expression of power. He may apologize to the victim, ask for forgiveness, he may re-contact the victim; he is a "gentleman rapist" who lacks a social and sexual capability to interact with women. According to Merrill, this rapist is most likely to confess when the moral seriousness of the crime is minimized and his "nice guy" image, based on how "nicely" he treated the victim, is emphasized. The *power assertive* type of rapist commits the crime to dominate the victim. He shows no concern for the well-being of the victim. He is likely to use a moderate to excessive amount of force on the victim. This type of rapist will rape when he needs a woman. This type of rapist is most likely to respond favorably during an interrogation when investigators flatter him, allow him to brag about himself and his prowess, and blame his victim. The *anger retaliatory* rapist, who commits rape for the purposes of revenge and anger and who often uses excessive force on the victim, and the *anger excitation* rapist, whose primary motive is to inflict pain and suffering on the victim and who most often uses brutal force on the victim, are most likely to respond to *unemotional* themes in an interrogation setting. Most productive, according to Merrill, is to convince the suspect that his guilt has been proved and that he has no choice but to admit it (Hazelwood and Burgess 1995).

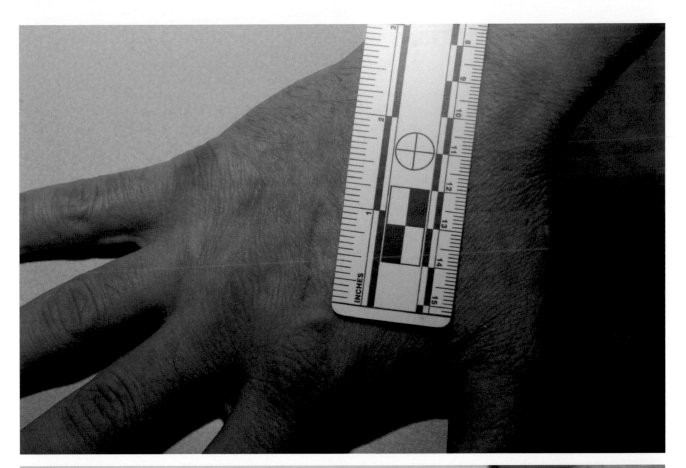

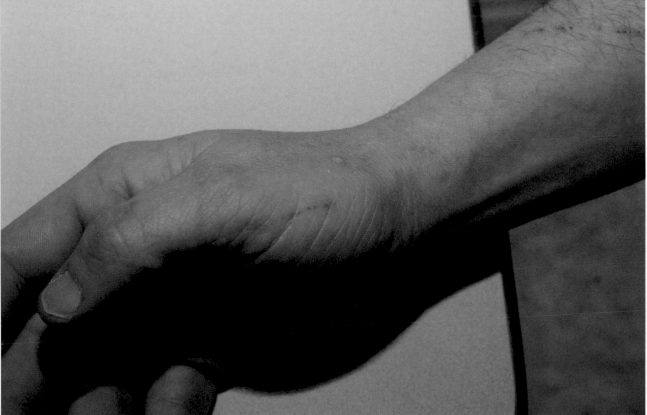

PHOTO 11.10–11.11: In violent crimes such as rapes, injuries on a suspect may be informative; however, it must be understood that injuries are circumstantial evidence at best and that they may have been sustained in ways other than in the commission of a crime.

●●● Other Sources of Evidence and Information in Sexual Assault Investigations

As with homicides, rapes committed by offenders who are strangers to victims pose a serious challenge for the police. It is likely that any rapist who attacks a stranger is, or could become, a serial rapist. According to statistics provided by Rossmo (2000), 44 percent of serial rapists are strangers to their victims. In these instances and other stranger rape cases, the information provided by a victim about the assailant may be of limited value in actually identifying the culprit. Once again, with these crimes, and as discussed in previous chapters, it is imperative that the police use all the means at their disposal for identifying and apprehending these perpetrators, including DNA banks, tip lines, media alerts, crime analysis, computer databanks, sex offender registries, and psychological profiles.

●●● False Allegations

A final comment with regard to rape investigations relates to the issue of *false* rape allegations. It is not unheard of that "victims" deliberately make up stories of rape that did not actually occur. There are many possible motives for a false report of a rape: to seek revenge on a person named as the assailant, to get attention, to receive medical treatment and/or drugs, to create an alibi, to favor child custody decisions, for profit (e.g., civil law suit or extortion), or to explain a pregnancy or the contraction of a sexually transmitted disease, among others. Such allegation may or may not include information about who committed the "rape." Particularly concerning are those cases where the victim identifies the person who committed the (false) crime. Left undetected, this false information has the potential to have devastating consequences for the person identified as the perpetrator. It is for this reason that investigators must be aware of this possibility and take steps to protect against it.

In some cases, the falseness of the allegation is clear. For example, in one jurisdiction, during the course of two weeks, the police were called by a woman who reported that she had been raped sixty-eight times . . . by Elvis Presley. The woman had a history of severe mental illness, and there was no other evidence to substantiate her claims. The police had good reason to believe that these allegations were not true. Of course, not all false allegations are as obvious as in this case.

Another type of false allegation involves reports of sexual assaults that actually do not constitute a violation of the law. For example, in one case, a woman called the police department to report a rape. When officers arrived at her location to investigate, she explained to the officers that she had consensual sexual intercourse with her boyfriend, but her boyfriend refused to wear a condom so she wanted to have him arrested. Officers had to explain that refusing to use a condom did not constitute a sexual assault. This is not a false allegation as much as it is just confusion about the law.

The fact of the matter is that a small percentage of rape allegations are suspected and substantiated as being false. Crowley (1999) estimates this percentage to be approximately 8 percent of all reported rapes; other estimates are closer to 2 percent (U.S. Department of Justice 2001). False rape allegations are probably less common than false burglary or robbery allegations. When investigating any crime, investigators must be aware of accounts provided by victims that just do not seem to make sense and that appear suspicious. Aiken et al. (1995) identify numerous possible red flags of false rape allegations. Of course, as any of these circumstances may actually be valid, great caution needs to be taken in drawing conclusions from them; the more of these circumstances that are present, the more caution needs to be exercised in evaluating the complaint. These red flags include:

- A history of mental or emotional problems

- Previous similar allegations

- A delayed report (although many victims delay reporting for legitimate reasons)

- No description of assailant or an unusually vague or detailed description of the assailant

- The involvement of more than one assailant

- The inability to tell investigators where the crime occurred, or changing where the crime occurred

- The inability to provide details regarding the sexual acts involved

- Extensive injuries, but a lack of concern about them

- No injuries to sensitive areas

- Injuries made by fingernails

- Injuries claimed to be defense wounds, although their nature does not indicate that they are defense wounds

- The condition of clothing worn at the time of the attack not fitting with the injuries sustained

While investigators need to be aware of these possibilities and motives, "It must be remembered that even those who are emotionally prone to make a false allegation can be raped. Basic principles of police professionalism require that officers who investigate rapes remain objective and compassionate" (Aiken et al. 1995, p. 238).

●●● Varieties and Characteristics of Other Assaults

The FBI's *Uniform Crime Report* defines two types of assaults that do not involve sexual contact: aggravated assault and simple assault. Aggravated assault refers to an "attack by one person upon another for the purpose of inflicting severe or aggravated bodily injury" (FBI 2012). Such injuries include broken bones, broken teeth, and loss of consciousness. Included in this category are attacks with a weapon or other means that may likely produce death or great bodily harm. Attempted murder is considered an aggravated assault, according to the FBI. Many aggravated assaults are nonfatal shootings, and many nonfatal shootings are gang-related.

Exhibit 11.1 What Is a Gang-Related Crime?

There is not a separate type of crime called gang-related crime. The simple fact of the matter is that gang members are disproportionately involved in all serious violent crime, especially murder, nonfatal shootings (especially drive-by shootings), and robbery. Gangs are also heavily involved in drug trafficking and dealing. Murders and nonfatal shootings committed by gangs are most often for the purpose of retaliation and counter-retaliation, protecting the territory of drug sales, and enhancing the status and reputation of the gang (Dedel 2007). However, not all crimes committed by members of gangs are best considered gang-related. Different police departments define *gang-related* differently. For example, the Los Angeles Police Department uses a broad definition and classifies a crime as gang-related if the victim or offender is a known gang member. However, the Chicago Police Department identifies a gang-related crime only when the crime has (or appears to have) a gang-related motive. Just because a gang member commits a crime does not make it gang-related (Dedel 2007).

As it is sometimes said, the difference between an aggravated assault and a homicide can be measured in *inches* (i.e., in a shooting, referring to whether or not the bullet struck a vital organ), *miles* (referring to the proximity of the victim to the nearest hospital), and *minutes* (referring to how quickly medical attention is received). Simple assaults include all other types of assaults that do not involve a weapon or serious injuries. As with sexual assaults, states may define and categorize assaults differently than the FBI.

In most jurisdictions—large, medium, and small—aggravated assault is the most common FBI index violent crime. Not surprisingly, the demographic profile of aggravated assault victims is similar to homicide victims, although a greater proportion of aggravated assault victims are female compared to homicide victims. Aggravated assault victims also tend to be younger than homicide victims. Victims of simple assaults tend to be even younger than victims of aggravated assault and are even more likely to be female (many instances of domestic violence are included as simple assaults) (Bureau of Justice Statistics 2011). As with homicide, the circumstance most likely to lead to an assault is an argument (Bureau of Justice Statistics 2005).

With regard to the relationship between the victim and the offender, approximately half of aggravated assault victims reported that they knew the attacker. This proportion is larger than in homicides but smaller than in rapes and other sexual assaults (i.e., sexual assault victims are the most likely to know the perpetrator; homicide victims are the least likely to have known the perpetrator). It is even more likely that the victim and offender know each other in simple assaults than in aggravated assaults (Bureau of Justice Statistics 2005). Again, this may be largely a function of the large proportion of domestic violence incidents in this category. It is much more likely that there is a relationship between the victim and the offender when the victim is female than when the victim is male (Bureau of Justice Statistics 2005). Aggravated assaults most often involve weapons such as clubs or other objects (33 percent), followed by personal weapons such as hands or feet (27 percent), firearms (21 percent), and knives and other cutting instruments (19 percent) (FBI 2012).

The circumstances during which aggravated (and simple) assaults typically take place contribute to the relatively high clearance rate for the crime. Particularly important is that there is face-to-face contact between the victim and the offender and that the offender is often known to the victim. Overall, approximately 57 percent of aggravated assaults reported to the police were cleared by the police in 2011, a slightly lower rate than that of homicide, but a higher rate than rape (FBI 2012). The largest proportion of people arrested for aggravated and simple assault are between twenty-five and twenty-nine years of age, just as with homicide and rape. However, juveniles have the highest proportional involvement in aggravated assaults compared to all other violent crimes (FBI 2012).

●●● Investigative Considerations With Other Assaults

As noted, aggravated and other nonsexual assaults are usually investigated in the same manner as murder, except that instead of a dead body there is a live witness. If the crime occurred in a private place, such as in a residence, most often there is a relationship between the victim and the offender, and the identity of the offender may be relatively easy to discern. If the crime occurred in a public place, such as on a street or in a tavern, there may be witnesses who may be able to provide critical information to investigators regarding the identity of the assailant. In either case, battery victims are likely to be able to provide critical information about the incident and the identity of the offender. However, in some instances, such as drive-by shootings, this may not be the case.

Like other victims of violent crime, victims of assault may also be emotionally traumatized by the incident. As such, care and compassion is necessary in interviewing and collecting evidence from these victims. A successful investigation may depend heavily on victim cooperation, and there is no better way to alienate a victim than through insensitive actions. As with sexual assault victims, the bodies of other assault victims must also be considered crime scenes. Although the procedures for collecting evidence may be less intrusive when the attack was not sexual, victims may still be reluctant to cooperate in this manner.

ANTI-SNITCHING NORMS AND RELUCTANT WITNESSES

A serious challenge to productive investigations, especially nonfatal shooting investigations, is the anti-snitching mindset among some witnesses. Simply stated, snitching, or providing information to the police to help an investigation, violates an unwritten rule that exists in many urban and other neighborhoods (Morris 2010). To be a "rat," "narc," "squealer," or "tattler," has never been a positive thing, but the label of "snitch" has taken on new meaning and prominence in the last ten years (Woldoff and Weiss 2010). The violation of this rule has real consequences, popularly explained by the slogans "Snitches end up in ditches" (Morris 2010) and "Snitches get stitches" (Woldoff and Weiss 2010). These subtle or more explicit threats are also known as witness intimidation (see Exhibit 11.2). (For a media discussion of the anti-snitching phenomenon, see the 2007 *60 Minutes* TV show available at www.cbsnews.com/video/watch/?id=2715238n.)

Exhibit 11.2 The Problem of Witness Intimidation

Intimidation of witnesses can take many different forms. According to Finn and Healy (1996) it most often includes the following:

- Physical violence (e.g., homicides, drive-by shootings, physical assaults)

- Explicit threats of physical violence (against not only the witness but friends and family of the witness)

- Implicit threats (e.g., gang members parked outside the witness's house, nuisance phone calls)

- Property damage (e.g., shootings into a witness's house, arson)

- Courtroom intimidation (e.g., threatening looks or gestures at a witness, a courtroom with many gang members present (pp. 6–7)

Finn and Healy also list four factors that increase the chances that a witness will be intimidated:

- The crime in question was violent.

- The defendant has a personal connection to the witness.

- The defendant lives near the witness.

- The witness is especially vulnerable (e.g., he or she is elderly or is a recent or illegal immigrant). (p. 8)

Finn and Healy state that the perpetrators of witness intimidation are usually not the defendants themselves; they are more often:

- Fellow gang members of the defendant

- Friends of the defendant

- Relatives of the defendant

Witness intimidation is a complex and multifaceted problem that is difficult to solve. Most measures designed to deal with the problem are within the control of judges and prosecutors. These measures can include vigorous prosecution of witness intimidation and the establishment of witness protection programs. However, according to Finn and Healy, investigators can also play a role in minimizing the significance of witness intimidation by adhering to the following guidelines:

- Don't talk to witnesses at the scene; they may fear being seen "cooperating" with the police.

- Don't appear at the door of potential (or actual) witnesses, which may label them as snitches and increase their reluctance to cooperate with the investigation. Arrange interviews at a neutral place.

- Witnesses will often say that they will talk to you but will not go to court. Tell them that is all right and get all the information you can anyway. You can always consider subpoenaing an individual later as a hostile witness, if necessary.

- Tell witnesses that they have vital information and let them know what can be done for them. Use salesmanship, because they may not believe you at first. Tell witnesses specifically what you can do to protect them. (p. 18)

PHOTO 11.12: The anti-snitching code is an obstacle in many violent crime investigations and is most often encountered in nonfatal shootings, especially those that involve gang members.

As noted, the anti-snitching phenomenon is most likely to reveal itself in nonfatal shootings, especially those that involve gang members. Anti-snitching norms may also be encountered in homicide investigations, but it is often less of an issue in these investigations because the seriousness of a murder may outweigh witnesses' concerns for their safety and well-being.

Even *victims* of nonfatal shootings are often unwilling to provide information to the police. Some of this reluctance may be due to the victim's own role in the crime (e.g., drug sale disputes and debts). It may also be due to an ongoing retaliation escalation in which the dispute is viewed by the parties as being private and to be settled among themselves without interference from the police. But, undoubtedly, much of it also has to do with anti-snitching norms. In fact, one of the reasons for recent declines in clearances of violent crime, especially homicides and assaults, maybe the "no snitching" code (Woldoff and Weiss 2010).

Clearly, the reluctance of witnesses to cooperate with the police because of cultural influences and consequences is a difficult obstacle for individual investigators to overcome. The larger issue is the relationship between the police and the community—the overall negative views that some citizens have of the police and the corresponding general distrust of the police. In any case, investigators should be aware of anti-snitching norms and understand the reasons for, and importance of, confidentiality and/or anonymity among witnesses. In some instances, critical information may be obtained from witnesses only with promises of protection, such as that provided through witness protection programs. Witness protection programs typically involve providing financial assistance and temporary (or permanent) relocation of witnesses in exchange for information and testimony (Dedel 2007).

●●● Domestic Violence and Child Abuse

Although not separate crimes per se, assaults of intimate partners and children (i.e., domestic violence and child abuse) involve unique circumstances and investigative issues. While the investigation of these crimes certainly has its challenges, the identification of the perpetrator is typically not one of them. In domestic violence incidents, the offender is known to the victim—most often it is an intimate partner of the victim (hence, intimate partner violence or IPV). In the overwhelming majority of child abuse cases, the offender is also related to the victim (typically a parent or stepparent) and is responsible for the care of the child.

DOMESTIC (OR INTIMATE PARTNER) VIOLENCE

Domestic violence involves assaultive behaviors among current or former intimate partners (Sampson 2007). Domestic violence tends to be dramatically under-reported; women report approximately 25 percent of all such assaults that occur; it has been estimated that men report only about 2 percent (Sampson 2007). Most domestic violence incidents involve pushing, slapping, and hitting; in most instances, medical treatment for injuries is not required or sought. Nevertheless, of course, IPV can be deadly. Intimate partner homicides make up 40 percent to 50 percent of all murders of women in the United States (Campbell et al. 2003). In addition, there is a high correlation between spousal abuse and child abuse; where there is one, there is likely to be the other. Although IPV is a serious and complicated problem, there is evidence that in recent years its frequency has declined at a rate consistent with the overall violent crime rate. The decline in IPV has been attributed to many factors, including the increasing ease of divorce, declining marriage rates, and improved victim advocacy options.

Females between the age of sixteen and twenty-four are at the highest risk of domestic violence victimization. Although IPV occurs among all demographic groups, it is most frequently experienced by lower-income African American females. Being young, black, low income, divorced or separated, a resident of rental housing, and a resident of an urban area have all been associated with higher rates of IPV among women (Sampson 2007).

As noted, given the relationship between the victim and the offender, the identification of the offender is not usually an issue in the investigation. Depending on the circumstances and seriousness of the incident, the investigation may end with the patrol officers' initial investigation and the on-scene arrest of the

PHOTO 11.13: Many cases of domestic violence, or intimate partner violence, go unreported. Many victims are reluctant to leave their abusers and plead with the police not to arrest the offender.

offender. In more serious incidents, other investigators may become involved. In either instance, the victim is the primary source of information and evidence in the investigation. The victim's statement about the incident and the documentation of the victim's injuries that resulted from the incident are most critical. The suspect's statement and other information from other witnesses may also be valuable.

Often the most common challenge with domestic assault investigations is obtaining the cooperation of the victim. Police officers can tell many stories about domestic violence victims who plead that the offender not be arrested. And often, after the offender is released from arrest, the victim continues to cohabitate with the offender. Several explanations have been offered as to why victims resist leaving an abuser (Sampson 2007, pp. 9–10). These explanations provide insight into the psychology of domestic abuse victims and may assist investigators when working with reluctant victims in investigations.

- Cycle of violence. Three cyclical phases in physically abusive intimate relationships keep a woman in the relationship: (1) a tension-building phase that includes minor physical and verbal abuse, (2) an acute battering phase, and (3) a makeup or honeymoon phase. The honeymoon phase lulls an abused woman into staying with her abuser and the cycle repeats itself.

- Battered woman syndrome. A woman is so fearful from experiencing cycles of violence that she no longer believes escape is possible.

- Stockholm syndrome. A battered woman is essentially a hostage to her batterer. She develops a bond with, and shows support for and kindness to, her captor, perhaps because of her unfamiliarity with more normal relationships.

- Traumatic bonding theory. A battered woman experiences unhealthy or anxious attachments to her parents, who abused or neglected her. The woman develops unhealthy attachments in her adult relationships and accepts intermittent violence from her intimate partner. She believes the affection and claims of remorse that follow because she needs positive acceptance from, and bonding with, the batterer.

- Psychological entrapment theory. A woman feels she has invested so much in the relationship she is willing to tolerate the battering to save it.

- Multifactor ecological perspective. Staying in physically abusive relationships is the result of a combination of factors, including family history, personal relationships, societal norms, and social and cultural factors.

Over the years, there has been much debate about the effectiveness of arresting offenders in misdemeanor domestic violence incidents. There is no debate about the necessity of arresting offenders in serious domestic violence incidents. Briefly, a study conducted in Minneapolis in the 1980s concluded that "arrest works best" in deterring offenders from committing future incidents of domestic violence. After this study, several replications were conducted in other cities using different methodologies. Some studies came to the same conclusion as the Minneapolis study, some found that arrest did not deter offenders, and others found that arrest actually led to an increase in offending. The most sophisticated of the replications found that arrest produces a deterrent effect among some offenders (e.g., those who are employed) but not others (e.g., those who are not employed).

Restraining orders are sometimes associated with domestic violence incidents. Restraining orders (or stay away orders or injunctions) are issued by a judge upon request by a victim, who is referred to as the petitioner. Usually in a court hearing, the petitioner presents reasons (evidence) for why the offender, called the respondent, should be ordered to stay away from the petitioner. If, as a result of the hearing, a restraining order is issued by the judge, then the respondent is ordered to stay away and to not have contact with the petitioner on a permanent basis or for a specified period of time. If the restraining order is violated and this violation is brought to the attention of the police, the respondent can be arrested and charged with violating the terms of the restraining order. In this way, the restraining order may deter an offender from committing future instances of IPV (Benitez et al. 2010). Indeed, research shows that restraining orders are associated with a reduced risk of violence toward the victim (Benitez et al. 2010). However, there is also a substantial chance that a restraining order will be violated, with the greatest risk of this being soon after the initiation of the order. In fact, the issuance of a restraining order may lead to the escalation of violence against the victim (Benitez et al. 2010; Moracco et al. 2010). Clearly, restraining orders are not a panacea to the problem of IPV. As an attempt to add value to restraining orders, some states have added a requirement that upon issuance of a restraining order, the respondent must surrender any firearms in his or her possession. The impact of these firearm surrender orders is yet to be determined.

CHILD ABUSE

Like IPV, child abuse is a very difficult problem to effectively address. As described by Dedel (2009, p. 3), child abuse has several different forms:

- Physical abuse, which may range in severity from minor bruising to death

- Sexual abuse, involving varying degrees of coercion and violence

- Neglect, ranging from the failure to provide food, clothing, or shelter to the failure to provide medical care, supervision, or schooling

- Emotional abuse, which involves actions which cause psychological trauma

Approximately two-thirds of substantiated maltreatment cases relate to neglect, followed by physical abuse (16 percent), sexual abuse (9 percent), and emotional abuse (7 percent) (Dedel 2009). Approximately 75 percent of children who die from abuse are under four years of age (Dedel 2009).

According to Dedel (2009, p. 8), the characteristics of victims vary by the type of maltreatment:

- The risk of physical abuse decreases as the child gets older, although adolescents are also victims of it. Boys and girls are equally at risk of minor physical abuse, although boys are slightly more likely to sustain serious injuries. Physical abuse occurs disproportionately among economically disadvantaged families. Income also affects the severity of abuse.

- Children are at highest risk of sexual abuse from age seven to twelve, although sexual abuse among very young children does occur and is often undetected because of their inability to communicate what is happening to them. Sexual abuse victims tend to be selected because they are vulnerable in some way (e.g., very young, passive, quiet, needy). Girls are significantly more likely to be sexually abused than boys, although it is possible that boys are simply less likely to report their victimization.

- The risk of neglect generally declines with age. The mean age of victims of neglect is six years old. Boys and girls are equally at risk of neglect.

Similarly, the characteristics of offenders also vary by the type of maltreatment (Dedel 2009, pp. 10–11):

- Caretakers who physically abuse their children tend to experience high stress (e.g., from being a single parent, health problems, unemployment, poverty) and may have poorly developed coping skills. They may also struggle with personality factors such as low self-esteem, poor impulse control, depression, anxiety, and low frustration tolerance. Their expectations for their child may exceed the child's developmental capacity. As a result, they may not interact well with their child and tend to use more punitive discipline. Perhaps because mothers spend more time with their children, perpetrators are slightly more likely to be female than male. Further, normal adolescent defiance and rebellion increases family tension and may frustrate parents, who respond with excessive punishment. When confronted, physically abusive caretakers tend to offer illogical, unconvincing, or contradictory explanations for the child's injury.

- Sexual abusers are usually in a position of authority or trust over their victims. They are usually male and typically in their early thirties, although a significant proportion are adolescents, such as siblings or babysitters. Offenders who victimize family members tend to have only one or two victims (usually female), while nonrelative offenders tend to have a much larger number of victims (usually male). Their feelings of inadequacy, depression, isolation, rigid values, and deviant arousal patterns contribute to their offending. Once they have selected a vulnerable victim, perpetrators generally "groom" the victim by progressing from nonsexual touching to sexual activity. They may use their authority to force their victims to participate, or they may use various forms of enticements and coercion. Using bribes, threats, isolation, or physical aggression, perpetrators also persuade their victims to remain silent about the abuse so that other adults cannot intervene. Sexual abusers tend to rationalize and minimize their behavior, deny the sexual intent, or project blame onto the victim. That said, most sexual abusers are not attracted exclusively to children (that is, they are also sexually attracted to adults), and they have relatively low recidivism rates, particularly as they get older.

- Single female caretakers are mostly likely to be reported for neglecting their children. Younger mothers, those with large families, and those who experienced neglect themselves are also more likely to neglect their children's needs. Economic hardship and isolation from social activities and peers are also contributing factors. Offenders may also have a substance abuse problem that limits their ability to care for themselves and creates a chaotic lifestyle that compromises their parenting abilities.

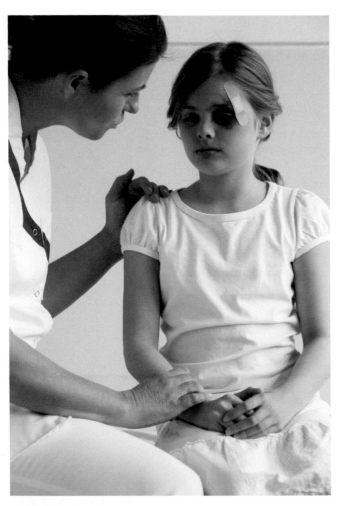

PHOTO 11.14: Child abuse cases can be very difficult to investigate. One significant challenge is discovering that abuse has occurred. In addition, special skills and techniques are necessary when conducting interviews of children.

From an investigative standpoint, child abuse poses several challenges. The first is determining whether the injuries sustained by the child were as a result of an accident or were intentionally inflicted. Second, because the victim is a child, investigators need to understand children's unique emotional and psychological needs, responses to such trauma, and cognitive development, and they need to be able to effectively communicate with these victims. Third, child abuse almost always occurs in private, and the offenders usually try to hide evidence of the crimes, perhaps by hiding the child (e.g., keeping the child home from school, failing to seek medical attention for the child). These actions on the part of the abuser may make the discovery of the crime more difficult. In this regard, states have laws in place that require certain people (e.g., medical personnel, teachers, mental health professionals, social workers, law enforcement officers, and other professionals who have frequent contact with children) to report suspected abuse or neglect. Some states require *any* person that suspects abuse to report it. Many state laws also specifically state that a report must be made if maltreatment is even suspected (versus confirmed), and the laws specify penalties for the failure to report.

When it comes to investigating allegations of suspected child abuse, police agencies usually have help in the form of local child protective services agencies. In fact, state laws most often require that reports be made to child protective services, although some require reports to be made to the local law enforcement agency, and some give the reporter discretion to whom the allegation is reported. Very few states require that all reports be made to a law enforcement agency (Dedel 2009). While child protective service agencies may most often take the lead in investigating allegations of maltreatment and abuse, police departments are responsible for investigating those cases that involve serious injuries to, or the death of, a child. Of course, unlike child protective service workers, the police have the ability to make arrests. The police are also sometimes called upon to assist child protective services staff when conducting home visits, investigating other allegation of child abuse, or when removing children from the home due to an immediate danger to the child (Dedel 2009). Given the significance of the problem and the unique demands of addressing child abuse, child protective services workers are in a position to focus on the issue. They have training and expertise in the detection of child abuse, interacting with child victims, interviewing young children, and recognizing the behaviors of abusing and nonabusing parents (Dedel 2009).

Given that one of the most significant investigative challenges associated with child abuse is the difficulty in discovering that it has occurred, it is necessary for the police to be on the lookout for evidence of such crimes. Police officers in schools, officers who respond to calls for service, and investigators who conduct other investigations often have contact and interactions with children. When an injured child is encountered, it is necessary for the officer to ask questions of the child and others about how the injury occurred and be aware of unusual, improbable, or conflicting explanations. It is also the responsibility of the police to investigate allegations of abuse that are brought to their attention and/or or notify child protective services of the report (Dedel 2009).

Especially noteworthy with regard to the investigation of child abuse is the importance of appropriate interviewing skills. Not only can poor interviewing skills cause additional trauma to child victims, they can also lead to inaccurate understandings of the facts of the incident. In particular, child victims are generally very susceptible to leading questions and irrelevant information. As explained by Dedel (2009, p. 24), the accuracy of information obtained from child victims can be improved when investigators adhere to the following guidelines:

- Make the interview setting child-friendly

- Recognize the developmental capabilities of children of different ages

- Exercise patience when asking the child to explain what happened

- Avoid "why" questions and focus instead on clear, open-ended questions about salient events

- Make efforts to offset any guilt the victim may experience for "causing trouble."

It is necessary that investigators who work child abuse cases receive extensive training on the development of interviewing skills and techniques for child victims. Training should also focus on legal issues, child development, evidence gathering, and the dynamics of child abuse (Dedel 2009).

MAIN POINTS

1. Forcible rape refers to "the penetration, no matter how slight, of the vagina or anus with any body part or object, or oral penetration by a sex organ of another person, without the consent of the victim." Most states use more inclusive definitions to include other forms and circumstances of sexual assault.

2. Most sexual assault victims are young and female. Some sexual assaults result in physical injuries to the victim and are committed by an offender who is a family member, intimate partner, friend, or acquaintance.

3. The circumstances in which most sexual assaults occur are favorable for their solution. In particular, face-to-face contact between the victim and the offender and the presence of a relationship between the victim and the offender can help investigators identify the perpetrator.

4. The most important source of information in a sexual assault investigation is usually the victim. In particular, critical information about the crime is often obtained from the investigator's interview of the victim and from a forensic medical examination of the victim.

5. Upon first contact and interview with investigators, different victims may have different emotional dispositions. It is a myth that victims are always hysterical and crying after a rape. Most victims are in a state of shock and disbelief.

6. The emotional and physical trauma of the sexual assault may last for weeks, months, years, or even a lifetime.

7. If information is to be produced about the offender, it is most likely to come from the victim. Physical evidence can be used to establish sexual contact/intercourse and may lead to the identification or confirmation of the perpetrator. The victim's statement that the sexual acts were not consensual, along with documentation of injuries to the victim, the use of a weapon, and other circumstances of the crime, can establish lack of consent. That the acts actually occurred can also be established by the victim's detailed statement of what transpired and/or a confession from the perpetrator.

8. If the assault was not committed by someone the victim knew or was acquainted with, and/or the victim is not able to provide a name of the suspect, then the task of identifying the perpetrator is likely to be more challenging. In these cases, details from the victim regarding the characteristics of the perpetrator may be especially useful.

9. Along with obtaining descriptive information about the offender from the victim, it is important that investigators ask about the nature and circumstances of the sexual attack. This information may provide investigators with insight into the type of person who committed the crime, his method of operation (MO) and signature, other clues about his identity, and effective interrogation strategies.

10. Forensic examinations of victims are conducted at hospitals and are performed by either a physician or a nurse who has received special training in forensic matters. Nurses with such training are referred to as sexual assault nurse examiners (or SANEs). The primary objectives of forensic examinations of sexual assault victims are to document injuries caused by the assault, recover biological evidence present as a result of the assault, and to provide treatment for injuries sustained as a result of the assault.

11. In addition to examining the victim of a sexual assault for physical evidence, it is important for investigators also to search for and collect evidence from crime scenes. It is around crime scenes that physical evidence and witnesses may be located. In a rape, there may be many crime scenes, both primary and secondary.

12. Rohypnol and GHB are two of the most common date rape drugs. Although their forms are different, their effects are similar. Victims who have ingested these drugs have severe memory distortions.

13. If a suspect can be named by the victim, then biological evidence recovered from the victim or from the crime scene may be immediately used for comparison purposes. If the suspect is not known, DNA can be searched in a DNA data bank. Furthermore, once identified, the suspect may be required to undergo a forensic examination to document any injuries; collect saliva, blood, and hair specimens; and seize the clothing worn at the time of the attack or that contains suspected evidence.

14. Interrogation of the suspect may produce information that confirms that the suspect is the perpetrator. Rapists with different motivations may respond differently to various themes in an interrogation.

15. A small percentage of rape allegations are suspected and substantiated as false. When investigating any crime, investigators must be aware of accounts provided by victims that just do not seem to make sense and that appear suspicious. There are various red flags of false rape allegations.

16. Aggravated assault refers to an attack by one person upon another for the purpose of inflicting

severe or aggravated bodily injury. Many aggravated assaults are nonfatal shootings. Simple assaults include all other types of assaults that do not involve a weapon or serious injuries.

17. The difference between an aggravated assault and a homicide can be measured in inches, miles, and minutes.

18. The demographic profile of aggravated assault victims is similar to that of homicide victims, although a greater proportion of aggravated assault victims are female compared to homicide victims. Aggravated assault victims also tend to be younger than homicide victims. Victims of simple assaults tend to be even younger than victims of aggravated assault and are even more likely to be female.

19. The circumstances during which aggravated and simple assaults typically take place contribute to the relatively high clearance rate for the crime. Particularly important is that there is face-to-face contact between the victim and the offender and that the offender is often known to the victim.

20. A serious challenge to productive assault investigations, especially in nonfatal shootings, is the anti-snitching mindset among some witnesses.

21. Snitching, or providing information to the police, violates an unwritten rule that exists in many urban and other neighborhoods. While loyalty to peers and reluctance to get peers into trouble is valued among most people, the anti-snitching "rule" has become a prominent high-profile issue at least partially as a result of hip-hop music and the underground media.

22. Domestic or intimate partner violence (IPV) involves assaultive behaviors among current or former intimate partners. While most instances of it do not require medical attention, IPV can be deadly. IPV accounts for a large proportion of all murders of women in the United States.

23. Often the most common challenge in domestic assault investigations is obtaining the cooperation of the victim in the investigation and especially in the prosecution of the perpetrator.

24. Several explanations have been offered as to why victims resist leaving an abuser, including the cycle of violence, battered woman syndrome, Stockholm syndrome, traumatic bonding theory, psychological entrapment theory, and multifactor ecological perspective.

25. Restraining orders are a strategy to prevent domestic violence incidents. Restraining orders are issued by a judge upon request by a victim. They order the abuser to not have contact with the victim. If the restraining order is violated, the abuser can be arrested. Restraining orders have limited effectiveness.

26. Child abuse can take several different forms: physical abuse, sexual abuse, emotional abuse, and neglect.

27. From an investigative standpoint, child abuse poses several challenges, including determining the cause of injuries, obtaining reliable information from child victims, and identifying possible instances of abuse.

28. When it comes to allegations of suspected child abuse, police agencies usually have help in the form of the local child protective services agencies. Child protective services workers have training and expertise in the detection of child abuse, interacting with child victims, interviewing young children, and recognizing the behaviors of abusing and nonabusing parents.

IMPORTANT TERMS

Aggravated assault	Child neglect	Power assertive rapists
Anger excitation rapists	Contact rapists	Power reassurance rapists
Anger retaliatory rapists	Domestic violence	Rape
Anti-snitching "rules"	False allegation	Rapists' modus operandi (MO)
Child abuse	Intimate partner violence (IPV)	Reference samples

Restraining orders

Rohypnol and GHB

Serial rape

Sexual aggressor rapists

Sexual assault

Sexual assault evidence kit

Sexual assault nurse examiners (SANEs)

Simple assault

Specimen samples

Theories of the continuation of IPV

Toxicology screen

Witness protection programs

QUESTIONS FOR DISCUSSION AND REVIEW

1. What are the varieties and characteristics of rape and other sexual assaults? What are the characteristics of victims and offenders?

2. What are the short-term and longer-term psychological and physical responses experienced by sexual assault victims?

3. What critical information may be provided by a victim as the result of an investigative interview?

4. What is the potential value of physical evidence in sexual assault investigations?

5. What are Rohypnol and GHB? What are their effects and how might they affect sexual assault investigations?

6. How might the interrogation of a sexual assault suspect be made more productive if the

investigator has an understanding of the suspect's motive in committing the crime?

7. What are the varieties and characteristics of aggravated and simple assaults?

8. What is the anti-snitching code and when is it most likely to present itself?

9. What are the characteristics of domestic violence or IPV?

10. What are the most challenging and least challenging aspects of domestic violence investigations?

11. What are the characteristics and types of child abuse? What are the common characteristics of victims and offenders?

12. What are the most challenging and least challenging aspects of child abuse investigations?

▶ STUDENT STUDY SITE

Visit **www.sagepub.com/brandl3e** to access additional study tools including eFlashcards, web quizzes, web resources, video resources, and SAGE journal articles.

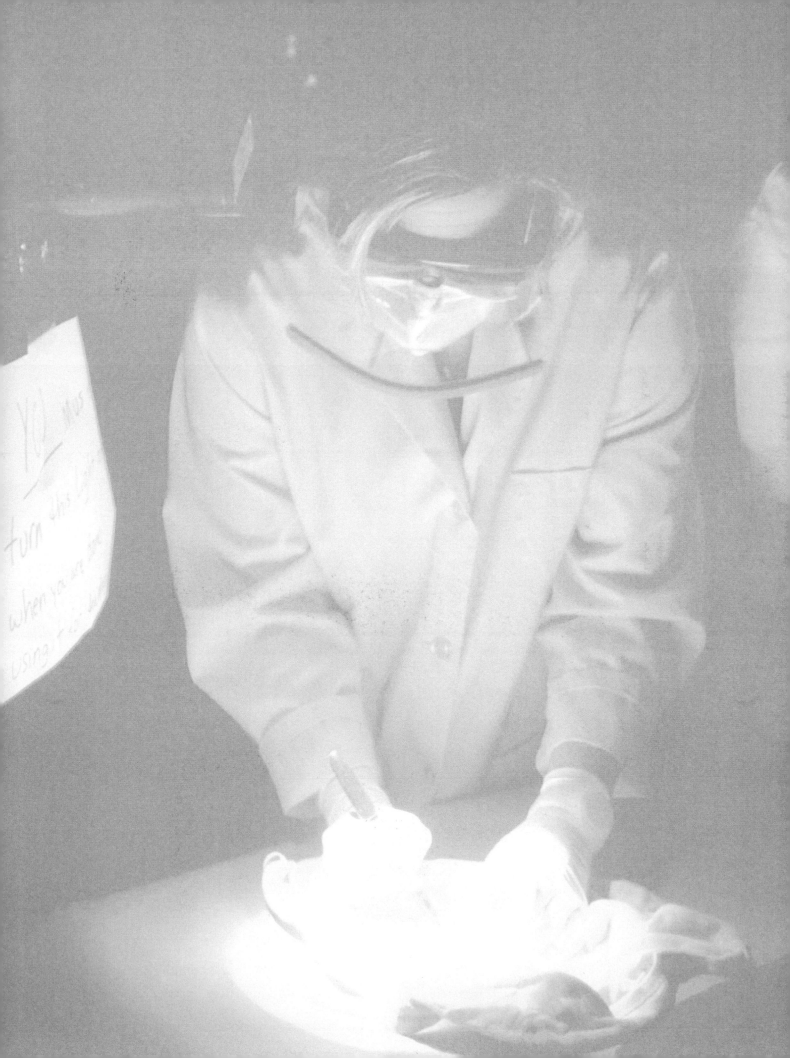

12

The Investigation of Robbery

Objectives

After reading this chapter you will be able to:

- Identify the varieties and characteristics of robbery, and explain why robberies typically have a relatively low rate of solvability

- Discuss the potential value of eyewitness identifications, hold-up alarms, and CCTV video surveillance cameras in robberies and identify the common limitations of the cameras

- Discuss what might be inferred about the robbery perpetrator based on the target that was selected to be robbed and the amount of planning that appeared to be present in the robbery

- Compare the differences in MO of an amateur and a professional bank robber

- Explain the potential investigative value of the robber's verbal activity during the robbery

- Describe how the perpetrator's weapon and disguise may represent leads in a robbery investigation

- Identify the types of physical evidence that may be present in robberies

- Identify the property of most interest to robbers and the circumstances in which the property taken may provide value to the investigation

- Discuss the interrogation approach that is most likely to be effective with robbers

- Discuss other possible sources of evidence and information in robbery investigations

From the **CASE FILE**

A Surprise Attack on a Pair of Restaurant Robbers

At about midnight, Glendale Police were called to Kopp's Restaurant. An armed robbery had just occurred. It was a few minutes after midnight when the manager of the restaurant and two other employees were in the process of locking up and leaving work. Suddenly, two black men wearing bandanas over their faces burst through the rear door. One of the men, the taller of the two, held a gun to the head of one of the employees; the other robber, who was carrying a black backpack, grabbed the manager and pushed him down the steps (photo 12.1) to the manager's office in the basement. The taller robber, and the employee he had in his grasp, followed down the steps. The manager told the police that the stairway and basement were dark, but the robber who was taking him down the steps seemed to know where he was going. Once in the manager's office, the shorter robber demanded that the manager open the safe (photo 12.2; photo 12.3). The taller robber demanded, "Get the door open or I'm going to kill him," referring to the employee. The manager opened the safe and both employees got on the floor as instructed. The shorter robber then filled up the backpack with money from the safe.

Unknown to the robbers, another employee was upstairs in the restaurant and heard the commotion. He realized they were being robbed. He armed himself with a metal trash-compacting rod (photo 12.4), and, as the robbers were running up the steps toward the door to make their exit with the backpack full of cash, he hit one of them in the head with the rod. The robber was knocked down some of the steps and dropped the backpack full of cash (photo 12.5; photo 12.6). The blow to the head also caused blood to splatter onto the nearby wall and the cash that had spilled on the steps (photo 12.7; photo 12.8). The employee who struck the robber then hurried down the steps and hid. The injured robber hollered at his partner to shoot the employee who had hit him. The uninjured robber, who had already made his exit from the restaurant, returned and assisted in getting his partner up the steps. They also gathered some of the cash that had fallen out of the backpack. Both of the perpetrators

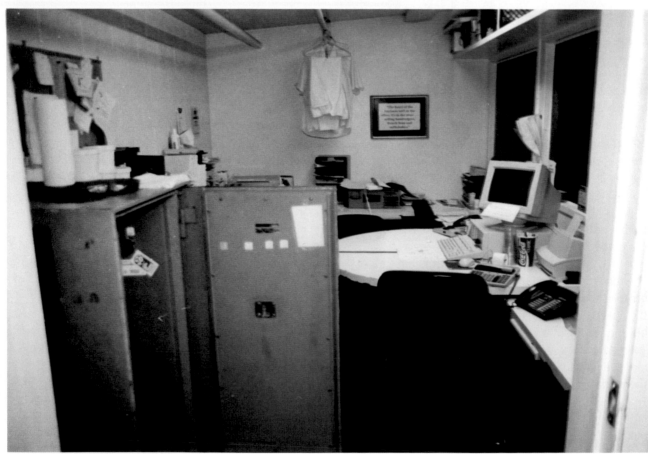

then fled through the back door (photo 12.9), leaving the backpack behind. One of the suspects dropped his cap on the way out (photo 12.10).

The manager reported that the shorter robber was approximately 5'8", had a medium build, was of medium complexion, and was wearing a bandana and white mask over his nose and mouth. The taller robber with the gun was about 5'11", had a thin build, and wore a dark bandana over his face. The manager told police that a total of $1,891 was actually taken; the cash and coins that were still in the backpack and scattered on the stairs and basement floor amounted to $3,746. He told police that neither he nor any of the other employees consented to being robbed by the two masked robbers.

Investigators had blood and a cap from one of the perpetrators and a partial description of each of them.

The blood on the wall, steps, coins, and cash was collected and sent to the crime lab for analysis and for a search in the DNA data bank. Since the perpetrators of business robberies (especially restaurant robberies) are often former employees, a list of such persons was created and descriptions were compared. A composite drawing of the suspect with the gun was developed and sent to area law enforcement agencies (see composite sketch). Media releases about the crime were prepared and disseminated. The search for the robbers was on.

The day after the robbery, three people came to the restaurant and ordered food. One of the employees who was robbed the previous night was working, and he thought that one of these men looked like one of the robbers. The employees got the license plate number of the vehicle the customers were driving and immediately reported it to the police. The

Exhibit 12.1   Composite Sketch of the Taller Robber With the Gun

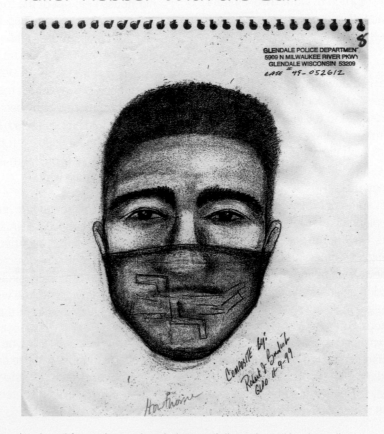

A composite sketch that was developed from witness descriptions and disseminated by the police.

police located the vehicle and interviewed each of the occupants. They were questioned and, with their consent, investigators obtained buccal DNA swabs from each of them so their DNA could be compared with the DNA evidence collected from the crime scene.

Three days later, while the Glendale police were checking former employees and waiting on the DNA results, a police officer in a neighboring jurisdiction received information from a confidential informant that two men, Dewayne Young and Peter Hawthorne, were involved in the robbery of the Kopp's Restaurant in Glendale. The informant provided some details about the incident, and told the officer that Young received a large gash to his head as a result of the robbery. This information was immediately transmitted to the Glendale police. Investigators then checked on the whereabouts of the two named suspects and found that Young was currently in jail on a drug charge. Investigators also discovered that Young used to be an employee at Kopp's several years ago, until he was fired. The Kopp's manager told police that one night when Young was working, $1,200 was taken from the safe. All employees were ordered to take a polygraph to find out who had stolen the money, but Young never showed up and never returned to work. Investigators visited Young in jail. Indeed, he had a 1–½" long scar on his forehead, closed with stitches, but he refused to talk to investigators.

Investigators then tracked down Peter Hawthorne and arrested him. After he was told why he had been arrested, Hawthorne agreed to tell investigators about his role in the robbery. Hawthorne explained that Young was friends with his girlfriend. Young told Hawthorne that he used to work at Kopp's and that they had a lot of money there. He asked Hawthorne if he wanted to go get some of it. Hawthorne said that Young had been planning on robbing the restaurant for months. Hawthorne said they went to the restaurant in Young's 4Runner the night before they robbed it, but they saw a police car parked in the area so they decided against robbing it then. They came back the next night in Young's vehicle and the police car was not there. Young told him, "It is going down." Hawthorne explained that he was wearing a white and black bandana and a red hat. Young was wearing a white bandana over his face and a gray cap. Young wanted to wear the bandana to cover his gold teeth. Hawthorne told the detectives what happened

after he and Young entered the restaurant. He then explained what happened as they were fleeing the restaurant:

> We leave. I go up the steps first with the gun still out. I hit the back door and it swings open and I run all the way to the parking lot. The door is barely closing and I could hear Dewayne yelling "Shoot 'em, Quan. Shoot 'em Quan." Quan is my nickname. I run back to the door, I see Dewayne flipping an employee down the stairs. Later when we were talking about it, we realized a third employee was waiting upstairs. When Dewayne was putting the money in the book bag, I told him to zip it shut, but he didn't. He was holding it by the top. So when Dewayne got hit, he spills the money. He went down 4–5 stairs and tried to pick it up. He couldn't get all of it because the dude was lying on the book bag. We flee the scene. I saw Dewayne was bleeding from his head. He was bleeding bad. I told him I would drive, but he doesn't let me. We leave the parking lot and Dewayne drives right over the curb. I'm guessing he's kind of knocked out, because he's swerving all the way. We went to Dewayne's girlfriend's house. When we got to her house I got out of the truck and threw-up. I was so scared and nervous. I never did anything like this before. After a while I thought 'what did I get myself into?' I went into the house and threw-up some more. . . . Dewayne was counting the money. Dewayne told me that he thought he should get more money because he got his head busted. I told him go ahead, I was glad it was over. I got about $500. I left the gun there with Dewayne. . . . If I could turn it all around, I would never have done it.

After questioning Hawthorne, police obtained a search warrant to collect buccal DNA swabs from Dewayne Young, who was still in jail. That DNA was collected and compared to that recovered from the crime scene. It matched. The composite sketch that was developed was of Peter Hawthorne. The witnesses were not able to make identifications from the photo lineups.

Peter Hawthorne and Dewayne Young were both found guilty of armed robbery while concealing identity. Hawthorne received a sentence of twenty years in prison; Young received a sentence of ten years in prison.

PHOTO 12.11–12.12: These photo lineups were created and shown to the robbery victims. None of them were able to identify Hawthorne or Young as the perpetrators. In photo lineup #1814, Hawthorne is in the top middle. In photo lineup #1813, Young is in the lower left.

Case Considerations and Points for Discussion ●━━━━━━━━━━━━━━━

- What was the most important evidence in the case that led to the identification of Young and Hawthorne as possible suspects? What was the role of the police in developing this information? What evidence was most useful in proving that Young and Hawthorne actually committed the robbery?

- What was the biggest mistake made by Young and Hawthorne in committing this robbery? Why?

- What do you think was the single most important action of investigators that led to this crime being solved?

●●● Varieties and Characteristics of Robbery

Robbery refers to "the taking or attempting to take anything of value from the care, custody, or control of a person or persons by force, threat of force, violence, and/or by putting the victim in fear" (FBI 2012). To establish that a robbery has occurred, the victim must state that property was taken by force and without permission.

In most jurisdictions, robbery is the second most common violent crime; only aggravated assault usually occurs more frequently. As with murder, there are typically more robberies and a higher robbery rate (i.e., the number of robberies per 100,000 persons) in large urban areas than in smaller cities, suburbs, or rural areas. Because robbery is a serious and relatively frequent crime, and because the circumstances of the crime are such that a suspect is seldom immediately identifiable, police departments that experience robberies at a high rate typically allocate a large proportion of investigative resources to them.

There are many situations in which a robbery may occur (Monk et al. 2010; Scott 2001; Smith 2005). For example, there are street robberies (e.g., robbery of pedestrians, robbery of people using automated teller machines, drug-related robberies), commercial robberies (e.g., robbery of banks, gas stations, and convenience stores), vehicle-related robberies (e.g., robbery of armored trucks and taxi drivers, carjacking), and home invasion robberies. Since each type of robbery occurs in a different setting and has unique characteristics, the investigative response to each type of robbery will also vary.

In 2011, street robbery accounted for nearly 44 percent of all robberies known to the police (FBI 2012), followed by robberies of commercial establishments (22 percent), and robberies of persons in residences (17 percent). In 2011, the average loss that resulted from each robbery was $1,153. Bank robberies involved the greatest average loss at $4,704 per incident, followed by other business robberies ($1,783), residential robberies ($1,489), convenience store robberies ($890), and street robberies ($785) (FBI 2012; see Table 12.1).

TABLE 12.1 Relative Frequency of Robbery and Amount of Loss

TYPE OF ROBBERY	FREQUENCY (%)	AVERAGE $ VALUE OF LOSS
Street robbery	43.8	$785
Residential robbery	17.0	$1,489
Other business robbery	13.0	$1,783
Gas station/convenience store robbery	7.5	$890
Bank robbery	2.0	$4,704
Other robbery	16.8	$1,050

Source: Federal Bureau of Investigations. 2012. *Crime in the United States, 2011 Uniform Crime Reports.* Washington, DC: U.S. Department of Justice.

Robbery offenders and victims are most often young and male, especially in street robberies. The largest proportion of those arrested for robbery are between the ages of sixteen and twenty-one, and approximately 88 percent are male (FBI 2012). The largest proportion of robbery victims are between the ages of eighteen and twenty. More than 69 percent of robbery victims are male (Bureau of Justice Statistics 2005). Among all violent crimes, robbery is least likely to involve victims and offenders who know each other. In only 28 percent of robberies is there a relationship between the victim and the offender (Bureau of Justice Statistics 2011). Robberies that occur between people who know each other often involve illicit goods (e.g., drug-related robberies) and are the least likely to be reported to the police (Bureau of Justice Statistics 2005).

Robberies are most often committed with a weapon (armed robbery); approximately 42 percent are committed with strong-arm tactics. Guns are most often used in armed robberies (71 percent; FBI 2012). A street robbery committed with strong-arm tactics is sometimes referred to as a mugging.

The circumstances in which most robberies occur are generally not favorable for their solution. Even though there is often face-to-face contact between the victim and the offender, the victim may not be able to provide the information necessary for the police to identify and apprehend the perpetrator because usually the victim and offender are strangers. Usually little physical evidence is left behind at robbery scenes. Indeed, of all violent crimes, robberies have the lowest clearance rate. Nationally, in 2011, only approximately 29 percent of all robberies were cleared (FBI 2012). In general, as with many other crimes, smaller departments in rural areas tend to have the highest clearance rate for robberies; large departments tend to have the lowest clearance rate (FBI 2012).

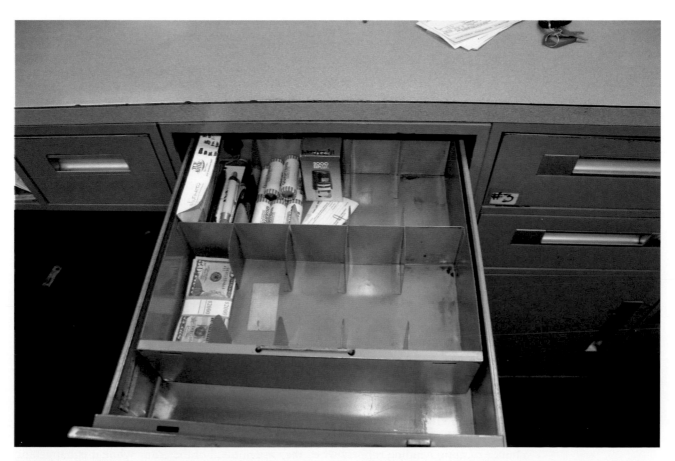

PHOTO 12.13: Often there is little physical evidence to be found at a robbery scene. Pictured here is a bank drawer from which cash was stolen.

MYTHS & MISCONCEPTIONS 12.1

Only the Best and Smartest Robbers Rob Banks

As often portrayed in the media and in movies, banks robberies are committed by smart and extremely violent criminals who plan their crimes down to the last detail. As a result of their superior criminal capabilities and meticulous planning, they get away with tens or even hundreds of thousands of dollars. In reality, very few bank robberies happen like this. While there may be great incentives among some criminals to rob banks (after all, banks are "where the cash is at"), there are also good reasons among even the most motivated robbers to avoid banks. As it turns out, the average take in a bank robbery is less than $5,000, and some of the cash may be stained by dye packs (see below) or otherwise unusable. Further, most bank robbers are apprehended, if not immediately then eventually. While about 20 percent of all robberies are solved, approximately 60 percent of bank robberies are solved (Weisel 2007), similar to the clearance rate of murder. The conviction rate for bank robbery is also very high, at about 93 percent (Weisel 2007). The higher rate of bank robbery clearances (and convictions) is because these crimes are investigated very thoroughly, they are reported as soon as they occur, they occur during daylight hours, they involve witnesses, and many of them have surveillance camera images as well as other evidence that can be used to identify perpetrators (Weisel 2007). For most people inclined to commit robberies, banks robberies are just too risky. That would also explain why just 2 percent of all robberies involve banks. In the criminal world, there are just too many other easier ways to "get paid." As an experienced robbery detective explained, "Only the dumb or desperate rob banks."

●●● Investigative Considerations With Robbery

There has been more research and experimentation on robbery *prevention* strategies than on robbery *apprehension* strategies. For instance, to prevent street robberies, it has been recommended that police agencies deploy foot and directed patrol in frequent robbery locations, that robbery awareness campaigns be used to educate citizens about the risks of robbery victimization, that safe transportation options be provided to reduce pedestrian traffic at high-risk times and places, and that lighting be increased at dark high-risk places, just to name a few such strategies (Monk et al. 2010). Indeed, given the (lack of) evidence available in the aftermath of most robberies, it may be easier and more cost effective to try to prevent robberies from occurring than trying to apprehend offenders after the fact. As the adage goes, "An ounce of prevention is worth a pound of cure." (See Scott 2001, Altizio and York 2007, Smith 2005, Weisel 2007, and Monk et al. 2010 for discussions regarding the prevention of robbery.) Nevertheless, of course, for those robberies not prevented, efforts at apprehension must be made. Discussed in more detail below is the evidence that may be available in robberies—evidence that that may lead to the apprehension of the perpetrator.

●●● Holdup Alarms and a Fast Police Response

Alarms have more to do with apprehension than prevention. Approximately 98 percent of banks that are robbed have an alarm system, but obviously banks are still robbed. The real value of an alarm is that it may lead to a fast police response. The police have the best chance of apprehending robbers when they are notified of the crime while it is happening and they respond quickly to the scene, thereby allowing for an on-scene apprehension.

Compared with burglar alarms, bank and store holdup alarms are much less likely to be false. They also call attention to the need for victims to contact the police immediately after a robbery has occurred.

The importance of a quick police response to a robbery scene also calls attention to related police procedures (Rice 1998). Robberies are often identified as one of the most potentially dangerous situations for the police. As a result, a top priority in responding to such calls must be the protection of officers' and victims' safety at the scene. Squad arrivals should not be visible or audible from inside the scene, as this may lead to panic and violence on the part of the perpetrator. Typically, emergency lights, but not sirens, should be used. This also requires extra travel precautions on the part of responding officers. When police are within blocks of the scene, emergency lights should also be deactivated. Ideally, responding officers will have information about the perpetrator, including his or her description and mode and direction of travel from the scene. Officers should always assume that the perpetrator is armed and that there may be more than one perpetrator involved. As officers arrive, the entire area around the scene should be monitored, and officers should be aware of persons and vehicles leaving the area, and of other vehicles in the area. Officers should watch for robbery lookouts and getaway cars. Robbers are just as likely to walk from a robbery scene as they are to run because running is likely to draw more attention (Wright and Decker 1997). Officers must consider all possibilities and always use extraordinary caution. When securing the scene, victims and witnesses should be separated and immediately questioned regarding the description of the perpetrators. Officers should be aware that descriptions of clothing worn by the perpetrator can be misleading because clothing can be quickly changed and discarded.

Various strategies are available to the police for proactively dealing with robberies. Based on crime analysis, the police may establish decoy or stakeout operations, or they may increase police presence in those areas most likely to experience robberies. It is in these ways that the police may be better able to respond quickly to robberies when they occur.

EYEWITNESS IDENTIFICATIONS AND CCTV

Eyewitness descriptions of the perpetrator are typically the best evidence available in robberies. However, as discussed in Chapter 6, this evidence is certainly not foolproof or without its limitations. Depending on the victim and the circumstances of the crime, it may be possible for the victim or witnesses to provide details in order for investigators to develop a composite picture of the perpetrator. In addition, the victim or witnesses may be able to provide a description of the getaway car, if one was used. The composite picture or description of the car may then be advertised via the media, and information relating to the crime may be obtained by the police via a tip line or other avenue. Recall that this was the primary investigative approach used by the police in the robbery investigation discussed in the introduction to this chapter, and critical information about the robbery was provided by a confidential informant as a result. In some cases, the victim or witnesses may also be able to provide other details about people loitering in the area prior to the robbery. This information may also provide leads for investigators to pursue.

If images of the perpetrator were recorded on closed circuit television (CCTV) security surveillance camera video, which is standard with robberies of banks and other commercial establishments, including some taxis, but uncommon in other types of robberies, then those images may also be shown in media alerts in order to generate useful leads about the identity of the perpetrator. Exterior surveillance cameras may be of benefit in recording images of the entrance and getaway of the perpetrator and/or the perpetrator's vehicle. There are a variety of different types of surveillance systems, which have varying degrees of reliability. These include constantly recording cameras, cameras that record over previously recorded images on a time loop, surveillance cameras that have to be activated by employees, surveillance cameras that show recorded images on a screen that can be seen by the would-be offender, and broadband internet video that can be viewed in real time by the police (Weisel 2007). "Smart" cameras, such as facial recognition cameras, are also available and are being used more often in certain locations (e.g., casinos).

Although the images caught on cameras have certainly led to the identification and apprehension of robbers, there are at least two frequently encountered problems with surveillance video. First, many robbers of commercial establishments are aware that security cameras are present and, as a result, they may wear a disguise to hide their identity (Wright and Decker 1997). Or, depending on the placement of the camera, prior to the robbery the perpetrator may render the camera useless (e.g., using spray paint or shaving cream to cover the camera lens). Second, more so in some commercial establishments than with banks, some security camera video images are of such poor quality—often due to old equipment—that they may be nearly worthless. It is also not uncommon that cameras are in place but do not work (as in the robbery of the gas station described in the introduction to Chapter 6). In other instances, the cameras may be operational but poorly placed. Despite these common problems, video images can still be useful. Although facial characteristics of the perpetrator may not be evident, distinctive clothing and other characteristics may be, and this may be enough to generate useful leads.

Perpetrators sometimes visit, or "case," the business establishment as a "customer" prior to robbing the place. It is in this manner that perpetrators may become more familiar with the place and more comfortable being there prior to the time of the actual robbery. A review of earlier security camera video footage by the victim or witnesses may lead to a particular "customer" being recognized as the perpetrator, and the perpetrator may not be in disguise at this point.

PHOTO 12.14: The woman in the white hat is robbing the bank. What value might this photo provide in the investigation?

PHOTO 12.15: Many video surveillance systems in place today do not provide high-quality images. What value might this photo provide in the investigation?

The real-time monitoring of street surveillance cameras by the police may hold promise as a strategy by which to collect evidence in street robberies, but these systems can be expensive to purchase, operate, and maintain. Research also suggests that when these cameras can be seen by would-be offenders, the offenders often respond by simply moving their criminal activities (e.g., drug selling) to places outside the view of the camera. Surveillance cameras placed in unmarked parked police cars may be an effective countermeasure to this criminal adaptation.

●●● Modus Operandi

Victims and witnesses (as well as security camera footage) may also be able to provide information to the police to substantiate the offender's MO and signature. This information can be used by investigators to link robberies together and to the same perpetrator, to clear crimes when an offender is identified and apprehended, and to provide other clues as to the characteristics of the perpetrator. In particular, it may be meaningful to understand the target of the robbery, the apparent degree of planning involved in committing the robbery, how the robber approached the target, what was said by the robber (or written, in the case of a robbery note), the nature of the demand(s), the weapons used, the type of force used, and the method of the departure. Several of these dimensions of robbery MO are discussed below.

MOTION : POST-ALARM

C28[GAS STATION]8/27/2012 1:45:14 PM

PHOTO 12.16: Some video cameras produce very clear photographs. Shown here is a subject who is about to rob the Citgo gas station. The subject's vehicle is also seen.

THE MEANING OF TARGET SELECTION

Generally speaking, targets (victims) that are unguarded, in places that are familiar to the offender, and where escape routes are known and clear to the offender, represent the most attractive places/people to rob. Of course, these perceptions depend on the perpetrator. As discussed earlier in *Criminal Investigation*, offenders generally do not travel far to commit their crimes—they tend to commit crimes in proximity to where they live. People are most comfortable in the areas around their homes and tend to do most things in this area. So too it is with robbers. Some offenders lack transportation and therefore commit their robberies within walking distance of where they live. In general, younger robbers tend to commit robberies in closer proximity to their homes than older robbers, but differences in travel distance may depend on several other factors, such as access to, or availability of, public transportation.

The degree of knowledge or familiarity the robber appeared to have about the place that was robbed is an important aspect of offender MO. For example, robberies of businesses, particularly restaurants, are often committed by former disgruntled employees (or by the associates of these former employees) who were fired. These individuals may have feelings of anger and a desire for revenge, and they also have the knowledge of the inner workings of the business (e.g., closing procedures, location of the safe, amount of money in the safe, knowledge of who has the combination to the safe, etc.) that is necessary to commit a successful robbery. It is prudent for investigators to consider employees and recently fired employees as possible suspects, especially when it appears that the perpetrator had "inside" knowledge about how best to commit the crime. Recall that in the case discussed in the introduction to this chapter, the manager of the restaurant told police during their initial investigation that it appeared that one of the robbers was familiar with the restaurant because he was able to navigate his way to the basement in the dark and knew that the basement was where the safe was kept. Sure enough, one of the robbers was a former employee of the restaurant.

The apparent degree of planning involved in committing the robbery may also provide a clue regarding the offender's level of experience, knowledge, and age. Specifically, as with many other crimes, robberies that appear to have been well planned are usually perpetrated by older and more experienced offenders (Feeney 1999; Wright and Decker 1997). More experienced offenders are, by definition, likely to be *serial* offenders. Well-planned robberies usually involve more than one person, are committed with a weapon, are committed using a disguise, and involve a getaway car. Robberies that are not well planned are more likely to involve younger offenders, and younger offenders are likely to talk about their crimes with one another and with others. If others report these overheard conversations to the police, good leads may result. Even bank robberies are most often committed by amateurs. Approximately 80 percent of bank robbers act alone, 72 percent are unarmed, and about 60 percent do not use disguises. Additionally, approximately 80 percent of arrested bank robbers do not have previous convictions for bank robbery (Weisel 2007; see Table 12.2).

TABLE *12.2*   Distinguishing Professional and Amateur Bank Robbers

	PROFESSIONAL	AMATEUR
Offenders	• Multiple offenders with division of labor • Shows evidence of planning • May be older • Prior bank robbery convictions • Travels farther to rob banks	• Solitary offender • Drug or alcohol use likely • No prior bank crime • Lives near bank target
Violence	• Aggressive takeover with loud verbal demands • Visible weapons, especially guns • Intimidation, physical or verbal threats	• Note passed to teller or simple verbal demand • Waits in line • No weapon
Defeat security	• Uses a disguise • Disables or obscures surveillance cameras • Demands that dye packs be left out, alarms not be activated, or police not be called	• No attempt
Robbery success	• Hits multiple teller windows • Larger amounts stolen • Lower percentage of money recovered • More successful robberies • Fewer cases cleared • Longer time from offense to case clearance	• Single teller window victimized • Lower amount stolen • Higher percentage of money recovered • More failed robberies • Shorter time from offense to case clearance, including more same-day arrests • Case clearance more likely
Robbery timing	• Targets banks when few customers are present, such as opening time • Targets banks early in the week	• Targets banks when numerous customers are present, such as around midday • Targets banks near closing or on Friday
Target selection	• Previous robbery occurred there • Busy road near intersection • Multidirectional traffic • Corner locations, multiple vehicle exits	• Previous robbery occurred there • Heavy pedestrian traffic or adjacent to dense multifamily residences • Parcels without barriers • Parcels with egress obscured
Getaway	• Via car	• On foot or bicycle

Source: Adopted from Deborah L. Weisel. 2007. *Bank Robbery.* Problem-Oriented Guides for Police Series: Problem-Specific Guide No. 48. Washington, DC: U.S. Department of Justice.

THE ROBBER'S APPROACH AND DEPARTURE

How the robber approaches the victim is another important dimension of MO, particularly for street robbers. Weisel (2007) identifies several possibilities:

- *Confrontations,* in which the offender demands money or property from the victim through verbal commands. Violence may follow if compliance is not provided.

- *Blitzes,* in which the offender uses violence first to gain control over the victim. Once this is accomplished, the robbery occurs.

- *Cons,* in which the offender first uses a distraction to then surprise the victim with the robbery demand (e.g., asking the victim for a cigarette before robbing him or her).

- *Snatch-thefts,* in which no communication or interaction occurs before the robbery; the offender simply grabs the property (e.g., purse) and flees.

Altizio and York (2007) explain that convenience store robbers generally use one of two approaches: the *straight* approach, in which the robber demands money immediately upon entering the store, or the *customer* approach, in which the robber demands money after entering the store and spending time making a purchase.

Similarly, how does the robber end the robbery event? By running away? Demanding that the victim run away? Having the victim walk away in a certain direction? Having the victim close his or her eyes and count to ten? Sometimes bank robbers in particular feel the need to make a dramatic sort of exit as they leave the bank. As seen in the photo below, in one case, the robber lit a smoke bomb in the bank prior to his departure. The particulars of the robber's departure may be an important aspect of MO and may assist in linking several crimes to a particular perpetrator.

PHOTO 12.17: Bank robbers set off smoke bombs before leaving the bank—a very unique MO that helped investigators link several bank robberies to the same perpetrators.

PHOTO 12.18–12.19: Here are two bank robbery notes believed to have been written by the same suspect in two different robberies. These notes could be used to link the same perpetrator to the crimes through handwriting analysis and/or possible DNA left on the notes.

VERBAL ACTIVITY OF THE ROBBER

What was said by the robber (or written, in the case of a robbery note) before, during, and after the robbery may be a strong indicator of MO. "Where's the money at?," "I want your money!," Give me your money!," and "Give me your cash now!" are similar demands but are also quite unique. Repeated use of one particular phrase may be the common denominator among robberies committed by the same offender. Sort of like how people feel comfortable in certain places, people also feel comfortable using certain words. They are likely to use those same words repeatedly in normal conversation, and in robberies. Words and expressions may also reveal peculiarities about the offender. Intelligent people may have a broader vocabulary than less intelligent people, young people may use different words than older people, and people who live in one part of the country may use different words than people who live in another part. In one recent series of robberies of gas stations and convenience stores in several different cities in a metropolitan area, the robber wore different clothing and covered much of his face in different ways, but he always stated to the clerk or attendant "Give me the money! Do you think this is a joke?" When the offender was eventually apprehended, several robberies were attributed to him and were cleared, partially based on his spoken words. The nature of the demand may also be rather unique. For example, consider the street robber that demanded, "Give me your money and take off your pants!" This is a rather strange demand among robbers and, along with similar descriptions of the perpetrator, provided investigators a good basis to conclude that the robberies were committed by the same person.

Robbery notes, most often used in bank robberies, may also provide useful evidence in the investigation. The note itself may contain fingerprints or DNA, or if the note is taken by the offender after the robbery, the note might later be found in the offender's possession or vehicle. The style of handwriting or penmanship of the note may be used in a handwriting comparison when a suspect is identified. The words used, and the spelling of those words, may be revealing.

THE WEAPON AND DISGUISE USED

Another potentially valuable lead in robbery investigations may be the identification and discovery of the weapon used to commit the crime. In particular, if a gun is used in the crime and can be described by the victim or witnesses, or if the gun was fired by the robber at the scene and ballistics tests reveal information about the gun, then investigators may be able to link the robbery to the person in possession of the gun if that gun is eventually seized by the police for some reason.

Usually a robber uses a disguise to make the identification of his or her face more difficult. An elaborate disguise may be more likely to be used by a more experienced or professional robber. A useful question to consider may be, what is it that the disguise might cover? A wig could be used to cover a bald head or a unique hair color or style. A bandana covering the mouth or face may be used to cover unique aspects of those features. Recall in the case introduction to this chapter that the perpetrators wore bandanas over their faces because one of them had gold teeth. Discarded and recovered disguises may link perpetrators to their crimes.

●●● Physical Evidence

Leads may be developed in a robbery investigation through physical evidence recovered from the scene. Of course, physical evidence is usually best at confirming the identity of a suspect who has previously been identified by some other means. In addition, robbery crime scenes are often not very extensive, and usually little physical evidence is available. The chapter introduction clearly illustrates this point. The robbers were first identified through

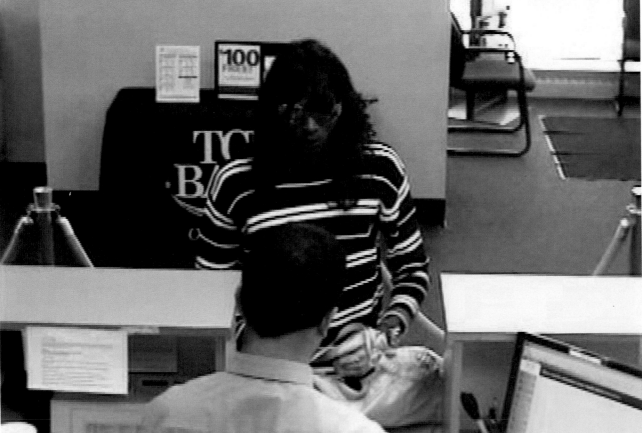

PHOTO 12.20–12.23: This man, disguised as a woman, is robbing the bank. Later, the police stopped the suspect's vehicle and discovered a wig in the front seat. This wig was used to link the suspect to one robbery, and then other evidence linked him to a second robbery he committed while wearing a different wig.

information provided by a confidential informant; once identified, a DNA comparison was made between one of the robbers and his blood that was left at the scene. This information, along with a confession, led to the perpetrators' conviction.

However, despite the fact that little physical evidence may be produced as a result of the crime, it is still critical that investigators search for such evidence. Fingerprints may be recovered from cash registers, countertops, entrance/exit doors, dropped cash, or from other items touched by the perpetrator before, during, or after the robbery. Demand notes may be recovered. In addition, in a surprising number of cases, the perpetrator leaves other valuable evidence behind (e.g., billfold, identification card, car keys, and clothing), or these items are lost along the escape route. As a result, it is important that investigators conduct thorough searches of robbery crime scenes and suspected escape routes.

Recall from Chapter 9 how the Washington, D.C., snipers were identified. In a robbery/homicide at a Montgomery, Alabama, liquor store committed several weeks prior to the shootings in Washington, police recovered a fingerprint from a gun catalog that the perpetrator was reportedly looking at in the store prior to the robbery. Along with a tip from the sniper himself, this fingerprint was eventually used to identify John Malvo as the perpetrator of the robbery/homicide in Montgomery. This ultimately led to his identification as one of the snipers in Washington. Even though it is uncommon at robbery scenes, physical evidence can definitely make a difference (see Case in Point 12.1).

The use of dye packs in bank robberies may prove useful in bank robbery investigations and may best be considered physical evidence. Dye packs are used by banks to prevent stolen money from being used, and thus they function as a robbery prevention strategy. Dye packs are contained in certain designated packs of bills and are placed into a bag by a teller with the other cash taken in a robbery. As the robber exits the building, a radio transmitter in the stack of bills is activated, and within seconds the dye pack explodes. Red dye is released and the package often burns. The dye may also stain the clothing and hands of the perpetrator. Finding cash stained in this manner, or finding a person stained in this manner, may lead to the identification of a robber. In this sense, using dye packs may also serve as an apprehension strategy. Sometimes dye packs are supplemented by tear gas, which is also triggered as the robber flees the bank exit doors. The tear gas is supposed to cause the robber to drop the money and be temporarily incapacitated (Weisel 2007).

●●● The Property Taken in the Robbery

Yet another source of leads in a robbery investigation may come from the money or property taken. If the items taken in a robbery can be found, the perpetrator may be identified. The primary motivation for robbery is money, and cash is what is most often taken (Wright and Decker 1997). Simply stated, robbery is all about the cash. This fact may also explain the recent increase in home robberies. If robbers want to go to where the cash is, houses often contain more cash than billfolds or purses. Most often, stolen money is used to buy drugs and alcohol, to gamble, and to buy clothes (Wright and Decker 1997). This direct and quick "payoff" is identified as part of the attractiveness of the crime to robbers. As stated by one robber:

> Robbery is the quickest money. Robbery is the most money you gonna get fast. . . . Burglary you gonna have to sell the merchandise and get the money. Drugs, you gonna have to deal with too many people, [a] bunch of people. You gonna sell a $50 or $100 bag to him, a $50 or $100 bag to him, it takes too long. But if you find where the cash money is and just go take it, you get it on all one wad. No problem. I've tried burglary, I've tried drug selling . . . the money is too slow. (Wright and Decker 1997, pp. 51–52)

CASE in POINT 12.1 — The Thief That "Blew It"

The owner of a jewelry store called 911 to report that someone had just grabbed four diamonds worth approximately $150,000 and fled from the store. When interviewed by the police, the witness explained that the man came into the store and asked about large diamonds, claiming that he was interested because he was going to purchase an engagement ring and wanted to get just the right diamond. The owner of the store led him to a room where she displayed for him four diamonds. After looking at them briefly, he grabbed them and fled out the front door of the store. She told police that he sped away on a dark-colored bicycle. She and another employee were able to provide a detailed description of the thief: He was described as being 5'6" or 5'7", with curly, dark brown hair down to his neck. He had large hands and short fingernails. He was wearing a black leather jacket down to his thighs, a striped polo shirt, black jeans, a gold necklace with a boxing gloves pendant on it, a gold watch, and a black beret type hat. She said that he said that he owned a construction company, but she did not think he sounded intelligent enough to actually own a business.

The two witnesses were further interviewed, and composite sketches were developed based on the descriptions they provided. Meanwhile, the table at which the suspect sat prior to grabbing the diamonds was processed for fingerprints, as was the front door through which he fled. Several prints were recovered from the front door. The bicycle was also found a short distance from the store; it too was examined for evidence.

Then, as explained by the lead investigator in his report:

> After I returned to the police department to process the evidence, I received a phone call from Officer Scannell who was with Mary Husar and creating a composite of the suspect. According to Scannell, Mary Husar had thought of something, which she forgot to disclose earlier. According to Officer Scannell, Mary Husar remembered that at one point while dealing with the actor, he had asked to use a Kleenex to blow his nose. Mary stated that she had handed the subject a Kleenex at which time he blew his nose and discarded the tissue into the garbage can in the side room. Mary Husar stated that the tissue, which was the only one in the garbage can, was still there. I returned to the Husar's store and collected the tissue, which supposedly contained nasal secretions from the actor. The tissue was processed as evidence and later taken to the crime lab for DNA testing.

While the DNA from the tissue was being analyzed, the fingerprints recovered from the door were submitted through a local AFIS system, as well as IAFIS, but there was no match.

There was a sticker on the bike from a bike shop 200 miles away; the bike shop was contacted, and investigators learned who had purchased the bike from the store. That person was located, but he said that the bike was stolen seven years ago from his garage (which was also located about 200 miles from the jewelry store).

One of the composite sketches was disseminated in the media, which led to several people being identified as possible suspects. Each person resembled the sketch but also had a strong alibi. The DNA profile was developed from the Kleenex and a search was made of the state's DNA data bank, but there was no match. The investigation appeared to be dead in the water.

About four months later, investigators received a phone call from another police department in the area. Investigators at this department said that they had a similar robbery of a jewelry store and that they had developed a suspect in the robbery. They sent a photo of the suspect to the investigators in the jewelry store robbery, who conducted a photo lineup with the witnesses from the store. The women at the store were unable to make an identification.

About two years later, investigators received a phone call from officers at a police department in a neighboring state about 250 miles away. These officers told investigators that they had a similar jewelry store robbery and had identified a suspect in the crime: Anthony Volpendesto. That suspect, they told investigators, was currently in prison on other charges. Another photo array was conducted with the two witnesses at the jewelry store; this time both identified the suspect. The DNA profile from the tissue was then sent to the neighboring state, and a search was conducted in their DNA data bank. There was a hit: Anthony Volpendesto. Investigators went to the prison with a warrant to obtain Volpendesto's DNA. They obtained buccal swabs and then submitted them to the crime lab for analysis. The DNA from the swabs matched the DNA from the Kleenex tissue.

After three years, the case was solved. If the witness had not remembered that the thief blew his nose, it is unlikely that a conviction would have been obtained, or perhaps even unlikely that the crime would have been solved. Volpendesto was sentenced to seven years in prison with an additional five years of extended supervision. He was also ordered to pay $27,500 restitution to Husar's jewelry store. Below are the two composite sketches (Exhibit 12.1 and Exhibit 12.2) that were developed of the perpetrator from the jewelry store witnesses, both done by the same artist.

It is very difficult for the police to recover stolen cash; it is typically spent immediately after it is stolen. Even in bank robberies, 80 percent of the stolen money is never recovered (Weisel 2007). It is possible, but extremely unlikely, that robbers might deposit stolen money into a bank account. More likely, but still not common, the sudden access to a large amount of money may be noticeable to the perpetrator's friends, associates, or family members, and this may prompt a tip to the police. As noted, yet another possibility is for the police to recover cash that has been stained as a result of an exploding dye pack. Other stolen property—taken as a result of robberies, burglaries, or other thefts—is also usually very difficult to find. Offenders may show off jewelry or other items taken in a robbery, however, and this might prompt a tip to the police. Another possibility is that the police may discover suspected stolen property (e.g., credit cards, identification card, a purse, or dye-stained cash) in the possession of an offender, and this property may then be linked to a particular crime victim.

Interestingly, stolen cell phones provide a good opportunity for investigative leads. When cell phones are stolen it is usually for one or two reasons: (1) to prevent the victim from quickly calling the police to report the robbery or (2) so the robber has a cell phone to use or sell. A surprising number of street robberies have been solved as a result of the robber using the stolen cell phone to call friends and associates. Cell phone numbers can be tracked, and important questions can be asked of the individuals who received the calls from the robber.

As discussed in more detail in Chapter 13, the process of converting property into cash is usually not very visible to the police. Few successful robbery investigations have had this development as the key to solving the case.

●●● Interrogation Considerations

Finally, with regard to the most productive interrogation strategies to use with robbers, it is important to realize that most robbers are generally angry, hostile, and desperate, and they generally have a strong attachment to the street culture (Wright and Decker 1997). They

Exhibit 12.2

Exhibit 12.3

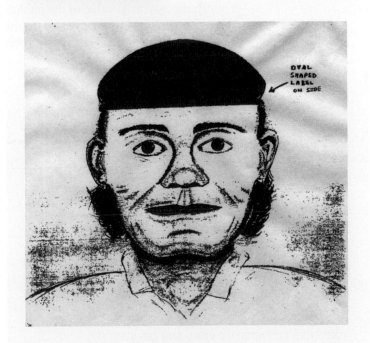

are unlikely to have feelings of guilt about their crimes. Accordingly, the most effective interrogation approach with robbery suspects is the nonemotional approach (recall Chapter 7). Minimizing the seriousness of the crime and convincing the suspect that his or her guilt has been, or will be, proved is likely to be most productive in obtaining useful information from the suspect during the interrogation.

••• Other Strategies and Sources of Information

Given the often-encountered challenges of investigating robberies, investigators may need to use other strategies and sources of information in identifying and apprehending the perpetrators. Several of these possibilities are briefly discussed here.

First, because there is a high rate of recidivism among robbery offenders, it makes sense to monitor the whereabouts of previously convicted robbers. In particular, probation and parole officers can be asked to notify the local police department when previously convicted robbery offenders are released back into the community. Detailed information about each offender, including his or her photograph, description, MO from previous robberies, and address, can be collected and made available for investigative purposes (Weisel 2007).

With specific regard to bank robberies, tracking devices may be useful. An electronic GPS tracking device that is placed among packs of bills taken by the robber could send a signal to the police as to the location of the money (and the offender). If it was known among would-be bank robbers that tracking devices were routinely used, these devices might prevent bank robberies from occurring. And even if they do not prevent robberies, the devices could certainly aid in the apprehension of bank robbers (Weisel 2007).

In bank robberies and possibly in other commercial robberies, the use of bait money could be useful for investigative purposes. Bait money is cash with sequential serial numbers that have been recorded by the bank or business. When the money is spent, the police attempt to track the source of the money, which can hopefully lead them to the robber. You may recall the introduction to Chapter 2 where the use of bait money led to the identification of the person responsible for the kidnapping of the Lindbergh baby in the 1920s.

Finally, the potential value of the publication of information on high-profile robberies and the use of tip lines to receive tips on these crimes cannot be underestimated. Citizens are often afraid of being caught up in a robbery, especially in a bank, store, restaurant, or their home, and they may be willing and interested in providing information to the police about such crimes when they have it.

MAIN POINTS ●━━━━━━━━━━━━━━━━━━━━━━━━━━━━━━━━━━━━

1. Robbery refers to "the taking or attempting to take anything of value from the care, custody, or control of a person or persons by force, threat of force, violence, and/or by putting the victim in fear." To establish that a robbery has occurred, the victim must state that property was taken by force and without permission.

2. There are several types of robberies: street robberies, convenience store and gas station robberies, vehicle-related robberies, bank robberies, and home invasion robberies. Street robberies are the most common; bank robberies are the least common.

3. The circumstances in which most robberies occur are not favorable for their solution; in particular, although there typically is face-to-face contact with the perpetrator, the perpetrator and victim usually do not know each other.

4. The value of a holdup alarm is not in preventing robberies but in apprehending robbers. Robbery holdup alarms are not likely to be false, and they provide for a fast police response.

5. Robberies have often been identified as one of the most potentially dangerous situations for the police. As a result, a top priority in responding to such calls must be the protection of officers' and victims' safety at the scene.

6. Typically, eyewitness descriptions of the perpetrator are the best evidence available in robberies. When available, security surveillance video may also be extremely useful.

7. The MO and signature of the robber may be used by investigators to link robberies together and to the same perpetrator, to clear crimes when an offender is identified and apprehended, and to provide other clues as to the characteristics of the perpetrator. In this regard, it may be meaningful to understand the target of the robbery, the apparent degree of planning involved in committing the robbery, how the robber approached the target, what was said by the robber, the nature of the demand(s), the weapons and disguise used, and the nature and method of the robber's departure.

8. The perpetrator's apparent familiarity with the target and the degree of planning involved in committing a robbery may also provide clues about the offender, especially his or her experience as a robber and age.

9. A street robber's approach can take several different forms: confrontations, blitzes, cons, and snatch-thefts. A convenience store robber's approach MO can be straight or through pretending to be a customer.

10. Usually a robber uses a disguise to make the identification of his or her face more difficult. An elaborate disguise may be more likely to be used by a more experienced or professional robber. A useful question to consider is, what is it that the disguise might be hiding?

11. The use of dye packs in bank robberies may prove useful in such investigations and may best constitute physical evidence. Dye packs are contained in certain designated packs of bills and are placed into a bag by a teller with the other cash taken in a robbery. As the robber exits the building, the dye pack is programmed to explode, staining the bills and the perpetrator.

12. If the items taken in a robbery can be found, the perpetrator may be identified. The primary motivation for robbery is money, and cash is what is most often taken. Most often stolen money is used to buy drugs and alcohol, to gamble, and to buy clothes. Stolen cash is seldom recovered by the police.

13. Most robbers are generally angry, hostile, and desperate. They are unlikely to have feelings of guilt about their crimes. Accordingly, the most effective interrogation approach with robbery suspects is likely to be the nonemotional approach.

14. Monitoring previously convicted robbers, using bait money, and using tip lines may be useful strategies in identifying and apprehending robbery offenders.

IMPORTANT TERMS

Armed robbery

Bait money

Blitzes

Closed circuit television (CCTV)

Commercial robbery

Confrontations

Cons

Dimensions of robbery MO

Dye packs

Home invasion robbery

Mugging

Prevention versus apprehension

Professional versus amateur robbers

Robbery

Snatch-thefts

Street robbery

Strong-arm robbery

Vehicle-related robbery

QUESTIONS FOR DISCUSSION AND REVIEW

1. What are the major types and characteristics of robbery?

2. Why do robberies typically have a relatively low rate of solvability?

3. What is the value of robbery holdup alarms?

4. What procedures should police officers use when approaching robbery scenes?

5. What is the potential value of eyewitness identifications and CCTV video surveillance cameras in robberies? What are the common limitations of such cameras?

6. What might be inferred about a robbery perpetrator based on the target that was selected to be robbed and the amount of planning that appeared to be present in the robbery?

7. How do the MOs of an amateur and professional bank robber differ? Why are bank robberies more likely than other robberies to be solved?

8. What is the potential investigative value of the robber's verbal activity during the robbery?

9. What types of types of physical evidence may be present at robbery crime scenes?

10. What property is of most interest to robbers? Why?

11. What interrogation approach is most likely to be effective with robbers? Why?

12. What other evidence may be available in robbery investigations?

 STUDENT STUDY SITE

Visit **www.sagepub.com/brandl3e** to access additional study tools including eFlashcards, web quizzes, web resources, video resources, and SAGE journal articles.

13

The Investigation of Burglary, Vehicle Theft, Arson, and Other Property Crimes

Objectives

After reading this chapter you will be able to:

- Discuss the characteristics and varieties of burglaries and explain the difficulties of investigating burglaries

- Identify the five primary aspects of a burglary offender's MO

- Discuss the potential value of physical evidence and informants in burglary investigations

- Discuss the characteristics and varieties of motor vehicle theft identify potential value

- of physical evidence in those investigations

- Identify the various methods of stealing a vehicle and what inferences may be made about the offender on this basis

- Discuss the characteristics and varieties of arson and describe the unique challenges of investigating arson

- Discuss how establishing a motive for the arson may be useful in an investigation and

- identify the various arson motives

- Discuss the characteristics and varieties of larceny theft

- Discuss the challenges of investigating larceny and explain why investigating this crime often takes low priority in police departments

- Discuss interrogation considerations with arsonists, burglars, and other thieves

From the CASE FILE
Dad and Daughter Go to Work

During November and December of 2011, Middleville police responded to approximately 1,000 burglary incidents. At least three of these burglaries were committed by the same perpetrator, and one of those three was committed by the perpetrator and his daughter. These three cases and their corresponding investigations are described here. These cases highlight the value of the stolen property in a burglary investigation, as well as the roles of victims and witnesses, computer data systems, physical evidence, and interrogations.

On November 30, 2011, the Middleville police were called to 8021 W. Tripoli Avenue for a burglary complaint. Upon arrival, officers spoke with Dustin Maas, who stated that he left the house for work at about 10:40 a.m. and returned at approximately 3:15 p.m. When he arrived home, he discovered that the window on the rear door of the house was broken. He entered the home, armed himself with a knife, and proceeded to check if anyone was in the house.

Finding no one in the house, he proceeded to his bedroom and saw that his HP laptop computer, Dell computer, and iPod were missing. He then called his mother to tell her what had occurred. Dustin's mother, Pam Mrozinski, was also on scene when the police arrived. She reported to officers that approximately thirty pieces of jewelry valued at about $50,000 were taken from her bedroom. An itemized list and description of the stolen jewelry was provided to the police. Pam explained that one of the missing pieces was a very unique ring. It was described as yellow gold, with a teardrop shape and ¾ carat diamonds set on a black background.

A neighborhood canvass of the area was conducted. One of the three neighbors contacted reported that at about 11:00 a.m. she saw a white vehicle parked at the west end of the alley. Photographs of the scene were taken. Using black magnetic powder, fingerprints were searched for, but no usable prints were found.

PHOTO 13.1: Entry to the house was obtained by breaking the glass on the door and either opening the door from the inside or crawling through the window.

On December 7, investigators entered the description of the teardrop gold diamond ring into the state's computer system, which contains information on all reported secondhand sales transactions of merchandise at jewelry stores and pawnshops. It was discovered that a ring matching this description was sold to Robert Haak Diamonds the day of the burglary (November 30) by a James C. Hilton in transaction #6818. Hilton's address was listed as 2787 Swann Ave. in Middleville. During this transaction, eleven other rings, three bracelets, and three necklaces were also sold to the store by Hilton. Investigators obtained photographs of the jewelry from the computer system and then showed them to the victim. Upon viewing the photographs, the victim identified all twelve rings and other items as belonging to her. The

jewelry store was contacted and advised to hold all of the items in transaction #6818. The next step was to locate and question James Hilton.

The next day, December 8, Middleville police were called to another burglary. This one was at 4598 S. 42nd Street. The victim, Audra Raade, told police that about 2:00 p.m. she was at home. She was not feeling well and was laying on the couch in her living room. She heard someone knock at her front door and ring the doorbell. She said that she got up, looked outside, but did not feel well enough to answer the door. She said she saw a white car that she did not recognize parked in front of her house. She went back to the couch and fell asleep. She then heard glass break. She woke up, ran out of the house to the neighbor's house, and called the police. Upon reentering the house with the police officers, she discovered that jewelry and a blanket were missing from her bedroom. An inventory listing of missing jewelry was recorded. A canvass of neighbors revealed no additional information. Fingerprints at the point of entry were searched for, but none were found.

The next day, December 9, a burglary was reported at 5209 E. Fillmore Avenue. The victim reported that when she came home from work at about 12:40 p.m., she found the side door window smashed and the door open. She went in, noticed things out of place, and then ran to the neighbors, at which point she called the police. She told officers that a homemade pie was missing from the kitchen counter, as was a potholder that was on top of the stove. The paper plate the pie had been on was found in the front yard. She noticed that in the living room the television had been unplugged and moved. In the den, the drawers to the dresser were open, and a camera, two cell phones, and a handheld game system were missing. In her bedroom, her jewelry box was empty. Missing were several rings, chains, pendants, and bracelets. Officers obtained an itemized list of all the missing property. Photographs of the scene were taken, and latent prints from the living room television were obtained. A neighborhood canvass was conducted, but the two neighbors who were home did not see or hear anything out of the ordinary.

PHOTO 13.2: The bedroom from which the jewelry was taken.

PHOTO 13.3: The stolen computer was taken from this table.

PHOTO 13.4: Similar to the previous burglary, the window of the door was broken in order to gain entry.

PHOTO 13.5: Again, a door window was broken to gain entry.

PHOTO 13.6: Jewelry was stolen from this jewelry box.

PHOTO 13.7–13.8: Fingerprints were found on the big-screen TV at one of the crime scenes.

At about 4:00 p.m. on December 9, about three hours after this last burglary on E. Fillmore occurred, detectives who were investigating the first burglary on Tripoli Avenue went to James Hilton's home to talk to him about that burglary. At the house, investigators first spoke to Alyssa Hilton, the daughter of James Hilton. She stated that her father was not at home but allowed detectives to search the residence. After sever minutes of searching, James was found hiding inside a small wicker trunk in the upstairs bedroom. He was taken into custody and transported to the police station for questioning.

After being read his Miranda rights, Hilton agreed to answer the detectives' questions. He first told investigators that the jewelry that he sold to the jewelry store was his own personal jewelry that he had owned for many years. When investigators told him that they knew this was a lie, he changed his story and said that he actually bought the jewelry on Craigslist from a "Slovakian" guy named "Christian." He was adamant that this was the truth. As they were not making any progress, investigators returned Hilton to his jail cell. The next day he was questioned again. He continued to deny involvement in the burglary, although he admitted that when he purchased the jewelry from "Christian," he knew it was stolen. He also admitted using the cash he obtained for the jewelry to buy heroin from a guy named "Jaco." Then he told investigators that the jewelry he sold at the jewelry store actually came from "Jaco," not "Christian." That was all he had to say. Later on December 10, Hilton was questioned yet again. This time Hilton stated that he was involved in several burglaries during the past couple of weeks. He stated that one of these burglaries was on Fillmore. He stated that he knocked on the door and when no one answered he broke out a window on the door and reached through the door to unlock it. He stated that he took a strawberry pie, a camera, a cell phone, a GPS system, and some jewelry. He stated that he traded some of the items for heroin from Jackie Alvarado (aka "Jaco"). He also confessed to the burglaries that occurred on S. 42nd Street and on Tripoli Avenue. Hilton stated that he remembered the burglary on Tripoli Avenue because the house had a large fence around the backyard and because he got the largest amount of jewelry from there. He stated that he sold the jewelry he got from this house for about $2,300 (recall the victim estimated the value of the jewelry at about $50,000). He stated that with each of the burglaries he used his wife's white Grand Prix car and that all of the homes he broke into were chosen by him at random. He stated that he did not know anyone who lived in these homes. Hilton stated that he sold the stolen jewelry at various stores and used the money to buy heroin from Alvarado. He sold the other items to Alvarado for heroin.

Subsequent to Hilton's confession, a search was conducted of the jewelry and pawnshop record system for all transactions performed by Hilton. Several transactions at local jewelry stores were identified. The associated stolen jewelry was recovered and returned to its owners. All told, nearly three-quarters of the jewelry stolen in the three burglaries was recovered. The residence of Jackie Alvarado was also searched, although none of the stolen property was found. Alvarado was arrested for possession of heroin.

James Hilton was found guilty of three counts of burglary and sentenced to three years in prison (via a plea bargain). Jackie Alverado was found guilty of possession of heroin with intent to deliver and was also sentenced to three years in prison via a plea bargain.

One question remained: Whose prints were on the television at the Fillmore Avenue burglary? They were not from James Hilton. On April 25, 2012, as police worked through the backlog of cases, those prints were entered into the AFIS system and were subsequently identified as being from Alyssa Hilton, James's daughter. Her prints were in the AFIS system as a result of a previous theft conviction. On May 10, 2012, Alyssa Hilton was located, arrested, and questioned. After being informed of her constitutional rights, she told investigators that on the day of that burglary she was driving around with her father looking for a house to burglarize. She stated that her father needed money. She stated that her father parked the white Grand Prix on the street in front of the victim's residence. She went up to the side door with her father and saw him break the window of the door. She entered the residence with her father. Her father went upstairs; she went to the living room. She stated that there was a large window in the living room with a television in front of the window. She looked out the window and crouched down so she would not be seen. She stated that her fingerprints must have been on the television because she leaned on the television when she crouched down. She stated that her father brought a small duffle bag with him to carry the stolen property. She denied taking or carrying any property from the victim's residence. Alyssa Hilton was not charged for her role in the burglary.

Case Considerations and Points for Discussion

- What was the most important evidence in these burglaries that led to the identification of James Hilton as the perpetrator? Where did this evidence come from? What was the role of the police in identifying and collecting this evidence? What was the value of the physical evidence in the investigation? Of the witnesses?

- What were the most significant mistakes made by the perpetrator(s) in these burglaries? Why? In your assessment, did the police make any mistakes in investigating these burglaries? If yes, what were they? And why?

- As discussed several times in *Criminal Investigation,* investigators can learn something from just about every investigation. What do you think should be the biggest lessons learned by the police as a result of these burglary investigations?

●●● Varieties and Characteristics of Burglaries

The FBI defines burglary as "the unlawful entry of a structure to commit a felony or theft" (www.fbi.gov/about-us/cjis/ucr/crime-in-the.u.s/2011/crime-in-the-u.s.-2011/property-crime/burglary). Use of force to gain entry is not required to classify an offense as burglary. To establish that a burglary has occurred, there must be evidence of entry, evidence of theft from the structure, or evidence of a felony having occurred there, and the owner of the structure must state that entry was obtained without permission. Individual states may provide different definitions and classifications.

Burglary is a relatively frequent and serious property crime. In smaller police departments in particular, the investigation of burglaries uses a large proportion of investigative resources. Approximately 75 percent of burglaries are residential (e.g., houses, apartments), and most of these (53 percent) occur during daylight hours when residents are typically not at home. Of the nonresidential burglaries, approximately 65 percent occur during the nighttime hours when the establishment is closed. In 2011, the average reported loss per burglary was $2,185—approximately the same in residential and nonresidential burglaries. July is the month that sees the most burglaries; February the least. The most common items taken in burglaries are things that can be easily converted to cash and that can be easily carried away by perpetrators. This can include guns, jewelry, small electronics, and, of course, cash (Wright and Decker 1994).

From the perspective of burglary victims, the crime is often traumatic for at least two reasons: first, their property has been stolen, and second, their personal territory has been invaded. Because of insurance reimbursement, the emotional consequences and fear associated with the intrusion may be more significant than the property loss. Victims often view their burglary as a serious crime and, consequently, they may expect that the police will investigate the incident to the fullest extent, that the perpetrator will be apprehended, and that the stolen property will be recovered. However, the fact of the matter is that relatively few burglaries are actually solved (13 percent), and seldom is stolen property recovered (FBI 2012). Like with many other crimes, smaller cities tend to have a higher clearance rate for burglaries than larger cities.

Of the burglaries that are cleared, juveniles are disproportionately involved as perpetrators. This is the case in other property crimes as well. In 2011, 21 percent of the individuals arrested for burglary were younger than eighteen; 35 percent of arrestees (the largest proportion) were between eighteen and twenty-four. With regard to gender, about 85 percent of those arrested were male. Finally, nationally, approximately 67 percent of individuals arrested for burglary were white, nearly 28 percent were black, and other races accounted for approximately 2 percent (FBI 2012).

●●● Investigative Considerations
With Burglary

As evidenced by the low clearance rate, burglary is a difficult crime to solve. Generally speaking, it may be more cost effective to try to prevent burglaries from occurring in the first place than to rely on apprehension efforts. Much has been written about the effectiveness of various efforts in the prevention of burglaries (e.g., see Weisel 2004).

Burglaries are usually discovered only after the crime has occurred and the perpetrator has fled. In fact, one of the many problems associated with investigating burglaries is that it is often difficult to determine precisely when the crime occurred. This makes it more difficult to collect usable information from witnesses and to associate the suspect with the scene at a particular time, if a suspect is identified. In addition, given the typical lag between when the crime occurred and when it becomes known to the police, offenders are afforded more time to dispose of property. Furthermore, there are usually no eyewitnesses to a burglary. Physical evidence may not be found and/or collected. In short, most burglaries do not produce sufficient evidence for a perpetrator to be identified and apprehended.

So what are the possible keys to a successful burglary investigation? Physical evidence may be of great value, and it is important to look for this evidence, but there is a good chance it does not exist. The same is true for eyewitnesses. As shown in the case example presented in the introduction to this chapter, the property taken in the burglary may play an important role in the investigation, although it must also be understood that seldom is stolen

PHOTO 13.9: What might you infer about the offender that committed the burglary of this house, based on this photo?

property ever found. Other witnesses and informants may also play a role in successful burglary investigations, if they are identified or come forward. The perpetrator's MO is also potentially important.

●●● Burglar Alarms and the Initial Police Response

One might think that burglar alarms would be useful in that the police could respond quickly to them and make on-scene arrests as a result. However, unfortunately, burglar alarms seldom play an important role in burglary investigations. There are at least three reasons for this. First, some types of alarms can be easily foiled by knowledgeable burglars. Second, unlike holdup alarms in robberies, most burglar alarms are false. In fact, some estimates are that between 94 percent and 98 percent of alarm calls are false. As a result, many police departments do not even respond to such alarms (Sampson 2002). Third, many burglars have reported that they avoid places with alarms (Wright and Decker 1994). As such, alarms may be effective in prevention but not in apprehension. The bottom line is that burglar alarms usually do not contribute significantly to burglary investigations.

Most often, burglaries are discovered by residents when they return home or when employees show up at their place of business for work in the morning. Sometimes the police are notified by an alarm service company of a verified illegal entry. In any case, when the police are notified of a suspected burglary, it may be unknown if the burglary is in progress or if it happened some time ago (i.e., the burglary is "cold"). If there is any doubt, officers should respond as if the perpetrator is still on scene or in the area. A fast police response may lead to an on-scene apprehension, although it is more likely that the perpetrator would still be in the area or in the process of getting away. As such, it is important that officers be on the lookout for possible perpetrators. Whereas street robbers are likely to flee on foot, burglars are more likely to use a car. This has much to do with the type of property taken (e.g., a wallet versus a big-screen TV) and the logistical issues of transporting that property. The vehicle used by a burglar may be parked near the residence or several block away. There may or may not be a getaway driver. The description of vehicles parked and being driven in the area should be noted. License plate readers (LPRs; see below) may be quite useful in these situations.

Upon their arrival, it may be necessary for the police first to verify entry (the victim may have already confirmed entry, as in the cases presented in the introduction) and whether a perpetrator is inside or not. This is the process of "clearing" a building. If feasible and practical, a police canine may be useful in this regard. At this time, it is also necessary that the structure be observed from all sides to prevent an unobserved escape by the perpetrator. Although burglars tend not to be armed or violent (if they had violent tendencies, they would probably commit robberies), officers should take corresponding precautions in clearing the structure.

As usual, and as discussed in detail in Chapter 5, care should be taken when conducting a search of the scene. In accordance with Locard's Exchange Principle, officers should assume that evidence will be found. As discussed below, if physical evidence such as fingerprints or DNA is present, it is most likely to be found at the point of entry and/or the point of exit (e.g., door knobs, broken glass). However, of course, it may be found wherever it appears that the perpetrator was present. Officers should also be aware of other items such as tools and clothing that do not seem to belong where they are located; those items may have been left behind by the perpetrator. Also, as in other investigations, it is important that a neighborhood canvass be conducted. Neighbors may have heard or seen something that relates to the crime, but they may not realize that this is the case.

Descriptions of vehicles and possible suspects may be developed as a result of the canvass, as may other evidence. These are basic investigative activities that should be performed in all burglaries.

●●● The Burglar's Modus Operandi

A burglary offender's MO can be revealed in several ways, all of which can be determined through an examination of the scene and from information provided by the victim. The following information should be considered when determining a burglar's MO:

- Inferences about how and why the perpetrator selected this particular target

- The perpetrator's method of entry

- The type of property taken and not taken

- The apparent amount of planning that took place prior to the burglary

- How the perpetrator searched for property

Once MO has been established, it can be used by investigators to link burglaries together and to the same perpetrator, to help clear crimes when an offender is identified and apprehended, and to provide other clues as to the characteristics of the perpetrator.

THE PERPETRATOR'S METHOD OF TARGET SELECTION

Clues as to who committed the burglary may come in the form of information about how the target of the burglary was selected. Research has shown that the selection of a burglary target is rarely a spur-of-the-moment decision. Burglars usually have some knowledge about the contents of a target and the routine of the occupants before actually committing the burglary. According to Wright and Decker (1994), based on their study of burglars in Saint Louis, information about a target most commonly comes from the offender's own observations of it (62 percent of burglars stated that this was usually how they learned of the target and its contents). These offenders reported that they watched a specific dwelling for some time before burglarizing it and, most often, these places were discovered during the course of the burglar's normal living activities. As explained by one offender in Wright and Decker, "We'll pick a house; we'll be just walking around and stuff and we pick a house. . . . You see, it's real simple and easy, you know. It's got to be a house we done watched for a while" (p. 78).

The second most common way that burglars obtained information about the target was by knowing the occupants (21 percent). According to Wright and Decker, many burglars spoke of burglarizing neighbors or their drug dealers, or stated that they had jobs that brought them into potential target homes (e.g., as delivery people or cleaning people). One of Wright and Decker's subjects explained, "When I was reconnecting the cable line, I overheard the lady talking on the telephone and saying that they be out of town for a few days. And when I heard that, I knew what time it was, time to come back and help them out; watch they house for them" (p. 68). Only a few burglars (6 percent) stated that they usually learned of a target from information provided by someone else.

This knowledge of how burglars choose targets underscores the importance of investigators questioning victims about their neighbors, about people seen in the area, about workers who may have had recent access to the premises, or, in the case of business burglaries, about suspicious current employees or recently fired employees. Information about such subjects may turn into productive leads. Most burglars try hard to avoid entering occupied houses. Accordingly, investigators should also ask victims questions about whether anyone approached the house or knocked on the door and about people making odd or unusual phone calls to the residence.

THE PERPETRATOR'S METHOD OF ENTRY

About two-thirds of burglaries involved forced entry (Weisel 2004). Windows, doors, and patio doors are common entry points. Burglars most often use screwdrivers or crowbars to pry open doors or windows, or they may simply break a window or kick in a door. In the other one-third of cases, the offenders do not force entry; they enter through unlocked or open windows and doors. Offenders may simply test many doors until they find one open. The entry point depends largely on the structure of the house and the visibility of windows and doors (Weisel 2004). The method used to gain entry into the premises may be a good indicator of the perpetrator's skill, experience, and other characteristics. For instance, a burglar who picks a lock or one who does little damage to a window frame when using a crowbar to gain entry into a residence is generally more experienced than a burglar who kicks in a door or smashes a window.

THE PERPETRATOR'S DEGREE OF PRE-OFFENSE PLANNING

Often a distinction is made between novice, professional, and mid-range burglary offenders. Compared to novice burglars, professional burglars tend to be more experienced, steal property of greater value, and are willing to commit potentially higher-risk burglaries. These offenders tend to engage in more pre-offense planning than novice offenders. It is also more likely that experienced burglars are older. Experienced burglars are also more likely to commit crimes farther away from their homes (Weisel 2004). On the other hand, burglaries committed by novice offenders are usually poorly planned. Their crimes are likely to be spontaneous events motivated by fun and excitement. Novices tend to be younger, make minimal gains from burglaries, and burglarize nearby dwellings. They tend to avoid places with dogs, alarms, or locks.

Evidence that a burglary was poorly planned might be that no tools were used to gain entry (to bring tools is to plan) or that risk factors did not appear to be considered in committing the crime (e.g., noise was not minimized when gaining entry). Novice offenders are more likely than professional offenders to commit crimes near their homes or on walking routes to or from other destinations. Mid-range burglars most often fall between novice offenders and more experienced offenders in terms of their methods and characteristics. One defining characteristic of mid-range burglars is that they more often work alone than do the others (Weisel 2004). An important distinguishing feature between the types of burglars is their outlet for stolen goods. Professionals tend to have well-established outlets (e.g., fences), whereas novices do not.

It is noteworthy that juveniles, including juvenile burglars, tend to commit crimes in groups. Among some groups of juveniles, status may be enhanced through criminal behavior. This objective, however, is obtained only if others are told about the crimes that were committed or if the crimes are discussed among the perpetrators themselves. These conversations can be overheard, people can notify the police about these conversations, and good leads may result. Consideration of this possibility calls attention to the importance of tip lines and police officers in schools. Police school liaison and resource officers, as well as other officers in frequent contact with juveniles, are in a good position to develop, receive, or otherwise obtain information about criminal activity from students.

HOW THE BURGLAR SEARCHED FOR PROPERTY

The perpetrator's actions in searching for property may also be an indicator of his or her knowledge of the contents of the premises. For instance, ransacking is either an act of vandalism (and is most likely committed by juveniles) or it is a result of trying to find property

PHOTO 13.10–13.13: In this particular burglary, a brick was used to break a window through which the perpetrator(s) entered the house. The brick came from the landscaping of the house. What might this MO suggest about the perpetrator?

to steal. If one knows where desired property is located or hidden, there is little need for ransacking. In one case, a home in an upscale suburb was burglarized and approximately $60,000 of jewelry, coins, and other property was taken. The only item in the house that was disturbed was a dresser—specifically the third drawer of a four-drawer dresser—and the property was taken from this drawer. The drawer was pried open with a crowbar-type instrument. Given this MO, it appeared that the burglar knew exactly where the desired property was located. Investigators eventually arrested the housekeeper who worked at the house and her son.

THE PERPETRATOR'S CHOICE OF PROPERTY

The type of property that was stolen may also hold clues about the characteristics of the burglar. Most houses have a lot of things that could be taken, and burglars have to make choices. It would be difficult to take everything. What do they decide to take? What do they leave behind? Certain items are "CRAVED" by offenders more than others (see Felson and Boba 2010). These items are *c*oncealable, *r*emovable, *a*vailable, *v*aluable, *e*njoyable, and *d*isposable. Just about all burglars have an interest in taking small electronic items such as iPods or iPads, but few have an interest in washing machines. Offenders also tend to steal what they know, either because they like it or they know the value of it. For example, expensive art and jewelry is probably not of much interest to young or novice offenders, but video games and systems may be. The Mozart CD may not be taken, but the Rihanna CD would be. The Twinkies are taken, but the T-bone steak in the freezer is not. The Nike Air Force Max shoes are gone, but the Santoni Quisps remain. Other conclusions may be inferred as well. The big-screen television was taken? More than one person was involved. Several big-screen televisions were taken? The perpetrators used a van or a truck.

PHOTO 13.14: In a burglary investigation, it is important to determine not only what was taken but what was *not* taken. This can give investigators clues about the characteristics of the perpetrator.

••• The Investigative Value of the Stolen Property

In many solved burglaries, the recovery of the stolen property by the police had something to do with the identification of the perpetrator. If investigators can find the property, then they may find the thief.

Studies have shown that many burglars commit their crimes primarily for the purpose of supporting a drug habit (Wright and Decker 1994), particularly heroin addiction (Weisel 2004). Interestingly, some studies have suggested that burglars are most likely to use heroin, whereas robbers are most like to use cocaine. In either case, of course, cash is most often the best way to buy drugs (although property or sex is sometimes used as well). However, unfortunately for burglars, seldom is cash available to be taken in burglaries. As explained by burglars and robbers themselves, a disadvantage of committing burglaries compared to robberies is that with burglaries, property is most often stolen and that property needs to be converted to cash in order to be most useful. An additional major problem for burglars is that they can only expect to receive pennies on the dollar when they convert property to cash. A thief may need to steal $100 worth of goods to get $5 or $10 in cash. This is because there are usually significant "markdowns" taken in the process of converting the property to cash. There may be markdowns on the property as a result of damage done to it while stealing it, as a result of it being used, as a result of it being stolen, and as a result of the burglar's need to get rid of it quickly (Felson and Boba 2010). Recall that in the case example presented in the introduction to this chapter, the burglar received approximately $2,300 for jewelry that had an estimated value of $50,000.

The process of turning property into cash involves various degrees of risk (and effort) for offenders, and various degrees of opportunity for investigators (Table 13.1). The difficulty for the police is that the process is usually not very visible and occurs quickly after the property is taken. Property is usually converted into cash within hours of the crime (Wright and Decker 1994). In addition, to have even a remote chance of the property being recovered, the victim must be able to provide a detailed description of it.

There are at least five ways that offenders can convert property to cash (Wright and Decker 1994). The most common method is to sell the property to a friend, acquaintance, or relative. This is a low-risk and low-effort option for the burglar and, unfortunately for the police, it is not very visible. According to one of Wright and Decker's burglars: "Well, let's just say [I sell what I steal] to friends. . . . I mean I can't sell it to anybody else off the street cause that's basically just publicizing me" (p. 185). The buyer may realize that the property is stolen, but he or she has an incentive to keep the transaction quiet because if the property is discovered by the police, it would be confiscated.

The second option, and a frequently used one, is to trade the property for illicit drugs. Again, this is a low-visibility and low-effort process, and it highlights the importance of investigators searching drug houses for stolen property that could be traced back to particular burglary victims. Depending on the particular items stolen, this option may yield the least amount of value for the stolen property. More usable items such as electronics would be more likely disposed of in this manner than items such as rings and necklaces.

The third option for the burglar involves selling the property to a professional fence, which is a person who knowingly buys and sells stolen goods. As reported by Wright and Decker (1994), this option is used by more sophisticated burglars. Most burglars do not know a professional fence and would not know how to find one if they had to. The fact that fences are used as frequently as they are, however, means there is opportunity for the police to recover stolen goods and make arrests through undercover fencing operations.

A fourth option involves selling the stolen property to a pawnshop or secondhand store. As seen in the chapter introduction, the disadvantage of this option for burglars is that pawnshops and other stores that buy secondhand merchandise are highly visible and subject to police scrutiny. In many jurisdictions, operators of these stores are required by law to record transactions and take fingerprints and/or photographs of individuals who sell property. In addition, even if burglars are able to find a pawnshop that is willing to over-look the rules, it is unlikely that easily traceable property (e.g., anything with a serial num-ber) would be accepted. Of course, the disadvantage for burglars is the advantage for the police. If the police routinely monitor the property being purchased by stores in their juris-diction, useful information may be developed. Unfortunately for the police, disposing of property through pawnshops is usually not a common method for burglars. Unless a well-maintained and well-funded computer system is available, monitoring the sales prac-tices of secondhand stores could be a daunting task for the police. At the extreme, consider the city of Los Angeles. Los Angeles has approximately 120 licensed pawn shops and 4,000 other secondhand dealers. Of the millions of transactions that occur at these places, only a small percentage likely involves stolen merchandise.

A fifth but seldom-used option is selling property to strangers. There are many opportunities for these sorts of sales (e.g., Craigslist, eBay, swap meets, flea markets), and the markdowns are likely to be less in these types of sales than in others. However, the disposal of property in this manner involves much more effort on the part of the burglar and is time consuming. This defeats the purpose of committing the crime in the first place, as the whole idea behind committing the crime is to get quick money with minimal effort (Felson and Boba 2010). Furthermore, as noted, this type of transaction is potentially risky for the burglar.

The final and least common option is that the burglar keeps the stolen property for his or her own use. This is also risky and also defeats a primary reason for committing the bur-glary in the first place—to get money.

In short, finding the stolen property offers investigators a chance of finding the perpetrator. However, burglars tend to avoid risk in disposing of property, thus providing limited oppor-tunities for the police (see Table 13.1).

PHOTO 13.15: Retail stores that buy secondhand property offer an opportunity for burglars and other thieves to convert stolen property to cash, although this is a relatively risky option for offenders.

TABLE 13.1	Methods of Converting Stolen Property to Cash: Effort, Risk, and Reward		
METHOD	**LEVEL OF EFFORT**	**LEVEL OF REWARD**	**AMOUNT OF POTENTIAL RISK/ POLICE VISIBILITY**
Sell to a friend	Low	Low	Low
Trade for drugs	Low	Low	Low
Sell to a fence	Moderate	Moderate	Moderate
Sell to a pawnshop	Moderate	Moderate	High
Sell to strangers	High	High	High

●●● Physical Evidence

In burglaries, physical evidence most often takes the form of tool marks from screwdrivers or crowbars used to pry open doors and windows, other evidence at the point of entry or exit (e.g., fingerprints, footprints), or other items that belong to the perpetrator that are left at the scene. Additionally, in cases where things are broken, such as window glass, there may be blood. Any of these items could be valuable in identifying the perpetrator, but seldom are they found or collected. Burglary scenes are seldom processed for DNA evidence. Recent research, however, suggests that when DNA is collected from burglary scenes, more than twice as many perpetrators are identified and apprehended and more than twice as many cases are accepted for prosecution (Ritter 2008). So why aren't more police departments doing it? Cost. On average, it costs an additional $1,400 to collect and process DNA evidence from burglary scenes, $4,502 to identify the burglar who otherwise would not have been identified, and $14,169 to arrest a burglar who otherwise would not have been identified (Ritter 2008). Clearly, when it comes to crime solving, there are trade-offs. This research had several other interesting findings: perpetrators were five times more likely to be identified through DNA evidence than through fingerprints, blood was more effective at solving these crimes than other biological evidence, and evidence collected by evidence technicians was no more likely to result in an identification of the perpetrator than when the evidence was collected by patrol officers.

There is reason to believe that physical evidence (biological and otherwise) would be found at burglary scenes if scenes were more thoroughly searched. Most burglars claim that they are typically inside a premise no longer than a few minutes, that their stress levels are high, and that they are in a hurry while committing the burglary. As stated by one burglar, "I be shakin' when I'm [doing a burglary] cause, you know, I have a feelin' that I'll be caught. But I'm tryin' not to think about that and have faith in what I'm doin'" (Wright and Decker 1994, p. 128). The burglar's potential haste inside a premise creates the possibility that he or she will make mistakes. Clearly, this fact underscores the importance of a thorough crime scene search by investigators. At the least, in the haste of looking for valuables and fleeing the residence, personal items such as a billfold, keys, or clothing may be dropped by the perpetrator, or other physical evidence may be left behind. Depending on the nature of the evidence, it could be useful in an investigation. As seen in the introduction to the chapter, the perpetrator who left her fingerprints on the television may not have even realized at the time that she touched the television, given her immediate concern with serving as a lookout for her father.

Once inside premises, burglars try to minimize the amount of time they spend there. This is simply a risk reduction strategy. The burglars in Wright and Decker's study (1994) reported that they immediately go to the master bedroom in search of property. They commonly search dressers, bedside tables, the bed, and the bedroom closet. The second most common place to search for valuables is the kitchen, followed by the bathrooms. As a result, these are also good places for investigators to search for fingerprints and other evidence.

●●● Informants

In the course of an investigation, it is possible that individuals unconnected to the burglary but who have knowledge of the burglary, the perpetrators, or the property taken in a burglary, might contact or be otherwise located by the police. Criminals tend to know other criminals. There may be competition (and jealousy) among them. As a result, it is little wonder that informants can be a valuable source of information in criminal investigations—even burglary investigations. Regardless of the informant's motivation, such information may be the key to identifying the perpetrator(s).

●●● Other Considerations in Burglary Investigations

Many burglars tend to be prolific, committing large numbers of crimes. Wright and Decker (1994) found that 35 percent of their sample of burglars committed more than eleven burglaries a year (20 percent of these committed more than forty-nine burglaries a year). In addition, the burglars in their study were involved in a variety of other crimes as well—including theft, robbery, assault, and murder—although to a lesser extent than burglary. Through the course of an investigation, if a perpetrator is linked to a burglary, the investigative challenge is to determine the other crimes for which he or she is responsible. In this way, it is possible to clear many crimes and potentially recover a lot of property with just one arrest. Again, the property found in possession of the offender may be traceable to particular crimes and be useful in attributing responsibility for those crimes.

●●● Varieties and Characteristics of Vehicle Theft

Motor vehicle theft refers to "the theft, or attempted theft, of a motor vehicle and includes the stealing of automobiles, trucks, buses, motorcycles, motor scooters, snowmobiles," and so forth (FBI 2012). To establish that a vehicle theft has actually occurred, the police need to determine that the vehicle was taken from the owner without the owner's consent.

In many jurisdictions, vehicle thefts and burglaries occur at about the same rate. Accordingly, about equal investigative resources are allocated to them. Seventy-four percent of vehicle thefts involve automobiles (FBI 2012), and most of these occur for the purpose of joyriding (Keister 2007; Fleming 1999). The largest percentage of vehicles are stolen while parked on a street outside the victim's home (Bureau of Justice Statistics 2012a), simply because that is where most cars are parked. However, hour for hour, cars parked in parking lots and structures are at most risk of being stolen (Clarke 2010). The average value of motor vehicles reported stolen in 2011 was $6,089 (FBI 2012). Urban areas generally have a much higher rate of vehicle theft than rural areas. Cities near major water ports (e.g., Miami) and in proximity to the Mexican border (e.g., San Diego) typically experience the highest vehicle theft rates in the country. Indeed, according to Aldridge (2007), about 33 percent of all recorded vehicle thefts in the United States occurred in the four states bordering Mexico (California, Arizona, New Mexico, and Texas), even though these states only account for about 23 percent of all vehicles in the country.

Motor vehicle thefts have one of the highest reporting rates (approximately 83 percent of vehicle thefts are reported to the police) but one of the lowest clearance rates. Interestingly, even though about one-half of stolen vehicles are eventually located, in only about 12 percent of such crimes are offenders identified and arrested (FBI 2012). Of the vehicle thefts in which an arrest is made, juveniles are often the perpetrators and the purpose of the theft was a joyride. In 2011, nearly 21 percent of the individuals arrested for vehicle theft were younger than eighteen. Nearly 46 percent of those arrested were younger than twenty-five. With regard to gender and race of arrestees, approximately 82 percent of those arrested were male, and about 64 percent of arrestees were white.

MYTHS & MISCONCEPTIONS *13.1*

Expensive Cars Are the Most Frequently Stolen

In contrast to media portrayals of vehicle theft—and what may seem to make most sense—the vehicles that are most frequently stolen are not new, expensive, or even all that desirable. Rather, they are the ones that are common on the road and that do not have factory installed antitheft technology, thus making them easier to steal. According to the National Insurance Crime Bureau, the cars listed below were the most frequently stolen vehicles in 2012:

- 1994 Honda Accord
- 1998 Honda Civic
- 2006 Ford F Series Truck

- 1991 Toyota Camry
- 2000 Dodge Caravan
- 1994 Accura Integra
- 1999 Chevrolet Silverado Truck
- 2004 Dodge Ram Truck
- 2002 Ford Explorer
- 1994 Nissan Sentra

Clearly, among most auto thieves, ease of theft is a more important consideration than style or value.

••• Investigative Considerations With Vehicle Theft

Similar to burglaries, and as indicated by their low clearance rate, vehicle thefts are difficult to solve. Usually they occur very quickly, usually there are no eyewitnesses to the crime, and, unless the vehicle is recovered, there is likely to be no physical evidence (and seldom is there usable physical evidence even if the vehicle *is* recovered). Even though most stolen vehicles are recovered, many are not recovered intact, and there is usually little information available that will lead to the identification and apprehension of the perpetrators. As such, prevention is generally a more productive approach to the problem of vehicle theft than is apprehension. Prevention efforts range from the simple, such as not leaving keys in the ignition of an unattended car, to the more sophisticated, such as the use of car alarms, fuel cutoffs, or other devices such as LoJack® or OnStar® that can be installed on vehicles to identify their locations and assist in their recovery if they are stolen.

Overall, the best chance of apprehending the thief occurs if the vehicle is located. And to be realistic, even then the odds are still not very good; in only about 20 percent of thefts where the vehicle is found is an arrest made. If a vehicle is located without a driver, there is a chance that evidence and clues might be present, including physical evidence inside the vehicle. A better chance to apprehend the thief comes if the police can locate the vehicle while it is being driven. The best chance at apprehending the thief is to locate the vehicle while it is being driven *by the thief who stole it*. In the scheme of things, seldom does that happen. Unless the vehicle is discovered, investigators may only be able to draw conclusions about the offender based on the offender's MO. Again, this is not much, but it is something. As with other types of investigations, MO can be used by investigators to link vehicle thefts together and to the same perpetrator, to help clear crimes when an offender is identified and apprehended, and to provide other clues as to the characteristics of the perpetrator.

POLICE OFFICERS ON THE LOOKOUT, VINS, AND LICENSE PLATE READER (LPR) TECHNOLOGY

As noted, even if the stolen vehicle is recovered, there is a good chance that this will not lead to the apprehension of the person who took it. Many vehicles are stolen for the purpose of joyriding, and when the ride is over, the car is simply abandoned and not found in the possession of anyone. One of the best ways to apprehend a motor vehicle thief is to find the perpetrator when he or she is still driving the vehicle. Because of their presence on the streets, patrol officers are in a good position to be on the lookout for stolen vehicles. While on patrol, officers can query license plate numbers of suspicious vehicles in their license plate registration computer system to see if the vehicle has been reported stolen. There are several good indicators that a vehicle may have been stolen. These indicators include:

- The vehicle being operated without ignition keys, or the use of material to disguise the lack of missing keys

- A broken or otherwise exposed steering column

- Broken window glass

- Dirty license plates/tags on a clean car or clean plates on a dirty car (indicating false or stolen plates)

- Expensive car parts on an inexpensive car or inexpensive parts on an expensive car

- A missing trunk lock

- VINs on the same vehicle that do not match

- A license plate that does not register to the make, year, and model of the vehicle it is on

Along with license plate numbers, the vehicle identification number (VIN) of a vehicle is useful when identifying the vehicle as being stolen. Every vehicle has a unique VIN. On car models newer than 1981, the number consists of seventeen numbers and letters. On automobiles, the number is usually located on the front driver's side dashboard and can be seen through the front window. On some models, the number is located where the driver's side door latches to the vehicle body. The VIN is also normally printed on the vehicle title. The VIN may also be located on certain engine and other parts of the vehicle. When a vehicle is reported stolen to the police, the vehicle's VIN is entered into the NCIC database. When a suspected stolen vehicle is recovered, NCIC can be queried with the VIN to see if the vehicle has, in fact, been reported stolen. With the discovery of the stolen vehicle, leads in the investigation may be developed.

Technology, particularly license plate reader cameras (LPRs), may also assist in the discovery of stolen vehicles. License plate readers are "smart" cameras that are linked to stolen vehicle license plate databases. The camera can be mounted either on a stationary base or on mobile police cars. These devices continuously scan and capture images of license plates on cars that are moving or that are parked. They can signal when a scanned plate has been reported stolen (Stauffer and Bonfanti 2006). Some LPR systems can also be queried for license plate numbers (and partial numbers) and can indicate when and where the license

PHOTO 13.16: Every vehicle has a unique vehicle identification number (VIN), and this number can be useful in identifying a suspected stolen vehicle.

plate was recorded. They may also be able to produce images of the vehicle in question. There has not yet been any systematic research that has examined the effectiveness of LPRs, but accounts provided by some agencies have not been especially encouraging. The systems are expensive and can be foiled (e.g., when a plastic cover is placed over the plate). However, upgrades and evolution of the technology may reduce the significance of these limitations (Petrossian and Clarke 2011).

PHYSICAL EVIDENCE

A stolen vehicle that has been recovered may contain property and physical evidence that can be linked to a particular suspect. The presence of such evidence may assist in identifying the person who stole the vehicle. Accordingly, recovered stolen vehicles should be processed as crime scenes. The vehicle should be impounded and an inventory of all items in the vehicle should be made. The vehicle and items located in it can be processed for fingerprints and/or DNA. Common locations for DNA and fingerprint evidence in a vehicle include the steering wheel, dashboard, seats, and rearview mirror. In some cases the perpetrator(s) may take actions to render the interior worthless as a source of physical evidence. For example, in one recent case, before abandoning the vehicle, the perpetrators spayed what appeared to be WD-40 throughout the entire interior of the vehicle. In another case, the vehicle's interior was set on fire. These actions could make the recovery of useful physical evidence more difficult, if not impossible.

PHOTO 13.17–13.21: Items found in a recovered car, damage to the car, or, in this case, graffiti writing in the car may provide clues as to the identity of the perpetrator. How might the evidence photographed here be useful in the investigation of this vehicle theft?

MODUS OPERANDI: THE MOTIVE FOR, AND METHOD OF, THEFT

The way in which the vehicle was stolen may be evidence in a motor vehicle investigation. Investigators may be able to identify the method used to steal the car from the information provided by the victim or upon recovery of the car. In particular, the perpetrator's MO may reflect the degree of planning involved in the crime and the sophistication of the thief. As with burglaries, more sophisticated methods are usually used by older, more experienced, criminals. Generally speaking, the least sophisticated methods of stealing vehicles are the most commonly used. For example, less sophisticated methods involve offenders using keys that have been left in the ignition, finding a spare key hidden on the outside of the car, commandeering a running but unattended car, or stealing keys from a car owner. In most of these instances, vehicle theft is a crime of opportunity; the thief is on foot and sees an opportunity to steal a vehicle. If the thief is on foot, chances are that the thief is in proximity to where he or she lives. As such, one may infer that when a less sophisticated method is used to steal a vehicle, the offender is young and lives in the area. Again, it may not be much information, but it is a start.

More sophisticated methods of vehicle theft involve hot-wiring a car by breaking open (or "peeling") the steering column and bypassing the ignition to start the car, stealing keys from a parking lot attendant, towing the car away, or doing a "bump and run" (when one individual bumps a target vehicle on the road and, when the motorist gets out of the vehicle, the thief enters the car and drives away). Perhaps the most sophisticated (and least common) method involves obtaining the ignition code number from the vehicle and making a duplicate key with a portable key maker. Perpetrators who use these methods are more likely to be older and to live farther way from the site of the crime.

PHOTO 13.22: This vehicle was stolen by bypassing (and removing) the ignition.

The method used to steal the car may relate to the motive for stealing it. There are two primary motivations for stealing vehicles: joyriding and profit (although vehicles are stolen for other reasons, like to use as a getaway car, this is relatively infrequent). Joyriding is most likely associated with less sophisticated methods of theft and is most common among young perpetrators. They are most likely to steal a car when the opportunity presents itself and for purposes of fun and excitement. As noted, cars used for joyriding are usually recovered, although not necessarily in complete form or in the same condition as when they were taken. As is the case with burglaries committed by juveniles, juveniles are likely to talk about having stolen a vehicle, and this represents an opportunity for the police.

The other primary motivation for vehicle theft is more instrumental in nature: profit. First, it is not unheard of that a vehicle owner would dispose of his or her car (through a sale or other means) and then report it as stolen in order to collect insurance settlement. Insurance fraud is always a possibility, and investigators must be aware of it.

Second, thieves who steal vehicles for profit are more likely to use more sophisticated methods to steal the vehicle than are thieves who steal a car for convenience or fun. Perpetrators can convert stolen vehicles into cash in a number of ways. Once again, each method reflects differences in the skill and sophistication level of the perpetrator. Offenders can attempt to sell the car outright after slight or major modifications to it, they can strip the car and sell its parts, they can transport or simply drive the vehicle out of the country, or they can use a combination of these options (e.g., they can steal cars and then sell them to someone who transports them). Most common among these options involves the stolen vehicle being

PHOTO 13.23: A stolen vehicle is recovered by the police in an alley. Police can make inferences about the characteristics of the perpetrator and his or her motive based on the discovery of the vehicle at this location and in this manner.

stripped at a "chop shop." The car parts are then sold to salvage yards or dishonest body repair shops. These places can make money by buying the stolen car parts at a deep discount. Some parts of vehicles are quite valuable, including air bags, high-intensity headlamps, and catalytic converters (Keister 2007). A frequent target are "ordinary" cars; the more common the car, the larger the market for its parts. Police monitoring of car part and body shop outlets may produce useful leads in auto theft investigations.

Selling cars overseas is probably the most profitable means of converting stolen cars into cash, but is also the most difficult. The National Insurance Crime Bureau (NICB) estimates that 30 to 35 percent of unrecovered stolen vehicles are exported out of the country. Oversees buyers will often pay double the original purchase price for a quality automobile. Vehicle thieves may be sophisticated and devious enough to get around U.S. Customs procedures. The easiest and most common method is to simply drive the stolen vehicle across the border—the Mexican border in particular. If the car is driven across the border before it is reported stolen, it is very unlikely that the offender will ever be apprehended (Petrossian and Clarke 2011). Once the car is in Mexico, it can be taken to a chop shop, be shipped to points beyond, or be sold and used in Mexico. It is estimated that between 70 and 80 percent of vehicles stolen in southern border cities end up in Mexico (Ethridge and Gonzalez 1996).

CASE in POINT 13.1　Finding Your Stolen Car on eBay

In 1970, Robert Russell's 1967 Austin-Healey was stolen while it was parked in front of his house in Philadelphia. Although the police were unable to recover the vehicle, Russell never gave up looking for his car. In 2012, he was searching eBay and saw what he thought was his car listed for sale by a Beverly Hills, California, car dealership. Russell still had the car's title, and, with the assistance of the Philadelphia police, the car was impounded and returned to him.

Source: "Robert Russell Found His Own Car, Stolen 42 Years Ago, on eBay." (2012). Huffington Post. July 15. www.huffingtonpost.com/2012/07/15/robert-russell-found-stolen-austin-healy-car-ebay-years-theft_n_1674198.html.

EYEWITNESSES AND SURVEILLANCE CAMERAS

Depending on the method used to steal the vehicle and the location from which the car was taken, there may be eyewitnesses to the crime, but it may be difficult to find them. If there are no eyewitnesses to the actual theft of the vehicle, there may be eyewitnesses to related events, such as the theft of the keys that allowed for the theft of the vehicle.

As noted, most vehicle thefts occur when cars are parked on the street near the owner's property. This fact is not surprising because this is where cars are most often located. However, the risk of theft, per hour parked, is greatest when cars are left unattended in parking lots. Particularly susceptible are cars in park-and-ride lots, downtown parking lots, shopping mall parking lots, and college parking lots (Clarke 2010). Once again, these are potentially busy areas where thefts may be witnessed by other parking patrons or captured on parking lot surveillance cameras. If the captured images of the perpetrator are clear enough, they may represent useful evidence in the investigations. If the only image captured by the camera is the vehicle being driven away, or of the license plate of the vehicle being driven away, of course this will not be very useful.

THE USE OF BAIT CARS

Given the difficulties in apprehending vehicle thieves, creative strategies may be called for. One such strategy is the use of bait cars. Essentially a decoy undercover operation, a car is placed on a street in plain view. The keys may be left in the ignition, or the engine may be left running. Undercover officers watch the car, and when a perpetrator attempts to steal it, they can apprehend the offender in the act. In some instances, sensing and GPS devices are placed on the car to signal when the car is moved and where it is located. The bait car may also be equipped with an engine "kill" switch that allows officers to remotely turn the engine off, thereby eliminating the possibility of a high-speed pursuit. This strategy is likely to be most effective (and least controversial) when used in an area experiencing a high rate of vehicle thefts (Keister 2007). Petrossian and Clarke (2011) reported that in 2003, authorities in Scottsdale, Arizona, deployed thirty bait vehicles, and by 2005 the use of this strategy led to 100 arrests. Most often such strategies are most effective at identifying young offenders interested in taking the car for a joyride. Depending on the technology used, these strategies can also be expensive to staff and operate (Stauffer and Bonfanti 2006).

INVESTIGATIVE TASK FORCES

Given the magnitude of the auto theft problem in the southern border areas, and the difficulty of investigating such crimes, several agencies have developed and operate comprehensive auto theft task forces. For example, consider the San Diego County Regional Auto Theft Task Force (RATT). Authorities in San Diego County developed RATT to combat individuals believed to be transporting stolen vehicles through Mexico to Guatemala and El Salvador (Casey 1995). RATT was a multifaceted response that included education, crime analysis, and law enforcement. Specifically, investigators identified and monitored chop shops in the San Diego area, developed their own undercover chop shop, and developed informants by infiltrating car theft rings. Between July 1992 and February 1995, RATT detectives recovered more than 780 stolen vehicles and made more than 100 arrests. A related investigation conducted by federal and state agents in California resulted in the arrest of twenty-eight suspects who ran an auto theft ring that shipped vehicles and parts from the Sacramento area to Russia and Eastern Europe (Organized Crime Digest 2000).

Another task force, named STATETF, used similar strategies with similar results (Ethridge and Gonzalez 1996). As in San Diego, the problem in south Texas is that a vehicle can be stolen and driven to Mexico even before the owner realizes that the car is missing. Investigators assigned to STATETF conducted surveillance of areas where auto thefts often occurred—parking lots at shopping malls, hospitals, grocery stores, movie theaters, and discount stores—so that they were in a position to take action as the crimes were occurring. They routinely inspected junkyards, vehicle repair shops, and used car lots to identify stolen autos and stolen auto parts. They developed and used informants to obtain information on auto theft rings. In addition, investigators went undercover as sellers and buyers of stolen vehicles.

In 1994, the Texas Department of Public Safety created the Border Auto Theft Information Center (BATIC), which acted as a communication link between United States and Mexican law enforcement. Bilingual personnel staffed a hotline that was accessible twenty-four hours a day, seven days a week to U.S. and Mexican law enforcement agencies in an attempt to provide real-time information on recent vehicle thefts. In addition, the program involved working with U.S. Customs to identify stolen vehicles, training Mexican officers on how to identify stolen vehicles, and working with these agencies in recovering stolen vehicles from Mexico (Petrossian and Clarke 2011).

No question, vehicle theft, particularly organized vehicle theft, is a difficult matter to investigate. RATT, STATETF, and BATIC are examples of proactive investigative responses to the problem.

●●● Varieties and Characteristics of Arson

Arson refers to "the willful or malicious burning or attempting to burn, with or without intent to defraud, a dwelling, house, public building, motor vehicle or aircraft, personal property, of another, etc" (FBI 2012). Fires that are simply suspicious or of unknown origin are not considered arson. To establish that arson has occurred, there must be evidence of the fire being deliberately set for the purpose of causing harm. One of the most common ways to help establish that arson has occurred is to confirm the use of an accelerant in setting the fire. Accelerants include gasoline, kerosene, and lighter fluid.

In most jurisdictions, arson is a relatively uncommon crime; however, the consequences of it can be serious. Property loss associated with arson can be considerable, and the possibility of the loss of life as a result of the fire is present. In 2011, the average property loss in arson crimes was just more than $13,000 per incident (FBI 2012). Structural losses averaged nearly $24,000, and losses associated with mobile property (e.g., automobiles) averaged just more than $7,000 per incident. Motor vehicles are the most common type of property burned in arson, followed by single-family homes (see Table 13.2). Larger cities (i.e., those with more than 250,000 inhabitants) generally have a higher rate of arson than smaller cities. This national trend may not represent the experience of individual jurisdictions, given their potentially unique conditions and circumstances.

In 2011, the clearance rate for arson was approximately 20 percent (FBI 2012), which is slightly higher than the rate for burglaries and auto thefts. As with other property crimes, smaller cities tend to have a higher clearance rate for arson than larger cities. Clearance rates are highest when arson involves community or public (e.g., schools) structures, and lowest when it involves motor vehicles (see Table 13.2). Of the cases of arson that are cleared, juveniles are involved as perpetrators at a higher rate than in other types of property crime. In 2011, 41 percent of the individuals arrested for arson were younger than eighteen. With regard to gender, more than 82 percent of those arrested were male. Finally, approximately 72 percent of individuals arrested for arson were white (FBI 2012). Of all FBI index crime arrests, whites are most highly represented in the crime of arson.

TABLE 13.2	Arson by Type of Property, Amount of Loss, and Clearances, 2011		
TYPE OF PROPERTY	**% OF TOTAL**	**AVERAGE $ LOSS**	**% CLEARED**
Total	100.0	13,196	19.9
Total structure	45.9	23,918	24.0
Single residential	22.2	24,990	22.6
Other residential	7.1	22,690	26.3
Storage	3.2	16,911	21.5
Industrial/ manufacturing	0.4	68,349	18.2
Other commercial	3.6	37,855	19.7
Community/public	4.4	26,610	36.2
Other structure	4.9	9,508	21.5
Total mobile	23.9	7,016	10.1
Motor vehicles	22.7	6,580	9.6
Other mobile	1.3	14,848	18.2
Other	30.2	1,813	21.3

Source: Federal Bureau of Investigation. 2012. *Crime in the United States, 2011 Uniform Crime Reports.* Washington, DC: U.S. Department of Justice.

••• Investigative Considerations With Arson

Little question, arson is a difficult crime to solve and poses unique challenges to investigators. In particular, the investigations associated with arson are unusual in that considerable time and effort are devoted to determining simply whether a crime was committed. Furthermore, the fire often (but not always) destroys critical physical evidence that could assist in determining whether it was maliciously and willfully set, and, if it was, in identifying and apprehending the perpetrator. Fire investigations are also often hindered by the lack of witnesses or the inability to locate them. Further complicating matters are that personnel from several agencies have interest and authority in fire prevention, control, and investigation. In particular, fire department personnel typically have the expertise in understanding fires and have responsibility for investigating fires in order to determine their cause. Law enforcement personnel have knowledge of the law and criminal investigation procedures and have responsibility for investigating arson in order to determine who committed the crime. The split responsibility in arson investigations has the potential to create conflict and coordination issues. What begins as a fire investigation conducted by the fire department may end as an arson investigation conducted by the police. The necessary involvement of representatives from other agencies, including rescue and emergency medical services, hazardous materials teams, utility company personnel, and health and safety officers, may create further challenges for communication, coordination, and control in such investigations. For all of these reasons, determining whether a fire resulted

PHOTO 13.24: Arson occurs when a person burns or attempts to burn property with the deliberate purpose of causing harm. Arson is a challenging crime to investigate as it can be difficult to determine if a fire is the result of arson. Also, often valuable evidence is destroyed in the fire.

from arson may be difficult, and determining who is responsible for the crime may pose additional challenges.

RESPONDING TO THE FIRE SCENE: INITIAL INVESTIGATIVE ACTIVITIES

The goals of the initial responders at a fire scene are to prevent harm to individuals who may be threatened by the fire, render aid to any people who have been injured, and extinguish the fire. It is also important for first responders to be aware of unusual circumstances or unusual activities of people at or around the scene. These observations may later prove to be relevant and informative in a criminal investigation. First responders should also be aware of possible evidence (e.g., shoeprints, broken windows) and either take reasonable efforts to preserve such evidence or make a mental note of it (National Institute of Justice 2000b). Observations must be communicated to investigators. It is also critical that first responders establish security and control of the scene. This is to prevent the unnecessary loss of evidence as well as to ensure safety. It must be understood that ensuring the safety of civilians and public safety personnel is the most important objective for first responders. In short, "The actions of first responders at a fire scene are not only critical to saving lives and suppressing fires; they also set the stage for the investigators arriving to process the scene by establishing a controlled security perimeter and initiating documentation of the scene" (National Institute of Justice 2000b, p. 19).

When investigators arrive, the goals become oriented toward the collection of evidence. In the early stages of a fire investigation, evidence is used to determine the cause of the fire. At this point, the evidence at a fire scene is not necessary *criminal* evidence; the evidence may simply help establish the cause of the fire. When the fire is determined to be as a result of arson, the evidence becomes *criminal* evidence and the investigation becomes a *criminal* investigation.

In the first stages of a fire investigation, several tasks are critical (see National Institute of Justice 2000b). The value of performing these tasks, which are listed below, will be especially evident if (or when) the fire is determined to be as a result of arson:

- Contact and communicate with first responders as to the status of the scene and activities performed.

- Establish the scope, size, and boundaries of the scene.

- Identify and interview individuals (possibly witnesses) at the scene; identify possible witnesses through a neighborhood canvass.

- Evaluate and determine the security access to the scene prior to and during the fire. "The investigator should determine whether the building or vehicle was intact and secure and if intrusion alarms or fire detection and suppression systems were operational at the time of the fire. This information

helps to establish factors such as ventilation conditions, possible fire development timelines and scenarios, and whether vandalism of the property or systems occurred prior to the fire" (National Institute of Justice 2000b, p. 24).

- Identify what is needed in order to collect evidence from the scene.

- Photograph (and videotape, if available) the exterior and, when safe, the interior of the structure. If possible, the crowd and the fire in progress should also be recorded. A scene sketch should also be created and should include dimensions of the structure and scene.

After documenting the scene, the next step is to process the scene:

- Identify, collect, and preserve evidence. Special care should be taken to collect evidence in any areas where

the fire may have first started (see indicators discussed below). Evidence should be collected in accordance with agencies' laboratory policies and procedures.

- Prevent evidence contamination by wearing clean gloves and garments and using clean tools and instruments when collecting evidence. Access to the scene should also be controlled and limited.

- Evidence must be packaged and transported in accordance with standard best practices (see Chapter 5).

- Establish and maintain the chain of custody.

EVIDENCE TO DETERMINE THE CAUSE OF THE FIRE

At a fire scene, evidence is collected in order to first determine the cause of the fire. Then, if the cause is determined to be arson, the evidence may be used to establish that a crime occurred and may be helpful in identifying who committed the crime. Determining the cause of the fire is usually a primary responsibility of fire department personnel. When the cause of a fire is suspicious at the outset, fire department personnel may assist investigators or provide direction in the detection of evidence at the scene.

Fires can be classified into several categories based on their cause:

- Natural (e.g., caused by lightning, heat from the sun)

- Accidental (e.g., stove fires, children playing with matches)

- Suspicious (e.g., not natural or accidental, but arson cannot be proved)

- Incendiary (i.e., arson; fires determined to be set deliberately and maliciously)

- Of unknown origin (when the cause of the fire cannot be established)

Legally, the presumption is that all fires have natural or accidental causes. There must be proof that the burning was the result of arson (that the fire was maliciously and willfully set) in order for it to be considered arson. On average, 16 percent of all reported fires are the result of arson (National Institute of Justice 2000b). The cause of a fire is most often established through statements of witnesses and the physical analysis of the fire scene. Arson in particular is most often established with evidence that an accelerant was used to cause the burning; however, this determination is also difficult as not all fires that involve an accelerant are arson.

To determine the cause of a fire, it is first necessary to identify *where* the fire started—in other words, to identify the point of origin. Most basically, for a fire to occur, it needs a source of heat and material to burn. The place that these two ingredients come together is referred to as the *point of origin of the fire*. In addition, items and other materials located at the point of origin may be informative regarding the cause of the fire and whether it was a result of arson. For example, items such as a timer (part of an ignition device) or newspaper (material ignited) located at the point of origin—and where they may not belong—may raise suspicions about the possibility of arson. The identification of the point of origin may be relatively easy or quite difficult depending on the amount of destruction caused by the fire. Generally, the more devastation there is to the property as a result of the fire, the more difficult it is to identify the origin (and cause) of the fire (see Bennett and Hess [1984] for a dated but still outstanding discussion of arson investigations).

The point of origin and the cause of the fire may be established by interviewing witnesses and firefighters, reviewing video surveillance camera images, reconstructing and examining the pattern of the fire, examining objects in the structure, and/or by locating the area of the structure with the most destruction from the fire. Statements of witnesses and firefighters regarding the fire are critical. For instance, investigators may learn about suspicious activity around the scene prior to the discovery of the fire (e.g., that juveniles were seen running from the scene). They may learn the presumed cause of the fire (e.g., that it was caused by careless smoking). From firefighters, investigators may learn about the condition of the fire on their arrival at the scene, the color of the smoke, the color of the flames, the location of the flames, the condition of doors and windows on arrival, whether people were present at the scene, whether there were suspicious persons or vehicles at or leaving the scene, the method of entry by fire department personnel, the removal of any property by fire department personnel, any unusual aspects of the fire, and the nature of the fire spread.

An examination of the fire pattern is likely to provide critical clues regarding the cause and origin of the fire and, ultimately, whether the fire was deliberately set. Most fundamental, it is instructive to examine what was burned in relation to what was not burned. For example, in an isolated fire it may be relatively easy to determine the point of origin because it would be what sustained damage from the fire (e.g., a reclining chair). A V-shaped pattern of flame staining and destruction often emanates from items that were on fire. In a fire that caused more extensive damage, it may be instructive to examine the layering of material and debris on the floor. If, for example, broken glass from a window is discovered on the floor and is covered by other burned material, it may indicate that the window was broken before the fire started and before the heat of the fire could have caused the glass to break. Also in this example, the distance of the glass from the window and the location of the glass in relation to the window, as well as the characteristics of the broken glass, could indicate whether the glass was broken prior to the fire (e.g., as a result of an incendiary device being thrown through the window), because of the fire, or as a result of actions taken by firefighters. In addition, the point of origin of a fire may be identified by tracing the fire from where the least damage occurred to where the most damage occurred. Areas that sustain the heaviest fire damage tend to indicate the point where the fire started.

An examination of objects in the structure may also provide clues regarding the origin (and cause) of the fire. Again, in general, objects that show the heaviest burning and charring damage tend to be at or near the point of origin. Identification of metal items that have melted can provide a basis for determining the heat of the fire. Various types of materials cause various heat intensities. For example, flammable liquids produce fires with extraordinary heat. In addition, an examination of furniture springs may be revealing regarding the nature and cause of a fire. Furniture springs are likely to sag as a result of a fire only when the fire originated from inside the cushions or from a fire external to the furniture that was intensified by a fire accelerant. Examination of light bulbs may also provide a clue regarding the heat of the fire and the direction from which it originated. Light bulbs tend to expand on the side that faces the source of the heat. In addition, hot and fast-moving fires (indicated by degree of destruction, white or blue-white flames, and black smoke) are usually associated with the presence of accelerants.

With regard to locating the area of the structure with the most destruction from the fire, burn indicators (the impact of fire on material) may be revealing. There are many factors that can influence the amount of char on wood; however, in general, the deeper the char, the longer the material was exposed to the fire. An area characterized by the deepest char may signal the point of origin of the fire. In most cases, the area that sustained the most intense burning is the point of origin.

As noted, the clearest indication of arson is the presence of flammable liquid at the point of origin; however, the presence of a flammable liquid does not necessarily mean that the fire was willfully and maliciously set. The associated circumstances are critical considerations. The presence of an accelerant can be positively detected through a variety of means, including human smell, scientific testing devices, and with canines that are trained to detect the odor of accelerants.

EVIDENCE TO DETERMINE WHO COMMITTED THE ARSON

It is one thing to determine that a fire was a result of arson; it is quite another to find the person who set it. As with burglaries, there are unlikely to be eyewitnesses to the crime of arson, although other people may come forward who have critical knowledge of the crime and/or the perpetrator. Video surveillance may contain images of people who were in the area before, during, or after the fire. Besides the evidence associated with the fire itself, physical evidence may play a relatively small role in arson investigations. Investigators should be mindful of the possibility that physical evidence exists, but they should also be aware that the fire and the measures taken to extinguish it can easily lead to the loss of such evidence. Because of the typical lack of evidence regarding who committed the crime, consideration of the motivation of the arsonist becomes an important aspect of the investigation. If it can be determined *why* someone would have wished to burn a structure or other property, it may provide a clue as *who* may have committed the crime. Evidence that associates the person with the scene may then be collected.

The motivations for arson are many (see Douglas et al. 1992). Arson may be an expression of anger or revenge. It is critical to determine whether, from the victim's point of view, there is anyone who may have sought revenge by destroying the victim's property. Did anyone make any prior threats about destroying the property? An ex-boyfriend? An ex-employee? An angry neighbor? When considering revenge as a possible motive, investigators should look to the relationships the owner of the property has with others. It is interesting that when female subjects commit arson it is usually for this reason and the items burned usually belong to a former boyfriend or husband. When a male subject sets a fire that is motivated by revenge, the target is usually a residence or business.

In addition, arson may be an act of terrorism—an organized effort aimed at creating fear and guided by political or other beliefs. For example, federal agents believe that the 2007 southern California wildfires, which resulted in more than $1 billion in lost property and displaced more than a million people, were intentionally set and probably perpetrated by members of the al-Qaeda terrorist group (Hagmann 2007; Schwartz 2012). And many instances have occurred over the years in which homes of African American ministers and churches were set ablaze. These cases represent hate crimes or terrorism (Bowes 2013).

Arson may be an act of vandalism. If this is the case, it would likely point to younger offenders, usually acting in a group, who live in the neighborhood or area where the fire occurred. As discussed earlier with regard to burglaries and vehicle thefts, young offenders are likely to talk about their actions among themselves and with others, and this may offer an opportunity for the police to identify them. Young, amateur offenders are also most likely to use flammable liquids to start a fire and not use a timing device. It is not uncommon that when flammable liquids are used, the person setting the fire gets burned in the process. As such, it may be productive for investigators to make inquiries regarding treatment for burns at medical facilities after a suspected case of arson is identified. More sophisticated and older arsonists are more likely to use some form of delayed ignition, such as candles, flares, cigarettes, or timers, to start a fire. Remnants of these items may be found at the point of origin.

Arson may be committed to conceal another crime, to destroy evidence in another crime, or simply to mislead investigators (i.e., staging). Most often, offenders are unsuccessful at concealing crimes through arson. However, it is essential that investigators are aware of the possibility in searching the arson crime scene. Evidence of other crimes at an arson scene may be obvious (e.g., a dead body with gunshot wounds to the back). Large amounts of liquid accelerants are often present at such scenes (Holmes and Holmes 2009). Usually the related crime offers more informative leads regarding who was responsible for it than the arson.

Another motivation for arson is profit. The basis for profit in arson is usually insurance fraud. Therefore, it is important for investigators to ask who would financially benefit if this property was destroyed. Was the property insured? For how long was it insured? Was it over-insured? What is the financial situation of the victim? Answers to these questions may be revealing and may lead investigators to the "victim" as the perpetrator or to a "hired torch"—an individual who was hired by the "victim" to set the fire and destroy the property. Other evidence of an "inside job" includes the absence of personal items from the fire scene, the absence of personal records and books, missing tools, pets that have been removed, an empty refrigerator or freezer, or an increase in insurance just prior to the fire.

Arson may also be committed for the perpetrator's emotional satisfaction. This motivation is often referred to as *pyromania*. A pyromaniac is described as having a compulsive need to set fires. In this sense, an outward, evidence-based motivation may not be evident to investigators. Offenders with this motivation are the most prolific at fire starting. Targets are often randomly selected. Fires are often set in haste and most often at night. In addition, the fire may have been set to allow the arsonist to be a hero. From an investigative standpoint, it is interesting that these offenders have reported that they were the ones who discovered the fire and informed the police, stayed at the scene as a spectator, and even assisted with first aid or rescuing victims. These offenders are likely to have an arrest record and to have committed the arson by themselves (Rider 1980a; Rider 1980b). When all the possibilities are considered by investigators, some motives may appear more likely than others and good leads may be developed. There is little question that the identification of an offender's probable motivation can be a powerful tool in guiding an arson investigation.

●●● Varieties and Characteristics of Larceny

Larceny refers to "the unlawful taking, carrying, leading, or riding away of property from the possession or constructive possession of another. It includes crimes such as shoplifting, pocket-picking, purse snatching, thefts from motor vehicles, thefts of motor vehicle parts and accessories, bicycle thefts, etc." (FBI 2012). To establish that larceny has occurred, there must be evidence of possession of the property by the victim and a statement from the victim that the property was taken without permission.

Larceny is the most common type of property crime. The most common form of larceny is theft from motor vehicles (24.8 percent), followed by shoplifting (17.5 percent) (see Table 13.3). The average dollar value per larceny offense in 2011 was $987, with thefts from buildings involving the highest property loss ($1,443) and shoplifting the lowest ($199).

TABLE 13.3   Types of Larceny Theft, 2011

TYPE OF THEFT	% OF TOTAL
Pocket-picking	0.4
Purse snatching	0.4
Shoplifting	17.5
From motor vehicles	24.8
Motor vehicle accessories	8.1
Bicycles	3.5
From buildings	11.8
From coin-op machines	0.3
Other	33.1
Total	100.0

Source: Federal Bureau of Investigation. 2012. *Crime in the United States, 2011 Uniform Crime Reports*. Washington, DC: U.S. Department of Justice.

Generally, small communities with large shopping malls have the highest rates of larceny. This is because of the frequency of shoplifting in relation to the number of people who live in the community. Overall, just more than 21 percent of larcenies were cleared in 2011. This figure overstates police success in solving larcenies because virtually all shoplifting crimes that are known to the police are cleared (the theft is observed and the perpetrator is apprehended at the store), which makes the clearance rate for this type of theft close to 100 percent (FBI 2012).

As with other property crimes, larceny is difficult to solve, as demonstrated by the low clearance rate. Of the larcenies that are cleared, juveniles are disproportionately involved as perpetrators, although to a lesser extent than in other property crimes. In 2011, 20 percent of the individuals arrested for larceny were younger than eighteen. With regard to gender, 62 percent of those arrested were male. Of all property crime, female subjects have the greatest representation in larcenies (arrests); 43 percent of those arrested were female. Finally, nationally, 69 percent of individuals arrested for larceny were white (FBI 2012).

••• Investigative Considerations With Larceny

With larcenies, there are usually few leads for the police to pursue. Larcenies are usually discovered only after the crime has occurred and the perpetrator has had ample time to flee with the property. Furthermore, there are usually no eyewitnesses to the crime, no usable physical evidence, and generally few other good leads for an investigator to pursue. There is little variation in motive; thieves usually steal property that they can use for their own benefit. As a result, it may be more difficult to find and trace property taken during a larceny compared with property taken during a burglary. In addition, the property taken during a larceny may not be remarkable or noticeable to others (as opposed to the perpetrator driving a new car without explanation) or may not be otherwise identifiable (e.g., no serial number). Because such crimes typically involve relatively small losses and provide few leads for investigators to pursue, relatively few investigative resources are allocated to the investigation of larceny offenses. Police departments that have a telephone reporting unit dispose of a majority of larceny complaints in this way. As such, only a report is completed, there is no investigation of the crime. The primary exceptions would be if the property loss was large or if good leads were present that would make it likely that the perpetrator could be identified. In short, larceny poses a tremendous challenge to investigators because of its frequency and because little evidence is usually produced during the commission of the crime. It may be necessary for investigators to search for such evidence, but the reality is that due to the pressure of other, more serious, cases, larcenies receive low priority.

Exhibit 13.1 Crime Solvers Press Release

Prince William County, Virginia . . . The Prince William County Police Department needs your help in locating suspects involved in a series of larcenies. There has been a recent increase in wallet and purse larcenies throughout the County, although most of the incidents have occurred in eastern Prince William County. There have been 22 reported incidents since May 26th. Detectives believe more than one group of suspects is involved in these cases. The incidents have occurred in grocery stores, restaurants, hardware stores and discount stores. Some victims have had wallets taken from purses left in shopping carts. Some wallets have been taken from purses hanging on chairs in restaurants. Descriptions of suspects were provided after stolen credit cards were used from these incidents.

These are the descriptions of suspects that were provided:

1. Hispanic male, 23–30 years old, 5'8", 160 lbs. with a second Hispanic male driving a gray or silver Honda 4 door.

2. Hispanic female, 30–40 years old, 5'5", 140 lbs. with a Hispanic male 40–50 years old, 5'9", 200 lbs. and a Hispanic male 30–40 years old, 6'0", 170 lbs.

3. Black female, 28 years old, 5'4", 135 lbs. black and gold framed glasses.

4. White female with a white male, 24–26 years old, 5'8", 150 lbs.

5. Black male, 21–33 years old, 5'11", 150 lbs. with a black female, 20–30 years old, 5'5", 140 lbs. with blond hair.

6. White male, 50–60 years old, 6'0", 200 lbs.

Citizens should be aware of these incidents and not leave purses unattended at any time, but especially in restaurants, stores, and shopping carts. If anyone knows the identity of the suspects, or has information about these cases, please call Prince William County Crime Solvers at 703–670–3700. You don't have to give your name, just the information. You could earn up to a $1,000 cash reward.

●●● Interrogation Considerations With Burglars, Arsonists, and Other Thieves

As discussed in detail in Chapter 7, the most effective interrogation strategies to be used with a suspect will depend largely on the characteristics of the suspect. This is true regardless of the type of crime in question. Particularly important is the extent of criminal experience of the suspect. If the suspect is an experienced nonemotional offender, he or she will most likely respond to factual themes (e.g., "There is no point denying your involvement, we have you on surveillance video"). If the suspect is an emotional offender, other strategies may be most effective (e.g., showing sympathy, blaming others, flattery). Of course, when multiple offenders are believed to be involved, one offender can be "played" against the other (e.g., "T-Bone confessed but said you are the one who actually took all the shoes"). While confessions of burglary suspects can be extremely valuable, due to the other challenges in such investigations, suspects to interrogate may not be identified.

MAIN POINTS ●

1. Burglary refers to "the unlawful entry of a structure to commit a felony or theft. Use of force to gain entry is not required to classify an offense as burglary." To establish that a burglary has occurred, there must be evidence of entry, evidence of theft from the structure, or evidence of a felony having occurred in the structure, and the owner of the structure must state that entry was obtained without permission.

2. Burglary is a difficult crime to solve. Burglaries are usually discovered only after the crime has occurred and the perpetrator has fled. There are usually no eyewitnesses to the crime, and physical evidence may not be found and/or collected.

These factors help explain why only 13 percent of burglaries are solved.

3. Burglar alarms seldom play an important role in burglary investigations because some types of alarms can be easily foiled by knowledgeable burglars, most burglar alarms are false, and many burglars avoid places with alarms.

4. A burglary offender's MO can be revealed in several ways, all of which can be determined through an examination of the scene and from information provided by the victim. They include inferences about how and why the perpetrator selected this particular target, the perpetrator's method of entry,

the type of property taken, the apparent amount of planning that took place prior to the burglary, and how the perpetrator searched for property. MO can be used by investigators to link burglaries together and to the same perpetrator, to help clear crimes when an offender is identified and apprehended, and to provide other clues as to the characteristics of the perpetrator.

5. Compared to novice officers, professional burglars tend to be older, more experienced, steal property of greater value, engage in more pre-offense planning, commit crimes farther away from their homes, and are willing to commit potentially higher-risk burglaries.

6. The perpetrator's actions in searching for property may also be an indicator of his or her knowledge of the contents of the premises. For instance, ransacking is either an act of vandalism (and most likely committed by juveniles) or it is a result of trying to find property to steal.

7. The type of property that was actually stolen may also hold clues about the characteristics of the burglar. Most houses have a lot of things that could be taken, and burglars have to make choices. Certain items are "CRAVED" by offenders more than others. These items are *c*oncealable, *r*emovable, *a*vailable, *v*aluable, *e*njoyable, and *d*isposable.

8. The process of turning property into cash involves various degrees of risk (and effort) for offenders and various degrees of opportunity for investigators. There are at least five ways that offenders can convert property to cash: sell the property to a friend, trade for goods, sell to a fence, sell to a pawnshop, or sell to strangers.

9. In burglaries, physical evidence most often takes the form of tool marks from screwdrivers or crowbars used to pry open doors and windows, other evidence at the point of entry or exit (e.g., fingerprints, footprints), or other items that belong to the perpetrator that are left at the scene. Additionally, in cases where things are broken (e.g., glass from a window), blood may be present.

10. Although burglary scenes are seldom processed for DNA evidence, recent research suggests that when DNA is collected from burglary scenes, more than twice as many perpetrators are identified and apprehended and more than twice as many cases are accepted for prosecution.

11. Motor vehicle theft refers to "the theft, or attempted theft, of a motor vehicle and includes the stealing of automobiles, trucks, buses, motorcycles, motor scooters, snowmobiles," and so forth. To establish that a vehicle theft has actually occurred, the police need to determine that the vehicle was taken from the owner without the owner's consent.

12. Motor vehicle thefts have one of the highest reporting rates but one of the lowest clearance rates. In only about 12 percent of such crimes are offenders identified and arrested.

13. The best chance to apprehend a motor vehicle thief is to locate the vehicle while it is being driven by the thief who stole it. Police officers on the lookout for stolen vehicles and the use of automated license plate readers may be most effective in this regard.

14. A stolen vehicle that has been recovered may contain property and physical evidence that can be linked to particular suspects. Accordingly, a recovered stolen vehicle should be processed as a crime scene.

15. Unless a stolen vehicle is recovered, the way in which it was stolen may be the only evidence in a motor vehicle investigation. The perpetrator's MO may reflect the degree of planning involved in the crime and the sophistication of the thief.

16. There are two primary motivations for stealing vehicles: joyriding and profit. Joyriding is most likely associated with less sophisticated methods of theft and is more common among young perpetrators. Thieves who steal vehicles for profit are more likely to use more sophisticated methods to steal the vehicle and are more likely to be professionals.

17. Perpetrators can convert stolen vehicles into cash in a number of ways. Offenders can attempt to sell the car outright after slight or major modifications to it, they can strip the car and sell its parts, they can transport or simply drive the vehicle out of the country, or they can use any such combination of these options. Selling cars overseas is probably the most profitable means of converting stolen cars into cash, but is also the most difficult.

18. The use of a bait car involves placing the car on a street in plain view. The keys may be left in the ignition, or the engine may be left running. Undercover officers watch the car and, when a perpetrator attempts to steal it, they apprehend the offender in the act. Investigative task forces have also been used to combat vehicle theft in places that experience that crime at a high rate.

19. Arson refers to "the willful or malicious burning or attempting to burn, with or without intent to defraud, a dwelling, house, public building, motor vehicle or aircraft, personal property, of another, etc." To establish that arson has occurred, there must be evidence of the fire being deliberately set for the purpose of causing harm.

20. Arson is a difficult crime to solve and poses unique challenges to investigators.

21. In the early stages of a fire investigation, the evidence at a fire scene is not necessary *criminal* evidence; the evidence may simply help establish the cause of the fire. When the fire is determined to be as a result of arson, the evidence becomes *criminal* evidence and the investigation becomes a *criminal* investigation.

22. Fires can be classified into several categories based on their cause: natural, accidental, suspicious, incendiary (i.e., arson), or of unknown origin. Legally, the presumption is that all fires have natural or accidental causes until proven otherwise. Approximately 16 percent of all reported fires are the result of arson.

23. To determine the cause of a fire, it is first necessary to identify *where* the fire started—in other words, to identify the point of origin. For a fire to occur, it needs a source of heat and material to burn.

24. An examination of a fire pattern is likely to provide critical clues regarding the cause and origin of the fire and, ultimately, whether the fire was deliberately set.

25. The clearest indication of arson is the presence of flammable liquid at the point of origin; however, the presence of a flammable liquid does not necessarily mean that the fire was willfully and maliciously set.

26. Because of the typical lack of evidence regarding who committed the crime, consideration of the motivation of an arsonist may be an important aspect of the investigation. The possible motives for arson are many, including anger, terrorism, vandalism, to conceal another crime, profit, or pyromania.

27. Larceny refers to "the unlawful taking, carrying, leading, or riding away of property from the possession or constructive possession of another. It includes crimes such as shoplifting, pocket-picking, purse snatching, thefts from motor vehicles, thefts of motor vehicle parts and accessories, bicycle thefts, etc." To establish that larceny has occurred, there must be evidence of possession of the property by the victim and a statement from the victim that the property was taken without permission.

28. With larcenies, usually there are few leads for the police to pursue. Larcenies are usually discovered only after the crime has occurred, there are usually no eyewitnesses to the crime or usable physical evidence, and generally few other good leads exist for an investigator to pursue. There is little variation in motive, and the property taken may not be remarkable or traceable. Relatively few investigative resources are allocated to the investigation of larceny offenses.

IMPORTANT TERMS

Arson	Causes of fire	Joyriding
Bait car	Chop shop	Larceny
"Bump and run"	"Cold" burglary	License plate reader (LPR)
Burglar alarms	"CRAVED" property	Locard's Exchange Principle
Burglary	Fire pattern	Motor vehicle theft
Burglary modus operandi (MO)	Incendiary	Novice, professional, and mid-range burglars

"Peeling"	Professional fence	Stolen property "markdowns"
Point of origin	Pyromania	Vehicle identification number (VIN)

QUESTIONS FOR DISCUSSION AND REVIEW

1. What are the major characteristics and varieties of burglaries?

2. What is the value of burglar alarms in burglary investigations?

3. How should patrol officers respond to burglary scenes?

4. What are the five primary aspects of a burglary offender's MO?

5. What are the inferences that can be made about the burglary offender based on how and why the perpetrator selected a particular target, the method of entry, the type of property taken (and not taken), how the perpetrator searched for property, and the apparent amount of planning that took place prior to the burglary?

6. What property is "CRAVED" by burglars? What are the six ways by which property can be converted to cash? Why do some methods have greater risks for burglars than others?

7. What is the potential value of physical evidence in burglary investigations? What is the potential value of informants in burglary investigations?

8. What are the major characteristics and varieties of motor vehicle theft?

9. What is the best way to identify a vehicle thief? How can police officers on the lookout, vehicle identification numbers (VINs), and license plate reader (LPR) technology be useful in motor vehicle theft investigations?

10. What is the potential value of physical evidence in motor vehicle theft investigations?

11. What are the two primary motives for vehicle theft and what inferences may be made about the offender on this basis? What are the various methods of stealing a vehicle and what inferences may be made about the offender on this basis?

12. What are bait cars and vehicle theft task forces? How might they be useful in vehicle theft investigations?

13. What are the major characteristics and varieties of arson?

14. What are the unique challenges of arson investigations?

15. What should be the initial activities of first responders at fire scenes? What is the potential importance of these activities?

16. What are the five ways by which the cause of fires can be classified?

17. How can the cause of a fire be established? What is the value of establishing the origin of a fire?

18. What are the possible motives for arson? How might establishing a motive for the arson be useful in an investigation?

19. What are the major characteristics and varieties of larceny theft?

20. What are the challenges of investigating larceny? Why do larceny investigations often take low priority in police departments?

21. What are the factors to consider when conducting interrogations of burglars, arsonists, and other thieves?

14

Digital Evidence and the Investigation of Fraud and Other Computer-Related Crimes

Objectives

After reading this chapter you will be able to:

- Define fraud and identity theft, and name several of their major forms

- Identify the challenges associated with the investigation of identity theft, and explain how it should be documented and investigated by police

- Define the following types of fraud: check and credit/debit card fraud, and prescription fraud and identify how they can be investigated

- Identify the most important sources of information and evidence in various fraud investigations

- Define cyber-attacks and its various forms

- Define cyber-bullying and harassment and explain why it is an important area of concern for the police

- Define the crimes that constitute child pornography and identify how those crimes are most often discovered

- Discuss the essential role of digital evidence in child pornography investigations

- Discuss digital evidence as a unique form of evidence in criminal investigations, and identify it's various sources

- Identify the legal basis for the search and seizure of electronic devices and discuss the procedures for properly collecting and handling electronic items that may contain digital evidence

From the CASE FILE

An Internet Chat With an Undercover Officer

In December of 2008, Gary Becker, the fifty-one-year-old mayor of Racine, Wisconsin, population 80,000, brought his personal computer to work at city hall and asked a computer technician to see if he could fix the problems that Becker was having with it. While fixing the computer, the technician discovered what appeared to be child pornography on its hard drive. The technician contacted the police to alert them of his discovery. After obtaining a search warrant, investigators collected the images from the computer. Investigators were also informed that approximately two years prior, Becker had another of his personally owned computers serviced by a city computer technician, and a disk which contained files from the computer had been created by the technician who worked on the computer. When the investigator now examined that disk, another similar pornographic image was discovered. Investigators also discovered evidence of over 1,800 online chats, many of which were sexually explicit and appeared to involve juveniles. Investigators determined that the user's profile was "WISC_GARY" and that his screen name was "m reed." Subsequent to that discovery, on January 12, 2009, an investigator had an approximately two-hour online conversation with "m reed," except "m reed" thought he was conversing with a fourteen-year-old girl. Presented below is a transcript of that conversation (edited for length). Gary Becker is "m reed" and the undercover investigator is "Hope ulikeme14." (Warning: Disturbing content.)

4:10 p.m.:

m reed: how r u doing honey? Have u been a good girl lately?

No response

m reed: r u still teasing the men?

No response

m reed: how is sweet little hope doing today???

Hope Ulikeme14: hi reed sorry I was doing my homework b4

Hope Ulikeme14: lemme kno if u wanna chat later ttyl

10:15 p.m.:

m reed: r u done with ur home-work honey

Hope ulikeme14: yes thanks

m reed: hey cutie

Hope ulikeme14: hiya

m reed: all done studying??

Hope ulikeme14: yea school sucks

m reed: what grade r u in?

Hope ulikeme14: 8th did u c my profile

m reed: just double checking

m reed: have u ever dated an older man

Hope ulikeme14: like what u mean

m reed: have u every been with an older man

Hope ulikeme14: oh that yea

m reed: what did u do with him or what did he do with u

Hope ulikeme14: like everything I gues

m reed: how old was he how young were u

Hope ulikeme14: it was last summer I was 13

Hope ulikeme14: it was one of my moms bf's

m reed: lucky him

m reed: how old is ur mom

Hope ulikeme14: 40

m reed: is she a bitch or a nice mom

Hope ulikeme14: I think shes a bitch threats me like som litle kid

*****More conversation about her mom, dating, and her mom's boyfriend**

m reed: what is ur body like hon

m reed: how developed r u

Hope ulikeme14: not very im kinda thin

m reed: that is ok young girls r all sexy

Hopeulikeme14: thank you

m reed: or most are anyway

Hopeulikeme14: u r sweet

m reed: was he the first guy u fucked

Hope ulikeme14: yeah

m reed: did u know he wanted u

m reed: had you been flirting with him behind moms back?

Hope ulikeme14: for sure

Hope ulikeme14: u just know the way I guy looks at u

Hope ulikeme14: he got me drunk 2

m reed: u were nervous

m reed: or did you want a cock badly

Hope ulikeme14: not really cuz I was drunk

*****More conversation about her mom and her mom's boy-friend**

M reed: what do you like to do hope

Hope ulikeme14: I like going to the mall chillin with my gfs u kno

m reed: spending lots of money??

Hope ulikeme14: if I had it!!! Lol

m reed: I wold treat u

Hope ulikeme14: awesome wher u live

m reed: Wisconsin and u

Hope ulikeme14: get out r u kidng

m reed: honest

m reed: what about u

Hope ulikeme14: me 2 kinda by milwauke

m reed: sweet

m reed: where abouts

Hope ulikeme14: u know wher Brookfield square is

Hope ulikeme14: it is a mall

m reed: of course

m reed: do u shop at the victoria's secret there

m reed: or r u too young yet

Hope ulikeme14: I like lookin in there 4 sure!

m reed: I luv shopping for lingerie with girls or women

*****More discussion about lingerie**

m reed: do u wear a regular bra yet or still a trainer??

Hope ulikeme14: just a 32a):

m reed: why the frown

Hope ulikeme14: guys like big tits u kno

m reed: sexiness is a state of mind all tits are sexy they do not have to be big

Hope ulikeme14: u r like SO sweet

*****More discussion about lingerie and underwear and the Victoria's Secret catalogue online.**

*****Discussion about their height and weight and her previous sexual experiences with boys; explicit sexual questions from "m reed."**

Hope ulikeme14: so r u really from Milwaukee 2

m reed: nearby

Hope ulikeme14: awesum

Hope ulikeme14: this is like destiny lol

m reed: u r so cute and adorable

m reed: I could just eat u up

m reed: love u all day

Hope ulikeme14: mmmm

Hope ulikeme: u make me feel so nice

m reed: u r so nice honey

m reed: does it make u wet to chat like this with an older man

Hope ulikeme14: what do u think

m reed: smile

m reed: how wet r u

Hope ulikeme14: kinda sorta

m reed: I wish I was there to make u kinda sorta dripping

Hope ulikeme14: nice

m reed: lick u till u cum

Hope ulikeme14: so it is cool that im 14?

Hope ulikeme14: u r a doll and a half

m reed: so it is cool that I am 48???

Hope ulikeme14: age don't matter to me yur heart is beautiful

m reed: thanxs baby u too

*****More explicit chat about sexual activities that "m reed" would like to perform with her.**

*****Questions about her school, clothes that she likes to wear, sharing of photographs, her previous sexual activities, and what he is going to buy for her when they go shopping at Victoria's Secret.**

Hope ulikeme14: what if I calld u

m reed: what time

Hope ulikeme14: after school I guess

m reed: or do you just want to meet at the mall

Hope ulikeme14: that wold be awesum

m reed: what time is good for u

Hope ulikeme14: I could get a ride from school

Hope ulikeme14: like 330

m reed: cool

m reed: where is a good place to meet

Hope ulikeme14: u been to Brookfield square b4

m reed: it has been awhile

Hope ulikeme14: u know where it is

m reed: yes

Hope ulikeme14: they have this really cool new food court

m reed: k

Hope ulikeme14: its kind of back in the mall

m reed: I am sure I can find it

Hope ulikeme14: not 2 far from victoria's

m reed: convenient

Hope ulikeme14: totally

Hope ulikeme14: how do I kno it is u

m reed: I will find u

Hope ulikeme14: I have no pic of u

Hope ulikeme14: ok

m reed: cool

M reed: what time will u have to be home by

Hope ulikeme14: 530 or 6. Ill tell my mom ill get a ride from a friends mom or something

Hope ulikeme14: shes 2 stupid not 2 believe me

m reed: I can drop u off

m reed: hopefully she will not see

Hope ulikeme14: it wuld have to be down the block but that is sweet of u

*****More explicit chat about sexual activities that he would like to perform with her.**

m reed: it will be hard to keep my hands off u in public

Hope ulikeme14: well do u have anything else in mind

m reed: what do u mean

Hope ulikeme14: in private duh LOL

m reed: I would luve to geta hotel room

m reed: and have lots of fun with u

Hope ulikeme14: wow u r such a tease

*****More explicit chat about sexual activities that he would like to perform with her.**

m reed: sitting on my lap in the hotel room

m reed: just chattinwith u

m reed: I am going to go jerk off when we r done

Hope ulikeme14: wow

Hope ulikeme14: u make me so hot

m reed: as u sit on my lap facing me

m reed: I lift ur shirt up over ur lil titties

*****More sexually explicit chat.**

Hope ulikeme14: r u serious about the mall????

m reed: I will try

m reed: I have a meeting downtown earlier

m reed: what r u going to wear?

m reed: what color top?

Hope ulikeme14: jeans and a green jacket with a furry collar

Hope ulikeme14: should I call u

m reed: what will u tell ur friend

m reed: I am calling this married older guy to hook up??

Hope ulikeme14: I dunno no one asks y

Hope ulikeme14: LOL

Hope ulikeme14: u r 2 funny

Hope ulikeme14: friends that u kno

m reed: I kno

m reed: it may be too soon

m reed: I have to be very careful u kno

Hope ulikeme14: ok

Hope ulikeme14: shold I go there or no

m reed: yes, I will try to be there but I may not make it

Hope ulikeme14: that is ok

m reed: I really want to meet u and talk

Hope ulikeme14: I gues but ill freeze walkin home

m reed: u2

m reed: I will do everything ican to be there for u

*****More discussion about arrangements to meet the next day

. . .

Hope ulikeme14: OK babe

Hope ulikeme14: miss u

m reed: u too

m reed: what time is school out, 3????

Hope ulikeme14: yeah so just after or as soon as I find a friend

Hope ulikeme14: I cant wait

m reed: cool talk to u then

m reed: nite hope

Hope ulikeme14: nite sweetie!

Hope ulikeme14: x's o's

m reed: u too hon

m reed has signed out. (1/13/2009 1:17 AM)

The next afternoon an investigator posing as "Hope ulikeme14" called "m reed" at the phone number he provided. "Hope ulikeme14" told "m reed" that she would be at the food court until 6:00 p.m. Approximately one hour later "Hope ulikeme14" called "m reed" again. At that time "m reed" told her that he would be there in about thirty minutes. Investigators gathered at the mall food court. At about 5:30 p.m. an individual known to be Gary Becker was seen by investigators at the food court. As written in the criminal complaint, the agent

> approached Gary Becker and asked him if he was Mr. Reed, whereupon Becker turned around and identified himself as Gary Becker. The Agent states that he informed Becker that

he had received a complaint from a mother about improper internet use by her daughter. After being advised of his Miranda rights, Becker explained that he was at Brookfield Square Mall to eat and shop at Victoria's Secret to get items for his wife. . . . Becker initially stated that he was not Mr. Reed; however, Becker later admitted that he was Mr. Reed and admitted that his Yahoo screen name is WISC_GARY . . . and the chat log was his.

Gary Becker resigned as mayor on January 20, 2010, the same day his wife filed for divorce. He pled guilty to attempted second degree sexual assault of a child and child enticement. Five other felonies were dropped. He was sentenced to three years in prison.

Case Considerations and Points for Discussion ●

- What was the most important development in this case that led authorities to Gary Becker? What was the role of the police in developing this information?

- Keeping in mind that "Hope ulikeme14" was really a police investigator, what did the investigator say, or not say, during this conversation to get "m reed" to go to the shopping mall to meet? Overall, how would you characterize the conversational approach taken by "Hope ulikeme14?" From a legal perspective, why do you think the investigator took this approach?

- From an ethical standpoint and from your point of view, is this type of investigation proper? Why or why not? As discussed, "m reed" was targeted by investigators because he earlier was discovered to have images of child pornography on his computer and because he had previously engaged in sexually explicit online chats with juveniles. Does this fact make a difference when judging the ethics of this sort of investigative strategy?

The purpose of this chapter is threefold: to discuss (1) the crime of fraud and its investigation; (2) other crimes where a computer or other electronic device is, or may be, used to commit the crime; and (3) computers as a source of evidence in criminal investigations. An electronic device may be used in various types of crimes. In particular, *cybercrimes* are crimes that *require* the use of a computer for their commission (e.g., distribution of computer viruses, hacking, online solicitation of juveniles for sex), and *computer-facilitated crimes* are those that often, but not always, involve a computer in their commission (e.g., identity theft, bullying). There are also crimes in which a computer was used in some way and therefore may contain evidence related to that crime. This chapter begins with a discussion of fraud and the investigative issues associated with it. It then examines other computer-facilitated crimes and cybercrimes and issues unique to their investigation. The chapter concludes with a discussion of digital evidence and electronic evidence more generally.

●●● Fraud and Its Investigation

Fraud is a general and encompassing term that refers to "all the ways one person can falsely represent a fact to another in order to induce that person to surrender something of value" (IRS 1993). Several types of fraud offenses are listed below:

- *Tax evasion* occurs when a person or corporation provides deceptive information to avoid paying taxes.

- *Bribery* occurs when anything of value is offered in exchange for influence in decisions or actions of the taker.

- *Embezzlement* occurs when a person who is entrusted with the money of a business uses it for his or her own use and benefit.

- *Forgery* involves the use of a false document or instrument to defraud the recipient. Types of forgery include counterfeit checks, the unauthorized use of credit cards, false medical prescriptions, and counterfeit merchandise.

- *Blackmail* involves a demand for money to avoid bodily harm, destruction of property, or the disclosure of secrets.

- *Extortion* occurs when one person obtains property from another as a result of actual or threatened force or fear or by using the authority of an official office (e.g., acting as a police officer).

- A *kickback* occurs when a person who sells an item pays the buyer part of the proceeds from that sale.

- *Racketeering* refers to operating an illegal business for personal profit.

- *Insider trading* occurs when a person uses privileged "inside" information to profit through the trading of stock in a publicly held corporation.

- *Money laundering* refers to the investment of illegally obtained money (e.g., through drug sales, racketeering) into legitimate businesses so that the original source of the money cannot be established.

- *Investment fraud* occurs when an individual obtains money from another under the false pretext of a legitimate investment.

- *Insurance fraud* refers to when car accidents and injuries are staged, reported property damage is bogus, property damage is self-inflicted (e.g., arson), or even when one's death is fraudulently reported to collect insurance benefits.

- *Welfare and food stamp fraud* involves obtaining or using welfare benefits or food stamps illegally.

- *Internet fraud* can take a variety of forms, the most common of which is auction fraud, in which the property being bid on is misrepresented or not provided with a winning bid. In addition, the Internet provides opportunities for many other forms of fraud (e.g., credit card fraud, investment fraud, etc.) (see IRS 1993).

Although this is a long list, it is just a start. A multitude of other illegal actions can be best defined as fraud: medical/health care fraud, worker's compensation fraud, journalism fraud, standardized test (SAT, GRE) fraud, psychic fraud, construction contract fraud, automobile accident fraud, charity fraud, and so on. The FBI's *Uniform Crime Report* identifies three related crimes—forgery, fraud, and embezzlement—and classifies them as Part II crimes. As Part II crimes, few details are provided about them. The report states that offenders arrested for forgery, fraud, and embezzlement are similar in their characteristics: approximately 66 percent are white, 33 percent are under the age of twenty-five, and the near majority are male.

It is safe to say that opportunities for fraud are more prevalent today than ever before, and that trend may continue. As such, it is likely that more and more investigative resources will be devoted to the investigation of fraud-type offenses. The discussion presented here focuses most directly on three significant types of fraud that are commonly brought to the attention of the police: identity theft, check and credit/debit card fraud, and prescription fraud.

IDENTITY THEFT

Most broadly defined, identity theft occurs when one person steals the personal information of another and uses it without permission. More specifically, four types of identity theft are often identified: criminal identity theft (posing as another person when apprehended for a crime), financial identity theft (using another's identity to obtain credit, goods, and services), identity cloning (using another's information to assume his or her identity in daily life), and medical identity theft (using another's identity to obtain medical care or drugs) (see the Identity Theft Resource Center at www.idtheftcenter.org/).

Typically, identity theft has a financial motive. For instance, offenders may use a stolen identity in order to open cell phone accounts in the victim's name, open bank accounts in the victim's name and write worthless checks from those accounts, open new credit cards using the victim's name, take out auto loans or mortgages in the victim's name, submit false income tax returns to obtain refunds, or obtain social security payments (often using identities of people who have died). Identity theft is also sometimes motivated by a desire to get revenge or to cause embarrassment; these types of incidents may also be considered cases of cyberbullying or cyberharassment (see Case in Point 14.1).

Identify theft usually depends on first obtaining protected information about a person such as birth date, address, or social security number. Documentation such as energy or telephone bills with account numbers, bank or credit card statements with account numbers, or convenience checks can also be used to steal another's identity. To obtain this information, offenders can do the following:

- Steal wallets or purses

- Steal mail in various ways, from simply taking it from unsecured mailboxes to submitting a fraudulent change of address form to the post office to have a person's mail redirected

- Search through garbage or dumpsters ("dumpster diving")

- Obtain a victim's credit report by posing as someone who is legally permitted to do so, such as a landlord or employer

- Work with employees of firms that maintain client or employee records to illegally obtain those records, or, if they are employees, access the information themselves

CASE in POINT 14.1   "Visit Me!"

Julie Mathews (not her real name) called the police to report that she was receiving phone calls from unknown men who were interested in having sex with her. She explained to the police she had learned from some of the men that they were responding to her Craigslist ad and that some told her they were just following up on her responses to *their* ads. She told the police that she had also discovered a Facebook profile with her photo and personal information. Only one problem . . . Julie had not posted an ad, responded to any ads, or created the Facebook profile.

The Craigslist ad read as follows (phone number was changed):

> Under 30. Freaky, yet shy off the bat. Willing to try any-thing. Clubbing has become so boring—same types of people and situations. Sales is my profession—and now I need to learn to sell myself!
>
> Eight eight one seven four nine zero zero two one
>
> Julie

Prior to contacting the police, Julie had contacted Craigslist and made a complaint about the ad. Craigslist had removed the ad and forwarded to Julie the information they had regarding the poster, including the Yahoo! e-mail address that was used to post the ad and the Internet Protocol (IP) logs for the poster. Julie gave this information to investigators. Upon receiving the information, the investigator served subpoenas upon Yahoo! Inc. and Time Warner Cable to obtain information on the billing address for the IP address connected to the Craigslist ad.

The Facebook profile included a photo of Julie, her full name, her birthday, her place of employment, and her home address, which was one block from where she actually lived. The profile read as follows (names, dates, and places have been changed):

> Sex: Female
>
> Birthday: August 12, 1984
>
> Hometown: Greenfield, Texas
>
> Political Views: an uptight bitch
>
> Religious Views: Does God hate whores?

Activities: When I take the time, I will walk my dog, but generally I leave it to my landlord to take care of. I like naughty activities.

Interests: S&M, Anal, Taboo issues, etc.

Favorite Music: I'm generally a loose kinda chick, so all depends on my mood

Favorite TV Shows: My interests are not allowed on TV

Favorite Movies: Movies that entail my interests

Favorite Books: Books? No way. Give me a sassy raunchy dirty mag!

About Me: Visit me at work and let me give ya my "sales talk" . . . but we will know what you are visiting me for. Quality Cabinets on Mitchell Street in Greenfield. Ask the receptionist for Julie.

On her Wall, Julie Mathews wrote at 8:52 a.m. on August 24, 2010:

2167 S. 18th Street, Apt A

Greenfield, TX

Visit me!

Julie Mathews wrote at 8:58 am on August 24, 2010:

I want it, and want it bad!

The investigator sent a subpoena to Facebook.com requesting the posting information for the profile and requesting that the profile information be removed from public view.

The next day the investigator received the results of the Time Warner Cable Company subpoena, which revealed the billing information for the IP address in connection with the Craigslist ad. It was traced to Scot Ashur, 976 S. Pine Street, Greenfield, Texas. The investigator then spoke with Julie and asked her if she knew anyone with the first name "Scot." She thought for a moment then told the investigator that a person she used to work with at Quality Cabinets, Dianna Ashur, was married to a guy named "Scot" with one "t." She told investigators that Dianna blamed her for being fired from the company. Dianna had been Julie's receptionist. Julie told investigators that Dianna would have had access to her address, phone number, and other information through payroll records.

Later that day, investigators went to the home of the Ashurs and spoke with Scot and Dianna separately. Upon talking with Dianna, one of the investigators informed her that he was investigating something that had happened on the computer involving the posting of Craigslist ads, and he asked her if she knew what he was taking about. Dianna immediately told the detective that she answered several Craigslist ads while pretending to be someone else, a former co-worker named Julie Mathews. Upon speaking with Scot, it did not appear that he was aware of what his wife had done. Dianna was then informed that she was under arrest for unlawful use of an individual's identifying information. She then told the detectives and her husband that she would not have done it if she had known it was illegal. Detectives seized the computer. At the police station, a Mirandized interrogation of Dianna was conducted. At that time she admitted to creating the Facebook profile, responding to and creating the Craigslist ads, and using the victim's identifying information to do so.

- Burglarize homes or businesses to find personal information on forms or computers
- Hack into corporate computers, steal customer and employee data, and then sell that data to other identity thieves
- Contact credit card issuers and change the billing address for an account so the victim does not realize immediately that purchases are being fraudulently being made on the account
- Buy identities and/or credit cards obtained by other offenders
- Buy or create counterfeit documents such as birth certificates, visas, or passports
- Buy false or counterfeit IDs on the Internet
- Create counterfeit checks and credit or debit cards using another person's name
- Steal PINS and user IDs by various means, including tricking Internet users into giving their passwords and other personal information via fraudulent e-mails (see Exhibit 14.1).

Exhibit 14.1   "Your Account Has Won $1,000,000.00"

Everyone who has an e-mail account has probably received an e-mail like the one below, although you may need to check your spam folder to find it. If you found it, hopefully you did not believe it. This is not a legitimate e-mail. Rather, it is very likely an attempt to obtain personal identifying information in order to facilitate an identity theft.

NOT SPAM (((((Congratulations ** Your Account Has Won $1,000,000.00

From: MASTER CARD notificationcentermastercard@yahoo.com

Subject: NOT SPAM (((((Congratulations **Your Account Has Won $1,000,000.00

Reply To: MASTER CARD <m_international@aol.com>

YOUR EMAIL WON $1,000,000.00. OPEN ATTACHMENT FOR DETAILS. SEND ALL INFORMATION'S TO (M_INTERNATIONAL@AOL.COM) FOR CLAIM IMMEDIATELY.

MasterCard_eng_E_lottery2013. . . . docx 687 KB

Given the odd e-mail addresses and the grammatical errors, it is not difficult to identity this message as being bogus. Also, if you won $1,000,000, you probably would receive more than an e-mail notification. And when was the last time someone won $1,000,000 from their credit card company? The reality is that most police departments would be unlikely to investigate this e-mail unless financial harm had been done to the recipient because of it. Most police departments just have too many more pressing crimes to investigate. Further, since the sender of the e-mail is probably on the other side of the planet, there is little that a local police department could reasonably do to investigate.

As is the case with fraud in general, police departments are increasingly being informed of incidents of identity theft. Due to the Fair and Accurate Credit Transactions Act (FACT Act), consumers are entitled to free annual access to their credit history, which may lead to increased detection of identity theft incidents (see Exhibit 14.2). Additionally, credit reporting agencies now require that victims report such incidents to the police as part of an identity theft affidavit; this practice is also contributing to increased reporting of identity theft crimes (Newman 2004b).

Exhibit 14.2   What Does the FACT Act Do?

The FACT Act provides consumers, companies, consumer reporting agencies, and regulators with important new tools that expand access to credit and other financial services for all Americans, enhance the accuracy of consumers' financial information, and help fight identity theft. These reforms make permanent the uniform national standards of our credit markets and institute new, strong consumer protection and free credit reports.

The Fair and Accurate Credit Transactions Act of 2003 will accomplish the following priorities to help ensure that Americans of every income level and background are able to build good credit and confront the problem of identity theft and receive free credit reports.

1. Ensuring that lenders make decisions on loans based on full and fair credit histories, and not on discriminatory stereotypes. In 1996, uniform national standards were established to set clear rules on what credit agencies were entitled to include in individual credit reports, and now more than a million Americans have credit as a result. This legislation makes those national standards permanent.

2. Improving the quality of credit information and protecting consumers against identity theft. Giving consumers the right to their credit report free of charge every year. Consumers will be able to review a free report every year for unauthorized activity, including activity that might be the result of identity theft.

3. Helping prevent identity theft before it occurs by requiring merchants to leave all but the last five digits of a credit card number off store receipts. This law will make sure that slips of paper that most people throw away do not contain their credit card number, a key to their financial identities.

4. Creating a national system of fraud detection to make identity thieves more likely to be caught. Previously, victims would have to make phone calls to all of their credit card companies and three major credit rating agencies to alert them to the crime. Now consumers will only need to make one call to receive advice, set off a nationwide fraud alert, and protect their credit standing.

5. Establishing a nationwide system of fraud alerts for consumers to place on their credit files. Credit reporting agencies that receive such alerts from customers will now be obliged to follow procedures to ensure that any future requests are by the true consumer, not an identity thief posing as the consumer. The law also will enable active duty military personnel to place special alerts on their files when they are deployed overseas.

6. Requiring regulators to devise a list of red flag indicators of identity theft, drawn from the patterns and practices of identity thieves. Regulators will be required to evaluate the use of these red flag indicators in their compliance examinations of financial institutions and impose fines where disregard of red flags has resulted in losses to customers.

7. Requiring lenders and credit agencies to take action before a victim even knows a crime has occurred. With oversight by bank regulators, the credit agencies will draw up a set of guidelines to identify patterns common to identity theft and develop methods to stop identity theft before it can cause major damage.

Source: Adapted from www.factact.us/factact_002.htm.

Identity theft investigations range from the relatively simple (as in Case in Point 14.1) to the daunting and complicated. One reason that these investigations can be complicated is that there is the potential for many jurisdictions and agencies to be involved. For instance, the victim may live in one jurisdiction, the theft may have occurred in another jurisdiction, the credit card company may be in another jurisdiction, the credit card may have been used illegally in yet another jurisdiction, and the offender may live in still another jurisdiction. The theft may actually involve many crimes. As such, the investigation of identity theft may be investigated by many agencies, including local police departments, the U.S. Secret Service, the Postal Inspection Service, the FBI, Homeland Security, local government offices, and motor vehicle departments, among others, depending on the nature of the theft and associated crimes (Newman 2004b). The Secret Service has primary responsibility for investigating identity theft, but it does not accept cases unless there is over $200,000 in loss and victims from multiple states are involved. Identity theft investigations may be further complicated in that the full extent of the crime, and the extent of the damage done, may be unknown and only discovered by the victim incrementally. On the positive side, in most identity theft cases the victim knows who is responsible for the crime (Newman 2004b), although the victim may not realize it at the time the crime is discovered.

Local police departments usually have primary responsibility for documenting and investigating identity theft complaints. Police departments get many such complaints. Legally, the location of the identity theft is the victim's residence (Dadisho 2005), so victims should be referred to the law enforcement agency that has jurisdiction over their residence. Then, if it is determined that the crime(s) associated with the identity theft occurred in another jurisdiction, the case may be referred to that agency for investigation. Identity theft reports should be taken in person, not telephonically, in order for the police to verify the identity of the victim. Victims should be asked for identification and should be asked to provide any relevant documents pertaining to the identity theft complaint (Dadisho 2005). The preliminary investigation report should include when the victim discovered the fraud, a list of the fraudulent activity discovered to date, and information about the thief, if known (Newman 2004b). Investigators should also include with the report copies of documents that relate to the identity theft allegation (e.g., credit reports, invoices, bank statements) and a copy of the victim's identification (e.g., driver's license). The notifications made by the victim to financial institutions and credit reporting agencies should also be noted in the report. The report should be signed by the victim (Dadisho 2005). Efforts should be made to detect and avoid duplicate reporting of the same crime. To this end, other involved agencies should be contacted and advised.

The victims should be provided a copy of the police report, which will allow him or her to move forward in filing an identity theft affidavit (Newman 2004b). The victim should also be provided with information about the necessary steps to address the damage done as a result of the theft (see Exhibit 14.3). For example, victims should be referred to "Identity Theft: What to Do if It Happens to You" on the Privacy Rights Clearinghouse Web site (www.privacyrights.org/fs/fs17a.htm) and the Federal Trade Commission's (FTC) Web site (www.consumer.gov/idtheft). The victim's complaint information should be entered into the FTC's Identity Theft Data Clearinghouse, or the victim should be advised to file a complaint with the FTC directly by calling 1–877–ID–THEFT or visiting www.consumer.gov/idtheft. Putting the complaint into the national database will allow investigators from across the county to link complaints about the same offender together, which may facilitate successful apprehension and prosecution (Newman 2004b).

Subsequent investigative activities will vary substantially based on the particulars of the crime. Typically, a good place to begin is with the financial and credit bureau documents or the credit card/bank statements that show the fraudulent charges. These documents will provide information about the time and place of the fraudulent activities and may link known suspects to the crime (Dadisho 2005). Several national databases may also be useful

Exhibit 14.3 Advice for Identity Theft Victims

The Federal Trade Commission recommends that victims take the following steps as soon as possible upon discovery of identity theft (see http://www.ftc.gov/opa/2002/02/idtheft.shtm):

1. Contact the fraud departments of each of the three major credit bureaus and report the theft. Ask that a "fraud alert" be placed on your file and that no new credit be granted without your approval.

   - Equifax: (800) 525-6285
   - Experian: (888) 397-3742
   - Trans Union: (800) 680-7289

2. For any accounts that have been fraudulently accessed or opened, contact the security department of the appropriate creditor or financial institution. Close these accounts. Put passwords (**not** your mother's maiden name or Social Security number) on any new accounts you open.

3. File a report with local police or the police where the identity theft took place. Get the report number or a copy of the report in case the bank, credit card company or others need proof of the crime later.

4. Call the ID Theft Clearinghouse toll-free at **1.877.ID.THEFT (1.877.438.4338)** to report the theft. Counselors will take your complaint and advise you on how to deal with the credit-related problems that could result from ID theft. The Identity Theft Hotline and the ID Theft Website (www.ftc.gov/idtheft) give you **one** place to report the theft to the federal government and receive helpful information.

The Federal Trade Commission can be contacted toll-free at 877–ID–THEFT (877–438–4338) or online at www.consumer.gov/idtheft.

Source: www.factact.us/factact_006.htm.

---

when investigating identity theft complaints. E-Information is a free Internet site operated by the U.S. Secret Service that is available to law enforcement agencies and investigators (see www2.einformation.usss.gov/eInformation/home.seam). The resources available at E-Information Network include the following:

- Bank identification listings
- Credit card information
- Counterfeit check database
- Genuine and counterfeit identification document database
- Cybercrime resources
- Fraudulent document database

FinCEN (Financial Crimes Enforcement Network; www.fincen.gov) is another potentially useful intelligence and information resource to use when investigating identity theft and other financial crimes. Through FinCEN, authorized users can access nearly forty different databases in three main categories: law enforcement, financial, and commercial. The databases include AutoTrack, LexisNexis, the Social Security Administration Death Master File, and several databases of the Drug Enforcement Administration, FBI, and IRS. The FTC Consumer Sentinel (www.ftc.gov/sentinel/) may also be a potentially useful resource when investigating identity theft (see Exhibit 14.4).

Obviously, a primary goal of the investigation is to identify the person(s) responsible for the identity theft. However, another important objective is to search for and find other victims associated with a particular offender. When additional victims are attributed to the same offender, available evidence can be pooled and additional resources for the investigation (e.g., multi-agency task forces, involvement of the U.S. Secret Service) may be mobilized (Dadisho 2005).

Exhibit 14.4   The FTC Consumer Sentinel

Consumer Sentinel is the unique investigative cyber tool that provides members of the Consumer Sentinel Network with access to millions of consumer complaints. Consumer Sentinel includes complaints about:

- Identity theft
- Do-not-call registry violations
- Computers, the Internet, and online auctions
- Telemarketing scams
- Advance-fee loans and credit scams

- Immigration services
- Sweepstakes, lotteries, and prizes
- Business opportunities and work-at-home schemes
- Health and weight loss products
- Debt collection, credit reports, and financial matters

Consumer Sentinel is based on the premise that sharing information can make law enforcement even more effective. To that end, the Consumer Sentinel Network provides law enforcement members with access to complaints provided directly to the Federal Trade Commission by consumers, as well as providing members with access to complaints shared by data contributors.

Source: Adapted from www.ftc.gov/sentinel/.

PHOTO 14.1: The elderly are often a target of fraud and identify theft.

Exhibit 14.5 What Identity Thieves Do with Your Information and How They Do It

Identity thieves frequently open new accounts in your name. They often apply for new credit cards using your information, make charges, and leave bills unpaid. It is also common for them to set up telephone or utility service in your name and not pay for it. Some victims have found that identity thieves applied for loans, apartments, and mortgages. Thieves have also been known to print counterfeit checks in a victim's name.

Thieves also often access your existing accounts. They may take money from your bank accounts, make charges on your credit cards, and use your checks and credit to make down payments for cars, furniture, and other expensive items. They may even file for government benefits, including unemployment insurance and tax refunds.

Unfortunately, thieves often use a stolen identity again and again. It is very common for victims to learn that thieves have opened and accessed numerous accounts, often over a long span of time.

Four out of five victims have no idea how an identity thief obtained their personal information. Of those who think they know what happened, many believe the identity theft occurred when their purse or wallet was stolen or lost. Thieves also steal identities from the trash—this is called "dumpster diving"—which can occur at home, at work, or at a business. Mail can be stolen from your home mailbox, from a drop box, at a business, and even directly from postal workers. Home computers can be infected with viruses that transmit your data to thieves.

Group identity theft has become a major problem for consumers. A thief gains access to a place that keeps records for many people. Targets have included stores, fitness centers, car dealers, schools, hospitals, and even credit bureaus. Thieves may either use the stolen identities themselves or sell them to other criminals.

"Pretexting" is a method of identity theft that is on the rise. The identity thief poses as a legitimate representative of a survey firm, bank, Internet service provider, employer, landlord, or even a government agency. The thief contacts you to reveal your information, usually by asking you to "verify" some data.

Victims of identity theft often find that someone they know has committed the crime. Roommates, hired help, and landlords all have access to your home, and it is possible for them to access private information. Identity theft within families is also fairly common. This causes particular difficulties because victims may be reluctant to notify the authorities or press charges. People are especially vulnerable when ending relationships with roommates and spouses.

Identity theft often goes undetected. Within a month of being committed, half of the crimes still remain unnoticed. One in ten stays hidden for two or more years. Identity thieves may change "your" address on an account so that you won't ever receive bills with the fraudulent charges on them. They will often pay the minimum balances on accounts they have opened to avoid calling attention to the account and having it cut off. They may even use the identities of children or persons who are deceased so that the crime is less likely to be noticed.

Source: Adapted from the Federal Reserve Bank of Boston (www.bos.frb.org/consumer/identity/idtheft.pdf).

CHECK AND CREDIT/DEBIT CARD FRAUD

One common and relatively simple form of identity theft involves check and credit/debit card fraud. Credit/debit card fraud usually involves stealing a card and then using it to make unauthorized purchases. Credit cards are often used fraudulently more than debit cards. Debit cards, which involve the automatic deduction of money from the card owner's bank account upon purchase, may require the entry of a personal identification number (PIN) upon making a purchase. The PIN is not printed on the card. This security feature is often enough to thwart the fraudulent use of debit cards. When debit cards are used fraudulently it may involve forcing the account owner to disclose the PIN, which would then make the crime a robbery.

Some security measures may prevent the fraudulent use of a credit card, debit card, or personal check. For example, some retailers require that the buyer provide a fingerprint upon use of a card or a personal check. Some retailers require a customer who uses a card or check to provide a signature that is then compared with the signature on the card (for a card purchase) or on a driver's license (for purchase with a check). These security measures, along with alert salespersons, could assist in the prevention of this type of fraud or assist in the investigation of those offenses that are not prevented.

In order to use a credit/debit card or personal check fraudulently, the offender must, of course, first obtain the check or card (or card number) that is to be used fraudulently. There are a multitude of methods by which an offender may obtain checks and cards for fraudulent purposes:

- An employee can record a customer's credit card number at the time of a transaction.

- Counterfeit checks and cards can be made.

- A fraudulent credit card application with someone else's name (which would also constitute identity theft) can be completed.

- Checks and credit cards can be intercepted in the mail or stolen from mailboxes.

- Another person's credit card number or PIN can be obtained through trickery; for example, by "shimming" (watching as the person enters the number) or "skimming" (using a device to electronically read numbers from a credit/debit card, most often used on ATMs).

- A company database can be hacked to obtain credit card numbers.

- Bogus Web sites that request credit card and other personal information can be created.

Once the offender has the card or check, there are several ways by which he or she may fraudulently use it. Five of the most common methods are discussed here (Newman 2004a). First, a common and simple ploy is the passing and cashing of worthless checks. For example, Bob knowingly writes a personal check from his (or another person's) nearly empty checking account to his friend Dan. Dan then takes the check to a different bank and cashes it, receiving cash. Bob and Dan share the proceeds.

Second, an offender can alter the name on a check or the amount of a check in order to cash it or in order to receive more cash than intended. For example, Barb Smith could alter a check written to "Bob Smith" so she could cash it. Or "four hundred" dollars could be changed to "fourteen hundred" dollars.

Third, an offender can present a fraudulent/stolen check or card at checkout in order to make a purchase. In some instances, the sales clerk may attempt to verify that the person presenting the check or card is the actual account holder. Given bank rules and regulations, more scrutiny may be given to checks than to credit cards. The retail outlet that accepts a fraudulent check may be held liable for the purchase, as the bank is unlikely to honor the check if it detects a forgery. However, retailers are generally not responsible for fraudulent credit card usage. Upon the successful purchase of merchandise, the offender is likely to either sell the property to someone for cash or return the goods to the store for a refund in cash (Newman 2004b). An increasingly common variant of this MO involves the offender repeatedly using a credit card to obtain gasoline at a gas station. The offender obtains a card and notifies his or her friends to meet at the gas station to fill up their cars with gasoline. The offender uses the card ("pay at the pump") to purchase gasoline for the multiple cars and then collects cash from the others in exchange for the gasoline.

Fourth, offenders can make a card-not-present purchase, as would be done when making a purchase via telephone or the Internet. This method allows the offender to avoid scrutiny from the salesperson at the point of sale. To make a card-not-present purchase, the offender needs to have the credit card number and the security code printed on the back of the card.

For offenders, one of the difficulties associated with making fraudulent card-not-present purchases is that the items purchased usually need to be shipped. Some Internet point-of-sale programs only allow items to be shipped to the address on the credit card. If the items are to be shipped to a different address (i.e., the address of the offender), that would obviously increase the traceability of the purchase to the offender. To avoid this problem, it is not unheard of that offenders have the item shipped to the card owner but then steal it before the victim takes possession of it (e.g., steal it from the mailbox or doorstep). Card-not-present purchases account for a fast-growing proportion of all credit card fraud (Newman 2004). Similar opportunities and difficulties exist for offenders with the use of electronic checks. Generally, only the account owner's name, the bank routing number, and bank account number is needed to allow such as transaction.

Fifth, offenders can order an item with a legitimate credit card but then deny ordering and/or receiving the item (Newman 2004). Postal package tracking and requiring signatures upon delivery may reduce these opportunities for offenders or provide a basis upon which to investigate them.

A large percentage of credit card thefts and fraud are not reported to the police, although credit card companies are increasingly likely to require notification of the police. Most often with credit cards, customers are not liable for any unauthorized purchases, thereby minimizing the need of the victim to report the theft/use to the police, only to the credit card company. However, banks may be more likely to hold customers or retailers liable for fraudulent use of debit cards and checks, so these crimes more often come to the attention of the police. Depending on the workload of the police department and the amount of loss involved, the simple reality is that these sorts of crimes may not be a priority. As such, the investigation may receive little time or be referred back to the bank, credit card company, or retailer.

When check/card fraud crimes are investigated, there are several possible courses of action for investigators to pursue. First, it is important to obtain a hard copy of the check (or of the electronic signature in the case of a credit card) that was forged or altered, or any other fraudulent documents associated with the fraud (e.g., the credit card application). These documents can help establish that a crime occurred, provide a basis for handwriting analysis comparisons, and may even contain fingerprints or DNA. Second, if the fraud was facilitated by a theft, burglary, or robbery, a successful investigation of that crime may lead to the offender who committed the fraud. Third, when burglars, robbers, and other offenders are identified, a search of items in their possession may reveal stolen checks or cards that were used fraudulently, thereby linking one offender to many crimes. Fourth, from the credit card statement or the canceled or returned check, the date, place, and possibly the time the card or check was used should be able to be determined. With this information, it may be possible to obtain information about the offender from the salesperson who conducted the transaction and to examine security cameras at the store to find the image of the person who fraudulently made the purchase. Of course, depending on the number of days that video can be stored on the recording technology prior to deletion, an examination of the security camera footage may need to occur without delay. Clearly, the sooner the better (see Case in Point 14.2).

Finally, as in burglaries and robberies, a potentially useful investigative activity is to try to locate the property that was fraudulently purchased (see Chapter 13). If the property is found, the offender may be identified as well. Pawnshops, secondhand stores, other retail stores, and online auctions are common outlets for fraudulently purchased merchandise.

PRESCRIPTION FRAUD

Prescription drug fraud, and the misuse of those drugs, is a significant law enforcement problem. Law enforcement agencies increasingly identify *prescription* drugs as their greatest drug control challenge (Wartell and LaVigne 2004). In a nationwide survey conducted

CASE *in* POINT 14.2   Theft, Theft, Purchase, and Arrest

A woman was attending her child's swimming class at the local fitness center. She placed her key ring on the chair next to her while she watched the activities in the pool. At one point she got up to get a drink, and when she came back her keys were missing. She immediately went outside, checked on her car, and saw that her purse was missing from her car. She then notified the police. The police reasoned that the culprit took the keys and then quickly proceeded outside and used the door lock activation button on the car key to sound the car's horn and find the vehicle in the parking lot. The thief then discreetly, and without notice, took the purse from the car. The victim called the credit card companies to deactivate her credit cards. She was informed at that time that a purchase had just been authorized at a local electronic store for a GPS unit and other items, with a total cost of nearly $600. Approximately thirty minutes had elapsed from the time the keys were stolen to when the purchase was made at the store.

The victim told the police what the credit card company had just told her; they immediately responded to the store and obtained a description of the person who had just purchased the GPS unit and other items, as well as security camera footage from inside the store that showed this person buying the merchandise and from outside the store that showed the person's vehicle. From that video, a license plate number was obtained, and from this investigators obtained the name and address of the registered driver of the vehicle. The police went to the subject's home and found the person who drove that vehicle and matched the description of the customer who bought the items at the store just minutes earlier. Police searched the trunk of the subject's car and found some of the property that had been fraudulently purchased at the store. The subject was arrested and charged with theft and fraudulent use of a credit card.

in 2010, approximately seven million people reported illegally using prescription drugs in the previous month (Wartell and LaVigne 2004). Another study found that illegally obtained prescription drugs were the second most common form of drugs used among young people; only marijuana was used more frequently (Wartell and LaVigne 2004). In many of these instances, the prescription drugs were obtained via fraud. The true extent of prescription drug fraud and abuse is largely unknown simply because it is not often brought to the attention of the police. Most often, when it is, it is because a pharmacy calls the police to alert them to the possibility. For example, in one recent case, a pharmacy received a handwritten prescription order for OxyContin that did not seem legitimate; the number of tabs, the number of refills, and the characteristics of the person requesting the prescription raised questions. The pharmacy contacted the doctor's office from where the prescription was supposedly ordered; the doctor's office had no knowledge of the patient or that prescription. The pharmacy then contacted the police. In the meantime, while the subject was waiting for his prescription to be filled at the store, the police arrived and questioned the man. He was eventually arrested for fraud.

The most common prescription drugs that are misused and fraudulently obtained are pain relievers such as Vicodin® (hydrocodone), OxyContin® (oxycodone), Lorcet®, Dilaudid®, Percocet®, Soma®, Darvocet®, and morphine. Prescription stimulants prescribed for attention deficit/hyperactivity disorder (ADHD), such as Adderall® and Ritalin®, are also increasingly common, particularly among college students who use them to improve focus and studying (Wartell and LaVigne 2004).

In addition to outright theft through burglaries, robberies, or other means, offenders can obtain prescription drugs in numerous fraudulent ways (Wartell and LaVigne 2004). Offenders can forge prescriptions or alter a prescription to increase the quantity, dosage, or number of allowed refills. To do this, they can steal or counterfeit prescription pads from physicians, impersonate medical staff and call in false prescriptions to pharmacies, visit multiple doctors to obtain multiple prescriptions ("doctor shopping"), or purchase drugs illegally on the Internet.

Part of the difficulty in investigating prescription drug fraud and misuse is that offenders who obtain the drugs are usually most interested in using the drugs themselves, not selling the drugs to others. This essentially eliminates one of the primary strategies used by investigators when investigating drug trafficking, the undercover "buy-bust." As such, it is generally much easier to prevent prescription drug fraud than to investigate it. The police should serve as educators and inform physicians and pharmacists about the methods used in fraudulently obtaining prescriptions, the importance of checking the patient's request and the doctor's prescription order, the value in using tamper-resistant prescription pads, and the benefits of electronically transmitting prescriptions directly to the pharmacist. Such practices may eliminate many of the opportunities to illegally obtain prescription drugs.

Another complicating dimension of this type of investigation is that in most instances, it is not known immediately if the drugs were obtained by the subject through a legitimate prescription, obtained by the subject through fraud, illegally obtained by the subject from someone else who had a legitimate prescription, or illegally obtained by the subject from someone who obtained the drugs through fraud. Further, even if the subject in possession of the drugs is able to provide the prescription order to investigators or is able to provide a labeled prescription bottle with his or her name on it, it still may not be easy to determine if that prescription was obtained fraudulently. As such, an investigation may need to be conducted to simply determine the legality of the prescription.

The investigation of prescription fraud is highly dependent on the particular circumstances associated with the fraud. An investigative inquiry into possible prescription fraud usually begins with either (1) the discovery of the suspected illegal drugs by a third party (e.g., a friend or associate of the offender) who then notifies the police, (2) the discovery of the

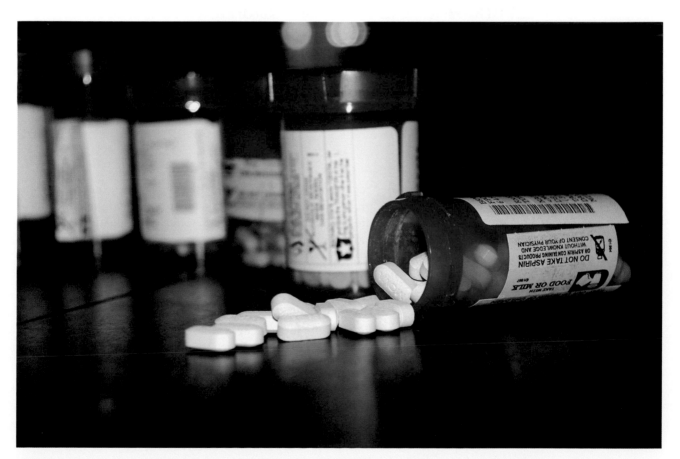

PHOTO 14.2: Prescription drug fraud is a major challenge for investigators. Often the crime is not brought to the attention of the police, and it can be difficult to determine if a prescription is legitimately linked to a particular person or not.

illegal drugs by the police (e.g., during a search), or, (3) as noted above, with the discovery by a doctor's office or pharmacy of the fraudulent actions to obtain the drugs and the resulting notification of the police. In any case, the fundamental investigative task is to first establish that the drugs were obtained and possessed illegally and then trace the drugs, or fraudulent actions, to the source, to an offender. If a labeled prescription bottle is recovered and there is question about the legality of the prescription, the prescription should be able to be traced to a particular pharmacy through the information contained on the label. The pharmacy is likely to have additional information about the patient/offender and the prescription that was filled. That information may be useful by itself in identifying the offender, or it could identify the physician who ordered the prescription or whose prescription pad was used to forge the prescription order. In any case, the physician's office may be able to provide additional information about the offender. If the time and place of the fraudulent prescription sale can be determined, it may be possible to examine security camera video to find the image of the person who fraudulently obtained the drugs.

If only the prescription drugs are discovered in possession of the subject, then investigators may be dependent on obtaining information from the actual subject or his or her parents, friends, associates, or co-workers in order to identify the legality of the prescription drugs and their source. Regardless of the particulars of the investigation, it is likely that physicians, nurses, and pharmacists will provide critical information about the prescription and the offender.

●●● Varieties of Computer-Facilitated Crime and Their Investigation

Some criminals use crowbars to commit their crimes; some use computers. As discussed, many types of fraud are facilitated through the use of computers. Other crimes, such as cybercrimes, sometimes involve "attacks" on computers and computer systems. Besides fraud and cyberattacks, there are many other types of crimes that involve computers, such as the distribution and possession of child pornography, the solicitation of minors for sex (as described in the introduction to this chapter), and cyberbullying, among others.

CYBERATTACKS

Cyberattack investigations can be highly technical and rely on advanced expertise in computer hardware and software. As such, presented here is only a very brief introduction to the topic. Entire textbooks are devoted to the issue of cyberattack investigations, and even those just touch on the potential complexity of the topic.

"Cyber-attacks are crimes in which the computer system is the target. Cyber-attacks consist of computer viruses, denial of service attacks, and electronic vandalism or sabotage" (Bureau of Justice Statistics 2008). Other cyber-related incidents include spyware, adware, hacking, phishing, spoofing, and pinging (see Exhibit 14.6). These attacks most often involve businesses. The National Computer Security Survey revealed that 67 percent of businesses experienced some form of cyberattack in 2005 (Bureau of Justice Statistics 2008), and most cyberattacks involved a computer virus infection or other related incident (e.g., hacking, spoofing, etc.). Only 15 percent of victimized businesses reported incidents to law enforcement, and when such incidents were reported they usually involved embezzlement, fraud, and theft of personal or financial data. In other instances, the events were reported internally or to another organization. As these crimes become more frequent and their consequences more severe, it is likely that law enforcement agencies will become increasingly involved in their investigation.

Exhibit 14.6 Types of Cyberattacks

A *denial of service attack* is designed to overwhelm a Web site in order to slow the transactions performed on the site or to crash it altogether. Amazon.com has experienced several denial of service attacks over the years, leading to loss of business and frustrated customers.

A computer *virus* is a computer program that is designed to disable or shut down a single computer. A *worm* is designed to travel to other computers in the network for the same purpose. The "ILOVEYOU" virus was one of the most widespread computer viruses. It spread via e-mail when unsuspecting recipients opened an attachment to the e-mail.

Spyware is software that collects and sends information about computer usage to another person or computer without the computer user's consent. The "cookies" maintained on a computer system are the most common and least harmful form of spyware.

Hacking involves the infiltration of a computer or computer system in order to gain control of that system. In 2013, hackers gained control of the Associated Press Twitter account and tweeted that there were explosions at the White House and that the president was injured.

Phishing (pronounced "fishing") involves obtaining usernames, passwords, and other personal information through trickery. Exhibit 14.1 is an example of a phishing scheme.

Spoofing involves one person masquerading as another through information distortion. Spoofing occurs when it appears that an e-mail was sent from an address from which it was not actually sent, or when a phone call is received from a number that was not actually used to make the call.

CYBERBULLYING AND HARASSMENT

Bullying can be defined as physical aggression (e.g., pushing, shoving) or verbal abuse (e.g., name calling) among individuals, both adult and juvenile. It occurs at school, on the playground, and at work. However, all sorts of additional opportunities for harassment and bullying are now possible due to the Internet, particularly through social networking sites, but also through e-mail and text messaging. Cyberbullying may involve sending or posting mean and inaccurate messages, starting and circulating rumors, stealing e-mail passwords, and sending messages. With the Internet, bullying can occur anytime, anywhere. It can occur every day, all day. Rumors and other false information can be spread among hundreds or thousands of people instantly. Fortunately for the investigation of cyberbullying and other computer-facilitated crimes, there is no such thing as anonymity on the Internet.

Research has shown that online victimization is quite common: 10 percent to 42 percent of college students have experienced some form of online victimization; some estimates among adolescents are higher (see Henson et al. 2011 for a review), and some are lower (Pelfrey and Weber 2013). Online victimization, especially bullying, is not any less significant in its consequences than other forms of bullying. Studies have shown that bullying corresponds to higher levels of depression among adolescent victims, especially among girls (Turner et al. 2013). Bullying is also associated with reduced academic performance, association with deviant peers, and involvement in violence (see Turner et al. 2013 for a review). Depression can have other negative effects, including suicide (Case in Point 14.3). Given the consequences, online victimization is an important and legitimate area of police involvement.

Although bullying and harassment are serious forms of conduct, only sometimes do they constitute criminal behavior. This depends on state law. For example, even some high-profile instances of online harassment have not resulted in criminal charges. For example, in 2012, Manti Te'o, the football player from the University of Notre Dame, fell victim to a "catfishing" hoax in which someone created an alternative identity and pretended to be someone that they were not. Te'o thought of this person as his girlfriend. No criminal

CASE *in* POINT 14.3 — "You Are a Bad Person and Everybody Hates You"

Megan Meier was fourteen years old and thrilled the day she received a friend request on MySpace from a sixteen-year-old boy named Josh Evans. Although she did not know him, she begged her parents to allow her to add him as a friend, and they agreed. Josh told Megan that he was from Florida and had just recently moved to Missouri, near to where Megan lived in O'Fallon. He told her that he was homeschooled and that he played the guitar and drums. He said that his dad left him, his mom, and his two brothers when he was seven years old. He seemed like a nice boy. Megan had attention deficit disorder; she was heavy and had tried to lose weight. She had dealt with depression. Megan decided to no longer be friends with a girlfriend who lived down the street, but she was thrilled with her new friend Josh. Megan was happy. Megan thought Josh was a great friend. She looked forward to her after-school chats with him.

Then, on October 15, 2006, Megan received a very upsetting message from Josh. It said "I don't know if I want to be friends with you anymore because I've heard that you are not very nice to your friends." The next day, Megan logged onto her MySpace account again and was horrified by what she saw posted from Josh and others. "Megan Meier is a slut." "Megan Meier is fat." Megan was hysterical and in tears. And the posts kept coming and coming. Megan fired back with vulgar posts of her own. Distraught, Megan went to her room and hung herself in her closet. She was discovered by her mom. Megan died the next day. On the day she died, Megan's father logged onto her MySpace account and viewed what he believed to be the last message seen by Megan. It was from Josh: "Everybody in O'Fallon knows how you are. You are a bad person and everybody hates you. Have a shitty rest of your life. The world would be a better place without you."

Six weeks after Megan died, a neighbor told Megan's mom that "Josh Evans" was not a real person. He was created by the parents of Megan's old friend, the one that Megan had earlier decided to not be friends with. The last message that was sent to Megan was from her former friend. The police were notified and they investigated. The former friend's mom who created the account explained to the police that she created the account just to find out what Megan was saying about her daughter online. She told police that somehow other people found out the password to the account and used it to send the mean messages to Megan. The FBI also investigated but were unable to retrieve from the computer the electronic messages received by Megan on the day she committed suicide. No criminal charges have been filed in connection with Megan's death. (For more information, see www.meganmeierfoundation.org.)

charges were issued in that case. Case in Point 14.3 is another "catfishing" example—one with a tragic ending—and no criminal charges were issued in this case either. Although there has been no attempt to identify the exact extent of cyberbullying, it is reasonable to conclude that most instances of cyberbullying occur in schools, especially middle and high schools. School resource officers typically learn of such instances and deal with them outside of the legal system.

"Sextortion" is probably best considered a form of cyberbullying. It is much more likely to lead to criminal charges. Sextortion usually involves a subject voluntarily providing another person (of true identity such as a boyfriend or a person assuming a false identity) compromising photos of himself or herself. Then, at some point, the person who received the photos threatens to distribute those photos unless the victim agrees to some other demand. This behavior is criminal. As shown in Case in Point 14.4, the collection of digital evidence is critical in the investigation of cyberbullying cases.

CHILD PORNOGRAPHY

Child pornography has become a much more significant problem as a result of the Internet. For the person who so desires, the Internet can transform a computer into a pornography superstore. As explained by Wortley and Smallbone (2012, p. 9), the Internet

- permits access to vast quantities of pornographic images from around the world;

- makes pornography instantly available at any time or place;

- allows pornography to be accessed (apparently) anonymously and privately;

- facilitates direct communication and image sharing among users;

- delivers pornography relatively inexpensively;

- provides images that are of high digital quality, do not deteriorate, and can be conveniently stored; and

- provides for a variety of formats (pictures, videos, sound), as well as the potential for real-time and interactive experiences.

With specific regard to child pornography, there are three distinct forms of illegal behavior: (1) production of the pornographic images, (2) distribution of the pornographic images, and (3) downloading/possession of the pornographic images. Offenders may be involved in one or any combinations of these behaviors. The production, distribution, and downloading of pornographic materials that involve adults is not, in most places, illegal. However, when it involves children, it is.

Production refers to the creation of pornographic images. Images can be produced professionally or, more commonly, amateurs can document the abuse of children to which they have access or control. Cell phone and Web cameras may facilitate the creation of the content. The production of child pornography typically comes to light with evidence of abuse or the discovery of hidden cameras used to record children.

Distribution involves the dissemination of pornographic images. Using the Internet, child pornography can be easily distributed around the world by uploading it onto Web sites; it can also be shared via e-mail, instant messages, newsgroups, bulletin boards, chat rooms, and peer-to-peer (P2P) networks (Wortley and Smallbone 2012). Due to efforts to police child pornography on the Internet, such Web sites are often quickly closed upon discovery. In addition, the exchange of pornography via e-mail or chat rooms is risky for offenders because of the possibility of undercover police operations (such as in the introduction to the chapter). Nevertheless, trafficking in child pornography continues on the Internet and through other means.

Downloading involves accessing and viewing child pornography via the Internet. Any images accessed through a computer or other electronic device may constitute downloading, including opening spam and clicking on pop-up links. Accidentally accessing a child pornography Web site may also constitute downloading. In most cases, however, users must deliberately search Web sites for child pornography or subscribe to groups dedicated to child pornography in order to find it and download it. Some analysts have noted that genuine child pornography is uncommon in open areas of the Internet and that most child pornography is downloaded via newsgroups and chat rooms. Access to such sites may be closed and require paying a fee or using a password (Wortley and Smallbone 2012). The possession/downloading of child pornography often comes to light as a result of another person's observation of the computer or of the contents of the computer's hard drive (as was the case in the introduction to the chapter) or through other police operations.

In the detection and investigation of the production, distribution, or possession of child pornography, electronic (digital) evidence is, once again, likely to be the centerpiece of the investigation. In particular, images accessed on a computer can be retrieved from the computer's hard drive. A record of log files (who logged on to the computer and when), modem logs (when a computer was connected to the Internet), Web browser history (online activity on the computer), and e-mail and chat logs can also be retrieved from a forensic examination of the computer (see below). Digital cameras and mobile phones may also contain evidence of child pornography that can be recovered from memory cards installed in the devices. Internet Service Providers (ISPs) maintain records of Internet Protocol (IP) addresses,

CASE *in* POINT 14.4 — "I'm Going to Send out the Photos Unless . . ."

Tony Scarver (not his real name) was a high school senior who was picked on a lot. Bullied. Made fun of. The brunt of many jokes. But Tony fought back, in a nasty, criminal sort of way. Tony created the fictitious Facebook profile of a girl named "Kayla," who supposedly attended the same high school as Tony. Through Facebook, "Kayla" lured unsuspecting boys from the high school and middle school to take nude and other sexually explicit photographs of themselves and send those photos to "her." Often the boys asked "Kayla" to send a nude photo of herself first. "Kayla" usually complied, sending a photo of a girl with her face cropped from the photo. Thirty boys in total fell into the trap; some were as young as thirteen. After the boys took photos of themselves and sent them to "Kayla," seven of the boys received texts from "her." In each instance, "she" told the boy that "she" was going to send out the photos to everyone unless they would agree to allow "her" friend, Tony Scarver, to "suck him off." After the boy received the text from "Kayla," Tony would text the victim and tell the unsuspecting boy that he was sure that "Kayla" would delete the photos if the boy agreed to "her" demand. Tony and the boy would make arrangements to meet in the bathroom at the public library. Tony brought a camera to photograph the sex acts, saying that "Kayla needed

proof" that the boys actually did it. On more than one occasion, Tony told the victim after the meeting that he accidently deleted the photos and that they would need to do it again.

One day during the time that these meetings were occurring, the principal and two teachers at the high school received an e-mail that there was a bomb in the school. The police were notified. Via the Internet Protocol (IP) address associated with the e-mail, the e-mail was traced to a computer in the public library. A library employee identified Tony Scarver as the person who was using the computer at the time that bomb scare e-mail was sent. As the police were talking with Tony about the bomb scare, a boy came forward to the police and told them that he was being forced to engage in sex with Tony Scarver. Due to these allegations, additional investigation was conducted. Tony's computers and cell phone were seized and examined. Nude and other images of the thirty boys were recovered from the hard drive of the computer, and the texts sent to the boys were obtained from Tony's phone. As a result, the full extent of Tony's crimes became known. Tony Scarver pled guilty to repeated sexual assault of a child, while numerous other counts were dismissed. He was sentenced to twelve years in prison.

---

which are unique to each computer and can be linked to subscriber names and billing addresses, and when and what files were accessed with those computers. Finally, through the use of "digger engine" software, investigators may monitor the online and chat room activity of offenders though the recording of IP addresses (Wortley and Smallbone 2012).

As a prerequisite for effective child pornography investigations, it has been recommended that investigators acquire the special technical expertise required to collect and process electronic evidence. In addition, ISPs play a critical role in child pornography investigations, as well as in other Internet-related investigations. As such, it is important the police develop a good relationship with ISPs in order to work together to effectively combat these crimes.

To proactively combat child pornography on the Internet, the police can locate child pornography sites and take the necessary steps to have them removed. Investigators can conduct undercover sting operations by entering pedophile newsgroups or chat rooms posing as pedophiles and request that child pornography images be e-mailed from others in the group. Alternatively, they may enter associated chat rooms posing as children and identify offenders who may send or request pornographic images, or they may suggest a meeting for sexual purposes. Another option is for the police to place ads on the Internet for the sale of pornography and then conduct "buy-bust" operations. Investigators may establish Internet "honey trap" sites that claim to contain child pornography but are really designed to identity the IP addresses or credit card numbers of those who access the site. The investigation of seemingly unrelated crimes may include the search and seizure of computers and other electronic devices. Such searches may reveal not only evidence of the crime in question but also other crimes, including the creation, distribution, or possession of child pornography.

Child pornography crimes often come to light as the result of information provided to the police from members of the public who either alert the police to content on a Web site or to the actual involvement of a subject in child pornography crimes; from computer technicians who work on a customer's computer and, in the process, discover such images; or from victims who report abuse to the police. Additionally, child pornographers may be identified as a result of an arrest of other offenders, or, as mentioned, the police may identify evidence of child pornography when investigating other crimes. In any case, once the crime has been discovered, evidence of it is likely to be in digital form.

●●● Digital Evidence

Digital evidence is "information and data of value to an investigation that is stored on, received, or transmitted by an electronic device" (National Institute of Justice 2008, p. ix). As defined by the National Research Council (2009, p. 179), the analysis of digital evidence "deals with gathering, processing, and interpreting digital evidence, such as electronic documents, lists of phone numbers and call logs, records of a device's location at a given time, e-mails, photographs, and more," including databases, Internet browsing history, chat logs, friend lists, and calendars.

Along with desktop, laptop, and tablet computers, other devices that may contain digital evidence include cell phones, GPS devises, digital cameras, video cameras, surveillance equipment, computer servers, video game systems, MP3 players (e.g., iPods), external hard drives, and other storage devices (e.g., thumb drives). These devices serve as electronic filing cabinets that may contain evidence related to various types of crimes. In this era of information and computerization, many of our daily activities are, in some way, recorded digitally: where we went, when we went there, what we did when we got there, who we spoke with, and what we said. This applies to criminals as well, except with criminals this information may constitute criminal evidence. Given the proliferation of electronic devices, it is not an exaggeration that nearly every crime could have digital evidence associated with it. Sometimes digital evidence is the primary evidence in a criminal investigation (see Case in Point 14.5).

Of course, before an electronic device can be analyzed and digital evidence collected from it, the device first has to be identified as being at least potentially relevant in an investigation. For instance, a technician has to notify the authorities of the child pornography on a computer, parents have to notify the police of the video that makes fun of what happened to their daughter (Case in Point 14.5), or a boy has to come forward and notify the police that he was forced to engage in sexual acts (Case in Point 14.4).

Another important way by which crimes can be traced to a particular computer, and thus perhaps a particular person, is through the identification of the Internet Protocol (IP) address of the computer. This is usually most relevant in cases where a computer was used to send e-mails or to engage in other Internet activities. The tracing of an IP address was an important part of the investigations described in Case in Point 14.1 and Case in Point 14.4. Most fundamentally, an IP address is an identifying number that is associated with a computer. However, there is much variation in the assignment of IP addresses; IP addresses on computers can change (dynamic), remain the same (static), or be shared by several computers. An IP address can be potentially useful for criminal investigation purposes because it can be obtained from a Web site that maintains a log of IP addresses that accessed that site. Once an IP address is in hand, that address can be linked to the Internet Service Provider (ISP) that connects that computer to the Internet. That ISP can then provide the billing

CASE *in* POINT 14.5   "She Is So Raped"

Text messages sent with cell phones and photos and video taken with cell phones played a critical role in the 2013 conviction of two high school football players in Ohio for the crime of rape. Trent Mays, seventeen, and Ma'lik Richmond, sixteen, were found guilty of raping a drunken sixteen-year-old girl at party. A critical issue at the trial was that the girl was too intoxicated to consent to the acts and too intoxicated to resist. The text messages, video, and photos spoke directly to these issues.

The crime was first brought to the attention of authorities by the victim's parents, who learned that a video that made fun of the girl and her assault had been posted on YouTube by some of the teens who attended the party. In that video the victim was referred to as "the dead girl," and one attendee commented, "She is so raped." A photo showing the two defendants carrying the girl out of a house by her arms and legs was posted on Instagram. Subsequent to these discoveries, cell phones from seventeen of the teens were seized by the police. Approximately 350,000 text messages were recovered from the phones and analyzed, as were hundreds of thousands of photos, videos, tweets, and other posts. Two photos of a nude girl were recovered from the cell phone that belonged to Mays. As reported in the media, some of the text conversations recovered from Mays' phone included the following:

Friend of Mays:	Did u do it?
Mays:	No, lol. She could barely move.
From another friend:	How dead is she?
Mays:	Not at all, she's looking for her phone.
Mays:	I'm pissed all I got was a hand job, though. I should have raped since everyone thinks I did.

From the victim's phone to a friend:

Victim:	What the fuck? Who was there? What happened to me?

Victim:	I swear to God I don't remember anything. I remember at one point hearing Trent telling me to do something, but I said no.

Later, the victim texted Mays:

Victim:	Ok, tell me right now what the fuck happened last night and don't lie to me. We need to talk about this right now.
Mays:	Nothing happen last night. You [sexual act] last night and that's it.
Victim:	OK, that's not all that happened. Tell me the truth now.

Later, the victim e-mailed Mays:

Victim:	Why the fuck would you let that happen to me? Seriously, you have no fuckin respect.

Later, Mays texted a friend:

Mays:	Dude, I'm so fuckin scared. Her dad knows where we brought her. If we are questioned, just say she was really drunk and we were trying to keep her safe.

It was only as a result of the digital evidence that investigators were able to reconstruct the past and determine, at the very least, what the participants were saying about the incident prior to the involvement of the police.

(Note: Although the defendants were juveniles, their names were widely used in court documents and media stories. Their names are provided here as well.)

For additional details see Carter et al. (2013a), Carter et al. (2013b), Almasy (2013), Wetzel (2013), and Richardson (2013).

---

name and address associated with that IP address. It is in this way that the identification of an IP address may lead to the name and addresses of the person who controls or uses that computer.

As with any search and seizure, there must be a legal basis for the collection of electronic equipment and the search for digital evidence. There is not a digital evidence exception to the search warrant requirement. Normally, electronic devices are seized either as a result of consent, plain view, or the execution of a search warrant. As discussed in Chapter 4, cell phones may be seized and searched incident to lawful arrest (Bulzomi 2007).

In most cases, electronic items that are believed to contain digital evidence can be collected using standard equipment and tools, although caution needs to be exercised to avoid altering or destroying the evidence. Tools that may produce or emit static electricity and magnetic devices should not be used near electronic items. Mobile devices such as cell phones should be collected, transported, and stored in frequency-shielding materials such as aluminum foil to prevent the phones from receiving calls, tests messages, or other signals that may alter or destroy the evidence. To prevent damage from moisture, under no circumstances should phones or other electronic devices be packaged in plastic bags. If the phone was on when discovered, it should be left on. If it was off, it should be left off (National Institute of Justice 2008).

The place where the electronic items were located should be treated as a crime scene. As such, appropriate precautions and security measures, as well as documentation of the scene (noting especially the location of electronic equipment and connections of the device), are necessary to preserve the integrity of the scene. The device should be photographed and the corresponding cables and connections should be labeled and noted prior to disconnection. Additional technical procedures are outlined in the National Institute of Justice (2008) work titled *Electronic Crime Scene Investigation: A Guide for First Responders*. It must also be remembered that physical evidence on the devices (e.g., fingerprints) may be important evidence in the investigation, and efforts should be made to preserve and collect it.

When seizing computers, different procedures should be employed depending on whether the computer is on or off, whether computer experts are available on scene, whether the computer is part of a business network, and whether electronic evidence is visible onscreen (National Institute of Justice 2008). Generally speaking, if the computer is off, it should not be turned on. If it is on, it should not be touched or moved unless it appears that files are being deleted. In this case, the computer should be immediately disconnected from the power source. If the computer is on and not in the process of deleting files, the computer should be turned off but only under the direction of a trained digital evidence expert. If the computer is off, it can be unplugged and carefully transported for forensic analysis. Any external storage devices should also be seized (e.g., thumb drives, CDs). Although this is standard practice, some data (e.g., recently typed passwords) may be lost when the device is turned off (National Institute of Justice 2008). Investigators should be aware of all possible devices that may contain digital evidence related to the investigation.

Along with the digital evidence, information from those persons who have access or ownership of the devices will also likely prove to be useful in the investigation. As such, the following information should be collected from them (National Institute of Justice 2008, p. 17):

- Names of all users of the computers and devices
- All computer and Internet user information
- All login names and user account names
- Purpose and uses of the computers and devices
- All passwords
- Any automated applications in use
- Type of Internet access used
- Any offsite storage
- Internet service provider
- Installed software documentation
- All e-mail accounts
- Security provisions in use
- Web mail account information
- Data access restrictions in place
- All instant messaging screen names
- All destructive devices or software in use
- Social networking Web site account information
- Any other relevant information

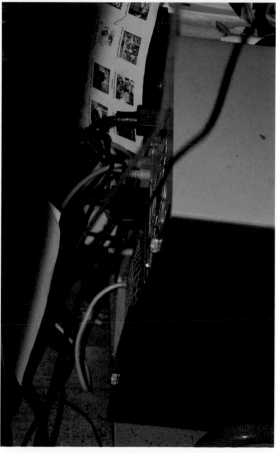

PHOTO 14.3–14.7: These crime scene photographs relate to a low-tech counterfeiting operation. The computer and printer were critical evidence in the investigation.

Although specific details regarding the collection of digital evidence are beyond the scope of this chapter, the basics are highlighted here (National Research Council 2009). Normally, digital evidence is contained in the memory of the device. There are several types of memory, and different devices have different types of memory. Magnetic memory includes hard drives, floppy discs, and tapes. Optical memory includes compact discs (CDs) and digital versatile discs (DVDs). Electronic memory consists of USB flash drives, memory cards, and flash memory microchips.

The analysis of a computer for the collection of digital evidence involves several steps. First, all the data on the storage device, most often a hard drive of the computer, is copied to a new, blank hard drive. The imaged hard drive can then be compared to the original hard drive to verify the accuracy of the imaged hard drive. Electronically, every file is then given a unique identifying number. The imaged hard drive is then examined for saved computer files that may relate to the case at hand. These logical files are most often photographs, documents, spreadsheets, and e-mails that have been saved by the user in various folders and directories. Logical files are patent files. Next, the imaged hard drive is examined for files that have been deleted. These data are physical files on the hard drive, but they are not logically available on the computer operating system; these files are latent (sort of like how latent fingerprints are not visible until they are made visible).

Finally, systems files that were created by the computer operating system are examined. These files have been described as sort of like a surveillance tape that shows user activity on the computer and files that were changed by the user. The goal of the examination of the contents of the hard drive is to "find files with probative information and to discover information about when and how these files came to be on the computer" (National Research Council 2009).

As digital evidence has become relevant in more investigations, the field of forensic digital evidence has continued to evolve. It used to be that a police officer with an interest in computers would be designated as the digital evidence expert in the department. Now the techniques and standards of digital evidence collection have become more rigorous and scientific. Individuals who are designated as digital evidence collection experts should expect to receive considerable training regarding the collection and analysis of the evidence. Nevertheless, challenges remain. According to the National Research Council (2009, p. 181), these include the following:

- The digital evidence community does not have an agreed-upon certification program or list of qualifications for digital forensic examiners.

- Some agencies still treat the examination of digital evidence as an investigative rather than a forensic activity.

- There is wide variability in, and uncertainty about, the education, experience, and training of those practicing this discipline.

With increased use of computers and other digital devices in our daily lives, digital evidence has become more and more significant in criminal investigations. Digital evidence can be quite powerful. It has the unique ability to cast light onto past conversations, statements, and behaviors of victims and offenders. Although the presence of digital evidence may not be obvious and its collection is quite technical, investigators should always be mindful of the possible role it may play in criminal investigations.

MAIN POINTS

1. Fraud refers to all the ways one person can falsely represent a fact to another in order to induce that person to surrender something of value. There are many different types of fraud, only limited by offenders' imaginations.

2. Identity theft is a common form of fraud that occurs when one person steals the personal information of another and uses it without permission. Typically, identity theft has a financial motive, but it may have other motives as well, such as revenge.

3. There are many ways by which offenders can steal personal information. And there are many ways by which that personal information can be used in order for the offender to profit from it.

4. The Fair and Accurate Credit Transactions Act of 2003 (the FACT Act) provides consumers with rights and helps to detect and combat identity theft.

5. Identity theft investigations can be quite complicated depending on the extent of the theft and the number of agencies that may be involved.

6. Local police departments usually have primary responsibility for documenting and investigating identity theft complaints.

7. The preliminary investigation report should include when the victim discovered the fraud, the fraudulent activity discovered to date, and information about the thief, if known. Other documentation related to the theft should also be included. The victim should be provided with information about the necessary steps to address the damage done as a result of the theft.

8. Several national databases may be useful when investigating allegations of identity theft.

9. There are several common ways offenders may fraudulently use checks or credit/debit cards. These include the passing and cashing of worthless checks, presenting a fraudulent/stolen check or card at checkout to make a purchase, making a card-not-present purchase, or ordering an item with a legitimate credit card but then denying ordering and/or receiving the item.

10. When check/card fraud crimes are investigated, there are several possible courses of action for investigators to pursue depending on the particulars of the crime.

11. Prescription drug fraud, and the misuse of those drugs, is a significant law enforcement problem. Law enforcement agencies increasingly identify prescription drugs as their greatest drug control challenge.

12. Part of the difficulty in investigating prescription drug fraud and misuse is that offenders who obtain the drugs are usually most interested in using the drugs themselves, not selling the drugs to others.

13. Another complicating dimension of this type of investigation is that in most instances, it is not known immediately if the drugs were obtained by the subject legitimately or through fraud.

14. The investigation of prescription fraud is highly dependent on the particular circumstances associated with the fraud and almost always involves obtaining critical information from doctors' offices and pharmacies.

15. Cyberattacks are crimes in which the computer system is the target. Cyberattacks consist of computer viruses, denial of service attacks, electronic vandalism or sabotage, spyware, adware, hacking, phishing, spoofing, and pinging. These attacks most often involve businesses and are very seldom reported to law enforcement.

16. Bullying has traditionally been defined in terms of physical aggression, verbal abuse, or other negative relational behaviors among individuals, both adult and juvenile. Cyberbullying may involve sending or posting mean and inaccurate messages, starting and circulating rumors, stealing e-mail passwords, and sending messages. Due to Internet access, bullying can occur anytime and anywhere.

17. The consequences of bullying can be significant and tragic and, as a result, these behaviors may be of police concern.

18. "Catfishing" and "sextortion" are best considered examples of cyberbullying.

19 With regard to child pornography, there are three distinct forms of illegal behavior: (1) production of the pornographic images, (2) distribution of the pornographic images, and (3) downloading/possession of the pornographic images.

20. In detecting and investigating the production, distribution, or possession of child pornography, electronic (digital) evidence is usually the centerpiece of the investigation.

21. Digital evidence is information and data of value to an investigation that are stored on, received by, or transmitted by an electronic device.

22. Along with desktop, laptop, and tablet computers, other devices that may contain digital evidence include cell phones, GPS devises, digital cameras, video cameras, surveillance equipment, computer servers, video game systems, MP3 players (e.g., iPods), external hard drives, and other storage devices (e.g., thumb drives).

23. Internet Protocol (IP) addresses are an important form of digital evidence. An IP address is an identifying number that is associated with a computer. IP addresses can be obtained from Web sites and linked to Internet Service Providers (ISP). ISPs have records of names and addresses associated with computer IP addresses.

24. When seizing computers, different procedures should be employed depending on whether the computer is on or off, whether computer seizure experts are available on scene, whether the computer is part of a business network, and whether electronic evidence is visible onscreen.

25. Along with the digital evidence, information from those persons who have access or ownership of the devices will also likely prove to be useful in the investigation.

26. Digital evidence is contained in the memory of the device. The collection of evidence from the memory of the device involves several technical steps, from the imaging of the memory to the analysis of the memory.

27. With the increased use of computers and other digital devices in our daily lives, digital evidence has become more and more significant and common in criminal investigations.

IMPORTANT TERMS ●───────────────────────────

Buy-bust strategy	Dumpster driving	Internet Protocol (IP) address
Card not present purchase	E-Information	
Catfishing	Fair and Accurate Credit Transitions Act (FACT Act)	Magnetic memory
Child pornography		Optical memory
Computer memory	FinCEN	Spyware
Computer viruses	Fraud	Passing and cashing
Computer-facilitated crime	FTC Consumer Sentinel	Phishing
Cyberattacks	Hacking	Pretexting
Cyberbullying	Identity cloning	Sextortion
Cybercrime	Identity theft	Shimming
Digital evidence	Imaged hard drive	Skimming
Doctor shopping	Internet Service Provider (ISP)	Spoofing

QUESTIONS FOR DISCUSSION AND REVIEW

1. What is fraud? What are some of the various types of fraud?

2. What is identity theft? What forms may it take? What are typical motives for identity theft?

3. What are the challenges associated with the investigation of identity theft?

4. How should identity theft be documented and investigated by the police? What sources of information are available for investigators in identity theft investigations?

5. What actions should victims be advised to take when they discover the theft of their identity?

6. What is check and credit/debit card fraud? What are the common ways by which it occurs?

7. How can check and credit/debit card fraud be investigated?

8. What is prescription fraud? What are the ways by which it is committed?

9. What are the difficulties associated with detecting and investigating prescription fraud?

10. What are the most important sources of information and evidence in prescription fraud investigations?

11. What are cyberattacks? What forms may they take?

12. What is cyberbullying and harassment? Why is this an important area of concern for the police?

13. What crimes constitute child pornography? How is child pornography most often discovered?

14. What is the essential role of digital evidence in child pornography investigations?

15. What is digital evidence? Why is it a unique form of evidence in criminal investigations?

16. What are the various sources of digital evidence in criminal investigations?

17. What are Internet Protocol (IP) addresses? How can they be obtained and used as evidence?

18. What is the legal basis for the search and seizure of electronic devices?

19. What are the procedures for collecting digital evidence from computers?

▶ STUDENT STUDY SITE

Visit **www.sagepub.com/brandl3e** to access additional study tools including eFlashcards, web quizzes, web resources, video resources, and SAGE journal articles.

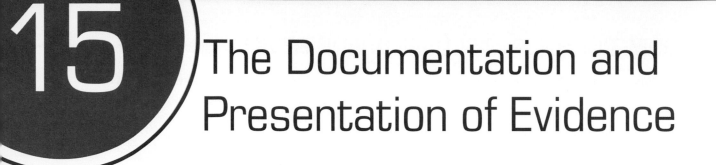

15

The Documentation and Presentation of Evidence

Objectives

After reading this chapter you will be able to:

- Describe the court process as an adversarial process and explain the role of defense attorneys, prosecuting attorneys, judges, and the police in the adversarial process

- Discuss the importance and value of a vigorous defense for defendants

- Explain the various ways in which police misconduct and incompetence can lead to miscarriages of justice

- Discuss the role and importance of investigative reports in criminal investigations and the court process

- Identify the guidelines to be used when writing investigative reports

- Define the role of lay and expert witnesses in court, and the controversies of using experts in court

- Identify the steps or stages of the trial process, and the two main questions addressed in the trial

- Discuss the purpose of the cross-examination and evaluate the tactics commonly used by defense attorneys when cross-examining investigator witnesses

- Identify the guidelines regarding testimony in court

From the CASE FILE
A Horror Story With a Happy Ending

On July 17, 1982, a twenty-seven year-old woman was walking home from a shopping center in Hanover, Virginia, when a man riding a bicycle abducted her and carried her into a nearby wooded area where he raped, beat, and sodomized her. The victim reported the incident to the police and told investigators that one of the statements made by the perpetrator during the assault was "I got me a white girl at home." A police officer immediately suspected that the perpetrator might be Marvin Anderson because Anderson was the only black man the officer knew who lived with a white woman. Anderson did not have a mug shot photo on file at the police department because he had never been arrested. The officer obtained a color employment photograph card of Anderson from Anderson's employer. The color identification card, along with six black-and-white mug shots of other individuals, was shown to the victim. The victim identified Anderson as the man who attacked her. Within an hour of this identification, a live lineup was conducted and she identified Anderson again. Anderson was the only individual who was in the photo array as well as in the live lineup. Anderson was arrested.

The case went to trial in 1983. At the trial, the victim testified in detail about the assault. She explained that the offender pried her mouth open and inserted his penis, forced her to consume fecal matter, and urinated on her. She again identified Anderson as the perpetrator. The serology analysis was uninformative; it could not include or exclude Anderson as the assailant. The defense presented an alibi for Anderson (that he was at home with his girlfriend) but failed to present evidence about a different suspect—John Lincoln. The bicycle that the offender used was identified by the owner, and he stated that Lincoln had stolen it from him about thirty minutes before the rape. Anderson requested that his lawyer question the owner of the bicycle and Lincoln as witnesses, but his lawyer refused. The all-white jury convicted Anderson of rape, forcible sodomy, abduction, and robbery. He was sentenced to 210 years in prison. (It was later discovered that Anderson's lawyer had previously defended John Lincoln in a rape case; Lincoln was acquitted in that case.)

Five years later, in 1988, John Lincoln came forward and confessed to the crime for which Anderson was convicted. Lincoln provided details of the crime under oath in court, but the judge, who had also presided over the original trial, rejected Lincoln's confession and refused to vacate Anderson's conviction. Anderson then requested that the newly discovered DNA analysis be performed on the semen evidence, but he was told that the evidence had been thrown away. All hope seemed lost. In 1994, Anderson contacted the Innocence Project and his case was accepted. Lawyers got busy trying to find the physical evidence in the case, but every avenue was a dead end. Finally, in 1997, Anderson was paroled after spending fifteen years in prison. He continued to maintain his innocence.

In 2001, Innocence Project attorneys were advised that physical evidence in the case had been found. The director of the Virginia Division of Forensic Science notified the attorneys that sperm and semen samples recovered from the victim had been located in a laboratory notebook of the criminalist who originally analyzed the evidence in 1982. The retention of evidence in this manner was not in accordance with agency policy. If the swabs had been returned to the sexual assault evidence kit, they would have been thrown out. A request for DNA analysis on the evidence was made. Attorneys were informed that the analysis would be performed only under court order or by order of the Virginia governor, neither of which was granted. A legal battle ensued. Later that year, DNA analysis was finally conducted on the evidence. On December 6, 2001, the results were in: the DNA analysis excluded Anderson as the perpetrator. When the DNA profile was compared to those in the Virginia DNA database, two matches were obtained. One was of John Lincoln, who was in prison for an unrelated conviction. The identity of the other man has not been released.

On August 21, 2002, the governor of Virginia granted Marvin Anderson a full pardon. He was a convicted sex offender no more. (For more information, see innocenceproject.org.)

Case Considerations and Points for Discussion

- What evidence led to the arrest and conviction of Marvin Anderson as the perpetrator of the rape?

- What mistakes did the police make in conducting the investigation? If it was not for these mistakes, do you think Marvin Anderson would have been arrested and convicted?

- Something can be learned from every investigation—more in some investigations than in others. What do you think should be the biggest lessons learned by the police as a result of the investigation, conviction, and the vacated conviction of Marvin Anderson?

Most of this book has been devoted to a discussion of how criminal investigations should be conducted, how evidence should be collected, the role and functions of evidence, the strengths and weaknesses of evidence, and the collection of evidence in particular types of crimes. This chapter takes a different focus. This chapter discusses issues relating to the documentation of evidence in reports and the presentation of evidence in court through testimony. It also examines the trial process and the outcomes of that process.

The information in this chapter is important for students of criminal investigation for several reasons. First, the identification and apprehension of offenders is not the end of the criminal justice process. As discussed in Chapter 1, in order to achieve a reduction in crime, offenders have to be deterred or incapacitated, and this largely depends on *convictions* being obtained in court, not on arrests. Arrests are a good start, but convictions are what really matters. Further, successful prosecutions are based on good evidence and, as such, successful prosecutions depend on competent and thorough investigations. Consequently, investigators should be knowledgeable about the process involved in adjudicating offenders and obtaining convictions.

Second, the evidence used by prosecutors in court is documented in police reports. Evidence, and the associated testimony of investigators involved with a case, may only be as good as the reports completed by those investigators. As such, the value and importance of well-written and thorough reports cannot be underestimated.

PHOTO 15.1: Marvin Anderson spent many years in jail for a crime he did not commit. He was eventually exonerated by DNA analysis of the evidence in the crime.

Third, to be most effective, police investigators should be as familiar with the court process as they are with the criminal investigation process. They should feel as comfortable and competent on a witness stand as they do at a crime scene. Again, this is simply because the job of investigators does not end with an arrest being made. They have important responsibilities in assisting the prosecutor in preparing the case for court and testifying.

Fourth, investigators must understand that although they play an important role in the prosecution of offenders, many other people do as well. If a case results in a bad outcome (e.g., a guilty defendant is not convicted or an innocent defendant is convicted), investigators should be able to maintain perspective. They may or may not share responsibility for that outcome.

Finally, and relatedly, given the seriousness of a conviction and what happens to offenders upon conviction, investigators should appreciate the tragedy of bad judicial outcomes, regardless of who is responsible for those outcomes. The work of criminal investigators is extremely important and mistakes can be tragic. Investigators must understand the seriousness of their work.

●●● The Adversarial Process

The court process in the United States can be described as being adversarial in nature. It can be viewed as a contest or even a game (Dershowitz 1982), albeit a serious one, in which defense attorneys and prosecuting attorneys are opponents. Indeed, defense attorneys and prosecuting attorneys present conflicting arguments, or conflicting versions of the truth, in court in an effort to win the "game." The judge is supposed to be a neutral referee in the contest, making sure that rules of the game are enforced fairly. Police investigators are a part of the prosecution team. The role of investigators is to collect the evidence in the case and, on the basis of probable cause, to identify and apprehend the individual who committed the crime. The prosecution then presents evidence collected by the police in court to convince a judge or jury, beyond a reasonable doubt, that a crime occurred and that the defendant committed it.

The role of the defense attorney is to probe, test, and question the evidence presented by the prosecutor. Defense attorneys provide alternative explanations for the evidence and present other evidence in an attempt to establish reasonable doubt. It is in this way that the quality and integrity of the evidence in the case is tested and defendants are represented. As such, the provision of a legal defense is no less important for a guilty defendant than it is for an innocent one. After all, it is only through the legal process that it is determined who is guilty and who is not. As explained by Dershowitz (1982), "Defending the guilty and the despised—even freeing some of them—is a small price to pay for our liberties. Imagine a system where the guilty and the despised—or at least those so regarded by the powers that be—were not entitled to representation!" (p. xiv).

At times it may seem that the prosecution team is at a disadvantage in the game. Defense attorneys do not have to prove anything to win; the burden of proof is entirely on the prosecution. In addition, the prosecution and the police have to follow and abide by numerous rules in collecting and presenting evidence. The police have to tell the truth in court or face the consequences of perjury. Defense attorneys can develop alternative explanations for the evidence. The prosecution has to share all evidence in the case with the defense counsel. Indeed, the prosecution does have some disadvantages, but, all things considered, they also have some major advantages. Most importantly, the prosecution has the full authority and power of the government on its side. The prosecution usually has significantly more resources at its disposal for evidence collection, analysis, and presentation, including resources for trial consultants, expert witnesses, and a legal staff. Only with the relatively rare wealthy defendant are the players in equal standing in terms of resources available.

Police officers and investigators often express contempt toward the judicial process and defense attorneys in particular. Some studies have shown that dealing with the courts, and testifying in particular, is one of the more stressful aspects of a police officer's job (Miller 2006; Brown and Campbell 1994). One reason for this is that judges and defense attorneys are in a position and have the responsibility to review and question the actions of police officers. Defense attorneys often test the evidence in the case by testing the police. As such, police officers may see defense attorneys as being on the side of criminals and as an obstacle to justice. Clearly, defense attorneys are adversaries to the police/prosecution team.

Although problematic from the perspective of individual officers, from a judicial perspective, the process of testing the evidence is necessary to increase the chances of a fair and just outcome. The lack of a vigorous defense is one of the common features in many miscarriage-of-justice cases, as seen in the introduction to this chapter (and as discussed later). It must be noted, however, that an adequate test of the evidence through a vigorous defense is not a guarantee that fairness and justice will prevail. Defense attorneys may mount a vigorous defense and their clients may still be convicted for crimes they did not commit. In addition, on probably quite rare occasions, a vigorous test of the evidence can actually result in justice being denied—in a guilty subject being set free. Because all defendants—both guilty and innocent—are entitled to a vigorous test of the evidence, this is a risk that is inherent in the process and, as argued by Dershowitz (1982), is a small price to pay for our civil liberties. It is the nature of the game.

PHOTO 15.2: Defense attorneys question investigators about how they conducted an investigation. Investigators must be prepared to answer these questions.

●●● Errors in Justice Outcomes

THE SERIOUSNESS OF ERRORS IN JUSTICE OUTCOMES

Miscarriages of justice, be they in the form of innocent subjects being punished or guilty subjects going free, are serious. If a guilty person goes free, that person has avoided punishment and justice is denied for the victim and for society. That person is also free to offend again. If an innocent person is convicted, it will have devastating effects on that person's life. Imagine the horror. Imagine the police showing up at your house accusing you of committing a serious crime. Imagine being arrested. But you did not commit the crime. Imagine being placed in handcuffs and put in the back seat of a police car, transported to the police station, and interrogated. Imagine being fingerprinted, searched, and put in jail. But you did not commit the crime. Think about your appearances in court. Think about the trial and the jury's verdict of guilty. But you did not commit the crime! Imagine going to prison. Think about the first night in prison, the first week, the first month, the first year. Five years. Ten years. Twenty years. *But you did not commit the crime!* Can you imagine a worse nightmare? Probably not. If that is not bad enough, when an innocent person is arrested and convicted, it means that the person who actually committed the crime is still free to offend, possibly raping, robbing, or murdering more victims. Criminal investigators should keep this in mind every day. Investigators should be passionate

A Question of Ethics

?

Why Is It Okay to Lie Sometimes but Not Other Times?

The rules for proper investigative conduct vary by the situation. For example, while it is legally acceptable for investigators to lie to suspects in the interrogation room, it is not legal for them to lie to the judge or jury in the courtroom. Why is this so?

The sloppy evidence collection procedures compounded the problem. In particular, four significant mistakes were made in handling the physical evidence in the Simpson case. Briefly, first, the police used a blanket from Nicole's house to cover the bodies. This cast doubt on the hair and fiber evidence said to have been recovered from the bodies. Second, from the records kept, it appeared that some of the blood drawn from O. J. for DNA analysis was missing. Third, it was determined that Detective Vannatter took the blood drawn from O. J. back to the crime scene. Finally, some of the blood evidence at the crime scene was only first recovered weeks after the homicides had occurred. Clearly, these errors, together with the lies, cast a shadow on all of the evidence. It is no wonder that the jurors found reasonable doubt.

PROSECUTORIAL MISCONDUCT AND INCOMPETENCE

Another reason for bad judicial outcomes is prosecutorial misconduct and incompetence. Prosecutors exercise considerable discretion in deciding how cases should be processed and prosecuted. When this discretion is abused or incompetently used, when exculpatory evidence is suppressed, when evidence is destroyed, when witnesses who are known to be unreliable and to be offering perjured testimony are used, or when evidence is fabricated, the rules of the game are violated and justice may likely be sacrificed.

DEFENSE ATTORNEY MISCONDUCT AND INCOMPETENCE

The U.S. Constitution requires that those individuals accused of crimes be afforded legal counsel and be provided a vigorous defense. As noted earlier, without this ingredient, the adversarial process ceases to exist. The game becomes totally lopsided. If there is no possibility that the evidence in a case will be tested, police and prosecutors may misbehave with impunity. An unjust outcome may be the result. This issue is of most concern with defense attorneys who represent indigent clients. Common are incredible caseloads that prevent attorneys from spending the time on each case that it requires. Lack of time to prepare a defense may have obvious implications.

The case of Jimmy Ray Bromgard illustrates the extreme of defense counsel incompetence. In 1987, Bromgard was convicted of raping an eight-year-old girl and was sentenced to forty years in prison. In 2002, after already serving nearly sixteen years in prison, he was exonerated on the basis of DNA testing that proved he did not commit the crime. During Bromgard's original trial, his attorney conducted no investigation, did not give an opening statement, did not prepare a closing statement, questioned no witnesses, did not file an appeal, and presented no expert testimony to refute the (fraudulent) testimony of the prosecution's forensic expert witness. Beside this forensic testimony and a tentative identification of Bromgard by the witness, there was no evidence against Bromgard (see www.innocenceproject.org).

At the other extreme, it may be reasonable to ask whether a vigorous defense can go too far. In the O. J. Simpson case, the defense attorneys were criticized a number of times for their actions. In particular, race was made a major issue; in fact, from the perspective of some people, it was unjustifiably the *central* issue. One of the most controversial actions occurred when defense attorney Johnny Cochran compared Mark Fuhrman with Adolf Hitler during his closing arguments:

> There was another man not too long ago in the world who had these same views, who wanted to burn people, who had racist views and ultimately had the power over people in his country. People didn't care. People said he is just crazy. He is just a

half-baked painter. They didn't do anything about it. This man, this scourge, became one of the worst people in the history of this world. Adolf Hitler, because people didn't care or didn't try to stop him. He had the power over his racism and his anti-religion. Nobody wanted to stop him and it ended up in World War II. And so Fuhrman, Fuhrman wants to take all black people now and burn them or bomb them. That is genocidal racism. (Dershowitz 1996; p. 119)

Another example of a controversial action on the part of the defense attorneys was that, for all practical purposes, Simpson's house was "staged" prior to the visit by the jurors: the picture of Simpson and his white girlfriend at the time was taken down and replaced with a Norman Rockwell picture of a black girl being escorted to a southern school by federal marshals, photographs of Simpson and his white golfing buddies were replaced with pictures of black people, and a bible was placed on a table in the living room. All these changes were part of a "redecoration" of Simpson's house (Dershowitz 1996). Neither the reference to Adolf Hitler nor the staging, however, was ruled to be unlawful by the judge.

INEPT JUDGES

We all know what happens when referees are biased and favor one team over the other. It is no longer a fair game. So it is with the game of justice. Judges who allow police, prosecutorial, or defense misconduct are working against the desired outcome of justice. Examples abound of uninformed and biased legal decisions made by judges. Most judges are elected, and they realize that criticism from a challenger that they are "soft on crime" may cost them their reelection. Judges are generally reluctant to enforce the technicalities of the law and to take action against prosecutors and the police (e.g., for perjury).

INCOMPETENT AND CORRUPT EXPERT WITNESSES

The testimony provided by experts in court can be quite influential on the final outcome of a case. Unfortunately, due to the manner in which experts are often compensated and the process by which they are hired, they may have incentive to provide testimony that is not necessarily truthful. For example, Dr. Ralph Erdmann was a medical examiner who traveled from county to county in Texas to conduct autopsies. He claimed to have performed more than 400 autopsies a year for more than ten years. The case that exposed his misconduct involved a man who was found dead in his home. Erdmann indicated that the autopsy revealed that the man died as a result of a cocaine overdose. The man's family did not agree with this conclusion. In reviewing the autopsy report, it was noted that the man's spleen had been examined and weighed. The only problem was that the man's spleen had been removed four years earlier! On further examination of the body, no autopsy incision marks were found. A subsequent—and complete—autopsy showed that the man died of a heart attack. Investigation into other autopsies that Erdmann claimed to have performed indicated that many were not conducted. In 1992, Erdmann pleaded no contest to seven felony counts involving fraudulent autopsies (Teitell 1994).

In another case, Andrea Yates, a mother who drowned her five young children in the bathtub of her Texas home in 2001 and who was subsequently convicted and sentenced to life in prison, was ordered to receive a new trial because of faulty expert witness testimony. The state's forensic psychologist expert testified Yates was not insane at the time of the murders. He explained that there was a similar crime portrayed on a recent episode of *Law and Order*. In that episode, the defendant was found insane. The expert implied that Yates may have gotten the idea for the crime from the show. However, no such episode existed (Casey 2005).

As yet another example, consider Case in Point 15.2.

CASE *in* POINT 15.2   The Case of Glen Woodall

In 1987, the residents of Huntington, West Virginia, were on edge. In separate incidents, two women had been abducted at knife point from a shopping mall parking lot. The perpetrator repeatedly raped each of the victims and robbed them of jewelry. Although the perpetrator wore a ski mask and forced the victims to close their eyes, both victims caught glimpses of the attacker, and one of them was able to provide a partial description of him. Both victims were able to describe his clothing, and both told the police that the perpetrator was uncircumcised.

As the police began their search for the rapist, their attention focused on Glen Woodall, who worked at a cemetery across the street from the mall where the abductions took place. The physical description of the perpetrator provided by the victims matched Woodall, and a police search of his house revealed clothing similar to that described by the victims. On the basis of this evidence, Woodall was arrested. During a pre-trial hearing, Woodall's defense counsel requested that a DNA test be performed on the evidence in the case. The judge denied the request because DNA analysis was not yet a proven science. At the trial, the prosecution presented

evidence, including chemical tests conducted by a state police chemist, Fred Zain, that showed Woodall's blood secretions matched secretions in the semen recovered from the victims, that body and facial hair removed from a victim's car was consistent with Woodall's hair, and that a unique smell of the perpetrator noted by the victims was consistent with the smell found at Woodall's workplace. On the basis of the evidence, Woodall was convicted of sexual assault, sexual abuse, kidnapping, and aggravated battery. He was sentenced to two life terms plus 203 to 335 years in prison.

After the trial, Woodall's defense counsel once again requested that DNA tests be performed on the evidence in the case, and this time the request was granted. The results of the test, however, were determined to be inconclusive. On appeal, further DNA tests were conducted, and these tests positively excluded Woodall as the perpetrator. As a result, in 1992, his conviction on all charges was vacated. Woodall was free after spending five years in prison. Subsequent to the verdict reversal, the state police chemist who testified at the trial, Fred Zain, was investigated and indicted for providing perjured testimony in criminal cases, including Woodall's.

PERJURED AND UNRELIABLE TESTIMONY BY LAY WITNESSES

Witnesses may have a variety of reasons for providing intentionally misleading or erroneous information to the police. The reasons could include a desire to get revenge on an enemy, to cover their own illegal behaviors, or to protect someone they care about. In addition, even well-meaning witnesses have the ability to provide seriously misleading information, particularly through eyewitness identification testimony. Examples of faulty eyewitness testimony are plentiful, and the ramifications of those identifications are clear when reviewing cases of false convictions. As discussed in Chapter 6, this problem can be at least partially remedied by changes in eyewitness identification procedures.

INEPT JURIES

Another possible reason for a wrongful conviction is an inept jury. The trial process depends heavily on juries to consider the evidence in the case conscientiously and carefully and reach a decision based on instructions provided by the judge. In many respects, the jury is the final link in the justice chain. If the jurors do not make decisions in good faith, bad outcomes may result. Good faith may be inhibited by fear for their personal safety, fear for others' safety, or concern about the ramifications of their verdict. Jurors may also be affected by extraneous information and evidence. It is important to remember that juries almost always play a passive role in the trial process. They are there to hear and consider the evidence as it is presented. Jurors can only work with the evidence they are presented.

PHOTO 15.3: Lay witnesses often play a critical role in investigations and as witnesses in court.

●●● The Value and Importance of Investigative Reports

Reports are written documents that contain information relating to a criminal incident and investigation. They are used to document the particulars of a crime and the investigation. As illustrated in the police report included in the introduction to Chapter 6 and the excerpts of police reports provided in Chapters 10, 11, 12, and 13, investigative reports typically contain information about the criminal incident (e.g., who, what, where, when, and sometimes why and how); activities performed in the investigation; and the evidence that resulted from the activities performed. This could include, for example, witness statements and identifications, the presence of physical evidence recovered from the crime scene, and/or the confession obtained by the perpetrator. Investigative reports may also include details on the offender's MO and descriptions of the suspect, the suspect's vehicle, and the property taken. Incident reports are most often written by patrol officers at the conclusion of the initial investigation. Supplementary reports most often consist of a narrative that describes in more detail the leads in the case, the source of the leads, the result of the leads, and statements from witnesses and suspects. Supplementary reports are most often completed by detectives on an ongoing basis throughout the duration of a follow-up investigation.

Report writing is an *extremely* important skill and activity for police officers and detectives. Investigative reports reflect the writer's education, intellect, training, and competence as an investigator, similar to how the papers you write in college are a reflection of your capabilities as a student. Most police departments do not "grade" officers' reports; however, reports are usually reviewed by supervisors for style, form, completeness, and accuracy. Indeed, contrary to what is portrayed in television detective dramas, a considerable amount of investigators' time is spent simply reading and writing reports.

Investigative reports may be read by numerous people for various reasons. Certainly other police officers, investigators, and supervisors read reports, and so will prosecuting attorneys, defense attorneys, judges, citizens, the media, and others. Each person who reads the report may have a different reason for doing so. In particular, police supervisors may read reports in order to determine whether the case should receive a follow-up investigation and in order to manage progress and activities in investigations. Investigators may read reports to determine what has been done in the investigation and what activities still need to be performed. Investigators often review their own reports when testifying in court in order to refresh their memory of the crime and the investigation. Prosecutors will read reports to become familiar with the conduct of the investigation and the evidence in the case. They use reports in order to determine whether charges should be pursued against a suspect and, if so, what those charges should be. They also use them to prepare cases for trial. Like prosecuting attorneys, defense attorneys read investigators' reports to become familiar with the investigation and the evidence in the case. Defense attorneys often question investigators about their reports when the investigators testify in court. Finally, judges may review reports to familiarize themselves with the evidence in the case, to understand how the investigation was conducted, and to review the legality of officers' and investigators' conduct.

For all these reasons, it is critically important that reports be written well, that they be accurate, that they be complete, and that they be in proper form. Given the importance of report writing, police officers and investigators typically receive numerous hours of training regarding the technical aspects and requirements of report writing in their respective agencies. Briefly, several basic rules can be identified for writing good reports (also see Orthmann and Hess 2013):

- Reports should be well organized. The narrative of the report should identify, in chronological order, the activities that were performed by the investigator who wrote the report, and it should identify the information/evidence obtained as a result of those activities.

- Reports should be factual, specific, and detailed. Opinions, personal beliefs, and summary conclusions should not be included in reports. Conclusions may not be justified, they may be ambiguous, and they may be misinterpreted. For example, instead of writing, "She then confessed to the crime," the words she actually spoke should be included in the report.

- Reports should be written in past tense, first person, and active voice. For example, "I then spoke with Mr. Roberts. He stated that he was at home with his two children between 6:00 p.m. and 7:00 p.m." is preferred over, "Mr. Roberts was then spoken to. He states that between 6:00 p.m. and 7:00 p.m., he was at home with his two children." Do you see a problem with the second statement?

- Reports should be accurate. Details matter. Details minimize the possibility for misinterpretation and confusion. Even basic things such as misspellings of names, incorrect date of births, and wrong addresses can be significant, especially when the report is in the hands of a defense attorney who wishes to question the competency of an investigator. "Little" errors can lead to big problems.

- Reports should be objective. All facts that appear relevant should be included, regardless if they support the case or not. In addition, the words used in the report should also be objective. The best way to ensure objectivity in word choice is to be as factual as possible. Instead of writing, "Mr. Roberts had the appearance of a gang member," write, "Mr. Roberts had a tattoo which read 'Vice Lords' on his chest." Instead of writing,

"Mr. Roberts *claimed* that he was at home," write simply, "Mr. Roberts *stated* that he was at home." Interestingly, the word "stated" is probably one of the most common words included in investigative reports.

- Reports should be written in Standard English. The rules of the English language apply to investigative reports (see Strunk and White 1979 for the rules of writing).

Across agencies, reporting and record-keeping processes and policies vary considerably, as do the actual reports that are completed by investigators. In most agencies, the process is largely computer automated, so reports can be typed on computers or dictated. In some agencies, reports are handwritten. Some agencies store and process reports electronically, others manually. The one consistent dimension across agencies regarding investigative reports is that much of investigators' time is spent reading and writing them.

••• The Value and Importance of Investigative Testimony

All evidence presented in court is delivered through, or accompanied by, testimony—statements made in court by individuals sworn under oath to tell the truth. Witnesses provide testimony. Witnesses can be classified as either lay witnesses or expert witnesses. Lay witnesses can testify only to the facts of the case as they see them. Lay witnesses testify regarding their actions and observations. To the extent that judgments can be offered by lay witnesses, the judgments are related to the particular case at hand, such as when a witness says, "In my judgment, he was intoxicated when he said he was going to kill her. He was slurring his words." Police officers and investigators are usually, but not always, considered lay witnesses in court. Expert witnesses, on the other hand, can express their opinions in court and can discuss hypothetical scenarios. Expert witnesses are usually persons who are skilled or knowledgeable on a particular subject. Their testimony is supposed to educate the jury or judge on a particular issue that may not be understood by lay persons. An expert's opinion is advisory to the jury.

••• Expert Testimony

The use of expert witnesses in court is quite controversial. Expert witnesses are most often hired and compensated by either the defense counsel or the prosecution. In trying to advocate either the guilt or innocence of the defendant, the attorneys, of course, desire testimony from an expert that supports their respective position. It is likely that if an expert is not able to offer a supportive opinion, the attorney will look for a different expert who could provide such testimony. As such, if an expert witness cannot offer testimony to support the attorney's position, that expert will not be hired. Although one may legitimately question the appropriateness of this arrangement, what is even more problematic is that experts may have considerable economic reasons to conform their opinions to the position of the attorney who is requesting such testimony. Expert witnesses are often compensated very well. It is quite common for expert witnesses to receive $300 to $400 an hour or more for their work on a case. Sometimes experts are considered hired guns, not conveyors of the truth.

Seldom are scientific opinions uniformly and unambiguously supportive of a one-sided conclusion. Attorneys who request the testimony of experts must realize that this is, in fact, the case. Accordingly, the most desirable and ethically defensible role for the expert is that of an impartial educator who comes to a conclusion and provides testimony based on a well-informed understanding of the issue in question. In practice, the expert's testimony that supports the desired position is usually elicited during the direct examination of the witness, and a more balanced view emerges as a result of the cross-examination. In addition, jurors and judges may find the background, experience, credentials, and expertise of expert witnesses relevant in judging their credibility and their believability.

The use of expert testimony in legal proceedings is also potentially problematic for other reasons as well. In particular, the sometimes-complicated opinions offered by the expert may be misunderstood by jurors. Indeed, because testimony of an expert witness may be shaped by the questions asked by the prosecution and defense attorneys, there is considerable opportunity for testimony from even a well-intended impartial expert to be misunderstood. In addition, although it is possible that a fair, honest, and knowledgeable expert could provide an accurate opinion based on the available scientific research on the issue, it is also possible that this opinion could be invalidated sometime in the future by subsequent research on, and later knowledge of, the issue. In essence, how can experts testify regarding the "truth" when "truth" in science is always changing? An understanding of these issues may provide a better appreciation of the role of expert testimony in the legal process.

●●● Testimony of Investigators

As noted, investigators are usually considered lay witnesses in court. Their primary role is to describe what they did in conducting an investigation and the evidence that resulted from those activities. In many ways, the relatively limited scope of their testimony makes their job in court a little easier. As lay witnesses, they do not have to form, justify, or defend their opinions. As lay witnesses, they are required to *not* express their opinions. They just have to tell the truth. Nevertheless, the testimony of investigators in court is critical. The lead investigator on the case is often one of the most important witnesses in the presentation of the prosecution's case. Without a believable or credible investigator, a conviction will likely not be possible.

TESTIMONY AT THE DEPOSITION, PRELIMINARY HEARING, AND TRIAL

There are three situations in which investigators may be required to provide testimony relating to the investigations they conducted. First, in some cases, and in some states, investigators may be required to provide testimony in a deposition. A deposition occurs out of court and before a trial. It provides a lawyer an opportunity to question a witness under oath to learn what testimony that witness may provide in court. A commonly stated rule for attorneys is to never ask a question in court to which they do not already know the answer. A deposition allows for attorneys to find out answers to questions prior to court. Depositions can be stressful for witnesses because the scope of the questioning can be wide. There is basically no topic or issue that is off limits in a deposition. As a result, depositions often take much longer than testimony provided in court. Along with written reports, defense attorneys can attempt to use deposition testimony to contradict the courtroom testimony of investigators.

The second situation in which investigators may be required to provide testimony is in a preliminary hearing. A preliminary hearing is one of the first steps in the court process. It can be described as a mini-trial. The purpose of the preliminary hearing is for the prosecutor to prove that (1) a crime occurred and (2) that the defendant committed it. The standard of proof is probable cause, the same standard as in an arrest. However, in a preliminary hearing, the probable cause is to be determined by a judge. Because the standard of proof is lesser at the preliminary hearing than at the trial, less evidence needs to be offered at a preliminary hearing. Many times the evidence includes only testimony from the victim and the police officers or other investigators who conducted the investigation.

If the judge determines that there is probable cause that a crime occurred and that the defendant committed it, and if there is not a plea bargain agreed upon by the prosecution and the defense, then a trial will occur. An investigator will also provide testimony at the trial. A trial may either be a bench trial, in which the judge determines the verdict, or a jury trial, in which a jury determines the verdict. A typical trial has several steps or stages:

- Jury selection, also known as the voir dire

- The opening statement of the prosecution, in which the prosecutor presents an overview of the evidence that is supposed to lead the jury to a guilty verdict

- The opening statement of the defense attorney, which explains why the jurors should arrive at a not guilty verdict

- The presentation of the prosecution's case though direct examination of witnesses; after each witness the defense attorney can cross-examine the witness. There may also be a redirect and a recross examination of any or all witnesses.

- Presentation of the defense case through a direct examination of

witnesses; after each witness the prosecuting attorney can cross-examine the witness. There may also be a redirect and a recross examination of any or all witnesses.

- Closing statements, first presented by the prosecution then by the defense. Each closing statement is a summary of the evidence presented and an explanation as to why a guilty verdict or a not guilty verdict should be reached.

- Instructions to the jury by the judge that explain what the jurors are expected to do and the decisions they need to make

- Jury deliberates in private.

- Reading of the verdict in court with the defendant and attorneys present

Investigators almost always testify as part of the prosecution's case. As such, the prosecuting attorney conducts a direct examination of the investigator to elicit the facts of the case and the corresponding evidence against the defendant. Questions asked of investigators during the direct examination usually begin with "who," "what," "when," "where," "how," and sometimes "why." At the conclusion of the direct examination, the defense attorney has the opportunity to question the investigator in a cross-examination.

THE CROSS-EXAMINATION

To test the evidence, defense attorneys often "test" the police. This test occurs during a cross-examination when the defense attorney asks questions of the investigator. This is the opportunity for the defense attorney to score points with the prosecutor's evidence. The cross-examination is usually the most difficult, frustrating, and stressful aspect of testifying. The best way to overcome this is to understand the tactics of the defense attorney and be prepared for them.

The goal of the cross-examination for the defense attorney is to convince the jury or judge that the investigator should not be believed or that certain evidence presented by the investigator should not be believed. In essence, the goal is to "impeach" the witness. A defense attorney can attempt to impeach a police witness in several ways (Stutler 1997). First, the defense attorney may use leading questions in an attempt to put words in the witness's mouth. Leading questions suggest the answer in the question itself. To the weary and poorly prepared, leading questions can make answering questions easier. But the easy answers may very well be incorrect. Questions that begin, "Isn't true that . . ." or "Wouldn't you agree that . . ." are questions that are designed to prompt certain answers. Investigators must be aware of this tactic and that it may (but not always) signal trouble ahead.

Second, the defense attorney may try to anger, badger, or simply annoy the investigator. As discussed below, emotion on the part of the investigator can undercut his or her believability.

Third, the defense attorney may ask difficult and slanted questions of investigators where the answer may not necessarily sound good. Examples would be, "Have you ever made a mistake in an investigation?," "Have you lied before?," or "Have you rehearsed your testimony with the prosecutor?" These and all other such questions should be answered truthfully. Honesty translates into credibility among jurors. If there is an objection or clarification that needs to be made, that should be left to the prosecutor.

Fourth, the defense attorney may question the witness about the legality of the actions taken, the investigator's knowledge of the law, and the legal justifications for the actions taken. This line of questioning can be used to lay a foundation for an argument that the evidence was collected unlawfully.

Fifth, the defense attorney can attempt to discredit the investigator by attacking the quality and accuracy of the investigator's reports. Defense attorneys know that some police officers refer to their reports as "lie sheets" and treat them as such. The task of the defense attorney is to find the lies. As such, an investigator's testimony in court may only be as good as his or her reports.

Relatedly, defense attorneys may look for inconsistencies within the reports or inconsistencies between the investigator's reports and accounts provided by other officers, witnesses, or victims. Any testimony from anyone that is inconsistent with what is contained in an investigator's reports is very likely to be an area of interest and questioning by defense attorneys. Consider the following exchange:

DEFENSE ATTORNEY: Officer, did you search for fingerprints at the time of your initial investigation of the robbery?

OFFICER: I did not.

DEFENSE ATTORNEY: Indeed, there is no such reference to such an activity in your report, is there?

OFFICER: No, there is not.

DEFENSE ATTORNEY: We heard from the bank manager, however, that you did dust for fingerprints. He was 100 percent sure that you did. Why wasn't this in your report, officer? Do you not remember whether or not you conducted a thorough investigation in this robbery?

Clearly the intent of such an exchange is to try to discredit the officer based on a perceived discrepancy between the victim's account and the officer's account. The discrepancy may be small, relatively insignificant, and even explainable, but it may be the focus of questioning nonetheless. Or, at the very least, the intent may be to confuse or fluster the investigator through the use of double negative, repetitive, or compound questions. Investigators should simply speak to their actions and knowledge. Generally speaking, investigators should *not* try to explain discrepancies on their own. The prosecuting attorney can ask questions of the witness, or of another witness, in order to clarify. Investigators should not be surprised if they are accused of lying when such a discrepancy is discovered or when a mistake in testimony (or a report) is identified. In such an instance, it must be understood and explained that a mistake is unintentional, a lie is not.

Another method used to impeach an investigator is to call into question statements of fact and opinions, if any of these have been stated in reports. Recall how earlier it was discussed that opinions and conclusions should not be provided in investigative reports and that reports should report facts as specifically as possible. The following exchange demonstrates why:

DEFENSE ATTORNEY: Officer, you wrote on page two of your report that "entry was gained through the bedroom window that was left unlocked." Is that correct?

OFFICER: Yes.

DEFENSE ATTORNEY: How do you know that the window was not locked?

OFFICER: Because it appeared to me that if the lock on the window was locked, the window would have to have been broken in order to open it. And the window was not broken.

DEFENSE ATTORNEY: Do you realize, officer, that the lock on the window was broken prior to the incident in question?

OFFICER: No.

DEFENSE ATTORNEY: That window could not have been locked because the lock did not work. Did you put that in your report, officer? Did you put in your report that the lock was broken? What else didn't you put in your report, officer?

During this exchange, the defense attorney is not even contesting whether the window was locked. The defense attorney is just highlighting the fact that the officer did not know that the lock was broken. From here, the defense attorney suggests that the investigation was incompetently performed. The intent on the part of the defense attorney is to discredit the officer by questioning a seemingly simple statement that might not have even had an important role in the investigation. Although objections might be raised by the prosecuting attorney regarding this line of questioning, the damage may already have been done. The lesson here is that investigators should draw conclusions and write their reports very carefully.

PHOTO 15.4: Defense attorneys attempt to impeach investigator witnesses in court. Some of the methods used to do this include asking leading or difficult questions, annoying the investigator, and calling the investigator's integrity into question.

Defense attorneys may also attempt to impeach an investigator witness by calling into question the investigator's honesty and credibility. If the defense attorney can show that the investigator lacks honesty or credibility, then the opportunity exists for the defense attorney to call into question the honesty and credibility of the investigator with regard to the current case. Consider how the defense attorneys cast a shadow on the evidence discovered by Mark Fuhrman in the O. J. Simpson investigation based on Fuhrman's past conduct and his attempt to cover up that bad behavior through perjury. It is not unheard of that defense attorneys request and receive access to the personnel files of the police officers who conducted the investigation in an attempt to find evidence of previous misconduct that might relate to those officers' conduct in the current investigation.

Finally, defense attorneys may also try to confuse or otherwise fluster investigators. They may ask confusing or complex questions (e.g., "Is it not true that you didn't search for and collect fingerprints?"), they may try to trick investigators by deliberately mischaracterizing or summarizing previous testimony, they may ask for a yes or no answer to a question that requires explanation, or they may take a friendly tone and ask leading questions in order to lull the investigator into careless answers. Understanding the strategies commonly used by defense attorneys in cross-examining investigators may help investigators in preparing for their testimony. As stated in Stutler (1997), "Indeed, the right time for law enforcement officers to contemplate the defense's strategy is at the beginning of an investigation, not while they are sitting on the witness stand." (p. 5).

Several guidelines have been suggested for investigators to follow in order to most effectively testify in court (Department of Homeland Security 2010; Miller 2006). These include:

- Tell the truth. This should go without saying as lying on the witness stand is a crime. If a mistake or misstatement is made in the testimony provided, correct it as soon as possible.

- Be prepared. Review the case, your notes, reports, and other documents associated with the case prior to your testimony. In court, reports can be used to refresh your memory about particular details of the case. Do not memorize your testimony as this is not convincing.

- Stick to the facts and avoid opinions. Speak to your personal knowledge—what you did, saw, or heard. Let other witnesses speak for what they saw and did.

- Answer the question asked, no more, no less.

- Be mindful of nonverbal communication and be serious. Avoid laughing or smiling. Avoid any negative or inappropriate gestures and facial expressions. Any behavior that indicates hostility, annoyance, or anxiety should also be avoided.

- Be respectful of the defense attorney, judge, prosecuting attorney, the jury, and others. The attorneys should be addressed as "sir" or "ma'am," the judge as "your Honor."

- Speak directly, clearly, and confidently. Speak clearly and loudly enough to be easily heard. Maintain eye contact. If the judge asks the question, look at the judge when answering. When an attorney asks a question, look at the jury when answering. Speak in terms understood by the jury (i.e., avoid "cop talk").

- Listen and think before you speak. Do not look to anyone else for an answer to the questions you are asked. If you did not understand

A Question of Ethics ?

Why So Many Legal Rules?

The American trial process and the jury system is a rather strange way to determine the truth—a method unlike any other. It is an odd method of truth finding because the rules (e.g., the exclusionary rule, double jeopardy, evidence beyond a reasonable doubt to convict) are so artificial, so "made up." Another oddity is that the evidence presented to the jury is not necessarily inclusive of all evidence collected by investigators. The rules regarding the admissibility of information are very strict with regard to the defendant's criminal history, his or her right to remain silent, his or her attempts to plea bargain in the present case, and other evidence that was collected but not introduced at trial. So the question is, why in the American trial process does it seem like there are so many rules that protect the rights of the accused and make it more difficult to obtain convictions?

the question, ask for it to be repeated. If you do not know the answer to the question, say "I do not know." If you do not remember, say "I do not remember."

- Be professional. This includes how you dress and how you speak. Avoid slang. Dress should be in accordance with agency policy regarding proper attire in court.

- Keeping these guidelines in mind will provide for a clear and effective presentation of evidence in the case.

A final comment about testimony relates to those issues that an investigator should be sure to *not* volunteer when testifying (Department of Homeland Security 2010). First, an investigator should not comment about the defendant's prior criminal history. There are strict rules regarding the admission of this information in court. Second, investigators should also not comment about the defendant's Miranda rights. Defendants have the right to remain silent and to have an attorney present during questioning. Neither of these rights, if invoked, constitutes evidence. Any testimony about the defendant's Miranda rights should be in direct response to questions that asked about that exact information. Similarly, investigators must not provide any testimony about the defendant's attempts to negotiate a plea bargain. Unsuccessful plea bargain negotiations are not evidence. Finally, no testimony should be offered with regard to evidence that has been ruled inadmissible by the judge. For example, if evidence was collected as a result of a search that was ruled to be unconstitutional, there is to be no mention of that search or the resulting evidence. If an interrogation was ruled to be illegal, there must be no mention of that interrogation or the resulting confession.

MAIN POINTS

1. The court process in the United States is adversarial in nature. Defense attorneys and prosecuting attorneys present conflicting versions of the truth in court. The judge is supposed to be a neutral referee in the contest.

2. Police investigators are a part of the prosecution team. Investigators collect evidence and establish, with probable cause, who committed the crime. The prosecution then presents this evidence in court to convince a judge or jury, beyond a reasonable doubt, that (1) a crime occurred and (2) that the defendant committed it.

3. Defense attorneys "test" the evidence in the case, often by "testing" the conduct of the police in collecting the evidence. This is necessary to increase the chances of a fair and just outcome.

4. Miscarriages of justice, be they in the form of innocent subjects being punished or guilty subjects going free, are serious. If a guilty person goes free, that person has avoided punishment and justice is denied for the victim and for society. That person is also free to offend again. If an innocent person is

convicted, it will have devastating effects on that person's life and the person responsible for the crime remains free to offend again.

5. False convictions may occur for a variety of reasons: police misconduct and incompetence, prosecutorial misconduct and incompetence, defense attorney misconduct and incompetence, inept judges, incompetent and corrupt expert witnesses, perjured or unreliable testimony from lay witnesses, and inept juries.

6. Reports are written documents that contain information relating to a criminal incident and its investigation. They are used to document the particulars of a crime and the investigation. Investigative reports may be read by numerous people, each for a different purpose.

7. Several guidelines can be offered with regard to effective report writing: reports should be well organized; they should be factual, specific, and detailed; they should be written in past tense, first person, and active voice; they should be accurate and objective; and they should be written in Standard English.

8. All evidence presented in court is delivered through, or accompanied by, testimony—statements made in court by individuals under oath to tell the truth. Witnesses provide testimony. Lay witnesses can testify only to the facts of the case as they see them. Expert witnesses can express their opinions in court. Expert witnesses are usually persons who are skilled or knowledgeable in a particular subject.

9. The use of expert witnesses in court is controversial for several reasons.

10. Police officers and investigators are usually considered lay witnesses in court. Their role is to describe the investigation they conducted and the evidence that resulted from the investigation.

11. There are three situations in which investigators may be required to provide testimony relating to the investigations they conducted: in a deposition, at a preliminary hearing, and at a trial.

12. Defense attorneys often "test" the police during a cross-examination when the defense attorney asks questions of the investigator. The cross-examination is usually the most difficult aspect of testifying. The best way to overcome this is to understand the tactics of the defense attorney and to be prepared for them.

13. The purpose of the cross-examination of an investigator is to convince the jury that the investigator should not be believed—to "impeach" the investigator. A defense attorney can attempt to impeach a police witness in several ways, including by asking leading questions, asking difficult or confusing questions, attacking the credibly of the investigator, and focusing on inconsistencies in testimony, among others.

14. Several guidelines can be offered with regard to effective testimony: tell the truth; be prepared; stick to the facts and avoid opinions; answer the question asked; be mindful of nonverbal communication and be serious; be respectful; speak directly, clearly, and confidently; listen and think before you speak; and be professional, including in your attire.

15. When testifying, investigators must avoid comment about the defendant's prior criminal history, the defendant's Miranda rights and that he or she invoked them, the defendant's attempts to negotiate a plea bargain, and any evidence that has been ruled inadmissible by the judge. Each of these actions may be grounds for a mistrial.

IMPORTANT TERMS

Adversarial process	Impeachment	Past tense, first person, and active voice
Bench trial	Incident report	Police perjury
Cross-examination	Jury trial	Preliminary hearing
Deposition	Lay witness	Supplemental report
Exoneration	Leading question	Testimony
Expert witness	Miscarriage of justice	Voir dire process

QUESTIONS FOR DISCUSSION AND REVIEW

1. Why is the court process an adversarial one? What is the role of the defense attorney, prosecuting attorney, judge, and the police in the process?

2. Why are errors in justice outcomes a serious problem?

3. Why is a vigorous defense for defendants necessary in the judicial process?

4. Why are accurate, thorough, and well-written investigative reports so important in the criminal investigation and court process?

5. What are the rules to follow when writing investigative reports?

6. What are the situations in which investigators may be required to provide testimony?

7. Why is it important for investigators to be as comfortable and competent on the witness stand as they are at crime scenes?

8. What are the steps or stages of the trial process and what are the two main questions addressed in the trial?

9. What is the purpose of the cross examination? What tactics are commonly used by defense attorneys when cross-examining investigator witnesses?

10. What are the rules to follow when providing testimony in court?

STUDENT STUDY SITE

Visit **www.sagepub.com/brandl3e** to access additional study tools including eFlashcards, web quizzes, web resources, video resources, and SAGE journal articles.

16

Terrorism, Technology, and the Future of Criminal Investigation

Objectives

After reading this chapter you will be able to:

- Summarize the investigation of the terrorist hijackings on September 11, 2001

- Describe the three "eras" of policing in the United States

- Discuss terrorism as a "new" criminal threat

- Discuss technology as a "new" demand on the police

- Explain what is meant by the "militarization" of the police

- Discuss how, in the future, DNA may become more useful as a tool in identifying criminals

- Identify the various emerging technologies of biometrics

- Identify and discuss other emerging crime detection

and criminal investigation technologies

- Discuss the factors that may inhibit the incorporation of technology into criminal investigations

From the **CASE FILE**
The Day the World Changed[1]

Nineteen motivated men. A few box cutters. Four hijacked commercial airplanes. Sixty thousand gallons of jet fuel. Logistical and training support from the al-Qaeda terrorist organization. Several hundred thousand dollars. The World Trade Center and the Pentagon, filled with people. On September 11, 2001, these ingredients came together to create a disaster of previously unseen proportions. The criminal investigation that followed was arguably the largest and most complex in history. In fact, in many respects, it has actually become a multitude of interrelated investigations, all of which represent the War on Terror. The attacks of September 11 led to the creation of the Department of Homeland Security and to a massive reorganization of federal law enforcement agencies. Information uncovered led to investigations in numerous foreign countries and to war in Afghanistan. The global pursuit of terrorists led to war in Iraq. Given the magnitude of the event, summarizing it in just a few pages is difficult, to say the least. To complicate matters even more, many of the details are still of a classified nature. Given its significance, however, any informed discussion of the future of American criminal investigations would be incomplete without it.

On September 11, 2001, at 7:59 a.m., American Airlines Flight 11 departed Boston Logan Airport en route to Los Angeles with ninety-two people aboard. It was flown into the north tower of the World Trade Center at 8:45 a.m. At 8:14 a.m., United Airlines Flight 175 left Boston Logan en route to Los Angeles with sixty-five people aboard. It struck the south tower of the World Trade Center at 9:03 a.m. At 8:10 a.m., American Flight 77 left Dulles International Airport in Washington, D.C., for Los Angeles with sixty-four people aboard. It was flown into the Pentagon at 9:39 a.m. United Flight 93 left Newark International Airport en route to San Francisco at 8:01 a.m. with forty-four people aboard. It crashed in a cornfield in Pennsylvania at 10:03 a.m. It is believed that it was headed for the White House or the U.S. Capitol Building before passengers attempted to take control of the aircraft from the hijackers. In total, more than 3,000 people were killed as a result of the terrorist acts.

It was known by authorities even before the first plane crashed into the World Trade Center that at least three planes were under the control of hijackers. Passengers and crew on the planes made phone calls to loved

---

1. This discussion is based largely on Fainaru (2002a), Fainaru (2002b), Isikoff and Klaidman (2002), and Schmidt and Eggen (2002).

ones after the planes were hijacked. The phone calls made from the planes described the hijackers as "Arab men" with knives. One was said to have a red box strapped to his chest that was believed to be a bomb. In addition to the information gained from the frantic phone calls, it was also clear from communications received by air traffic controllers from some of the planes that hijackings were in progress. As the planes crashed, one by one, the enormity of the situation became obvious to everyone.

The first objective of investigators in the wake of the hijackings was to stop or interrupt any additional hijackings. Air travel on September 11 was ordered to a halt. Planes that were in the air were ordered to land, and planes on the ground were prohibited from taking off. All grounded planes were then searched and passenger flight manifests examined. Box cutters were found hidden on two other airplanes. Investigators believed at the time that, indeed, other planes had been intended to be hijacked. It appeared that the hijackers had accomplices. Investigators discovered that two Middle Eastern men who had been on a flight from Newark to San Antonio boarded an Amtrak train to San Antonio after their flight landed in St. Louis because of the hijackings. These men were detained in Texas, and the police found box cutters, a large quantity of cash, and hair coloring in their possession, among other items. Reportedly, these men were later released without charges. Other investigations began on airport workers in an effort to identify who might have assisted in the terrorist plot.

The second objective was to determine the identities of the dead hijackers. To do so, the passenger manifests from each of the hijacked planes were collected. From the information provided by passengers and crew before the planes crashed, investigators were already confident that they knew the hijackers were Middle Eastern men. Several Arab names appeared on the manifests for Flight 93, Flight 11, Flight 175, and Flight 77.[2] With the manifests in hand, investigators had names of suspects.[3] The airlines were also able to provide information to investigators about when and how these individuals purchased their tickets: all were one-way tickets, several were purchased with the same credit card,

and most were purchased shortly before the flights. The credit card records and flight manifests led investigators to addresses in Florida, New Jersey, and California. Investigations were conducted in each of these places on the suspected individuals. Meanwhile, it was discovered that a suitcase checked for Flight 11 at Boston Logan by Mohamed Atta, one of the individuals identified as a hijacker, did not make the flight. The suitcase was opened and numerous items of interest were found, including a suicide note, a copy of the Koran, an instructional video on flying commercial airliners, a fuel consumption calculator, a letter containing instructions to the hijackers in Arabic, and other personal belongings.

At about this same time, after hearing about the hijackers, an individual contacted the police and told them about an argument that he had with several Arab men in the parking lot at the Boston airport the morning of September 11. He described the car they were driving as a white Mitsubishi. The police found the car in the airport parking garage. One of the items of interest seized from the car was a flight training manual written in Arabic. Similarly, another vehicle identified as belonging to the hijackers was seized from Dulles International Airport. Inside that vehicle the police found a Washington, D.C., area map. Written on the map was the first name and phone number of Mohamed Abdi. When authorities contacted Abdi, he could not explain why his name was in the possession of the hijackers, nor could investigators establish a link between Abdi and the hijackers. Also found in the car was a letter identical to the one found in Atta's suitcase. Days later, another copy of the same letter was found at the crash site of Flight 93 in Pennsylvania. A rental car that was believed to have been used by the hijackers was recovered from the Portland, Maine, airport (several hijackers made a connecting flight in Boston). Most leads led investigators to Florida. Searches of the hijackers' residences, along with interviews with landlords and neighbors, led to the discovery that many of the suspected hijackers had been enrolled in flight schools in Florida and other places in the country. It was discovered that the hijackers lived low-key, low-profile lives; they did not stand out in any significant way.

---

2. As it turned out, eighteen of the nineteen hijackers' names were listed on the manifests. Hani Saleh Hanjour was not listed on the Flight 77 manifest because he may not have had a ticket.

3. It was determined later that many of the hijackers used names obtained from stolen identities of individuals in Saudi Arabia, used aliases, or had common Middle Eastern names. This factor in itself added an extra dimension of complexity to the investigation.

Further investigation of visa and immigration records revealed that none of the hijackers was born in America, nor were they American citizens. All were in the United States either legally on student or business travel visas, or illegally on expired visas or without visas. At least one lived in the United States as far back as 1990, when he had taken an English class in Arizona, and another had attended flight school in the United States as early as 1997.

As the investigation progressed, investigators discovered that a man already in police custody was likely a player in the plot. Zacarias Moussaoui had been arrested by the INS on immigration charges August 17, 2001, after an instructor at a flight school in Minnesota became suspicious of him. Reportedly, Moussaoui was only interested in learning how to turn an aircraft; he was not interested in takeoffs or landings. It was believed by investigators that Moussaoui was to be the fifth hijacker aboard Flight 93. In 2006, Moussaoui was convicted on several counts of conspiracy to aid terrorists and was sentenced to life in prison without parole.

With the hijackers identified, analysts at the Central Intelligence Agency (CIA) realized that they had prior knowledge of several of these individuals and had actually been monitoring their foreign travels as far back as 2000. In the bombing of the U.S. Embassy in Nairobi, Africa, in 1998, one of the terrorists—the man who drove the truck filled with explosives to the embassy—was apprehended. He was questioned by the FBI and provided information about an al-Qaeda safe house in Yemen, a "logistics center" of sorts where the African embassy bombings were planned. The CIA monitored the house and intercepted phone conversations that alerted agents to a January 2000 meeting of al-Qaeda terrorist operatives in Malaysia. Of the twelve individuals who attended the meeting, two were identified as Khalid Almihdhar and Nawaf Alhazmi. The CIA knew that when Almihdhar and Alhazmi left the meeting in Malaysia, they were headed for the United States.[4]

In an attempt to identify others who supported the hijackers, the FBI sent a notice to all U.S. banks requesting information on any transactions that involved twenty-one individuals on the FBI suspect list, nineteen of whom were believed to be the actual hijackers. Also included on this list were numerous addresses associated with the names. Reportedly, no large cash transfers were uncovered. Later attempts to "follow the money" were more productive. Most of the money received by the hijackers while in the United States appeared to have had a single overseas source.

In tracing the activities of each of the hijackers through credit card receipts, airline records, flight school records and enrollments, housing rental records, and INS records, investigators were led to Hamburg, Germany, where Atta and several of the other hijackers had earlier shared an apartment and attended the same university. The investigation in Germany led authorities to believe that the hijacking plan was probably first discussed and planned at that time. From there, travel by several of these individuals to Afghanistan and Pakistan, among other places, was uncovered. Links between the hijackers and the al-Qaeda terrorist group led by Osama bin Laden became clear. In October 2001, the United States invaded Afghanistan in search of bin Laden and his associates. Nearly ten years later, on May 2, 2011, bin Laden was killed in Pakistan (see below).

During the course of the early investigation, countless other leads, many of which were false or otherwise unexplained, were developed. For example:

• Khalid S. S. Al Draibi was stopped by police ten miles north of Dulles International Airport twelve hours after the planes crashed in New York and Washington. He was driving on the highway with a completely flat tire. When his car was searched, flight training manuals were found. Further investigation revealed that since he had arrived in the United States in 1997, he had used ten variations of his name, three social security numbers, and drivers' licenses from five different states. After intensive investigation, his only charge was for lying on a visa application. He was deported in 2002.

---

4. Almihdhar and Alhazmi were two of the hijackers aboard Flight 77, which was flown into the Pentagon. Representatives of the FBI have said that they were not told by the CIA that these two individuals came to the United States. Representatives of the CIA have said that they did, in fact, provide this information to the FBI. Apparently, what neither the CIA or the FBI knew at the time was that both of these men were already living in San Diego for two months prior to the meeting in Malaysia. In mid-2000, Almihdhar left the United States for the Middle East. While he was away, his visa expired, but the State Department consulate in Saudi Arabia issued him a new one. He returned to the United States on July 4, 2001. Meanwhile, Alhazmi moved to Phoenix and stayed with Hani Hanjour, who is believed to have piloted Flight 77. They moved to New Jersey on August 25.

• It was discovered that two of the hijackers used credit cards that belonged to Dr. Al Badr Al-Hazmi, a radiologist who lived in Texas, for various purchases. Interestingly, Al-Hazmi was missing from work on September 11 without explanation. It was eventually determined that he was a victim of theft and had no connection to the hijackers.

• Ahmed Badawi, a travel agent in Orlando who sold plane tickets to several of the hijackers, wired money on their behalf, and cashed their checks, was also identified as a possible accomplice, but he was also eventually released without charges.

• Nabil al-Marabh was arrested September 30, 2001, in Chicago, where he was working as a clerk in a liquor store. It was believed by the FBI that in the 1990s, al-Marabh had stayed at a home in Pakistan that was known to be used by terrorists. It was discovered by authorities that he lied about his relationship with a man sentenced to death in Jordan for plotting to blow up a hotel on New Year's Day in 2000. At the time he was arrested by the FBI, al-Marabh was found to have in his possession $22,000 in cash and gems worth $25,000. It was determined that he entered the United States illegally at a crossing near Niagara Falls on June 27, 2001. He was deported on September 4, 2002, without further prosecution.

• In 2002, federal agents began investigating a fraudulent scheme whereby foreign (primarily Middle Eastern) students hired other people to take their Test of English as a Foreign Language (TOEFL) exams, which are often required of international students for admission into American colleges and universities. Agents conducted a search of a Virginia address where the suspected leader of the scheme, Fahad Alhajri, lived, and they found flight manuals, flight school catalogs, a diagram of a plane striking the World Trade Center, a postcard with aerial pictures of the Pentagon, photos of people inside the World Trade Center, and a Rolodex of oil refineries. After extensive investigation, investigators came to the conclusion that Alhajri was not involved in the September 11 plot.

With associations made between the hijackers and Osama bin Laden's al-Qaeda terrorist group, the investigation into September 11 went global. As a result of the wars in Afghanistan and Iraq and raids of suspected terrorist hideouts in Afghanistan and Pakistan, many leaders and planners in the al-Qaeda group have been apprehended or killed, including, of course, Osama bin Laden. As a result of interrogations conducted of suspected al-Qaeda operatives from 2002 to 2006, the CIA learned the name of an individual who served as bin Laden's personal courier. Through wiretaps, surveillance, and other intelligence, the courier was eventually tracked to a large compound in Pakistan in 2010. The CIA reasoned that it was the sort of place where bin Laden might live. The CIA watched the three-story house from a neighboring residence. The compound had no Internet or phone service, and the occupants of the house buried their garbage in their yard. As investigators were reasonably certain that bin Laden was in the compound, on May 2, 2011, a highly trained SEAL team descended on the compound from helicopters, found Osama bin Laden inside, and shot and killed him (Mazzetti and Cooper 2011; Shane and Savage 2011). The courier and several others were also killed during the raid. The identity of bin Laden was initially confirmed by one of his wives in the compound when she called him by name during the raid. Positive identification was later made as a result of comparing DNA from the body to that which was previously collected from one of bin Laden's sisters.

There were many other operatives captured or killed prior to bin Laden. For example, on September 11, 2002, authorities in Pakistan captured Ramzi Binalshibh in a raid conducted by the FBI, CIA, and Pakistani police. Binalshibh was known by authorities as being instrumental in the planning of the September 11 hijackings. It is believed that he shared an apartment with Atta in Hamburg, that he wired money to Moussaoui and hijacker Marwan Al-Shehhi when they were in the United States, and that he attended the January 2000 meeting in Malaysia. It was also known that Binalshibh attempted to obtain a visa for entry into the United States four times between May and October 2000. In all likelihood, Binalshibh was to be the twentieth hijacker. But with Binalshibh unable to gain entry into the United States, Moussaoui may then have been designated to take his place; however, as noted, Moussaoui was unable to participate because he was arrested on immigration charges in August 2001.[5]

As another example, in Yemen in October 2002, a U.S. Predator drone (an unmanned aerial aircraft) operated by the CIA fired a missile at a car in which Qaed Salim Sinan al-Harethi was an occupant, killing him and five

---

5. It remains unclear who was intended to be the twentieth hijacker. Investigators have identified at least five al-Qaeda members who may have been designated as such.

others who were in the car. Al-Harethi was known to be Osama bin Laden's top lieutenant in Yemen.

Along with ongoing arrests of suspected al-Qaeda terrorists and commanders overseas, arrests were also made in the United States. For example, based on information uncovered as a result of the arrest of al-Marabh in Chicago, the police were led to a previous address of his in Detroit. Police raided the apartment in which he used to live and arrested several men. A search of the apartment revealed maps of the Detroit International Airport and security passes for the airport. The men arrested were eventually charged with conspiring to aid terrorists. In September 2002, the FBI arrested six men who allegedly comprised a terrorist cell in New York State. They were charged with supporting bin Laden's al-Qaeda network. In October 2002, six additional U.S. citizens were arrested and accused of traveling to Afghanistan after September 11, 2001, for purposes of joining the al-Qaeda fight against America. In December 2002, FBI agents raided a software firm in Boston because of suspicion that its owners were funneling money to terrorists while doing business with sensitive U.S. agencies, including the FBI, the North Atlantic Treaty Organization (NATO), and the IRS. In 2006, seven men were arrested and charged with conspiring with al-Qaeda to blow up Chicago's Sears Tower and an FBI building in Florida (Sherman 2006). In addition to these high-profile, well-publicized arrests, a multitude of other people in the United States have been arrested for immigration violations and have been deported.

Since 2001, there have been several terrorist incidents in the United States. The 2013 bombings at the Boston Marathon killed three people and injured nearly 200 others. In 2010, a bomb was ignited in a car parked in New York's Times Square, but it failed to detonate. In 2009, a Nigerian man on a flight from Amsterdam to Detroit attempted to set off an explosion with materials concealed in his underwear. Also in 2009, a U.S. Army major shot and killed thirteen people and wounded more than thirty others at Fort Hood

PHOTO 16.1: September 11, 2001, changed the world in many ways, some of which are yet to be realized.

in Texas (although, officially, the U.S. government has not defined this as an act of terrorism). The rest of the world has seen hundreds of successful terrorist acts since 2001, and many of these acts have led to the death of Americans. Examples of these include the 2002 Bali nightclub bombings (over 200 people killed), the 2004 Madrid train bombing (191 killed), the 2005 London bus and train bombings (fifty-two killed), the 2006 Egypt car bombs (eighty-eight killed), the 2007 Algeria car bombs (over sixty people killed), and the 2012 attack on the American consulate in Benghazi, Libya (which killed the U.S. ambassador and three others). No doubt, terrorism is alive and well, as is the war against it.

Case Considerations and Points for Discussion

- By all accounts, the investigation into the September 11, 2001, hijackings was a massive undertaking. Where did the investigation begin? What were the first questions that needed to be answered? What evidence was collected to answer these initial questions?

- From the information available and provided here, what were the most significant successes

and failures of the authorities in preventing and investigating the September 11, 2001, hijackings and related events?

- What do you suppose were the biggest lessons learned by the authorities as a result of the investigations associated with the hijackings of September 11, 2001?

A Question of Ethics

(?)

Information at Any Cost?

In the years subsequent to 2001, it has been reported that the CIA used various extraordinary methods to obtain information from certain suspected al-Qaeda operatives, including so-called waterboarding (Walsh 2009). Waterboarding involves restraining a subject, covering the subject's face with cloth, and then pouring water onto the subject's mouth and nose. Waterboarding creates the sensation of drowning. Because the subject is unable to breath, it has the potential to cause injuries and brain damage. Some people define waterboarding as a method of torture. The information about the identity and location of Osama bin Laden's courier may have been obtained from subjects in this way. The question is this: From your perspective, under what circumstances, if any, would the use of torture be acceptable as a way of obtaining critical information in a criminal investigation? Why?

••• History as a Guide to the Future

One reason for studying history is that it may serve as a guide to the future. In fact, some people argue that history tends to repeat itself, so to know the past is to know the future. Knowing the future is useful, as this can help us prepare for it.

CRISIS AND CHANGE IN POLICE HISTORY

American policing has progressed through three eras: the political era, the reform era, and the community problem-solving era (Kelling and Moore 1988). During the political era, from the mid-1800s to the early 1900s, politicians controlled virtually every aspect of policing, including the hiring and firing of officers and what officers did while they were at work. The police were corrupt and generally inefficient. Methods of criminal identification were crude and ineffective. The political era came to an end as a result of a technological and crime crisis: in particular, due to the use of automobiles in the early 1900s, criminals were able to commit crimes in one jurisdiction and flee to another, causing major problems for the police. With the early 1900s also came a rise in concern about serious crime, gangsters, communists, and kidnapping. The police at the time could not effectively deal with the new demands, and authorities realized that a new way of policing was required.

The new way of policing in the early 1900s took the form of the reform era. Technology was an important element of this era. Automobiles allowed the police to institute preventive vehicle patrols and to offer fast responses to crime scenes as a way to make more arrests. The patrol cars also removed officers from close day-to-day contact with citizens and allowed them to patrol anonymously through communities. The two-way radio allowed police supervisors to monitor and direct the activities of officers on the streets. State and federal law enforcement agencies were created to assist local police departments. More scientific methods of criminal detection and identification were developed; detectives became indispensable in solving crimes.

This style of policing worked well until the 1960s. With the assassination of President John F. Kennedy (and others), the antiwar and race-related riots, the counterculture movement, researchers questioning the strategies of preventive patrol and detectives as crime solvers, and the doubling of the crime rate from 1960 to 1970, the police found themselves in the midst of another crisis. And yet again, crisis led to change.

This time the new style of policing took the form of the community problem-solving era, which remains the predominant style of policing today. During this era, efforts have been made by the police to recognize the indispensable role of citizens in criminal investigations and to embrace the notion that police and citizens "coproduce" crime prevention. Technology plays a significant role in methods of criminal identification and investigation.

It is reasonable to expect that the community problem-solving era of policing will not last forever. It too will come to an end. If history repeats itself, it will come to an end probably because of a crisis, a crisis caused by new crime and technological demands being placed on the police. What might these new demands be? What will be the new style of policing and the new approach to criminal investigations? It is these questions that are addressed in this last chapter.

••• The Future of Policing and Criminal Investigation

As we continue to move into the twenty-first century, technology continues to advance. With the adoption of the Internet, individual citizens have widespread and immediate access to information. The "information revolution" is affecting every aspect of human life. Crime also continues to change and become more sophisticated. With these changes, there are once again significant new demands on the police. Given how new demands have prompted changes in the past, it may be reasonable to expect that these demands will lead to changes in the future, especially in criminal investigations.

TERRORISM AND TECHNOLOGY

Many of the new demands on the police today are related to crime and technology. With regard to crime in particular, it is clear from history that as society becomes more complex, so does crime. Indeed, over time, crime has become more devious, organized, specialized, and complex (Marx 1988). Further, as society has become more global, so has crime. The globalization trend has spawned world wars, global and continental currencies, global trade agreements, and so forth. These two trends—increasingly devious and sophisticated crimes and globalization—may point to *terrorism* as the new significant crime-related demand on the police.

Defining terrorism is difficult, especially given the number of terrorist organizations and the wide range of goals associated with these groups. The FBI defines terrorism as "the unlawful use of force or violence against persons or property to intimidate or coerce a government, the civilian population, or any segment thereof, in furtherance of political or social objectives" (www.fbi.gov/albuquerque/about-us/what-we-investigate). There are hundreds of other definitions, ranging from criminal activity designed to inflict mass casualties to acts motivated by political goals which are designed to cause fear. Terrorism can also be classified as being internationally based (committed by foreigners or foreign nationals) or domestic (committed by American citizens). Whether terrorism is perpetrated by foreigners or American citizens may have direct implications on the motivation for the acts. Domestic-based terrorism is usually motivated by antigovernment, anti-abortion, or anti-equality sentiment, or by just plain hate. Terrorism perpetrated by foreigners is typically motivated by extreme religious views and hatred toward the United States. When terrorists receive funding, support, training, or protection from governments, terrorism is said to be state-sponsored. Individuals acting on their own without attachment to a terrorist group are often referred to as lone wolves.

Regardless of the method, motive, or target, terrorism is hardly a new phenomenon, but it has taken on new meaning since September 11. International terrorist incidents have become much more frequent since the late 1960s, and this frequency has increased further since the mid-1990s (U.S. Department of State 2001) and even more since 2001. Acts of terrorism directed against the United States by foreign interests is most directly related to American support for Israel and American involvement in Middle Eastern political affairs. The United States is the global superpower, and attacks on it can glean attention for groups that wish to advance a particular cause (Kelley 1998). Given the hatred of the United States by some foreign interests, acts of terrorism directed against the country are not surprising.

Of course, on September 11, 2001, terrorism came to the United States in a big way. Those events made it clear that America is not immune to major terrorist actions, even on our own soil. The 2013 attack at the Boston Marathon was a reminder of this. In the aftermath of that event, a police officer was killed by the perpetrators, one of the perpetrators was killed by the police, and the entire city of Boston and its suburbs were shut down

Exhibit 16.1 Terrorist's Tools and Targets

The Global Terrorism Database (GTD), maintained at the University of Maryland, includes data on terrorist incidents from 1970 to 2010. According to the GTD, approximately 45 percent of all incidents involved the use of bombs/explosives (Johnson 2013). Armed assaults accounted for 26 percent of terrorist attacks, and assassinations accounted for 15 percent. All other methods accounted for 14 percent of attacks.

Bombs have many benefits for terrorists: they are dramatic, potentially devastating, can cause horrific injuries, and draw a lot of media attention. They are potentially more destructive than guns or knives. They can create mass causalities with no warning. The blasts are indiscriminate. Bombs come in all shapes and varieties, including letter bombs (e.g., Unabomber), backpack bombs (e.g., Boston Marathon bombing), suitcase bombs (e.g., Pan Am Flight 103 in 1988), and truck and car bombs (e.g., Oklahoma City Federal Building bombing). The most recent variety, which has not yet appeared in the United States, is in the form of a suicide bomb; in this type of attack an individual detonates explosives attached to his or her body: This has been referred to as the "poor-man's smart bomb" and is especially difficult to defend against (Kronenwetter 2004).

With regard to the favorite targets of terrorists, Johnson (2013) reports that the GDT shows that the most common terrorist targets are as follows:

- Private citizens and property (22 percent of all attacks)
- Businesses (15 percent)
- Government (13 percent)
- Military (12 percent)
- The police (12 percent)
- All other targets accounted for 38 percent of attacks.

while authorities searched for the second bomber. Bus and taxi service was suspended, businesses were closed, the airport was shut down, and citizens were ordered to "shelter in place" (to take refuge inside their home in an interior room; see www.nationalterroralert.com/shelterinplace/).

Other serious threats may loom, and they are not hypothetical. If public gatherings such as a marathon can be attacked, then no public place can be completely safe. If commercial airliners can be turned into missiles to destroy skyscrapers filled with people, then bioterrorism and the use of nuclear bombs for terrorist purposes could be a possibility. Given the new threats, new methods may need to be used to confront them.

Law enforcement and other governmental agencies received their share of criticism regarding the inability to foresee September 11, rightfully so or not. For years it was known that terrorist planned to use airplanes in attacks. In 1995 investigators discovered and interrupted a terrorist plot to blow up eleven American jetliners over the Pacific Ocean and crash a light aircraft loaded with explosives into CIA headquarters. Al-Qaeda terrorists hijacked an Air France flight as it prepared to leave Algeria for Paris (presumably to crash it into the Eiffel Tower), but commandos stormed the plane during a refueling stop and killed the terrorists. Several informants in the investigation of the 1988 African embassy bombings spoke of al-Qaeda's interest in flight training. And Islamic terrorists planned to use an airplane to kill President George W. Bush in July 2001 in Italy. Additionally, a multitude of intelligence reports were received by the CIA that spoke of the interest of al-Qaeda in hijacking American airplanes and flying them into various high-profile targets. The list of warning signs was a long one. Despite this knowledge, government officials described September 11 as "a new type of attack that had not been foreseen" (Fainaru 2002a; p. a09). Simply stated, the inability to prevent what happened on September 11 may have been a failure in information management. In response, major changes have been made, and continue to be made, by American law enforcement agencies in order to deal with the new and ever-present threat. In particular, these agencies have been increasingly incorporating an intelligence-gathering function into their operations and are adopting technology at a fast rate.

Unfortunately, law enforcement agencies were once again criticized in the aftermath of the 2013 Boston Marathon bombing for not "connecting the dots" and preventing the attack. It was revealed that the FBI had previously interviewed one of the suspects, Tamerlan Tsarnaev, because of his affiliation with Islamic extremists, that the FBI had received information from Russian authorities about Tsarnaev's earlier suspicious travels to Russia, and that the FBI had Tsarnaev and his mother on a terrorism watch list. Additionally, Tsarnaev apparently created and posted jihadist videos on YouTube and made a large fireworks purchase in New Hampshire, presumably for constructing the bombs (see www.nydailynews.com/opinion/evil-article-1.1325514). Over time, such criticisms could turn into a crisis—a crisis that might prompt changes.

Might the international terrorist threat to the United States just quietly disappear? Probably not. There are good reasons to believe that the threat will continue. One such reason is the demographics of Middle Eastern countries. For instance, in Saudi Arabia, 70 percent of the population is twenty-five years of age or younger—the age group most likely to become involved in terrorist activity. This situation will not change soon because almost one-half the population is younger than the age of fifteen. Further, the decline of the central authority of political heads of state in Middle Eastern countries is troubling. It is this type of political environment that can serve as a haven for terrorist groups. As explained by Kaplan (2002), "The experience of neighboring Yemen, with its brazen highwaymen and rampant kidnappings, may be what Saudi Arabia can look forward to—and that's the optimistic view" (p. 55). Furthermore, American power, influence, and foreign policy, which are the source of much of the hatred directed against the United States, are not likely to change. As a result, the terrorist threat is likely to be with us for a while.

Along with the rise in terrorism, another trend that may have implications for crime and the future of criminal investigations is the rapid discovery and deployment of technology. As was the case with electricity, the telephone, the automobile, and the airplane, the technology of today dramatically affects the nature of our lives. As has been the case throughout history, technology can also place incredible demands on the police. The most significant technology of today and of the future is the Internet. The Internet is a global computerized network that allows for the exchange and dissemination of information.

The Internet has the potential to change *everything*. The Internet will continue to affect everything from the nature of work and where people live ("going to work" may eventually become as uncommon as "dialing the phone") to methods of governing, the nature of medical care, the content and delivery of education, the structure of families, how we communicate with each other, and media and entertainment. But the Internet has a dark side: it has created a multitude of criminal opportunities. The Internet can be used to disseminate information of hate through Web sites and e-mail. It can be used to disseminate other unlawful materials (e.g., child pornography) and facilitate related crimes (e.g., chat rooms and Web sites used to identify intended victims). It can be used as an educational tool for terrorists (e.g., sites that instruct how to build a bomb), to perform acts of terrorism (e.g., cyberterrorism), and to facilitate communication among criminals. The Internet can be used to gain illegal access to and steal protected governmental and corporate information (e.g., hacking). It can be used to distribute computer viruses to disable Internet infrastructure. It can be used to facilitate fraud and identity theft (as discussed in Chapter 14). Complicating matters even further, with the Internet, the perpetrator and victim may not even be in the same country. And today, the Internet is still in its infancy. No question, the Internet poses a tremendous challenge to law enforcement today and in the future.

Exhibit 16.2 Terrorist Group Structure

Unlike most street gangs, operational-level terrorists tend to keep a low profile. This helps them escape identification and detection. The organization of terrorist cells is usually such that few people know everything that is being planned and carried out. For instance, it is unlikely that the four groups of people who hijacked each plane on September 11, 2001, knew each other. It is in this way that detection of one group (and operation) would prevent the identification of the entire group (and operation).

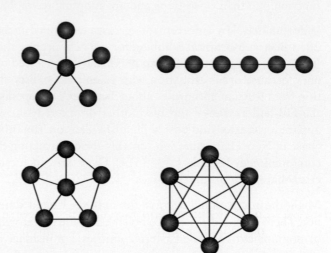

A terrorist group will consist of numerous such cells, perhaps each in a different location and with a different purpose. Some members of the cell may be responsible for gathering intelligence, some for providing support, and some for actually carrying out the acts.

THE "NEW" POLICE

In the face of the "new" crime and technological demands, what might be the next adaptation for the police and criminal investigations? When crimes are simple and local, detection strategies are simple and local. When crimes are complex and global, detection strategies are complex and global (Marx 1988). As such, at a minimum it seems reasonable to predict that criminal investigations of the future will likely be more complex and global than in the past. To support the increased scope of police operations, it is likely that more resources and legal authority will be provided to law enforcement agencies, and particularly to *federal* law enforcement agencies, to deal with global crime. This point was made clear with the federal antiterror bill—the 2001 USA PATRIOT Act (Uniting and Strengthening America by Providing Appropriate Tools Required to Intercept and Obstruct Terrorism). The PATRIOT Act was written and signed into law in October 2001, in the wake of September 11. The act is complex and comprehensive (it contains nearly 350 pages of text) and consists of ten sections. The act's provisions include the following (Congressional Research Service 2001):

- Gives additional power and authority to law enforcement officers to gather evidence relating to electronic communications, including phone calls, e-mail, and Internet activity, and allows for the increased scope of wiretaps

- Amends money laundering laws

- Changes immigration law to prevent terrorists from entering the United States and to allow for the detention and deportation of foreign terrorist suspects

- Expands law enforcement officers' ability to seize individuals' records held by a third party (e.g., doctors, libraries, Internet service providers)

On signing the bill, President Bush stated, "We're dealing with terrorists who operate by highly sophisticated methods and technologies, some of which were not even available when our existing laws were written. The bill before me takes into account the new realities and dangers posed by terrorists."

Interestingly, in June 2013, the country was shocked to learn that the U.S. government was collecting information about domestic phone calls and Internet activity of overseas residents—information "leaked" by a former federal contractor, Edward Snowden. Federal prosecutors have charged Snowden with espionage and theft of government property. However, given the parameters of the PATRIOT Act, these revelations should hardly be surprising.

In addition to legislative changes that will allow for new criminal investigation methods, massive resources are being allocated to federal agencies for the purposes of enhancing homeland security. The greatest proportion of the money is being spent on national security, border security, and transportation security. With the increased resources devoted to federal law enforcement efforts, a decline in federal funding to local police agencies is expected.

Regardless of these shifting priorities, citizens will remain powerful players in the police enterprise and in fighting crime. Nowhere will this be more apparent than with the role of citizens as sources of information. Reward and tip lines will become increasingly important as the police continue to rely on citizens for information about crimes and the people who committed them. This includes the investigation of terrorism. The Department of Homeland Security media campaign, "If You See Something, Say Something," speaks directly to the issue. For example, in the aftermath of the 2013 Boston Marathon bombings, after surveillance video images of the two bombers at the marathon were released, the two suspects were quickly identified as Dzhokhar Tsarnaev and his brother Tamerlan Tsarnaev. Approximately twenty-four hours later, one of the suspects had been killed by the police and the other was taken into custody after a massive but brief manhunt. Authorities found Dzhokhar hiding in a boat parked in a backyard after the boat's owner called the police to report that he saw someone hiding in it. In the failed 2010 Times Square car bomb plot, it was street vendors that alerted the police to the suspicious vehicle.

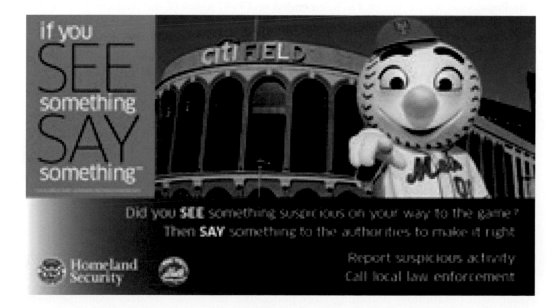

PHOTO 16.2: In the future, citizens will be expected to continue to assist law enforcement by bringing suspicious activity to the attention of police.

Exhibit 16.3 Seven Signs of Terrorist Activity

The Michigan State Police created a video to help identify individuals who might be planning a terrorist attack (Johnson 3013). The seven signs consist of the following:

- Surveillance: watching, photographing a possible target

- Elicitation: attempting to gain information about a person, place, or operation

- Tests of security: taking action to cause a security response in order to learn about the security response

- Acquiring supplies: theft or purchase of chemicals, explosives, weapons, identification, etc. needed in order to carry out the attack

- Suspicious people who don't belong: people displaying behaviors that do not fit in the situation or at that place

- Dry runs: rehearsals of the attack, necessary actions before and after the attack

- Deploying assets/getting into position: putting into place the necessary instruments for the attack (weapons, bombs)

Investigations of the future may also reflect the continuation of another trend already in place: the lines separating the police and the military will become increasingly blurry. In particular, the police will become more military-like and the military will become more police-like. With regard to the military becoming more police-like, since September 11 there have been numerous instances of the military becoming involved in domestic law enforcement activities. For example, an immediate response to September 11 was the placement of fully equipped National Guard personnel in airports to provide security. The U.S. Air Force operated air patrols over numerous cities in an effort to enforce airspace restrictions and to protect cities from any additional terrorist airplane attacks. In November 2002, the Department of Defense provided aircraft surveillance to assist federal, state, and local law enforcement authorities in the investigation of the sniper shootings in the Washington, D.C., area. In recent years, efforts to tighten security at the United States–Mexican border have included the deployment of National Guard troops. The National Guard has also been used to assist local police in dealing with hurricanes and other natural disasters. In the wake of the 2013 Boston bombings, the National Guard was deployed in the city to provide security and transportation services.

The Posse Comitatus Act of 1878, amended in 1994, restricts the participation of the military in domestic law enforcement activities. The navy and the marines are included in the Posse Comitatus Act as a result of a 1992 Department of Defense regulation. The original intent of the act was to end the use of federal troops in policing state elections of the former Confederate states. There are several important exclusions to the act, including the following:

- The use of National Guard forces

- The use of federal troops to quell domestic violence, by presidential order

- The use of military personnel to provide for aerial photographs and surveillance

- The use of military personnel to combat the War on Drugs

- The use of the Coast Guard

- The use of navy resources to assist the Coast Guard

Additional revisions and exceptions to the Posse Comitatus Act may be forthcoming, such as the use of the military to combat the War on Terror.

Along with the military becoming more police-like, the police are also becoming more military-like. Police organizations in America are already quasi-military in structure and

PHOTO 16.3: The Boston police search for a suspect in the Boston Marathon bombings.

function; however, the parallels are becoming even clearer and will likely become even stronger in the future. During the last few decades in America, a gradual and now more rapid adaptation of the police into military roles has occurred. The War on Terror is being fought by both police forces and the military. As the police function evolves, law enforcement agencies may be "democratic and participatory" (community oriented) in peacetime but "highly centralized and authoritarian" (military-like) during times of unrest (Toffler 1980).

Military tactics and technologies are increasingly being used by police departments. This trend is what Kraska and Kappeler (1997) refer to as the "militarization of the police." Much law enforcement technology, and civilian technology for that matter, has its beginnings in defense contract work. Consider the development of technologies such as radar, two-way radios, night vision, sensor technologies (including gunshot detection), and even the Internet. All were born at least in part through defense grants and contracts. The diffusion of military technologies into local law enforcement is likely to continue.

THE NEW TECHNOLOGY OF CRIME DETECTION AND CRIMINAL INVESTIGATION

Technology not only makes certain types of crime possible, it also provides the police with new tools for fighting these, and other, crimes. It is likely that the discovery and adoption of technology for crime detection and investigative purposes will continue to progress at an accelerated pace. Much of the significant new crime-fighting technology will focus on identification (e.g., biometrics), "seeing" and scanning, computer/Internet applications, and information management and access.

THE TECHNOLOGY OF IDENTIFICATION AND FORENSIC SCIENCE

Biometrics refers to technologies that are capable of identifying a person by measuring a feature of that person's unique physical characteristics (Moradoff 2010). Although the concept of biometrics has appeared only relatively recently, attempts at identifying people based on their characteristics have been around for a long time (e.g., recall Bertillonage from Chapter 2). Of course, most significant today is the science of DNA. DNA analysis was first applied to criminal investigations in the late 1980s. Since that time, it has become a widely used and powerful tool in criminal investigations and prosecutions. However, the value of DNA for purposes of criminal identification depends on having a suspect for comparison. With the development of CODIS, a nationwide DNA network that includes DNA samples from *convicted* offenders and crime scenes, DNA has become a more useful tool for identifying suspects. DNA as a tool of criminal identification still has major limitations, however. In the near future, the United States may follow the lead of England, which collects and stores DNA samples from all *arrested* offenders (not just some convicted offenders) and solves a much greater proportion of crime through DNA matches than does the United States (Williams and Johnson 2005; Asplen 2003). On the more distant horizon may be the construction and operation of a massive DNA databank that would include DNA from every individual who resides, or was born, in the United States. The technology to store this amount of data is available, but legal and ethical issues have inhibited the development of such a system. Of course, with such an arrangement, DNA would become a much more effective tool for identifying perpetrators.

Progress continues to be made on the science of collecting and analyzing DNA. New technologies are being developed that will allow DNA to be collected from difficult environments (e.g., evidence exposed to fire and chemicals; Tontarski et al. 2009) and allow it to be analyzed more efficiently and more quickly at lower cost. Miniaturization of DNA collection and testing devices will allow DNA evidence to be collected and analyzed at the crime scene and will allow for crimes to be solved via DNA analysis more quickly. Technology is being developed and tested whereby DNA can be analyzed at a cost of $20 per test, compared to the current cost of $600 to $1,600 (Nunn 2001). Indeed, as technology evolves, on-the-spot field testing (versus laboratory testing) will be common practice.

DNA technology is also advancing whereby physical characteristics of individuals can be determined on the basis of a DNA profile. This emerging field of scientific inquiry is referred to as DNA intelligence or DNA phenotyping. To date, this application has been limited to identifying sex, hair color, eye color, and race of the subject from DNA, but future applications may involve other externally visible characteristics (Walsh et al. 2011; Walsh et al. 2013).

The technology that supports fingerprints as a method of identification is also likely to continue to evolve. In many police departments today the old system of using ink and paper for fingerprinting has been replaced with optical sensing or other electronic methods. In the future, the verification and identification of suspects may be performed through portable fingerprint collection technologies. Fingerprint collection at crime scenes will also likely become more efficient and less labor intensive as a result of improved fingerprint collection technology. Technologies are continuing to be developed that allow fingerprints to be recovered from difficult surfaces such as skin and burned items, and from items exposed to water, weather, and sunshine (Brown et al. 2009).

As for the comparison of fingerprints for purposes of criminal identification, IAFIS provides for nationwide access to computerized fingerprint files. AFISs are also being improved to provide faster and more accurate search results. Fingerprints are likely to continue to be used in other applications as well. For instance, fingerprint scanning devices have been developed to take the place of passwords on computers and locks on doors. Palm recognition, iris recognition, and retinal recognition devices have also been developed for similar purposes. Application of voiceprint (and speaker recognition) technology in the field may be on the near horizon.

Facial recognition systems are also being used as a method of identification and will continue to evolve. Facial recognition systems go beyond passive camera surveillance and include a capability whereby the system can capture a facial image on camera and compare it to digital images stored in a reference database. Ideally, when a match is made, the operator of the system is alerted. In the United States, facial recognition systems have been deployed in casinos for several years, assisting security personnel in identifying and apprehending known gambling cheats and scam artists. Facial recognition systems have also been implemented on a limited basis in airports, on public streets, and in sports stadiums. As is the case with other technologies, these systems raise a multitude of issues with regard to privacy. In addition, research on these systems has demonstrated numerous reliability problems, as false identifications are sometimes made (Moradoff 2010). However, given the potential value and usefulness of the technology, it is likely that efforts to refine it will continue.

Future biometric technologies may include heartbeat and pulse recognition, voice biometrics, and handwritten signature recognition. Of these, voice biometrics probably has the greatest potential application. Common today are telephone response systems whereby navigation can be made via speech prompts. Another example is Apple's Siri, a program that is able to search the Internet via speech prompts. Much more sophisticated however, are systems that can recognize individuals' *voices* for purposes of identification. While such applications have been deployed, additional work remains to be done to improve the reliability of the technology (Moradoff 2010).

Implantable microchips are another technology that could serve an important identification function, most likely in the distant future. This technology is already in existence, but to date has only limited application. The implantable chip is about the size of a grain of rice and has been used in the United States to track and identify house pets, livestock, and fish. Similar technology has been incorporated into a wristwatch-type device that, when linked to a global positioning system, can transmit information on body temperature, pulse, and location of the person who is wearing it. This system is sold in the United States as a way to monitor the whereabouts of Alzheimer's patients, children, and parolees. It is conceivable that a future application of the technology will involve under-the-skin placement, with the chip providing readable information on an individual's identity, whereabouts, and other critical information.

? A Question of Ethics

Why Are Some Biometric Technologies So Controversial?

The development and use of DNA databases that include the entire population, facial recognition systems, and especially implantable identification microchips may have the ability to dramatically improve the ability of the police to identify and apprehend criminals. At the same time, they are extremely controversial. Why? As a society, shouldn't we take whatever steps necessary to prevent crime and keep our society safe?

THE TECHNOLOGY OF "SEEING"

Technological advances are also being made in the technology of "seeing." Perhaps most significant is the use of low-level x-rays to facilitate the detection of weapons, explosives, drugs, and other contraband. For example, although we are all very familiar with walk-through metal detectors, a more recent technology includes devices that allow one to see through clothing and to see items that may be hidden under clothing. Right now, these systems are deployed at airports, but future installations may include shopping malls, schools, and other public buildings. Similar technologies have been developed that allow

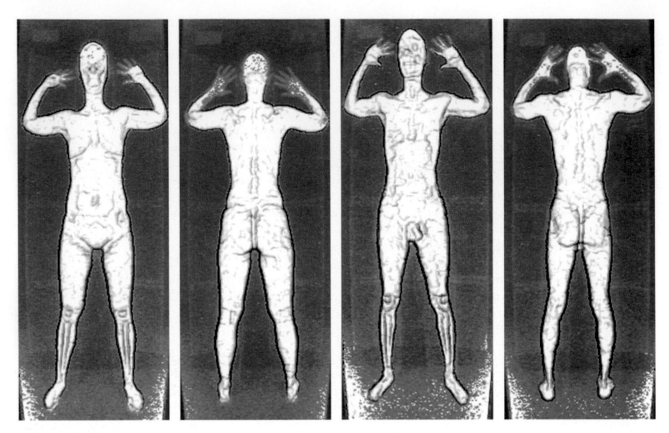

PHOTO 16.4: Technology that sees through clothing is useful in detecting weapons and other contraband, but allegations have been made that it invades privacy.

one to see through luggage to search for explosives and to see through cargo containers. Future applications may also include portable or handheld devices to detect not only metal weapons but also other contraband.

Many urban police departments presently deploy gunshot detection systems. These units are mounted on buildings or poles and have the capability to detect gunshots in a defined geographic area. Ideally, these systems could shorten police response times to shooting incidents and thus allow for more on-scene apprehensions of offenders. Current systems are deployed at a cost in the range of $40,000 per square mile (Walker 2013). It is likely that in the future the cost of the systems will decline and deployment of these systems in urban areas will increase.

Thermal imaging technology, which can detect heat inside closed structures, thus allowing one to see through walls and barriers, already exists but has encountered several legal obstacles in its use. Right now, this technology is most often used to detect indoor marijuana farms, to assist in search and rescue operations, and to detect fleeing suspects and find missing persons (Laba 1996). Successful navigation of legal issues will allow the police to effectively use this technology in many other situations. As a result, it could become a very powerful tool of crime detection and evidence collection (Nunn 2003). The next generation of this technology will be in the form of a flashlight-sized device that, when shined on a wall, projects the image behind it (Nunn 2001).

It is certainly not a stretch of the imagination to predict that the use of closed circuit television (CCTV) surveillance will increase dramatically in the future in the United States. Again, the United States may follow the lead of the United Kingdom in this regard. The UK has an estimated 4.2 million cameras in place (Moradoff 2010)—nearly 500,000 in London alone. It has been suggested that the typical Britain is filmed by about 300 cameras every day. In

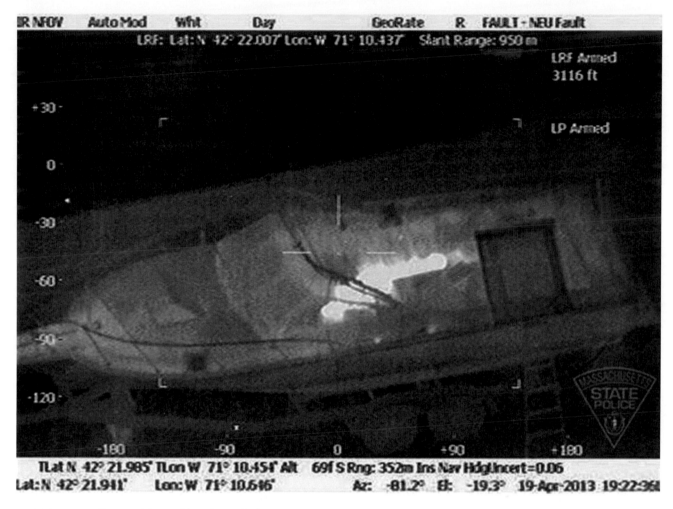

PHOTO 16.5: Police used thermal imaging to find Dzhokhar Tsarnaev, one of the Boston Marathon bombers, hiding in a covered boat located in the backyard of a citizen's house.

comparison, it is estimated that all of Boston has approximately 150 cameras installed throughout the city, mostly downtown, along with those installed at private businesses and residences. Most common now is the installation of cameras at intersections and roadways as an efficient way to remotely enforce traffic laws, particularly speeding (Nunn 2001). However, as discussed earlier in *Criminal Investigation,* and as clearly demonstrated in the 2013 Boston Marathon bombing investigation, surveillance cameras can be a very powerful investigative tool. Compared to many other technologies, they are also relatively inexpensive to purchase, operate, and maintain.

In addition to CCTV, the use of unmanned aerial vehicles (UAVs) with camera technology may see future widespread applications in law enforcement. UAVs, or drones, have been a mainstay on the battlefields in Iraq and Afghanistan during the War on Terror. Some of those UAVs have been equipped with not only cameras for surveillance but also missiles to destroy terrorist targets. The CIA has reportedly been using dragonfly-sized UAVs for spying for many years (Brown 2008). Law enforcement has already begun experimenting with such technology; the Miami-Dade Police Department, U.S. Customs and Border Protection, and the FBI are early adopters of the technology and use it primarily for surveillance and search operations (Brown 2008). Pending approval of the Federal Aviation Administration, UAVs are set to be deployed by many additional law enforcement agencies. UAVs will continue to get smaller, becoming typically the size of a small bird. This technology will take video surveillance evidence to a new level—literally (Reed 2008).

PHOTO 16.6: Analysis of video surveillance camera footage in the area of the Boston Marathon bombings revealed the images of the two suspects, one of whom is seen here. Reportedly, video surveillance showed one of the suspects putting one of the backpack bombs in place.

Like "seeing" technology, "sniffing" technology will also continue to develop. Electronic "sniffer" microchips are designed to detect microscopic amounts of substances, including chemicals, explosives, radiation, and drugs. In the future, it is likely that this technology will replace canines. Systems could also be mounted on buildings or have mobile applications. This technology would be particularly useful when paired with facial recognition cameras.

Other systems are being developed to improve upon current polygraph technology and to even "read minds" (see www.LiveScience.com). Experimentation is being conducted with "smart" cameras that can detect increased body temperature, high pulse and blood pressure, and heavy respiration, all of which are indicators of stress and deception (Kolbel and Selter 2010). This application may be particularly useful in detecting drug smugglers and people with terrorist intentions in airports. With regard to lie detection, the emerging technology of brain scans "revolutionize lie detection because they bypass unreliable physiological indicators of anxiety . . . focusing instead directly on the brain states provoking those physical reactions" (Kerr et al. 2008, p. 369). The theory underlying this approach is sometimes referred to as brain-fingerprinting. The brain produces identifiable electric signals when processing a memory (Kerr et al. 2008). As such, one such method under investigation involves the subject being shown relevant words and photographs (e.g., a murder weapon) and measuring the associated brain activity through an electroencephalogram (EEG). If the subject is shown something that is recognized, the EEG will detect and record the associated brain reactions. This technique may also have application in conducting eyewitness identifications. Similar experimentation has been conducted using magnetic resonance imaging (MRI) machines (Kozel et al. 2009).

TECHNOLOGIES FOR COMPUTER AND INTERNET APPLICATIONS

Other investigative tools are also being deployed to deal more effectively with Internet and computer-related crimes. For example, technology has been developed to search e-mail traffic for specific senders, recipients, and keywords. Law enforcement can direct computer viruses to particular individuals (via e-mail) to record keystrokes made by the user, which is especially useful when investigating child pornographers and hackers. Technology to effectively track the location of cell phones is also continuing to progress. It is likely that related technologies will be developed and existing technologies will be improved to effectively confront related crimes.

TECHNOLOGIES FOR INFORMATION MANAGEMENT AND ACCESS

One of the primary functions of technology in the workplace is to enhance productivity by making work tasks less time consuming. Technology will continue to have such effects on criminal investigations and policing more generally. Common today is the use of laptop computers in police cars for communication and deployment purposes. In the future, police personnel may have immediate access to a multitude of information through portable or wearable computers—information such as photographs of suspects and photographs of stolen property, as well as fingerprint and DNA databases. Officers and investigators will be able to construct and conduct photographic lineups with computers in their vehicles. Voice recognition, now in its infancy, will likely control these technologies (Reed 2008).

Other efforts are underway to create massive databases for criminal intelligence purposes—systems that combine law enforcement records with commercially available collections of personal information (O'Harrow 2003). Such a system, for example, would be able to identify the name and address of every brown-haired male over 200 lbs. that owns a white four-door vehicle and who has a criminal record in a particular city. Sounds like the technology available only on television shows today!

••• The Implications of Technology on Crime Detection and Criminal Investigation

Little question, the technology discussed here and its widespread adaptation may produce a significant reaction from the public, mostly as it relates to the issue of privacy. Indeed, it is likely that most future legal challenges that relate to technology will center on privacy issues (Moradoff 2010). For example, the law relating to the constitutionality of strip and body cavity searches is well developed; however, do digital five-second body examinations through the use of low-level x-rays alter notions of privacy and expectations of it? Do surveillance devices that see through walls alter the meaning of search and seizure? What are the parameters of privacy in e-mail? The courts have begun to address these questions, but clearly technology has opened a new set of issues relating to the reasonable expectation of privacy.

Along with these privacy concerns, another factor that may inhibit the incorporation of the newest technology into criminal investigation operations is cost. Law enforcement agencies are dependent on tax revenue for their operations. Much debate and concern about the level of taxation exists in the United States, and there is a lot of competition for those tax dollars. Clearly there are real-world concerns that may limit the capabilities and effectiveness of criminal investigations.

MAIN POINTS

1. One reason for studying history is that it may serve as a guide to the future. The purpose of studying the future is to prepare for it.

2. American policing has progressed through three eras: the political era, the reform era, and the community problem-solving era.

3. The political era and the reform era ended as the result of a crisis. The community problem-solving era may end in a similar fashion.

4. The most significant new demands on the police of the future may be related to terrorism and technology.

5. Defining terrorism is difficult given the number of terrorist organizations and the range of goals associated with these groups. The FBI defines terrorism as "the unlawful use of force or violence against persons or property to intimidate or coerce a government, the civilian population, or any segment thereof, in furtherance of political or social objectives."

6. Terrorist groups are organized into cells. Cells are organized to limit knowledge of, and communication with, other cell members.

7. Bombs are the most common weapon of terrorist groups, and private citizens are the most common target.

8. It seems reasonable to predict that criminal investigations of the future will likely be more complex and global than in the past. In addition, the lines separating the police and the military will become increasingly blurry.

9. Technology not only makes certain types of crime possible, it also provides the police with new tools for fighting these, and other, crimes. Much of the new crime-fighting technology will focus on identification (e.g., biometrics), "seeing," computer/ Internet applications, and information management and access.

10. Biometrics refers to technologies that are capable of identifying a person by measuring a feature of a person's unique physical characteristics.

11. DNA technology, as applied to criminal investigations, is in its infancy. DNA could become a more powerful tool of criminal investigations if the number of DNA samples contained in DNA databases is expanded, if collection and analysis capabilities become more efficient, and if DNA phrenotyping is further developed and used.

12. Facial recognition systems go beyond passive camera surveillance and include a capability whereby the system can capture a facial image on camera and compare it to digital images stored in a reference database.

13. Future biometric technologies may include the ability to recognize a person's heartbeat and pulse, voice biometrics, and handwritten signature recognition.

14. Implantable microchips are another technology that could serve an important identification function, most likely in the distant future.

15. Technological advances are also being made in the technology of "seeing." Perhaps most significant is the use of low-level x-rays to facilitate the detection of weapons, explosives, drugs, and other contraband. Right now, this technology is deployed in airports. In the future, other places may use this technology to replace metal detectors.

16. It is likely that the use of closed circuit television (CCTV) surveillance will increase dramatically in the future in the United States. In addition to CCTV, the use of unmanned aerial vehicles (UAVs) with camera technology may see future widespread applications in law enforcement.

17. Other technologies are being developed to improve upon current polygraph technology and to "read minds." Other investigative tools are also being deployed to deal more effectively with Internet and computer-related crimes and to create and manage information.

18. It is likely that most legal challenges of the future that relate to technology will center on privacy issues.

19. Along with privacy concerns, the costs associated with developing and adopting technology may inhibit the incorporation of technology in law enforcement agencies.

20. Effective criminal investigations must be balanced with the real-world concerns of individual privacy and cost.

IMPORTANT TERMS

Biometrics	DNA intelligence or phrenotyping	Terrorism
Brain-fingerprinting	Facial recognition cameras	Terrorist group and cell structures
Closed circuit television (CCTV)	Militarization of the police	Thermal imaging
Combined DNA Index System (CODIS)	Posse Comitatus Act	Unmanned aerial vehicles (UAVs)
	Privacy issues	USA PATRIOT Act of 2001

QUESTIONS FOR DISCUSSION AND REVIEW

1. What are the three historical eras of policing in the United States? What caused the change from one era to another?

2. What is terrorism and why might it be a "new" significant threat?

3. How are terrorist groups/cells structured and organized? Why?

4. What are the most common tools and targets of terrorists?

5. What are the seven signs of terrorist activity?

6. What new technology may represent a significant demand on the police and why?

7. What is meant by the militarization of the police?

8. How may DNA become even more useful as a tool in identifying criminals?

9. What is biometrics? How might such technology make criminal investigations more effective?

10. What are some of the other emerging crime detection and criminal investigation technologies?

11. What are the limitations and drawbacks of new technologies in crime detection and criminal investigation?

 STUDENT STUDY SITE

Visit **www.sagepub.com/brandl3e** to access additional study tools including eFlashcards, web quizzes, web resources, video resources, and SAGE journal articles.

Appendix

Capstone Case

Presented here is the description of a serial homicide investigation in the 1960s that involved the sexually motivated murders of seven mostly college-aged women in Michigan. The discussion provided here draws primarily on Keyes (1976). The case is longer and more detailed than the other From the Case File chapter introductions. It can serve as a capstone discussion of many issues covered in *Criminal Investigation*, including the basic problems of criminal investigation, the value of eyewitness identifications, the value of other evidence, the potential value of DNA evidence, and how proof can be established. Questions for discussion and review are presented at the conclusion of the case.

Capstone **CASE**
The Coed Murders

The nightmare began on the evening of July 10, 1967, when nineteen-year-old Mary Fleszar did not return to her apartment, which was located just a few blocks from the Eastern Michigan University (EMU) campus in Ypsilanti, Michigan. Mary was a student at the university. As is the case in most missing person investigations, the first task for investigators was to determine when and where she was last seen. In reconstructing the last known whereabouts of Mary, an EMU police officer recalled seeing a girl matching her description walking near campus at about 8:45 p.m. the night before she was reported missing. She was alone. Another witness reported that he saw the girl at about 9:00 p.m. that same night in the same area, walking on the sidewalk. The witness reported that a car drove up next to her and stopped. According to report the witness gave, the only person in the vehicle was "a young man," and the vehicle was "bluish-gray in color, possibly a Chevy." The witness said that it appeared that the young man inside the car said something to Mary, she shook her head, and the car drove off. Shortly thereafter, the same car passed the witness's house again and pulled into a driveway

in front of Mary, blocking her path. Mary walked around the back of the car and continued down the sidewalk. The car pulled out of the driveway and, with a squeal of the tires, drove down the street. At this point, the witness lost sight of Mary and the vehicle. Mary Fleszar was never again seen alive.

On August 7, 1967, a heavily decomposed nude body was found on farmland two miles north of Ypsilanti. Through dental records, the body was identified as Mary Fleszar. It was clear to investigators that, given the area in which the body was found (an open field) and the circumstances of her disappearance, the cause of death was certainly not natural, accidental, or suicide. In addition, given the area in which the body was found and the fact that no clothes were found in the vicinity, in all probability she was not killed where she was found. Her body had probably been dumped there. With the identity of the decedent determined and the crime established as a homicide, the next questions for investigators became, who killed her? And where was she killed? Matted grass around the body and the positioning of the body suggested that the corpse had been moved several times. Did the killer return to the scene or was the body moved by animals? The autopsy conducted on the body of Mary Fleszer revealed that she had been stabbed approximately thirty times and that she had been severely beaten. It could not be determined if she had been sexually assaulted. Most puzzling was that the girl's feet were missing and her lower leg bones had been apparently smashed. Wild animals may have been able to carry away the feet, but only the killer could have crushed her leg bones.

Two days before the funeral for Mary, one of the maintenance men at the funeral home reported to the police that an individual in a bluish-gray Chevy came to the funeral home and asked to take pictures of the corpse, but this person was not carrying a camera. This was certainly of extraordinary interest to investigators, but the worker could only describe this man as "sort of young, sort of ordinary looking." Investigators had no good leads into who caused Mary's death. The description of the vehicle possibly involved in the crime was the most promising lead, but even that was nearly worthless.

To the relief of residents, students, parents, and the police, throughout the spring of 1968 there were no more murders. It appeared that the murder of Mary was an isolated event. How wrong this was. On Monday, July 1, 1968, a second EMU student, twenty-two-year-old Joan Schell, was reported missing. Police determined from several eyewitnesses, one of whom was her friend, that she was last seen at a bus stop when a car with three men stopped and talked to her. The car was described as a late-model two-door with a red body and a black vinyl top. One of the men in the car was described as being in his twenties, about six feet tall, clean-cut, good-looking, and dark-haired. He was wearing a green T-shirt. After what appeared to be a brief conversation between Joan and the men, Joan got into the car and the car drove off. One of the witnesses told the police that he saw one of the men in the car in the EMU Union at about 11:00 p.m. that evening, after the building was closed. In checking this possible lead, the police found no signs of forced entry into the Union, indicating that whoever this was must have had a key.

The disappearance was, of course, front-page news. Joan's boyfriend, Dickie Shantz, who was absent without leave from his army base at the time of Joan's disappearance, was questioned by investigators but eventually cleared. Other friends and acquaintances of Joan were also questioned but dismissed as possible suspects. On Friday, four days after she was reported missing, the body of Joan Schell was found at a nearby construction site. The body was nude and covered with dried blood, although no blood was found in the area around her body. Most unusual about the body was that the top one-third was in an advanced state of decomposition, but the bottom two-thirds were well preserved. In addition, the grass around the corpse was trampled, perhaps indicating that the body was recently disposed of. Where was she killed? And where was the body kept until it was disposed of? The autopsy provided few answers. It revealed that Joan was stabbed twenty-five times, including once into the side of her head, with a knife about four inches long. Due to the presence of semen and related injuries, it was determined that she had been sexually assaulted.

At this point, a task force was created to coordinate the activities of the five police agencies involved in the investigation, and a reward for information relating to the arrest of the killer was established. With few good leads to pursue, a major goal on the part of investigators was to find where Joan's body was kept prior to being dumped at the construction site. Investigators needed a crime scene—one that would provide them with evidence. A sketch of the individual with whom Joan was last seen was prepared and disseminated through the media. Two EMU students came forward to the police and told them that they saw Joan with an individual by the name of John Collins the night she disappeared. Interestingly, John was a student at EMU and held a part-time job at the Union (Joan also worked part-time at the Union). The information provided by these witnesses did not match the information provided by the other witnesses, but, not to leave any stone unturned, police found and interviewed John. Investigators learned that he drove a DeSoto, and it was neither red nor black. John told the detectives that he was not in the city when Joan disappeared and that he was the nephew of a Michigan State Police officer. Another apparent dead end.

On the morning of March 21, 1969, the dead body of a young woman was found in a cemetery located about four miles outside Ypsilanti. The woman who discovered the body lived near the cemetery, and she told the police that she saw a white station wagon leave the cemetery at about midnight the previous night. Another witness reported that he saw a late-model green station wagon cruising around the cemetery the night before the discovery of the body.

Through items contained in an overnight case found near the body, the victim was identified as Jane Mixer, a twenty-three-year-old law student at the University of Michigan. The victim was fully clothed and appeared to be deliberately and carefully placed in line with a grave marker. One of her shoes rested on her lower abdomen. The victim had two gunshot wounds to her head and a tightly bound noose from a nylon stocking around her neck. Was there any significance to the shoe on her abdomen? Why was she placed at this particular grave site? And where was she killed? The autopsy revealed that she died from the gunshot wounds to her head; the noose was placed around her neck after she was already dead. It was also determined that the victim was currently in her menstrual period and that she had not been sexually assaulted.

In tracking the last activities of Jane, the police learned that she had posted a note requesting a ride home on the ride board at the University of Michigan Student Union. In searching her apartment, the police discovered on her desk a note that read "David Hanson Lvg. 6:30 PM" and a checkmark by "David Hanson" in the phonebook. The police thought they had a big break. They quickly found David Hanson, but he told investigators that he was in theater rehearsal at 6:30 the night Jane disappeared, that he had no knowledge of her or her attempt to find a ride home, and that he drove a green Volkswagen. Yet another dead end. The police figured that the killer probably saw the ride request posted by Jane and called her claiming to be David Hanson, saying he would give her a ride home and would pick her up at 6:30 p.m. He was late, so she looked in the phone book, called David Hanson, and found that he was not at home. Probably just minutes later, the killer, believed to be David Hanson by Jane, showed up at her apartment, and Jane left with him and was never seen alive again. Once again, the police had few leads to pursue in the investigation. And they still did not even have a crime scene. Investigators spoke with Jane's boyfriend and other acquaintances, but they were all cleared of any wrongdoing. They also checked and interviewed all the other David Hansons in the area, but to no avail.

The situation was only to get worse. Four days later, on March 25, 1969, the nude and beaten body of Maralynn Skelton, sixteen, was found. The body was found in a remote rural area one-quarter mile from where Joan Schell's body was found the previous summer. The victim had been severely beaten to death and had numerous welts covering her body, as if she

had been flogged by a belt with a large buckle. She sustained massive head injuries. Other marks on her hands and feet indicated that she had been bound, probably during the beating. A piece of dark blue cloth was found deep in her throat. But most revolting was a tree branch that protruded from her vagina. All her clothes were piled neatly nearby except for her underwear. In searching for witnesses in the area, the police found one person who heard someone scream a few nights prior to the discovery of the body. Another witness saw a red car in the area, and another saw a small, white, two-door car in the area. The police determined that the last place Maralynn was known to be alive was a nearby shopping center. She called a friend from the shopping center to see if the friend could pick her up. No other witnesses saw or heard anything of Maralynn after that phone call.

The media began to refer to the four homicides as the "coed murders." Indeed, the similarities between the cases were striking. Only the murder of Jane Mixer appeared substantially different (death as the result of a gunshot). But to the dismay of everyone involved, the investigation of the four homicides seemed to be going nowhere. The major problem in the investigation was a lack of *good* information. At this point, six jurisdictions were involved in the investigation, and twenty persons were assigned to the investigative task force. The task force received and considered a substantial amount of information, including the possible relevance of other unsolved homicides in other jurisdictions in the state and across the country. One promising suspect that came to the attention of the police was a man by the name of David Parker. He was a suspect in the Boston Strangler homicides and was, coincidently, a graduate student at the University of Michigan at the time of the murders. He even had a connection with a David Hansen (with an "e"). But after much investigation, it was determined that he was not in the area when some of the murders occurred. Things were not going well for investigators. They still did not even have a crime scene.

On April 16, 1969, a month after the murder of Maralynn Skelton, the body of thirteen-year-old Dawn Basom was discovered in a remote residential area outside Ypsilanti. The girl had been reported missing the night before and had disappeared within a half mile of her home as she was walking on the sidewalk. When found, she was clad only in her bra and blouse. It was determined that she had been dead for less than twelve hours. She had been strangled with a black electrical cord, which was still tightly knotted around her neck. It also appeared that she had been repeatedly slashed across her torso, gagged, and raped. Later, the police found some of her clothes in the area, as if they had been tossed from a moving vehicle.

Then the police finally got a break, but it did not turn out to be as big as they hoped. While searching for witnesses to the murder of Dawn Basom and for a place where she, or any of the other women, may have been murdered, a police officer came across an abandoned farmhouse. The farmhouse was just outside Ypsilanti and close to where some of the bodies had been found. In searching the farmhouse, the officer discovered some women's clothes, jewelry, and, in the basement, blood and a black electrical cord—a black electrical cord that matched the one used to strangle Dawn Basom. A crime scene at last! The basement of the house, it was reasoned, could also have been a naturally cool place in which to preserve a human body (the body of Joan Schell). The police set up a stakeout operation at the farmhouse and hoped that the killer would return, perhaps with another victim. The police had difficulties in keeping the discovery and stakeout of the farmhouse a secret, but they hoped for the best. After a week of watching the farmhouse, nothing unusual was observed. Investigators went into the farmhouse once again and discovered, to their surprise, another earring in the basement (later determined to belong to Maralynn Skelton) and a piece of a blouse (that belonged to Dawn Basom). This meant four things: (1) the killer had returned to the farmhouse, (2) at least some of the murders were probably committed by the same person, (3) the killer was keeping personal items from the victims as souvenirs, and (4) the stakeout did not work very well. A few days later, a fire broke out in the barn and destroyed it, but the house was undamaged. Police quickly arrested the arsonist, Robert Gross, but after questioning and a polygraph, it was determined by investigators that he was not involved in the homicides. Shortly after the fire and the arrest of Robert Gross, a reporter from the *Ypsilanti Press,* John Cobb, found five plump lilacs on the driveway of the farmhouse. Cobb brought the discovery to the attention of the police, and the police found it strange that only he noticed these flowers, even though many police officers were in the area. The police wondered if the five lilacs represented the five dead girls. Did the killer return again? Could the reporter be the killer? The police had found a crime scene, but they still had more questions than answers.

There seemed to be no end to the nightmare. On June 9, 1969, the body of a woman was discovered in the rarely used driveway of another deserted farm in the area. The body was partially clad in a torn blouse and skirt. On the ground next to the body were torn underwear and pantyhose, the pantyhose slashed through the crotch. She had been stabbed multiple times, as though her killer was in a frenzy, but a single gunshot to her head was what caused her death. Her throat was cut, but it appeared that this had occurred after her death. She had been sexually assaulted. Once again, it did not appear that she was killed where her body was found. In canvassing the area, investigators found shoes, buttons from a coat, and blood in the same general area where several of the other bodies were found. All these items were matched to the unidentified body. After several days with the body still not identified, the police placed a photograph of the dead woman's face in the newspaper in hopes that someone would recognize her. Sure enough, the victim's roommate came forward and identified her as Alice Kalom, a twenty-three-year-old University of Michigan student. At about this same time, Alice's parents read the story in the newspaper; they identified Alice's body later that same day. The police were unable to track the last activities of Alice. Understandably, investigators were extremely frustrated. They had six homicide victims and no suspects. They had some evidence to believe that most, if not all, the crimes were related (MO), and they had numerous incomplete descriptions of vehicles that could have been involved. This was not much.

After this sixth homicide, a *Detroit Free Press* reporter contacted Peter Harkos, a well-known psychic (the same psychic who identified the wrong person as the culprit in the Boston Strangler case) and asked if he could provide a telepathic composite of the killer. The reporter met with Harkos in California, and Harkos provided a description. He said the killer was five foot seven, brilliant, maybe a student, loved cars, drove a motorcycle, had one eye that was bigger than the other, had a knife, and worked in gardens. He also said that there would be more victims. Reluctantly, the police later met with Harkos in Michigan, and he provided to them accurate descriptions of some of the crime scenes, including details not previously released, but none of the information provided new leads for the police to pursue.

At 11:15 p.m. on Wednesday, July 23, 1969, Karen Beineman, a nineteen-year-old EMU student, was reported missing after curfew at her dorm. Her roommates were the last to see her. She left school to go to downtown Ypsilanti to a wig shop, Wigs by Joan, that afternoon. The police went to the wig shop with a photograph of Karen, and two ladies who worked at the shop remembered that Karen was there and left with a guy on a motorcycle. They described this man as "nice-looking, clean-cut, short dark hair, early twenties, nice build, about six feet tall, and . . . wearing a green and yellow striped shirt." The bike was "big, loud, and shiny, dark blue, possibly a Honda." The police put out an all-points bulletin for the missing girl, had a composite sketch drawn of the man last seen with her, and got a list of registrations for all motorcycles in the Ypsilanti area. The police located another witness who saw the girl on the motorcycle, and she said the bike was definitely a Triumph.

Meanwhile, a new Ypsilanti police officer who had just graduated from EMU received a briefing on the missing girl and remembered that he saw a man in a striped shirt on a motorcycle talking to a girl on the street on the afternoon in question. He did not remember the man's name but knew that he was associated with the Theta Chi fraternity. He decided to go to the fraternity house and ask some questions. He learned from the other guys at the house that a person by the name of John Collins matched the description but that he did not live at the house anymore. The officer went to where John was said to live, and he found John working on one of four motorcycles in the garage. The officer asked John if he saw anyone that looked like him driving around picking up girls that Wednesday afternoon. John said that he saw nothing of the sort. Before leaving, the officer wrote down the license plate numbers of each of John's motorcycles, and John got angry, demanding, "What the hell are you doing that for? Bug off and play policeman somewhere else" (Keyes 1976; p. 204). Then the officer found a girl that he knew was a friend of John's and asked her if she had a photo of John that he could borrow. She did, and he took it to the wig shop. One of the ladies said that the man in the photo was definitely the guy seen on the motorcycle with the missing girl; the other lady said that it was "pretty close." With the positive identification, John Collins became a prime suspect in the disappearance of Karen Beineman.

Within minutes of John Collins being identified as a suspect, the body of Karen Beineman was found. The nude body was discovered in a residential area of Ypsilanti, approximately twenty feet down a gully embankment. The discovery was treated as top secret. Based on previous crimes, the police believed that the killer often returned to see the dead bodies, and they

hoped that he would do so again. The police removed the body, replaced it with a store mannequin, and set up Operation Stakeout. They hoped this stakeout would work better than the last one. As it grew dark on that hot, rainy night, the police hid in the nearby bushes and waited for the killer to return. After a few hours, an individual was seen by the police running from the area, but before the police could notify each other as to what was seen and the direction in which the man was running, the person had vanished. Thinking that maybe the person had been able to get close enough to touch the body, the police checked for fingerprints on the mannequin, but the only ones recovered were those of the district attorney who had set the mannequin in place.

The autopsy on the body revealed that Karen had been dead for about three days, probably killed on Wednesday at about 3:00 p.m. (she was seen riding away on the motorcycle at about 1:00 p.m.). She had been strangled and severely beaten, and semen was present. Her chest and breasts had been severely mutilated, as if they had been burned with some type of a liquid or acid. It appeared that she also had been bound, as evidenced by ligature marks on her wrists and ankles. Burlap material was found in her throat. Recovered from the victim's vagina were her underwear. On closer examination of the underwear, a most interesting discovery was made: in the underwear were tiny head hair clippings. Where did they come from? Was Karen Beineman killed in a barber shop?

Meanwhile, the police maintained surveillance on their prime suspect, John Collins. Other young women came forward to the police and said that the man pictured in the composite had tried to get them to go for a ride. Another said that John offered her $50 if he could take pictures of her. With the evidence mounting against John, two young Ypsilanti police officers took it upon themselves to question him. They accused him of Karen's murder, and, in the process, told him what they knew about the crime. John provided an alibi to the officers and told them that his uncle, David Leik, a Michigan State Police officer, would not be happy that they were making such accusations of him. This premature questioning of John Collins turned out to be another big mistake—one of many in the investigation.

During the next several days, the police spent time verifying John's alibi for the date and time of the disappearance and murder of Karen, and it seemed to hold up. Why? Was it true? Or did he have time and forewarning enough to create an alibi? The police continued to uncover evidence that at least indirectly suggested that John Collins was the coed killer. The task force, however, was in turmoil, and it was believed by many that the investigation was being poorly managed. As a result, just as the case was to break wide open, the governor of Michigan assigned responsibility of the investigation to the Michigan State Police. The *Detroit Free Press* headline read "The Keystone Kops Get Help."

At about this same time, David Leik's wife went to the basement of her Ypsilanti home to do the laundry after a twelve-day vacation out of town. She noticed something quite strange—dried black paint on the basement floor and also on a ladder. On a shirt hanging in the basement were several small, brownish spots. She also noticed other items either missing or out of place. She wondered if John, her nephew, had any knowledge about the condition of the basement, as he was the only one with access to the house while the Leiks were on vacation. She called David at the state police office and told him about the basement. Shortly thereafter, David was told by his supervisor at the state police post that John was a suspect in the murder of Karen Beineman. Although he found this nearly impossible to believe, David told his supervisor about what his wife found in his basement. They agreed that the crime lab should examine the basement, just to be sure.

Upon examining the basement, investigators carefully scraped the black paint off the floor, expecting that under this paint was going to be blood. An initial test was immediately conducted on the drops visible under the paint, and they were determined to be . . . not blood! David then remembered that a varnish stain was on the floor, dripped there while he was doing a project a long time ago. Then, while on his hands and knees on the basement floor, one of the investigators looked under the washing machine and found several blonde head hair clippings; clippings that were similar, it seemed, to those found in Karen's underwear that were recovered from her body. Next, several drops of blood were recovered from the shirt hanging in the basement. The police finally had what they believed was a good crime scene, and John Collins was the only one who had had access to it. Evidence was falling into place. The hair clippings were in the basement because that was where Mrs. Leik always trimmed her children's hair. The police reasoned that Karen was in the basement, and while she was being tortured and killed, her underwear was on the floor. The hair got in her underwear, and John then put the underwear in her vagina. Then, when cleaning the basement after he killed Karen, John

noticed what he thought was a stubborn stain of blood and, not being able to remove it, decided to paint over it. John made a mistake; the stain was varnish and it had been there previously. When John was questioned and confronted with his mistake, he "drew a sharp breath that caught in his throat, and then, as though a plug had been dislodged, the tears spilled out and ran down his cheeks" (Keyes 1976; p. 283).

John Collins was arrested, and a search warrant was issued for his apartment and car. A black paint spray can, .22 caliber shells, and several knives were recovered from his apartment, but the police did not find what they were really hoping to find. All along, the police believed that the killer was taking and keeping souvenirs from his victims, but they found nothing of the sort in his apartment. Later it was learned from one of John's roommates that after being prematurely questioned by the two officers, John carried out of the apartment a box that could have contained items that belonged to the victims. The police conducted a lineup for the purpose of having the wig shop workers identify John as the man seen with Karen. The police interrogated Donald Baker, a friend of John's, and Donald provided information that destroyed John's alibi, portrayed him as a thief who committed burglaries and stole motorcycle parts. Donald also said that John often carried a knife on his motorcycle.

The trial of John Collins for the murder of Karen Beineman began June 2, 1970. The prosecution had three primary objectives—three points to prove. First, the prosecution sought to prove that Karen was last seen with John Collins near the wig shop on his motorcycle. The eyewitnesses were used to establish this point. Second, prosecutors needed to establish that Karen was in the basement of the Leik house and was probably killed there. The primary evidence used to establish this link was the hair found in the basement and the hair in Karen's underwear found in her vagina. Third, it needed to be established that John was the only one who had access to the home at the time the crime occurred there.

The defense offered three counterpoints. First, they questioned the procedures used by the police to identify John as the man last seen with the victim. It was argued that the lineup identification of John was invalid because the witnesses were earlier shown a single picture of John as the perpetrator. It was argued that this biased the witnesses' perceptions and identification. Second, the defense raised questions about the actual whereabouts of John during the critical time period in question and argued, through witnesses,

Exhibit A.1 — The Triangle of Evidence in the Investigation and Prosecution of John Collins

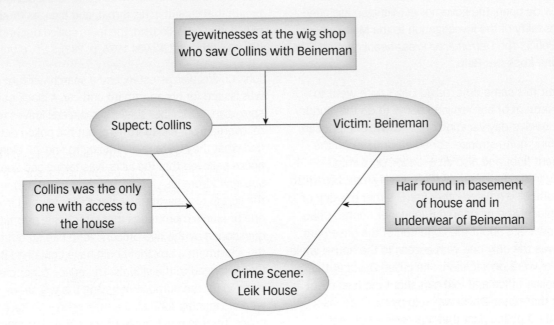

that John had a valid alibi. As a result, it was argued, he could not have possibly committed the crime. Finally, the defense questioned the methods used to confirm that the victim was in fact in the basement. They questioned the results of the hair and blood comparison analysis (remember, this case took place before the discovery of DNA analysis). The trial lasted seventeen days and fifty-seven witnesses provided testimony. John Collins did not testify. After five days of deliberation, the jury found John guilty of the murder of Karen Beineman. He was sentenced to life in prison without the possibility of parole (Keyes 1976).

Some people question why John Collins was never tried for any of the other homicides that were believed to be part of the series. The probable and most likely reason was that the prosecutors did not believe that they had enough evidence to prove beyond a reasonable doubt that John committed these crimes. There was little physical evidence that associated John with the other murders. It has also been reported that the prosecutor held back some evidence and did not pursue the other homicide charges in the event that John was found not guilty of the murder of Karen Beineman or he successfully petitioned for a new trial, which he requested in 1988 (James 1991).

At least one of the seven murders was not committed by John Collins. On November 25, 2004, Gary

Leiterman, sixty-two, was charged with the murder of Jane Mixer, the victim who arranged for a ride with "David Hanson" and whose body was found at the cemetery. Leiterman was subsequently found guilty and sentenced to mandatory life in prison for this murder. The conviction was made possible by advances in crime technology. Upon prompting from the victim's relatives, authorities had entered the DNA profile of Jane's killer into the Michigan State DNA database. The DNA was obtained from evidence recovered from the victim that had been stored for many years. The print matched that of Leiterman, whose DNA profile was in the database because of an earlier conviction for prescription fraud. It is not clear if DNA evidence is still available for analysis in any of the other homicide cases.

John Collins maintains that he did not commit the murder of Karen Beineman or any of the other murders in which he is suspected. In 1980, he changed his name to John Chapman. While in prison, he has attempted to escape at least twice. He remains incarcerated in Michigan.

Also:

- See "oldnews.aadl.org/taxonomy/term/2558" for an archive listing of news clippings relating to the trial and incarceration of John Collins.

- Search YouTube for "Kelly & Company John Norman Collins" for a five-part series on the case and an interview with John Collins.

- Search for "John Collins, MDOC number 126833" on the Michigan State Department of Corrections Web site at http://mdocweb.state.mi.us/otis2/otis2.html.

QUESTIONS FOR DISCUSSION AND REVIEW

1. Previously in *Criminal Investigation,* it was explained that there are often several basic problems with criminal evidence: (1) at the time evidence is collected, it is unknown if it relates to the crime; (2) at the time evidence is collected, it is unknown if the evidence is accurate; and (3) the evidence is not always as it seems to be. Provide an example of each of these issues being present in this case.

2. As discussed, there are various forms and functions of evidence in criminal investigations. Provide an example of each of the following in this case: (1) corpus delicti evidence, (2) identification evidence, (3) behavioral evidence, and (4) associative evidence.

3. In the investigation of the murder of Karen Bieneman, the police identified John Collins as the suspect, Karen as the victim, and the Leiks' house as the place where Karen was killed. What specific pieces of evidence linked these people and this place?

4. In the investigation of the murder of Karen Beineman, give examples of direct evidence and circumstantial evidence. Also, give examples of inculpatory and exculpatory evidence. Was there any direct evidence to allow one to conclude that John Collins killed Karen Beineman?

5. During the investigation, the police discovered what they thought to be two crime scenes. Identify these two places. One of the scenes was much more useful (and valuable) than the other. Explain why.

6. These crimes and their investigation occurred in the 1960s, prior to the discovery of DNA and DNA printing for criminal investigation purposes. Consider and discuss how this investigation may have differed if it was conducted today. What might have been different about the investigation? Be specific. What important aspects of the investigation would have likely remained unchanged?

7. How was John Collins first identified as a prime suspect in the murder of Karen Beineman? How was his name developed and how was he linked to the missing girl? John's name came up in the investigation prior to becoming a suspect in the murder of Karen. Explain what evidence led to this development.

8. This investigation occurred prior to the widespread understanding of psychological profiling. Based on the crimes that were committed and how they were committed, what could have been inferred about the characteristics of the killer? Did the crime scenes more closely reflect those of an organized serial killer or a disorganized killer? What value might this psychological profile have been in the investigation?

9. As discussed, a psychic was used in the investigation. Was any of the information that he provided accurate? Was it relevant? What value, if any, did he provide to the investigation?

10. Identify the most significant mistakes that John Collins made in committing these crimes, especially the murder of Karen Beineman. Explain.

11. Identify and discuss the mistakes that detectives made in investigating these murders.

12. Overall, identify and discuss the one dimension of this investigation that would have differed the most if it was conducted today rather than in the 1960s.

13. Based on the evidence collected throughout the investigation and the interview of John Collins (the YouTube videos cited above), do you think John was guilty of the murder of Karen Beineman? Any or all of the other girls? Why or why not?

References

Adams, Susan H. 1996. "Statement Analysis: What Do Suspects' Words Really Reveal?" *FBI Law Enforcement Bulletin* 65(10): 12–20.

Aiken, Margaret M., Ann Wolbert Burgess, and Robert R. Hazelwood. 1995. "False Rape Allegations." In *Practical Aspects of Rape Investigation: A Multidisciplinary Approach*, edited by Robert R. Hazelwood and Ann Wolbert Burgess, 219–240. Boca Raton, FL: CRC Press.

Ainsworth, Janet E. 1998. "In a Different Register: The Pragmatics of Powerlessness in Police Interrogations." In *The Miranda Debate: Law, Justice, and Policing*, edited by George C. Leo and George C. Thomas. Boston: Northeastern University Press.

Akin, Louis L. 2005. "Blood Splatter Interpretation at Crime and Accident Scenes: A Basic Approach." *FBI Law Enforcement Bulletin* 74(2): 21–24.

Aldridge, C. D. 2007. "'Bait Vehicle' Technologies and Motor Vehicle Theft along the Southwest Border." Report funded by the Justice and Safety Center of Eastern Kentucky University, performed by the NLECTC/Border Research and Technology Center, a program of the National Institute of Justice.

Almasy, Steve. 2013. "Two Teens Found Guilty in Steubenville Rape Case." CNN Justice. CNN.com. March 17. www.cnn.com/2013/03/17/justice/ohio-steubenville-case.

Alter, Jonathan, and Mark Starr. 1990. "Race and Hype in a Divided City." *Newsweek*, January 22, 2.

Altizio, Alicia, and Diana York. 2007. *Robbery of Convenience Stores*. Problem-Oriented Guides for Police Series: Problem-Specific Guide No. 49. Washington, DC: U.S. Department of Justice.

Areh, Igor. 2011. "Gender-Related Differences in Eyewitness Testimony." *Personality & Individual Differences* 50(5): 559–563.

Asplen, Christopher H. 2003. *The Application of DNA Technology in England and Wales*. Washington, DC: U.S. Department of Justice.

Baker, James, N. 1990. "Boston: A Deadly Family Affair." *Newsweek*, January 15, 3.

Baker, Liva. 1983. *Miranda: Crime, Law, and Politics*. New York: Atheneum.

Ball, Larry, D. 1978. *The United States Marshals of New Mexico and Arizona Territories, 1846–1912*. Albuquerque: University of New Mexico Press.

Band, Stephen R., and Donald C. Sheehan. 1999. "Managing Undercover Stress: The Supervisor's Role." *FBI Law Enforcement Bulletin* 68(2): 1–6.

Bartol, Curt R., and Anne M. Bartol. 2013. *Criminal and Behavioral Profiling*. Thousand Oaks, CA: Sage.

Baskin, Deborah, and Ira Sommers. 2010. "The Influence of Forensic Evidence on the Case Outcomes of Homicide Incidents." *Journal of Criminal Justice* 38(6): 1,141–1,149.

———. 2012. "The Influence of Forensic Evidence on the Case Outcomes of Assault and Robbery Incidents." *Criminal Justice Policy Review* 23(2): 186–210.

Ben-Shakhar, Gershon, Maya Bar-Hillel, and Mordechai Kremnitzer. 2002. "Trial by Polygraph: Reconsidering the Use of the Guilty Knowledge Technique in Court." *Law and Human Behavior* 26(5): 527–541.

Benitez, Christopher, Dale McNiel, and Renee Binder. 2010. "Do Protection Orders Protect?" *Journal of the American Academy of Psychiatry & the Law* 38(3): 376–385.

Bennett, Wayne W., and Karen Hess. 1984. *Investigating Arson*. Springfield, IL: Charles C. Thomas.

Bennett, Margo, and John E. Hess. 1991. "Cognitive Interviewing." *FBI Law Enforcement Bulletin* 60(3): 8–13.

Benoit, Carl. 2008. "Questioning 'Authority': Fourth Amendment Consent Searches." *FBI Law Enforcement Bulletin* 77(7): 23–32.

———. 2011. "The 'Public Safety' Exception to Miranda." *FBI Law Enforcement Bulletin* 80(2): 25–32.

Blackledge, Robert D. 1996. "Condom Trace Evidence: A New Factor in Sexual Assault Investigations." *FBI Law Enforcement Bulletin* 65(2): 12–16.

Blinkhorn, Steve. 1988. "Lie Detection as a Psychometric Procedure." In *The Polygraph Test: Lies, Truth, and Science,* edited by Anthony Gale, 29–39. London: Sage.

Botsch, Robert. 2008. "Developing Street Sources: Tips for Patrol Officers." *FBI Law Enforcement Bulletin* 77(9): 24–27.

Bowes, Mark. 2013. "Chesterfield Police Investigating Arson, Vandalism at Minister's Home." *Richmond Times Dispatch.* March 20. www.timesdispatch.com/news/latest-news/chesterfield-police-investigating-arson-vandalism-at-minister-s-home/article_67c95de4–9176–11e2–9e89–001a4bcf6878.html.

Brandl, Steven G. 2004. "The Relationship between Circumstances, Evidence, Investigative Effort, and the Outcome of Homicide Investigations." Paper presented at the annual Academy of Criminal Justice Sciences meeting, Las Vegas, NV.

Brandl, Steven G., and James Frank. 1994. "The Relationship between Evidence, Detective Effort, and the Disposition of Burglary and Robbery Investigations." *American Journal of Police* 13(3): 149–168.

Breed, Allen G. 2002. "Two Men in Custody in Sniper Hunt." Associated Press News Archive. October 21. www.apnewsarchive.com/2002/Two-Men-in-Custody-in-Sniper-Hunt/id-109906a3a8f2fb62605b5c1dba200480.

Brown, Adam, Daniel Sommerville, Brian Reedy, Ronald Shimmon, and Mark Tahtouh. 2009. "Revisiting the Thermal Development of Latent Fingerprints on Porous Surfaces: New Aspects and Refinements." *Journal of Forensic Sciences* 54(1): 114–121.

Brown, Jennifer M., and Elizabeth A. Campbell. 1994. *Stress and Policing: Sources and Strategies.* New York: John Wiley and Sons.

Brown, Tom. 2008. "Spy-in-the-Sky Drone Sets Sights on Miami." Reuters. March 26. www.reuters.com/article/2008/03/26/us-usa-security-drones-idUSN1929797920080326.

Bulzomi, Michael. 2007. "Search Incident to Arrest in the Age of Personal Electronics." *FBI Law Enforcement Bulletin* 76(9): 26–32.

Bureau of Justice Statistics. 2002a. *Survey of DNA Crime Laboratories, 2001.* Washington, DC: U.S. Department of Justice.

———. 2002b. *Rape and Sexual Assault: Reporting to Police and Medical Attention, 1992–2000.* Washington, DC: U.S. Department of Justice.

———. 2003. *Reporting Crime to the Police, 1992–2000.* Washington, DC: U.S. Department of Justice.

———. 2005. *Criminal Victimization, 2004.* Washington, DC: U.S. Department of Justice.

———. 2008. *Cybercrime against Businesses.* Washington, DC: U.S. Department of Justice.

———. 2010. *Criminal Victimization, 2009.* Washington, DC: U.S. Department of Justice.

———. 2011. *Criminal Victimization, 2010.* Washington, DC: U.S. Department of Justice.

———. 2012a. *Criminal Victimization, 2011.* Washington, DC: U.S. Department of Justice.

———. 2012b. *Violent Victimization Committed by Strangers, 1993–2010.* Washington, DC: U.S. Department of Justice.

———. 2012c. *Census of Publicly Funded Forensic Crime Laboratories, 2009.* Washington, DC: U.S. Department of Justice.

———. 2013. *Female Victims of Sexual Violence, 1994–2010.* Washington, DC: U.S. Department of Justice.

Burgess, Ann Wolbert, and Robert R. Hazelwood. 1995. "The Victim's Perspective." In *Practical Aspects of Rape Investigation: A Multidisciplinary Approach,* edited by Robert R. Hazelwood and Ann Wolbert Burgess, 27–42. Boca Raton, FL: CRC Press LLC.

Campbell, J. C., D. Webster, J. Koziol-McLain, C. R. Block, D. Campbell, M. A. Curry, F. Gary, J. McFarlane, C. Sachs, P. Sharps, Y. Ulrich, and S. A. Wilt. 2003. "Assessing Risk Factors for Intimate Partner Homicide." *National Institute of Justice Journal* 250: 14–19.

Canter, Philip. 2000. "Using a Geographic Information System for Tactical Crime Analysis." In *Analyzing Crime Pattern: Frontiers of Practice,* edited by Victor Goldsmith et al. Thousand Oaks, CA: Sage.

Carroll, Douglas. 1988. "How Accurate Is Polygraph Lie Detection?" In *The Polygraph Test: Lies, Truth, and Science,* edited by Anthony Gale. London: Sage.

Carter, Chelsea J., Poppy Harlow, and Brian Vitagliano. 2013a. "Ohio Rape Trial Focuses on Text Messages: Case Has Cast Unwelcome Spotlight on Ohio Town." WCVB Boston. March 14. www.wcvb.com/news/national/Ohio-rape-trial-focuses-on-texts-messages/-/9848944/19313512/-/item/0/-/p8aur3z/-/index.html.

———. 2013b. "Steubenville Rape Trial Focuses on Text Messages, Cell Phone Pictures." CNN Justice. CNN.com. March 14. www.cnn.com/2013/03/14/justice/ohio-steubenville-case.

Casey, Rick. 2005. "Yates Wins: Shrink Was Delusional." *Houston Chronicle,* January 7.

Casey, Steven J. 1995. "Car Thieves Smell a RATT." *FBI Law Enforcement Bulletin* 64(11): 1–4.

Cassell, Paul G. 1998. "Miranda Social Costs: An Empirical Reassessment." In *The Miranda Debate: Law, Justice, and Policing,* edited by George C. Leo and George C. Thomas. Boston: Northeastern University Press.

Cassell, Paul G., and Bret S. Hayman. 1998. "Police Interrogation in the 1990s: An Empirical Study of the Effects of Miranda." In *The Miranda Debate: Law, Justice, and Policing,* edited by George C. Leo and George C. Thomas. Boston: Northeastern University Press.

Castleman, Terry L. 2000. *Death Investigation: A Handbook for Police Officers.* Springfield, IL: Charles C. Thomas.

Christiaansen, R. E., J. D. Sweeny, and K. Ochalek. 1983. "Influencing Eyewitness Descriptions." *Law and Human Behavior* 7(1): 59–65.

Clark, M. Wesley. 2009. "Searching Cell Phones Seized Incident to Arrest." *FBI Law Enforcement Bulletin* 78(2): 25–32.

Clark, S. C., Ernst, M. F., Haglund, W. D., and Jentzen, J. M. 1996. *Medicolegal Death Investigation.* Big Rapids, MI: Occupational Research and Assessment, Inc.

Clarke, Ronald V. 2010. *Thefts of and from Cars in Parking Facilities.* Problem-Oriented Guides for Police Series: Problem-Specific Guide No. 10. Washington, DC: U.S. Department of Justice.

Cohen, Bernard, and Jan Chaiken. 1987. *Investigators Who Perform Well.* Washington, DC: U.S. Department of Justice.

Constable, George, ed. 1987. *Mysteries of the Unknown: Psychic Powers.* Alexandria, VA: Time-Life Books.

Conti, Philip M. 1977. *The Pennsylvania State Police: A History of Service to the Commonwealth, 1905 to Present.* Harrisburg, PA: Stackpole.

Council on Scientific Affairs. 1985. "Scientific Status of Refreshing Recollection by the Use of Hypnosis." *Journal of the American Medical Association* 253(13): 1,918–1,923.

Congressional Research Service. 2001. *Terrorism: Section by Section Analysis of the USA PATRIOT Act.* Washington, DC: Congressional Research Service, The Library of Congress.

Crowley, Sharon R. 1999. *Sexual Assault: The Medical Legal Examination.* Stamford, CT: Appleton and Lange.

Cunningham, Larry. 1999. "Taking on Testifying: The Prosecutor's Response to In-Court Police Deception." *Criminal Justice Ethics* 18(1): 26–40.

Dabney, Dean. 2010. "Observations Regarding Key Operational Realities in a Compstat Model of Policing." *Justice Quarterly* 27(1): 28–51.

Dadisho, Ed. 2005. "Identity Theft and the Police Response: The Investigation." *Police Chief* 72 (1). Available online at www.policechiefmagazine.org/magazine/index.cfm?fuseaction=display_arch&article_id=493&issue_id=12005.

Damphousse, Kelly R. 2008. "Voice Stress Analysis: Only 15 Percent of Lies about Drug use Detected in Field Test." *National Institute of Justice Journal* 259: 8–12.

Damphousse, Kelly R., and Brent L. Smith. 1998. "The Internet: A Terrorist Medium for the 21st Century." In *The Future of Terrorism: Violence in the New Millennium,* edited by Harvey W. Kushner. Thousand Oaks, CA: Sage.

Davis, Ann, Maureen Tkacik, and Andrea Petersen. 2002. "Nation of Tipsters Answers FBI's Call." *The Wall Street Journal,* November 21.

Davis, Robert C., Carl Jensen, and Karin E. Kitchens. 2011. *Cold Case Investigations: An Analysis of Current Procedures and Factors Associated with Successful Outcomes.* Santa Monica: RAND.

Dedel, Kelly. 2007. *Drive-By Shootings.* Problem-Oriented Guides for Police Series: Problem-Specific Guide No. 47. Washington, DC: U.S. Department of Justice.

———. 2009. *Child Abuse and Neglect in the Home.* Problem-Oriented Guides for Police Series: Problem-Specific Guide No. 55. Washington, DC: U.S. Department of Justice.

Department of Homeland Security. 2010. *Legal Division Handbook.* Glynco, GA: Federal Law Enforcement Training Center.

del Carmen, Rolando V. 1995. *Criminal Procedure: Law and Practice.* Belmont: Wadsworth.

———. 2003. *Criminal Procedure: Law and Practice,* 6th ed. Belmont: Wadsworth.

Dershowitz, Alan M. 1982. *The Best Defense.* New York: Random House.

———. 1996. *Reasonable Doubts: The Criminal Justice System and the O. J. Simpson Case.* New York: Simon & Schuster.

Deslauriers-Varin, Nadine, Patrick Lussier, and Michel St-Yves. 2011. "Confessing Their Crime: Factors Influencing the Offender's Decision to Confess to the Police." *Justice Quarterly* 28(1): 113–145.

Devery, Christopher. 2010. "Criminal Profiling and Criminal Investigation." *Journal of Contemporary Criminal Justice* 26(4): 393–409.

Dillon, Jeff, and Steve Perez. 2002. "On Tape, Westerfield Describes Meandering Trip." *San Diego Union Tribune,* June 12.

Dilworth, Donald C. 1977. *Identification Wanted: Development of the American Criminal Identification System, 1893–1943.* Gaithersburg, MD: International Association of Chiefs of Police.

Dix, Jay, and Michael Graham. 2000. *Time of Death, Decomposition and Identification: An Atlas.* Cause of Death Atlas Series. Boca Raton, FL: CRC Press.

Doan, Brandy, and Brent Snook. 2008. "A Failure to Find Empirical Support for the Homology Assumption in Criminal Profiling." *Journal of Police & Criminal Psychology* 23(2): 61–70.

Douglas, John. 2000. *The Cases That Haunt Us.* New York: Scribner.

———. 1996. *Unabomber: On the Trail of America's Most Wanted Serial Killer.* New York: Pocket Books.

Douglas, John E., Ann W. Burgess, and Robert Ressler. 1992. *Crime Classification Manual.* New York: Lexington.

Douglas, John E., and Corinne Munn. 1992. "Violent Crime Scene Analysis: Modus Operandi, Signature, and Staging." *FBI Law Enforcement Bulletin* 61(2): 1–10.

Douglas, John, Robert K. Ressler, Ann W. Burgess, and Carol R. Hartman. 1986. "Criminal Profiling from Crime Scene Analysis." *Behavioral Sciences and the Law* 4(4): 401–421.

Dowden, Craig, Craig Bennell, and Sarah Bloomfield. 2007. "Advances in Offender Profiling: A Systematic Review of the Profiling Literature Published over the Past Three Decades." *Journal of Police and Criminal Psychology* 22(1): 44–56.

Dreeke, Robin, and Joe Navarro. 2009. "Behavioral Mirroring in Interviewing." *FBI Law Enforcement Bulletin* 78(12): 1–10.

Eck, John E. 1983. *Solving Crimes: The Investigation of Burglary and Robbery.* Washington, DC: Police Executive Research Forum.

Egger, Steven A. 1998. *The Killers among Us: An Examination of Serial Murder and Its Investigation.* Upper Saddle River, NJ: Prentice Hall.

Elaad, Eitan, and Murray Kleiner. 1990. "Effects of Polygraph Chart Interpreter Experience on Psychological Detection of Deception." *Journal of Police Science and Administration* 17: 115–123.

Ellis, Hadyn D. 1984. "Practical Aspects of Face Memory." In *Eyewitness Testimony: Psychological Perspectives,* edited by Gary L. Wells and Elizabeth F. Loftus. Cambridge: Cambridge University Press.

Ethridge, Philip A., and Raul Gonzalez. 1996. "Combating Vehicle Theft along the Texas Border." *FBI Law Enforcement Bulletin* 65(1): 10–13.

Fainaru, Steve. 2002a. "Clues Pointed to Changing Terrorist Tactics. *The Washington Post,* May 19, A09.

———. 2002b. "September 11 Detainee Is Ordered Deported." *The Washington Post,* September 4, A10.

Federal Bureau of Investigation. 2000. *FBI Laboratory 2000.* Washington, DC: U.S. Department of Justice.

———. 2004. ViCap Alert. *FBI Law Enforcement Bulletin* 73(10): 13. Washington DC: U.S. Department of Justice.

———. 2006. ViCap Alert. *FBI Law Enforcement Bulletin* 75(2): 23. Washington DC: U.S. Department of Justice.

———. 2007. *Handbook of Forensic Services.* Washington, DC: U.S. Department of Justice.

———. 2012. *Crime in the United States, 2011 Uniform Crime Reports.* Washington, DC: U.S. Department of Justice.

Feeney, Floyd. 1999. "Robbers and Decision Makers." In *In Their Own Words: Criminals on Crime,* edited by Paul Cromwell. Los Angeles: Roxbury.

Felson, Marcus, and Rachel Boba. 2010. *Crime and Everyday Life.* Thousand Oaks, CA: Sage.

Ferkenhoff, Eric. 2002. "Man Held Mistakenly Is Dropped as Suspect." *The Chicago Tribune,* June 9.

Finn, Peter, and Kerry Murphy Healy. 1996. Preventing Gang- and Drug-Related Witness Intimidation. Washington, DC: National Institute of Justice.

Fisher, Jim. 1994. *The Lindbergh Case.* New Brunswick, NJ: Rutgers University Press.

Fisher, Ronald P., and R. Edward Geiselman. 1992. *Memory-Enhancing Techniques for Investigative Interviewing: The Cognitive Interview.* Springfield, IL: Charles C. Thomas.

Fisher, Ronald P., R. Edward Geiselman, and Michael Amador. 1989. "Field Test of the Cognitive Interview: Enhancing the Recollection of Actual Victims and Witnesses of Crime." *Journal of Applied Psychology* 74(5): 722–727.

Fisher, Ronald P., R. Edward Geiselman, and David S. Raymond. 1987. "Critical Analysis of Police Interview Techniques." *Journal of Police Science and Administration* 15(3): 177–185.

Fleming, Zachary. 1999. "The Thrill of It All: Youthful Offenders and Auto Theft." In *In Their Own Words: Criminals on Crime,* edited by Paul Cromwell. Los Angeles: Roxbury.

Fredrickson, Darin D., and Raymond P. Siljander. 2004. *Street Drug Investigation: A Practical Guide for Plainclothes and Uniformed Personnel.* Springfield, IL: Charles C. Thomas.

Fuhrman, Mark. 1997. *Murder in Brentwood.* Washington, DC: Regnery Publishing.

Gaensslen, R. E. 2003. How Do I Become a Forensic Scientist? Educators Pathways to Forensic Science Careers. *Analytical and Bioanalytical Chemistry* 376(8): 1,151–1,155.

Garner, Brian A., ed. 2000. *Black's Law Dictionary.* St. Paul, MN: West.

Geberth, Vernon J. 1996. *Practical Homicide Investigation: Tactics, Procedures, and Forensic Techniques.* Boca Raton, FL: CRC Press.

Geiselman, R. Edward, and Ronald P. Fisher. 1989. "The Cognitive Interview Technique for Victims and Witnesses of Crime." In *Psychological Methods in Criminal Investigation and Evidence,* edited by David C. Raskin. New York: Springer.

General Accounting Office. 1979. *Report of the Comptroller General of the United States, Impact of the Exclusionary Rule on Federal Criminal Prosecutions.* Washington, DC: U.S. Government Printing Office.

Gentry, Curt. 1991. *J. Edgar Hoover: The Man and the Secrets.* New York: Penguin Books.

Goff, M. Lee. 2000. *A Fly for the Prosecution: How Insect Evidence Helps Solve Crimes.* Cambridge, MA: Harvard University Press.

Goldenson, Robert M. 1984. *Longman Dictionary of Psychology and Psychiatry.* New York: Longman.

Goldstein, Herman. 1987. "Toward Community Oriented Policing: Potential, Basic Requirements, and Threshold Questions." *Crime and Delinquency* 33(1): 6–30.

Gonzalez, Richard, Phoebe C. Ellsworth, and Maceo Pembroke. 1993. "Response Biases in Lineups and Showups." *Journal of Personality and Social Psychology* 64(4): 525–537.

Goodman, Gail S., and Annette Hahn. 1987. "Evaluating Eyewitness Testimony." In *Handbook of Forensic Psychology,* edited by Irving B. Weiner and Allen K. Hess. New York: John Wiley and Sons.

Green, Sara Jean. 2012. "Seattle Police Outreach Asks, 'Who Killed Me?'" *The Seattle Times.* September 18. http://seattletimes.com/html/localnews/2019186576_unsolvedhomicides18m. html.

Greenwood, Peter W., Jan M. Chaiken, and Joan Petersilia. 1977. *The Criminal Investigation Process.* Lexington: D. C. Heath.

Griffin, Timothy, Monica Miller, Jeffrey Hoppe, Amy Rebideaux, and Rachel Hammack. 2007. "A Preliminary Examination of AMBER Alert's Effects." *Criminal Justice Policy Review* 18(4): 378–394.

Gudjonsson, Gisli H. 1992. *The Psychology of Interrogations, Confessions, and Testimony.* New York: John Wiley and Sons.

Hagmann, Doug. 2007. "Domestic Terrorism . . . California Arson Fires Easier than Hijacking Planes." Canada Free Press. October 25. www.canadafreepress.com/index.php/article/362.

Haller, Mark H. 1976. "Historical Roots of Police Behavior: Chicago, 1890–1925." *Law and Society Review* 10(2): 303–323.

Haskell, Neal, and Christine Haskell. 2002. "Forensic Entomology." *Law and Order* 50 (5): 58–63.

Hayeslip, David, and Malcolm Russell-Einhorn. 2003. "Evaluating Multi-Jurisdictional Drug Enforcement Task Forces." *National Institute of Justice Journal* 250: 40–42.

Hazelwood, Robert R. 1995. Analyzing Rape and Profiling the Offender. In *Practical Aspects of Rape Investigation: A Multidisciplinary Approach,* edited by Robert R. Hazelwood and Ann Wolbert Burgess. Boca Raton, FL: CRC Press.

Hazelwood, Robert R., and Ann Wolbert Burgess. 1995. "The Behavioral-Oriented Interview of Rape Victims: The Key to Profiling." In *Practical Aspects of Rape Investigation: A Multidisciplinary Approach,* edited by Robert R. Hazelwood and Ann Wolbert Burgess. Boca Raton, FL: CRC Press.

Hazelwood, Robert R., Park Elliot Dietz, and Janet Warren. 1992. "The Criminal Sexual Sadist." *FBI Law Enforcement Bulletin* 61(2): 12–20.

Hazelwood, Robert R., and Janet Warren. 1989. "The Serial Rapist: His Characteristics and Victims, Conclusion." *FBI Law Enforcement Bulletin* 58(2): 18–25.

Hendrie, Edward M. 1998. "Warrantless Entries to Arrest: Constitutional Considerations." *FBI Law Enforcement Bulletin* 67(9): 25–32.

Henson, Billy, Bradford W. Reyns, and Bonnie S. Fisher. 2011. "Security in the 21st Century: Examining the Link between Online Social Network Activity, Piracy, and Interpersonal Victimization." *Criminal Justice Review* 36(3): 253–268.

Holcomb, Jayme. 2006. "Knock and Talks." *FBI Law Enforcement Bulletin* 75(8): 22–32.

Holliday, Robyn E., Joyce E. Humphries, Rebecca Milne, Amina Memon, Lucy Houlder, Amy Lyons, and Ray Bull. 2012. "Reducing Misinformation Effects in Older Adults with Cognitive Interview Mnemonics." *Psychology and Aging* 27(4): 1,191–1,203.

Holmes, Ronald M., and Stephen T. Holmes. 2009. *Profiling Violent Crimes: An Investigative Tool.* 4th ed. Thousand Oaks, CA: Sage.

Homant, Robert J., and Daniel B. Kennedy. 1998. "Psychological Aspects of Crime Scene Profiling: Validity Research." *Criminal Justice and Behavior* 25(3): 319–343.

Horvath, Frank. 1982. "Detecting Deception: The Promise and the Reality of Voice Stress Analysis." *Journal of Forensic Sciences* 27(2): 340–351.

Inbau, Fred E., John E. Reid, Joseph P. Buckley, and Brian C. Jayne. 2013. *Criminal Interrogations and Confessions.* Burlington, MA: Jones & Bartlett Learning.

Internal Revenue Service. 1993. *Financial Investigations: A Financial Approach to Detecting and Resolving Crimes.* Washington, DC: U.S. Government Printing Office.

Isenberg, Alice R. 2002. "Forensic Mitochondrial DNA Analysis: A Different Crime-Solving Tool." *FBI Law Enforcement Bulletin* 71(8): 16–22.

Isenberg, Alice R., and Jodi M. Moore. 1999. "Mitochondrial DNA Analysis at the F.B.I. Laboratory." *Forensic Science Communications* 1(2). Available online at www.fbi.gov/about-us/lab/forensic-science-communications/fsc/july1999/dnalist.htm/dnatext.htm#Introduction.

Isikoff, Michael, and Daniel Klaidman. 2002. "The Hijackers We Let Escape." *Newsweek,* June 10, 19–28.

James, Earl. 1991. *Catching Serial Killers: Learning from Past Killer Investigations.* Lansing, MI: International Forensic Services.

Janikowski, Richard. 2006. The Myth That the Exclusionary Rule Allows Many Criminals to Escape Justice. In *Demystifying Crime and Criminal Justice,* edited by Robert M. Bohm and Jeffrey T. Walker. Los Angeles: Roxbury.

Johnson, Paul, and Robin Williams. 2007. "Internationalizing New Technologies of Crime Control: Forensic DNA Databasing and Datasharing in the European Union." *Policing & Society* 17(2): 103–118.

Johnson, Ross. 2013. *Antiterrorism and Threat Response: Planning and Implementation.* Boca Raton, FL: CRC Press.

Jones, Charlotte-Foltz. 1991. *Mistakes That Worked: 40 Familiar Inventions and How They Came to Be.* New York: Doubleday.

Jonsson, Patrik. 2007. "The Police Lineup Is Becoming Suspect Practice." *The Christian Science Monitor.* February 6. www.csmonitor.com/2007/0206/p01s02-usju.html.

Kaplan, Robert D. 2002. "The World in 2005: Hidden in Plain Sight." *The Atlantic Monthly* 286(3): 54–56.

Kassin, Saul M., Christine C. Goldstein, and Kenneth Savitsky. 2003. "Behavioral Confirmation in the Interrogation Room: On the Dangers of Presuming Guilt." *Law and Human Behavior* 27(2): 187–203.

Kassin, Saul M., and Gisli H. Gudjonsson. 2004. "The Psychology of Confessions: A Review of the Literature and Issues." *Psychological Science in the Public Interest* 5(2): 35–67.

Kassin, Saul M., and Rebecca J. Norwick. 2004. "Why People Waive Their Miranda Rights: The Power of Innocence." *Law and Human Behavior* 28(2): 211–221.

Keister, Todd. 2007. *Thefts of and from Cars on Residential Streets and Driveways.* Problem-Oriented Guides for Police Series: Problem-Specific Guide No. 46. Washington, DC: U.S. Department of Justice.

Kelling, George L., and Mark H. Moore. 1988. "The Evolving Strategy of Policing." *Perspectives on Policing* 4: 1–15. Washington, DC: National Institute of Justice.

Kelling, George L., Tony Pate, Duane Dieckman, and Charles E. Brown. 1974. *The Kansas City Preventive Patrol Experiment.* Washington, DC: Police Foundation.

Kelley, Robert J. 1998. "Armed Prophets and Extremists: Islamic Fundamentalism." In *The Future of Terrorism: Violence in the New Millennium,* edited by Harvey W. Kushner. Thousand Oaks, CA: Sage.

Kelly, John F., and Phillip Wearne. 1998. *Tainting Evidence: Inside the Scandals at the FBI Crime Lab.* New York: Free Press.

Keppel, Robert D., and Joseph G. Weis. 1993. *Improving the Investigation of Violent Crime: The Homicide Investigation and Tracking System. Research in Brief.* Washington, DC: National Institute of Justice.

———. 1994. "Time and Distance as Solvability Factors in Murder Cases." *Journal of Forensic Sciences* 39(2): 386–400.

Kerr, Ian, Max Binnie, and Cynthia Aoki. 2008. "Tessling on My Brain: The Future of Lie Detection and Brain Privacy in the Criminal Justice System." *Canadian Journal of Criminology & Criminal Justice* 50(8): 367–387.

Keyes, Edward. 1976. *Michigan Murders.* New York: Readers Digest Press.

Kiley, William P. 1998. "The Advanced Criminal Investigation Course: An Innovative Approach to Detective In-Service Training." *FBI Law Enforcement Bulletin* 67(10): 16–18.

Klockars, Carl B. 1985. *The Idea of Police.* Beverly Hills, CA: Sage.

Kocsis, Richard, and Harvey J. Irwin. 1998. "The Psychological Profile of Serial Offenders and a Redefinition of the Misnomer of Serial Crime." *Psychiatry, Psychology and the Law* 5(2): 197–213.

Kocsis, Richard, Jenny Middledorp, and Anne Karpin. 2008. "Taking Stock of Accuracy in Criminal Profiling: The Theoretical Quandary for Investigative Psychology." *Journal of Forensic Psychology Practice* 8(3): 244–261.

Kohlmeier, R. E., C. A. McMahan, and V. J .M. DiMaio. 2001. "Suicide by Firearms." *American Journal of Forensic Medical Pathology* 22(4): 337–340.

Kolbel, Ralf, and Susanne Selter. 2010. "Hostile Intent—The Terrorist's Achilles Heel? Observations on Pre-Crime Surveillance by Means of Thought Recognition." *European Journal of Crime, Criminal Law and Criminal Justice* 18(3): 237–259.

Kovaleski, Serge F., and Sari Horwitz. 2002. "In Letter, Killer Makes Demands and Threats." *Washington Post,* October 26, A14.

Kozel, F. Andrew, Kevin Johnson, Emily Grenesko, Steven Laken, Samet Kose, Xinghua Lu, Dean Pollina, Andrew Ryan, and Mark George. 2009. "Functional MRI Detection of Deception after Committing a Mock Sabotage Crime." *Journal of Forensic Sciences* 54(1): 220–231.

Kraska, Peter B., and Victor E. Kappeler. 1997. "Militarizing American Police: The Rise and Normalization of Paramilitary Units." *Social Problems* 44(1): 1–18.

Kuykendall, Jack. 1986. "The Municipal Police Detective: An Historical Analysis." *Criminology* 24(1): 175–200.

Laba, Jonathan Todd. 1996. "If You Can't Stand the Heat, Get out of the Drug Business: Thermal Imagers, Emerging Technologies, and the Fourth Amendment." *California Law Review* 84(5): 1,437–1,486.

Lamb, Michael E., Yael Orbach, Kathleen J. Sternberg, Irit Hershkowitz, and Dvora Horowitz. 2000. "Accuracy of Investigators' Verbatim Notes of Their Forensic Interviews with Alleged Child Abuse Victims." *Law and Human Behavior* 24(6): 699–708.

Lane, Roger. 1967. *Policing the City: Boston 1822–1885.* Cambridge, MA: Harvard University Press.

Larocque, Marc. 2013. "Fire at Vacant Raynham House Labeled Arson." Wicked Local Raynham. March 26. www.wickedlocal.com/raynham/news/x694781265/Fire-at-vacant-Raynham-house-called-arson#axzz2WIoCWGwd.

Lassiter, G. Daniel, Andrew L. Geers, Ian M. Handley, Paul E. Weiland, and Patrick J. Munhall. 2002. "Videotaped Interrogations and Confessions: A Simple Change in Camera Perspective Alters Verdicts in Simulated Trials." *Journal of Applied Psychology* 87(5): 867–874.

Laughery, Kenneth R., and Richard H. Fowler. 1980. "Sketch Artist and Identi-Kit Procedures for Recalling Faces." *Journal of Applied Psychology* 65(3): 307–316.

Lavine, Emanuel. 1930. *The Third Degree: A Detailed and Appalling Exposé of Police Brutality.* New York: Garden City Publishing.

Leo, Richard A. 1992. "From Coercion to Deception: The Changing Nature of Police Interrogations in America." *Crime, Law, and Social Change* 18(1): 35–59.

———. 1996. "Inside the Interrogation Room." *Journal of Criminal Law and Criminology* 86(2): 266–303.

———. 1998a. "The Impact of Miranda Revisited." In *The Miranda Debate: Law, Justice, and Policing,* edited by George C. Leo and George C. Thomas. Boston: Northeastern University Press.

———. 1998b. "Miranda and the Problem of False Confessions." In *The Miranda Debate: Law, Justice, and Policing,* edited by George C. Leo and George C. Thomas. Boston: Northeastern University Press.

———. 2008. *Police Interrogation and American Justice.* Cambridge: Harvard University Press.

Leo, Richard A., and Richard J. Ofshe. 1998. "The Consequences of False Confessions: Deprivations of Liberty and Miscarriages of Justice in the Age of Psychological Interrogations." *Journal of Criminal Law and Criminology* 88(2): 429–496.

Lindsay, D. Stephen. 1994. "Memory Source Monitoring and Eyewitness Testimony." In *Adult Eyewitness Testimony: Current Trends and Developments,* edited by David Frank Ross et al. Cambridge: Cambridge University Press.

Loftus, Elizabeth F., Edith L. Greene, and James M. Doyle. 1989. "The Psychology of Eyewitness Testimony." In *Psychological Methods in Criminal Investigation and Evidence,* edited by David C. Raskin. New York: Springer.

Loftus, Elizabeth F., and John C. Palmer. 1974. "Reconstruction of Automobile Destruction: An Example of the Interaction between Language and Memory." *Journal of Verbal Learning and Verbal Behavior* 13: 585–589.

Lykken, David. 1981. *A Tremor in the Blood: Uses and Abuses of the Lie Detector.* New York: McGraw-Hill.

———. 1998. *A Tremor in the Blood: Uses and Abuses of the Lie Detector.* 2nd ed. Reading, MA: Perseus Publishing.

Malone, Patrick A. 1998. "'You Have the Right to Remain Silent': Miranda after Twenty Years." In *The Miranda Debate: Law, Justice, and Policing,* edited by George C. Leo and George C. Thomas. Boston: Northeastern University Press.

Maltz, Michael D., Andrew C. Gordon, and Warren Friedman. 1991. *Mapping Crime in Its Community Setting.* New York: Springer-Verlag.

Mancusi, Stephen. 2010. *The Police Composite Sketch.* New York: Humana Press.

Martin, Christine. 1994. *Illinois Municipal Officers' Perceptions of Police Ethics.* Chicago: Criminal Justice Information Authority.

Marx, Gary. 1988. *Undercover: Police Surveillance in America.* Berkeley: University of California Press.

Mazzetti, Mark, and Helene Cooper. 2011. "Detective Work on Courier Led to Breakthrough on Bin Laden." *The New York Times.* May 2. www.nytimes.com/2011/05/02/world/asia/02reconstruct-capture-osama-bin-laden.html.

McGough, Maureen. 2012. "To Err Is Human: Using Science to Reduce Mistaken Eyewitness Identifications in Police Lineups." *National Institute of Justice Journal* 270: 30–34.

McGuire, Philip G. 2000. "The New York City Police Department COMSTAT Process: Mapping for Analysis, Evaluation, and Accountability." In *Analyzing Crime Patterns: Frontiers of Practice,* edited by Victor Goldsmith et al. Thousand Oaks, CA: Sage.

McIver, J. P. 1981. "Criminal Mobility: A Review of Empirical Studies." In *Crime Spillover,* edited by Simon Hakim and George F. Rengert. Beverly Hills, CA: Sage.

McNeil Jr., Donald G., and Pam Belluck. 2011. "Experts Say DNA Match Is Likely a Parent or Child." *The New York Times.* May 2. www.nytimes.com/2011/05/03/science/03dna.html.

Merrill, William F. 1995. "The Art of Interrogating Rapists." *FBI Law Enforcement Bulletin* 64(1): 8–12.

Miller, George I. 1987. "Observations on Police Undercover Work." *Criminology* 25(1): 27–47.

Miller, J. Mitchell. 2011. "Becoming an Informant." *Justice Quarterly* 28(2): 203–220.

Miller, Laurence. 2006. "On the Spot: Testifying in Court for Law Enforcement Officers." *FBI Law Enforcement Bulletin* 75(10): 1–7.

Miron, Murray S., and John E. Douglas. 1979. "Threat Analysis: The Psycholinguistic Approach." *FBI Law Enforcement Bulletin* 48(9): 5–9.

Mitchell, Jacqueline. 2008. "What Your Car Says to the Opposite Sex." *Forbes.* February 5. www.forbes.com/2008/02/05/cars-sex-signals-forbeslife-lovebiz08-cx_jm_0205oppositesex.html.

Monk, Khadija M., Justin A. Heinonen, and John E. Eck. 2010. *Street Robbery.* Problem-Oriented Guides for Police Series: Problem-Specific Guide No. 59. Washington, DC: U.S. Department of Justice

Moracco, Kathryn E., Kathryn Andersen, Rebecca M. Buchanan, Christina Espersen, J. Michael Bowling, and Courtney Duffy. 2010. "Who Are the Defendants in Domestic Violence Protection Order Cases?" *Violence against Women* 16(11): 1,201–1,223.

Moradoff, Nissan. 2010. "Biometrics: Proliferation and Constraints to Emerging and New Technologies." *Security Journal* 23(4): 276–298.

Morgan, Charles A., Gary Hazlett, Anthony Doran, Stephan Garrett, Gary Hoyt, Paul Thomas, Madelon Baranoski, and Steven M Southwick. 2004. "Accuracy of Eyewitness Memory for Persons Encountered During Exposure to Highly Intense Stress." *International Journal of Law and Psychiatry* 27(3): 265–279.

Morganthau, Tom, and Tom Masland. 1993. "The New Terrorism." *Newsweek,* July 5, 18.

Moreau, Dale M., and P. David Bigbee. 1995. "Major Physical Evidence in Sexual Assault Investigations." In *Practical Aspects of Rape Investigation: A Multidisciplinary Approach,* edited by Robert R. Hazelwood and Ann Wolbert Burgess. Boca Raton, FL: CRC Press.

Morris, Edward W. 2010. "'Snitches End Up in Ditches' and Other Cautionary Tales." *Journal of Contemporary Criminal Justice* 26(3): 254–272.

Mount, Harry A. 1990. "Criminal Informants: An Administrator's Dream or Nightmare." *FBI Law Enforcement Bulletin* 59(12): 12–16.

Muller, Gallus. 1889. *Alphonse Bertillon's Instructions for Taking Descriptions for the Identification of Criminals and Others* [translation of 1889 work]. Chicago: American Bertillon Prison Bureau.

Murray, Robert K. 1955. *Red Scare*. New York: McGraw-Hill.

Myers, Kenneth A. 2011. Searches of Motor Vehicles Incident to Arrest in a Post-Gant World. *FBI Law Enforcement Bulletin*. 80(4): 24–32.

Napier, Michael R., and Susan H. Adams. 1998. "Magic Words to Obtain Confessions." *FBI Law Enforcement Bulletin* 67(10): 11–15.

Nardulli, Peter F. 1983. "The Societal Costs of the Exclusionary Rule: An Empirical Assessment." *American Bar Foundation Research Journal* 8(3): 585–609.

National Gang Intelligence Center. 2011. *National Gang Threat Assessment*. Washington, DC: U.S. Department of Justice.

National Institute of Justice. 1996. *Convicted by Juries, Exonerated by Science: Case Studies in the Use of DNA Evidence to Establish Innocence After Trial*. Washington, DC: U.S. Department of Justice.

———. 1999a. *Eyewitness Evidence: A Guide for Law Enforcement*. Washington, DC: U.S. Department of Justice.

———. 1999b. *What Every Law Enforcement Officer Should Know about DNA Evidence*. Washington, DC: U.S. Department of Justice.

———. 2000a. *Crime Scene Investigation: A Guide for Law Enforcement*. Washington, DC: U.S. Department of Justice.

———. 2000b. *Fire and Arson Scene Evidence: A Guide for Public Safety Personnel*. Washington, DC: U.S. Department of Justice.

———. 2001. *Understanding DNA Evidence: A Guide for Victim Service Providers*. Washington, DC: U.S. Department of Justice.

———. 2003a. "DNA Evidence: What Law Enforcement Officers Should Know." *National Institute of Justice Journal* 249: 1–15.

———. 2003b. *Eyewitness Evidence: A Trainer's Manual for Law Enforcement*. Washington, DC: U.S. Department of Justice.

———. 2008. *Electronic Crime Scene Investigation: A Guide for First Responders*. Washington, DC: U.S. Department of Justice.

———. 2012. *DNA for the Defense Bar*. Washington, DC: U.S. Department of Justice. Office of Justice Programs.

National Research Council. 2009. *Strengthening Forensic Science in the United States: A Path Forward*. Washington, DC: The National Academic Press.

Navarro, Joe. 2004. "Testifying in the Theater of the Courtroom." *FBI Law Enforcement Bulletin* 73(9): 26–30.

Nelson, Scott A. 1989. "Crime-Time Television." *FBI Law Enforcement Bulletin* 58(8): 1–9.

Newman, Graeme R. 2004a. *Check and Card Fraud*. Problem-Oriented Guides for Police Series: Problem-Specific Guide No. 21. Washington, DC: U.S. Department of Justice.

———. 2004b. *Identity Theft*. Problem-Oriented Guides for Police Series: Problem-Specific Guide No. 25. Washington, DC: U.S. Department of Justice.

Newton, Christopher. 2002. "FBI to Profile al-Qaida Prisoners." *Associated Press*, August 9.

Ney, Tara. 1988. "Expressing Your Emotions and Controlling Feelings." In *The Polygraph Test: Lies, Truth, and Science,* edited by Anthony Gale. London: Sage.

Nunn, Samuel. 2001. "Cities, Space, and the New World of Urban Law Enforcement Technologies." *Journal of Urban Affairs* 23(3–4): 259–278.

———. 2003a. "Seeking Tools for the War on Terror: A Critical Assessment of Emerging Technologies in Law Enforcement." *Policing: An International Journal of Police Strategies & Management* 26(3): 454–472.

O'Harrow Jr., Robert. 2003. "U.S. Backs Florida's New Counterterrorism Database." *The Washington Post,* August 6.

Olson, E. A., and G. L. Wells. 2004. "What Makes a Good Alibi? A Proposed Taxonomy." *Law and Human Behavior* 28: 157–176.

Organized Crime Digest. 2000. *Federal, State Agents Break Up Ring Stealing Cars for Russia, East Europe*. Vol. 21: 1–2.

Orne, Martin T., David A. Soskis, David F. Dinges, and Emily Carota Orne. 1984. "Hypnotically Induced Testimony." In *Eyewitness Testimony: Psychological Perspectives,* edited by Gery L. Wells and Elizabeth F. Loftus. Cambridge: Cambridge University Press.

Orthmann, Christine Hess, and Karen Matison Hess. 2013. *Criminal Investigation.* Clifton Park, NY: Cengage.

O'Toole, Mary Ellen. 1999. "Criminal Profiling: The FBI Uses Criminal Investigative Analysis to Solve Crimes." *Corrections Today* 61(1): 44–47.

Owen, David. 2000. *Hidden Evidence: 40 True Crimes and How Forensic Science Helped Solved Them.* Buffalo, NY: Firefly.

Patterson, Debra. 2011. "The Impact of Detectives' Manner of Questioning on Rape Victims' Disclosure." *Violence against Women* 17(11): 1,349–1,373.

Pelfrey, William V., and Nicole L Weber. 2013. Keyboard Gangsters: Analysis of Incidents and Correlates of Cyberbullying in a Large Urban Student Population. *Deviant Behavior* 34(1): 68–84.

Peterson, Jonathan, and Robert L. Jackson. 2001. "Look-Alike Letters Provide Clues." *Los Angeles Times,* October 24.

Petherick, Wayne. 2009. *Serial Crime: Theoretical and Practical Issues in Behavioral Profiling.* Burlington, MA: Elsevier, Inc.

Petrossian, Gohar, and Ronald V. Clarke. 2011. *Export of Stolen Vehicles across Land Borders.* Problem-Oriented Guides for Police Series: Problem-Specific Guide No. 63. Washington, DC: U.S. Department of Justice.

Pettry, Michael. 2011. "The Emergency Aid Exception to the Fourth Amendment's Warrant Requirement." *FBI Law Enforcement Bulletin* 80(3): 26–32.

Pinizzotto, Anthony J. 1984. "Forensic Psychology: Criminal Personality Profiling." *Journal of Police Science and Administration* 12(1): 32–39.

Pinizzotto, Anthony J., and Norman J. Finkel. 1990. "Criminal Personality Profiling: An Outcome and Process Study." *Law and Human Behavior* 14(3): 215–232.

Pittel, Stephen, and Laila Spina. 2011. "Investigating Drug-Facilitated Sexual Assault." In *Rape Investigation Handbook,* edited by John O. Savino and Brent E. Turvey. Amsterdam: Elsevier Inc.

Porter, Bruce. 1983. "Mind Hunters." *Psychology Today* 17(4): 44–52.

Porter, Stephen, and John C. Yuille. 1996. "The Language of Deceit: An Investigation of the Verbal Clues and Deception in the Interrogation Context." *Law and Human Behavior* 20(4): 443–458.

Potter, Angela. 2002. "Who Will Get the Sniper Reward Money?" *Associated Press,* November 26.

Prough, Todd. 2009. "Investigating Opiate-Overdose Deaths." *FBI Law Enforcement Bulletin* 78(4): 27–31.

Rabon, Don. 1994. *Investigative Discourse Analysis.* Durham, NC: Carolina Academic Press.

RAND Corporation. 2001. *Challenges and Choices for Crime-Fighting Technology: Federal Support of State and Local Law Enforcement.* Santa Monica: RAND.

Raskin, David C., and Charles R. Honts. 2002. "The Comparison Question Test." In *Handbook of Polygraph Testing,* edited by Murray Kleiner. San Diego: Academic Press.

Rattner, Arye. 1988. "Convicted but Innocent: Wrongful Conviction and the Criminal Justice System." *Law and Human Behavior* 12(3): 283–293.

Reed, Ben. 2008. "Future Technology in Law Enforcement." *FBI Law Enforcement Bulletin* 77(5): 15–21.

Regini, Charles L. 1997. "The Cold Case Concept." *FBI Law Enforcement Bulletin* 66(8): 1–6.

Reiser, Martin. 1989. "Investigative Hypnosis." In *Psychological Methods in Criminal Investigation and Evidence,* edited by David C. Raskin. New York: Springer.

Ressler, Robert K., and Ann W. Burgess. 1985. "Crime Scene and Profile Characteristics of Organized and Disorganized Murderers." *FBI Law Enforcement Bulletin* 54(8): 18–25.

Rhodes, Henry T. F. 1968. *Alphonse Bertillon: Father of Scientific Detection.* New York: Greenwood Press.

Rice, Thomas. 1998. "When You're First at a Robbery Scene." *Police* 22(5): 38–41.

Richardson, Cara. 2013. "Text Messages Key Evidence in Steubenville Rape Trial." *USA Today.* March 14. www.centralohio.com/usatoday/article/1987471.

Rider, Anthony Olen. 1980a. "The Firesetter: A Psychological Profile, Part I." *FBI Law Enforcement Bulletin* 49(6): 6–13.

———. 1980b. "The Firesetter: A Psychological Profile, Part II." *FBI Law Enforcement Bulletin* 49(7): 6–17.

Ritter, Nancy. 2008. "DNA Solves Property Crimes (But Are We Ready for That?)." *National Institute of Justice Journal* 261: 2–12.

Rosenbaum, Dennis P., Arthur J. Lurigio, and Paul P. Lavrakas. 1989. "Enhancing Citizen Participation on Solving Serious Crime: A National Evaluation of Crime Stoppers Programs." *Crime and Delinquency* 35(3): 401–420.

Rossmo, D. Kim. 2000. *Geographic Profiling.* Boca Raton, FL: CRC Press.

————. 2006a. "Criminal Investigative Failures: Avoiding the Pitfalls." *FBI Law Enforcement Bulletin* 75(9): 1–8.

————. 2006b. "Criminal Investigative Failures: Avoiding the Pitfalls (Part Two)." *FBI Law Enforcement Bulletin* 75(10): 12–19.

Roth, Alex. 2002a. "Experts Agree Defense Team for Westerfield Has a Hard Task." *San Diego Union Tribune*, March 14.

————. 2002b. "Uncoiled Hose Aroused Suspicion, Police Testify." *San Diego Union Tribune*, June 12.

Rudd, Jonathan. 2010. "You Have to Speak Up to Remain Silent: The Supreme Court Revisits the Miranda Right to Silence." *FBI Law Enforcement Bulletin* 79(9): 1–3.

Sampson, Rana. 2002. *False Burglar Alarms*. Problem-Oriented Guides for Police Series: Problem-Specific Guide No. 5. Washington, DC: U.S. Department of Justice.

————. 2007. *Domestic Violence*. Problem-Oriented Guides for Police Series: Problem-Specific Guide No. 45. Washington, DC: U.S. Department of Justice.

Sanders, Glenn S., and William L. Simmons. 1983. "Use of Hypnosis to Enhance Eyewitness Accuracy: Does It Work?" *Journal of Applied Psychology* 68(1): 70–77.

Sandoval, Vincent A., and Susan H. Adams. 2001. "Subtle Skills for Building Rapport: Using Neuro-Linguistic Programming in the Interview Room." *FBI Law Enforcement Bulletin* 70(8): 1–5.

Savino, John O., and Brent E. Turvey. 2005. "Interviewing Suspects and Victims." In *Rape Investigation Handbook*, edited by John O. Savino and Brent E. Turvey. Amsterdam: Elsevier Inc.

————. 2005b. "Processing the Rape Crime Scene." In *Rape Investigation Handbook*, edited by John O. Savino, and Brent E. Turvey. Amsterdam: Elsevier Inc.

Schafer, John R. and Joe Navarro. 2010. *Advanced Interviewing Techniques: Proven Strategies for Law Enforcement, Military, and Security Personnel*. Springfield, IL: Charles C. Thomas.

Scheflin, Alan W., and Jerrold Lee Shapiro. 1989. *Trance on Trial*. New York: Guilford Press.

Schmidt, Susan, and Dan Eggen. 2002. "Suspected Planner of 9/11 Attacks Captured in Pakistan After Gunfight." *The Washington Post*, September 14, A1.

Schott, Richard. 2009. "The Supreme Court Reexamines Search Incident to Lawful Arrest." *FBI Law Enforcement Bulletin* 78(7): 22–31.

Schroeder, David, and Michael White. 2009. "Exploring the Use of DNA Evidence in Homicide Investigations: Implications for Detective Work and Case Clearance." *Police Quarterly* 12(3): 319–242.

Schulhofer, Stephen J. 1998. "Miranda's Practical Effect: Substantial Benefits and Vanishingly Small Societal Costs." In *The Miranda Debate: Law, Justice, and Policing*, edited by George C. Leo and George C. Thomas. Boston: Northeastern University Press.

Schulte, Brigid, and Sylvia Moreno. 2002. "Who Will Get $500,000 for Tip Leading to Suspect?" *The Washington Post*, October 26, A16.

Schwartz, Ian. 2012. "Al-Qaida Touts Forest Arson as Terrorism." KRQE News. May 3. www.krqe.com/dpp/news/environment/al-qaida-touts-forest-arson-as-terror.

Scott, Michael S. 2001. *Robbery at Automated Teller Machines*. Problem-Oriented Guides for Police Series: Problem-Specific Guide No. 8. Washington, DC: U.S. Department of Justice.

Semmler, Carolyn, Neil Brewer, and Gary L. Wells. 2004. "Effects of Postidentification Feedback on Eyewitness Identification and Nonidentification Confidence." *Journal of Applied Psychology* 89(2): 334–346.

Serrano, Richard A. 1998. *One of Ours: Timothy McVeigh and the Oklahoma City Bombing*. New York: W. W. Norton.

Shane, Scott, and Charlie Savage. 2011. "Bin Laden Raid Revives Debate on Value of Torture." *The New York Times*, May 3. www.nytimes.com/2011/05/04/us/politics/04torture.html?_r=0.

Sherman, Mark. 2006. "Sears Tower Terror Plot Foiled." *Chicago Sun Times*, June 23.

Sherman, Lawrence, Patrick Gartin, and Michael Buerger. 1989. "Hot Spots of Predatory Crime: Routine Activities and the Criminology of Place." *Criminology* 27(1): 27–56.

Simon, David. 1998. "Homicide: A Year on the Killing Streets." In *The Miranda Debate: Law, Justice, and Policing*, edited by George C. Leo and George C. Thomas. Boston: Northeastern University Press.

Skolnick, Jerome H., and James J. Fyfe. 1993. *Above the Law: Police and the Excessive Use of Force*. New York: Free Press.

Smith, Martha. 2005. *Robbery of Taxi Cab Drivers*. Problem-Oriented Guides for Police Series: Problem-Specific Guide No. 34. Washington, DC: U.S. Department of Justice

Smith, Sharon S., and Roger W. Shuy. 2002. "Forensic Psycholinguistics: Using Language Analysis for Identifying and Assessing Offenders." *FBI Law Enforcement Bulletin* 71(4): 16–21.

Snook, Brent, Richard Cullen, Craig Bennell, Paul Taylor, and Paul Gendreau. 2008. "The Criminal Profiling Illusion: What's behind the Smoke and Mirrors?" *Criminal Justice & Behavior* 35(10): 1,257–1,276.

Stauffer, Eric, and Monica S. Bonfanti. 2006. *Forensic Investigation of Stolen-Recovered and Other Crime-Related Vehicles*. Amsterdam: Elsevier.

Steblay, Nancy, Jennifer Dysart, Solomon Fulero, and R. C. L. Lindsay. 2003. "Eyewitness Accuracy Rates in Police Showup and Lineup Presentations: A Meta-Analytic Comparison." *Law and Human Behavior* 27(5): 523–540.

Steblay, Nancy K., Jennifer E. Dysart, and Gary L. Wells. 2011. "Seventy-Two Tests of the Sequential Lineup Superiority Effect: A Meta-Analysis and Policy Discussion." *Psychology, Public Policy, and Law* 17(1): 99–139.

Steblay, Nancy Mehrkens, and Robert K. Bothwell. 1994. "Evidence for Hypnotically Refreshed Testimony: The View from the Laboratory." *Law and Human Behavior* 18(6): 635–651.

Stutler, Thomas R. 1997. "Stand and Deliver: Cross-Examination Strategies for Law Enforcement." *FBI Law Enforcement Bulletin* 66(9): 1–5.

Strunk, William, and E. B. White. 1979. *The Elements of Style*. New York: Macmillian.

Sullivan, Thomas P. 2004. *Police Experiences with Recording Custodial Interrogations*. Chicago: Northwestern University School of Law.

Sutton, Michael. 2010. *Stolen Goods Markets*. Problem-Oriented Guides for Police Series: Problem-Specific Guide No. 57. Washington, DC: U.S. Department of Justice.

Sutton, Paul. 1986. "The Fourth Amendment in Action: An Empirical View of the Search Warrant Process." *Criminal Law Bulletin* 22(5): 405–429.

TECH Beat. 2013. *Inmates Provide Anonymous Tips with Face Crook*. Washington, DC: National Law Enforcement and Corrections Technology Center System.

Teitell, Beth. 1994. "Experts: Faked Forensics 'Surprisingly Widespread.'" *Boston Herald,* July 31.

Thomas, George C. 1998. "Miranda: The Crime, the Man, and the Law of Confessions." In *The Miranda Debate: Law, Justice, and Policing,* George C. Leo and George C. Thomas. Boston: Northeastern University Press.

Toffler, Alvin. 1980. *The Third Wave*. New York: William Marrow.

Tonkin, Matthew, John Bond, and Jessica Woodhams. 2009. "Fashion Conscious Burglars? Testing the Principles of Offender Profiling with Footwear Impressions Recovered at Domestic Burglaries." *Psychology, Crime & Law* 15(4): 327–345.

Tontarski, Karolyn, Kyle Hoskins, Tani Watkins, Leanora Brun-Conti, and Amy Michaud. 2009. "Chemical Enhancement Techniques of Bloodstain Patterns and DNA Recovery after Fire Exposure." *Journal of Forensic Sciences* 54(1): 37–48.

Trager, Jennifer, and JoAnne Brewster. 2001. "The Effectiveness of Psychological Profiles." *Journal of Police and Criminal Psychology* 16(1): 20–25.

Trimpe, Michael. 2011. "The Current Status of GSR Examinations." *FBI Law Enforcement Bulletin* 80(5): 24–32.

Turner, Michael, Lyn Exum, Robert Brame, and Thomas Holt. 2013. "Bullying Victimization and Adolescent Mental Health: General and Typological Effects across Sex." *Journal of Criminal Justice* 41(1): 53–59.

Turvey, Brent E. 2005. "Rapist Modus Operandi and Motive." In *Rape Investigation Handbook*, edited by John O. Savino and Brent E. Turvey. Amsterdam: Elsevier Inc.

Uchida, Craig D., and Timothy S. Bynum. 1991. "Search Warrants, Motions to Suppress, and 'Lost Cases': The Effects of the Exclusionary Rule in Seven Jurisdictions." *Journal of Criminal Law and Criminology* 81(4): 1,034–1,066.

U.S. Department of Justice. 2001. *First Response to Victims of Crime*. Washington, DC: Office of Justice Programs, Office for Victims of Crime.

———. 2008. *Electronic Crime Scene Investigation: A Guide for First Responders*. Washington, DC: National Institute of Justice.

U.S. Department of State. 2001. *Significant Terrorists Incidents, 1961–2001: A Chronology*. Washington, DC: U.S. Department of State.

Vallano, Jonathan, and Nadja Schreiber Compo. 2011. "A Comfortable Witness Is a Good Witness: Rapport-Building and Susceptibility to Misinformation in an Investigative Mock-Crime Interview." *Applied Cognitive Psychology* 25(6): 960–970.

Verschuere, Bruno, Gershon Ben-Shakhar, and Ewout Meijer. 2011. *Memory Detection: Theory and Application of the Concealed Information Test*. Cambridge: Cambridge University Press.

Vessel, David. 1998. "Conducting Successful Interrogations." *FBI Law Enforcement Bulletin* 67(10): 1–6.

Wagstaff, Graham F. 2009. "Is There a Future for Investigative Hypnosis?" *Journal of Investigative Psychology & Offender Profiling* 6(1): 43–57.

Walker, Don. 2013. "Police Officials Detail High-Tech Shot Sensors in High Crime Areas." *Milwaukee Journal Sentinel.* January 24. www.jsonline.com/news/milwaukee/police-officials-detail-hightech-shot-sensors-in-high-crime-areas-bn8gp6i-188247881.html.

Walker-Holcomb, Jayme. 2004. "Consent Searches." *FBI Law Enforcement Bulletin* 73(2): 22–32.

Walker, Samuel, and Charles M. Katz. 2012. *The Police in America.* New York: McGraw-Hill.

Waller, George. 1961. *Kidnap: The Story of the Lindbergh Case.* New York: Dial Press.

Walsh, Bryan. 2009. "Waterboarding: A Mental and Physical Trauma." *TIME Magazine.* April 20. www.time.com/time/nation/article/0,8599,1892721,00.html.

Walsh, Susan, Fan Liu, Kaye Ballantyne, Mannis van Oven, Oscar Lao, and Manfred Kayser. 2011. "IrisPlex: A Sensitive DNA Tool for Accurate Prediction of Blue and Brown Eye Colour in the Absence of Ancestry Information." *Forensic Science International: Genetics* 5(3): 170–180.

Walsh, Susan, Fan Liu, Andreas Wollstein, Leda Kovatsi, Arwin Ralf, Agnieszka Kosiniak-Kamysz, Wojciech Branicki, and Manfred Kayser. 2013. "The HIrisPlex System for Simultaneous Prediction of Hair and Eye Colour from DNA." *Forensic Science International: Genetics* 7(1): 98–115.

Walters, Stan B. 1996. *Principles of Kinesic Interview and Interrogation.* Boca Raton, FL: CRC Press.

Waltz, Jon R. 1997. *Introduction to Criminal Evidence.* Chicago: Nelson Hall.

Wartell, Julie, and Nancy G. La Vigne 2004. *Prescription Fraud.* Problem-Oriented Guides for Police Series: Problem-Specific Guide No. 24. Washington, DC: U.S. Department of Justice.

Weisel, Deborah Lamm. 2002. *Burglary of Single-Family Houses.* Problem-Oriented Guides for Police Series: Problem-Specific Guide No. 18. Washington, DC: U.S. Department of Justice.

Weisel, Deborah L. 2007. *Bank Robbery.* Problem-Oriented Guides for Police Series: Problem-Specific Guide No. 48. Washington, DC: U.S. Department of Justice.

Wellford, Charles, and James Cronin. 1999. *An Analysis of Variables Affecting the Clearance of Homicides: A Multistate Study.* Washington, DC: Justice Research and Statistics Association.

Wells, Gary L. 1993. "What Do We Know About Eyewitness Identification?" *American Psychologist* 48(5): 553–571.

Wells, Gary L., and Amy L. Bradfield. 1998. "'Good. You Identified the Suspect': Feedback to Eyewitnesses Distorts Their Reports of the Witnessing Experience." *Journal of Applied Psychology* 83(3): 360–376.

Wells, Gary L., Steve D. Charman, and Elizabeth A. Olson. 2005. "Building Face Composites Can Harm Lineup Identification Performance." *Journal of Experimental Psychology: Applied* 11(3): 147–156.

Wells, Gary L., and Elizabeth A. Olson. 2003. "Eyewitness Testimony." *Annual Review of Psychology* 54: 277–295.

Wells, Gary L., Mark Small, Steven Penrod, Roy S. Malpass, Soloman M. Fulero, and C. A. E. Brimacombe. 1998. "Eyewitness Identification Procedures: Recommendations for Lineups and Photospreads." *Law and Human Behavior* 22(6): 603–647.

Wells, Jeffery D., Francesco Introna Jr., Giancarlo Di Vella, Carlo P. Campobasso, Jack Hayes, and Felix A. H. Sperling. 2001. "Human and Insect Mitochondrial DNA Analysis from Maggots." *Journal of Forensic Science* 46(3): 685–687.

Wetzel, Dan. 2013. "Steubenville Suspect's Text Messages Paint Disturbing Picture of Night of Alleged Rape." Yahoo! Sports. March 15. http://sports.yahoo.com/news/highschool—steubenville-suspects—text-messages-paint-disturbing-picture-of-night-of-alleged-rape—according-to-prosecutors-053236470.html.

White, John, David Lester, Matthew Gentile, and Juliana Rosenbleeth. 2011. "The Utilization of Forensic Science and Criminal Profiling for Capturing Serial Killers." *Forensic Science International* 209(1–3): 160–165.

White, Peter J. 1998. *Crime Scene to Court: The Essentials of Forensic Science.* Cambridge: Royal Society of Chemistry, Information Services.

White, Russ. 2008. "MSU Researcher Creates System Helping Police to Match Tattoos to Suspects." Michigan State University. May 28. http://msutoday.msu.edu/news/2008/msu-researcher-creates-system-helping-police-to-match-tattoos-to-suspects/.

Wilcock, Rachel, Ray Bull, and Rebecca Milne. 2008. *Witness Identification in Criminal Cases: Psychology and Practice.* New York: Oxford University Press, Inc.

Williams, R., and Paul Johnson. 2005. "Inclusiveness, Effectiveness and Intrusiveness: Issues in the Developing Uses of DNA Profiling in Support of Criminal Investigations." *Journal of Law, Medicine and Ethics* 33(3): 545–558.

Willmer, M. 1970. *Crime and Information Theory.* Edinburgh: University of Edinburgh Press.

Witzig, Eric W. 2003. "The New ViCap: More User-Friendly and Used by More Agencies." *FBI Law Enforcement Bulletin* 72(6): 1–7.

Woldoff, Rachael A., and Karen G. Weiss. 2010. "Stop Snitchin': Exploring Definitions of the Snitch and Implications for Urban Black Communities." *Journal of Criminal Justice and Popular Culture* 17(1): 184–223.

Wortley, Richard, and Stephen Smallbone. 2012. *Child Pornography on the Internet*. Problem-Oriented Guides for Police Series: Problem-Specific Guide No. 41. Washington, DC: U.S. Department of Justice.

Wright, Richard T., and Scott H. Decker. 1994. *Burglars on the Job: Street Life and Residential Break-ins*. Boston: Northeastern University Press.

———. 1997. *Armed Robbers in Action*. Boston: Northeastern University Press.

Yarmey, A. Daniel, Meagan J. Yarmey, and A. Linda Yarmey. 1996. "Accuracy of Eyewitness Identifications in Showups and Lineups." *Law and Human Behavior* 20(4): 459–476.

Zalman, Marvin. 2000. "Criminal Justice and the Future of Civil Liberties." *Criminal Justice Review* 25(2): 181–206.

———. 2002. *Criminal Procedure: Constitution and Society*. Upper Saddle River, NJ: Prentice Hall.

Zeman, David, and Ben Schmitt. 2002. "How Justice Failed Eddie Joe Lloyd." *Detroit Free Press*, October 24.

Zhu, Bi, Chuansheng Chen, Elizabeth Loftus, Qinghua He, Chunhui Chen, Xuemei Lei, Chongde Lin, and Qi Dong. 2012. "Brief Exposure to Misinformation Can Lead to Long-Term False Memories." *Applied Cognitive Psychology* 26(2): 301–307.

Zuckerman, Miron, Richard Koestner, and Audrey O. Alton. 1984. "Learning to Detect Deception." *Journal of Personality and Social Psychology* 46(3): 519–528.

Zulawski, David E., and Douglas E. Wicklander. 1992. *Practical Aspects of Interview and Interrogation*. New York: Elsevier.

Index

About the Author

Steven G. Brandl (Ph.D., Michigan State University, 1991) is an associate professor in the Department of Criminal Justice at the University of Wisconsin, Milwaukee. Professor Brandl teaches numerous graduate and undergraduate courses including Criminal Evidence and Investigation, Criminal Psychology, Police Administration, and Issues in Police Practice and Policy, among others. His research interests include police decision-making and behavior, police use of force, the hazards of police work, the relationship between the police and the community, criminal investigation, and program evaluation.

He has conducted numerous research projects and consulted with the Milwaukee Police Department and suburban police departments as well as other major metropolitan police departments on forensic science and policing issues. Besides this textbook, he is the author of numerous articles in professional journals, co-editor of *The Police in America: Classic and Contemporary Readings and Voices From the Field,* and a frequent presenter at regional and national professional conferences.

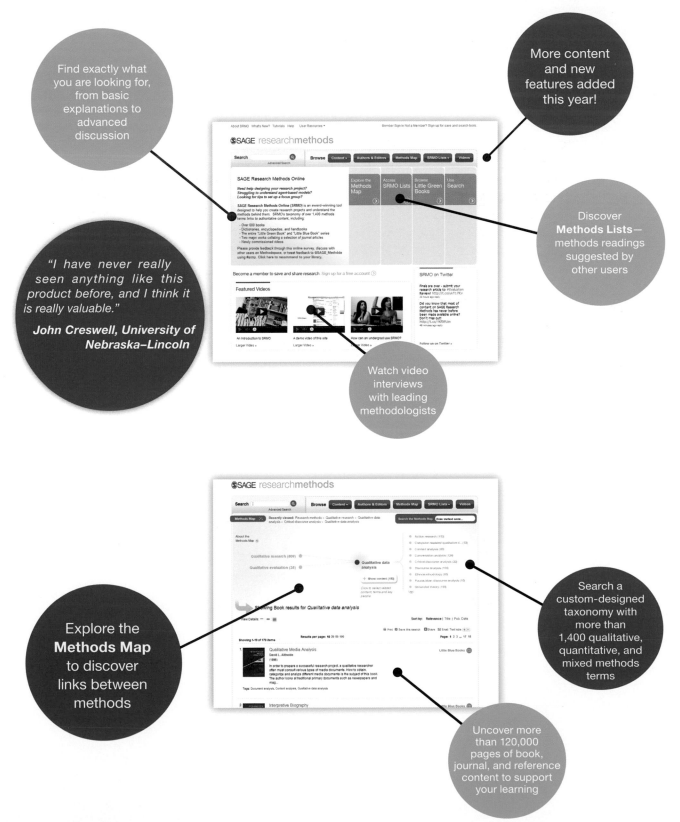